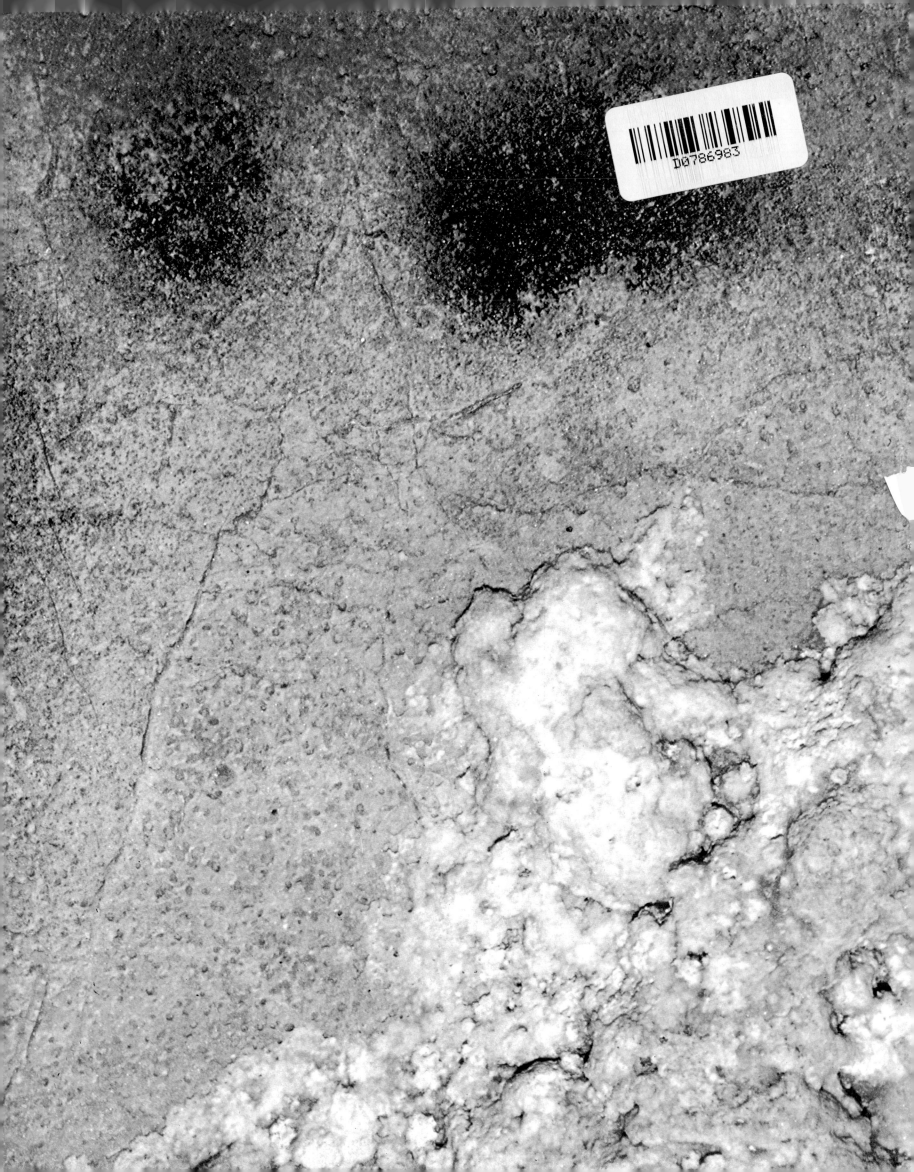

TREASURES OF PREHISTORIC ART

TREASURES OF

André Leroi-Gourhan

PREHISTORIC ART

HARRY N. ABRAMS, INC., Publishers, New York

Translated from the French by Norbert Guterman

Patricia Egan *and* Alice Roberts · *Editors*

International Standard Book Number: 0-8109-0426-8

Library of Congress Catalog Card Number: 67-22851

Published in association with Editions d'Art Lucien Mazenod, Paris

Printed and bound in France

TREASURES OF PREHISTORIC ART

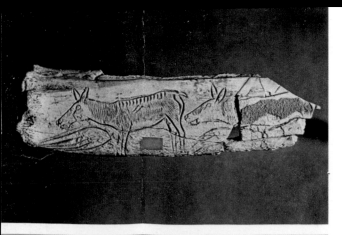

3   LE CHAFFAUD. *Engraved hinds.*

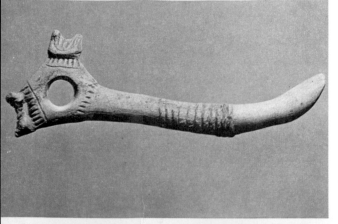

4   LAUGERIE BASSE. *Pierced staff.*

5   ARUDY. *Horse's head carved in silhouette.*

6   BRASSEMPOUY. *Woman's head, ivory.*

7   LAUSSEL. *Engraved slab, female figures.*

CONTENTS

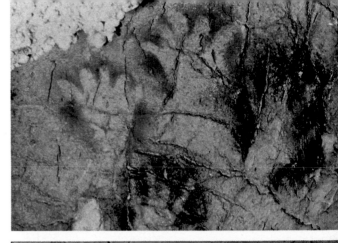

8   GARGAS. *Negative hands on wall.*

9   NIAUX. *Panel of signs.*

10   LASCAUX. *Horse and signs.*

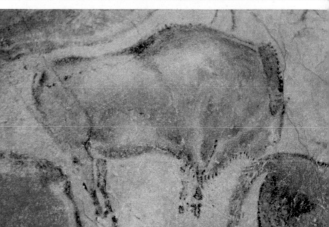

11   ROUFFIGNAC. *Mammoth.*

12   ALTAMIRA. *Bison on the Painted Ceiling.*

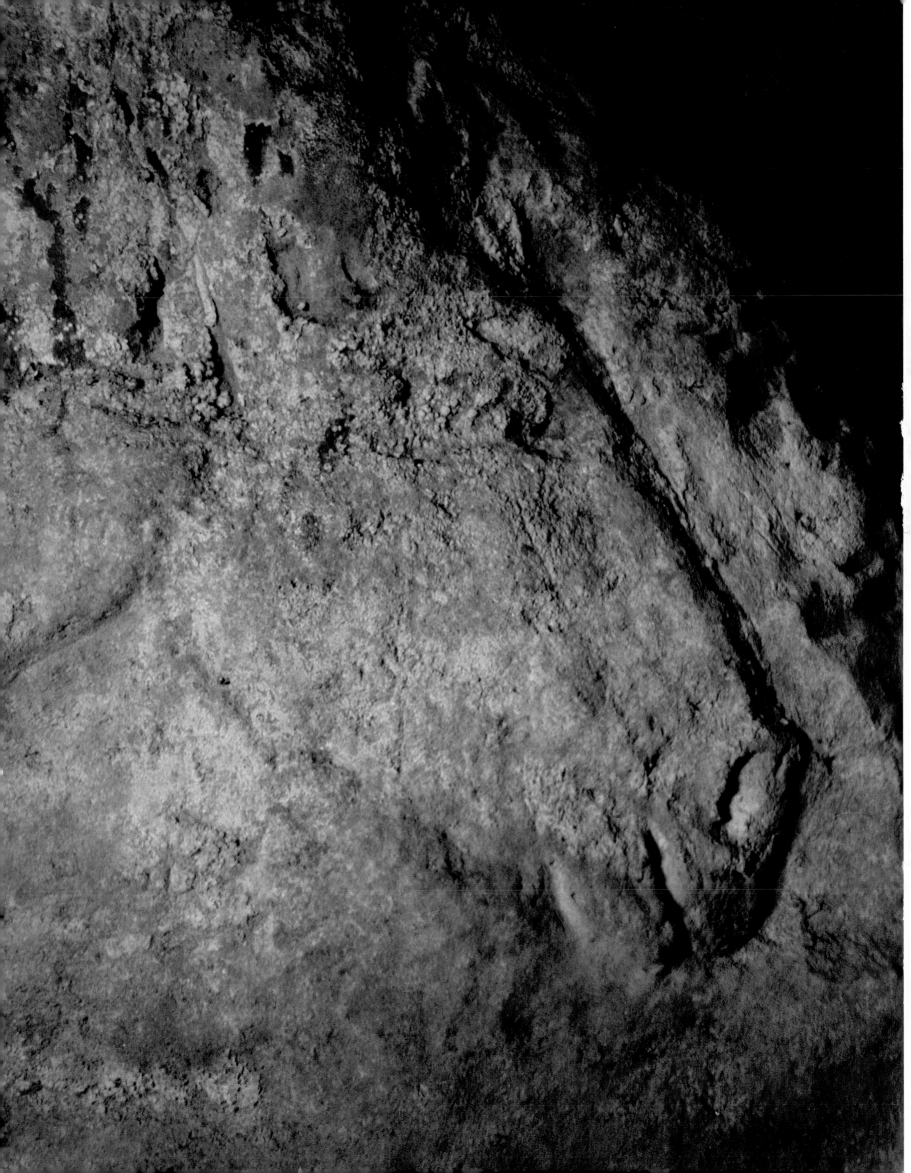

AUTHOR'S FOREWORD

Opposite page
13 COMMARQUE. *Horse's head in low relief.*

THIS book had a fairly long history even before its publication. It was in 1947 that Lucien Mazenod and I first discussed the project of a work on prehistoric art; it remained in the air for several years, and only in 1956 did it begin to take shape. "Do the book as you see fit; I'll see to its publication"—this offer of Lucien Mazenod's represents the real origin of this book, so unlike the usual art book, which is presented as the product of friendly cooperation between myself and the publisher, for to him fell the task of taming the monster my pen had brought into being.

After it was decided to publish, the team was easily assembled. Jean Vertut had for several years been interested in the photography of caves, and he needed only to adapt his speleological training to the photographing of works on the cave walls. The third member of our team was the Rev. R. P. Hours, who had long been a colleague on our field trips. In some cases the three of us worked together, or we were joined by members of the group excavating Arcy-sur-Cure. Eventually, Michel Brézillon joined our original group. During the academic vacations, we explored nearly every known cave and rock shelter in France and Spain, section by section. Each of us had a well-defined role. Jean Vertut and his assistants took the photographs. Father Hours, who was in charge of our schedule and itineraries, also took over the major part of the documentary preparation, a task he shared with Michel Brézillon. My own responsibility was to make the record of the layout and contents of each cave, and I often took a photographic record of my own. All of us joined in deciphering the cave-wall figures, and of the numerous discussions we held while sitting on the damp ground, I recall only one real difference of opinion; that concerned a certain sign painted over one of the bison in the Marsoulas cave. Our whole group, which occasionally numbered more than ten, contributed to systematically covering the cave walls, and (as our hypotheses concerning the positioning of the works took on shape) all began to search for figures and signs more and more methodically. We visited the majority of sites twice, and our work as a team enabled us to assemble our documentation in so relatively short a time. I must emphasize the fact that Abbé Henri Breuil, not in the flesh but in the form of his scholarly legacy, was our constant companion in the field; I am far more indebted to him than may be evident from this book, in which I have often taken a position different from his. We were also guided by a number of other authors, whose writings we actually took along with us into the caves. I hope I have done justice to them all in my accounts and in the bibliography.

nentation of the decorated objects took place under the same conditions of shared labor, most

caves, but we had our home base at the Château de Morigny where Mme. de Saint-Périer

zling treasures from Isturitz and Lespugue. We went back there whenever our thinking de-

e evidence. The greater part of the illustrations of decorated objects come from Morigny and

in-en-Laye.

full "corpus" of its subject) has merit as a source of artistic satisfaction and as a collection

ucien Mazenod, Jean Vertut, the field team, and all who opened their doors to us, as it does

n the publisher so imprudently granted me in the writing of the book, I alone am to blame if

labyrinth of hypotheses spun out over entire chapters. My initial project was simple enough:

European prehistoric art with photographs. Abbé Breuil devoted many works to describing

several times he outlined a chronology of the works without being tempted to draw a systemat-

was room for just such a work. Having assimilated the available literature, I began in 1957

ding good examples of the necessary cases in point. But I did not find the cultural chaos

ver the walls in disorder by successive generations of hunters. Neither Lascaux nor Altamira

ather, I was impressed by the unity each of the sets of figures embodies. It no longer seemed

ions in order to make out the chronological divisions. Almost from the first visits, the cave as

han the dating problems. My new thinking first crystallized in connection with Le Portel, on

nction with Abbé Breuil's excellent publication on that site. Not only did I come to believe

(except in accidental instances), but a real order seemed to me to be reflected in the arrange-

his might be was as yet confused in my mind. At this point both Mme. Laming-Emperaire and

n the same track. After an exchange of ideas, we decided not to be influenced by each other,

es, the better to compare our eventual findings, at least until she completed La Signification

the book she was at that time still writing. When we finally compared notes, we saw that if we had both "gone off the track," at least we had done so with the same sense o

least a certain interest. Her grasp of the importance of the bison/horse pairing pointed in the s

results, and her assertion of the elaborate character of Paleolithic compositions coincided wi

analysis had brought to light. It was at about this time that I came to the realization tha

chronology in the decorated caves, and my two preoccupations—with stylistic evolution, and

the groups of figures—merged into one.

This work can represent only one stage in a continuing investigation, and I am firmly

at the same time I feel that it reflects some considerable part of the actual truth. Chronologica

and moved up or down on the time scale; some more articulate theory than this one of paired g

account of the motivation underlying the compositions. All scientific work must be taken as

especially in a field where there is no written word to guide us. There is, however, a solid

guide us, and at the risk of wearying the reader, I have been anxious to present as many fact

cases of museums and on the cave walls the works are to be seen; for those who will take t

the problems posed by the art of the caves and rethink them once again.

ACKNOWLEDGMENTS

IT would be nearly impossible to express thanks to everyone who has helped us to complete this study and assemble all these works, but we should like to acknowledge especial gratitude to the following: Dr. J. Allain, for objects from the cave at Saint-Marcel; M. Altayrac, in charge of the cave at Le Mas d'Azil; MM. Max and Louis Bégouën, owners of Le Tuc d'Audoubert and Les Trois Frères; M. Bétirac, for objects from Bruniquel; MM. Bouchet and Laplace Jauretche, for our visits to the caves of Etcheberriko-Karbia and Isturitz (lower cave); MM. Castanet, father and son, for aid and assistance at Sergeac; MM. Couderc and Astruc, for assistance at Pergouset; M. Clastres, M. and Mme. Daubisse, and M. André David, for many long sessions at Niaux, Font-de-Gaume, and Pech Merle; MM. de Faccio and Versaveaud, for aid at Villars; M. A. Delporte, for the female figure from Tursac; Dr. Drouot and MM. Huchard, Gayte, and Escalon de Fonton, for help in the caves of the Gard and the Ardèche valleys; Dr. and Mme. Gaussen, who own Le Gabillou; M. Mario Grande, for assistance at Santimamine; the estate of Dr. Lalanne, for the low reliefs at Laussel; M. le Chanoine Lémozi, for his collections in the museum at Cabrerets; M. Mazet, for assistance at Cougnac; M. le Procureur Méroc, for greatly facilitating our work in the region of Lot, MM. Plassard, Nougier, and Romain Robert, for assistance at Rouffignac; M. Elie Peyrony, curator of the museum at Les Eyzies, for facilitating our work both in the museum and the Dordogne caves; M. Felipe Puente, guide at various El Castillo caves; M. Rauzi, for assistance at Bédeilhac; M. F. Trombe, owner of Montespan; MM. Vézian, father and son, owners of Le Portel; the managers or director of the caves at Bara-Bahau, Gargas, and Lascaux.

As for official institutions, we feel duty bound to acknowledge our gratitude to the Direction de l'Architecture; the Musée de l'Homme; the museum at Saint-Germain-en-Laye; the Musée d'Aquitaine at Bordeaux; the museums at Brive, Périgueux, Roanne, and Santander; the Direction of Spanish Prehistoric Antiquities; and the various foreign institutions which contributed to the photographic documentation.

Lastly, our most heartfelt thanks go to Mme. la Comtesse de Saint-Périer; the number of works from her collection illustrated in this book shows the extent to which she was involved in its realization.

THE PHOTOGRAPHS

All black-and-white photographs are by Jean Vertut, unless otherwise noted. All color photographs are by Jean Vertut, except for the following: 6, 24, 103, 105, A. Leroi-Gourhan; 24, Musée de l'Homme; 57, Jean-Dominique Lajoux; 74, 96, Hinz.

Part One: Descriptions and Theories

1. THE DISCOVERY OF PREHISTORIC ART

14 LE CHAFFAUD, *Engraved hinds*

1. THE DISCOVERY OF PREHISTORIC ART

ALL works dealing with prehistory recount the episodes that marked the discovery of prehistoric art. From them we learn that around 1834, several years before the official birth of prehistory, in a cave at Le Chaffaud, in the department of the Vienne, France, A. Brouillet found a bone showing two incised hinds.[1] At about the same time, François Major, a native of Geneva, discovered two Magdalenian decorated objects at Veyrier, at the foot of Mont Salève. The bone with the hinds from Le Chaffaud attracted little notice because there was as yet no way of dating such finds. Attributed to the "Celts," it was merely the first casualty caused by a mounting passion for exploring caves; right down to the twentieth century, hundreds of works were unearthed in this spirit, and scientists today are still having trouble assigning them reasonably exact dates. We must not, of course, hold it against these men that they destroyed most of the evidence for the science they founded: we can only be sorry that they were lucky enough to discover so many of the greatest prehistoric art treasures. By 1860 or 1870 the conviction had become current that objects showing images of mammoths, reindeer, and wild horses were the work of the people who had lived among them. Within a few years, finds made at Massat, Lourdes, Bruniquel, La Madeleine, Laugerie Basse, and a little later at Brassempouy and Le Mas d'Azil, yielded most of the decorated objects yet discovered. It will be evident later in this book that although this material has been dated approximately sufficient uncertainties remain to hamper research. Ever since, apart from the cave at Isturitz (Basses-Pyrénées, France), such decorated objects and small works of art as have been found have come to light one by one and have been much more accurately dated than the earlier, vastly more extensive finds. Unfortunately, even

[1] *fig. 14*

some of the most recently discovered sites have been scoured as recklessly as those discovered by the pioneers of our science. This means that the number of all-but-undatable finds has continued to mount, so that even today we are left with comparatively few chronological guideposts. This accounts to a great extent for our continuing troubles in establishing the chronology of prehistoric art.

² fig. 15

It was quite some time before the works of art on the cave walls were recognized as genuinely prehistoric. Every writer on the subject recounts what happened after Señor Marcelino de Sautuola explored the cave of Altamira² (Santander, Spain) in 1879. His five-year-old daughter, not as interested as her father was in the clay layers full of flints on the floor of the cave, noticed that there were animals painted on the ceiling. When De Sautuola suggested to the scientific world that these frescoes must go back to very ancient times, he was met with total disbelief. The same specialists who were willing to recognize bison incised on bones from the Lozère and the Pyrenees utterly refused to recognize the bison painted on the ceiling at Altamira as anything more than some stray cowherd's scrawls—if they were not outright forgeries. However, more and more such finds were made: between 1883 and 1901, between the Rhone and the Atlantic alone, hundreds of works of art in caves came to light—at the Chabot cave, Pair-non-Pair, La Mouthe, Marsoulas, Les Combarelles, Font-de-Gaume—and gradually the scientific world was completely won over. It was about this time that the Abbé Breuil's great career was launched, and until his death in 1961 it was he who documented and published the great majority of these finds. His perspicacity, technical skill, and conscientiousness are attested by the fact that most of them (frequently very hard to decipher) are even today known to the world solely through his drawings. The discovery of Lascaux (Dordogne, France) in 1940 for the first time gave ready access to a monumental collection which could be easily photographed; it has been since then that the world at large has become especially aware of prehistoric art.

PREHISTORIC ART, PALEOLITHIC ART

THE term "prehistoric art" is extremely vague. Prehistory begins with the earliest trace of man-made objects and ends at different periods in different regions of our globe—c. 3,000 B.C. in the eastern Mediterranean, and in the nineteenth century for the Eskimos. If a geological or climatic definition is adopted, prehistory—so far as the period presenting evidences of artistic activity is concerned—encompasses the end of the last glacial age and the beginning of the present climatic cycle. It is known with certainty that the gap between the last ice age and the temperate period corresponds to a gap in many areas of human activity, and in particular to the disappearance of cave art. From the point of view of tool-making, we distinguish, in the ages preceding the present climatic cycle, several stages of technical evolution; the totality of these stages is called the Paleolithic period, which was followed by the periods we designate as the Mesolithic and the Neolithic. Consequently, the part of prehistoric art dated roughly before 8,000 B.C. is Paleolithic. Since this book is intended to treat only the beginning of art, it is confined to Paleolithic art.

In what parts of the world do we find an art that can be reliably assigned to the Paleolithic Age? So far nothing of the kind has been discovered in America or Oceania. In Asia only one site has been found, near Lake Baikal, which has supplied a few decorated objects. This leaves Africa and Europe. In Africa thousands of prehistoric frescoes and engravings on rocks have been discovered, but the art objects are few. From the Atlas to the Hoggar, from the Hoggar to the Sudan, in Rhodesia, and in present-day South Africa, we find on walls of rock shelters fascinating processions of elephants, giraffes, hunters, and dancers. Are the earliest of these works Paleolithic in the sense here defined? Probably, but the whole matter has yet to be determined ac-

How the large black and red bison

on the Altamira ceiling

must have looked

to little Maria de Sautuola in 1879.

15   ALTAMIRA

The bison crowded together
on the Painted Ceiling are shown standing,
lying, or rolling in the dust.
Their movements are rendered
very realistically. The outlines
are drawn in black manganese;
within these, flat areas of graduated
red ocher are applied,
except to the limbs.

curately; we can speak with certainty of African prehistoric art, but only by hypothesis can we attribute any of it to the Paleolithic Age.

May we conclude, then, that Europe possesses the only art that is more than ten thousand years old? That Europe possesses such art is unquestionable, but that Europe alone possesses it remains subject to future discoveries. However, surveying all we have learned about the prehistory of the Mediterranean basin, we find that prehistoric western European art forms a coherent whole, with one center in southern France and another in northern (Cantabrian) Spain, and with border regions where the evidences are more scattered and marginal in character. There have been finds in Belgium, Germany, central Europe, Russia, and Italy, but these are few and far between, suggesting that these areas were frontier regions. A Paleolithic art may well be discovered some day in the Near East, China, Siberia, or Africa, but the only one we possess so far is the one that was centered in western Europe.

It could be claimed—and with a high degree of probability—that there were other major centers of Paleolithic art of which we may never know anything for purely material reasons. Most of the works of art produced by living primitive peoples and kept today in ethnographic museums are executed in wood, skins, feathers, and fabrics, none of which can survive extended or severe weathering. Except in advanced cultures, decorated objects in bone, ivory, or stone are relatively few in number and, for the most part, small in size. Two physical circumstances account for the fact that the Paleolithic art of the Franco-Cantabrian region has come down to us in some quantity: first, the decorated objects are fashioned from fragments of bone or soft stone; second, and more important, some of the works were stored in caves. As will become evident, Paleolithic man seems to have been under the sway of a complicated religious system which induced him to decorate his implements and the walls of his caves with symbolic figures, sometimes realistic, sometimes abstract to an astonishing degree. We may call attention here to the Australian aborigines, whose ritual practices are of a complexity that has engrossed ethnologists for the last sixty years: their arts consist of drawings in sand, feather ornaments, and a repertory of theatrical gestures, none of which leaves the slightest archaeological trace. Franco-Cantabrian Paleolithic people also must have expended an important part of their creative activity on perishable works. There is good reason to suppose that what has come down to us is the merest shadow of their actual achievement, for we find dozens of palettes for grinding ocher colors in places where there are no wall paintings, and at the strata where artifacts have been excavated Paleolithic ocher is found in fifty-pound deposits. Before embarking on an inventory of what has actually come down to us, we may in our mind's eye summon up admirably painted skins of horses or bison, marvelous wood sculptures, and dancing and singing people, their bodies painted with intricate designs in black, red, and white—all the panoply and vivacity of the great Magdalenian rituals, the major part of which must remain forever unknown. Not even the severest scientific criticism can frown upon such use of our imagination; after all, we know with certainty that these people possessed skins (zoologists tell us from just which animals), wood (studies of fossil pollen tell us the exact species), black pigment (manganese) and a variety of reds (iron oxides), and we also know that they had a complex religious system. Prehistory supplies just enough evidence to encourage such speculation, but even as we let ourselves go in these imaginative exercises, we are brought up short. The science of prehistory is extremely well equipped when it comes to providing certain details, such as in what direction the ocher was rubbed over the palette, but it can tell us nothing about what happened when the hand was raised to apply it. All the rest, if we assume that it existed, must be deduced from a patchwork of data gleaned from study of the aboriginal Australians, the Ainus, and the Amerindians. If we are to be perfectly truthful, we must confine ourselves to the surviving evidence and let it tell us what it can in fragments which are often incoherent.

Prehistoric art is thus no more than a remembered impression barely supported by a few hundred finds, the tiny remnant of a vanished whole, which happen to have come down to us because these objects were less perishable than the rest. Indeed, western Paleolithic art owes its survival to a combination of circumstances which may not have been present anywhere else.

Those who see primitive society as made up of widely separated wandering hordes tirelessly pursuing their quarry over vast empty reaches of tundra are due for a surprise. In western Europe, at least, where numerous geographical obstacles served to cut off regions one from another, stable traditions over many thousands of years led to the maturing of a symbolism absolutely continuous in development from the earliest artistic manifestations down to the end of the Magdalenian period. This continuity is all the more striking because the material equipment of the prehistoric cultures was periodically altered: this is what the scholarly division of prehistory into periods— Chatelperronian, Aurignacian, Gravettian, Solutrean, Magdalenian—brings to our attention. These divisions now and again give rise to popular notions of successive waves of prehistoric peoples appearing out of nowhere, sweeping away their predecessors, and triumphantly introducing a new civilization. However attractive to the imagination, this conception of repeated racial upheavals is probably without foundation in reality. It is as though some archaeologist of the future, attempting to make sense of our history in a dramatic manner, were to formulate the following chronological sequence: Age of the Bow, Age of the Crossbow, Age of the Musket, Age of the Rifle, Age of the Intercontinental Ballistic Missile, and so on. He would thereby call attention to successive changes in our military equipment, but meanwhile he would distract attention from the actual continuity of our languages and religious traditions over the same period. We must keep in mind the similar character of the divisions of prehistory. "Aurignacian" does not indicate a racial or ethnic type of man, or a language, but primarily a type of spear. Beneath the surface of sharp chronological divisions such as this, which are derived from technology (mostly from hunting techniques), everything else of which we now have evidence testifies to a continuity comparable to that linking twentieth-century western Europeans with their Merovingian ancestors. Moreover, the clearest evidence for this continuity is supplied by art. Attempts are still being made to discover a typically Solutrean or typically Magdalenian art, but in fact Paleolithic works follow one another in imperceptible gradations that submerge the technologists' divisions. The first thesis that we shall defend here is that the evolution of European Paleolithic art is homogeneous and continuous and that it implies the cultural continuity and homogeneity of the human groups that produced it. One or another type of weapon may have come in from the east or the south and been enthusiastically adopted while the thread of the religious traditions upon which artistic traditions were founded remained unbroken.

MOTIVES FOR THE CREATION OF ART

ART is not unrelated to the rest of life, and it is proper to ask why the men who hunted the mammoth also produced paintings and sculptures. Images captivate the curious in two ways: by the beauty they contain, and by the ideas they perpetuate. When we are dealing with the classical civilizations, whose modes of thinking are supposed to be familiar to those who admire the beauty of the forms in their art, we can for most purposes ignore the second. Not so where the art of prehistory is concerned.

Just as African art is sometimes judged from the point of view of modern French art, and the qualities discovered in it are not what were put there but what we are looking for, so some prehistorians, especially in the heroic age of their science, created a Magdalenian mentality very much like the mentality of a nineteenth-century urban middle-class man dressed up as a bison hunter. Between 1880 and the beginning of the twentieth century, when Gabriel de Mortillet, Émile Cartailhac, and Édouard Piette revealed the existence of engravings on reindeer antlers and on ivory, the prevailing ideas on "primitive man" were based on the implicit assumption that of course he had no religion. Having only just developed from the ape, he had not as yet (according to some) had time to attain sufficient moral maturity, or (according to others) to have become bogged down in superstition. Today we know that a good many millennia separate the Lascaux man from the epic age when monkeys learned to stand erect; chronologically speaking, the mere fifteen thousand years that separate Lascaux men from ourselves make them part of our own epoch. But the engravings of horses and reindeer had to be accounted for somehow, and the explanation chosen was the most harmless and also the poorest—that of art for art's sake.

The attitude of these pioneers in prehistory reflects a long philosophical tradition; though this attitude lasted no more than a few years, it bequeathed to scientific folklore (in no field richer than in prehistory) a certain number of clichés. Some of these clichés still persist—especially those of prehistoric "art schools," "sketchbooks," the circulation of models, and artists peddling effigies of bison. These legends were not elaborated without reference to established fact. The discovery at Limeuil (Dordogne, France) of a considerable number of limestone slabs showing admirably incised animal figures[3] whose legs or heads are often similar in outline suggested the idea of a Stone Age Montparnasse studio, where student drawings of the legs of an ibex or of the horns of an ox were corrected by the teacher. This notion might have been further corroborated by other findings: stones of various sizes that are incised with animals overlapping in no apparent order, piled up over one another to the point of illegibility, are extremely common. These might have been a sort of equivalent to "pages" of "sketchbooks," in which artists make quick on-the-spot notations. Yet the actual truth concerning both sorts of find seems very different today, and the question of engraved stones is treated at greater length later. Even the hypothesis that models were circulated was based on historical evidence: the fact that the small incised stone discovered at La Genière (Ain, France) shows a bison very closely resembling one of the bison painted on the walls of Font-de-Gaume (Dordogne). It would be more accurate, however, to say that it closely resembles one of the paintings of bison reproduced in the Abbé Breuil's book on Font-de-Gaume, and that some practical joker went to the trouble of copying it onto the small stone with the help of a good modern steel burin before he led the explorer to stumble upon this particular "find."

All the same, there is a real problem concerning the circulation of artistic traditions in Paleolithic times, and I shall have occasion to come back to the matter later on. In brief, the problem has two aspects. The first can be treated on the basis of what we know of recent or present-day primitive art: for instance, the Eskimos exhibit the same traditions in the representation of figures over many thousands of miles, but they never had a "school" or professional sculptors traveling over the Arctic wastes disseminating models. What did circulate among them were stories of hunters' exploits that had common interest and practical concern to all, and served to provide a common fund of representational themes. This was sufficient, as it was in the Paleolithic era, to give an underlying unity to what in fact amount to innumerable local variations. The second aspect of the problem of circulation of models is purely archaeological. It is physically impossible to decide whether two paintings side by side in the same cave are by the same hand. When we analyze the lines that render the horse or the bison, we find everywhere the same fundamental features, and these are of a common ethnic tradition, not an individual one. By contrast, there are no two caves in which we receive exactly the same impressions: this figure is from Font-de-Gaume, that one from Niaux, and—apart from that all-too-famous La Genière bison—we never encounter two identical images. When you come to think of it, it is very unlikely that two all-but-identical drawings will ever turn up. Approximately one hundred decorated caves is all we have, representing a time span of nearly fifteen thousand years: even supposing that masters in the art of painting bison hired themselves out, the odds that two works by the same artist will ever be discovered (even in caves only a few miles apart) are almost zero. Although it is certain that forms of representation were handed down from generation

[3] figs. 28, 85, 475–477

to generation, and incontestable that styles did circulate, the theory of "schools" is unprovable.

Attempts to explain prehistoric art on the basis of aesthetic feelings devoid of religious foundation eventually gave way to new explanatory systems. In her important work, *The Meaning of Paleolithic Art*, Mme. Laming-Emperaire pointed out that as early as 1865 the English anthropologist A. Taylor had touched upon the subject of affinities between prehistoric art and magic. This insight, however, had passed unnoticed until 1903, when Salomon Reinach, in his *Art and Magic*, formulated the problem in terms that are still generally accepted. Beginning with the Abbé Breuil, all prehistorians down to our own day have followed Reinach's lead.

It would be only too easy to criticize those who at the beginning of this century set out to construct a prehistoric man patched together from Australian, Eskimo, and Lapp components; it would also be most unfair. The scientific mind can build only on known facts: to be allowed to head the list of primitive peoples, Cro-Magnon man had first to submit his biography. He supplied us with chipped flints, ivory spears, and reindeer bones by the thousands, and with incised images of animals by the hundreds; he did not think of supplying us with so much as a hint as to the purpose these served. So ethnography was called upon to supply the living context which these surviving evidences presume. To the Abbé Breuil goes most of the credit for having tirelessly explored the primitive world known to his own day in search of data capable of restoring some sort of life, however artificially, to prehistoric man. We are indebted to him for nearly everything we have learned about Paleolithic art, as well as for the major part of the efforts yet made to explain it. Once restored to life, prehistoric man inevitably found his way into literature, and the composite image has taken on the status of historical reality. A new folklore about our ancestors was brought into being, though the earlier one involving "art schools" and "sketchbooks" did not entirely die out. Stone Age man, as restored by Breuil, has the merit of plausibility, at least. We see him as a hunter going down into a cave to paint a wounded bison on the walls—incontestable evidence of sympathetic magic. We see him painting signs, more or less geometric, which are interpreted by some as portrayals of his own dwellings, by others as animal snares or dwelling places of spirits. We see him reproducing the image of pregnant mares in order to secure the fertility of the game he hunts. We see him dancing, wearing a horned mask and a horse's tail, which implies the existence of imitative magic and incantations. We see him leading terrified youths down into the cave in order to show them his work, which implies the existence of a system of initiation. It is impossible to say how much of all this is fiction. Most of these hypotheses are reasonable; each is based on physical evidence that may constitute proof. The picture as a whole is even unassailable in the sense that almost nothing has been added to it over the past half-century. The ethnography of prehistory has withdrawn from the field, at least temporarily, to rest upon its hard-won half-certainties.

This creation of a living, intelligible prehistoric mankind marks a crucial stage; today, however, we may raise one methodological objection. To take what is known about prehistory and cast about for parallels in the life of present-day peoples does not throw light on the behavior of prehistoric man. All that is proved in this way—and this is not to belittle its importance—is that the behavior ascribable to prehistoric man falls within the same general patterns as the behavior of recent man; in other words, prehistoric man's behavior was human in the present-day sense. There really are Paleolithic bison marked with wounds, as today there are dolls stuck with pins for magic purposes; but when we count up the images of bison, we find fewer than 15 percent marked with wounds or with weapons sticking in them. What, then, was the purpose of the remaining 85 percent? To be sure, there are three or four instances of geometric signs placed over animals, and these may represent snares, but there are also hundreds of signs which are not placed over animals: where then is the proof that the Magdalenians practiced sympathetic magic? We shall see later what we are to make of images of "pregnant" animals. (Many stallions portrayed by Chinese painters are just as "pregnant" as the Magdalenian horses.) All our conjectures concerning the initiation of young hunters are based upon the existence of narrow heel prints near the modeled bison at Le Tuc d'Audoubert. The existence of initiation rites in the Paleolithic Age is by no means out of the question, but we do not appear to have found a really scientific means of proving it by the comparative method, at least not yet. All that the comparative method can do is to tell us that initiation rites exist among many peoples of the world today, and that consequently prehistoric man may also have had them; it cannot go further than that.

Through what means can we hope to grasp more than a shadow of the inner life of the Australian aborigines and the Eskimos, or, for that matter, of that of some witch still casting her spells deep in the European countryside? Can we perhaps try to question prehistoric man directly? It is hard for us to question the dead without putting our own answers in their mouths, except by using a procedure which makes a strict distinction between the historical evidence and our own explanatory hypotheses.

METHODOLOGY

ALTHOUGH this book is by its very nature intended as an introduction to Paleolithic art, it is so untraditional in its handling of crucial matters that some statement as to the methods employed is called for. Moreover, such a statement may help to show why so many artistic aspects of Paleolithic life have to be taken into account if a coherent prehistory of art is to be arrived at without recourse to historical parallels.

The fundamental condition of our investigation has been to make use, not of selected examples, but of all extant data, or at least of a sampling large enough to provide us with a sound quantitative basis. So far as cave art is concerned, I have exhaustively studied on the spot sixty-six of the approximately one hundred known caves and rock shelters; the rest are familiar to me through the archaeological literature. As for the decorated objects, it is impossible for anyone to make within normal time limits a complete inventory; a large number of objects are in private collections, some of these even clandestine, and except for the hundreds of objects I have studied in museums and special collections, I have had to make use of the scholarly publications.

Two practical problems are presented: the dating of cave works and of decorated objects, and the investigation of the possible relationships of historical evidence among them. It was necessary, for instance, to determine in what periods the reindeer appears and disappears in Paleolithic art, and the relative frequency with which this animal turns up on objects and on cave walls; it was also necessary to take note of the instances in which the reindeer is associated with representations of fish, the types of object on which it appears and does not appear, and the systematic or occasional character of its position at cave entrances and inside caves; further, it was necessary to test every hypothesis that this sort of investigation produced. The only suitable tool for this sort of factual survey and analysis is the punch-card tabulator and sorter, which facilitates the handling of large quantities of evidence and at the same time assures the objectivity of the dialogue between the latter-day scholar and the prehistoric artist. Without recourse to materials other than Paleolithic, questions can be addressed to the dead informant: he is of course mechanically limited in his replies by what has actually survived of his creations, but these replies are at least expressed in his own language, and not in the accents of nineteenth-century Tierra del Fuego or the contemporary Sudan.

The thorniest problem has been that of dating the works. Like all other aspects of our work, this has demanded the utmost honesty possible, including a refusal to accept traditional approaches when the evidence does not support them. Thus, we have become involved in a thorough-going revision of the whole subject of chronology, not just where individual works of art are concerned, but also in the matter of the historical evidence upon which dating is normally based—that is, the implements discovered at the site. Our results in this connection are perhaps more disappointing than might have been expected. Prehistoric man can tell us very accurately just how many bison he portrayed for every ibex, but he cannot tell us just when and in what order he portrayed them—at least not if the archaeologist who made the find failed to record the sequence of deposits or blithely mixed up the strata of different periods. In such cases, the incoherent message which the machine produces by sorting our tabulated evidence lets us conclude no more than that for a given site the technique of excavation was rather crude. Not all the early excavators were vandals, but in many cases their finds are usable only for the most cursory sort of dating. A hundred years ago the Marquis de la Vibraye explored the caves at Arcy-sur-Cure and observed three layers, which was remarkable at the time; half a century ago, the Abbé Parat, one of the finest explorers of his generation, observed six layers in some places, seven in others; today we find forty, and if a large part of the deposits had not disappeared, the total would probably be more than seventy.

If only, even for a dozen or two of the major sites containing works of art, we possessed accurate information as to the order of the successive deposits, we could achieve —taking into consideration that we are dealing here with material accumulated over many millennia—a degree of accuracy comparable to that of the historian of the Middle Ages. What prevents our investigation from achieving anything like this is the unreliability of the physical evidence. At the same time, the situation is by no means hopeless. The chronological ladder exists, but climbing it is still a rather risky business: some rungs are missing, and some of those that remain are frighteningly weak.

And yet dating the works has been a major concern. The Abbé Breuil devoted a considerable part of his time and energies to it. He concentrated on the material hardest to date, namely, cave art. A reindeer incised on a small plaque, found in a layer that also yielded hundreds of flints, is often easy to date, but a mammoth painted on a cave wall three feet or more above the ground is cut off from all chronological clues. By a method of cross references, the Abbé Breuil set up a system of dating which enabled him to distribute the cave works over the entire time span of the Upper Paleolithic. This system, which is still the only one we have, was never specifically explained in a study primarily concerned with it and containing all the arguments that might be adduced in its support. It was merely summarized in the preface to *Quatre cents siècles d'art pariétal (Four Hundred Centuries of Cave Art)* ; and as the theory was built up very gradually over a full half-century, it is sometimes hard to locate all Breuil's arguments for arranging the styles in a particular chronological sequence.

The method adopted here is different, in the sense that I have first of all tried to determine which cave works and decorated objects are dated beyond all possible dispute. This enabled me to establish with some degree of accuracy the time span of Paleolithic art (which is probably below previous estimates); to chart the evolution of styles among objects; to integrate the rare verifiable datings of cave art; and, by means of a method of cross-checking style and content, to suggest dates for previously undated cave works which show indisputable affinities with the datable works. A considerable number of works remain which could be fitted into this chronological scheme only with great uncertainty, but at present this is about as far as we can go.

2. KNOWN AND UNKNOWN IN PALEOLITHIC CHRONOLOGY

2. KNOWN AND UNKNOWN IN PALEOLITHIC CHRONOLOGY

THERE is no hope that art works in caves can ever be dated directly: they can be placed in time only by being related to an archaeological context. In a few especially valuable cases, deposits exactly at the foot of the works, or covering them partly or entirely, provide just such a context. The early Solutrean and Magdalenian sculptors sometimes executed their low reliefs in their own living quarters, on the back wall of the rock overhang of cave entrance or shelter. Those of their contemporaries who painted on walls situated deep inside the caves, however, made our task of dating their works extremely difficult by choosing spots remote from ordinary habitation for their sanctuaries. Thus cave art must, at least provisionally, be discussed separately: works in this category which we can date with certainty are not numerous enough to provide us with a chronological pattern. It is not deep inside the caves that we witness the birth of art, but at the entrances, in the piles of refuse conveniently (for our purposes) left behind by people who did not confine their artistic activity to decorating the dripping ceilings of the back chambers.

When he is inside his own home and treated with suitable deference, Paleolithic man speaks readily; we would know a great deal about him had only as few as ten dwelling sites been explored solely with a view to understanding the life of these people rather than with that of recovering their implements in the order they were "laid down" over the centuries. The latter is an operation that can be performed anywhere by digging vertically, as on a quarry face. If five sites containing works of art had been completely explored, the people who made engravings on stone would have disclosed a considerable part of their history. The only irreparable misfortune is that prehistoric sites were and still are excavated by persons without sufficient training and without the proper equipment, who practice research into prehistory as though it were a sport or a game.

GENEALOGY OF THE ARTISTS

To be complete, our story must begin before the appearance of the first engraved animal, for the most remarkable thing about the artistic career of the mammoth hunters is that we probably possess evidence of every stage in their development toward the mastery of form.

Acquiring artistic modes of thought, and above all that very specialized language which is the transcribing of forms in nature, did not happen overnight, by some especially gifted primitive's suddenly finding himself inspired one day to draw a rhinoceros on a rock and then teaching his children how to do it. Several millennia elapsed between the appearance of the first signs of aesthetic interest and the first known works of art as such.

According to one simplified view, which is no longer shared by specialists but still frequently appears in writings on the subject for the general reader, the close of the Paleolithic Age saw the decline of the Neanderthal people, who had been the carriers of the Mousterian culture, and the advent of modern man (embodied in the Cro-Magnon type). This new people brought with them the Aurignacian culture and the first manifestations of art. Whether explicitly or not, the transition from one human species to another was visualized as a tremendous upheaval, in the course of which Neanderthal man, still stooping, hairy, his eyes staring vacantly from under enormous superciliary ridges, was gradually driven out and superseded by a brilliant intruder who was taller and whose eyes sparkled with intelligence under a harmoniously curved forehead. The brutes still incompletely weaned from the original monkey were succeeded by present-day man, Homo sapiens, and art made its appearance. Today the facts appear to have been very different, and it is necessary to expound them at some length, particularly in order to introduce terms which often recur later.

At the beginning of the last relatively cold period which preceded the present-day climates, Neanderthal men had existed several tens of thousands of years. They were a very late product of human evolution, divided into several races, all of which are characterized to a more or less pronounced degree by low foreheads, deep eye sockets, and the coarse facial features with which we are familiar from reconstructions. Their culture, already remarkable for the diversity of its techniques, included the manufacture of flint implements, the real beginning of human industry. A considerably warmer period, which set in between forty thousand and sixty thousand years ago, marked in France the apogee of this Mousterian culture; during that time the earliest known fragments of red ocher made their appearance. Still very few and far between, these modest remnants of coloring matter are of major importance in human history because they push back the problem of the appearance of art to an epoch preceding our own. Nothing is known about how this ocher was used. At La Ferrassie (Dordogne), where ocher was first found, Denis Peyrony also discovered a limestone slab on which a few little cup-marks the size of a finger had been hollowed out. The first finds that were made in Late Paleolithic dwellings—several thousand years after the Mousterian culture—were again of ocher and stones with cup-marks.

During the last phase of the warm period important changes took place in implements, not because new implements replaced the old, but because the Mousterian forms evolved. This so-called post-Mousterian period is still little known, but its importance is apparent even now, because it is truly transitional between the Mousterian period and what is still called roughly the Aurignacian. The first bone implements make their appearance then. At Arcy-sur-Cure (Yonne), I discovered a number of odd objects picked up by the inhabitants of the Cave of the Hyena in the course of their wanderings. These include a thick spiraled shell of a fossil mollusk of the Mesozoic or Secondary era, a ball-shaped cluster of coral of the same epoch, and oddly shaped blocks of iron pyrites. They are not works of art, but the fact that natural forms were noticed by our zoological predecessors points to a degree of aesthetic interest. This is all the more striking because no interruption is perceptible in the subsequent ages: down to the Magdalenian period the artists continued to display bric-a-brac in their outdoor museums—blocks of pyrites, fossil shells, crystals of quartz and galena. There must surely be some connection between religion and this collecting of unusual objects, but if this is so the aesthetic implications are not thereby weakened, for natural and man-made forms are found side by side in the same religious setting, from the frescoes of Lascaux to the small pendants fashioned from fossils.

Thus, before Homo sapiens had taken his first steps, the range of what might be called "pre-artistic manifestations" is complete—ocher, cup-marks, and unusual natural forms permit us to put at least a faint halo around the flat skull of Neanderthal man. But are we still dealing with Neanderthal man? Perhaps this was the work of Homo sapiens, his successor? In actual fact, a gap of at least ten thousand years separates the latest of the known Neanderthal men from the earliest Homo sapiens; nothing is known about post-Mousterian man, and very little about man at the beginning of the Upper Paleolithic. The conflict between the two species of man went on for a long time, and future discoveries may show a development of physical types as uninterrupted as the aesthetic manifestations we are in process of uncovering. However that may be, Mousterian and post-Mousterian art have little in common—qualitatively or quantitatively—with the subsequent developments.

The next stage takes us to about 35,000 B.C. and corresponds to the Chatelperronian period (which is Breuil's Early Aurignacian and Peyrony's Lower Perigordian). Almost nothing is changed in the inventories of small objects—the post-Mousterians already had chipped flints, narrow knives with thick backs, small "scraping tools," bone awls, and ocher—but everything differs in quality, style, and variety. There is a profusion of bone and ivory objects, and ocher was transported by the hundreds of pounds. From the outset, the mastery of coloring stuffs is amazing: hard hematites, ferruginous clays, and crumbly red sandstone, the materials raw or baked in every tint from yellow ocher to dark violet, to which is now added the black dioxide of manganese. As yet no work of art containing figures has made its appearance, but a new step forward is made: we find many objects of personal adornment—bone fragments and teeth of foxes, bears, and deer fashioned to serve as pendants. The objects of greatest interest from our point of view are the engraved bone fragments. Arcy-sur-Cure—the site where the post-Mousterian and the Chatelperronian are best known—has yielded one thigh bone of a mammoth, cut off at both ends, and marked in the middle by three sets of parallel lines. Also, bone fragments with regularly spaced parallel incisions on the edge have been discovered. These last-named objects date from the later stages of the Upper Paleolithic and were long ago named "*marques de chasse*," "hunting tallies." Needless to say, nothing has been discovered to support this designation: the idea of the hunter conscientiously making a notch on his small stick every time he brought down a mammoth is more entertaining than plausible. Whatever the purpose of these objects, their occurrence throughout the Upper Paleolithic is a remarkable phenomenon —the earliest representation we have of a rhythmic arrangement with regular intervals, the beginning of the evolution that led to the ruler, the musical staff, the calendar, and the peristyle of the temple. The span of the Chatelperronian extends probably over several millennia, corresponding to the theoretical epoch of transition between the Mousterian culture of Neanderthal man and the cultures directly assigned to present-day man.

The earliest of these latter cultures is the Aurignacian proper (Breuil's Middle Aurignacian, Peyrony's Aurignacian I and II), defined by various types of implements characteristic of it, particularly lance points split at the base, from Aurignacian I, and those in the shape of a rather flat lozenge, from Aurignacian II.[1] So far as our subject is concerned, there is little to add. The use of ocher is particularly intensive: it is not unusual to find a layer of the cave floor impregnated with purplish red to a depth of eight inches. The size of these ocher deposits raises a problem not yet solved. The coloring is so intense that practically all the loose ground seems to consist of ocher. One can imagine that with it the Aurignacians regularly painted their bodies red, dyed their animal skins, coated their weapons, and sprinkled the ground of their dwellings, and that a paste of ocher was used for decorative purposes in every other phase of their domestic life. We must assume no less, if we are to account for the veritable mines of ocher on which some of them lived, without using it all up in the course of several centuries. It is certain that there were whole caves painted red: Dr. J. Allain discovered a small Magdalenian dwelling cave (at Saint-Marcel, Indre), the ceilings of which were coated with paint. It is also certain that they attached a religious meaning to ocher: the fact that has most impressed prehistorians is that they buried their dead in beds of ocher. We are less certain concerning other practices, but in 1958 we found at Arcy-sur-Cure, in a layer without ocher of the terminal Chatelperronian period, eight deposits, each consisting of several fragments of new and worn flints which had been encased in balls of ocher paste and placed on the ground (in places where ocher is uniformly distributed, it is hard to discover such evidences). Consequently, ocher served purposes other than painting. To return to the Aurignacians, their artistic equipment was not very different from that of their predecessors the Chatelperronians—ocher, manganese, fossils, unusual stones, pendants made of teeth or small disk-shaped bone fragments, and bones with regular incisions. Other elements make their appearance, as it were, more diffidently: there are a few awls

[1] *chart* VIII

16-22   SPEARS

*These provide our best clock for dating
the upper Paleolithic. The ones shown
here are of different periods, from
Aurignacian (second from right) to Late
Magdalenian (extreme left). Often carved
from the beam of the reindeer antler,
they were straightened while fresh,
but with time have resumed
their original curvature.*

decorated with lines forming a frieze of crosses or triangles. Thus, very slowly, over the millennia, the range of artistic manifestations increases, and the abstract decoration of objects makes its appearance.

According to the only incontestable evidence we as yet have, the appearance of the first unmistakable figures[2] may be assigned to Aurignacian I and II. The testimony is the more valuable because, as will be seen later, the features they present already hold in nucleus the entire subsequent symbolic range of Franco-Cantabrian art—animal figures in juxtaposition with sexual symbols.

[2] figs. 23, 249–255

This was the great moment when figurative art was born and began gradually to be differentiated from scribbles; these no doubt also had a figurative value, but they still depended upon the word, which gestures merely stressed or endowed with rhythm without transcribing it. Throughout animal evolution, especially that of the higher species, the motor nervous system of the face and that of the hand are closely coordinated —a coordination indispensable for feeding. In the case of man, this coordination attains a higher degree, that of verbal expression; the facial muscles are so organized that both sign language and articulate language become possible. The links between language and the hand remain close, and down to our own day gestures unconsciously accompany words. But the gesture does not rise to the height of language until it becomes drawing and writing: then thought can avail itself of two vectors, the facial organs and the hand; it rediscovers, in a sublimated form, the initial biological balance. Man certainly acquired language long before the Upper Paleolithic period, but the development of verbal tools most likely went hand in hand with the increased capacity for abstract thinking and the beginnings of graphic skills. We have indirect proof of this from the end of the Mousterian period onward, when the objects and the outer aspect of dwellings begin to arouse our awareness of living man, when coloring stuffs, objects of personal adornment, and rhythmic lines make their appearance. By the end of the Aurignacian, our impression of being close to fellow human beings is complete, and what we discover of the life of the cave dwellers is no more strange or puzzling than what we learn of still-living primitive peoples.

Two elements for the beginning of Western art are still missing: those of exact time and place. Archaeological dating of the earliest works is sufficiently precise: both at Isturitz and in the Dordogne, the characteristic decorated objects are spears split at the base (Aurignacian I) and lozenge-shaped spears (Aurignacian II). We can pin down the median date of the Aurignacian at about 30,000 B.C. The question of place raises a further problem, one which is unsolvable for the time being. Did the Aurignacians, from the Dordogne to the Pyrenees, invent figurative art when they incised stone slabs, or had they received it from elsewhere? Some day Paleolithic mankind may be discovered in other parts of the world who had already made animal drawings thousands of years before our own Paleolithic works. At present, the dates are too imprecise to hope to establish any priority based on a few thousand years; on the other hand, we do not know of works of art from other parts of the world that are approximately contemporaneous with ours. Finally, the emergence of figurative works was prepared by a very long evolution which is known to have been synchronic over a large part of Europe; there is reason to believe that the Franco-Cantabrian works made their appearance in a milieu that had attained the requisite maturity, and that the same phenomenon could have occurred at about the same time anywhere within the Aurignacian area.

EARLIEST DEVELOPMENTS

Down to the beginning of the twentieth century prehistorians divided the Late Paleolithic into two periods, the Solutrean and the Magdalenian; the names derive from two major sites, Solutré (Saône-et-Loire) and La Madeleine (Dordogne). At the

3 chart I

Congress of Monaco in 1906 the Abbé Breuil demonstrated that the Solutrean was preceded by cultures which were improperly lumped together in Magdalenian, and he reintroduced the term Aurignacian[3] (derived from the site of Aurignac in the Haute-Garonne). Since then, Breuil's Aurignacian has turned out to be a long sequence of different cultures, and he himself divided it into three periods: the Lower, Middle, and Upper Aurignacian. On the basis of detailed study of these cultures, Denis Peyrony concluded that they represented two major contemporaneous currents—the Perigordian and the Aurignacian proper. In the effort toward ever-greater accuracy, several prehistorians noticed that the Perigordians had almost nothing in common but the use of a knife with a thick back, and it became customary to divide (as we do here) the earlier part of the Upper Paleolithic into the Chatelperronian, the Aurignacian, and the Gravettian; in this way linguistic confusions are avoided, and we can distinguish three cultural groups which really are distinct. The Chatelperronian was still imbued with Mousterian traditions; the Gravettian was already caught up in the terminal stage of the Upper Paleolithic; between these two, the Aurignacian period plays somewhat the role of a hinge. It was precisely during this time of transition that the first definite figures made their appearance.

However, the term "different cultures" must be taken in a relative sense. Chronology is based upon technological innovations, and, like us, Paleolithic men were eager to adopt whatever made their life easier—a new model of spear, for example. Would we claim to be of a different race from our great-grandparents because we have supplanted the horse-drawn carriage with the automobile? We still use their furniture; their music and painting still have many admirers; their literature is very much our own. Nothing obliges us to suppose that Paleolithic men were different from us in this

4 figs. 16–22

respect. Although they changed their spears throughout their history[4]—a fact that is very useful to us for dating purposes—many other objects survived for a very long time, cutting across our chronological divisions. In their religious and aesthetic traditions, continuity is even more apparent: a single ascending curve describes the whole of the Upper Paleolithic, and its articulations do not always coincide with the divisions prehistorians have introduced. The latter have perhaps been insufficiently aware of the fact that cultural anthropology, which supplied us with detailed comparative data for the study of prehistoric man, has also made it possible to look upon prehistoric society as a living society wherein the evolution of technological skills did not necessarily

5 chart II

proceed at the same pace as the evolution of art and religion.[5]

From Aurignacian II onward, works of art are very slow to develop. The Gravettian covers a long time span, probably about ten thousand years. Barely a beginning has been made toward subdividing it: terminology is still chaotic (Gravettian; Perigordian III, IV, V; Proto-Magdalenian; Aurignacian V). Few works from this period

6 fig. 254

are known, but some slabs have been found at La Ferrassie,[6] where Aurignacian traditions lingered on for a long time. These stones are scarcely less crude than those of the preceding period.

Consequently our collection of the earliest works is limited; it comprises only representations of vulvas and drawings so rough that they are hard to decipher. These suggest none of the virtuosity of the classical period. Did men, even at this early epoch, create works of art in caves? We shall return to this question later, but we may say here that, although many figures on cave walls are regarded as Aurignacian, it is not settled. For these figures can be dated only on archaeological evidence or on the basis of their style; stratigraphic evidence does not exist for works on the walls of the caves, and the only dated finds are almost without exception those just mentioned. There can be no question of dating the latter on the basis of style: if we attempted this, then any formless drawing, of any epoch, would be presumably Aurignacian. On the other hand, it would be possible to say that the slabs from the Dordogne and the Pyrenees are the work of a few crude and backward sorcerers, and that cave art was already much more evolved in the Gravettian period. However, the evidence of the decorated objects from the period that followed would scarcely confirm such a hypothesis.

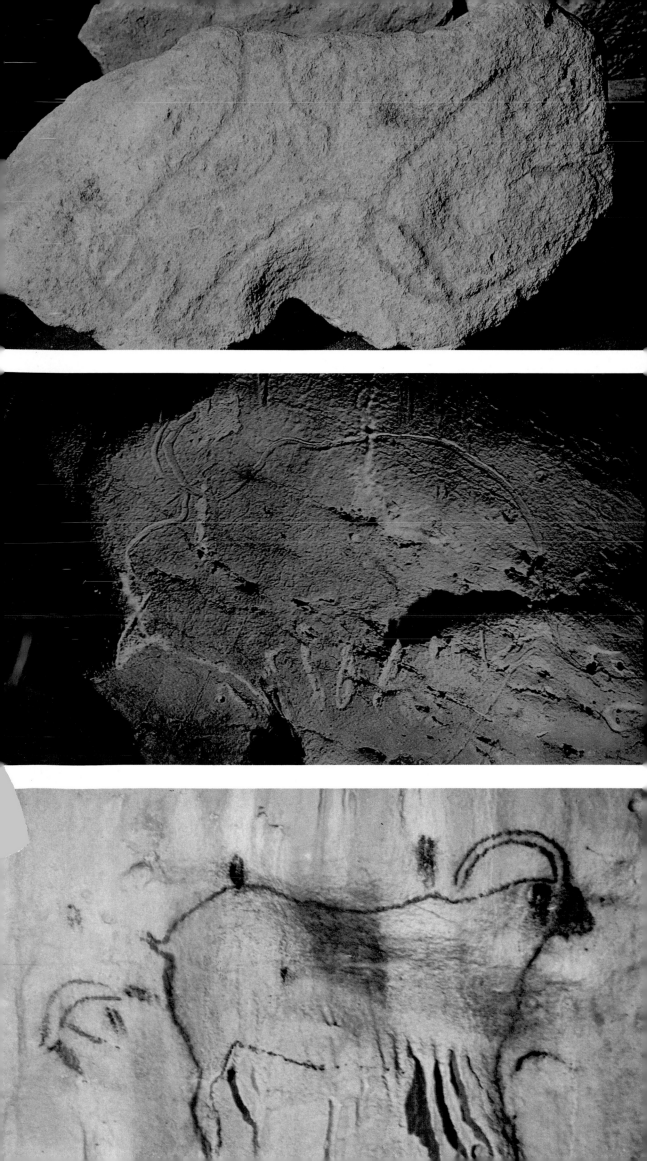

STYLE I

23 ABRI CELLIER
Slab incised with an animal head
and an irregular oval. About 13 in.
The drawing is stiff and the
figures are limited to essentials.

STYLE II

24 GARGAS
Bison drawn with finger on clay.
The cervico-dorsal curve is supplemented
with identifying details—hump,
horns, beard.

STYLE III

25 COUGNAC
Ibex in ocher. At left, the head
of another ibex. Signs in the form
of double strokes around the main figure.
About 30 in. The head and legs
are disproportionately small. Note
the rendering of the horns: in the main
figure, not in perspective;
in the head at left, semifrontal perspective.

The Middle Gravettian (Perigordian IV) is relatively well known; like the mature Gravettian (Perigordian V), it is marked by a cold, dry climate such as later marked the Solutrean and the first part of the Magdalenian. Works dated from the Middle Gravettian are few and remain in the tradition of the preceding periods. Some were found in the cave at Isturitz. These are plaquettes containing tangled outlines, but it is possible to discern identifiable animals, particularly cervids (animals of the deer family).

During the later Gravettian (Perigordian V), figurative art entered a new phase. Decorated objects appear in greater numbers in northern Spain and the Pyrenees and in the Charente. Still related stylistically to the rough sketches of the preceding periods, they show that images have become a permanent feature in the life of the hunters. A few figures deeply incised on blocks foreshadow the low reliefs of the next phase; spears with abstract decorations make their appearance, inaugurating the division of Paleolithic art into two aspects—that of expendable objects with schematic decorations, and that of objects and surfaces with elaborate figures.

Ever since D. Peyrony created the Perigordian, many works of art, especially of cave art, have been attributed to that period—for example, the engravings in the caves of Pair-non-Pair, La Grèze, and Gargas,[7] all of which contain figures of great artistic value. At Gargas, a pebble found in the mature Gravettian shows engravings in a style corresponding to others attributable to the same period from the Dordogne and the Basque region; the figures are in keeping with some of the engravings found in the cave, and Gargas seems to contain a cave group that is reasonably datable among the earliest. Pair-non-Pair probably belongs to the same epoch, judging from the testimony of A. Daleau, who started his exploration of the cave in 1874. The works there are certainly early, and in the same style as the preceding figures. As for Lascaux, despite the line Breuil took on this score, nothing would seem to let us assign the dozens of large figures there—in perfect stylistic agreement with works assigned to a later date—to an epoch for which stratigraphic archaeology supplies us no comparable works.

If, starting with the Aurignacian, we consider the two dozen decorated objects found *in situ* at well-defined age levels, and the few cave figures probably assignable to the period, it is hard to agree with traditional views concerning the existence of a well-developed Aurignacian art and of a Perigordian art skilled in the decoration of large sanctuaries. Rather, the picture to be drawn from these evidences is very coherent: for we find, in going from one incised slab to the next, from period to period, drawings progressively better organized, steadily increasing in number, and a style being created that is homogeneous for all the figures of the terminal stage of the Gravettian. At this point we already encounter cave works stylistically in keeping with the decorated objects—that is to say, still very primitive.

One question at least has been sufficiently elucidated: that of the female statuettes. The term "Aurignacian Venuses" is still in current use—it refers to small ivory or stone statuettes of which about twenty specimens are known. There is no certainty that any of them was found in a stratum as old as the Aurignacian. However, as will be seen later, it is extremely hard to determine the exact age of most of them; their chronological center seems to be located somewhere between the Late Gravettian and the Early Magdalenian—hence, possibly, in the period we have just quickly surveyed, and in the periods to be discussed next.

[7] *Cf. pp. 304–308*

MATURITY

THE period that follows falls approximately between 20,000 and 15,000 B.C.; it is marked by the development of the Solutrean cultures. The object characteristic of these cultures is a flint point, oval in shape and admirably chipped on both faces, which has been given the name "laurel leaf." Solutrean culture has especially lent itself to the learned game of plotting hypothetical migrations of peoples. Its laurel-leaf points turn up unexpectedly between the Gravettian and the Magdalenian, after a still obscure period (the terminal Aurignacian, Peyrony's proto-Magdalenian, the proto-Solutrean), and disappear so suddenly that one is almost compelled to view them as evidence of an invasion. Some think this invasion came from the east, others from the southwest; still others regard Africa or even Saône-et-Loire as the center from which this type of point spread. The laurel-leaf point certainly made its appearance at some particular moment, but this moment may be difficult to determine. What we actually see in France and in other European countries are oval points, at first only slightly chipped on one side, later chipped on both sides; they gradually get bigger and longer, and finally they disappear. Unless one assumes repeated waves of invaders, each eager to display its model of a new and more effective tool, one is inclined to infer a progressive general development of a manufacturing technique, which was for a time considered superior to the technique of manufacturing knives with thick backs, and later abandoned entirely for something else.

In the life of a society, models of weapons change very often, models of tools less often, and social institutions very seldom, while religious institutions continue unchanged for millennia. Since the beginning of this chapter—that is, since the Chatelperronian—we might have noted in turn thick cylindrical spears, spears split at the base, lozenge-shaped spears, spears oval in section. Now single-beveled spears make their appearance (at the same time as the laurel-leaf points), and several other models will appear before the end of the Magdalenian. On the other hand, awls have remained unchanged since the beginning. The pierced reindeer antler, still sometimes called *bâton de commandement*, which probably served to straighten out rods of bony matter, makes its appearance in the Aurignacian and is found throughout the Late Paleolithic. When we examine such evidences of material culture from a chronological point of view, Paleolithic Europe seems extraordinarily like present-day Europe—or, to be more accurate, like nineteenth-century Europe. A single religious system seems to underlie the works of art from Russia and the Ukraine to Spain, with local features that make it possible to distinguish the major areas; the store of technical objects with well-marked features is spread over each major area. Italy or Provence differs from Spain; France differs from the Pyrenees and the Low Countries, although from epoch to epoch one can sense a common developmental pattern. From time to time an innovation turns up, usually connected with the art of killing, and such an object comes to characterize an entire epoch as it spreads rapidly over a geographical area, occasionally even over the whole territory. None of this suggests the idea of small hordes wandering endlessly in pursuit of ever more distant quarry. A novelty might come from Russia or from Spain, but the people probably stayed within their respective cultural provinces century after century, kept up contact with their neighbors, were subject to invasion or invaded others from time to time, and moved about periodically within their traditional hunting grounds.

Consequently the Solutrean can be subdivided only with respect to a fraction of its material equipment; with respect to its art, it fits in naturally between the mature Gravettian and Early Magdalenian.

The important fact remains that a large number of dated low-relief sculptures are Solutrean, and it seems certain that there is a relationship between the two limits just mentioned. To gain a clearer understanding of this relationship we have unfortunately to go back to the arid domain of stratigraphy. Between the mature Gravettian (Perigordian V) and the Middle Magdalenian extends a period which is still rather little known. The stratigraphic sequences vary from one region to another. However, when we examine the artistic evidences, the dominant impression is one of peculiar unity: during the Solutrean, the archaic style matures and passes into a more classical style which comes to characterize the Solutrean and the Early Magdalenian uniformly over the Franco-Cantabrian area. The impression conveyed by these two considerations (stylistic unity and the rather confused diversity of chronological sequences from

EARLY STYLE IV

26 ALTAMIRA
Bison. Black manganese and ocher. About 6 ft. 5 in.
The body has the look of being suspended.
The coat is filled in with graduated ocher,
combined with conventional detailing.

EARLY STYLE IV

27 NIAUX
Horse in manganese modeled with hatching.
About 6 ft. 7 in.

LATE STYLE IV

28 LIMEUIL
Reindeer, feeding, engraved on a plaquette.
About 10 in. Realistic rendering
of form and movement has been mastered.

region to region) is that of the shortness of the whole period. The dates yielded by the measurement of carbon radioactivity (carbon-14) place the period from the Middle Solutrean to Magdalenian IV between 17,000 and 12,000 B.C. This estimate upsets traditional views in that it reduces by about five thousand years the period in which the major part of Paleolithic cave art was produced. The physicists' estimates must still be treated with caution, but, as will be seen later, they do away with most of the anomalies revealed by detailed stylistic study of the figures. Furthermore, if several millennia intervened between the chronological divisions we would hardly expect to find so many overlappings of tools and equipment from one to another. When one makes the attempt, as I shall do, to discover in the works the details of treatment that characterize a style, and when one compares one's results with the established chronological division, the impression of overlapping becomes still more unmistakable.

Without separating them from the Gravettian, the Solutrean and the Early and Middle Magdalenian must be considered to form a single artistic period. It is characterized by progressive development in the decoration of everyday objects, and this development reaches its peak in the Middle Magdalenian, lingering on for a time into terminal Magdalenian. The period of decorated caves falls chiefly between the Solutrean and the Magdalenian. During the Gravettian there already were a few deep-cut engravings on cave walls or on blocks at the cave entrances, or on the overhangs of rock shelters. The dated works are almost all situated in the areas receiving daylight. During the proto-Solutrean, this tradition seems to have persisted, at least in the Rhone basin, and several caves in the Ardèche still have deep-cut engravings in the lighted zone. During the Solutrean, the evolution leads to low relief, and low reliefs datable with certainty are still turning up in Magdalenian III. The sculptured works falling within this time span are among the largest, also the finest: Le Roc de Sers, Angles-sur-l'Anglin, Le Cap Blanc, Mouthiers.[8] It is now established that they were originally painted: traces of black and red are still visible on some of them.

[8] Cf. pp. 311, 343, 344-345

A problem arises once again: at what moment did the artists push into the dark depths of the caves in order to paint and engrave? It is probable that the tradition of outside sanctuaries is older than that of the interior ones, but several factors stand in the way of elucidation. There are no low reliefs in places that do not receive daylight, perhaps for technical reasons: the execution of a sculpture by the light of lamps burning animal fat would be extremely laborious. One can only suppose that beginning at a certain epoch the Paleolithic painters and engravers moved deeper inside the caves which their ancestors had already sculptured and decorated with paint at the entrances. But there are a few sanctuaries well inside caves which belong to the archaic style, such as at Gargas in the Pyrenees. At all events, it seems certain that while the first movement deeper into the caves may have occurred at an early date, the real invasion of the dark interiors was relatively late. These various questions will come up again in the course of these pages, for they are important and far from settled.

The cultural whole constituted by the Solutrean and the Early and Middle Magdalenian has a few solid chronological guideposts—among the most solid in all chronology. The low reliefs at Le Roc de Sers and those at Bourdeilles, to mention only the main ones, determine the Solutrean position; those at Angles-sur-l'Anglin and Le Cap Blanc the position in Magdalenian III. They are relatively close to each other in execution if not in style.

Next come two periods which are very important for the art that they include, and which correspond to the second mountain range that we must climb, starting with the Solutrean. These are Magdalenian III and Magdalenian IV. The exact nature of the relations between the two episodes within the Middle Magdalenian are still hard to define: the relevant layers are as a rule easy of access and, with few exceptions, were explored by the specialists during the time when the importance of stratigraphic details had not yet been realized, or the sites were simply plundered by Sunday archaeologists. The essential distinction between the two periods is based on two weapons—the spear and the harpoon. Beginning with Aurignacian V a so-called single-beveled spear is developed in various types; this is dominant in the Middle Magdalenian and then is replaced with a longer, "double-beveled" spear. The harpoons, in their turn, begin in the Middle Magdalenian. The early forms have short teeth, then the teeth become longer and occur in one row and in two rows until Magdalenian VI and beyond. The late single-beveled spear seems to correspond to Magdalenian III, the earliest double-beveled spears to Magdalenian IV, the developed harpoons and the last double-beveled spears to Magdalenian V and VI. In fact, the distinguishing features seem to be regional variations on the general theme; without ruling out the notion of progressive development, it may be more prudent (especially in view of the dubious character of many excavations) to speak merely, with respect to art, of Middle Magdalenian, it being understood that we are referring to Magdalenian III and IV.

It is only to be expected, of course, that such divisions do violence to the transitions, for the life of Paleolithic man was not a succession of abrupt jolts, but most likely marked by relative continuity. During the second part of the Middle Magdalenian the climate appears to have grown considerably warmer. This is the most luxuriant period of Franco-Cantabrian art: weapons and tools are generously decorated; the sanctuaries deep inside the caves come to know their splendor. The style reaches the point of a certain academism, often even of conventionalism—the abundant frescoes disclose a technique in which each animal species conforms to very precise conventional details. The profusion of decorated objects and plaquettes is particularly valuable, for the same conventions govern the minor works and provide fortunate cross references for the works on the cave walls.

The transition to the Late Magdalenian (Magdalenian V and VI) was also not abrupt, but a return of the cold climate seems to have affected the behavior of the latest Paleolithic men. Around 11,000 B.C., the double-beveled spears and the harpoons are at the height of their vogue. Objects are still richly decorated, but in a new style, closer to a photograph-like reality than the classical style had been and displaying a concern for realism occasionally carried to well-nigh anecdotal lengths, with galloping or grazing animals. The great period of interior sanctuaries comes to an end, and cave works move back to the entrances. The only dated cave of the period is that of Teyjat[9] where the incised images, still very fine, are executed on stalagmites near the entrance. The large incised slabs from Limeuil also date from this period. The first part of the terminal Magdalenian is consequently classical in quality yet novel in style. The last part is contemporary with the return of a warmer climate and marks the close of the Paleolithic age; art begins to regress at the moment when the last reindeer disappear from this region, about 9,000 B.C.

As presented here, the history of Paleolithic art departs from traditional views at many points. Each departure is defended in the chapters that follow. It must be kept in mind that the solid foundation on which new insights can be created was established by a very small number of men whose names recur continually. Wholly on their own, and often with very limited resources, they blazed trails through well-nigh virgin territory. Our admiration for them, and especially for the Abbé Breuil and Denis Peyrony, is beyond measure. If, in this book, I give the impression of frequently attacking their conclusions, this is essentially because there are scarcely any others to argue with, and because it is impossible to acknowledge on every page the lasting excellence and definitive nature of their contributions.

[9] *Cf. p. 339*

3. DECORATED WEAPONS, TO[
ORNAMENTS

3. DECORATED WEAPONS, TOOLS, AND ORNAMENTS

THE systematic presentation of Paleolithic works of art can be a tricky business. To classify them in strict chronological order would be misleading, since many excellent works would be eliminated merely because their position in time has not been determined within any particular subdivision of the Magdalenian period. As our purpose is not to present the entire corpus of Quaternary art but merely to supply enough examples to show what it was like, it is interesting to keep our eye on certain works of dubious parentage, for their value is precious as testimony to the total achievement. A strictly chronological framework would, moreover, tempt us (a temptation that others have not always strongly resisted) to assign uncertain finds to a specific epoch. Such a procedure might be harmless enough in any single case, but the cumulative effect of multiple instances thus established would be hopeless confusion.

Classification by subject might seem a safer approach: subjects varied very little in the course of the Upper Paleolithic, and one could assemble interesting sequences of bison, reindeer, etc. This approach is used principally to establish the significance of the subjects and to attempt a stylistic synthesis. However, there is also a hidden pitfall in a species-by-species presentation which many have fallen into before now. By treating separately the horse, the bison, the stag, one runs the risk of forgetting to ask if the artist or artists have not chosen to group them together on the same wall.

A third possibility would be to classify the works by technique, taking up engraving, sculpture, and painting in turn. Though apparently justified in a book on art, such a classification would lose sight of the possibility that the men of the Old Stone Age did not make the same distinctions among techniques that we do. It would be hard to fit into such a framework the sculptured and painted low reliefs at Angles-sur-l'Anglin, the bison painted over protuberances on the Altamira ceiling, and the horse at Font-de-Gaume painted so that the hindquarters stand out in the relief supplied by a stalactite. A great many animals are painted or engraved in hollows or over protuberances letting nature collaborate in the modeling of the body.

In order not to force the finds into a preconceived pattern and at the same time to avoid repetition as far as possible, I made an effort to discover how the works were classified—unconsciously of course—by the men of the Old Stone Age themselves. Study of the meaning of the works and the purposes they served provided a guiding thread. Statistical analysis makes it clear that in most cases the figurative outer wrapping is in keeping with its physical, material foundation.

This is why we shall not follow too slavishly the traditional division between decorated objects and cave art. The distinction is worth making in connection with determining the chronological distribution, but here it will be replaced by a distinction between objects of technical use and objects of religious use. This does not rule out religious decoration of technical objects, but it will be seen that subject and treatment set the latter apart.

Technical objects may be divided into three categories: expendable objects that were not expected to last, objects of lasting utility, and objects of personal adornment. The decoration on a spear which might be lost in the first bison encountered belongs in a different category from that on a spatula used daily, or from that on a pendant. Such distinctions account for the coexistence throughout the Upper Paleolithic of schematic, realistic, and abstract themes.

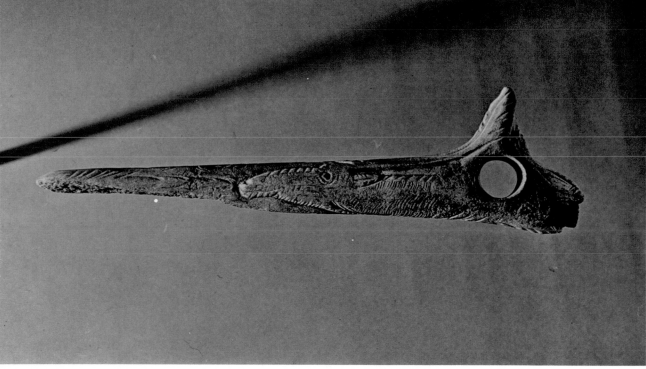

29 ISTURITZ
Horse engraved on a thick spear. 6 ³/₄ in.
The earliest dated utilitarian object
with realistic decoration (Gravettian,
c. 22,000 B.C.). The figure is in Style II
and is related to the horses engraved
on the walls of Pair-non-Pair and Gargas.
Collection Saint-Périer,
Château de Morigny.

30 LAUGERIE BASSE
Pierced staff from the Middle Magdalenian.
The main figure is a cervid in light relief.
The tip in front of the hole is carved as a bison head.
In front of the cervid's muzzle are three
overlapping ovals which represent
a barbed sign or a fish.
Musée de l'Homme, Paris

31 LAUGERIE HAUTE
Pierced staff with engraving of two facing
mammoths. Found in the levels of the period
between the Gravettian and the Solutrean
(Peyrony's proto-Magdalenian).
Probably the oldest pierced staff
with animal decoration. Flat projection
from photograph of original. Museum, Les Éyzies.

Religious art, too, falls into three distinct categories, not according to the subject treated or the apparent function, but probably according to the conditions in which they were used. The first category consists of statuettes; the second, of figures of a movable sort—on slabs, blocks, flat stones; the third encompasses cave art.

Within each division we shall follow a certain chronological order, beginning with works that are dated. It may seem idle to give attention to the frequently modest decoration of small objects instead of concentrating on major works of art, but the former hold considerable interest for the art historian. There is a kind of paradox in the presence, alongside one another in the same period, of realistic figures and of signs in which one notices, after examining a sufficient number of examples, that despite their extreme schematism they have lost nothing of what they represent. A whole series of psychological problems is raised by the contrast between the comparative stability of the animal figures and the evolution of the representations of human beings in the direction of a sort of pre-ideographic code.

EXPENDABLE WEAPONS

THE only objects of bony material which we can with certainty assign to the category of objects not expected to last are the points of weapons used in hunting—of spears and harpoons. These were subject to loss or breakage.

SPEARS

THAT a light throwing weapon was in use throughout the Upper Paleolithic is attested by the constant presence of pointed heads of bony substance, in shapes ranging in section from the cylindrical to a very flat oval. These vary in length from 2 to 12 inches, and in diameter from less than $\frac{1}{2}$ inch to about $1\frac{1}{4}$ inches. All are pointed at one end, with a variety of differently shaped bases—conical, tongue-shaped, or like the mouthpiece of a flute—with one or two bevelings. Many of them were broken while the bone was still fresh, by buckling or because the point of the weapon struck something hard.

The custom of decorating spears seems to have become current in the Gravettian. The excavations by R. de Saint-Périer at Isturitz have yielded a variety of these weapons, all from that period, which as a group present most of the problems concerning their decoration. One shows the finest figure on any decorated object of the Gravettian, a horse,[1] engraved with a few lines. Others are marked with double incisions or with short lines set in a row. A few broken spear heads were perforated as though to be transformed into pendants. It will be seen later that the animals represented on spears belong to certain definite species, the same that turn up in the deepest parts of the decorated caves—the horse, the rhinoceros, cervids, the ibex, fish—a fact that would seem to have symbolic implications. Especially interesting in this respect is the co-existence, already in the earliest examples, of naturalistic decoration and linear decoration having no apparent meaning. As Abbé Breuil showed authoritatively long ago, the schematic decoration of objects of use was derived from more detailed figurations, most often of fish and cervids. He saw it as a degenerative process, whereby initially realistic motifs, copied over and over again, by dint of repetition became unrecognizable. But from the outset we find schematic drawing, whereas weapons with realistic drawing are very rare. We may logically suppose simple drawings to have resulted from some simplifying process, but it is hardly possible to see them as the result of a gradual degeneration. Rather, it would appear that there was normal, continuous development both in the decoration of objects expected to last and in that of objects expected to be used for a short time only. We find the same sort of difference

[1] fi

when we compare very elaborate writing, such as hieroglyphics, with the Chinese characters having a cursive line, intended for minor uses. The two systems can be synchronous. In Paleolithic art we do not find elaborate decoration and schematic decoration on the same kind of object. The impression gained from examining a large number of specimens is that spears (at least some of them) had to be decorated with specific representations, but that these were considerably simplified in the case of objects fashioned by the dozen.

The instances of broken spear heads which were altered so they might be used as pendants stimulate the imagination. Do we have here weapons recovered from the bodies of particularly rare or dangerous animals? Or, since we find schematic signs also on pendants, do we have here merely the reutilization of an already decorated object? One might also wonder whether the simplified figures on the spears were marks of ownership. The idea of personal markings can be dismissed: when we examine contemporaneous spears found in a single cave, we are struck by the number of variations on so simple a theme as the oval. Of course, even minute variations could have served to indicate ownership, but it must be kept in mind that no set of absolutely identical spears has ever been found. On one occasion, while excavating at Saint-Marcel with Dr. Allain, I found a group of eleven Late Magdalenian spears that were unused and placed just as the hunter's hand had left them on the ground. Some were not decorated at all but the others were each decorated in a different manner.

Decoration of spears thus began in the Gravettian period. In the Solutrean, decoration is common on the big oval spears, and these are still found in the Early Magdalenian. In the Pyrenees and in Spain, Solutrean spears are fairly numerous and exhibit a curious peculiarity: the decoration extends down to the beveled base, where it would normally be concealed by the shaft. The same tradition of decorating large oval spears down to the base[2] lasts into the Early Magdalenian (I and II). In Spain, just as in the Dordogne and at the famous site of Le Placard in the Charente, we find these fashioned with great care, the size of a paper knife, and the striations at the base, indicating how they fit into the shaft, have an ornamental character. At Le Placard, the decoration is in some examples more realistic than we find elsewhere, showing fish, cervids, and a rhinoceros of simple but excellent execution. Subsequently this realism ceases to be found on the spears and does not recur until the Late Magdalenian.

In the Middle Magdalenian (III and IV) we find small spears with single beveling and the first long spears with double beveling. The striations at the beveled base are now no more than scratches for holding the weapon in its shaft. But the body of the spear is quite often decorated with grouped incisions, and occasionally (in the Pyrenees) with rows of protuberances. The decorative themes—"arrow" and "feather" forms, sequences of double lines—occur on the walls of caves decorated in the same period.

The Late Magdalenian (V and VI) employs the same themes, but there is a resurgence of naturalistic decoration, generally in the form of friezes of more or less simplified horses which are also found in the Pendo cave in Spain, in the Basque country at Isturitz, and at La Madeleine in the Dordogne.[3] At Laugerie Basse near Les Eyzies, one fragment was found that even shows the fish/horse theme, which is frequent on pierced staffs.

Mention must be made of an object often designated as a "chisel," frequent from the Middle Magdalenian onward, which is made from an old spear with double beveling, the point removed and the broken edge hammered flat; the beveled base looks as though it had actually been used as a wedge or splitting tool (not as a "chisel," for the beveling is not sharp enough to cut). The original decoration of the spear survives in some cases, as at Villepin (Dordogne), where one such object dating from the close of Magdalenian VI, just before the disappearance of figurative art, still shows a recognizable horse. The themes clearly portrayed are the horse, cervids, fish, and the rhinoceros.

Prehistorians use this term to designate rods made of reindeer horn, barbed on one or both sides, tapered at the base, and provided with one or two knobs for gripping purposes, or with a hole in the handle.[4] The point is normally sharp but the tip has often been much used. The utility of this object has not been completely clarified, though it seems to have served for fishing. Like the pronged harpoons used in salmon fishing by the Ainus in northern Japan and certain Indians and Eskimos, the head of the harpoon seems to have stuck in the fish; it was attached by a short thong to the shaft which the hunter held onto as to a fishing rod. In this way the operative bony portion of the weapon was less likely to be snapped off by the fish in its struggles. The weapon was not hurled but held in the hand as in spear-fishing. It must have served also to dig under stones and roots, which would account for the sometimes extremely blunted point.

4 figs. 175–177

We know that the first harpoons appeared at the end of the Middle Magdalenian, although their use extended beyond the Paleolithic. In their book *Les poissons, les batraciens et les reptiles dans l'art quaternaire (Fish, Amphibians, and Reptiles in Quaternary Art)*, H. Breuil and R. de Saint-Périer showed that the decoration of harpoons, most often very abstract, had the fish as its fundamental theme. Cases where even a slight degree of realism appears are rare, but on one Spanish example, at El Cueto del Rascaño, we recognize the theme of the cervid associated with the fish,[5] a theme then very common on other objects. As we saw earlier, one spear from Laugerie Basse (also Late Magdalenian) employed the horse/fish theme. Without these two examples we might be tempted to suppose that a spear decorated with the drawing of a horse was used in hunting horses, and that a harpoon showing a fish was used only for catching fish. But this interpretation is hard to accept when we are confronted with one drawing representing two such different animals; it is more natural to suppose that the theme had a symbolic rather than a purely technical meaning.

5 chart x

IMPLEMENTS OF LASTING UTILITY

Among surviving bone implements, we find a number of objects carefully decorated for the most part in a style altogether different from that characteristic of spears and harpoons. These are the pierced staffs, the spear-throwers, the spatulas, and the half-rounded rods, to which we may add shuttles and various bone tubes. Such designations are more or less arbitrary: the actual use of these objects is often different from what prehistorians at first supposed, or it is still unknown.

PIERCED STAFFS

Next to awls, the bone implement that turns up most regularly at every level of the Upper Paleolithic is the pierced staff.[6] It appears first in Aurignacian I and persists into the terminal Magdalenian. This is a piece of reindeer horn, cut at the branching of the antlers, with a round hole at its sturdiest point. In shape it brings to mind the present-day monkey wrench. As a rule, at least from a certain period onward, it is richly decorated.

6 figs. 30–32, 178–195; charts XI, XII

The name *bâton de commandement*, which was first given to this implement and is still occasionally used, is rather odd: it evokes some aged Magdalenian general directing, from the rear of his troops, an assault on a mammoth. By the end of the nineteenth century Eskimos and some Indians had been found to use a similar object for straightening out the wood or bone shafts of spears and arrows; in consequence, the implement was occasionally called a *redresseur de flèches*, an ambiguous translation of the English "arrow-straightener." Today it is more cautiously referred to as a perforated or pierced staff. I have tried to verify the uses of the pierced staff experimentally, and two considerations incline me to think that it did serve to straighten fresh reindeer horn and bone so as to fashion spears and harpoons; probably also to straighten shafts of wood. The first consideration is that reindeer antlers are naturally curved, and so cannot serve for spears without being straightened. However, many examples found at various archaeological levels are curved, a fact which suggests that they tended gradually to revert to their original curvature after having been straightened. The other consideration is that pierced staffs with especially small holes occur only at sites where the spears are especially thin and narrow.

Thus everything seems to indicate that the implement was in use as long as spears were made of reindeer horn, and that such implements must have been used frequently over a period of many years. This would account for its particularly careful decoration and for the fact that, together with the spear-thrower, the pierced staff is the Magdalenian art object *par excellence*.

As far as is known, pierced staffs first appeared in Aurignacian I: Denis Peyrony found a specimen at La Ferrassie. They became relatively common in the Gravettian and the Solutrean, and specimens have been found as far afield as the Ukraine. The earliest examples have little decoration, which is in keeping with the still relatively undeveloped decoration of spears. A Solutrean specimen from Bourdeilles exhibits doubled lines and parallel incisions; a Gravettian specimen from Arcy-sur-Cure shows deeply incised curved lines. In two specimens—one from La Ferrassie, and one among several from Isturitz—the handle shows a thickening at the end, which fairly clearly suggests the form of a phallus. This was to be the favorite decorative theme on pierced staffs throughout the Magdalenian.[7]

[7] *fig. 180; chart* XI

Indeed, there are many Middle and Late Magdalenian examples with the handle clearly carved as a phallus, sometimes abundantly decorated with signs or animals. The shape of the implement no doubt lent itself to such a representation, but, as we shall see shortly, male symbols were integrated in a system whereby the horse, the spear, and the signs having a masculine character are correlated in various ways with the bison, the wound, and the female signs. In the excellent pierced staff from the Pendo cave, dating probably from the Late Magdalenian, the general shape of the implement is simultaneously a horse's head and a phallus, the surface covered with a delicate tracery of heads of horses and hinds.[8]

[8] *fig. 190*

The evolution of nonphallic decoration is fairly hard to ascertain because a large number of fine specimens are only approximately dated. It is during Magdalenian IV that animal figures begin to appear on the surface of the implement, except for the isolated specimen from Laugerie Haute (Peyrony's proto-Magdalenian) that shows two facing mammoths.[9] During this period decoration is treated broadly, figures are few, and modeling very elaborate. Gradually, fine engraving begins to supplant deep incision and to delimit a raised field; subjects also become more complicated. In Magdalenian V and VI we arrive at objects covered with a network of small figures forming one composition, as on the plaquettes.

[9] *fig. 31*

The subjects represented on the pierced staffs are limited in number and show a statistical distribution like that of no other works.[10] The horse dominates, followed closely by the male figure, either shown in full or represented by the sexual parts only. Then come fish, the stag, reindeer, and—trailing far behind—the ibex, hind, bison, and an occasional isolated subject—mammoth, bear, lion. Of forty-one decorated staffs I examined, thirty-five have a male decoration (fourteen a phalliform handle), four show associated male and female subjects, two have only female subjects (bison). In other words, the most frequent subjects are those which are found in the caves in zones where male signs preponderate: this fact confirms our first impression of the "male" character of the tool for straightening spears. However, the possibility that the hole in the staff stood for a female symbol is not ruled out, nor that the example should

[10] *chart* VI

32   ISTURITZ (SALLE SAINT-MARTIN)
Fragment of a pierced staff from the Middle
Magdalenian. Bison head in light low relief
(head about 2 in.). Hatched modeling
in Early Style IV, identical
with the modeling in paintings at Niaux.
Collection Saint-Périer, Château de Morigny.

be attached to the general principle of juxtaposed sexual figures. When more than one subject is represented, the groupings, too, are of a different character from those we find in cave decorations. The most frequent combination is phallus/fish, and next in frequency is horse/reindeer. The isolated cases are similar in character: stag/fish, reindeer/fish, man/horse, horse/stag, horse/fish. In a few cases, however, we find the groupings of the cave-wall type: horse/hind, stag/hind. The most common grouping on the cave walls—horse/bison—does not appear, but the bison occurs alone in a number of instances,[11] some of them clear, like the extraordinary example from Isturitz, and the bison heads shown back to back on a specimen from Laugerie Basse. The latter supplies us with the significance of several pierced staffs that show, around the hole, two or three protuberances marked with parallel incisions or an incised circular crest—it most probably represents an ultimate stylization of the bison's mane.

The pierced staffs confirm the testimony of the spears. Elaborate decoration hardly appears before the Magdalenian, but that it arose out of a far older tradition is attested by scattered rough works that may go as far back as the Aurignacian. The invariability of the subjects represented, which we find in every category of object or on the cave walls, presupposes deep-rooted oral traditions and testifies to a precisely codified body of beliefs.

SPEAR-THROWERS

THE object now designated as a spear-thrower is the same that early authors called the *bâtonnet à crochet* or *crochet en bois de renne* (hooked rod, hook of reindeer horn), both of which terms describe it very well. It is a rod of reindeer horn sometimes the thickness of a thumb, with an oval perforation at one end, and at the other a hook or a broader carving of an animal with a hook incorporated in its body. This object has been likened to the thin stone slabs or hooked sticks used as throwing spears or harpoons at various periods by many peoples—Australians, New Guineans, Eskimos, and Amerindians (in the United States, Mexico, and Peru). Thus nothing prevents us from regarding the "hooked rods" as "spear-throwers"; on the other hand, there is no clear archaeological evidence that they were used as such. The presence of an eyelet on several extant specimens is rather hard to account for.

However that may be, the so-called spear-thrower was an object that was made to last, subjected to frequent use, and important: for from the moment it makes its appearance it becomes common wherever it is found at all. It is nonetheless noteworthy that the spear-thrower made of reindeer horn is very restricted both in space and time. Except for one find in Switzerland, it is confined to the region between the Pyrenees and the Dordogne, and to the period between Magdalenian IV and Magdalenian V. From the same period date the long spears with double beveling which are distributed over a far vaster geographical area than the spear-throwers: it would appear that something has escaped the prehistorians' perspicacity. If the object was actually used for throwing spears, the probability is that it was fashioned of reindeer horn only during a short period and within a circumscribed region; and that normally it was made of wood and thus has perished.

Although restricted in space and time, the spear-throwers have great stylistic and decorative unity. The plainest have the shape of a stick, the hook being formed by the forelock of a horse's head sculptured in low relief. These appear to be the latest type, as well as the type most widely distributed: they have been found in France in the departments of Ariège, Basses-Pyrénées, Tarn-et-Garonne, and Dordogne, and in Switzerland. The horse is invariably the main decorative element in this type of spear-thrower, but in two specimens, from Laugerie Basse and from La Madeleine (Magdalenian V), the stick shows in addition a cervid and a barbed sign that often serves as substitute for a fish. Thus we encounter the same group—horse/cervid/fish—that we found on the pierced staffs. Among the spear-throwers in the form of a hooked stick, we must mention a complete specimen from Gourdan which shows a little head generally supposed to be human, the hook being placed at the back of the neck.

The second type of decoration, of which there are numerous examples, might be called "animal with head turned back" or "animal with head cut off." To this type belong what are incontestably the finest decorated objects of Magdalenian art. To understand the very peculiar attitude in which the animals are represented, we must inquire into how the object was fashioned: this alone accounts for their position at the very tip of the stick with forelegs drawn up together, as though they were about to fall into the void. They are deliberately deprived of heads, or they crane their necks back to look at their tails where the hook is located.[13] For the spear-thrower to be sufficiently sturdy, the handle had to be carved out of the solidest part (in front or back) of the main stem of the reindeer antler. The hook, too, had to be made of solid tissue. This presented no special difficulty with the plain-stick type, but to produce the type with one end sufficiently large for an animal to be shaped out of it, the artist had to utilize the part of the main stem where the first or second tine of the antler branches off. When we trace the outline of a spear-thrower of the larger type over a complete antler,[14] we see that it can fit only by sacrificing the animal's head. This was the solution adopted in many specimens (from Les Trois Frères, Arudy, Isturitz), in which the body is cleanly cut off at the neck or terminates in a tenon. It looks as if a separate head must have been attached to the neck. One ibex head from Isturitz, unfortunately damaged, seems to have been used in this way. However, as will be seen later, in both decorated objects and cave art there are examples of animals whose heads have been deliberately omitted; thus it is hard to make a definitive statement.

Another solution consisted in engraving the backward-looking head on the animal's side: this is the case of the famous bison from La Madeleine, which is sticking out its tongue to lick its flank.[15] A still more ingenious solution consisted in sculpturing the entire animal but with head turned back, which masked the shortness of neck that the absence of material made necessary. This formula is illustrated by the complete spear-thrower from Le Mas d'Azil that shows "a fawn with head turned back." In this type of spear-thrower, the hook had to be placed relatively far from the hind parts, and since the fawn has a short tail, it was necessary to lengthen the body with an appendage that supports the hook. The imagination of the sculptor led him to a representation which to us seems completely surrealistic: the so-called fawn (it actually seems to be a young ibex) is raising its tail, and an enormous sausage of excrement is issuing from the posterior orifice. At the end of the sausage two birds are tenderly kissing; the hook is formed by the tail of the bird nearest the tip. Doctor Dorothy Garrod, in an excellent study of the spear-throwers, has shown that the subject found imitators; the same type of hook has been found at Arudy and at Bédeilhac,[16] but so transformed that it was incomprehensible without the model from Le Mas d'Azil.

The subjects represented on spear-throwers with enlarged heads are varied. Ibexes are frequent; the horse occurs only once, at Isturitz; the reindeer[17] appears at Arudy, showing the marks on the flanks characteristic of the Magdalenian treatment of this animal; the bison[18] occurs three times, the mammoth once (Bruniquel),[19] and the lion once (specimen from La Madeleine called "the hyena").[20]

Some spear-throwers are intermediate between the two preceding types or are too fragmentary to be defined with certainty. One from Le Mas d'Azil is in this last category. It represents an eel together with the tail of another fish, recalling the trout from Lourdes[21] and the bird from Le Mas d'Azil.

Two very remarkable finds each exhibit a rearing animal, seemingly about to bolt from the enlarged head of the reindeer-horn rod. One of these comes from old excavations at Laugerie Basse and represents a reindeer: it has often been referred to as a "dagger." The other, from Bruniquel, represents a horse in the same stance, and is one of the greatest Stone Age masterpieces.[22] This has an eyelet at the lower end, which proves it to be a spear-thrower. What is odd, even baffling to the investigator,

33 ARUDY

Spear-thrower of the "headless animal"
type. The animal is identifiable as an ibex
by its over-all outline and conventional
details of the coat. Museum,
Saint-Germain-en-Laye.

Diagram showing how spear-throwers
of this type were carved
out of reindeer antlers (figs. 33 and 34).

34 LES TROIS FRÈRES

Spear-thrower of the "headless animal" type.
Height 2 ³/₈ in. By using the part
of the antler where two tines come together
the artist was able to show two animals
playing or fighting. They are recognizable
as ibexes. The surface finish,
the definition of the withers by hatching,
and the way the spongy tissue was hollowed
out where the heads should be suggest
that separate pieces representing the heads
were glued on. H. Bégouen excavations,
Musée de l'Homme, Paris.

35 BRUNIQUEL

Spear-thrower carved with a leaping horse (see also
fig. 207). Dated Middle Magdalenian, the carving shows
all the details of Early Style IV hatched modeling like
that found on cave figures. Actual size. Bétirac
excavations, Museum, Saint-Germain-en-Laye.

is that neither this rod nor the rod with the reindeer has a hook for holding the butt of the spear.

The range of subjects represented on spear-throwers is very broad, comprising, in order of frequency, horse, ibex, fish, bison, reindeer, bird, mammoth, lion, and, probably, man; only the ox, the stag, the hind, and woman have still to be found to complete the list of most common subjects. The first three subjects do not figure in the bestiary of the region where the spear-throwers were found, at least not during the period covered by Magdalenian IV and V. Even more striking is the variety of subjects at the same site (ibex, horse, bison, bird, eel at Le Mas d'Azil; horse, bison, lion at La Madeleine) and, except on the stick-with-hook type, the absence of the paired animals that are so frequent on the pierced staffs.

SPATULAS[27]

THE terms "spatula" and "palette" are used to designate bone fragments in the general shape of an extended oval, fairly often ending in a narrower part forming a short handle or in a carving in the form of a fish tail. They are as a rule very carefully polished and most often decorated.

The use of these objects is unknown, and one may regard them as spatulas for mixing ocher on the palette, or as small spoons for picking the marrow out of bones, or as instruments of quite some other sort. It is even possible that they were used in an entirely different way; for example, they may have been suspended or fastened to wood or to animal skins, like the decorations on costumes and accessories of Siberian shamans. The earliest may go back to the Gravettian (one undecorated fragment exists at Arcy-sur-Cure) or to the early Solutrean (long palettes decorated on the handle were found in Russia at Kostienki I). However, like the preceding objects, they are abundant and richly decorated in the Middle Magdalenian; they remained in use to the end of the Late Magdalenian. Finally, objects of several different uses may have been grouped in this category. An argument in favor of multiple uses seems to me to rest in the fact that often, in the same period and in the same deposits, there are two opposed types of decoration—one very realistic, and the other abstract. One group partakes of the decorative type of the pierced staffs and the spear-throwers, whereas the other group is closer to the decoration on the objects to be suspended. Thus it is hard, when dealing with certain objects provided with a hole for hanging them up by or broken off at one end, to say whether they are palettes or some sort of pendant. These hard-to-classify objects will be treated again when we discuss pendants.

The most pronounced type is that of the spatula "with the fish," of which several specimens are known from sites spread from the Dordogne into Cantabrian Spain. Only a few of these were found during scientific excavations, but by a system of multiple cross-checking it is possible to assign them to around Magdalenian IV, the period to which are assigned, perhaps somewhat artificially, the bulk of works of art. The most explicit specimen comes from the Rey cave at Les Eyzies: it is a long palette curved like a sword blade with a fish engraved on it, the fish's tail carved into the "prehensile" shape of a handle.[24] The fish is of the Salmonidae family, a salmon or a trout. The other specimens are less clearly identifiable; the tails are not fully rendered, and the scales are reduced to a geometric pattern.[25] One of two palettes from Laugerie Basse represents an engraved horse in front of the fish's tail,[26] and the other has a horse on one side, a stylized fish on the other. Once again we find the horse/fish theme, to which the Magdalenians must have ascribed some specific meaning.

At Isturitz, in the layer corresponding to the Middle Magdalenian (III–IV), several spatulas were found. One[27] has the shape of a sword blade without a fish tail; on one side it shows a barbed sign and an ibex head, on the other a tiny schematized horse and the same barbed sign. The others have a hole at one end for hanging and might have been pendants; each shows a horse, and there is another fragment also showing a horse. Thus, as with the pierced staffs, spatula decoration seems to have been determined by the grouping of horse/fish/ibex/barbed sign. Finally we must mention a curious object, unfortunately broken off at both ends, which was found in the Bruniquel cave and seems to be akin to the spear-thrower with the rearing horse. In form, it resembles a spatula; engraved on it is the image of a man with circles that look like big buttons running vertically from neck to crotch.[28] These are probably not real buttons, but this representation of a man completes the similarity in decoration of the spatulas and the pierced staffs.

The latest spatulas and palettes (or smoothing tools, as they are sometimes called) belong to Magdalenian V–VI, and their decoration is perceptibly different. The fish spatula seems to have disappeared, and the complete specimens have a real handle (those from Fontalès, and from Pekarna in Moravia[29]). Decoration is much more generous, sometimes covering the entire surface—a feature not entirely compatible with the idea of objects of practical use. The themes represented are varied, falling into two categories of composition. On some we find again subjects belonging to the "male" group: reindeer/ibex/barbed sign at La Madeleine; horse/short strokes at Fontalès; bear/ibex at La Vache (Ariège). On others we find mixed subjects: at La Vache, for instance, one palette bears the head of a hind and the head of a bison feeding on plants shaped like barbed signs; at Pekarna we find a conventional grouping of the cave-painting type, bison/horse/ibex.

HALF-ROUNDED RODS

By this term (apt, since it describes the object accurately without commitment as to its uses), prehistorians designate strips of horn at most ¾ inch wide, sometimes more than 8 inches long, which were carved from the main stem of a reindeer antler.[30] The hard outer surface is rounded; the inside, spongy part has been cut flat. Very often the flat side is marked with grooves as if to make this roughening adhere to something, whereas the convex side is fairly often decorated. A full inventory of these rods, whether decorated or not, discloses a disparate variety—some are pointed, others end in an oval, or with a straight or diagonal cut. Decoration is especially notable for its absence of unity. Some of these objects show abstract motifs such as we mentioned in connection with spears, others bring to mind the more elaborate decoration of the palettes, or the pendants with schematic figures; still others showing figures engraved or in a raised field are the most meticulously executed and the most elaborate in all Paleolithic art. Lastly, some bear realistic representations of exceptional quality.

We have only one specific indication of the use of these objects. At Isturitz, E. Passemard found two nondecorated half-rounded rods glued together, thus constituting one large spear with double beveling. This throws light on the purpose of at least some of these implements; the half-rounded rods with decorations similar to those on the more expendable weapons were probably halves of spears. By the same token an important technical point is established. The firmest part of the reindeer antler is only a small fraction of an inch thick, and antlers of exceptional size would have been required for a spear to be cut that would not be weakened by the soft spongy tissue inside. By carving two half-spears out of the firmest tissue and then fitting them together, a technique similar to that used in the Japanese split-bamboo stick, it was possible to obtain a weapon whose resistance and resilience were considerably increased.

There remain, however, the many half-rounded rods that are too elaborately decorated to have served as component parts of a spear. Since the half-rounded rod is the result of a technical process, and is not itself an object, it seems clear enough that the same technique could have been applied to other objects, and thus our categories are made up of disparate elements.

The period in which the half-rounded rods were produced is rather sharply circum-scribed. The technique of splitting reindeer antlers in half-rounded parts seems to go back to the Gravettian culture, judging by a very few specimens. In the Early Magda-lenian there are at least two examples from Laugerie Basse of rods decorated in the spear style—that is, showing rows of small incisions—and capable of being assembled by twos into spear points. But the great period of their production, as for all decorated utilitarian objects that have come down to us, was Magdalenian IV–V. During Magda-lenian VI the technique seems to have been abandoned. A sufficient number of rods has been dated at La Madeleine, Isturitz, and Teyjat to establish that they were synchronous with the pierced staffs and the spear-throwers.

One type found at all the major sites just mentioned, and also at Laugerie Basse, is related to the usual spears from the same sites by clusters of short straight lines, by curves inserted between groups of three such lines to form chicken tracks, by chevron patterns, and zigzags.[31] As in the case of the spears, we sometimes notice that we are dealing with signs that are abridgments of the forms of art on more durable objects: bison represented by the oval of one eye and the curve of one horn (the resulting effect is that of a tadpole); rows of eyes; heads recognizable as those of cervids.[32] Again, we do not seem to be dealing with marks of ownership, but with simplified drawings comprehensible over a vast territory—the same forms occur with some variations from the Loire into Spain. That the engraver knew the meaning of this work is evident from the resurgences of realism that we see from time to time.

A second type is confined to the western Pyrenees—Lespugue, Arudy, Lourdes, and particularly Isturitz.[33] It includes some rather dissimilar objects, but all are character-ized by complicated decoration. One group from Isturitz shows interlocking lozenges, squares overlapping in the Greek Key pattern, and one specimen of the group probably discloses the meaning of all these schematic signs: a scattering of quadrangles marked with a short line inside, which occurs in cave art as the simplified representation of the female organs.[34] This subject is never found on spears, harpoons, pierced staffs, or spear-throwers, where the decoration is entirely "male"; it is also absent from the spatulas, while the half-rounded rods evidently belong to another category of objects altogether. Some are decorated with long parallel curves, occasionally mingled with barbed signs. Finally, at several Pyrenean sites, unusual half-rounded rods have been found, decorated with spirals formed from deep cutting.[35] On one of them, from Isturitz, a horse's head is clearly distinguishable within a group of circles and spirals. These last-named objects are as surprising in this part of the world as are the ivory bracelets and female statuettes decorated with a network of Greek Key borders and perfectly regular lozenges that have been found at Mezin in the Ukraine.

Our last category comprises the half-rounded rods with realistic decoration. Very few are known: one from Isturitz, dating from the Middle Magdalenian, shows an ibex's head accompanied by signs of the spear type; one from Laugerie Basse, probably dating from an adjacent period, shows two hinds' heads treated in the best manner of the pierced staffs.[36] A third specimen[37] comes from the middle layer at La Madeleine, and hence dates probably from Magdalenian V. Its decoration is peculiar: a vulva and a phallus are treated as a single decorative motif, accompanied by a bear's head. This is the freest sexual representation in all Paleolithic art, though it does not represent copulation, merely a conjunction of symbols. The fact is—and we shall go back to this (see p. 144)—there are two versions of the theme vulva/phallus/bear, the one realistic (as here), which comes from the Dordogne, the other, from Massat (Ariège), in which, on a well-known pierced staff, the bear's head is accompanied by the corresponding abstract signs—the oval and the barbed sign.

The half-rounded rods are thus probably surviving parts of objects that had various uses. A large percentage of them fit into the spear group by the character of their decoration, and we know that spears made of two such rods glued together actually existed. A small number of them have decoration of a distinctive type, very elaborate and abstract, which does not correspond to anything on objects of known use. Finally, a very few are decorated in the manner of the pierced staffs, showing realistic subjects of which the most interesting corresponds to a formula found in many specimens of cave art.

MISCELLANEOUS IMPLEMENTS

Among objects of technical use or presumed to have been of technical use, we should include the so-called chisels, awls, shuttles, decorated tubes, and lamps. All these are too few in number to provide a basis for systematic analysis. The chisels and awls are the same object, fairly frequent in the Late Magdalenian, and have been mentioned in connection with the spears: this is a spear with double beveling, broken off and then made reusable (perhaps as a wedge) by hammering the blunt end. Frequently some of the original decoration of the spear survives.

The shuttles are made of a solid fragment of the main stem of a reindeer antler, split at each end. In the Late Magdalenian at Saint-Marcel (Indre), Dr. J. Allain found some which show unmistakable traces of ligature and use, suggesting that they served as a handle for some sort of planing tool; a flint scraper may have been inserted in the cleft. They are most often decorated with the "tadpole" motif (an oval extended by a short straight line), which may represent either the eye of an animal and its horn or ear, or the bisexual motif of oval and straight line which appears on the half-rounded rod from La Madeleine and is frequently found in cave-wall art.

There are many hollow tubes made of bird bone; some have perforations and are thought to be flutes, others without holes are believed to be needle cases or containers for ocher coloring. Certain ones are decorated, and two are particularly noteworthy. The first comes from the Late Magdalenian layer at Saint-Marcel and may have served as a whistle or a bird-hunter's decoy; its decoration, in addition to the usual short lines, comprises a whole row of hinds' heads represented by the ears and the line of the muzzle. The second comes from the Spanish site of El Valle[38] and corresponds in style to small engravings of multiple subjects dating from the Late Magdalenian. It shows a stag, two horses, and a series of cross-ruled ovals such as usually represent fish. In other words, this object is decorated with "male" themes of the kind found on pierced staffs or spatulas of the same epoch. Finally, there are specimens of decorated stone lamps, such as the one from La Mouthe (Dordogne) with a fine ibex engraved on the bottom, or the one with handle decorated with male signs which the Abbé Glory discovered at Lascaux on the ground in the Shaft, at the foot of the fresco showing the disemboweled bison.

OBJECTS TO BE SUSPENDED

A whole class of prehistoric remains is constituted by objects provided with a hole for threading a cord through or with grooves for securing a binding with cord. One might call them "objects of personal adornment" or "pendants," but neither of these designations is adequate to characterize their varied uses and forms: all that we know definitely about them is that they were made to be suspended.

The objects so prepared for hanging (or stringing) can be roughly divided into natural objects (such as animal teeth), pendants (when oval or oblong in shape), "carved silhouettes," and disks.

A purely morphological or purely chronological classification of these varied objects is difficult to establish without undue repetition. A summary account of the general evolution is necessary before discussing the details.

As we saw in chapter 1, from the close of the Mousterian onward the collecting of

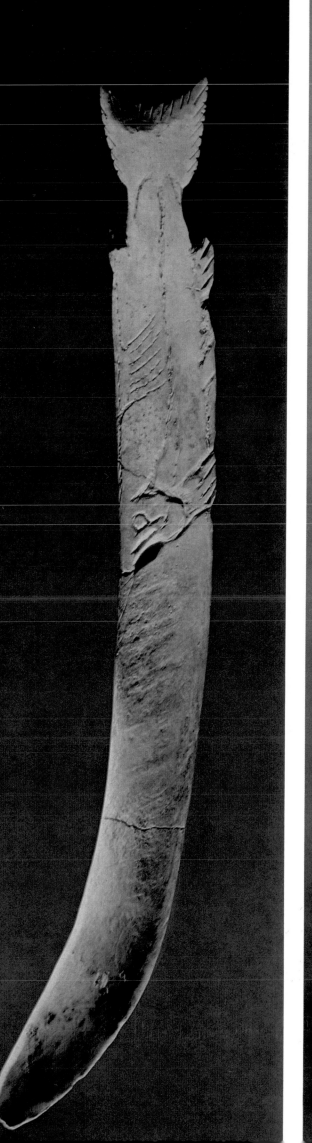

36 GROTTE REY, LES EYZIES
Spatula. Middle or Late Magdalenian.
The clearest example of the "fish"
spatula. 7 ³/₈ in. Museum,
Saint-Germain-en-Laye.

37 ISTURITZ
Spatula. The spatula themes (fish and horse)
belong to the category of male symbols.
This spatula, from the Middle Magdalenian
(c. 11,000 B.C.), confirms this:
there is a sequence of parallel chevrons,
an ibex head (with three short
lines indicating "breath"),
and one barbed sign. 7 ⁷/₈ in.
Collection Saint-Périer, Château de Morigny.

38-44   ISTURITZ

Decorated half-rounded rods.
The rods furthest at left have abstract
markings, the meaning of which
is as yet undecipherable.
The others, decorated with spirals
in sharp relief, are almost as impenetrable;
however, at the top of the second rod
from the right, note the outline
of the head of some herbivorous animal,
perhaps a hind. Despite the abstraction,
this type of decoration may have
a significance. Nearly actual size.
Collection Saint-Périer,
Château de Morigny.

natural oddities signaled mankind's earliest aesthetic or religious interest of which we have knowledge. The first objects to be suspended make their appearance at the beginning of the Chatelperronian. These are teeth of carnivorous or herbivorous animals, some of them provided with circular holes, others with a number of small grooves traced with a flint around the base of the tooth.[39] These occur until the end of the Magdalenian; the surface is often undecorated but, particularly in the Middle Magdalenian, it is sometimes marked with deep incisions. Incised decoration makes its appearance in the Chatelperronian—for example, the canine tooth of a stag found at Arcy-sur-Cure showing two incised chevrons.

PENDANTS

STAG canines (or "elks' teeth" as they were called when our grandfathers fancied them for wearing on a watch chain) were in demand from the beginning, and their popularity did not decline throughout the Upper Paleolithic. They seem to have enjoyed so much favor that, as early as the Chatelperronian, imitations of them were made of small reindeer bones having an approximately similar shape. In the same period we find fossils perforated so as to be hung or strung, as well as the first true pendants, which are rings carved in bone or ivory with an angular extension.[40] This type of ring-shaped pendant persists without much change down to the close of the Aurignacian.

In the Aurignacian appear the first notched pendants—ovals of bone or stone, the rims of which are notched with deep incisions or simply marked with thin lines around the edge. This type of pendant persists into the Middle Magdalenian. The notched pendants seem to be related to the oval pendants which are female sexual representations.

In the Middle Magdalenian, diversity of form and decoration reaches its peak, in keeping with the development of decorated objects in general. In addition to the objects just mentioned, we now find carved silhouettes of animal heads, and circular bone disks that show some kind of figure around the central hole. The Late Magdalenian contributes no new forms.

We may now examine the main types and what remains to be studied of their decoration. Ring-shaped pendants have now been discovered at Arcy-sur-Cure; their persistence there from the Chatelperronian to the close of the Aurignacian suggests that they were more than a purely local phenomenon. The two Chatelperronian specimens found in 1958 show the same large circular hole and two well-marked angles. In the Aurignacian, aside from the same type with angular protuberances, we find rings with pointed and two-lobed protuberances.

The notched pendants have been mentioned: from the Aurignacian onward they coexist with plain pendants of the same oval shape, which are often small pebbles of soft stone chosen for their form and simply perforated with a suspension hole. The plain form and the form with a border of parallel incisions may be the same object.

One may include among the pendants a certain number of small oval plaquettes of bony material which either have a hole for stringing, or may have had when intact. The most remarkable comes from Lalinde;[41] it measures $7\frac{1}{2}$ by $1\frac{5}{8}$ inches and was believed to be a so-called bull-roarer—the instrument from which the Australian aborigines, in particular, draw a humming sound by swinging it over their heads at the end of a string. It is a fact that a model made of the Lalinde specimen does work like a bull-roarer, emitting a fairly shrill sound. Consequently we may have here an instrument that was known to several peoples remote from one another; on the other hand, we know that a key may serve as a whistle, without being necessarily a musical instrument.

The great majority of decorated oval pendants date from the Middle Magdalenian. Some, of which it is not certain that they had a hole for stringing and may be fragments of palettes, form a homogeneous group from their decoration with barbed signs. They occur from the Dordogne to the Pyrenees. One of them, from Le Mas d'Azil, shows an engraving that seems to be a plant with stem, branches, and roots; but this could be the bisexual sign (barbed stem and oval) which we have already encountered several times. The same theme occurs on a pendant from Saint-Marcel having a barbed sign and a row of three circles inscribed within the notching of the rim. The little "ladybug" from Laugerie Basse, despite its similarity to the insect, is believed to be a female symbol in the form of a vertical line bordered with dots, inscribed within an oval of notched incisions. Two specimens, one from Marsoulas and one from Isturitz,[42] have only the incisions at the rim and bring to mind the small fish or sole carved in bone which was found at Lespugue.[43]

Finally, some pendants have realistic decoration. Two among them, both from Isturitz, underline the essentially sexual character of the symbols we find in this category of objects.[44] The first is a small tongue-shaped piece scalloped of interlocking ovals within which are inscribed signs of the chicken-track type, a stylized form of the common female symbol; the second is a carved bone phallus. Two pendants (from Lespugue,[45] and from Lortet) show engravings of snakes; two others very similar in decoration[46] (from Laugerie Basse and from Marsoulas) show in Dordogne and the Pyrenees the same very stylized engravings of ovals and fish.

On the whole, the decoration of the oval pendants is clearly of sexual inspiration, some male, others female, several bisexual. Their chronological grouping is fairly uncertain in its details. Except for a Solutrean stone pendant from Bourdeilles with the engraving of a reindeer,[47] the earliest specimens do not carry realistic motifs. In the Middle Magdalenian signs seem to predominate, and we see clearly that more explicit representation comes in with the approach of the Late Magdalenian—a phenomenon already mentioned in connection with other objects. Apart from sexual subjects and snakes, few other themes appear. One very confused engraving from El Pendo shows more or less clearly a cervid within a scattering of short lines; one pendant from Isturitz has a horse,[48] and another a bear;[49] some pendants in the shape of women in profile were found at Peterfels; and one object found a long time ago at Arcy-sur-Cure is supposed to represent a beetle, but could just as well be a female figure.

CARVED SILHOUETTES

THE carved silhouettes constitute a very special category narrowly circumscribed in time; their period corresponds to the mature Middle Magdalenian. Their known distribution in area is between the Dordogne and the Pyrenees. However, one carved silhouette was reportedly found in the first excavation at Saint-Marcel: this would extend the boundary north to the Loire. Thus, these silhouettes can be localized in the very center where the most important decorated objects were produced, and during the epoch of their greatest development.

The silhouettes are largely determined in appearance by the conditions of their fabrication. The hyoid bone in the head of the horse (and many other herbivores) is a thin Y-shape: by cutting off one branch and keeping the stem and the branch which forms the ear, one obtains a profile of a small horse's head; the contour needs only to be retouched and the eye and the mouth incised to make the work complete. One hole for hanging, sometimes two, are added last. These figurines 1 to 2 inches long are among the most spirited Paleolithic works; we appreciate them also for containing details which are found in cave art, thus helping to date the latter.

Most of them represent heads of horses[50]—as is suggested by the shape of the bone— but a few other subjects are known. At Le Mas d'Azil, the carved silhouette of a horse's skull is associated with the head of a living horse. Representations of skulls are quite exceptional in Paleolithic art, and besides this carved silhouette there is only one other specimen of a horse's skull, modeled on a fragment of an object, and also found at Le Mas d'Azil.[51] Also at that same site—which deserved to have been explored at some less "heroic" period—there is an ibex head carved in silhouette. One other is known at Isturitz;[52] it has two holes which seem to have been intended for fastening the object rather than for suspending it. Were it not for the thinness of the object, I should be tempted to see in it one of the heads that were added to spear-throwers carved with a headless animal. Finally, one small bone specimen found at Lespugue showing an unmistakable sole[53] may be regarded as a carved silhouette. It is not surprising that people and objects circulated between the coast and the central Pyrenees, considering the unity of mature Magdalenian art throughout the southwest, but this representation of an ocean fish is one of the rare tangible proofs that such circulation actually took place. In 1960 I called attention to two other fishes of the sole family, engraved on a block in a small chamber to the left of the Breuil Gallery at Le Mas d'Azil; we also know that a "turbot" figures in the cave decoration of La Pileta, near Gibraltar. It is possible that the sole, whose contours are those of the oval pendants bordered with thin lines, had a similar symbolic value.

Special mention must be made of G. Simonnet's discovery in the Labastide cave (Hautes-Pyrénées) shortly before the Second World War: this cave (which, incidentally, was plundered a few years ago) was decorated with engraved and painted figures; it also yielded an important series of engraved slabs (to be discussed later) which still occupied their original locations. Resuming excavations inside the cave, near the first engravings, Simmonet discovered a group of eighteen small carved silhouettes representing heads of ibexes, and a nineteenth representing the head of a bison. All the ibex heads were provided with holes for suspension. Apart from its artistic importance, this find is invaluable because it shows that the silhouettes may have been used in a series, like the elements of a necklace or some other arrangement for adornment. It also provides the only known example of a bison in this category.

DISKS

F ROM exactly the same epoch as the silhouettes carved from the hyoid bone, and at the same sites, we find a small object in the shape of a disk (about $1\frac{1}{2}$ inches in diameter), carved from the thin part of a shoulder blade and pierced with a little hole in the center. These round bone chips are nearly always decorated.

Several of them have a plain decoration consisting of lines radiating from the center, or of lines or dots around the rim. Over this decoration may be superimposed realistic subjects, or the latter may occur alone. The subjects represented are fairly varied. A disk found at Laugerie Basse shows a cow on one side and a calf on the other; a second disk has a hind on one side and a ruminant which may pass for a chamois on the other.[54] At Bruniquel in 1957, B. Bétirac discovered a disk decorated with an ibex;[55] at Raymonden there is a disk with mammoths on each side, at Isturitz one with a horse and bison, and at Le Mas d'Azil one with a reindeer. Also from the last-mentioned site, another disk, only half of which has survived, shows a strange combination: on one side there are bifurcated signs and short lines, plus a human creature with arms crossed and legs spread apart, seemingly pinned flat to the ground by what looks like a bear's paw. The other side[56] shows a man (his genitals clearly indicated) holding what may be a stick or spear on his upper arm; here too there are lines resembling a bear's paw. These figures seem to belong to a fairly frequent theme: we find it as a man attacked by a bison in the frieze at Le Roc de Sers, in the Shaft at Lascaux, in the cave at Villars, and on the pierced staff from Laugerie Basse. At Péchialet, it is a man attacked by a bear. The figures on the disks thus form a very eclectic group, recalling the figures on the cave walls where almost all the same actors reappear. It is possible that a number of these small objects constituted a set of coordinated figures like those on cave walls;

the various specimens so far discovered would then belong to such a set. Unfortunately our specimens have always turned up singly, at sites where the Magdalenians happened to leave them.

CONCLUSIONS

W<small>E</small> have now drawn up an inventory of the minor arts of the Upper Paleolithic, according to the present state of our knowledge. We see that the number of decorated objects is, all in all, very limited—spears, harpoons, pierced staffs, spear-throwers, spatulas, half-rounded rods, and objects to be hung or strung. Apart from a few objects known only from single specimens, this is the lot. We have not included needles, which, because of their size and function, could not be decorated, or such common implements as awls, wedges, and digging tools made from the ribs of large animals. Otherwise, practically all surviving bone objects fall within our divisions.

Several conclusions seem inescapable. The first is the characteristic lateness of figurative art in the Upper Paleolithic, at least on objects of practical use. The finds dating from before the Gravettian are extremely rare, and the decorations on them are rudimentary. Between the Gravettian and the second part of the Middle Magdalenian, the finds are substantial but relatively few in number. The great flowering occurs in the relatively short period of Magdalenian IV–V–VI, reaching its peak in Magdalenian IV–V.[57]

Another conclusion that seems important relates to the apparent specialization of decoration: it is realistic on objects expected to last, schematic on more expendable objects. This is an interesting point, for it suggests that the same themes were susceptible either of full treatment or of a treatment one might almost call "shorthand." It is advisable not to confuse this shorthand schematism with the schematic "degeneration" which Breuil showed conclusively to characterize works dating from the end of the Magdalenian. From the aesthetic and philosophical point of view, the existence of a system of symbolic representations in the Upper Paleolithic is highly instructive. We have become used to studying this phenomenon in the pictography and handwriting that cannot be assimilated to Paleolithic forms of representation but that are in a way equivalent to forms found, for instance, in Africa and among the Boni Negroes of French Guiana. Its employment by Paleolithic man in the decoration of useful objects will enable us to understand hitherto unexplainable elements in cave art, where symbolic signs occur constantly alongside explicit representations of animals.

This system of abbreviated representation is not a secondary phenomenon in Paleolithic art: the symbolic signs make their appearance at the outset, and the earliest were still in use during the last period. Nor is it a local phenomenon: from Spain into central Europe the same signs stand for the same figurative representations. These two facts suggest that from first to last the meaning of the signs, even of the most abstract ones, was clear to all who used them. This is proved by repeated revivals of realism in every period, but especially in the last one, when fish suddenly recover their tails and fins, and the barbed sign regains its male sexual character. Clearly such facts can only find their explanation in a body of generalized oral traditions, as may occur with a body of religious traditions.

There is also reason to suppose, in spite of the errors we may make in classifying what are often only fragments of the original objects, that decoration reflected specific notions as to the relative importance of the various figures. The bison does not appear on spears, nor is it usual on pierced staffs, whereas it is by far the most common animal on the plaquettes and the cave walls.[58] The horse, however, is the most usual animal—except on harpoons and half-rounded rods. The pendants show clearly a sexual character, whereas sexual signs are very rare on the spear-throwers. All this confirms the consistent character of the decoration and of the conscious figurative intentions (insofar

45   ISTURITZ (SALLE SAINT-MARTIN)
Ibex head. 2 ¹/₄ in. Middle Magdalenian.
The way the neck is broken off
and the carelessness of the perforations
suggest that this is a fragment
of a larger work. Collection Saint-Périer,
Château de Morigny.

46-47   ISTURITZ
Heads of horses carved in silhouette, 1 ³/₄ in.
and 2 ³/₄ in. The lower example belongs
to the most common type: in the majority
of examples from southwestern France
the details of modeling and coat
are stereotyped. The center head is a less
common type, but in comparison with fig. 45
and other specimens, we find here most
of the conventional details.
Collection Saint-Périer, Château de Morigny.

as they are discernible) of the hunters. Thus the only known authentically primitive art discloses the existence of a far more complex mentality than had been imagined.

Finally, the decorated objects provide us with our surest chronological guidelines. From a purely logical point of view, one might assume *a priori* that the most brilliant period of cave painting and engraving would correspond to the time of the richest minor arts. As we shall see later, the reality is not so neat, but there are good reasons to suppose that a great number of the richest underground sanctuaries date from the period when the minor arts were at their peak. This assertion, which scarcely conforms with accepted ideas, will find its proof in the objects themselves. In point of fact, the conventional character of the shorthand representations is paralleled by no less rigid conventions of realistic representation; details in the depiction of the animals' hair and hide recur throughout the range of the representations and they differ for each species. The horses on the spear-throwers or on the carved silhouettes, the ibexes and the reindeer, impose the existence during the Middle Magdalenian of a real syntax of drawing. This finding is far removed from the idea one might form of a primitive draftsman who, suddenly inspired by the sight of an appetizing bison, proceeds to draw it with his flint burin. When we examine these horses and bison carefully, it is obvious that they are just as "academic" as the horses in English sporting prints or in Chinese painting. This academism provides us with valuable pointers when we pass from the decorated objects to the art of the caves. For instance, the spear-thrower with the rearing horse discovered by Bétirac, which dates from Magdalenian IV, can serve as a key when it comes to interpreting the several dozens of horses painted or engraved in the caves. Every species of animal and every type of sign engraved on these objects is found again on the cave walls, and it is ultimately upon the objects that one of our two methods of dating the cave works will be based. This is why the inventory just presented was necessary. It is also why we have not insisted upon the details of style that will reappear in their proper place when the problems arise again.

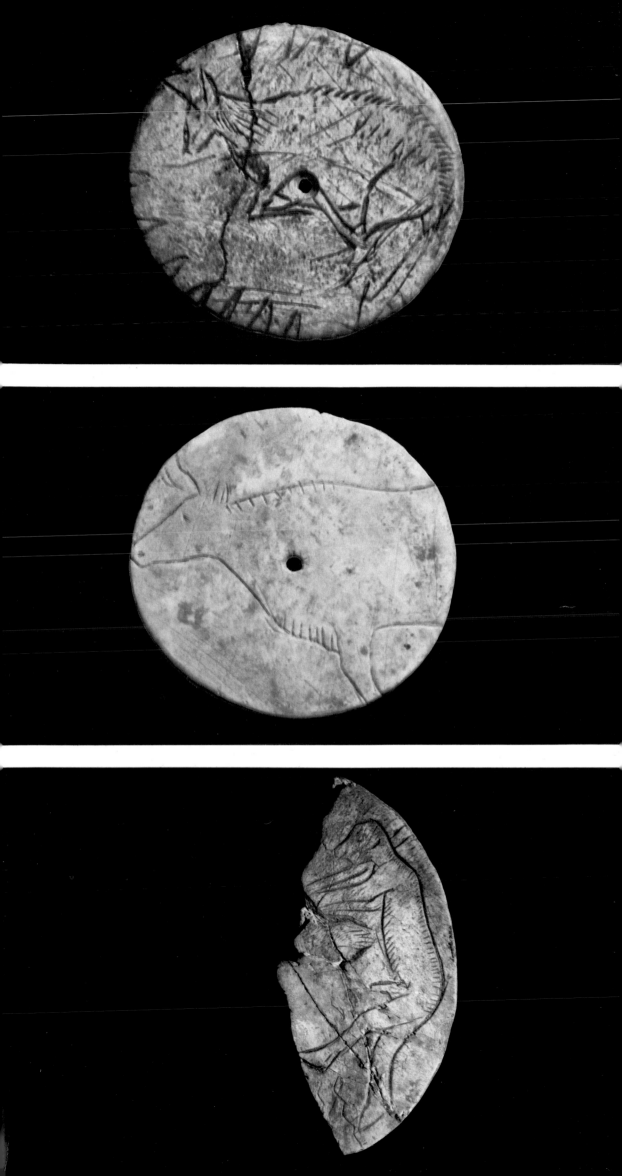

48 LAUGERIE BASSE
Disk carved from a shoulder bone. 1 $^1/_8$ in.
The animal represented on this side
seems to be a chamois.
Museum, Périgueux.

49 LAUGERIE BASSE
Disk engraved with an animal
resembling a cow.
Museum, Saint-Germain-en-Laye.

50 LE MAS D'AZIL
Carved bone disk. On this side is represented
a man apparently carrying some object
against his shoulder; a bear's paw is reaching
out toward his chest. On the other side
there is again a bear's paw, and a human
figure apparently lying on its stomach;
two forked signs, a row of strokes,
and a curved line are also part
of the composition. About 2 $^1/_8$ in.
Museum, Saint-Germain-en-Laye.

4. OBJECTS OF RELIGIOUS SIGNIFICANCE

51 LAUGERIE BASSE
Sculptured figure in reindeer horn representing a carnivorous animal, probably a bear. 3¹/₈ in. This figure is a good example of the difficulty of identifying subjects: if it was part of a spear-thrower, the position of the animal being dictated by the form of the object, the animal might well be a feline or perhaps a young ruminant; but if the shape reflects the animal's natural position, this can only be a bear. Museum, Saint-Germain-en-Laye.

4. OBJECTS OF RELIGIOUS SIGNIFICANCE

Besides objects of practical use, such as spears and pierced staffs, or of personal adornment, such as the disks, the minor arts include three categories of objects that apparently served no material purpose—statuettes, bone plaquettes, and engraved or painted stone plaquettes. We have seen the value of the objects of practical use for establishing a chronology of Paleolithic art; the religious objects are even more valuable on this score, as they lend themselves directly to comparison with the cave paintings and engravings. The reference to "religious uses" can surely cause no surprise; since the days when the engraved plaquettes were looked upon as "sketchbooks," the idea that they were connected with "magical" practices has become generally accepted. The proofs that are adduced are mostly extraneous, based on comparison with present-day primitives, for we still know virtually nothing about the actual practices associated with the statuettes and the plaquettes or, for that matter, with the cave frescoes. What will become clear from our descriptive analysis is that the statuettes, the plaquettes, and the figures in cave art were closely related; this suggests that the plaquettes were units belonging to sets—either in the sense that various figures were engraved on the same plaquette, or that a group was composed of several plaquettes, each showing a single figure. It has not so far been possible to supply material evidence for this hypothesis, since in most cases where groups of several plaquettes were discovered within a limited area the necessary observations could not be made or were overlooked; but occasionally groups of blocks that are larger than the easily handled plaquettes have been discovered, for instance, at Le Roc de Sers and at Teyjat. The inventory of the figures, and whatever can be reconstituted of their original grouping, leave no doubt as to the similarity of their arrangement with the cave-wall compositions, and the latter, of course, raise no questions as to the sequence of their subjects.

STATUETTES

STATUETTES are relatively rare in Paleolithic art, at least in the Franco-Cantabrian area. They are more abundant to the east, as far as southern Russia, and seem there to have taken the place of engraved plaquettes. Except for a few specimens, they are crowded within a relatively short period: most of those which can be reasonably well dated fall between the mature Gravettian and the Middle Magdalenian. To say "reasonably well" dated is no exaggeration, for the great majority of the figures in the round come either from Eastern European sites where, although they were found under favorable conditions, the dating is still difficult to synchronize accurately with Western datings, or from sites in the west where the conditions of discovery leave some room for chronological imagination.

ANIMALS

IN the west, statuettes of animals are very rare: about the only site worth considering is Laugerie Basse, where a bear in reindeer horn[1] was discovered, but under conditions as imprecise as those of the finding of the female statuette in the same place, and a considerable number of figurines found at Isturitz.[2] At Laugerie Basse there is little hope of narrowing down the chronology; our best guess is that the statuettes go back to the Middle Magdalenian. At Isturitz the data are more precise. E. Passemard explored the cave without paying attention to stratigraphic details, but he located the sculptured fragments in soft stone at the bottom of layer E (Solutrean). R. de Saint-Périer, who conducted very important excavations there, found sculptured figures in the Gravettian, and between the Solutrean and Magdalenian III–IV. Consequently the execution of figurines in the round might be extended into the Middle Magdalenian.

Animal sculpture is much more common in Central and Eastern Europe, where figurines of this type are contemporary with representations of the human female. At Vogelherd (Württemberg) a whole series of ivory statuettes was discovered—felines, a horse, a bison, a mammoth. Dolni Vestonice (Moravia) yielded figurines made of a paste of clay and ground bone, representing a feline,[3] a bear, a horse, a rhinoceros,[4] and a bird. Predmosti (Moravia) contributed one mammoth in a style very close to that of a mammoth in sandstone found in the Gravettian layer at Isturitz, and also to that of the figures at Kostienki, USSR, where the most numerous finds in this category were made. The Kostienki figurines are carved from some very soft rock and include several mammoths, fragments of a feline, a bear, a horse, a bird, and an indeterminate animal which was deliberately sculptured without a head. Cave art in Western Europe includes a sufficient number of headless animals to make this Russian specimen interesting.

In Eastern Europe, what the animal statuettes show tends to corroborate what will be indicated by the female statuettes discussed in the next paragraph: the animal sculpture may be dated from the period which includes, in our Western terminology, the close of the Gravettian, the Solutrean, and the first half of the Magdalenian. In Western Europe, sculpture seems to have appeared almost by accident, interest almost entirely having been centered on representation in low relief and in painting.

[1] fig. 51

[2] figs. 450, 459

[3] fig. 261 [4] fig. 262

FEMALE FIGURINES

THERE is copious literature on the so-called Stone Age Venuses or Aurignacian Venuses. When, as early as 1896–97, the first figurines representing prehistoric man—or at least his wife—came to light, they could hardly fail to attract a great deal of attention. The limited number of such figurines that are known have furnished material for many books and articles and for peculiar hypotheses. The forms of the female statuettes being for the most part extremely ample, they are sometimes called "steatopygous Venuses," or even "fat Venuses," terms rather more accurate though less flattering than "Aurignacian Venuses." The excessive prominence, in one or two instances, of the parts situated at the lower abdomen gave rise to the notion that Paleolithic women, like present-day Bushmen females, were especially fat in that section; it was even suggested that the Aurignacians and the Bushmen of South Africa may have been racially related. But steatopygy in Bushmen women seems to be an adaptation to the desert climate, like the hump of the camel or zebu, and the climatic conditions of Paleolithic Europe scarcely conform with such a hypothesis; moreover, as we shall see in discussing the artistic conventions involved, any attempt to conclude that Paleolithic woman must have resembled these statuettes would be like basing the anthropology of the modern Frenchwoman on works by Picasso or Bernard Buffet.

5 charts XLIV, XLV

The leading convention that characterizes these statuettes is the way breast, abdomen, and pelvic region are grouped approximately within a circle.[5] The rest of the body—toward the head and the feet—tapers gradually, even dwindles away along the vertical poles of the circle. As a result most of the figurines can be inscribed within a lozenge, the top of which is barely broken by a head that is usually reduced to a featureless button. In other words, it is a nonobjective representation, and anthropometric measurement in this case is out of the question.

The assigning of an exact chronology to the female statuettes is a difficult task. The traditional view is that they are Aurignacian, as Breuil suggested half a century ago. However, the Aurignacian has since then been defined more closely and a number of subdivisions introduced; we can say, without prejudice to Breuil's original dating, that the figurines made their first appearance somewhere within the boundaries of the Solutrean. What is the evidence that supports such a determination?

The number of "Venuses" so far unearthed is limited, and the conditions in which they were discovered are easy to establish. In the southwest, we have the fragments of ivory statuettes from Brassempouy (Landes). E. Piette, who discovered them in 1898, maintained that they were accompanied by "notched arrows" and "Solutrean leaves"; this best corresponds to what we call Late Solutrean. Breuil showed convincingly that they came from the level directly preceding the Solutrean; at that time this level was regarded as Aurignacian, but today it can just as probably be considered Gravettian or as belonging to the period between the Gravettian and the Solutrean. Unfortunately, exact stratigraphic determination remains unsatisfactory. Lespugue (Haute-Garonne) yielded the ivory statuette which, with one of those from Kostienki, is the masterpiece among the female figures:[6] Mme. de Saint-Périer, who took part in the excavation, told me that in her opinion it dates from within the limits of the Gravettian and the Solutrean periods. Unfortunately, no small object accompanied this figurine. Bédeilhac (Ariège) yielded a horse's tooth with a summarily sculptured head; it dates from an undetermined point in the Magdalenian. Le Mas d'Azil, also in the department of Ariège, yielded another horse's tooth with a female head and torso sculptured at the root; its dating is as uncertain as that of the other tooth. At Laugerie Basse early excavations disclosed a statuette, which has for some unknown reason come to be termed "the shameless Venus,"[7] also a figure in profile probably representing a man; neither can be reliably dated, but both are probably assignable to the period between Magdalenian III and Magdalenian VI. Also from the Dordogne we have the statuette found at Sireuil, a rather steatopygous female figure which may well be Paleolithic, but

6 figs. 52, 264

7 figs. 53, 433

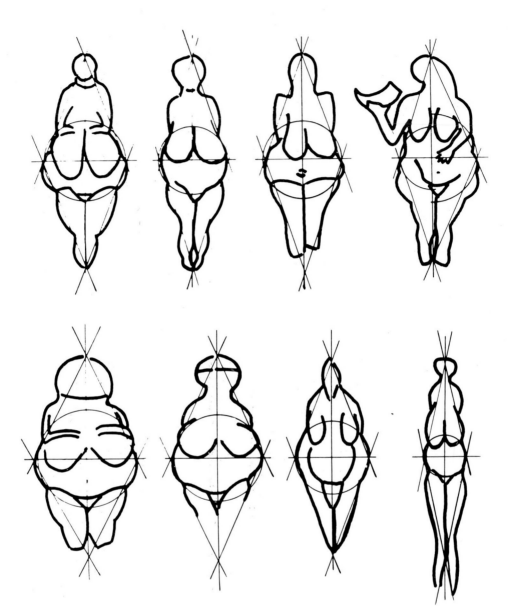

Diagrams, frontal view, of figures from (top row)
LESPUGUE, KOSTIENKI V, DOLNI
VESTONICE, LAUSSEL; *(second row)*
WILLENDORF, GAGARINO *(2 exs.)*, GRIMALDI.
*Note, especially in the works from Gagarino,
the stability of the design, regardless
of the variations in rendering
the proportions. On the basis of this,
the figures from Lespugue
and from Willendorf are entirely equivalent.*

52 LESPUGUE

Back view of female statuette carved
from a mammoth tusk. 5 ³/₄ in. Earlier
than the Solutrean level of the site.
Saint-Périer excavations,
Musée de l'Homme, Paris.

53 LAUGERIE BASSE

Statuette carved from mammoth tusk,
known as "the shameless Venus." 3 ¹/₈ in.
This remarkable work has not been
precisely dated. It comes from
an older excavation and was found
together with works from
Magdalenian III, IV, and V. It seems
never to have had a head; in this
respect it is related to a number
of Magdalenian figures (statuettes,
engravings, low reliefs) from Angles-sur-
l'Anglin, La Roche at Lalinde, and
Les Combarelles in France, Peterfels
in Germany, and Mezin in the Ukraine.
Seen from the side the figure
has the shape of a claviform sign.
Musée de l'Homme, Paris.

which, oddly enough, was discovered "by the side of a road." In 1958, at the Pataud rock shelter near Les Eyzies, H. L. Movius discovered a small low relief of a woman in the style of Brassempouy or Lespugue; it dates from the close of the Gravettian or from the period between the Gravettian and the Solutrean. In 1959 H. Delporte brought to light at Tursac (Dordogne) a very curious figure,[8] similar to that of Sireuil, in a level dating from approximately the same epoch.

[8] fig. 263

To the east of this region were discovered the Italian "Venuses," under circumstances even more peculiar, if that is possible, than those attending the French finds. In the course of the famous excavations at Balzi Rossi (near Ventimiglia) at the end of the nineteenth century, an antique dealer named Jullien unearthed several statuettes in soft stone.[9] Their authenticity, at first put in question, was defended with convincing arguments by the Abbé Breuil. Their chronological provenance remains strictly conjectural. The remarkable statuette from Savignano (province of Modena), sculptured in serpentine marble, was discovered in 1925 "in the course of digging foundations for a rural building," according to P. Graziozi, whose father has held on to the find. In 1940 another statuette was discovered "in a cave" at Chiozza (province of Reggio Emilia). Lastly, a small block in soft stone, about $1^1/_2$ inches long, vaguely cylindrical in shape, with two swellings at the base and a rounded protuberance in the center which might be regarded as a breast, was discovered under conditions so uncertain that even the place of the find is unknown. It has been dubbed "the Venus of Trasimeno." Thus, throughout all of Western Europe, the only dated finds are those at Lespugue, at the Abri Pataud, and at Tursac, all from within the Gravettian-Solutrean periods.

[9] fig. 265-267

At Willendorf, near Krems in Austria, in 1908, a small female statuette in stone[10] was discovered; it was found among tools and implements akin to those which in France we date to the close of the Gravettian. The figure is of the Lespugue type, a faceless head and hair treated in a pattern of lines marking out small rounded protuberances; the arms are folded over the breasts, the middle part of the body bulges excessively, and the short legs ended in minuscule feet, unfortunately broken off.

[10] fig. 268

In Moravia, at Dolni Vestonice, also in a Gravettian or Gravettian-Solutrean setting, several statuettes or fragments of statuettes were found. The most complete one[11] is modeled from a paste of clay and ground bone; although stylized, it belongs to the Lespugue and Willendorf type.

[11] fig. 269

In Silesia, at Petrkovice, a female torso sculptured in hematite was found in a Gravettian-looking context. We must look to the Don River valley in Russia to find the easternmost statuettes: at Gagarino near Tambov three almost complete figures were discovered in this "inter-Gravetto-Solutrean" environment of Eastern Europe, which is probably not too far removed in time from the comparable French one. They are very fine figurines in a style in every way equivalent to that of Lespugue. Even closer stylistically are four statuettes and numerous fragments from Kostienki I near Voronezh. The tools and implements accompanying them are of the proto-Solutrean type of Eastern Europe. The most complete of the statuettes has a faceless spherical head covered by a kind of hairnet, a flat chest from which enormous breasts droop down to the waist, a pendulous belly, small arms, and tapering legs: details that make it a close cousin to the famous statuette from Lespugue in the Pyrenees.

A few other eastern examples must be mentioned: first of all, the very schematic multiple figurines from Mezin (Ukraine), more recent in date than the other figurines from southern Russia. The lozenge-shape stylization is here pushed to the extreme; in the back, there is a protuberance covered with very schematic Greek-key patterns, in front a triangle, the apex of which points downward; the central mass has two tongue-shaped extensions, the longer one for the upper part of the body, the shorter one for the legs. A very similar figure, except for the geometric decoration, was found at Mauern (Bavaria) among Magdalenian remains. Finally the sites of Petersfels (Baden) and Pekarna (Moravia) have yielded some small bone figures carved to represent very schematically women in profile. We shall describe them in greater detail when we discuss the female figures in cave art.

The final tally, although rather unimpressive for the west, is definite on several important points. First of all, until we are more informed, it would be better to stop speaking of "Aurignacian Venuses"; the four western examples for which we have some chronological data are located in the period between the Gravettian and the Solutrean, and this is true for those found in Eastern Europe. No matter where found—Brassempouy, Lespugue, Abri Pataud, Willendorf, Dolni Vestonice, Gagarino, Kostienki—they are practically interchangeable, apart from their proportions. The most complete figures have the same treatment of the head, the same small arms folded over the breasts or pointing toward the belly, the same low breasts drooping like sacks to far below the waist, and the same legs ending in minuscule or nonexistent feet. If there is any time difference between the western and eastern statuettes, it cannot be very great. In both the western and eastern chronological sequences, these very special statuettes with highly conventionalized plastic features make their appearance at the same point of cultural evolution, having numerous coincidences in the tools and equipment they were found among; all are prior to a phase when realism gives way to symbolism in the representation of the female figure. In the east, the statuettes lead to the figures from Mauern and Mezin; in the west, the same symbols reappear in the large signs on the cave walls.

MALE FIGURINES

Male figurines are so few that they need only be mentioned. At Brassempouy, in addition to the female statuettes previously noted, there is a fragment of a statuette which is apparently male. At Laugerie Basse was found the profile of a man without legs which is closely related to certain cave figures. At Kostienki I, several heads in profile were discovered; they are of great interest because—exactly as they occur in western cave art—the faces are stylized like animal heads, a convention which has frequently led to the statement that they represent men wearing animal masks. In western cave art we encounter every possible stage between the approximately normal face and an astonishing representation of a face having a horizontal nose and muzzle-like lips.[12] As with the female statuettes, it is very interesting to see that the same stylistic convention exists at both ends of Europe.

[12] *chart* XXIX

When we survey all the finds, we are struck first by the small number of Paleolithic works in the round, and how widely scattered they are in the west. This scantiness may come down to a question of raw materials, as neither reindeer bone nor reindeer horn was very suitable; but Paleolithic man knew how to handle ivory and, at Kostienki, mammoth bone. It is also possible that there were sculptures in wood that have not come down to us. The only known works in wood are from the terminal Magdalenian; in North Germany (Ahrensburg, c. 8,500 B.C.), three stakes were discovered imbedded in peat; at the top of one of them, a human figure is very summarily carved. Finally it is possible—the over-all picture suggests it—that Franco-Cantabrian figurative systems were primarily focused on engraving, with its developments into deep-cut or low-relief techniques. The low reliefs date from the same epoch as the works in the round, and the temporary vogue for figures in relief may reflect the influence of the eastern cultural group. So many problems remain to be solved that all we can do at this time is formulate questions.

We have already had occasion to note that engraved or painted plaques or plaquettes provide our most valuable evidence for establishing the chronology of cave art. Because they occur without interruption throughout most of the Upper Paleolithic, there is no reason to suppose that they do not reflect the over-all development of figurative art, especially since the subjects on them are the same as those found on the cave walls. Whether the best chronological use has been made of them is doubtful, however, for two very different reasons. First, there are too many specimens of undefined age among the most famous engraved slabs, so that the fragile time scale established by the reliable specimens becomes cluttered with attributed dates. Second, the chronology based on the engraved and painted slabs does not always match the traditional attributions of cave art, in particular the prodigious antiquity presumed for certain frescoes.

The works on plaquettes vary in size as well as in the nature of their material. Some are of considerable dimensions, engraved on blocks or slabs about three feet in length; many are on fragments of soft stone or bone small enough to hold in the hand. Moreover, a certain distributive pattern is discernible: the small bone plaquettes become frequent only in the Middle Magdalenian, which begins the period when decorated objects are most abundant. In the case of some of these works, it is hard to say whether they may not have decorated larger objects of which only a fragment has come down to us; but the number of bone fragments more or less uniformly decorated, that obviously served no practical purpose, is sufficient to prove that bone slabs and stone slabs were contemporaneous.

FIRST PRIMITIVE PHASE (STYLE I)

The earliest figurative works belong to the category of engraved or painted stone slabs. Only one site yielded a stratigraphic series in the Aurignacian—La Ferrassie (Dordogne); but works from other sites (the Cellier and Castanet rock shelters, Isturitz, Arcy-sur-Cure) show that this case is not an exception. Nothing is known that can be dated prior to the Aurignacian, and at all our sites there is evidence of the extremely crude state of the representations. This continues for a long time, with a little progress discernible during the last phases of the Aurignacian, and all the known works dating from the earliest stage may be looked upon as belonging to the same primitive period.

The figurative expression is very unsure; several works can hardly be distinguished from the groups of jumbled lines that make their appearance in the Chatelperronian. At Isturitz, vague, undeterminable outlines are discernible; at La Ferrassie the figures are engraved more clearly, but the majority can be identified only with a great deal of difficulty. All we can say on the basis of the evidence dating from the epoch is that an effort was made to represent animals, and that they are in several cases accompanied by oval figures of a female sexual character.[13] In one case, rows of cup-marks accompany them (La Ferrassie, Aurignacian IV); at the Abri Cellier, vulvas and animal heads are accompanied by rows of strokes (Aurignacian I); at Arcy-sur-Cure (Reindeer Cave, layer VII) a schematic vulva is flanked by a row of short strokes (Aurignacian II). When we interpret these venerable but barely comprehensible documents in the light of the more explicit figures which succeed them, we realize that they belong to the same current: animal figures accompanied by female and male representations make up the core of all the later decorations on slabs and cave walls. We may also surmise that whenever several animals were represented they could be differentiated by species, probably already the groupings of animal species that constitute the art of the caves. Cave paintings have quite often been attributed to the Middle Aurignacian— that is, Peyrony's Aurignacian I and II: no reliable stratigraphic evidence, however, supports this hypothesis.

[13] *figs. 23, 249–255*

SECOND PRIMITIVE PHASE (STYLE II)

[14] fig. 258

IN the period that follows the Aurignacian, works are more abundant and link up directly with the crude figures from the terminal Aurignacian. The earliest dated figure comes from Laugerie Haute, where Peyrony found it in the old Gravettian (Perigordian III); it is a limestone tablet covered on both sides with barely legible thin lines out of which can be discerned on one side, two mammoths, and on the other, a head which might be that of a horse.[14] These figures are exactly what would be expected as a development out of the representations found in the terminal Aurignacian at La Ferrassie. At Gargas, an engraved pebble shows a lion and a bison; they can be made out clearly, but are still very summary. The same applies to the rhinoceros accompanied by a herbivore without horns or antlers from the Gravettian site at Les Rebières

[15] fig. 260

(Dordogne),[15] to the oxen and horses from El Parpallo (Spain), and to the slab and the plaquette from the Abri Labatut (Dordogne), on which the figures of horses are already more accomplished, but in the same representational line of the other sites. Finally, in two Gravettian levels at Isturitz, R. de Saint-Périer found several works; except for one probably representing a reindeer and another an ox, the figures are clear but

[16] fig. 259

the exact species is rather uncertain.[16]

On the strength of the documents, the earliest definite animal art is actually Gravettian: the animals have uniform stylistic traits which are found only on a very limited number of cave walls. If earlier cave works existed, their very primitive character would in any case make it hard to date them with certainty.

To say that no stylistic determination is possible in the primitive works would be incorrect, but the possible similarity of later works makes very risky any dating based solely on style. As for the works that are dated, the earliest that are not incomprehensible scrawls represent primarily animal heads and forequarters. This was noted by Breuil long ago, as was the cursory treatment of the feet in the majority of figures we here consider within the archaic period. The Gravettian figures also, in a considerable number of cases, consist of heads or foreparts. Those more fully treated have overdeveloped foreparts, communicating to the rest of the body a kind of forward and upward impulse which is most striking. I have grouped all the earliest dated figures under Style I, and those which are for the most part found in the Gravettian under Style II. It must be kept in mind, however, that actually the two primitive phases are linked together, and that, as we have already observed, changes in artistic style are not determined by changes in spears or scrapers.

ARCHAIC PERIOD (STYLE III)

THE linking of periods is just as real when we pass from the Gravettian to the Solutrean and then to the Early Magdalenian. We have already seen in chapter 2 that this intermediate period remains obscure, despite the striking character of the criteria that define its different aspects.

One thing is remarkable: when we consider the artistic works identifiable as Solutrean (from the proto-Solutrean to the terminal Solutrean), one group of them falls distinctly into Style II, and the other into Style III, although it is not always possible to draw a clear relationship between their stylistic features and the stage, more or less advanced, of the tools and equipment with which they were found. The reasons for this are the paucity of reliable data on the one hand, and on the other the circumstance that the figurative traditions in a region may have been independent of its technical traditions. This period, during which Paleolithic art attains maturity, is the more important because it was also the period of its greatest geographic dispersion.

The easternmost works—the female and animal statuettes previously discussed—

were located in the Don Valley. At Kostienki, which we may take as our point of reference, the figurative works are accompanied at two different levels by implements of a type parallel with the Solutrean or Gravettian. We have already mentioned that Eastern Europe has few engravings on slabs, and that statuettes predominate there—this fact may be connected with the development of low-relief sculpture in the west during the Solutrean and part of the Magdalenian. However, at Kostienki I, in a level that appears epi-Solutrean, one engraving of an ibex on a rib fragment was found, as well as a few fragments of engravings on soft stone including one female figure.

At the other end of Europe, Spain, in its Cantabrian and coastal sites, possesses Solutrean levels in which engraved and painted slabs are found. These finds suggest a number of general reflections. In the famous cave of El Parpallo in eastern Spain, painted and engraved slabs have been discovered which have been dated from the Gravettian to the Magdalenian, though it is not easy to distinguish between them solely on the basis of style. The Abbé Breuil reported the same engravings of hinds on bone plaquettes dating from the Solutrean at Altamira and from Magdalenian III at El Castillo, both in western Spain. If these facts could be confirmed by careful excavations they would show the real interlocking and the rapid succession of the chronological divisions in the period when great Paleolithic art came into being, for, in addition, the El Parpallo figures are in the archaic Style III, while the Cantabrian figures already emphatically belong to Style IV.

If we now pass to the French Solutrean, the data are fairly numerous and of a character intermediate between the Russian and the Spanish data. The pertinent sites are, from south to north: Lespugue and Isturitz in the Pyrenees, excavated by R. de Saint-Périer; Bourdeilles (Le Fourneau du Diable) in the Dordogne, excavated by D. Peyrony; Badegoule, also in the Dordogne, excavated by Dr. Cheynier, and Le Roc de Sers (Charente) excavated by Dr. Henri Martin. Unfortunately, Solutré (Saône-et-Loire) can only be mentioned in remembrance. On the whole, the works best represented are mature Solutrean, characterized by laurel-leaf points *à cran* ("notched"). What is striking is that works in low relief and in the round now occur regularly, among engravings on plaquettes that scarcely differ from those of the Early Magdalenian and the beginnings of the Middle Magdalenian. At Isturitz, E. Passemard and later R. de Saint-Périer discovered subjects treated in the round, and small low reliefs in soft stone, from the Solutrean to the Middle Magdalenian. At Bourdeilles, a small pendant of schist engraved with a reindeer[17] was found next to a large block on which several oxen are admirably rendered in low relief. At Le Roc de Sers, a few engravings on plaquettes were found in conjunction with the large blocks that bear a whole frieze of low reliefs. At Solutré itself, despite the carelessness of the early excavations, the two known works from the site—two small low reliefs in soft stone—are linked to the Solutrean. Furthermore, the famous reliefs supposed to be Aurignacian (that is, Gravettian) from Laussel (Dordogne) do not all have an absolutely certain stratigraphic position, and one of them was found in a relatively late Solutrean layer.

[17] *fig. 235*

The "Solutrean" group, which actually includes phases at each end, one in the Gravettian, the other in the Early Magdalenian, is thus of special interest because it marks the transition to the archaic style, or Style III. We shall come back to the characteristics of Style III when the evidence provided by cave art enables us to make a survey of all works in this style, but it is necessary to define them roughly here. The survey of Style I showed that in the beginning the figures were crude and usually limited to the head or foreparts. Style II, still very primitive, continued to stress the foreparts of animal bodies: arch-necked horses, bison with prodigiously swollen withers. Style III, which progressively supplants Style II, preserved the over-all arabesque design of primitive figures but introduced many conventions in treating details of limbs, musculature, and coat. The figures were gradually stabilized in a figurative code which in the Middle Magdalenian came to encompass the whole Franco-Cantabrian area. Some of these conventions were current as early as the Solutrean.[18]

[18] *charts XXXIX–XLIII*

Another point is important: the reliefs. If we exclude the figurines on Middle and

Late Magdalenian objects, there is a period in Paleolithic art which is marked by sculpture both in the round and in low relief. This is a relatively long period, centered around the Solutrean but running from the end of the Gravettian proper to the beginning of the Middle Magdalenian. Into this period which, according to carbon-14 dating, extended from 20,000 to 13,000 B.C., fall the female statuettes, the animal statuettes, the small low reliefs on plaques, the big sculptured flat stones and blocks, and the cave walls engraved all over with large animals. The various aspects of this art of sculpture are common to east and west, from the Don to the Pyrenees. Prehistorians were aware of some of the problems raised by this cultural community during the middle part of the Upper Paleolithic; two which particularly interested them were that of the origin of the Solutrean culture, and that of sculpture as the specifically Solutrean art. Concerning the origin of the Solutrean, hypotheses vary, and I have mentioned earlier that it is hard to choose among them. According to some, the Solutrean people came from the steppes of Central Asia; according to others, they came down from the slopes of the Pyrenees or across the Mediterranean. Such views rest on the assumption that the people—in this case, "the Solutreans"—were immigrants bringing with them a complete culture—namely, the Solutrean culture. Actually, the assumption of a migratory people is not needed; it is enough to assume that ideas and a few objects circulated from neighbor to neighbor, thus creating a cultural network —which necessarily comprises similarities and dissimilarities—throughout regions where the conditions of existence were roughly the same.

Another problem to which reference has already been made several times is that of the Early Magdalenian. Until careful excavations have been carried out at a sufficient number of sites, it will be hard to determine with any degree of certainty what is to be understood by the division between Early and Middle Magdalenian. When the Abbé Breuil introduced his six subdivisions of the Magdalenian, he clearly emphasized the lack of precision in the data then available. No real progress on this score has been made since, partly because excavators were more often eager to assign their finds to Breuil's Magdalenian IV or VI than to clarify the way the finds were actually disposed at every level and in each site.

The first perplexing question is that of Magdalenian I/II (or Dr. Cheynier's proto-Magdalenian). The decorated objects that have come down to us from this period are of little importance; apart from some handsome spears with decorated beveling, they are limited to a few engraved plaquettes, in particular one found at Laugerie Haute with two ibexes, and a pebble from Pech de la Boissière on which the same animal appears. We would willingly admit of an eclipse of the production of plaquette engravings in the Early Magdalenian, if we were sure that this "hiatus" is not merely created by shortcomings in archaeologists' methods and in the present chronological system.

[19] figs. 433, 485 CLASSICAL PERIOD (STYLE IV)[19]

MAGDALENIAN III is no less perplexing: its spears with single beveling, its cave walls sculptured in low relief, and its engraved slabs suggest a direct and normal continuation of the Solutrean. Unfortunately, there are again only a few sites that provide reliable data. The one richest in decorated objects is the Grotte de La Marche at Lussac-les-Châteaux (Vienne), which yielded several dozen decorated slabs and plaquettes. Although the excavations were made only recently, they were far from careful, and while some of the finds are admirable, they can be dated only approximately, like the finds made by the nineteenth-century pioneers. Moreover, the attributions in the published material vary from one subdivison of the Magdalenian to another. Fortunately, we have the excavations at Angles-sur-l'Anglin where Dorothy Garrod and Suzanne de Saint-Mathurin discovered excellent levels of Magdalenian III: though their detailed results are not yet published, what we already know makes it possible to define the situation around the Loire clearly enough. In that region Magdalenian IV, supposedly characterized by proto-harpoons with rudimentary barbs, is not clearly defined.

Farther south, in the Dordogne, at the sites near Laugerie Haute and at La Madeleine, Magdalenian III and IV appear to be distinguishable: in the first instance, there are the same spears as those found at Angles, and a scarcity of decorated objects; in the second, the spears are somewhat different, there are proto-harpoons, and a profusion of decorated objects. Still farther south, at Isturitz, for reasons apparently connected with excavation methods out of date even at the time, one passes from the Solutrean to a level at which spears like those at Angles, proto-harpoons, and a profusion of decorated objects are found side by side. Evidences from every stage of the Early and Middle Magdalenian are discernible there. In Spain the situation is even less clear. As for Isturitz (Basses-Pyrénées), the Abbé Breuil characterized the situation there as follows: "We know that in the majority of French sites in the Pyrenees Magdalenian IV follows the Solutrean without any interpolation of Magdalenian I–III." This remark implies that the Solutrean survived a long time in the Pyrenees; it could be as well interpreted by the shortness of the time span separating the two periods as by the absence of stratigraphic details.

Leaving aside these problems which scientific publications based on careful excavation may eventually settle by simply confirming the overlapping of the "leading fossils," it appears that there was an early "Magdalenian" episode which continues certain technical traditions of the Solutrean and is closely linked to it through features of its art. At the beginning of the Middle Magdalenian (Magdalenian III), decorated objects begin to be produced in larger numbers. An abundance of decorated objects and plaquettes characterizes the Middle Magdalenian and to an even greater extent the Late Magdalenian. Consequently there is a strong contrast between the early Magdalenian periods (Styles I, II, and III) and the following period (Style IV) in respect to the frequency of decorated plaquettes: 83 percent of them belong to Style IV. The ratio is inverted in cave art: the figures in Late Style IV are in the minority in relation to the earlier figures (Style III and Early Style IV). This suggests that decoration of the cave sanctuaries was gradually abandoned in favor of plaquette decoration. The moment when this development begins can be determined fairly accurately, as will be seen later. The themes characteristic of Magdalenian period III (bison/horse) continue into the beginning of period IV, sharing their predominance with the ibex and the stag. During the second half of period IV we observe a multiplication of mammoths in the caves (dated by decorated objects from Magdalenian IV), then of reindeer, with an occasional bear (though this is unusual). The reindeer and bears are identical with those on dozens of plaquettes contemporaneous with the harpoons. The proliferation of decorated plaquettes, then, occurred around Magdalenian V (c. 11,000 B.C.). There still remained for the minor arts about two thousand years of life.

So much space has had to be devoted to discussing the uncertainties of stratigraphic chronology because the major part of Paleolithic art occurs between the Solutrean and the Late Magdalenian, and because we should like to have a less slippery foundation for discerning the small steps in artistic evolution, and more solid clues for localizing certain finds at least to within five thousand years. Such a goal would be perfectly attainable if we had even four well-excavated sites in the whole of western Europe. Thanks to a few sites whose names recur constantly we can at least establish the principal lines. Up to this point the artistic development, based upon a few dated guideposts, appears coherent: the earliest figures from the Aurignacian (Style I) are consolidated in the Gravettian (Style II), assert themselves in the Solutrean, become abundant at the close of the Solutrean and during the Early Magdalenian (Style III), develop further during the Middle Magdalenian and the greater part of the Late Magdalenian (Style IV), only to undergo a final evolution which leads to their decline. This skeletal outline—or, to use a more flattering term, this framework—is apparently stable. However, it involves a certain disproportion which will probably be accounted for by future research: style analysis does not account for the considerable time span that is supposed to be covered by the first four Magdalenian periods, and we could not infer from the evidence of the objects alone the long lapse of time between the Solutrean at Le Roc de Sers and the sculptured spear-throwers of Magdalenian IV found in the Pyrenees. Did aesthetic canons stubbornly survive, as they occasionally do in religious art, or was there a rapid telescoping in the development of tools and equipment? For the time being it is best to leave this question open.

THE CLOSE OF THE MAGDALENIAN

A FTER the time span included within Magdalenian I to IV, which raises so many questions, an evolution takes place. During this period, at least in some sites, harpoons grow more numerous, and although decorated objects and engraved slabs remain abundant, their character changes. A more realistic style develops: conventional details disappear and the animals lose their hieratic attitudes, becoming more lively. A few realistic compositions of animal groups, even scenes combining animal and human figures, make their appearance. The famous engraved slabs from Limeuil[20] and the big slabs from Teyjat[21] are the best-dated evidences for this evolution, which was still producing great works in Magdalenian VI. This group of works, closely related to the group from Magdalenian IV, has been treated in this book as belonging to Late Style IV.

[20] figs. 28, 85
[21] figs. 99, 486

Toward the close of the Magdalenian, during Magdalenian VI, the groupings begin to break up and the figures to lose their proportions and contours. For instance, at Villepin[22] the latest engraved animals seem to fade with the merging of the Magdalenian into the Azilean, which prolongs the style in a physical environment resembling that of the present day.

[22] fig. 458

[23] charts VI, VII

THE SUBJECTS[23]

W E have thus far said little about the subjects treated in the decoration of slabs and plaquettes. A simple enumeration would suffice to show that they present every subject listed in Paleolithic art. It is more interesting to establish the importance of the various subjects. The most frequent is the reindeer (19 percent of the specimens); then the bison and the horse (12 percent each); and then, in the order given, the bear, the ibex, and the male human figure; less frequent are the ox, the hind, the female human figure; still less frequent are the stag, the bird, the feline, and the fish; the rhinoceros and the mammoth are rare; and quite exceptional are the chamois, the saiga antelope, the hare, and the grasshopper.

This classification does not agree with that covering the different groups of tools and equipment, especially the pierced staffs and the spear-throwers. It also differs from that of the animals in cave art, where the reindeer and the bear are less common, the mammoth and the stag more common. These differences are particularly instructive when the slabs are studied in chronological order: reindeer virtually disappear between the Solutrean and Magdalenian V, reappear toward the close of Magdalenian V, and remain until the end; bears become more numerous in the terminal period, when the reindeer reappear; mammoths occur especially in the periods prior to Magdalenian V. Consequently this difference can only be accounted for by a statistical reason, the strong increase in the number of plaquettes in Late Magdalenian art. It attests to two changes: the gradual turning away from cave-wall decoration in favor of the plaquettes, and the replacement of the big bovids and the feline as subjects by the reindeer and the bear.

When these facts are collated with the data obtained from methodical study of the cave-wall figures, we notice that the majority of caves with decorated walls date from exactly the period when the reindeer was dying out as a subject in the minor arts; and that in the Middle Magdalenian there is a coincidence between the decoration of household objects and that on the cave walls. This coincidence, together with the stylistic evidence and such finds as we can date, enables us to give an early date to the sanctuaries where mammoths turn up frequently; to the middle period, those caves where the bison and the stags are far from the cave entrances; and to the terminal period, those caves where we see the return of the mammoths and the proliferation of reindeer.

Decorated objects, taking together those of technical use and those of religious significance, provide us with a reliable guide through Paleolithic art, and its principal difficulties must be understood before we deal with the cave sanctuaries. We know that stratigraphic data concerning the sanctuaries is almost completely lacking; therefore the figures decorating them can be classified only in reference to some pre-established sequence. Cartailhac and Breuil, at a time when the efficacy of the stratigraphy of these dwellings was being discovered, planned to obtain a sequence of reference by using the superimposition of figures on the walls themselves: they assumed that the Paleolithic artists continually drew new figures on the same walls, just as walls of churches are repainted from time to time. This amounted to founding a system of mural stratigraphy which would need only to be compared with the stratigraphic evidence of objects to supply us with the key to dating cave art. Conclusive results were achieved in enough cases to serve as the basis for a referential sequence, but the method itself gave rise to many confusions, which have been pertinently pointed out by Annette Laming-Emperaire. For example, figures drawn at the same time and superimposed by the artist for compositional reasons place serious obstacles in the way of a clear-cut chronology.

The method followed in this book takes up an entirely different principle: it is based exclusively on the comparative sequence which the dated decorated objects provide. It is possible that objects and caves had entirely different iconographies, but it is harder to believe that each had an entirely different type of execution, and particularly that minor details of treatment recurred outside the cave at one epoch and inside the cave at another. Therefore, if the two sequences—the objects and the cave art—disclose the same variations in their evolution, it is more than probable that these variations are contemporaneous in the two sequences. Preliminary stratigraphic examination of the objects provides us with this fundamental safeguard.

On the artistic plane also, the stratigraphy of the decorated objects provides us with irreplaceable evidence that the history of the most primitive art known followed a normal, gradual course—that it was an art with a beginning, a long and varied flowering, and an end. The inventory of its subjects reveals an extraordinary stability in the thought that inspired them. Among the technical and religious objects, the relatively limited character of the themes, which constantly involve half a dozen animal species and representations of male and female principles, cannot be defined as clearly as we shall define it for cave art. But the persistence of these themes is reinforced by the different ways in which the various categories of objects are distributed, so that animals and men appear not so much as individuals than as symbols associated with the different functions of the objects.

This impression is further strengthened by the existence of a dual system of representation, symbolic and realistic, which develops in two parallel sequences throughout the full range of the Upper Paleolithic. It is even possible to ask whether symbolic representations did not precede realistic ones, since the earliest animal figures are no more than vague forms. As a matter of fact, the two methods of representation undergo a parallel development, and the maximum point of symbolic elaboration corresponds to the maximum point of realism or, rather, to the maximum conventionalization of realistic figures.

What armature of traditions could underlie a superstructure of figural representation at once so stable and so complicated? The objects alone cannot provide a satisfactory answer to this question, because *in situ* they are like pieces of a scattered jigsaw puzzle, each yielding only one element which cannot by itself be related to the whole. But cave art, set down forever on the walls in immutable compositions, can be asked to yield sequential developments that reflect more fully the thought that animated them.

5. THE MEANING OF CAVE ART

5. THE MEANING OF CAVE ART

[1] *chart* IV

THE distribution of cave art, compared with that of the minor arts, is more strictly limited both in space and, it seems, in time. The Paris Basin constitutes the northern boundary. To the east, if we discount the Italian finds, it does not extend beyond the Rhone Valley. The Atlantic Ocean constitutes the western boundary,[1] and Gibraltar the southern. Spain, central France, and southern France (from the Rhone Valley to the Atlantic) make up the entire territory of cave art, to which the term Franco-Cantabrian applies much more aptly than it does to the minor arts.

This situation is doubtless provisional, for we know that decorated objects from the Old Stone Age have been found as far east as the Ukraine and Russia, with other important discoveries in southern Germany and Belgium. Recently, in 1960, the Russians discovered painted animals (horses and mammoths) in the Kapova cave on the Belaya River which flows down from the Urals: this find extends the territory of European cave art more than 600 miles to the east. Consequently, further discoveries are possible. The decorated caves that have been discovered over the last fifteen years, however, following the rage for speleological exploration which has gripped Yugoslavia, Czechoslovakia, and Germany no less than France and Spain, are nearly all in regions where they would traditionally be expected to exist. The only exceptions so far are the Kapova cave in Russia, and, in Italy, the Romanelli cave (Otranto province), where a few very schematic figures were found, and some Sicilian caves of which the walls are decorated with quite remarkable animal and human figures.[2] The Italian form of groupings in these Sicilian caves, at Levanzo and Monte Pellegrino, show compositional features and themes common to the Franco-Cantabrian area, but treated in a different spirit. In the Kapova cave in Russia, the presence of bison, horses, mammoths, the rhinoceros, and symbolic signs points to an affinity with the west which we have already found in the statuettes.

[2] *fig. 710*

We must keep in mind the obvious fact that cave art exists only where there are caves; this in itself excludes large geographical areas, and the Paleolithic inhabitants of such areas must have used other sites for their sanctuaries. However, apart from the Ukraine and southern Russia, caves and rock shelters are to be found in a sufficient number of places that the empty ones do not weaken the argument for the regional character of cave art. When we leave aside the Soviet sites, which attest a close kinship with the west at about the Solutrean period but later apparently with a cultural complex different from the Franco-Cantabrian, one problem still remains: Magdalenian sites in Switzerland, Germany, and Belgium have yielded decorated objects, pierced staffs, spear-throwers, and plaques which are much akin to the Franco-Cantabrian, in caves or rock shelters whose walls were just as suitable for painting and engraving; why have no decorated caves been found in these countries? The question is hard to answer without reaffirming what seems to me to emerge from study of the Franco-Cantabrian evidence: if cave art is limited in space, it is also limited in time.

For a long time one could suppose that all the stages of the Late Paleolithic are represented on the cave walls of the west, but this is probably not the case. The earliest stage of the art seems to be missing: it is especially in the Gravettian that men began to execute decorations far inside the caves. These probably followed a long phase during which walls of rock shelters exposed to daylight—practically all of them later destroyed by the ice—were engraved with works in Style I, some few fragments of which have been picked up in the course of excavations. And just as the earliest works are largely missing, so are the latest. Many small thinly engraved figures long regarded as Magdalenian V–VI may have belonged to a much earlier stage, since at Angles-sur-l'Anglin the works of this type were buried by Middle Magdalenian layers. Wherever cave-wall figures dating incontestably from the Late Magdalenian have been found, they have been found at the cave entrances, in the daylight zone; incidentally, very few examples of such figures are known. Now, the Swiss and German stations which have yielded decorated objects are from the very phase when cave art seems to have ceased to be practiced in the Franco-Cantabrian area. Perhaps the most convincing proof of this is provided by the reindeer. The statement has become almost standard that the reindeer occurs very rarely in cave art, while it abounds in the art of Late Magdalenian decorated objects. Actually, the reindeer appears on decorated objects in two separate periods—at the beginning, between the Gravettian and the Early Magdalenian, and at the end, in Magdalenian V–VI. During the intermediate period, although reindeer bones keep turning up in the kitchen refuse of the dwellings, the animal appears only very rarely among the strictly limited cast of animal characters most frequently represented on walls and objects: its place was taken by the stag. In the Late Magdalenian the reindeer again appears on objects, but nothing of this recurrence is discernible on the cave walls, except among the latest decorations at a few sites, such as Les Combarelles, Font-de-Gaume, and Les Trois Frères. There is, however, one exception—of the type expressly made to prove the rule—and that is the Teyjat cave. This is thought to be the extremely rare case of a decorated cave of which the figures can be dated precisely—and it belongs incontestably to Magdalenian V–VI. But it is dated for the exact reason that the figures are not engraved on the walls but on large fragments of stalagmite; these were buried among the archaeological layers because they were in the inhabited portion of the cave, near the entrance, in the daylight zone.

The view we are advancing here, although it is not at all the usual one, confines the great age of decorated sanctuaries to the period between the Solutrean and the Late Magdalenian, its midpoint falling within Magdalenian III. As we shall see, there are decorations that go back to the Gravettian, and the Franco-Cantabrian area is so vast that local traditions could precede or survive this time scheme. However, the over-all pattern is so coherent that any major deviations from this norm are difficult to imagine.

METHOD OF DATING

UNTIL now the entire chronology of cave art has been founded on the works of the Abbé Breuil. These works are evidence of a considerable effort at systematization, and of an exceptional sense of form that enabled him to perceive features often lying beyond the reach of a method which was, after all, relatively simple and limited. Probably it was his extraordinary intuition and aesthetic sense that caused the method to serve as an instrument of verification rather than of research.

At a time when the dating possibilities afforded by a stratigraphic examination of the successive human occupations at a site were being discovered, Cartailhac, and Breuil who was then his pupil, had the idea of creating a stratigraphic system of dating the decorated walls: a study of the superimposition of the figures should make it possible to determine the older in relation to the more recent. I have already stated why this method, irreproachable in theory, is fairly unreliable in practice. There are isolated cases where a later figure is actually superimposed over a considerably earlier figure, but there are many more cases where the artist himself deliberately superimposed one figure over another. Mme. Laming-Emperaire has brought convincing proofs of this circumstance; the stratigraphic method is plainly not valid in such cases. At a time when it was thought that caves were secret places in which the hunters merely enumerated, one by one, the animals they hoped to kill, it was legitimate to make the most of the superimpositions. But when it appears, as I shall show presently, that the figures in a given cave form one whole, from the entrance to its innermost reaches, the most we can make of the superimpositions is that some figures were reworked or added in the course of time. Such corrections or additions are valuable for dating purposes, but unfortunately they do not as a rule encroach on older figures.

Cartailhac and Breuil were obviously on the right track when they proposed a stratigraphic approach to the works; some day this method of research will certainly be taken up again to achieve a progressively exact chronology. At the present stage I am dispensing with it. It is now possible to draw up an inventory of the great majority of the figures, but a complete and critical inventory of all the superimpositions would require setting up an entirely different research apparatus. Moreover, even when examining a single superimposition, it is by no means as easy as might be expected to determine which of two paintings or engravings lies atop the other. An inventory of superimpositions would probably introduce as many errors as fresh certainties.

In his enormous work surveying the whole of cave art, the Abbé Breuil had occasionally to decide that the older figure was the one whose style seemed to him to be the more archaic; that is, he was guided, in the last resort, by stylistic analysis. It is regrettable that he never devoted a work to the systematic exposition of the stylistic criteria which constituted the basis of his chronology. Except for his exposition of the general features of figure treatment in *Quatre cents siècles d'art pariétal* [*Four Hundred Centuries of Cave Art*], the work in which he sums up the development of Paleolithic engraving and painting, his stylistic criteria refer only to examples scattered throughout his studies published over half a century. Each case is generally enveloped in a context that suggests that things may be, in scientific matters, at once self-evident and relative; and thus we cannot reconstruct, strictly speaking, a grammar or syntax applicable to the whole.

TWISTED PERSPECTIVE

PERHAPS the most striking illustration in this connection is Breuil's criterion of "twisted perspective." This recurs continually in his writings, each time handled with moderation and caution but ultimately, when we add up the conclusions drawn from the various cases, proving of little value. Some of the oldest figures, like the bison at La Grèze, are shown with the body in profile and the horns spread out in frontal view. At first glance, this seems to provide a highly reliable stylistic criterion, one of those well-nigh infallible keys such as those that do turn up in the history of art in every period. He considers a bison in the cave at Le Portel, with both horns brought down toward the muzzle, to be an example of "twisted perspective," and for this reason the figure is classified as Aurignacian-Perigordian. But at La Loja in Spain, in a group that includes every possible type of horn and evidently engraved by one artist, a cow whose horns are represented exactly like those of the bison at Le Portel is dated, like the rest of the panel, "from the Magdalenian age"; the horns, we are told, are *en perspective à peine ou non tordue* ("in non-twisted or scarcely twisted perspective"). In Breuil's works we also find the term "semi-twisted perspective" used to characterize a type of horns which occurs throughout the period corresponding to our Style III, the type in which the foreground horn is shaped like the arc of a circle, while the background horn is S-shaped. At La Peña de Candamo, we are told, the oxen "are magnificently executed in the same semi-twisted perspective as the rock drawings of the [Spanish] Levant." But if the oxen at Candamo are really of the type described as "semi-twisted," those of the Spanish Levant are shown in twisted perspective and with symmetrically curving horns. The Lascaux oxen, dozens of which exhibit asymmetrical horns, are characterized in a different manner: "The horns, still in twisted perspective, nearly frontal in the previous sequence (large bulls), here show important variations in the drawing... the last two pairs of horns are still in twisted perspective but attenuated." This refers to bovids 19 and 24 in the Axial Gallery, which do not appear to differ noticeably from the large bulls, save perhaps that their horns are somewhat wider apart. But obscurity becomes total when we go back to the La Loja oxen (held to be Magdalenian): of four figures, one presents the horns in profile, two in semi-twisted perspective, and one completely frontal—that is, twisted—perspective. Now, what Breuil says about the perspective of the horns of oxen and bison or the antlers of stags is statistically exact;[3] among the criteria he discovered, this one is certainly most valuable. But statistical truth is only an indication, and each instance requires multiple cross-checking to establish the validity of the whole. Twisted perspective occurs in every period of art, down to our own day; semi-twisted perspective is the one the camera most often captures when one photographs a bovid whose head seems to be in profile. Our awareness on the one hand of the value of perspective as a criterion, and on the other of chronological disparities among figures having identical pairs of horns, obliges us to admit the ambiguity of the criterion taken by itself, and thus to seek other methods of discrimination.

[3] chart L

On these two seemingly fundamental points—superimpositions and stylistic criteria—I have been unable to continue the line taken by the Abbé Breuil; I should have had no choice but to repeat what he said that has served most students of prehistoric art for the last fifty years, or to undertake a laborious criticism of details that would be incompatible with the respect that is due his memory. I have never been his pupil, still less a disciple, but for twenty years I have profited from his knowledge often enough to conceive a true admiration for him. I may have been unable to convince him of certain facts which seem to me demonstrable, but I came late to the field, at a time when his system was already, to himself, a thing of the past. Therefore, the only course was to attempt an independent synthesis, and the reader has already seen the bases on which I felt I had to start anew on the inventory of datable art objects and to re-examine in person the majority of the known caves. Made cautious by nearly thirty years of experience as an anthropologist, I have also said why I have dispensed with anthropological parallels, setting aside what I know of the Australian aborigines or the Eskimos in order to avoid making the Magdalenians of western Europe into some mongrel progeny of the last primitives in the modern world. I could also add that I have had no recourse to my own imagination, since everything is contained in my topographic inventories of the caves and the data transferred to punch cards—a procedure that makes it possible mechanically to sort out all the bears, or all bears associated with bison, or the bears on spatulas, not to mention any subject occurring both on spatulas and on spear-throwers. Yet this statement would not be altogether true, for imagination is the foundation of scientific work; there is no escape from it, but the first use to which it should be put is to devise material means for keeping it within reasonable bounds. When the punch cards show that 90 percent of the bison are found, not at the entrances of caves or in the remotest reaches, but in the middle sections, we have a substantial fact on which to base the imagination but the imagination cannot create such a fact out of whole cloth.

THE IDEAL PALEOLITHIC SANCTUARY

Before attempting a chronology of the works of art (as I shall do in the last part of this book), it is necessary to establish what is found in a decorated cave, and the reasons for looking upon it as a sanctuary. The idea of mechanically transferring the disorder of caves onto cards, to see whether some sort of order would emerge, did not come to me quite spontaneously. Since 1947 I had been collecting data on decorated objects for this book, which was originally intended to present a chronology only. As I began to study the representations in the caves, I gradually became aware of repetitions—certain animals turned up next to each other too often for such associations to be explained only as chance. Above all, I realized the importance of the signs, everywhere present among the figures, and I began to make an inventory on regular file cards, by subject, in the customary manner. This was in addition to the punch cards on which I had long been recording, layer by layer, all the implements and all the art objects found at a given site. Then I went on to reconstruct whole caves, as the Abbé Breuil had done for several of them—Les Combarelles or Font-de-Gaume, for example—and I became sharply aware of the repeated occurrence of bison next to horses, of stags and ibexes in the deepest parts of the caves, and of the sequences of short strokes at both ends of the caves. This was the point at which Mme. Laming-Emperaire and I decided to compare the conclusions we had reached separately. What emerged from this exchange of views was more than reassuring; in her work, which was entirely independent of mine, she maintained that the cave-wall pictures were real compositions, not the casual additions that Paleolithic hunters had made over the course of millennia. She had found that bison invariably appeared in the neighborhood of horses; that lions were associated with horses in the deeper parts of the caves; and that women were regularly associated with bison. Moreover, she had noticed that certain combinations were sometimes repeated in the same cave, as if, she thought, they had originated in some mythological tale whose stereotype characters could be found everywhere, always in the same relationship. Such a convergence of results required us to create new working methods and to carry them as far as we could: I set out to re-examine all the figures in all the cave sanctuaries possible. It took me three years, with the help of Fr. Hours and Jean Vertut, to carry out this task. I prepared a punch-card index for each cave, section by section, in order to be able to test all the hypotheses concerning subjects and their positions. It would be too much to say that we reached a point where we could guess in advance the location and the nature of the pictures in a given section of a cave: the Paleolithic artist, although never contradicting himself, had at his disposal multiple and sometimes surprising solutions. However, on many occasions we surprised whomever was leading us by asking for missing subjects which he had, by force of habit, omitted to show because they were vague dots lost in some far gallery, or by telling him what we expected to find next in the cave he was about to show us.

An ideal cave would consist of a single corridor, along the walls of which Paleolithic artists, when they wished to execute a coherent design, lined up their figures one after the other. Such caves exist—for instance, La Croze at Gontran, Covalanas, Les Combarelles, the Axial Gallery at Lascaux, Le Gabillou, or Marsoulas. If the hypothesis that came to one's mind were always the simplest one I should have begun with these caves; moreover, others would have done so before me, for I would be guided by a kind of evidence that would not have escaped my predecessors. But in the present case, the facts only emerged after statistics had shown the variable frequencies between the subjects at entrances and in the remoter parts of the caves. Mme. Laming-Emperaire's discovery was remarkable considering the means she used, but it was of the same sort that I had noticed at the cave at Le Portel, where almost all the horses are in one gallery, almost all the bison in another, and all the signs in a third. Moreover, others had noticed this: in 1935, E. Bourdelle and P. Jeannel studied the horses at Le Portel from the zoological point of view and noted that they had been treated as a group. What could not be seen, however, was this: because horses normally occur with bison, the normal group is horse + bison. If at Le Portel there are twenty horses in one gallery and more than twenty bison in another, the necessary complement is found too: there is one horse among the bison, and one bison among the horses, as well as the minimum of indispensable signs.

Statistical exploration, then, led to the present scheme for bringing clarity into the seeming disorder with which the figures are strewn over the cave walls. The difficulty, however, was to set up a system of topographical divisions that would not prejudice or mask such actual order of the figures as may exist. In the case of an ideal cave, the risk is slight for one need only place the figures at the beginning, the middle, or the end of a sequence. As a rule, however, caves have nooks and crannies, side chambers running off in different directions; moreover, as Mme. Laming-Emperaire observed, the same composition may be repeated—occasionally more than five times. After a good deal of casting about, I adopted the following rule. The first figures and the last—usually isolated from the rest—are those at the entrance and at the back of the cave. In the in-between zone, topographical variations, such as narrow passages, bends, and passages connecting one chamber to another, served to establish my divisions; experiment showed that such topographical variations served Paleolithic artists for changes in the composition. Finally, I divided the central portion of each cave's decoration into panels (wherever such panels could be clearly made out), and within each panel or homogeneous group I distinguished between central figures and those surrounding them. This over-all scheme made it possible to separate out the other figures at the entrance of the cave, those at the beginning of each major composition, those on the periphery of the compositions, those which mark the end of each chamber or other portion of the cave, and those at the very back.[4] Many correlative facts were brought to light in this way, but when details were re-examined with reference to the first results, the system of grouping the figures disclosed an additional fact: the occurrence of minor "peripheral" subjects paired with typically "central" subjects. In other words, everything seems arranged according to a dualistic system: the signs and animals belonging to one group (A) frame or complement the signs and animals of group (B) that are all in the main panels. To take a simple example (which is also rather abstract), we may find a horse at the entrance and one at the back of the cave, also a horse at the entrance and at the exit of each chamber, and then, on the panels of the chambers, central bison each flanked by a small horse, and horses which enframe the whole. What we actually find is somewhat more complex, because group A will include several animals—horses with ibexes or stags—whereas group B will include only one species in each cave, usually the bison, sometimes the ox or the mammoth. We must also account for the subjects—such as men, lions, rhinoceroses, bears—that occur only at specific points, or those that form a small isolated group—such as the ox in bison caves, and the bison in ox caves.

This organization of the figures, which seem scattered at random over the wildly uneven surfaces of the cave walls, is so extraordinary that it must be shown in greater detail. By this route alone shall we reach toward the thoughts of these men who are the only people anywhere in the world, at any epoch, to have sheltered their works of art in the dank depths of caves.

[4] *chart* xv

THE ANIMALS

THE material used in this book comprises 2,188 animal figures distributed in the 66 decorated caves or rock shelters that I have studied on the spot,[5] among the 110 sites known at present. First of all it must be said that, statistically speaking, the number of species represented is much lower than the number of species known to have existed at the time. Paleolithic artists did not portray just any animal but animals of certain species, and these did not necessarily play an important part in their daily life. In order of frequency, I have counted 610 horses, 510 bison, 205 mammoths, 176 ibexes, 137 oxen, 135 hinds, 112 stags, 84 reindeer, 36 bears, 29 lions, and 16 rhinoceroses. Other animals are occasionally found, and the list may be completed with 8 large-horned deer, 3 undefined carnivores, 2 boars, 2 probable chamois, and 1 probable saiga antelope. Among the non-mammals, there are 6 birds, 8 fishes, and 9 monsters such as the composite animal at Lascaux (the so-called unicorn), the "antelopes" at Pech Merle, the "giraffes" at Lascaux and Le Gabillou, and the reindeer with palmate hoofs at Les Trois Frères.

[5] *chart* xvi

This list should be scrutinized from a geographical point of view. For instance, the majority of the 135 hinds come from Spanish caves, and the mammoths occur in a relatively small number of caves (50 percent of the mammoths are at Rouffignac in the Dordogne). However, a geographical breakdown reduces the regional totals to so few cases that they lose all statistical validity; it is still too soon to subdivide into ethnic zones developments occurring over many millennia. Hinds and mammoths have at least qualitative importance throughout the Franco-Cantabrian area, and the variations in frequency do not modify the over-all picture in which it is very clear that the main actors are the horse and the bison, the animals next in importance being the hinds, the mammoths, the oxen, the ibexes, and the stags. The relative unimportance of the reindeer is surprising, but we have already observed that the period of the decorated sanctuaries coincides with the decreasing representation of reindeer on decorated objects. Bears, lions, and rhinoceroses also play an important part, but as a rule there is only one representation of each per cave, and they are by no means represented in every cave.

The other animal species introduce special cases to which we shall come back later—such as local substitutions of the chamois for the ibex, and the intrusion of fish as a substitute for the barbed sign on decorated objects.

6 *chart* xix

If we now consider the animal species with respect to their topographical position within the caves, the results are extremely clear-cut.[6] Ninety-one percent of the bison, 92 percent of the oxen, 86 percent of the horses, and 58 percent of the mammoths occur in the central portions of the caves and rock shelters; in these areas the remaining species seem to have percentages of less than 10. Certain animals occur at the entrance, on the periphery of the central compositions, and at the back of the cave as well—these are the ibex ($9 + 65 + 21 = 95\%$) and the stag ($22 + 29 + 37 = 88\%$). The ratios are inverted between these two as "framing animals": stags appear more frequently at the entrance and at the back of the cave, ibexes more frequently in the vicinity of the bison and oxen.

The percentages of the rarer animals are in certain cases, significant. Seventy-one percent of the lions are at the back of the cave, but the lion may occur in the central composition, for instance at the Bayol cave and at La Baume Latrone. Of the bears, 60 percent are found on the periphery of the main compositions, and in passageways, but 17 percent are at the back of the caves. The case of the hind is special, for it occurs everywhere: in some regions, however, it seems have been regarded as one of the major herbivorous animals and thus placed at the center (for example, at Covalanas), while in others it had the role of a cervid and acted among the "framing animals" with the stag and the few representations of reindeer.

Consequently, topographical study discloses a clear division of the animals into three groups. The first comprises the large herbivores—bison, ox, mammoth, horse; the second, the small herbivores—stag and ibex; the third, the most dangerous animals—lion, bear, and rhinoceros, all of which occur by themselves in the rear portions of the caves.

This might almost suggest a cynegetic or hunters' division, a kind of technical classification of the species according to the risks involved or the amount of meat they can supply. But when the other figures have been brought into study, we shall see that such a division is very unlikely, and that underlying the figurative pattern is a dualistic classification. The first clue is provided by the horse: its most frequent position is at the center and, except at Arcy-sur-Cure, it is present wherever groups of large herbivores are present; but it never accompanies more than one of these herbivores (bison or ox)—a circumstance suggesting that in such cases the horse represents the other group of figures (B; see p. 111). Indeed, 12 percent of the horses are distributed in the parts of the cave where ibexes and stags are usually found, and this anomaly is so striking that when we visit a cave for the first time we ask ourselves, as we approach the remotest part, "will there be a horse?"

Here we may make a comparison with the decorated objects, on which the three "framing" or "complementary" animals—horse, ibex, and cervid—are in the overwhelming majority those found on such obviously male objects as spears, harpoons, spear-throwers, and the handles of pierced staffs. It may well be, then, that behind this topographical division there is a classification of animal species along two vectors—one comprising the horses, ibexes, cervids (stag and reindeer), and mammoths; and the other comprising the bison, oxen, and, occasionally, hinds. This first insight into the meaning of the sanctuaries will be amply confirmed when we come to examine the other figures.

THE HUMAN FIGURES

Representations of human beings are not very numerous. Various cross-checks seem to indicate that they make their appearance throughout the period of the cave sanctuaries, according to a system in which abstract representations are most frequently used.

Women are represented explicitly on slabs at Terme-Pialet and Laussel (Dordogne)[7] that date from the period between the Gravettian and the Solutrean; on the frieze at Angles-sur-l'Anglin (beginning of the Middle Magdalenian); at La Magdelaine (Tarn),[8] which is not reliably dated but has bison in the Angles style; on the engraved block from La Roche at Lalinde[9]; at Les Combarelles, which is also not dated reliably; and on the slab at the Couze railroad station (Dordogne), which is Middle Magdalenian. In many cases the representation of the human female in archaic or archaistic groups is confined to a vulva—for instance, at Pech Merle, Gargas, Ebbou (Ardèche), and Bédeilhac (Ariège). These female representations are often situated in the central area of the compositions, alone or accompanied by large herbivores: this constitutes a first confirmation of our impression that the division of the animals is on a sexual basis.

Representations of the human male are more numerous and rather varied in character. They may be profile silhouettes (for example, at Laussel, Les Combarelles, and La Peña de Los Hornos[10]; at Los Casares; at Pech Merle[11]; at Villars and Saint-Cirq[12]; at Cougnac[13]), ithyphallic figures (at Lascaux[14] and Le Portel[15]), isolated phalluses (at Ebbou, Les Combarelles, and Pech Merle), or faces in frontal or profile view (at Font-de-Gaume,[16] Rouffignac,[17] Les Combarelles,[18] Le Portel, Marsoulas,[19] Labastide, Altamira,[20] Angles-sur-l'Anglin). These figures have as large a chronological range as the female figures. Their topographical position is in nearly all cases at the back of the caves or on the periphery of a central composition—that is, inversely to the location of the female figures. In the remote portions of the caves are also found the male figures whose heads are provided with a pair of bovid or cervid horns, such as the famous "sorcerer" at Les Trois Frères,[21] the one at Le Gabillou,[22] and two less distinct figures, one at Font-de-Gaume and one at La Pasiega (Spain).

All these figures are placed in the vicinity of animals, or occasionally by themselves in some recess, but the striking fact is that their topographical positions are reversed: the males belong with the set of subjects found in the depths of the cave, the females with the subjects of the central sections. We may infer from the topographical division that the male human figures, the horses, the ibexes, and the stags form a group distinct from that of the female human figures, the bison, the oxen, and the mammoths. The division of the repertory of figures into a "male" group and a "female" group seems very probably to be a fact. However, two questions arise. What is the meaning of this dualistic system? Is there some real connection between the bison and the women, for example, or between the stags and the men? The first question may remain unanswered for a long time; as to the second, we shall be able only to specify the relationships between the two groups of figures that seem to constitute a single symbolic scheme.

[7] figs. 54, 55

[8] figs. 501, 502

[9] fig. 56

[10] figs. 270, 522, 689   [11] fig. 374
[12] figs. 358, 361   [13] fig. 384
[14] fig. 323   [15] fig. 391
[16] fig. 531   [17] fig. 343   [18] fig. 512
[19] figs. 567, 568   [20] figs. 402–404

[21] fig. 57   [22] fig. 58

54   TERME-PIALAT
Plaquette with two deeply incised
female figures. 8⁵/₈ in. The dating of
this work is relatively uncertain,
but it can be no later than Aurignacian
(the period between the Gravettian
and the Solutrean). Museum,
Périgueux.

GROUPINGS OF ANIMAL SPECIES

THE groupings of animal figures of different species is certainly one of the most characteristic features of Paleolithic art—a feature which was entirely overlooked until Mme. Laming-Emperaire published her work. Since the two caves in which she conducted her research, Lascaux and Pech Merle, are among those containing the clearest examples of these groupings, it is surprising that they have gone unnoticed by the dozens of other researchers who have passed before them. At Lascaux the most important section of each panel is occupied by oxen and horses—this occurs not only once but at least six times from the cave entrance to the back, in every chamber. At Pech Merle, the clearly delimited compositions repeat the themes of bison/horse and bison/mammoth at least six or seven times. Because I was investigating virtually all the caves and all the subjects represented, I had not arrived at so definite a distinction when I compared my results with Mme. Laming-Emperaire's. I had seen that the animals belonged to a limited number of species and that different formulas were used in different caves, some emphasizing the bison and others the ox, but that the number of possible combinations was fairly small and reflected a concern for group composition and for linkages between animal species. Realizing at once that discovery of the pairing ox/horse (at Lascaux) or bison/mammoth (Pech Merle) provides the first clue for interpreting the cave compositions, I began to make a statistical tabulation of all possible combinations among the different subjects. My tabulation not only confirmed Mme. Laming-Emperaire's discovery but disclosed in addition a whole network of relationships among animals, human figures, and signs, each set divided into two complementary groups.

The fundamental principle is that of pairing: let us not say "coupling," for there are no scenes of copulation in Paleolithic art. The idea of reproduction perhaps underlies the representation of paired figures but what we shall see subsequently does not absolutely establish this. Starting with the earliest figures, one has the impression of being faced with a system polished in the course of time—not unlike the older religions of our world, wherein there are male and female divinities whose actions do not overtly allude to sexual reproduction, but whose male and female qualities are indispensably complementary.

As we have seen, the central figure in cave art is a herbivore—in the great majority of cases it is the bison, less often the ox, in rare cases the hind. This central animal is almost always associated with the horse.[23] As early as 1924 Dr. L. Capitan and Abbé Jean Bouyssonie had been struck by the almost constant presence of the horse. In a study of numerous plaquettes from Limeuil, they made this valuable observation: "Let us note, however, that in almost all the drawings showing several figures the image of a horse can be made out." The numerical ratios between the two species of animals vary and do not yet seem to present any clear motivation; however, a kind of balance is suggested by the proportions. At Lascaux, for instance, the large bulls seem to be accompanied by small red bovids, while the large cows are surrounded by a small herd of horses. On the painted ceiling of Rouffignac, bison, horses, mammoths, and ibexes variously predominate, by size or number, in different parts of the caves. At Niaux and Les Trois Frères, one of these associated species is emphasized within each particular group.

The pairing principle is certainly fundamental, but it does not account for everything, for in a large number of cases the element of a third species is involved.[24] This is sometimes the ibex, sometimes the stag, and occasionally the mammoth. It is placed most often to one side, like the hind in the great ceiling at Altamira or the ibexes on two of the bison panels at Les Trois Frères. At Niaux, the ibexes are clearly subordinated to the bison and placed very close to some of the latter. In many cases a kind of hierarchy is discernible among the three species represented. The large herbivore not only occupies the central place but is larger in size than the others: at Lascaux, for instance, the oxen predominate on each panel by their dimensions; at Les Trois Frères, the main

23 *chart* XXIV

24 *chart* XXV

panel shows one bison within which are inscribed many small bison. In these cases the horse is smaller in size (Lascaux, Les Trois Frères, Niaux). Sometimes the horse even seems to be missing entirely, being indicated merely by a sketched dorsal line, as, for example, in the first panel on the left in the Black Salon at Niaux. The ibex is still smaller at Niaux, and at Les Trois Frères. The same treatment may occur when the mammoth completes the triad, as in the deep gallery at Altamira where a mammoth is represented only by its dorsal line at one side of a horse/bison group. A variation is supplied by occasional panels in which the complementary cast is enriched with a fourth element.[25]

[25] chart XXVI

The role of the mammoth is hard to unravel. In two cases it seems to be one of a central pair: at Arcy-sur-Cure it appears twice, in the vicinity of bison, without any other associated animal; at La Baume Latrone, it appears next to the horse and the feline. Apart from these highly untypical cases, which are also marginal geographically, the mammoth belongs to the group of animals complementary to the pairing bovid/horse, but its location and proportions vary. It may be found only at the entrance to the cave (Pair-non-Pair, Ebbou), in the remotest part (El Pindal, El Castillo, Altamira), or on the edge of a composition (Les Trois Frères). When it is integrated as a third element it may occur as an isolated subject within a composition (Gargas, Isturitz, Altamira, La Mouthe, Les Combarelles, La Croze at Gontran), or it may literally overwhelm the composition by the multitude of individuals associated with a single bison/horse pairing (Chabot, Pech Merle, Bernifal, Rouffignac).

So far we have discussed only the central associations that occur, often repeated several times in the same cave, whenever there is a pairing that includes one of the large herbivores of the bison-ox group. In short, these come down to a large-herbivore/horse pairing, plus a third element—ibex or cervid, or occasionally mammoth—which seems because of its subordinate position to serve as a kind of reminder of the pairings found at the entrance and at the back of the cave. Between the animals of the latter group (cervid-ibex, occasionally horse or mammoth) there is no complementary association but a kind of reduplication between symbols of the same order. As a matter of fact, we find caves showing one ibex or one stag or one horse (entrance and back may be identical or different), and caves showing two or even all three of these animals.

The complete list of possible groupings discloses extremely interesting linkages that confirm what has just been stated and help us to grasp other aspects of this curious problem. Among 2,151 figures, I have found 659 cases of pairing—the difference being explained by the fact that a single bison may be accompanied by several horses, and vice versa. The probability of error from confusing one group with another (in some caves the figures are extremely entangled) is approximately 20 percent; thus, to be on the safe side, I have regarded as normal only the associations that number above 30 percent of the cases.

The large herbivores of the series that seems to be fundamental present the following picture: the bison is associated with the horse in 64 percent of the cases, all other associations being less than 3 percent—that is, far below the margin of probable error. This method may be regarded as cruel and somewhat barbarous because it means omitting, for example, the bison/mammoth pairing which clearly exists at Pech Merle, but it serves primarily to disengage the main lines of development. The ox is associated with the horse in 49 percent of the cases, other associations being negligible. These are the only major pairings in the central series that involve animals of the second group (group B): thus it is safe to say that the bison and the ox are normally associated with the horse.

The animals found at the entrance and back of the cave, together with the central "framing animals," yield ratios which are equally characteristic. The horse achieves statistical validity only when it is a central animal, which is normal considering its marked predominance in large compositions (53 percent of the horses in groupings are linked with bison), but we also find it as a reinforcing element in the peripheral figures. Thirty-three percent of the stags are associated with horses, at the entrance and at the back of caves, but chiefly at the back. In 30 percent of the cases the stag is paired with the hind, which is very interesting, because these, along with the large-horned deer, are the only animals on the cave walls whose sex we can always distinguish with certainty. The ibex is associated with the horse in 40 percent of the cases. It throws a little light on the role played by the mammoth to note that the only substantial percentage it discloses (38 percent) is when it is linked with the bison: consequently it can often be topographically likened with the horse.

Can we speak of the more rare animals? The term "percentage" becomes purely formal when the total number is only 20, but at least it provides a clue which may or may not be helpful in an individual case. The 25 "associated" reindeer I l sted are associated with the mammoth in "32 percent" of the cases. The large-horne l deer, which occurs 6 times (Les Combarelles, Cougnac,[26] Gargas, Pair-non-Pair, Pech Merle), is represented 5 times with its hind. The lion is often represented very sketchily, but in 15 instances there can be hardly any doubt, and 7 others are probable in varying degree (Cap Blanc, El Castillo, Les Combarelles, Las Monedas—in a chimney, Pair-non-Pair, La Pasiega, Le Portel). Among the 15 figures which are certainly lions, 6 are associated with representations of horses (Les Combarelles, Font-de-Gaume, Labastide, Niaux, Pech Merle). In the 9 remaining cases, there is either no obvious association, or the feline is part of a composition of paired animals (Font-de-Gaume—engraving on clay, La Baume Latrone, Bayol, Angles, La Clotilde, Lascaux—4 felines).

[26] fig. 383

Thus the animal groupings seem to fall into two types: an association of a complementary type in the central part of the cave (bison/horse, for example); or an association of equivalent symbols in the peripheral area, such as at entrances and at the back of the caves (for example, horse/ibex/stag). What is certain is that one group, the peripheral animals, is represented in the central panels, whereas the bison/ox group never appears among the peripheral figures. This arrangement must be added to our tentative findings from the study of decorated objects which led to the hypothesis of a division of animal species into two groups.

To speak now of a "male" group and a "female" group is to get ahead of the argument; only after we discuss the problem of the signs will it become clear that there is a division along these lines. At this point we have only the merest inkling, from the distribution of subjects on the decorated objects. But before going farther we must dispel a possible misunderstanding concerning the sex of the animals. In general, we may say that their sex is not represented: it is almost astonishing to see how few of these animals can be identified with certainty as male or female. Writers refer on every possible occasion to "pregnant" mares, but it would be interesting to know just how anyone can distinguish a well-fed equine on a cave wall from a pregnant one. At a time when 50 percent of all prehistorians took it for granted that the purpose of the cave drawings was to encourage the fertility of game (and the other 50 percent believed that they represent magically slaughtered beasts) no one could be blamed for viewing every plump horse as pregnant. However, there is no material evidence to support this view.

When we try to reconstruct the attitude of Paleolithic man on the basis of his art, we are surprised from the outset by how little concerned he was to provide his animals with proper organs for guiding the prehistorian to decide their sex. The indications are absent, except in the case of a few bulls at Lascaux and one female bison on a panel at Les Trois Frères (and this in a bizarre composition where the bison, walking on her hind legs, follows a reindeer in the same attitude which waves its arms with palmate fingers, and precedes an evidently male creature that is half-bison, half-human). Other exceptions may still be found, but they are certainly not the rule, especially during the classical period.

Should we suppose that the figures have been conceived as sexless? This is unlikely, for a bull or bison often has a discreetly indicated sheath. Zoologists believe they can distinguish the males from the females among the oxen at Lascaux (exclusive of those bulls about which there is no possible doubt). It is entirely certain that, in the case of species which could not be drawn without indicating the sex, the secondary sexual characteristics suffice to show to which sex an animal belongs. In Spanish caves, stags and hinds are often found next to each other; there are large-horned deer in couples, the male with his immense antlers, the female without antlers; at Cougnac and Las Monedas couples of ibexes can be seen, the male with horns describing three-quarters of a circle, the female with small goatlike horns; among the reindeer, we sometimes find two subjects, one having very large antlers, the other rudimentary ones, which corresponds to the male and female characteristics of the species.

HUMAN FIGURES

Now we enter an even more fascinating domain, that of the self-portraits Paleolithic men have left behind. If we are to believe the evidence of the statuettes, the plaques, and the cave art, Paleolithic woman was a simple creature, naked, with curly hair, who lived with her hands clasped over her chest, her minuscule head rising serenely above distressingly sagging breasts and bulging thighs. As for Paleolithic man, his facial features extended into an animal snout with a bulbous nose, but he was otherwise unremarkable; like his mate, he maintained himself in the midst of a hostile nature clothed only in his convictions. In the depths of his cave, he sometimes assumed rather indecent attitudes and wore huge antlers or bison horns. Man and woman are occasionally shown in profile, bending forward as though bowing. This is all we know about them, and there is little doubt that the portraits they left us are somewhat idealized.

These few data, however, have been enough to give rise to several hypotheses—indeed, to a whole literature. I have already said what I think of the anthropological value of these figures: to regard their proportions as characteristic of a race would be as great an error as to take Bernard Buffet's faces as an index of the average Frenchman today. But some prehistorians have gone further—one Central European scholar worked out a detailed theory as to the Paleolithic technique of copulation. Here, once again, imagination is running far ahead of reality: there is not a single scene of human copulation in all Paleolithic art, not even a single instance of an ithyphallic figure in close proximity to a female figure. The only seeming exceptions are some engravings at Les Combarelles in which the hindquarters of two bison happen to be superimposed in such a way that they vaguely suggest a human couple[27]; a sculptured slab from Laussel which is so unintelligible that for the past half-century no consensus has been reached as to what is represented on it[28]; and an engraved plaquette from the cave at La Marche representing a woman in frontal view, which one prehistorian, making the most of a large number of stray lines, interprets as two human figures in profile in each other's arms.

[27] *chart* LV

[28] *fig. 273*

We have previously discussed the female statuettes and the pierced staffs with male decorations; but the study of human representations on cave walls must take into account everything represented on other objects and on plaquettes. Thus I shall now address myself to this matter as a whole.

REPRESENTATIONS OF WOMEN

Our survey of the statuettes of women has disclosed that they are widely distributed, from France to southern Russia and perhaps as far as Siberia. It has also shown that the forms are highly conventionalized, even in the figures that seem most realistic. The statuettes from Kostienki, Willendorf, and Dolni Vestonice, like those from Lespugue, Brassempouy, or the Abri Pataud, reflect a well-defined canon: the breasts, the belly, the pelvic region, and the thighs fall within a circle from which extend the tapering torso and legs. These latter portions of the anatomy are of such secondary importance that in Russia and in the Ukraine, between the Solutrean and the Magdalenian, they are eventually reduced to two thin sticks with no indication of details. What remains is a central mass on which the pubic triangle is engraved.

In the west, the engravings on plaquettes and on cave walls undergo a similar development: the earliest are complete figures of women or representations simply of the pelvic region or the vulva alone (these also occur at Kostienki I in a layer contemporary with the statuettes); only later are they replaced with abstract symbols. Among the complete examples, two types of representation occur—frontal and profile view—and each has its descendants among the abstract signs.

Women in frontal view are rare. We can mention only the low reliefs at Terme-Pialat (Aurignacian-Gravettian); those at Laussel (Gravettian-Solutrean); those at Angles-sur-l'Anglin (Magdalenian III) of which the torso and the legs are omitted, in keeping with the convention normal in that epoch; the surprising reclining women at La Magdelaine (Tarn) (Early Style IV, Middle Magdalenian); and the engraved plaquettes from the cave at La Marche, which may belong to Magdalenian III. Frontal representation thus seems limited in time to the early period. It is interesting to note that none occurs in the depths of the caves: this confirms the idea, which will be developed later, that the sanctuaries inside the caves are of later date than the sanctuaries at the entrances or beneath the rock shelters.

29 fig. 54

The women in profile view seem, in the west, to go back to the same epoch, judging by the slab from Terme-Pialat (Dordogne)[29] which dates from a highly developed stage of the Aurignacian, and shows the deeply incised outlines of one woman in frontal view and one in profile view. The pose of the latter is erect, and the contours are very similar to those of a statuette. The next specimen is later, since it was found in the Pech Merle cave; the dating of this cave presents difficulties, but one part of it seems to belong to the Solutrean and the other to the Early Magdalenian. On one of its ceilings there are several complete figures of women; they are shown in profile view, half-bent forward.[30]

30 fig. 382

The meaning of this inclination is not quite clear: Luquet was perhaps right to see in it an approximation of the line of the human figure to the dorsal line of an animal. In the last part of this book we shall see that the same dorsal line plus a few details of horns, trunk, or mane, is sufficient to define a bison or mammoth or horse, and that Paleolithic artists were so well aware of this that they engaged in plays on form, a sort of graphic punning. Thus Luquet's hypothesis may not be too far from the truth, particularly in view of the fact that at Pech Merle, near the bending women on the ceiling, we find the baffling group of bison/women that will be discussed later. We also find bending women at Les Combarelles, and it was these figures that gave rise to the astonishing hypothesis that Paleolithic women took this position when offering themselves to their mates. As a matter of fact there are at Les Combarelles, among figures of uncertain sex and simple coincidences of lines, three figures which are certainly female, shown in profile view, and without heads or legs.[31] The same highly schematized profiles are found on the Magdalenian slabs from La Roche at Lalinde[32] and the railroad station at Couze, which introduce us to the group of small figures on objects or plaquettes dating from Magdalenian IV–V.

31 fig. 514
32 fig. 56

The mature Middle Magdalenian and the beginning of the Late Magdalenian provide plaquettes having a fairly large number of female figures in profile view, almost all associated with animals; we shall return to these shortly. Unfortunately, almost all are broken. Among the isolated figures dating from the end of this period of Style III and the beginning of Style IV, we must mention a small plaquette from the Abri Murat (Lot),[33] which shows a bending woman with bison horns on her head; also the pendants from Petersfels in Germany, on which we find the same type of profile in zigzag, with no indication of head or legs.

33 fig. 434

Thus it seems that the representation of women's bodies is coherently distributed over two periods. The period of frontal representation includes, primarily, low reliefs of a type closely related to the statuettes (this is the early group, and is not represented in the caves). The period of profile representation of bending women is later, at least in the majority of cases. Only a few of these occur in the caves, but the type is almost abundant on decorated objects from the Middle and the Late Magdalenian.

VULVAR REPRESENTATIONS

THE presence of complete figures in the caves, however few they are, affords precious coordination in interpreting the wall compositions; but the whole system which the signs represent would probably have remained incomprehensible without the presence of figures that are limited to the representation of the female sexual parts. Even if we had no complete figures of women, we could still have established all that one can say on the subject of female representations.

The earliest works with figures that are reliably dated are those from the Abri Cellier in the Dordogne (Aurignacian I) and an incised slab from La Ferrassie (Aurignacian II), which, in addition to a few drawings of animal foreparts, include representations of vulvas.[34] Such representations are found at other Aurignacian sites in the Dordogne, particularly in the Castanet and Blanchard shelters. One fragmentary representation appears on a Gravettian plaquette from Isturitz. For the early decorated objects, judging from the finds accessible at present, the series ends around the proto-Solutrean of East European dating, for at Kostienki I, in addition to the well-known statuettes, there are curious little "medallions" in soft stone, semicircular in shape, the convex side of which apparently turned downward, showing in the hollow an oval representation of the nature of which we can hardly have any doubt. Among later objects, vulvar representations are rare and belong among the abstract signs rather than among the realistic figures (for instance, the small "ladybug" from Laugerie Basse), except for the engraved half-rounded rod from La Madeleine (Dordogne).[35] This shows a vulva, a phallus, and a bear's head arranged in a frieze, and is one of the keys to interpreting the abstract signs. This major work will be discussed again in connection with the signs.

In cave art, too, representations of the vulva are rare; there are not more than seven sites where such representations are unmistakable: Arcy-sur-Cure, Les Combarelles, and Pergouset[36]; Gargas, Pech Merle, Bédeilhac, and Ussat.

[34] figs. 249–254

[35] fig. 216

[36] figs. 513, 548, 557

MASCULINE REPRESENTATIONS

A survey of human representation in the Upper Paleolithic seems to show, as we move from epoch to epoch, that the proportion of male to female figures is wholly reversed. In the earliest period, statuettes and low reliefs of women are fairly numerous, then they grow scarce, giving way to abbreviated figures or signs. On the other hand, complete representations of men are rare in the early periods, and much more frequent in the caves during the peak period of the interior sanctuaries.

The earliest figures of men that we can place—though unfortunately not as accurately as we could wish—belong to the period between the Gravettian and the Solutrean and are far less characterized, according to sexual typology, than the statuettes and low reliefs of women from the same period. One fragment of a statuette from Brassempouy, the large statuette from Brno (Czechoslovakia), and the male figures in low relief at Laussel show they are masculine merely by a summary indication of the sexual organs. In the Solutrean there are two legible representations on low reliefs at Le Roc de Sers. At Angles (Magdalenian III) there is one fragment from a low relief showing a head in profile, which constitutes a transition toward the representations of faces in profile that we frequently find in decorated caves. It is impossible to discern a develop-

56 LA ROCHE AT LALINDE
*Schematic female figures engraved on
a slab. The size of the figures are
from 4 to 6 in. Magdalenian III.
Female figures reduced to the trunk are,
at other sites, associated with animals
in Early Style IV. These figures
at La Roche confirm the dating of a
part at least of Les Combarelles as
Middle Magdalenian.
Museum, Les Eyzies.*

57 LES TROIS FRÈRES
*The so-called Sorcerer. 29$^1/_2$ in.
The figure is partly painted, partly
engraved. Set in the highest and most
inaccessible spot in the "Sanctuary,"
it consists of a combination of male
symbols (man, cervid, horse).*

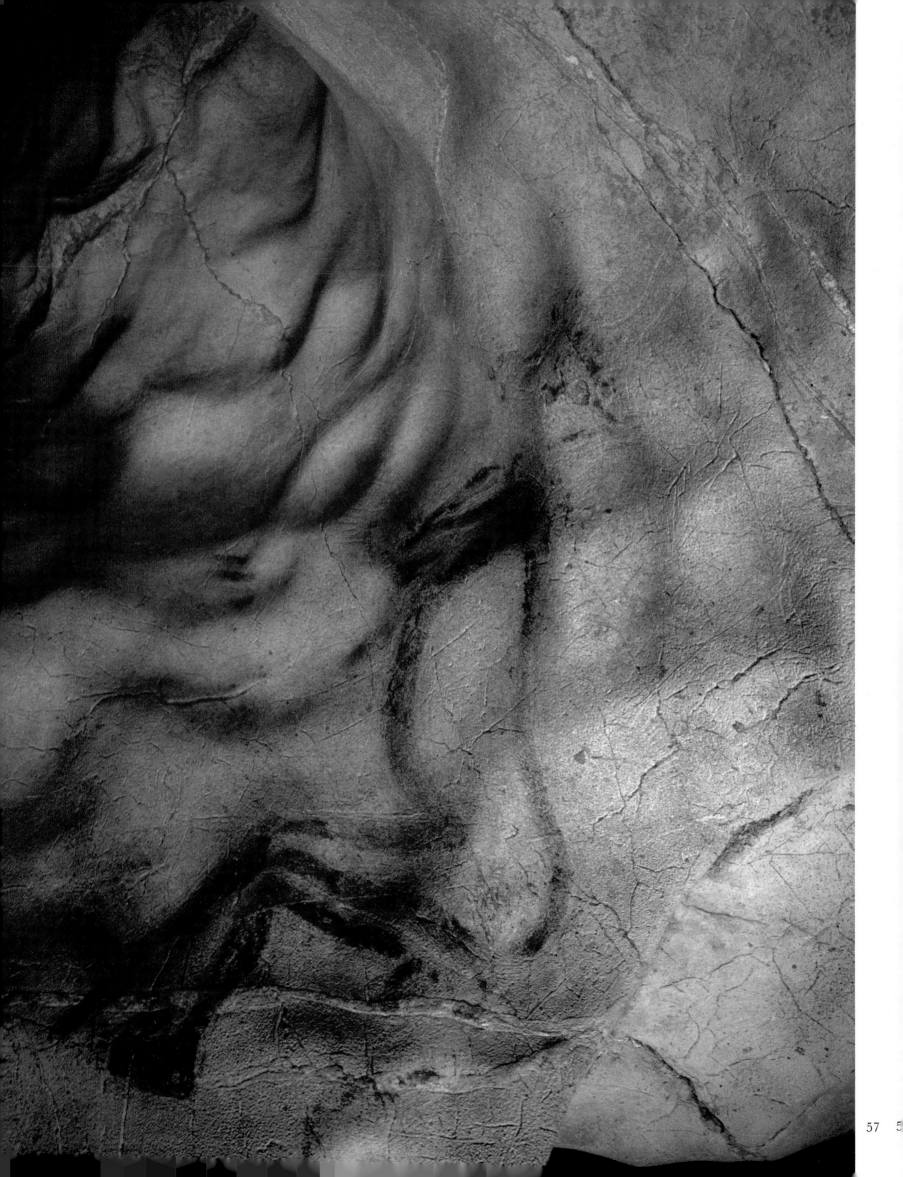

58   LE GABILLOU
Figure of a man with bison's head and tail, found in the group of engravings deepest in the cave.

59   MARSOULAS
Human face, frontal view. $7^7/_8$ in. The group of paintings and engravings at Marsoulas belong to the Middle Magdalenian, the period during which faces in frontal view are most in evidence.

mental tendency in these early figures, which for the most part are only fragmentary. The only fairly clear instance is that at Le Roc de Sers: showing a man carrying a long object, perhaps a spear, and fleeing before a charging bison. This is the rather frequent theme of a man at grips with a bison, illustrated in particular by the scene in the Shaft at Lascaux.

37 *chart* XXVIII

Fairly characteristic of male representations is the difficulty of reducing them to a system that makes sense. Mme. Laming-Emperaire attempted to show that male human beings most often occur in scenes of a tragic character, where they play the part of the vanquished. This is true of some figures[37]: at Le Roc de Sers (just mentioned); in the Shaft at Lascaux, where a man is shown lying on the ground, arms outstretched, in front of a wounded bison; on a reindeer antler from Laugerie Basse, whereon a man is lying with arms outstretched behind a bison pierced with a spear; at Villars, where, as in the Shaft at Lascaux, a man is raising his arms in front of a bison; on the slab at Le Péchialet, where a man, struck by a bear's paw, is shown lying on the ground. The three men at Cougnac and that at Pech Merle who are all stabbed with long spears are treated in a similar spirit. It is indeed remarkable that the few examples just listed, each involving a male human figure, make up almost all the narrative "scenes" known to Paleolithic art. The abstract character of the male figures is broken only by these exceptional treatments of the disarmed, vanquished man. At Lascaux, the contrast between the friezes of oxen and horses and the dramatic scene of the man thrown to the ground by the bison is so striking as to make some people believe that the episode depicted must actually have taken place and that the body of the hunter might be found by digging up the ground under the fresco. However, there are many other less dramatic representations, which can be roughly divided into the following categories: men bending forward, standing men, faces in frontal and in profile view, "ghosts," horned men, and phalluses.

The men shown bending forward correspond to the bending female figures previously discussed. In many cases they are represented with outstretched or lifted arms; this has been interpreted as a gesture of invocation. There is a small statuette from Laugerie Basse representing such a figure. On the engraved plaquettes, the figure of the man bending forward occurs relatively frequently (at Bédeilhac, Lourdes, and Isturitz, among others). An ithyphallic man carrying an oblong object on his shoulder is represented on a pierced disk from Le Mas d'Azil; he probably belongs to the theme of the vanquished man, but the disk is broken, and we can barely make out what seems to be a bear's paw. Finally, a thin bone plaquette from the Abri Murat shows three men, with elongated faces resembling animal muzzles, who seem to be walking one after the other.[38] In the caves, male figures bending forward or males with raised arms are relatively rare: there are several at Les Combarelles and at Altamira, and one at La Peña de los Hornos.[39]

38 *fig. 445*

39 *figs. 522, 689*

Standing men do not seem to form any very coherent category. In most cases the shape of the object made it necessary to increase the length of the figure. Among the known examples are a man with an erection represented on a pierced staff from Gourdan, and another on a bone fragment from La Madeleine (Dordogne).[40] The bone of a mammoth from La Colombière shows the upper part of the body of a bearded man with one arm held in front of him like a sleepwalker.[41] On a small spatula from Bruniquel is the figure of a man in frontal view; he has no arms and a row of small circles runs down from his neck to the pelvic region.[42] Finally, among the cave-wall decorations, we may mention the two small stalagmites projecting from the wall at Le Portel, which serve as penises for two men drawn in frontal view,[43] and some peculiar figures at Los Casares in Spain: one man standing up, apparently walking; a group of persons with turtle beaks; and a man lying diagonally, head down, who seems to be diving into a group of fishes.

40 *fig. 442*

41 *fig. 485*

42 *fig. 214*

43 *fig. 391*

Faces without bodies make up the majority of male representations. In the absence of other bodily details there is nothing to prove that these beardless faces are male rather than female. However, there are two reasons for supposing them to be male. The first is by inference, based on their locations in the cave—near the entrance, at the back, or on the periphery of panels—the usual positions for male symbols. The second reason is of an entirely different order. It was long believed that a number of the representations of men bending forward or of profile faces elongated into animal muzzles were images of masked men; anthropological comparisons led to conjectures either of dances in imitation of animal movements (which would account for the bodies being bent forward) or of a hunting technique whereby hunters disguised themselves the better to deceive their quarry. These hypotheses are not unreasonable, for it is quite likely that the men of the Stone Age were familiar with imitative dancing as well as with hunters disguised as animals. And yet the truth seems to be different: prehistoric art is a very conventional art, and it had its own canon of masculine beauty. We now have sufficient examples to prove that the male profile was rendered by exaggeratedly stressing the line of the nose.[44] In some cases (for example, the slab at Angles-sur-l'Anglin), the nose is merely up-tilted or even bulbous; on a plaquette from La Marche the profile, still recognizably human, shows a very long, almost horizontal nose, which gives the whole lower part of the face an exaggerated protrusion; finally, in several other figures, the whole face is elongated until it looks like an animal's snout or muzzle behind the nasal appendage. The resulting profile is very similar to that of statuettes from the Solomon Islands. We have enough Paleolithic female statuettes and engravings to know that women were not subjected to this peculiar stylization, and we have enough men represented with this snout and with unmistakable signs of their sex to conclude that the snout characterizes male figures.

On decorated objects the male face, either in frontal or profile view, is very rare, but we do find one on a small pierced staff from Saint-Marcel,[45] dating from the beginning of the Late Magdalenian. On plaquettes, however, we have several good examples[46] (La Marche, Isturitz, La Madeleine, Bédeilhac, Gourdan). In cave art male faces are more numerous than female figures. At Angles-sur-l'Anglin, apart from the slab already mentioned, there is one small face in frontal view on the margin of a group of three female torsos, and another, in profile, engraved on the right-hand side of the frieze; at Les Combarelles, at the end of each diverging gallery, a dozen faces in frontal or profile view are scattered among representations of men bending forward. At Font-de-Gaume,[47] Rouffignac,[48] Les Combarelles,[49] Marsoulas,[50] and Le Portel the male faces are found among the figures in remote portions of the caves.

One may ask what reasons, perhaps unconscious, determined a "bestial" stylization of the male face. It is possible, judging from the skulls we have of Late Paleolithic man, to maintain that his face was no more bestial than ours. The form of the nose is not known well, but its proportions were the same as ours today. Thus no attempt at realism was involved, and the Paleolithic nose is merely the inverse of the Greek nose—itself an abstraction. That some similarity to the faces of beasts may have been intended is not out of the question. In particular, it is not impossible that this peculiar profile corresponds to an allusion to the horse, the most frequent male symbol. At Isturitz (Magdalenian III–IV) there is a small bone plaquette covered with faces, four of which are quite legible. The first has the muzzle type of profile; the second has the same profile but with a pointed ear and reindeer antlers; the third is in frontal view; the fourth is simply a bear. In the combinations of figures that involve a male human being, a cervid, and a bear, we perceive a parallel with the figures at Pech Merle where women and bison are integrated in ambivalent outlines.

There is another type of figure, of undeterminable sex, which we shall regard as representing human faces—the so-called ghosts,[51] which occur only in cave art. Their topographic position is not too well determined; though mostly separated from the central figures, they are not invariably found apart from them as are the other figures already discussed. Their outline consists of a vaguely rounded bust in frontal view, the shoulders barely indicated, with two round eyes like those a cartoonist might draw to indicate a ghost peeping out of a shroud. The "ghost" at Le Portel is found at the back of one gallery[52]; at Cougnac, two or three ghosts are right in the middle of a chamber[53];

[44] *chart* xxix

[45] *fig. 191*

[46] *figs. 440–443*

[47] *fig. 531*   [48] *fig. 543*
[49] *fig. 522*   [50] *fig. 567*

[51] *chart* xxx

[52] *fig. 577*   [53] *fig. 386*

54 fig. 328

at Font-de-Gaume, near the point where the large panels begin, there is a figure made of a half-circle provided with two eyes; at Lascaux a ghost, flattened out like rolled pastry so that it seems very tall, is inserted between the legs of one of the stags in the Rotunda[54]; at Les Trois Frères there are at least two ghosts in the man/bison panel. The faces drawn on the ridges of the wall in the inner gallery at Altamira could be counted among these enigmatic figures.

55 fig. 626

It is hard to determine the meaning of those "ghosts" whose topographical placement is not very clear. In the sub-gallery at Les Trois Frères,[55] near the panels of tangled outlines, there are two figures very similar to our "ghosts"; they represent night birds, with bodies in profile view and heads with round eyes, similar to those just cited. Also, the "ghost" at Le Portel has an asymmetrical contour, one of its sides forming a bird's body in sketchy outline. But here, too, we are probably dealing with vagaries of form in which we are unable to detect the links Paleolithic man must have established among the various elements in his catalogue of symbols: also at Les Trois Frères, there are two large lions' heads with round eyes wide open, and one of the "ghosts" in the man/bison panel, placed very near the periphery, has two small round feline ears. This leads us back to the nearby cave of Le Portel where, at the end of the gallery of horses, opposite the most crowded panel, there is the bust of a creature in three-quarter view, with animal features and rounded eyes, which seems provided with a small round ear. The Abbé Breuil cautiously interpreted it as a "half-human head"; this particular "ghost," from both its position and its form, can represent either a lion or a man, especially since it is facing horses. This figure should be compared to the "cat" at Le Gabillou, which is represented frontally and in bust length.[56]

56 fig. 351

To the discussion about "ghosts" one might add the vague silhouettes which decorate a bone plaquette from Gourdan, and two other bone plaquettes, one from Raymonden (Dordogne) and one from Les Eyzies.[57] On these three objects there seem to be processions of men; in two cases the silhouettes are grouped with a bison to form a real scene, of which more later.

57 figs. 236, 446

Figures of men wearing horns or antlers on their heads make up a small group which has special interest because it also reveals something of the way the Paleolithic mind worked. Four among these figures are particularly legible: the "sorcerer"[58] and the "man/bison" at Les Trois Frères, the "man/bison" at Le Gabillou,[59] and the figure engraved on a plaquette found at Lourdes. The "sorcerer" is the most famous of these figures. Engraved and painted on a ceiling which dominates the "sanctuary" of the cave, above the most remarkable animal panels, he has the appearance of a man bending forward, his eyes big and round like those of a night bird (or a lion, or a "ghost"), cervid antlers on his head, and the ears and shoulders of a reindeer or a stag. The lower part of the back is provided with a horse's tail, below which the sexual parts are seen, rather human in shape, but located where a feline's would be. The Abbé Breuil interprets the figure as "the god of Les Trois Frères" (which is certainly more apt than "dancing sorcerer") and "the spirit governing hunting expeditions and the propagation of game." These particulars are hardly based on evidence, but it seems obvious that they contain part of the truth: this composite being in the innermost recess of the cave, with its anthropomorphic frame and the added features of cervid, horse, and probably lion, transmits in a concrete rendering something other than vague "magic."

58 fig. 57
59 fig. 58

Other "sorcerers" reflect a similar tendency in a less theatrical manner. The small figure on the plaquette from Lourdes is closely related to the "god" at Les Trois Frères; like the latter, it is bearded, and wears antlers and a horse's tail. The small figure at Le Gabillou and the two others at Les Trois Frères correspond to a different formula, that of bison features associated with the human male. The little man from Le Gabillou has a bison head and a long unidentifiable tail. He is standing, knees slightly bent, and next to him are two large rectangular female signs. At Les Trois Frères, one of the figures is a bison who seems to be dancing on one hind leg; the knee appears human but the leg is that of a bison; the very conspicuous sexual parts are those of a bison. The result is a somewhat puzzling figure. By contrast, the other figure brings strongly to mind the one at Le Gabillou: erect, one knee bent, ithyphallic, the arms in the shape of bison legs held out in front, it is following a strange creature with the body of a reindeer, very visibly provided with an anus and a prominent vulva. What we see at the level of the rump might be a very indistinct female silhouette, but this symbolism is not even needed to illustrate the proximity of two composite figures of the opposite sex.

Next come some vaguer silhouettes, which exhibit features both of the "ghosts" and the horned men. At Font-de-Gaume, in the back sector where stag, rhinoceros, lion, and horses are gathered, there is a very worn silhouette which could be that of a man in frontal view wearing a short antler on his head. At La Pasiega, in a remote recess which contains figures to be discussed later, we find an almost identical figure—the bust of a "ghost" wearing on its head something like bison horns. At Les Combarelles, at the turning where the engraved friezes begin, there is a little "ghost" with the body in profile, the head in frontal view, and round eyes; instead of arms it has mammoth's tusks. Finally, behind a pillar at the back of the Pech Merle ossuary, one can make out an extremely schematic figure which could be either a stag or a man with bison horns.

Representations of horned human figures on decorated objects are rare. We have already mentioned the plaquette from the Abri Murat showing a bending woman with bison horns,[60] and the one from Isturitz with four faces, among them a profile decorated with a reindeer antler, but the only object of technical use is the pierced staff from Teyjat. This object has already caused much ink to flow. The very skillful engraving on it shows the following picture: in the center is a horse (its male sexual parts visible), in front of the horse there is a hind's head, and behind the hind's ears there are three bands with small dots scattered over them. Under the horse are three very strange creatures, which look like skins for holding water, with uncertain long necks ending in heads which are neither a bird's nor a snake's. Behind the horse we see another tiny horse, a few short lines, and, seemingly flitting around the tiny horse, three tiny clusters of lines that support the little heads of a goat or a chamois, and finally two little human legs. This is one of several works from the very mature Magdalenian, which, like the processions of little men around the bison, may remain wrapped in mystery for a long time. If the waterskins with heads represent snakes, the picture, since it is on a pierced staff, could well be an accumulation of male symbols—horses, cervids, horned men, snakes. However, this object played an important part in the development of the *ratapa* theory. Salomon Reinach, trying to demonstrate the religious character of prehistoric art, thought that, like the *ratapas* of some Australian aborigines (ancestral spirits who are reincarnated by entering the body of a woman), the little imps are on the staff to assure the propagation of the horse species by flitting around the central horse-shaped animal. At that time, the attempt to prove the religious character of this work was meritorious, and we must not be too hard on a scientific legend that still fosters explanations concerning the religion of prehistoric man. And yet this fine stallion, which has been promoted to the rank of "pregnant mare" in so many books although the sheath is plainly visible, cannot really be pursued by these imps in search of their reincarnation. Apart from the fact that there are two imps too many for the purpose, nothing suggests that these little creatures with goats' heads are candidates for metempsychosis in the shape of foals.

To conclude our survey of representations of male human beings, the phallic representations have still to be mentioned. More than fifteen pierced staffs with phalliform handles are extant, dating from the period between the Gravettian and the terminal Magdalenian, but except for this implement representations on objects are rare. We may note the existence of a sandstone phallus, decorated with a barbed sign, at Farincourt, and a bone phallus at Isturitz (a phalliform pendant from the same site was mentioned on p. 78). The half-rounded rods from La Madeleine (Dordogne), which we shall discuss shortly, must also be noted here.

In cave art, phallic representations are even rarer. One phallus incised within a network of lines is present at the entrance to the Pech Merle ossuary, and another in group 67 at Les Combarelles. A semicylindrical mass in the middle part of the Bé-

[60] *fig. 434*

deilhac cave may also represent a phallus, scooped out of the surrounding clay with fingers, on the ground near two vulvas modeled in the clay.

GROUPINGS OF HUMAN FIGURES

We have seen that, on the whole, the distribution of human figures corresponds to the separation between the central and the lateral areas of the cave sanctuaries. What has been said previously concerning the groupings of animal species suggests that we may expect two possible combinations of these figures: female figures with complementary male figures in the central compositions, and human figures associated with animals. If the same type of relationship obtained in the great panels between women and men as between bison and horses, and if, on the other hand, the human figures at entrances and at the backs of the caves were exclusively male figures associated with ibexes, stags, and the rarer animals, this would appreciably confirm my earlier conclusions concerning the assimilation of these animals to male symbols.

There are very few male figures directly associated with female figures, and, as I have already said, no incontrovertible scene of copulation. In cave art, I know only of four pairings of male and female figures. At the entrance to the ossuary in Pech Merle, in a network of incised lines, one can make out a phallus and a vulva separated by an indistinct tangle of lines. At Les Combarelles, in a group showing two or three bending women and one "ghost," we see a vulvar oval and a phallus side by side; nearby, in a group of figures which seem male, we see a vulva superimposed on a horse.[61] Finally, in the frieze at Angles-sur-l'Anglin, a small face of a man in frontal view is sculptured above and apart from three female torsos.

The minor arts are no more lavish with documentation on this point. At La Madeleine (Dordogne) there is an incised pebble which shows on one side a man with an animalized face, and on the other a composite legless creature with one arm, a breast, and the head of a hornless herbivorous animal.[62] From La Madeleine, too, we have the indecent half-rounded rod which shows, separately but forming a single decorative theme, a vulva and a phallus facing a bear's head.[63] In short, associations of female with male human figures are as rare in decorated objects as in cave art.

Groupings with animals are far more frequent and instructive. I shall expound them very briefly here, because, although the system of man-animal relations in cave art is completely clarified by the interplay of abstract signs, a survey of realistic representations is useful because these are more expressive at first sight.

Here, then, are the examples we find of the groupings which cannot be fortuitous. On objects and in cave art, men are associated with the horse (male grouping) on two plaquettes, one from Bédeilhac, and the other from Isturitz[64]; with the horse and the snake on two pierced staffs, one from Teyjat, and one from La Madeleine[65]; with the bear on the disk from Le Mas d'Azil; with the bear and the reindeer on the incised bone from La Colombière[66]; with the stag, the ibex, and the mammoth on the walls at Cougnac.[67] All these associations are of male character. Men are associated with the bison in the scenes previously discussed in connection with the theme of a man facing a bison[68] or defeated by a bison (Lascaux, Villars, Laugerie Basse, Le Roc de Sers) and of man/bison (Les Trois Frères, Le Gabillou). To these must be added the two bone plaquettes from Les Eyzies[69] and Raymonden.[70] The former shows the forequarters of a bison and four forms that resemble alder trees bordering a kind of central path along which file nine small silhouettes carrying sticks on their shoulders. The motif of the man with a stick (or spear) over his shoulder has already appeared, in conjunction with the bison, in several scenes of the preceding type; but it is hard to find a link between the hunter lying on the ground at Lascaux and this peaceful procession of little men who seem to be walking toward a bison—they are so short they barely come up to the level of its fetlock. The other plaquette is no more explicit: we see seven little fellows disposed

[61] fig. 513

[62] fig. 441

[63] fig. 216

[64] fig. 443
[65] fig. 193

[66] fig. 485
[67] fig. 384

[68] chart xxviii

[69] fig. 446   [70] fig. 236

in two rows along the central path, which is occupied by a barbed sign; at one end of the path a bison's head and two legs seem to be lying on the ground, as though they had been cut off. One of the men carries over his shoulder not a stick or a spear but a kind of broom. Lacking more evidence, it is rash to try to interpret these objects, but apparently a "bison and hunter" theme exists, recurring in caves and on objects in various forms.

The groupings of women and animals are of a constant character. They go back to the very beginning of figurative art, since the earliest incised slabs at La Ferrassie and the Abri Cellier[71] show undefinable animals in close proximity to vulvas. As soon as the figures become completely definite, we see emerging the link between woman and bison, the recognition of which was the starting point of Mme. Laming-Emperaire's work. Dating from the period between the Gravettian and Magdalenian III, there is the low relief at Laussel of a woman holding a bison horn in her right hand[72] and the two bison which flank the female torsos at Angles-sur-l'Anglin. One of the two women at La Magdelaine (Tarn) is stretched out over a cornice on which a bison is sculptured[73]; at Bédeilhac, we twice find a bison and a vulva completely apart from the other figures; the same subject occurs at El Castillo. But the most extraordinary group is the one at Pech Merle already mentioned.[74] In a recess there, five figures display every conceivable transition from bison with raised tails (on the walls) to women bending over (on the ceiling). As we move from one figure to the next we see how the tail in the shape of a swan's neck is gradually turned into a neck and a head, how the hind legs move up from the ground to become pendulous breasts, how the hump of the withers is transformed into a rounded female rump. It is impossible to imagine a more striking illustration of the close affinity between these two symbols of the female category.

Decorated objects also provide good examples, such as "the woman with a reindeer" from Laugerie Basse—a broken plaquette which shows on one side a woman who is apparently pregnant but with no indication of breasts, and having the legs of a bison; on the other side is the complementary subject, a horse. At Les Trois Frères there is a plaquette which may well represent a woman with legs tucked under and a bison's leg.[75] Finally, at Isturitz was found a bone plaquette[76] decorated with a group as expressive as that of the women/bison at Pech Merle. One side shows two women who seem to be crawling in single file. The plaquette is broken; the head of the first woman is missing, and the second woman is seen only down to the beginning of the right breast. The thigh of the first figure is marked with a barbed sign which, as will be seen presently, is a male sign. The other side shows the forequarters of one bison and the hindquarters of another, both exactly symmetrical with the women; the flank of the bison which has been preserved is marked with two barbed signs. This work has already given rise to many commentaries. It is commonly interpreted as showing on the one side two bison hit by barbed harpoon points, and on the other side, a woman with a harpoon planted in her thigh, followed by a man who seems to crawl toward her with ill-concealed lust. That there are no harpoons here will be amply demonstrated, but it should be enough to recall that harpoons do not occur until Magdalenian V, that they have nothing to do with hunting land animals, and that there is no reason to ascribe unsavory nuptial customs to the Magdalenians. R. de Saint-Périer, who scrutinized the work closely, tells us that "the man" does not look ferocious, and that "the harpoon" may be no more than a symbol of ownership. This interpretation is perhaps closer to the truth, for we shall see later that the phallus, the barbed sign, and the throwing weapons were treated as equivalents. As for the female character of the second figure, despite its apparently clean-shaven skull, its sex is still harder to deny because under her right arm, at the spot where the plaquette is broken, we see the beginning of an outline of a pendulous breast identical with that of the headless woman.

Things would be simple indeed if all figures of women were peacefully associated with bison, but just as in the case of men paired with bison, there are instances where the polarization is reversed. At La Magdelaine (Tarn), opposite the woman shown reclining above a bison, there is another woman flanked by a horse.[77] At Les Combarelles,

[71] *figs. 253, 254*

[72] *fig. 271*

[73] *fig. 501*

[74] *figs. 367–371; chart* XLVIII

[75] *fig. 435*   [76] *figs. 436, 437*

[77] *figs. 500, 502*

vulvas incised on horses' flanks occur twice. At Gargas, a vulva and an animal which has been described as an elk without antlers but seems to be a horse in Style II (though an elk would do as well for the purpose of this argument) are found close to each other. Finally, on the ceiling at Pech Merle, several women have been engraved in juxtaposition with mammoths.[78] Whereas the most common case—woman with bison—marks a strengthening of the female symbol, on the plaquette from Laugerie Basse the horse comes in as the male element complementary to the woman/bison group; on the plaquette from Isturitz the complementary symbol is the barbed (male) sign.

[78] *fig. 382*

THE SIGNS

WE now enter the most fascinating area of Paleolithic art, the one which contradicts all customary ideas as to the simple-minded visual naturalism of the mammoth hunters: the abstract signs.

As early as the 1870s, when the theory of art for art's sake favored hypotheses concerning "pages" from the "sketchbooks" of Paleolithic artists, prehistorians began to notice that among the animal images there were certain signs. These were first observed on decorated objects, where, as a matter of fact, their occurrence is rare. The most striking example noted at the time was the pierced staff from Lortet, which is decorated with male symbols, stags, and fish, arranged in such a way that the composition may be taken to represent stags crossing a stream full of salmon. Behind the rump of one of the stags appear two lozenges, each of which is cut in half by a vertical line. These two little signs, which precede the first written characters by eight thousand years, should have prevented the next three generations of prehistorians from resting until the reason for their existence had been discovered. The history of the interpretation of the Lortet signs, however, is a good illustration of how science can, occasionally for a very long time indeed, become the prisoner of theories that were reasonable at one time. Édouard Piette, a highly valuable pioneer, believed—and rightly—that Paleolithic men were artists, but he saw them, perhaps, a bit too much in the guise of painters of his own day. To him, the meaning of the lozenges was perfectly obvious: these were artists' signatures. Subsequently, many of Piette's other theories were largely discredited, but his notion that Paleolithic artists "signed" their works survived peacefully amid scholars' collective indifference.

Signs occur very seldom on objects, at least such signs as did not become confused among stylizations of animals or decorative elements. It was their widespread occurrence in cave art that focused attention on the signs at the beginning of the twentieth century. The Abbé Breuil published drawings of a large number of them. Study of the Monte Castillo caves (El Castillo and La Pasiega) first aroused his interest—and consequently that of other prehistorians—in the strange configurations[79] which are found by the dozen in these two Spanish caves, in out-of-the-way corners and in the midst of the main panels. This fresh interest in the signs turned the tide of scholarly opinion, and the theory of signatures ceased to occur to anyone confronted by these odd markings: upstrokes and downstrokes, horizontal lines, and rectangles, the latter often compartmented like heraldic coats-of-arms. Comparative anthropology was very popular at the beginning of this century, and prehistorians looked for clues to the significance of the signs among primitive peoples of the modern world. Some interpreted the large rectangular or roof-shaped signs as houses—more accurately, as huts. Opinions varied as to whether these were simple huts of which structural details could be described, as at La Mouthe, or images of huts intended to "house" spirits (such as the *ratapas* who, it will be recalled, pester pregnant mares). Because certain of these signs are sometimes found on a bison, a mammoth, or the head of a hind, other prehistorians supposed that they must represent animal snares.[80] Someone even referred to those at Lascaux as coats-of-arms. As for the elongated signs with lateral protrusions, called "claviforms,"

[79] *fig. 61*

[80] *chart* LII

Breuil supposed that they represent missiles, perhaps boomerangs, and I admit that I was among those who, after the discovery of Lascaux, interpreted certain signs as spear-throwers.

The interpretation of the signs consequently developed toward viewing them as representations of objects: it was thought that the pictures on the walls portrayed the life of hunters (who occasionally danced with antlers on their heads), their wives, their dwellings, their weapons, and the animals they hunted. Everything seemed to constitute a coherent ensemble, and also to be consistent with the concepts attributed to the first men who expressed their ideas in pictures. This interpretation was all the more plausible because representations of this kind (dwellings, fields, harness, hand looms, weapons, etc.) are known in the cave art subsequent to the Paleolithic. A critical inventory of the signs would probably have long since eliminated this rationalistic view, but no one undertook such an inventory. Comfortably settled in a framework of "modern" explanations, prehistorians supposed that Paleolithic man went to the expense of installing warning signals in certain caves, to mark sharp turns and steep drops. At least this is how the black and red marks so often found in the connecting corridors between two chambers were interpreted.

When I began to list the figures by their location inside the caves, I had the animals primarily in mind, since the signs—except for the most elaborate ones—almost go unperceived: a dot on the wall, two or three strokes of ocher near a horse, a row of small dots. For all that, I listed them along with the animals, meticulously and without any preconceived ideas.

The real importance of the signs only emerged later, after an exploratory series of statistical tests.[81] Statistically, they proved to belong to two sets: one of single dots, rows of dots, short strokes, and barbed signs; the other of ovals, triangles, rectangles, and brace-shaped signs. Since one set occurs at the entrances and in the back-cave areas, and the other in the central portions, it became obvious that the two series correspond to the same system of distribution as the animal figures.

This was a statistical fact; consequently, it was necessary to examine critically such exceptions to this general rule as I could find. Exactly as it happens with the horses, an important number of signs of the first set (located at the entrances and the backs of the caves) turn up in the central groups. The rule of complementarity, according to which horses accompany bison in the central panels, thus applies also to these signs. When the subjects were re-examined one by one it was quickly evident that, generally speaking, every sign from the "enclosed" set on the central panels is matched by a sign of the "dot and stroke" set. And the converse was also entirely true: the signs from the "enclosed" set are just as rare at the entrances and in the back-cave areas as are bison and oxen.

When each set of signs was analyzed separately, it leaped to the eye that the ovals, triangles, and quadrangular signs were all more or less abstract variations on the vulvas which appear among the earliest works of prehistoric art. As for the dots and strokes, it was obvious that they are male signs, although their degree of abstraction is beyond any simple similarity of form. I suddenly recalled two decorated objects which had been published separately many times, and these furnished the final proof. The first is the half-rounded rod from La Madeleine already discussed, the second a pierced staff from the Massat cave.[82] Each shows the head of a bear on the right, but whereas the first shows most crudely a realistic phallus and vulva, the other, much more discreetly, shows in the same order a barbed sign and an oval. Additional proofs were supplied later from various sources: the sandstone phallus from Farincourt with a barbed sign; several pierced staffs with the same symbol; and, in the remote portion of the Lascaux cave called the Chamber of Felines, the barbed sign which also has two semicircular additions at one end, unmistakable enough.[83]

Having originally set out to classify the bison and mammoth figures in chronological order, I found myself in the end confronted with a system of unexpected complexity— the skeleton of a religious thought, as impervious to my understanding, moreover, as a

[81] *chart* XXXI

[82] *fig. 216*

[83] *chart* XXXVI

60 PECH MERLE
   Negative hand accompanied by dots.
   This group of markings is found at the
   entrance to the side chamber with the
   women/bison theme. At Pech—Merle,
   as at Gargas and El Castillo,
   hands in negative are often accompanied
   by dots.

61 EL CASTILLO
   Female quadrangular signs
   accompanied by complementary rows
   of male dots. The height of the signs
   ranges from 12 to 24 in.

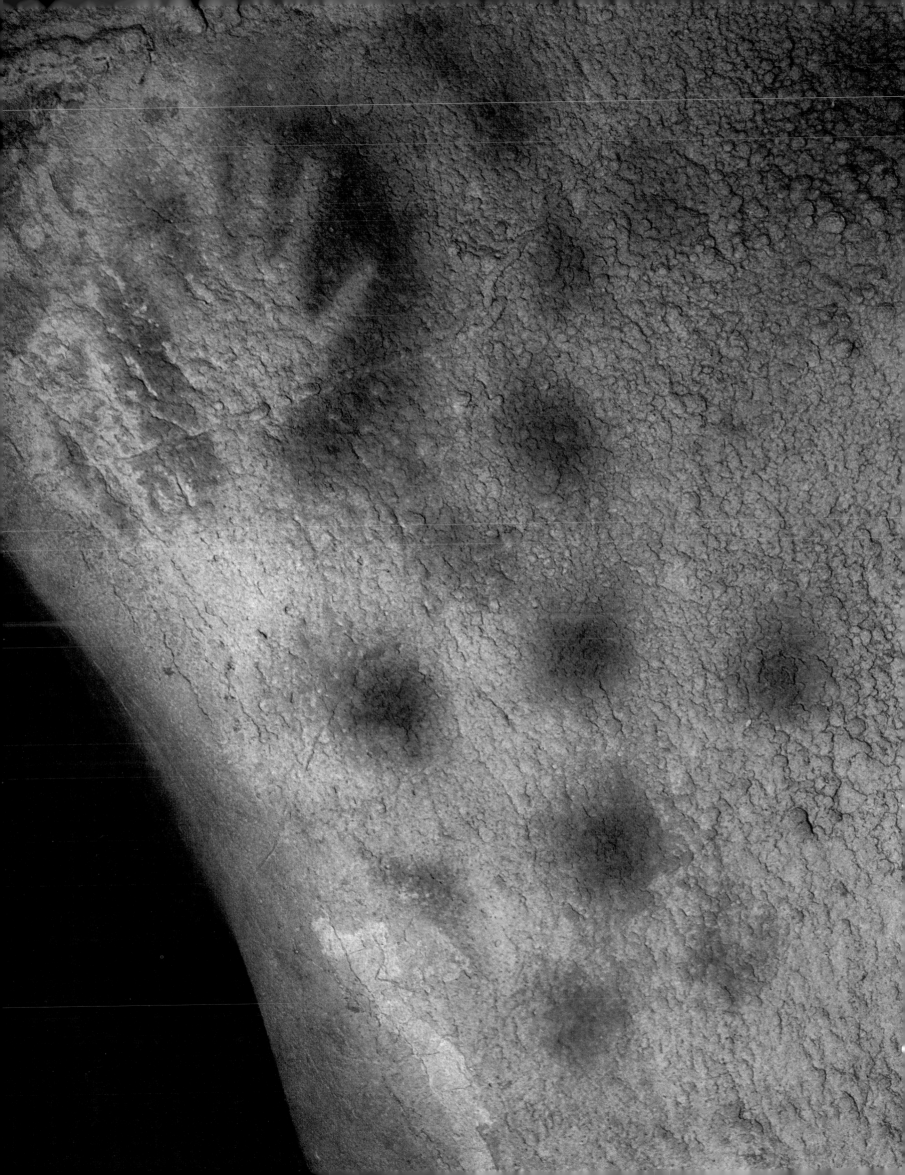

62

63

62 LA PASIEGA

Gallery B. Brace-shaped or early claviform signs close in style to the claviforms on the large ceiling at Altamira. About 16 in. Under the signs, on the right, are the schematized forequarters of a quadruped.

63 EL CASTILLO

Female signs in red, associated with a male barbed sign in black. The group is about 40 in. wide. No element permits this group to be directly dated; by comparison with other signs of the type, it may be placed in Early Style IV (Middle Magdalenian).

comparative study of the iconography of sixty cathedrals would be to an archaeologist from Mars. It is this framework that I have tried to grasp, eschewing all attempts at reconstruction. The reader may possibly be disappointed not to find a synthesis of Paleolithic religious thought in this book. Any such synthesis would be premature: a correlation of data from various sources will no doubt cast some light on the religion of the Upper Paleolithic, but today anything that we could say would be based on vague comparisons or limited to the reliable but utterly banal statement that there existed a religious system based on the opposition and complementarity of male and female values, expressed symbolically by animal figures and by more or less abstract signs.

What constituted for Paleolithic men the special heart and core of the caves is clearly the panels in the central part, dominated by animals from the female category and female signs, supplemented by animals from the male category and male signs. The entrance to the sanctuary, usually a narrow part of the cave, is decorated with male symbols, either animals or signs; the back of the cave, often a narrow tunnel, is decorated with the same signs, reinforced by horned men and the rarer animals (cave lion or rhinoceros). Although crowded with images this framework is quite simple; it leaves us completely in the dark concerning what we should like to know about the rites, and, let us say, about an underlying metaphysics. However, it rules out any simplistic idea concerning the religious system of Paleolithic men. It should be said, incidentally, that the religious thought of the most primitive peoples alive today—the Australian aborigines—is no less surprising. It is by arbitrarily assuming the perfection of our machine civilization that we establish a scale for the subtlety of thought, starting with ourselves and descending to the "savages."

THE FEMALE SIGNS

In respect to shape, the female signs can be divided into five groups: triangles, inverted triangles, ovals, rectangles, and claviforms.[84]

[84] *chart* XXXII

TRIANGLES

Triangles and inverted triangles are for the most part fairly realistic, often with a line running down the middle. There is a gradual transition in the successive representations of the pubic triangle in sculpture; from the woman at the left at La Magdelaine (Tarn) and the equally realistic triangle at Bédeilhac, to those found next to horses at Les Combarelles; then to triangles without any line down the middle (for example, at Las Monedas and Oulen); to the triangle without a base—the goose-track shape (Font-de-Gaume, El Castillo). The angle of the apex may be rounded (for example, at Bernifal), or the figure may take on the appearance of a bell as in the striking example at El Castillo.[85] An extreme example of the triangle without base is a sign in the form of an arrow point, the line in the middle standing for the shaft which may be more or less extended.

[85] *fig. 63*

RECTANGLES

Rectangles, divided by one or two vertical lines, are a frequent form in Style III. When there is only one dividing line, as at Le Gabillou, the similarity to pubic representation is clear, but the line may be doubled and the whole may ultimately develop into a rectangle divided into three equal parts (also at Le Gabillou, and at Lascaux), which is also occasionally divided horizontally to produce a checkerboard pattern. Furthermore, the line at the bottom or top of the rectangle may be missing, and this gives rise to a whole gamut of signs shaped like coats-of-arms or four-toothed combs. Outlines

144

may differ in the same cave (Le Gabillou, Lascaux, Marsoulas), and we cannot account for such differences by long lapses of time. A characteristic feature of all signs is the abundance of variations to be found within any one type, the pattern of variation often remaining very stable for each cave. Nor is it exceptional to find entirely empty rectangles (Chimeneas, Covalanas, Lascaux, La Pasiega, Santimamine). At Altamira and El Castillo a variant occurs: the rectangle takes on the look of an elongated oval, cut by two transverse lines. The caves with rectangular signs of various types are among those with the most homogeneous groups of figures. It is not uncommon to find in such caves rectangular as well as brace-shaped and claviform signs; many of these caves are among the best examples of Style III, or of Style III and early Style IV, such as Altamira (the "Black Sequence"), Le Gabillou, Lascaux, and Le Portel (Gallery 2).

LATTICE-SHAPED SIGNS

According to some, the lattice-shaped signs mark the final development of triangular signs; they are formed of a number of lines slanting in both directions, intersecting to form a grid. They occur in simple forms, such as the sign at Mazaculos (Spain) which is a zigzag of four lines. The large central sign at Labastide is made of six diagonal strokes crossed by a horizontal line, and there is a very similar one at Las Monedas. At Las Monedas, too, these diagonal lattice-shaped signs are found in the large panel of tangled lines at the entrance, but—and this is most interesting—the signs in this case imitate the appearance of certain portions of the cave wall that are deeply grooved with natural grids and lattice shapes. A flat stone on the ground under the large entrance panel has such natural grooves; its edges have been brightly polished by artificial means.

There are lattices made of crisscrossing horizontal and vertical lines—particularly at Arcy-sur-Cure, Les Combarelles, and Font-de-Gaume—which seem to be derived from rectangular signs.

TECTIFORM SIGNS

The so-called tectiform signs fall into two geographical groups. The first has so far been found only in the Cantabrian area of Spain (signs with a brace-shaped top); it is closely related to rectangular signs in the same area. The second group is confined to the region of Les Eyzies (Dordogne)—Font-de-Gaume, Les Combarelles, Bernifal, Rouffignac, Bara-Bahau—and is related to the regular (not inverted) triangle. The first group has been classified here as "brace-shaped signs," derived from the claviform signs; the second as derivations from the triangles.

OVAL SIGNS

The oval signs are the most numerous and fall into three types. The first type consists of two concentric ovals (La Croze at Gontran, Les Combarelles, Pair-non-Pair) or circles (Pair-non-Pair). The second type is an oval divided by a longitudinal line, occasionally projecting beyond one end (Les Combarelles, Pech Merle, Ebbou, Ussat). The third type is a simple oval, sometimes deformed into a "tear drop," or a circle. It occurs in all regions of Franco-Cantabrian art and in compositions of different periods: in the Périgord (Lascaux, Les Combarelles), in the Quercy (Pech Merle), in the Basque country (Isturitz, lower cave), in Spain (La Pasiega, Altamira, El Buxu), in the Ariège (Labastide, Le Portel, Les Trois Frères, Ussat), in the Ardèche (La Baume Latrone, Ebbou, Oulen). This type predominates in the chronologically latest compositions.

CLAVIFORM SIGNS

All the female signs discussed thus far—triangles, rectangles, and ovals or circles—constitute a single family, the representations of the female pubic triangle or vulva. Our last category, that of the claviform signs, has a different origin.

The claviform signs are the terminal form derived from the bending female figures discussed previously. The women at Les Combarelles consist merely of busts having no head or arms, legs having no feet, and voluminous representation of their posteriors. The incised figures at La Roche near Lalinde present tapering torsos and legs, and there is a sign at Villars where the lines of torso and legs are left open. These are the prototypes that lead to the claviform signs proper, which are strokes with a semicircular projection on one side or even simply a short line. Their distribution is typically Cantabrian and Pyrenean: Pindal, La Pasiega, Altamira, Le Portel, Les Trois Frères, Niaux. Lascaux, the only cave in the Périgord where claviforms occur, is an exception. From La Pasiega to the central Pyrenees the claviform signs overlap with the rectangular signs; one can follow their incidence by drawing a line that runs as far north on the map as the Périgord. Taken as a group, the sites where claviform and rectangular signs occur, separately or together, contain the majority of animal figures most clearly in Style III, and there is hardly any doubt that they all belong to the same chronological period, corresponding to the Early and Middle Magdalenian.

BRACE-SHAPED SIGNS

The brace-shaped signs syncretize the two lines of development. Chronologically placed between the rectangular and the claviform signs, they seem to combine features of both. Some are rectangles with brace-shaped tops, whereas others are closely related to the simplified outline of the female figure. Many details of their evolution remain to be clarified.

[86] *chart* xxxiii

MALE SIGNS[86]

When we study the evolutionary sequence of female signs, we note that even their most developed forms (for example, the "coats-of-arms" at Lascaux) preserve an obvious link with the realistic model. Not so with the male signs: without the engraved half-rounded rod from La Madeleine, and without the statistics as to caves where they are paired with female signs, their nature would be virtually incomprehensible. They are divided roughly into three groups: the barbed signs, the short strokes, and the rows of dots.

BARBED SIGNS

The barbed signs can be understood if we refer to the phallus with four little appendages on the half-rounded rod from La Madeleine (Dordogne). Two of these appendages might just conceivably be interpreted as hairs, but they seem rather to reflect some graphic convention having obscure meaning. The barbed sign in the Chamber of Felines at Lascaux provides a good transition for identifying the numerous "harpoons" or "feathered" signs found on decorated objects as well as in the cave art of the entire Franco-Cantabrian area. Some of these signs have the look of small stick figures of human beings: one vertical line, with four short straight lines imitating arms and legs.

SHORT STROKES (BÂTONNETS) AND DOTS

The short strokes are signs so simple that it is hard to reconstruct their lineage. However, at Le Gabillou we find a sign which might be taken as a feathered arrow: it consists of one vertical line with two short parallel strokes at each end; variants of the same sign occur at Lascaux.[87] An almost identical sign is found at Le Portel, and there is little doubt that it is related to the phallus from La Madeleine and to the "fish" in the Chamber of Felines at Lascaux.

[87] *fig. 65, chart* xxxvii

As for the single strokes and rows of dots, they are identified by referring to the principles governing the pairings of signs. The number of vulvas, ovals, triangles, claviform signs, or rectangular signs that occur regularly in close proximity to one or several strokes or rows of dots is great; and these can so well be correlated with pairings of realistic male and female figures, or with paired signs in which the male element is the barbed sign, that the male significance of the strokes and dots can be determined beyond possible doubt. This is further confirmed by the topographical distribution of the dots and the strokes, which follow the same rules that govern the distribution of other male signs. The short strokes occur sometimes singly, and sometimes several at a time, parallel to one another. Often the strokes are doubled, and whole groups of doubled short strokes are found.

Between the strokes and the rows of dots there is a whole range of forms hard to classify, such as wavy lines of small strokes, rake-shaped signs with numerous teeth, ladder-shaped signs, and the double line of "hyphens" at Altamira in a side chamber with four hidden elliptical signs divided into compartments. The dots exhibit exactly the same variations as the strokes; we find single rows, double rows, and series of parallel rows, which sometimes form spreads or splashes of dots. The oddest groups of this kind are found at Marsoulas, where we encounter successively an area of red dots forming the body of a bison whose head is represented in black, and a group of horizontal rows of dots from which vertical short strokes seem to be suspended.[88]

[88] *figs. 66, 569*

PAIRED SIGNS[89]

[89] *chart* xxxiv

We have seen that the signs correspond to what has been established for the animals and realistic human figures: the male signs are found almost exclusively at the point where the sanctuary begins, and in the remotest parts of the caves; they also appear in the transitions leading from one central composition to another. On the other hand, within the central compositions female signs are normally associated with signs of the male set.

We are so accustomed to the laws of perspective that there is something baffling in the freedom with which the Paleolithic images are arranged; it is nevertheless surprising that no one has ever noticed that the signs occur so frequently in pairs—for instance, an oval with a barbed sign, a rectangle with a row of dots, a triangle with a few strokes. Until now my efforts to discover a systematic arrangement in such pairings have been practically fruitless; oval or triangular signs, for example, may be associated with barbed signs, or with isolated or grouped strokes, or with dots, and no consistency seems to have been followed in these pairings, even in the same cave. On a single panel in the Chamber of Felines at Lascaux, for example, we see three rectangular signs of the same type, one associated with a barbed sign, the second with a stroke, and the third with a row of dots. At Niaux, the strokes and rows of dots are associated with identical claviforms, and for a time I wondered whether the strokes and dots might not have different meanings. This hypothesis is the more plausible because in a few instances (Labastide, La Cullalvera, and Oulen, for example) there are two different male signs for a single female sign. At Las Monedas a triangular sign is actually found near one barbed sign, three strokes, and a series of dots. If Paleolithic artists made use of nuances of meaning between this and that male sign, statistics do not confirm it; but all the same the question remains open. What is rather striking, moreover, is that a given type of female sign is characteristic for a given cave: Niaux has its claviforms; Lascaux, like El Castillo, has its "coats-of-arms"; La Pasiega has its brace-shaped signs. Wherever more than one type of female sign is found, we notice readily that we are dealing with different traditions and probably different periods: at Altamira, the claviform, the elliptical, and the quadrangular signs occur in different parts of the cave.

We have seen (and we shall come back to this) that in many sanctuaries the central composition is repeated twice or several times: when the female sign changes with each such repetition, as is the case at El Castillo, we may assume that the sections were added successively in the course of time.

HANDS

90 figs. 1, 8, 60, 64, 289–293, 366, 422

IN a certain number of caves impressions of hands have been found. Some, reported primarily from the Rhone area, are positive—that is, they were made by applying a hand coated with pigment against the wall: others, in the Franco-Cantabrian area, are negative—that is, executed by daubing color around a hand laid against the wall, fingers spread.[90]

The best-known group is that at the Gargas cave; it consists of nearly a hundred and fifty red and black hands. El Castillo contains about fifty hands, Tibiran and Pech Merle a dozen each. The other hands are either alone or in smaller groups—at the Bayol cave, La Baume Latrone, Rocamadour, Bernifal, Font-de-Gaume, and Le Portel. It can be seen that the distribution of the hands is wide, but only within a limited number of caves. Because the total incidence is small, it is difficult to apply statistical controls to hypotheses concerning their meaning.

The Abbé Breuil discovered long ago at Gargas and El Castillo that nine out of ten hands seemed to be left hands; this suggested that the owner was right-handed and put the palm of his left hand against the wall, using his right to surround it with color. Closer study of the impressions, however, tends to show that right hands, too, are present; they were placed with the back of the hand against the rock, which explains why certain ones occur in concavities of the wall where the palm-down method would not be practical. In most cases the hands are too small to have belonged to men: the majority seem to be women's hands, and some obviously belonged to children. The latter statement is corroborated by the fairly large number of imprints of children's feet discovered in clay, notably at the caves of Niaux, Aldène, and Pech Merle.

At Gargas, a considerable number of hands seem to have had fingers cut off or deformed. This has been explained as the result of "ritual" mutilations. But here again, closer scrutiny suggests that the person who put the back of his hand against the wall bent one or several fingers; the reason for this is not clear, but it did not have mutilation as its cause. In certain cases we can even see that the fingers, originally long, were later retouched to shorten them. At Gargas and Pech Merle rows of thumbs or fingers, bent to form hooks, are found near the hands.

Although the statistical evidence is insufficient for interpreting the "hands" theme, it seems to be possible to establish a certain number of facts. First of all, hands—by themselves or in groups—are paired with parallel strokes or with *ponctuations* (rows or splashes of dots); clear examples are found at Gargas, Rocamadour, Pech Merle, El Castillo, and Bernifal. Hands are also found next to central compositions or among the principal figures in them (Bayol cave, El Castillo, Pech Merle, Bernifal). Thus it is likely that when female hands were paired with male signs and placed in central panels, they must have performed the function of female signs.

GROUPINGS OF HUMAN FIGURES AND ANIMALS

WHAT has been disclosed about animals of the male category and of the female category, about male and female representations, and about the corresponding male and female signs gives some idea of the very involved yet highly organized system that governs combinations of figures from these categories. Had Paleolithic men been experienced in logical systems of thought and of numbers, speleologists exploring the cave sanctuaries might have discovered regular compositions, perhaps of a man and a woman with hands raised in gestures of protection, his over the horse, hers over the bison. However, modern iconographic principles are of no help in grasping the system according to which figures are organized in the caves; many of the errors committed by the older school of prehistorians no doubt stemmed from the excessively academic character of their training in art. We should look rather to medieval religious art: on the capitals of Romanesque columns, for instance, scenes may consist of many figures in an unrealistic space; a crowd may be represented by two heads, and the narrative be cut down to fit the given volume of the architectural mass; symbols and key figures may be repeated to fill available space; the same holy image may recur with different details, and the same scene may turn up in several basilicas, each time worked out according to a different formula. Or we should keep in mind the number of times that the Crucifixion may be represented in one small church, for all that one Christ is worshiped in all churches, and then imagine an archaeologist totally unacquainted with our civilization, trying to make sense of our all-pervasive but irrational symbolism —an empty cross, a crown of thorns, two juxtaposed Greek letters, or a fish, each one as meaningful as a scene containing 150 persons displaying contrasted emotions at the foot of the Crucifixion on Calvary. Some such effort is required to bring us close to Magdalenian thought and responsive to the flexibility that remains in the works that have come down to us.

There are a few "ideal" caves where the figurative elements are reduced to the minimum—they are like small country churches with only one cross over the altar and the Stations of the Cross along the walls. At La Meaza, for instance, Breuil found a single panel with just two signs, one male and one female; at Mazaculos, too, there is nothing but some lines forming a triangle and one row of dots. Among the slightly more elaborate caves, we may mention the small corridor-cave of Covalanas:[91] in the center [91] *fig. 140* there are three hinds and two rectangular signs that face a horse and a few strokes on the opposite wall; at the entrance there are four dots; at the back, two dots and a dorsal outline suggesting a horse; between the two ends of the cave, sixteen other hinds serve to fill the panels.

These modest sanctuaries that contain just three groups of representations (at the entrance, in the center, and at the back) are very different from sanctuaries such as El Castillo having chambers strung out over hundreds of yards and broken up by great masses of stone in the center portion, with recesses and intersecting corridors, where the over-all impression is of a baffling multitude of scattered figures. The distance between these two types is as great as that between a rural chapel and a city cathedral. To be sure, even here we find fairly reliable guideposts, such as a zone of bison and one of oxen, the stags and horses at the entrance, large paired signs in the recesses, and the corridor at the end with its rows of male dots, ibexes, and horses. But between these zones there are intermediate zones introducing a multitude of figures that form separate little sanctuaries, each with its horses and ibexes, and its female signs and barbed signs applied to a bison or an ox. To borrow another comparison from Christian churches—and, needless to say, I am referring only to the fairly similar over-all arrangement—a sanctuary like El Castillo is a little like a large church having many side chapels, each reproducing the features of the central sanctuary around which they are grouped. The parallelism here is only of form, not of content: there is nothing to suggest that the repetition of the general theme of a cave in perhaps ten separate small areas corresponds to a cult within which separate altars were each dedicated to a distinct divinity. After all, we have no direct evidence that the caves served as places of worship, let alone evidence for the worship of distinct deities. I am trying to explain that when we walk among these figures in which we can discern an order but not its meaning we find ourselves in a situation comparable to that of a Martian visitor wandering through an abandoned cathedral on this planet.

Under these circumstances, one must postulate a scale of nuances when seeking to establish a system governing the groupings of figures. This must be understood because, while the statistical evidence is incontrovertible, what is actually on the walls can, to our eye, be disconcerting. Even to speak of "the artist" may be misleading, for a given theme may have been elaborated by many hands over a long period. And "the artist" may have let one part of the theme stand for the whole. As we have seen, he sometimes contented himself with one pair of male and female signs (La Meaza); or he reduced secondary subjects to a mere indication (the dorsal outline of a horse in Panel IV of the Black Salon at Niaux); and he juxtaposed the figures to such a degree that the viewer is hard put to sort them out from one another. On the panels in the "sanctuary" at Les Trois Frères, for example, we can see clearly that the rhinoceros has been relegated to the extreme edge, but nevertheless it touches some of the bison that form a tapestry covering the entire wall. The viewer becomes the prisoner of his own way of seeing. If a panel contains no more than one bison, one horse, one woman, and one man, the situation is clear; but if it contains fifty figures apparently scattered at random, he is confronted with doubtful cases. Are the figures in the middle really associated with those on the periphery? To avoid extending an interpretation into uncertain regions, I make it my rule to consider associated figures to be grouped only when they are superimposed, or very close to one another.

Within these limits, we can find that the following groupings exist in, for example, the central panels: woman/bison, man/woman/bison, bison/horse, man/horse, man/woman/bison/horse, and, lastly, man/woman/bison/horse/ibex/stag. To look upon each combination as constituting a separate formula would be inexact, in the sense that in the numerous cases where such combinations of figures occur under the best conditions for observation, the complete formula includes two central pairs (woman/man and bison/horse) plus lateral or flanking animals (ibex or stag). But there are also cases, well placed for accurate observation, where we find the formula abbreviated, although there are no groupings that radically depart from it—never does man/stag serve as a central subject. If hundreds of decorated caves were statistically tabulated, and we had a precise and large-scale chronology, we surely could explain this diversity, which is hardly surprising over the course of several thousand years and over an area including half of western Europe. What is really surprising is that within so broad an area in space and time, the skeleton of the representational system should have remained unchanged.

If one point is solidly established, it is this: when the first cave sanctuaries made their appearance, the figurative system and the underlying ideology it presupposes had existed for several millennia. This is eloquently attested by the rock slabs or blocks at such early sites as La Ferrassie, the Abri Cellier, and the Abri Castanet, which are spread through the period between Aurignacian I and Aurignacian IV. Animals, vulvas, and series of short strokes figure on the earliest of these finds. Despite some gaps, the evidence is sufficiently complete that one may assert that not only was the system of pairings within the four basic subjects by then accomplished, but also that a system of symbolical representation of the sexes already existed prior to the representation of men and women as such.

64 PECH MERLE
*Horses in Early Style III, with
bodies covered with dots (right-hand
side of the group). Note the hands
in negative (especially the one under the
horse's belly, accompanied by a double
row of dots; see fig. 366).
On the horse's back is a fish of the
pike family painted in red, and there is a
circle on the chest. About $6^1/_2$ feet long.*

65 LE GABILLOU
*The largest of the central compositions
(Chamber K). It shows a bison in
Style III accompanied by a smaller
horse. The three verticals of a
quadrangular sign, and a male sign
of the barbed type closely related to
some of the signs at Lascaux, are
superimposed on the two animals.*

66 MARSOULAS
*Bison rendered as a spread of red dots,
at the lower right of the main
composition. One red barbed sign can
be seen underneath.*

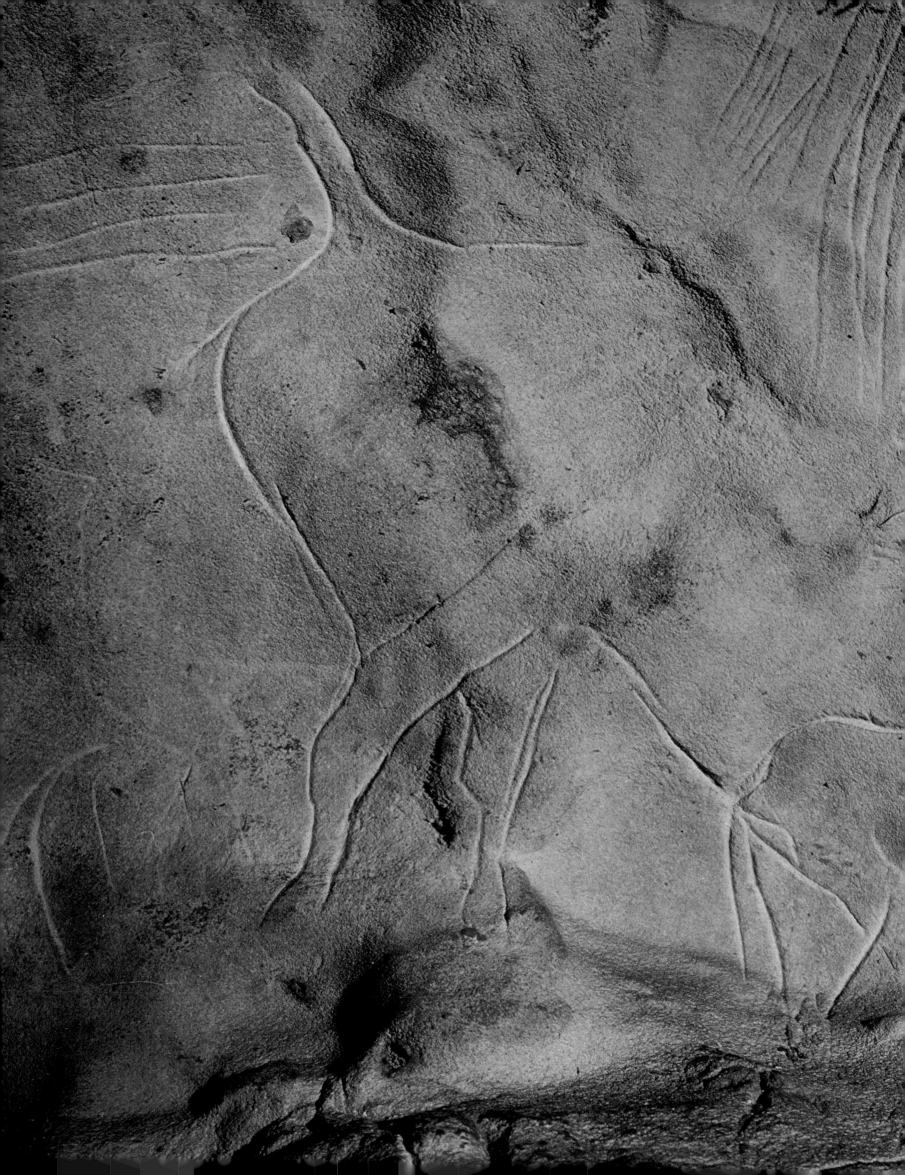

6. PALEOLITHIC SANCTUARIES

THE documentation section of this book contains charts covering the ways in which the different categories of associated figures are combined in various caves, as well as diagrams and on-the-site descriptions of a number of sanctuaries. There is, then, no need at this point to go into the technically involved matter of cave-by-cave variations from the statistically established over-all pattern of organization. I shall confine myself here to describing the latter in general terms.

EXTERIOR SANCTUARIES AND UNDERGROUND SANCTUARIES

THERE are two categories of cave compositions—those executed in daylight, either in rock shelters or at cave entrances, and those executed deep inside the caves where daylight does not penetrate. We have seen previously that sanctuaries receiving full or partial daylight consist largely of sculptured walls: Bourdeilles, Le Roc de Sers, Laussel, Le Cap Blanc, Commarque, La Magdelaine (Tarn), Angles-sur-l'Anglin, and Mouthiers. We have also seen that they belong to the early or middle phase of cave art, between the mature Gravettian and Magdalenian III, and that the human figures preserved in some of them include the finest examples we have of realistically represented women.

The sanctuaries deep inside the caves do not contain figures sculptured on the walls but only painted or engraved figures, with an occasional figure modeled in clay. Many weeks are required to sculpture a single figure in low relief, and it would have been arduous for the Paleolithic artist to spend so much time inside the caves working by the light of torches or lamps burning animal fat. However, in several dark interiors (for example, at Les Combarelles, Font-de-Gaume, Commarque), the deep-cut engraving creates a raised field, and the natural irregularities in the wall surfaces often produce the impression of low relief. We might assume that sanctuaries near the entrance, sculptured in relief, coexisted with the painted and engraved sanctuaries deep inside the cave: Mme. Laming-Emperaire goes so far as to suggest that these two types of representation marked a division between two different cultural areas. Far from excluding the probable existence of cultural differentiations within the Franco-Cantabrian region, I believe that a certain historical evolution took place, and that the underground sanctuaries are, for the most part, later than those located near the entrance. The stylistic reasons for this assertion are based on arguments which will be discussed later; but a survey of the relevant facts is necessary here.[1] More than twenty-five rock shelters and cave entrances with decorated walls are known, the best preserved being: in the Vienne and the Charente—Angles-sur-l'Anglin, Mouthiers, and Le Roc de Sers; in the Dordogne—Le Cap Blanc, Commarque, Saint-Cirq, Gorge d'Enfer, La Grèze, the Abri Labatut, Laussel, and the Abri Reverdit at Serjeac; La Magdelaine (Tarn); Pair-non-Pair (Gironde); Isturitz in the Pyrenees; La Peña de los Hornos in Cantabrian Spain; and, in the Ardèche, the caves of Chabot, Figuier, and Oulen. At some of these sites (Saint-Cirq, Isturitz, La Peña de los Hornos, Oulen) another sanctuary is found well underground, decorated with figures of a more recent character. Apparently, beginning in the Middle Magdalenian, there was a very considerable movement to-

[1] chart xx

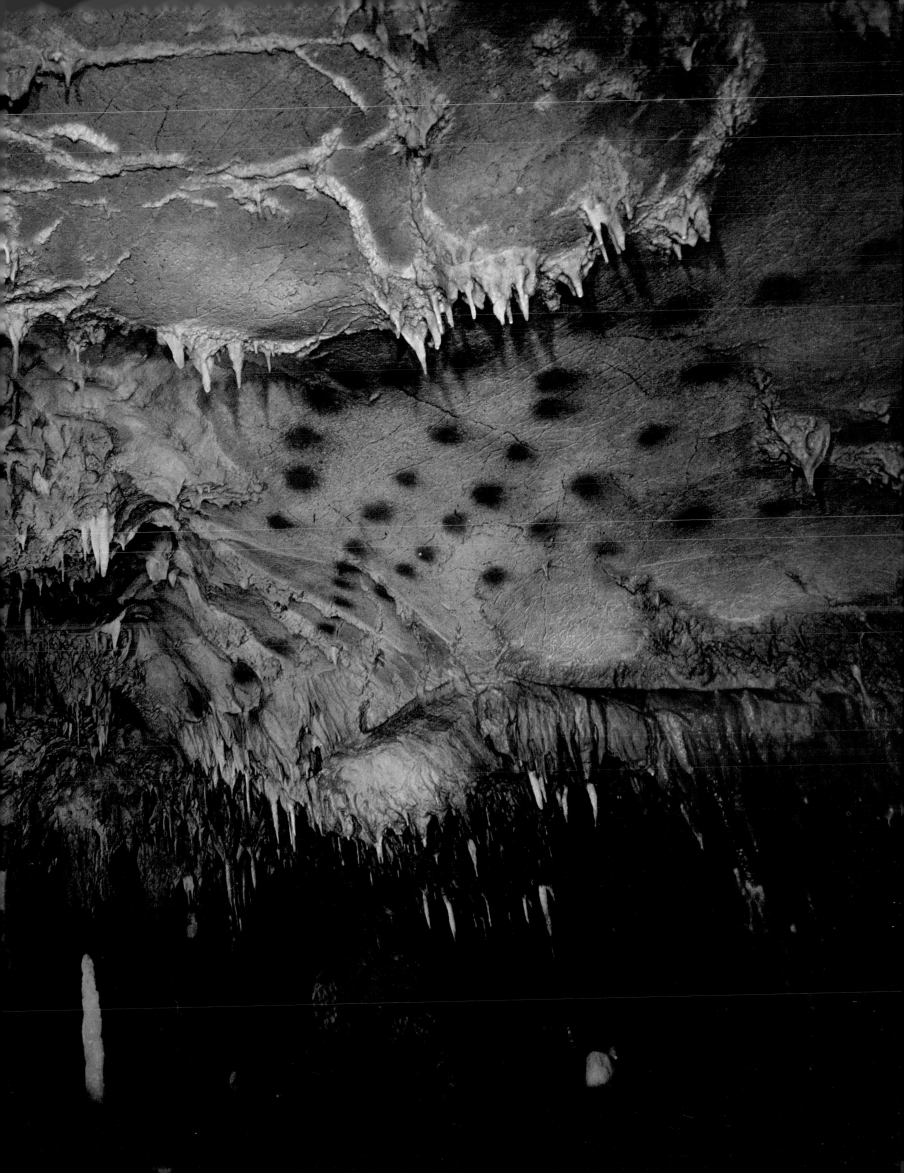

67 · PECH MERLE. *Entrance to Le Combel. Ceiling with red dots leading to the decorated chambers.*

68 PECH MERLE. *Black fresco in Late Style III. About 20 ft. long.*

69 LE CAP BLANC. *Frieze in low relief. Magdalenian III, Early Style IV. About 13 yds. long.*

70 NIAUX. *Groups of paintings in the Black Salon. Early Style IV. About 44 yds. long.*

71 SANTIMAMINE. *Main composition in the Round Chamber. About 8 ft. long.*

69

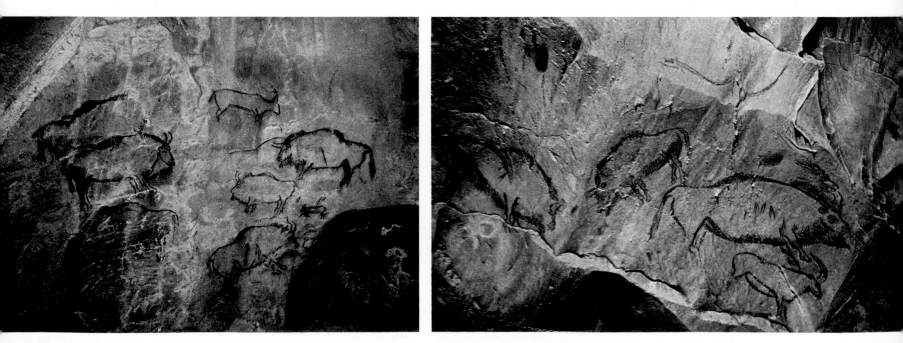

70

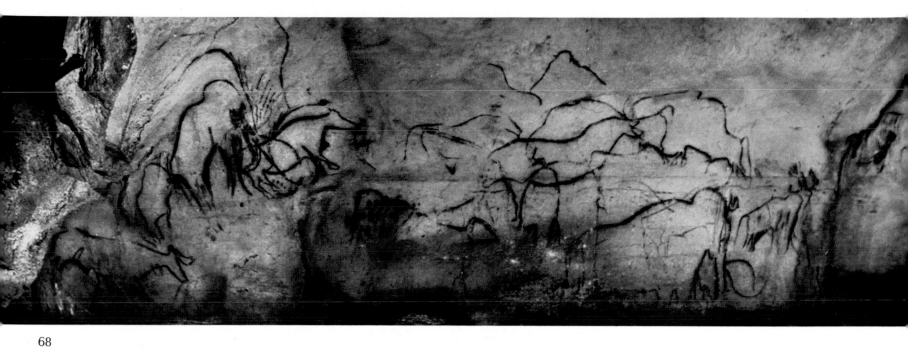

68

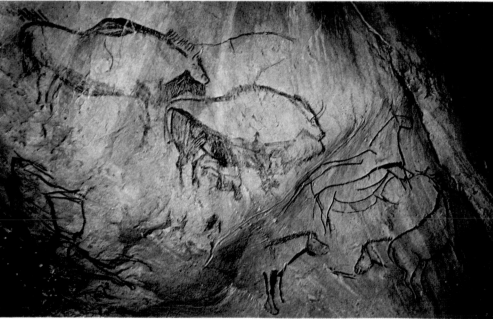

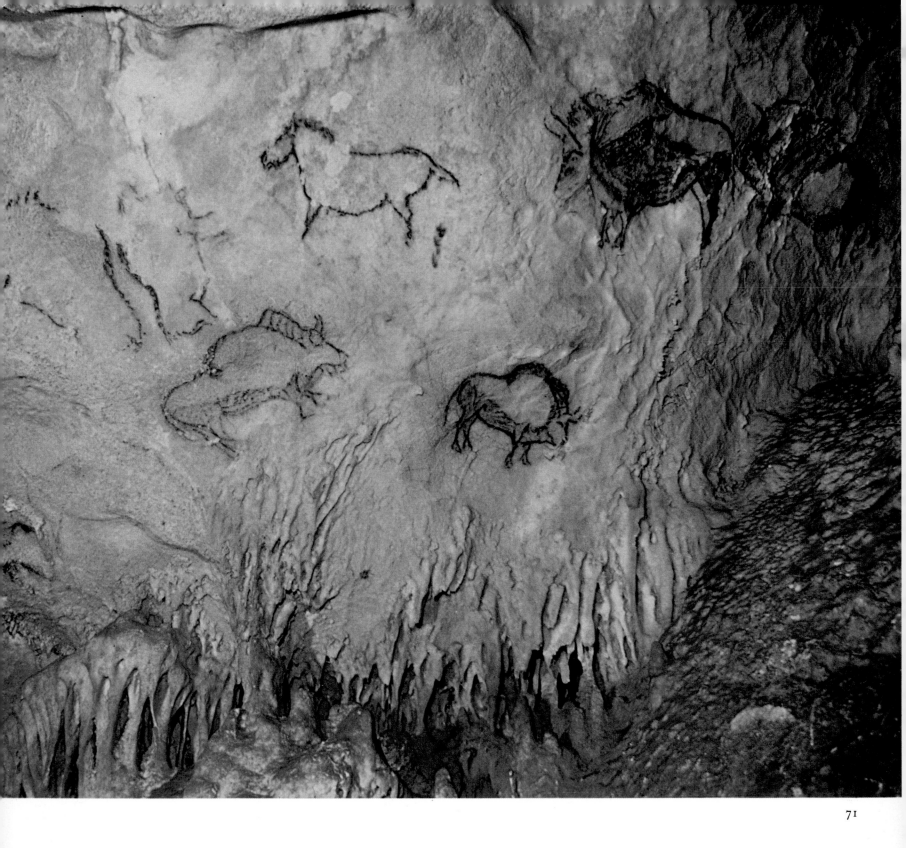

ward the cave interiors, away from the daylight. We have already seen that toward the close of the Paleolithic the sanctuaries moved back again to the cave entrances, and that the predilection for the dark interiors was relatively short-lived.

Does this imply that the cave interiors contain works executed only between the Middle Magdalenian and Magdalenian V? It is hard to answer this question on the basis of archaeological evidence, but toward the end of the Gravettian some sanctuaries seem to have been set up close to the areas reached by daylight—at Gargas, for example. However, this could be done only where lighting conditions were exceptionally favorable. I was able to ascertain that at Gargas, when full sunlight falls on the cave entrance, the interior is accessible without artificial light as far as the "semidome," even though the cave entrance is narrower today than it was then; it is possible to make one's way back from the "sanctuary" thanks to the light reflected from the right-hand wall in Hall II. In the Solutrean and Early Magdalenian, sanctuaries situated relatively far from the entrance are more numerous (Lascaux, Le Gabillou, Villars, El Castillo, La Pasiega). But the general rule remains valid: the majority of sanctuaries far inside the caves date from the middle part of the Magdalenian (Niaux, Rouffignac, Les Combarelles, Etcheberriko-Karbia, La Cullalvera).

Most of the sanctuaries in full daylight are in a poor state of preservation, and it is hard to establish the exact sequence of the figures. At Le Roc de Sers, where large chunks of wall have fallen onto the ground, we have a sufficient number of subjects to reconstruct a sizable portion of the classical sanctuary (including even a group showing a man struggling with a bison); unfortunately it has not been possible to reconstruct the original order accurately. By contrast, at Angles a very considerable part of the friezes have remained in place, and the sequence of the figures reproduces the order customary in the interior sanctuaries. The same applies to Le Cap Blanc.[2] At Pair-non-Pair, the panels receive dim light from the entrance and are arranged in an impeccable order: cervids at the entrance and in the back, with several repetitions of the theme ox/horse plus ibex. Consequently, what little we know shows that the daylight sanctuaries did not differ appreciably from the underground sanctuaries in respect to the order of subjects, and it is preferable to draw the over-all picture on the basis of the well-preserved compositions which have not been exposed to daylight.

Most of the interior sanctuaries do not begin at the cave entrance. The original shape and height of the underground opening and entrance area have often been greatly altered by rock falls and cave-ins, so it is hard to tell in any given case whether the system of decoration actually began at the last spot where daylight was visible, although in my work with Fr. Hours this turned out to be true in several caves—for example, Commarque, Labastide, La Cullalvera, La Croze at Gontran, and Saint-Cirq—where the lighting conditions at the back could not have been very different from what they are today. At La Croze, which is a very small cave, this spot is only a few yards inside the entrance; but at La Cullalvera and at Labastide the entrance can still be seen when one is more than 200 yards inside the cave. In many cases our rule certainly does not apply, for there are no figures at all until we come to the area of utter darkness, sometimes at a spot reached only after a very eventful journey. All the same, we cannot say that the Paleolithic people systematically concealed their works in cunningly hidden recesses which could be reached only after a perilous trip. This was occasionally the case, occasionally not; and though certain subjects have been knowingly placed in "chimneys," narrow clefts, or under very low ceilings, these choices are determined by both the nature of the subject and the character of the site. The impression one gets from repeated visits to the underground sanctuaries is that the Paleolithic artists took each cave for what it was and made the most of its peculiar features: singling out spots that appealed to them, making use sometimes of the whole cave, sometimes only of part of it. They were inclined to place certain subjects as far from the entrance as possible: they did this, for example, at Villars and at Rouffignac. At La Cullalvera[3] they took the trouble—incredible as this may seem—to scatter over an immense gallery, nearly a mile long, four small groups of figures that together form a decorative ensemble.

[2] fig. 144

[3] fig. 158

But probably the oddest of the underground sanctuaries is Etcheberriko-Karbia, a cave hidden in the mountains of the Basque country. The entrance to the cave is huge and would seem admirably suited for a fine set of wall decorations; but to reach the sanctuary a veritable expedition with full speleological equipment is required. One must toil for more than an hour, crossing little lakes, moving along narrow ledges, and climbing over slippery stalagmites several yards long, before reaching a low entrance that opens on a very narrow tunnel; the tunnel ends at a sheer cliff more than six feet high with no handholds. The sanctuary begins only on the other side of this cliff! It is even harder to get to the end: beyond the first composition, one must climb down a stalagmite fifteen feet high, skirt the edge of a precipice, and work down a twenty-seven-foot cleft to find the next composition. The last composition, a horse painted at the bottom of the cleft, is so placed on the edge of a sheer drop that we can only suppose that a colleague was holding the artist by the back of his garments over the void. It may be granted that some of the obstacles did not exist at that time, but at best this means that the little lakes were dry, for the other hurdles are matters of geological structure. As chart xx shows, except for La Baume Latrone and Villars, all the sanctuaries that are really hard to reach belong to Style IV.

The very term "sanctuary" suggests the question: who frequented these caves, and on what occasions? Here again it would be easier to answer if we had a sufficient number of examples and a better chronology. In the period when the sanctuaries were in parts of the caves receiving daylight, it is certain that people lived near them, and it is almost certain that in some caves—for example, Angles, Le Cap Blanc, Le Roc de Sers—they lived at the very foot of the decorations, which may have been concealed by a screen. As for the sanctuaries far inside, the question is very hard to answer precisely. The floors of the caves are sometimes covered with a thick layer of clay or rubble, but in several caves the very ground on which Paleolithic men walked has been preserved, and it shows very few footprints. Referring to Niaux, where the ground was intact and where footprints in the clay floor of one gallery are still visible, the Abbé Breuil said, "Nothing indicates that it was intensively frequented," and most underground sanctuaries suggest the same conclusion. Moreover, it seems that the deeper inside the cave a sanctuary is located, the less often did people visit it. Occasionally one suspects that only one expedition took place, perhaps just the one artist who went there to establish, once and for all, the sanctuary that was thenceforth known to exist deep under ground.

There are arguments against this conclusion, but they are not unanswerable. Many caves which are easy of access show traces of numerous visits in the form of the mysterious panels of scrawls that will be discussed presently. Although the subjects probably had a secret character, we know for certain that, during the Magdalenian as well as since the beginning, these same subjects were represented outside the sanctuary on stone plaquettes. It is possible that whereas the existence of the underground sanctuary was considered necessary, the rites connected with it were divided, in proportions that must have varied in each case, between the conveniently accessible plaquettes at the entrance and the interior portions of the caves which were more or less easy of access. The demonstration of this difficult point will be resumed in connection with the panels of scrawls.

FIGURES AT ENTRANCES, IN PASSAGEWAYS, AND IN THE BACK-CAVE AREAS

In a large number of cases, the area where the sanctuary begins is indicated by dots or short straight lines, either painted or engraved. The unvarying presence of these signs in cave after cave struck me at the outset of my investigations. We quickly noticed the regular recurrence of dots and strokes, not just at the beginning of the decorated area, but also at points of marked topographical change; these include turnings and especially

LASCAUX

LARGE PAINTED COMPOSITIONS

72 LASCAUX, THE ROTUNDA

*The composition is centered around two huge
aurochs facing each other. The one
on the right is a bull on whose shoulder
is a branched sign; facing the animal is
an incompletely rendered horse.
The aurochs on the left has no visible
sexual parts, but there is a sign in front
of its forehead and it is accompanied
by a large horse. Two other big bulls
follow the one on the right, and the damaged
head of another animal of the same species
is visible behind the aurochs on the left.
The group on the right is completed
by a string of little red aurochs;
the left-hand group includes a string
of little black horses. In the right-hand
group of bulls there is a bear
(not shown here), and bringing up the rear
of the left-hand group we find the "unicorn."
At the center, a group of small stags has been
inserted at the juncture of the two main groups.*

73 LASCAUX, THE AXIAL GALLERY, RIGHT-HAND
WALL

*This gallery contains two compositions
that echo each other on opposite walls.
A stag marks the entrance at the right,
and two facing ibexes bring up the rear.
There are four quadrangular signs,
each set in a different section
of the composition: in front of the stag,
over the "Chinese" horses, in front
of the reclining cow, and between
the ibexes. At the right of the
illustration is a red cow and the three
"Chinese" horses; at the left, the reclining
cow and a string of about a dozen little
horses. These two halves of the composition
correspond perfectly to the left side
of the composition in the Rotunda.
They are matched by the composition
(see figs. 319, 320) on the opposite wall:
a group of cows and little horses,
and a large black bull accompanied by cows.*

Wıтнın this framework of male symbols are inserted the large compositions, the most frequent type of which is based on the grouping comprising bison/horse with female-signs/male-signs. The fundamental fact is the existence of a characteristic grouping for each sanctuary. When a cave contains several compositions, the same formula is employed in each. Of the caves we have studied, 49 have as their basic theme ¹⁵ *chart* xvıı the bison in association with the horse.[15] At Montespan, the theme recurs in 11 compositions, at Les Combarelles it recurs 13 times, at Niaux 14, and at Gargas 19.

The caves in which the ox is associated with the horse are just as characteristic. Between them, the bison and the ox share the honors in the overwhelming majority of caves (70 out of 75 identifiable caves), but there are other formulas which fully confirm the deliberate and consistent character of the groupings in the central panels. For example, La Baume Latrone is a mammoth/horse cave, Covalanas a hind/horse cave. The latest of the dated caves, Teyjat, presents us, by way of exception, with a whole range of species, but these are grouped in an absolutely classical manner: bison/horse, ox/ horse, reindeer/horse. A similar flock, which does not alter the principle of pairing, is to be seen at Pech Merle, where the groupings are bison/horse, ox/horse, and bison/ mammoth.

I have already had occasion to mention an extremely interesting fact, namely, the presence of a supplementary ox/horse grouping in caves where the bison predominates: at Altamira, El Castillo, La Croze at Gontran, Le Gabillou, Font-de-Gaume, Les Combarelles, Niaux, and Santimamine, to mention only the most clear-cut cases. In each there is one section of the cave, or a panel, which shows an ox associated with a horse, in contrast to the repetition of the fundamental theme, the bison. In big caves, such as Les Combarelles,[16] Niaux,[17] and Altamira,[18] this single occurrence of the ox is very striking. It is even more striking that every ox cave contains, as well, a representation of the bison; at Lascaux,[19] for instance, the bison appears at the end of each big composition. Ebbou[20] is especially instructive in this respect: all the engravings in the cave are on the ox/horse theme; it is repeated three times, treated very homogeneously in the special Ardèche style which is related to certain works found in Italy. However, at two spots under low ceilings, beneath two panels showing oxen with horses, other Paleolithic artists have later engraved two bison in a Style IV that is closely related to that of Niaux, in complete contrast with the rest of the figures.

Finally we must mention central compositions with three or more species of animal: bison/horse + mammoth, for example, at Altamira, Bernifal, La Croze, and Gargas; a few caves, such as Pech Merle and El Pindal, have combinations that include the ibex, the stag, the hind, and sometimes the fish in their central compositions. These multiple-figure groupings which in a certain way recapitulate on one panel every animal species figured in the cave are often placed toward the back or in a side chamber, and as a rule they correspond to the last repetition of the theme before the terminal signs. This is the case in the "*camarin*" at Le Portel, where we find bison/horse/ibex/ stag + paired signs; at Niaux, where on panel ıv in the Black Salon are grouped bison/ horse/lion/ibex/stag; and at Lascaux, where the Chamber of Felines contains a profusion of small figures among which we find again bison/ox + horse/lion/stag/rhinoceros and paired signs.

¹⁶ fig. 147   ¹⁷ fig. 154   ¹⁸ fig. 132

¹⁹ fig. 125
²⁰ fig. 164

THE RELIGION OF PALEOLITHIC MAN

Iɴ regard to the meaning of this figurative scheme, of which we have been analyzing the details, it is not easy to promote conclusions that throw light on the underlying religious system it expressed. The hypothesis of bewitching the quarry, of picturing the animals to insure success in hunting them, is obviously insufficient. This theory originated in the fact that some animal figures show wound marks. However, the number of wounded animals is small—fewer than 10 percent of the animals represented— and the placement of these wounded animals was apparently chosen deliberately. At Niaux, their presence is most conspicuous; they occur on the panels (one or two wounded animals per panel) except for panel vi, in the Black Salon, where one of the bison is marked with paired signs. At Lascaux, one bison and two horses in the Nave and one feline in the Chamber of Felines show wounds. At El Castillo only one animal in the cave is clearly wounded; the same is true at Pech Merle. Moreover, the wound marks are often ambiguous, hard to distinguish from highly simplified female signs. The case that may seem clearest is that of the three animals in the Nave at Lascaux: the bison is marked with straight lines, and two of the horses with "arrows"—that is, marked with longer shafts having two short strokes at one end, resembling our ordinary road markers.[21] One of the felines in the Chamber of Felines bears eight such signs. Are we really dealing here with representations of a weapon? Apart from the fact that no type of spear with two barbs at the end is known from the period, this sign appears again at Lascaux, at the far end of the Chamber of Felines, in an unusual composition showing a headless animal (ibex or horse). Above it four parallel "arrows," tips in the air, point to four short strokes.[22] Now, when we consider the variants of the "arrow" and of the "wound marks," we become aware that these graphic markings can be assimilated to variant forms of the male and female signs. In other words, it is highly probable that Paleolithic men were expressing something like "spear is to penis" as "wound is to vulva." To be fully persuaded of this, it is enough to see that the bison in the central panel at Bernifal[23] is marked on its side, not with a "wound" and "arrows," but with an oval vulva in double outline and two pairs of short strokes. Thus a panel showing a horse and a wounded bison is found to be equivalent to a panel on which are shown a woman (or a quadrangular sign) and a man (or a barbed sign) accompanying the same animals. These examples show that the problem is not as simple as might have been thought, and that the signs of wounding are very probably related to sexual signs. It is not particularly surprising that the wound itself has been assimilated to a female representation, since we know that throwing weapons bear male symbols, but it rules out the hypothesis of the animals' simply being bewitched by the hunter.

We have referred in passing to headless animals.[24] It is hard to say whether there really is such a subject. Mme. Laming-Emperaire, following the Abbé Breuil on this point, observed that one of the bison on the Altamira ceiling was never completed, and on the basis of various other indications she thinks that this omission of the head may have been deliberate. For my part I have found few other examples: the headless animals at the back of the Chamber of Felines at Lascaux and in the back-cave area at Les Combarelles; at Niaux, one bison on the first panel in the Black Salon and the ibex by the terminal lake in the back-cave area; one ibex or perhaps cervid at Las Monedas; an unidentified painted animal at Bédeilhac; and one ibex (possibly) at the end of the terminal gallery at Altamira. I should not have attached any special importance to this problem had not a statuette of a herbivorous animal been discovered at Kostienki in the Don Valley, among the numerous statuettes in soft stone which form a group comparable to those on Franco-Cantabrian cave walls. Efimenko, who discovered the figurine, describes it as follows: "...an enigmatic little animal figure, clearly headless. The head never existed, as is evidenced by the frontal part of the figurine, which looks completed, that is to say, carefully finished, smoothed down, without a trace of deterioration."

But leaving open the question of headless animals—which by no means simplifies our attempt to discover the meaning of the figures—after we have ruled out the hypotheses of hunters' magic, of these being literal representations of trapped animals, or weapons and huts for spirits, or the simplistic symbolism of the pregnant animals, what hypothesis is left? Clearly, the core of the system rests upon the alternation, complementarity, or antagonism between male and female values, and one might think of "a fertility cult."

[21] *fig. 318*

[22] *chart* xxxvii

[23] *fig. 508*

[24] *chart* xxvii

If we weigh the matter carefully, this answer is at the same time satisfying and laughable, for there are few religions, primitive or evolved, that do not somewhere involve a confrontation of the same values, whether divine couples such as Jupiter and Juno are concerned, or principles such as *yang* and *yin*. There is little doubt that Paleolithic men were familiar with the division of the animal and human world into two opposite halves, or that they supposed the union of these halves to govern the economy of living beings. Did they conceive of this union the way we do, or in the fashion of Australian aborigines and Kanakas? Did they conceive of fertilization as biologists do, or did they suppose that the activity of the male only nourishes the spirit which has entered the body of the female? Theirs was probably some other explanation that we cannot imagine.

We have reconstructed a fundamental sexual division that is unrelated to the sexual character of the individuals; there is corroborative proof, perhaps, in the judicious restraint in associating the sexual signs with the figures. The erotic discretion of Paleolithic art, apart from certain rare human figures, may simply arise from the fact that the essence of the representations was not at all expressed in anatomical details. The cave as a whole does seem to have had a female symbolic character, which would explain the care with which narrow passages, oval-shaped areas, clefts, and the smaller cavities are marked in red, even sometimes painted entirely in red. This would also explain why these particular topographic features are marked with signs from the male set, which thereby become complementary. A few dots in the last small chamber of an immense cave then take on the same significance as the more complex groupings on the big panels, and this would account for the care with which, almost invariably, Paleolithic men placed some mark at the cave's innermost recess.

Talk of a "fertility cult" leads prehistorians (whose ideas on biology are inevitably those of our day) to imagine biological representations of fertility. Fifty years of literature on the subject leaves one with the feeling that the writers, aware of the role sexual representations might have played in Paleolithic thought, have tracked down every slightest attempt at realism, insisted on viewing the beasts as pregnant, and imputed equivocal attitudes to the "Venuses." As a matter of fact, Paleolithic art is fully as explicit as one might wish, but in a very different field from the one Western culture has lately taken to singling out.

Without overly forcing the evidence, we can view the whole of Paleolithic figurative art as the expression of ideas concerning the natural and the supernatural organization of the living world (the two might have been one in Paleolithic thought). Can we go further? It is possible that the truth corresponds to this frame of reference, which is still much too broad. To gain a dynamic understanding of the cave representations, one would still have to integrate into this framework the symbolism of the spear and the wound. Taken as symbols of sexual union and death, the spear and the wound would then be integrated into a cycle of life's renewal, the actors in which would form two parallel and complementary series: man/horse/spear, and woman/bison/wound.

In the last (though still provisional) analysis we arrive at the idea that Paleolithic people represented in the caves the two great categories of living creatures, the corresponding male and female symbols, and the symbols of death on which the hunters fed. In the central area of the cave, the system is expressed by groups of male symbols placed around the main female figures, whereas in the other parts of the sanctuary we find exclusively male representations, the complements, it seems, to the underground cavity itself.

We are very far from having solved all the difficulties, but we have the framework within which the figures are distributed, and it will always be possible to return to it as we revise our hypotheses. One point still remains unclear: why do the animals of the female group differ according to caves and regions? Investigations along this line promise to be doubly profitable, by casting light both on the meaning of the compositions and on the chronological evolution.[25]

The fact is that we have caves dedicated to the bison, the ox, the mammoth, and the

[25] *charts* XXI–XXIII

74 LASCAUX

The Scene in the Shaft. This episode,
known from other examples, is very probably
of a mythological or allegorical character.
The interpretation of it is likely
to be misleading: the man, the bird,
and the barbed sign have identical symbolic
values; the spear and the wound (here rendered
in the form of concentric ovals)
are complementary symbols. The bison
in this illustration is matched on the opposite
wall by a horse. Note the fairly advanced
style of the bison (Early IV) and the artificial
character of the connection between head
and withers. The beard, as if drawn
for an animal whose head projects forward,
is here in the middle of the forehead.

hind, and caves dedicated to the reindeer probably existed toward the end of the Paleolithic. Are we to look upon this choice as typifying the animal species in the forefront of the hunters' concerns at any given moment? Perhaps, but it has yet to be established that the hunters always represented the quarry currently most in view. The impression one gets is rather of traditions typical of a given epoch and region: the ox sanctuaries, except for Lascaux, seem to be located on the periphery of the Franco-Cantabrian area, and to be among the earliest; the bison sanctuaries, from the Poitou to the Périgord, are certainly old, and during the Middle Magdalenian they spread over an area that forms an inverted T into southwestern France and the Pyrenees. The mammoth sanctuaries (La Baume Latrone, Chabot), and those dedicated to the hind (Covalanas) are peripheral. In addition to these geographical data, which argue in favor of the existence of something more than a simple sampling of the representatives of the two sexual groups, there are two other pertinent facts: first of all, the presence in the central compositions of supplementary animals from the male group—ibexes, stags, mammoths; second, the existence of "ox chapels" within sanctuaries where bison predominate, and, correspondingly, "bison chapels" within the ox sanctuaries. Why was it necessary to have a few ibexes among the bison and the horses, and a few oxen in the bison caves?

Finally, it seems that in many cases individuals of both sexes of each species are represented. The sexual attributes are rarely defined, but the secondary characteristics (profile, horns, or antlers) are often very explicit. At Lascaux, bulls and cows form facing groups; at Teyjat and in southern Italy, bulls and cows follow one another; at La Pileta they are side by side. The sex of the horses is harder to make out, but fairly often they go in pairs. We find many stag-hind pairs (Spain), male and female reindeer (Les Combarelles, Teyjat, Font-de-Gaume), male and female large-horned deer (Les Combarelles, Pair-non-Pair, Cougnac), male and female ibexes (Gargas, Cougnac). We can imagine an ideal composition in which, like the paired male and female signs, one would find a pair of bovids associated with a pair of horses, this grouping completed by a pair of cervids or ibexes. This formula is not to be found anywhere with certainty, except at Levanzo and probably at Teyjat; in most cases it is worked out only in part.

The hypothesis of male and female entities, rulers of the male and the female spheres of life, is certainly oversimplified and incomplete; the hypothesis of the bison and the horse as the corresponding animal symbols in the same spheres is surely just as inadequate. Probably we are confronted with a system perhaps never formulated in rational terms of correspondence, equivalence, interchangeability, and complementarity among all the figures. For the time being it seems difficult to venture further in this direction, since the explanation cannot come from our imaginations, or from study of latter-day primitive peoples, but only from a new, more thorough analysis of our materials.

THE RITES

ONE might try to throw light on other aspects of the religious problem by examining such traces as may be left of rites which Paleolithic people supposedly performed in the caves. What exactly do we know about them? The sum of evidence in the sanctuaries as to what may have been religious practices is very modest. There are three reasons for this: the scanty evidences for such rites are scattered in odd corners of caves occasionally very large in size; the practical difficulties of systematic excavation in an environment which is often very irregular; and the gaps in the few excavations that have been carried out. We can make note of a few real finds at such caves as Gargas, Les Trois Frères, Labastide, Le Portel, Lascaux, and La Bouiche; the sum of the documents is very slight, taking into account that most of it has not been made the object of publication. Thanks, however, to Lascaux, Labastide, La Bouiche, and Le Portel, we know that some sanctuaries at least show signs of having been frequented quite intensively. This rapid survey of the most typical evidence will concentrate on the little that is known about the subterranean life led by the Paleolithic people.

At several rock shelters, where the sculptures were executed by daylight, we find traces of arrangements for the sanctuary. At the Fourneau du Diable (Bourdeilles), Denis Peyrony ascertained that the sector where the sculptured blocks were found had been brought into order by a sort of low wall constructed of broken rock, and that several holes for poles or posts had been dug in front of this man-made partition. The sanctuary thus formed a quadrilateral space open at the front, probably closed by a screen which masked the painted and sculptured blocks. A similar arrangement existed at La Madeleine (Dordogne) and at Laugerie Haute; here, too, we owe the observation to Peyrony's perspicacity. In the majority of these rock shelters, projecting rings carved from the stone were discovered on the walls and sometimes on the sculptures themselves;[26] what these were for is still very uncertain, since most of them have been broken, and the original order of their arrangement is hard to determine: they may have supported a screen in front of the decorations. Many hypotheses have been put forward on the subject of these rings: they are most often seen as the remains of some arrangement for attaching a tent to the walls, but some even see them as rings for tying up half-domesticated animals. Because they are often carved on sculptures, Mme. Laming-Emperaire rules out their practical use for holding a tent or screen. Whatever their actual usage, two observations are pertinent: we know of no arrangement in any underground sanctuary that closely or remotely resembles these rings; and we find many cases where a natural screen formed by a stalagmitic mass or a jutting rock has been put to decorative use for a composition. This procedure is seen most often in the Spanish caves: at El Castillo and at La Pasiega[27] narrow chambers containing signs are masked by columns decorated with animal compositions; at Las Chimeneas[28] the entrance animals are represented on successive vault-like springings in the ceiling and these are followed by several episodes of a composition on the ox theme; at El Pindal signs appear on short springings in front of the paintings. This utilization of successive planes to provide a sort of progression in the exposition of the central groups is certainly bound up with something very fundamental in Paleolithic art, for wherever caves present such natural features, they are exploited (Covalanas, La Peña de los Hornos, Las Monedas, Niaux, Oulen, Le Portel). What we still lack that might help us grasp the reasons for this practice is accurate observation of the physical disposition of the plaquettes found at the sanctuaries containing many of these works, such as Limeuil and Labastide; we must not forget that everything we have so far learned indicates a similar usage for the plaquettes in the shelters and the pictures on the cave walls. If the luck and scientific acumen of just one excavator were to reveal to us the topographic disposition of the plaquettes at some site where they had not been greatly disturbed, interesting general inferences could doubtless be drawn. In this connection, Russian excavations of a Paleolithic hut found at Mal'ta in Siberia discloses that the decorated objects and implements were divided into two groups, one found near each of the two hearths. Weapons and figurines representing birds were near the hearth at the right of the entrance; knives, scrapers, needles, awls, pendants, and female statuettes were near the hearth at the left. This remote Siberian site has been regarded for several decades as the only spot in Asia where we find an Upper Paleolithic culture comparable to that of western Europe, with its spears, its stone implements, and its female statuettes. It is all the more striking, therefore, to find there, thanks to methods of investigation adapted to the requirements of scientific archaeology, a division comparable to the one which I believe I have observed, by more indirect methods, in the western Paleolithic.

Inside the caves no traces of special arrangements are found; as a rule the natural environment was not altered, the over-all composition being adapted to it. One sometimes notes, as at Pech Merle, that stalactites were broken off to clear a passage, and in several caves, particularly at El Castillo and at Villars, slabs or flat stones placed by

[26] fig. 494

[27] figs. 134, 136–137
[28] fig. 131

nature or by man at the foot of certain compositions were covered with scrawls and unfinished animal outlines.

We mentioned earlier that footprints have survived only very exceptionally, where the ground did not become covered by sedimentation or the shoes of latterday visitors have not obliterated them. Those at Aldène, Montespan, Niaux, and Pech Merle tell us nothing about the rites that the original makers of the footprints may have performed. But it is impossible to speak of footprints without mentioning those at Le Tuc d'Audoubert. At the end of a gallery, 770 yards from the entrance, there are two bison modeled in clay which are among the very few known examples of sculpture found inside a cave; nearby there are a few piles of clay that may be the remains of other modeled figures, and a few sausage-shaped pieces perhaps representing male symbols. In the clay of a puddle-shaped depression covered by a thin film of stalagmite one can see about fifty heel imprints left by a youth who walked over this soft ground. The Abbé Breuil summed up the evidence with these words: "This track with about fifty human footprints evokes the thought of some initiation ceremony which was performed only once." The unusual way of walking with the weight on the heels and the fact that the imprints were beyond any doubt made by a youth provided the source material for a scenario based on the observations made by Breuil and Henri Bégouën, and occasionally one runs across other evocations of mysterious rites in which boys went out of a hall backward, walking on their heels.

One fact is very striking: practically all known footprints were made by young people. This of course argues strongly in favor of some sort of initiation ceremony. The long line of prints at Aldène suggests a group of youths running through the cave corridors; at Niaux and at Montespan, there are the tramplings of a few individuals at a point where the ceiling is low; in a puddle at Pech Merle, we have the footprints of a boy, perhaps accompanied by a woman, and the imprints of small heels in the puddle-shaped depression at Le Tuc d'Audoubert. Thus it is certain that children went inside the caves. Elsewhere the footprints are found at points well away from the normal route through the cave and (except for Aldène) in wet, clayey ground—one must wonder whether this does not simply attest to the fact that children like to step on places where the foot sinks in. Let us say that the children were carefree enough, however solemn the attendant circumstances may have been, to play around in mud puddles. As for the ritual of initiation, it is justified merely by the fact that young people penetrated the caves as far as the sanctuary.

Another important piece of evidence is the set of clay figures in the Montespan cave where we find several masses that have been completely deformed, a fairly recognizable relief[29] which seems to represent a horse (though it has been thought to be a feline), and a kind of clay sphinx without a head: this figure is riddled with holes which seem to have been made with a spear.[30] In another sector of this vast cave, we notice, engraved on the clay wall, a horse which is also riddled with marks of blows. According to the author of the find, N. Casteret, the skull of a bear cub was lying between the hoofs of the sculpture, which suggests that the latter may have been covered by a fresh hide of a bear cub with head attached, and subjected to ritual blows. Though very incomplete, the evidence of the Montespan bear and horse casts a little light on the nature of rites in the caves about which the cave-wall art tells us nothing definite. It must be noted, however, that the "slaughtered" figures—such as the wounded bison at Niaux and other caves, and the bear marked with small circles in the Trois Frères sanctuary— always appear singly within a group of intact figures. It is not impossible that in some sanctuaries a ritual took place, consisting of inflicting wounds on one or a small number of the images. This is the more plausible because it has not been established that the images were in fact stabbed with spears. When observed on the spot, the limitations of the space, the unchanging direction of the holes, and especially the rhythm and the precision disclosed by the grouping of the impacts, all suggest a systematic stabbing of the figures with a pointed object held in the hand, such as a dagger. This operation, which we can as well imagine in the setting of a theatrical ceremony as in the peaceful-

29 *fig. 648*

30 *figs. 646, 647*

ness of an artist painting the martyrdom of St. Sebastian for a country church (for we have only the material evidence), may be linked with the same process as the imposition of signs on certain figures. Indeed, when signs are superimposed over animal figures, it is obvious that the operation took place in two stages—first the animal was painted, then the signs were applied. When the signs are in a different color and when they recur elsewhere in the cave, as is the case at Niaux and at Marsoulas, we get the impression by cross-checking that the animal groups were painted at one time and the signs at another. In the Black Salon at Niaux (where all the animals, wounded or not, are painted in black, but all the signs are in red), we find two wounded bison in panel III which are marked in black, and one of them has two additional wound marks in red. Clearly, the evidence concerning rites is scanty and not very consistent.

Can we hope for some enlightenment from studying the objects (if any) found deposited in front of the images? In other words, are there evidences of offerings? Occasionally ocher has been found—for instance at Etcheberriko-Karbia. At Cougnac, a patch of ocher less than a foot square was found on the ground; it had been abandoned there, but nothing indicates more than neglect, whether voluntary or not.

The situation seems to be the same with respect to flint objects. From time to time a tool that was lost or forgotten is found on the ground, on a ledge, or in a recess of the cave: at Isturitz, for example, and at Etcheberriko-Karbia where a very pretty curved awl had been placed on a rock: At Labastide two blades were found in a cleft; at Arcy-sur-Cure a retouched blade was discovered stuck in the clay between two decorated chambers. In none of these cases can we speak of rites. At Lascaux long spears and a sculptured lamp were found at the bottom of the Shaft, but details as to their exact location are lacking, and we can only surmise that the objects were placed there for a religious purpose.

When a new cave is entered, hand lamps are often found. Thus several lamps and fragments of coloring matter were discovered on the cornices at Lascaux when it was first explored. In the same cave, at the bottom of the Shaft, Breuil and S. Blanc found a kind of depository of stones, some of which were naturally hollow and may have served as lamps or, as the Abbé Glory suggests, as torch holders. At Le Gabillou it was also noted that lamps were lying on the ground at the time the cave was discovered. At Cougnac a lamp was found on the ground, fairly close to the pile of ocher; it was lying upside down. If the initial discovery of such objects had been made under conditions of more exact recording, our task of assessing the materials would certainly be greatly facilitated.

Our survey thus yields very little in the way of precise information: Paleolithic people entered the caves with lamps made of hollow stones in which animal fat was burned, and sometimes left them there; they carried with them their pigments and their graving tools. Children accompanied them, at least on occasion, and they were barefoot. We know no more than this, aside from the fact that sometimes a kind of scaffolding would have been needed to reach the upper portions of the walls or the ceiling, and that, in caves having a unity of execution that suggests they were frequented only during a single period, the animal figures and the signs may have been set out in two or three successive series; this could perhaps be justified by religious reasons, but the reasons may also have been purely practical.

THE "UNFINISHED OUTLINES"

AFTER one has examined the large animal figures in a cave, taken separate note of the signs, and established a topographical breakdown of the sanctuary's various parts, there usually remains a not very promising residue of scrawls, of small figures timidly engraved one upon another, of partly preserved rows of short strokes, and of meanders traced with a flint or with fingers on soft portions of walls and ceilings. For the most part scholars merely mention these scrawls; they have rarely been reproduced, except when they were thought to be evidence of earlier or later decoration encrusting a composition dating from the middle epoch. Among these thankless figures we find the largest number of images that, when sketchily executed, are thought to be Aurignacian, or, when the delicate silhouette of a bison or horse emerges from the tangle of scrawled lines, to be terminal Magdalenian.

When I began my topographical investigations I had no preconceived ideas concerning these figures, which are as hard to copy by hand as to photograph; we more often noted their location than we recorded their details. Not until I completed my first tabulations did I become aware of the constant and regular character of the areas covered with sketchy, tangled figures. From that moment on we began systematically to look for the "panel of unfinished outlines" in each cave, and it must be said that our efforts have almost always been crowned with success.

The areas covered with meanders, clusters, "comet" shapes, rows of engraved short lines, and animal figures often incomplete but sometimes very delicately executed, are invariably found in the vicinity of the first large composition, between the signs or animals at the cave entrance and the first group of paired animals. In the sanctuaries having multiple compositions, one such area recurs in nearly every section; it was this repetition that first attracted my attention. The exact location is subject to variations: sometimes (the most frequent case) before we reach the central compositions, sometimes on the ceiling of the chamber containing the compositions, sometimes on surfaces underneath them—and in the latter case, fairly often on slabs or blocks placed slightly in front of the wall. One cave seems to be an exception—Lascaux; there the area of unfinished outlines is situated in the heart of the sanctuary, near the entrance into the Nave—but we do not know how the entrance toward the Rotunda of the Bulls was arranged in its original state.

There is little chronological progression to be seen in the areas of unfinished outlines: if in the earliest ones we seem to find primarily meanders or radiating lines, sometimes also including indistinct figures, executed on walls or ceilings that precede or face the central group, yet this same arrangement recurs in different epochs. The area thus covered is sometimes quite large. The most clear-cut example is Gargas[31] where the entire right-hand wall of the chamber between the first and the second section of central groups is covered by a compact network of scrawls traced with fingers on the soft surface. La Baume Latrone[32] presents an almost identical example: an entire ceiling and the adjacent walls before and around the central group of mammoth/horse + lion are covered with radiating lines and "macaroni," as Abbé Breuil christened them. At Pair-non-Pair the unfinished outlines and radiating lines are on the left-hand wall, facing the series of panels on the theme ox/horse + ibex; here we do not find meanders, but a host of curved lines corresponding to the dorsal contour of animals and two fairly distinct figures, one horse and one ox. In addition, there are rows of dots, clusters of strokes, and circular figures, the whole producing an utter tangle of indistinct lines; the execution is hasty, careless. The same impression is produced by the ceiling at Pech Merle[33] above the long frieze with the successive groups of mammoth/ox, bison/ horse, and bison/mammoth. Now and then an animal figure seems to emerge from this singular jumble, but never completely, except for two or three mammoths and three female figures which have continuous outlines, though they are by no means perfectly distinct from the rest. In the Ardèche is another example, the Chabot cave which is similar in arrangement to Pair-non-Pair—that is to say, it receives daylight and has two decorated walls. The wall on the right shows a series of figures on the ox/horse + mammoth theme; the wall facing it is covered for three or four yards with more or less complete outlines of mammoths, so many and so jumbled that one's first impression is of a series of vertical grooves, deep and noticeably parallel.[34] There are several other examples of walls decorated in this fashion—at Lascaux, where the ceiling of the Apse and the Nave are striped with long gashes, or at Rouffignac where the scratched outlines are too numerous to count. On these surfaces we find the same subjects as in the cen-

[31] fig. 124

[32] fig. 166

[33] figs. 129, 382

[34] fig. 714

tral compositions, but executed with less care, and most often reduced to the dorsal curves of animals and to scrawled signs, as though numerous individuals who were not necessarily very gifted in the art of engraving had superimposed reproductions of the central theme or merely traced meandering lines on the only available wall spaces near the major works.

The zone of unfinished outlines occurs on the ceiling only when the structure of the cave particularly lends itself to this arrangement; in many cases the area covered with scrawls is part of the wall near the central figures. However, a certain evolution is perceptible: in sanctuaries from the middle period (approximately, the Early and Middle Magdalenian), even where ceilings could have been used, these cursorily drawn figures appear on a wall or on flat blocks or stones placed near by.

At Altamira and El Castillo blocks covered with jumbled engravings are found at several points, but the most clear-cut case is that of Santimamine. In the chamber of that cave where the majority of the paintings is gathered, one wall is occupied by a composition of bison/horse/paired-signs that is one of the best anywhere on this theme. Opposite this wall, on a cascade of stalagmites and alongside various folds in the rock, are grouped the subjects normally found in the back-cave area—bear/ibexes/ stag. At the foot of the central composition is a hump of stalagmite the size of a large milestone, on which were engraved a number of bison crisscrossing in every direction, and also the forequarters of a bison painted in black.[35]

[35] fig. 661

In the majority of cases, the panel of unfinished outlines is found on a wall in the front part of the sanctuary, usually just past the first signs or animals at the entrance. This is the case at Niaux; after two short strokes, a first group of paired signs, and more short strokes, there then appears at the entrance to the Black Salon, with its extraordinary panels of black bison, a double panel that contains, not unfinished animal outlines, but a hodgepodge of symbolic signs in complete confusion—rows of dots, single short strokes and some drawn two at a time, claviforms, and marks resembling the imprint of a closed fist.[36]

[36] figs. 9, 588

At Labastide, the sanctuary begins at a ledge of rock from which one takes a last glimpse of the distant light from the cave entrance. Four or five short strokes mark the left-hand wall outside the entrance to a side gallery, and overhanging this entrance is a large block covered with unfinished engraved outlines. Among these we can make out horses, bison, and cervids, as well as rows of dots and strokes.[37] The central group is under this, inside the chamber.

[37] figs. 571, 572

At Las Chimeneas, the panels appear right after the two stags at the entrance: they are covered with incoherent scratches, radiating lines among which one can make out something like the rumps of unidentifiable animals. At the nearby cave of Las Monedas, as we approach the decorated portion, we find on one wall to the right a panel painted with vague outlines among which the dorsal line of a horse can be made out; on the opposite wall is a panel painted in black with the most surprising set of "doodlings" to be found in the entire Paleolithic. The figures include circles, rows of strokes, and lattice signs inspired by clefts in the rock, but the over-all effect is that of the figures, incoherent but linked by a common rhythm, which some people draw on paper while listening to the telephone.[38]

[38] fig. 678

In La Croze at Gontran, at the end of the daylight zone, we find a group of parallel strokes arranged in perpendicular sets to mark the sanctuary entrance; on the bell-shaped ceiling that follows, we see a tangle of curved lines, resembling dorsal lines, in addition to short strokes or hatchings; the main composition comes after this. I could extend this list almost indefinitely, pointing out that at Venta de la Perra (Spain), in the Vidal Gallery at Bédeilhac, or at Rocamadour, the entrance is marked by disorderly groups of incomplete figures. If I do insist on going on a bit longer, it is because this theory concerning the panels of unfinished outlines is, among the other theories expounded in this book, especially at odds with scientific traditions of prehistory. Thus, I can make my point only by supplying multiple examples which put the reader in a position to verify the hypothesis for himself. The verification is made the easier because several of the most accessible caves display this pattern with the greatest clarity.

At Font-de-Gaume, one entire gallery—the first lateral gallery—is occupied by unfinished animal figures set in no particular order. On emerging from this gallery, the visitor finds himself at the "Rubicon," a narrow passage beyond which the major compositions begin. At this very point we find, high up on the left, another panel of scratches, signs, and cursorily drawn animal outlines.[39] At Altamira the panels of unfinished outlines are repeated several times, at each resumption of the central groups: at the beginning of the ceiling with the big bison, as already mentioned; on a block just behind the recess with the oval signs; and toward the middle of the farther gallery, at Breuil's Group 52. At Les Combarelles there is one important zone of scratched scrawls preceding the first figures, and another at the beginning of the innermost gallery, where, before the stags, we see a series of curves, parallel strokes, and signs. At Pech Merle, apart from the ceiling already referred to, we find scrawls and tangled figures opposite the major groups in black—bison/horse and mammoth/bison; they are also visible between the gallery with the bear and the side chamber with the man pierced with spears, as well as just before the group of "dotted" horses; the most important group of jumbled figures is in the corridor leading to the ossuary and at the back of the latter. At Pech Merle every composition seems to have its panel of scrawls. The most extraordinary case is that of Lascaux. Ever since its discovery explorers have been struck by the contrast between the major part of the cave, which is decorated with majestic paintings of animals and signs, and the Apse above the Shaft where hundreds of small engraved figures crowd one another, intermixed with barbed signs, "comets," ovals, and series of parallel strokes, in apparently total disorder. These figures—and this is most unusual—are superimposed over a painted decoration in large measure damaged. This would suggest that the patternless decoration is later—perhaps very much later—than the large painted figures; however, some of the more clearly definable subjects, such as the stags and horses, disclose the same details of treatment as the large figures. The areas of scrawls must have been begun very early, additions being made throughout the life of the sanctuary.

These panels of figures, which have been attributed to a wide range of periods according to the degree of their awkwardness or accomplishment, are so constant a feature in the decorated caves that they cannot but be contemporaneous with the major compositions which they precede topographically. Their existence is surely linked with religious life, with the very conception of the sanctuary, since they are present even in the earliest decorated caves. These works, with their disorderly superimpositions of frequently incomplete figures covered with hatchings evoke most clearly the engraved plaquettes found in dwelling sites. Actually, these scratched zones constitute the most living element among the compositions having a fixed symbolic location in the cave decorations. In many cases they are located just where daylight ceases to enter, or close to this point, so they were easily accessible. Moreover, when we study them, we have the strong impression that here we are dealing with graffiti, not with works of art, even though their execution is sometimes remarkably good. This is why I have included them in this chapter on Paleolithic religion.

To the extent that the sanctuaries were frequented, an important part of the rites must have been performed in front of these panels, and the panels themselves can provide, to a certain degree, evidence of this frequentation. In some caves they hardly seem to exist; in others several square yards are covered with tangled figures. In some caves they are found next to imprints of hands (Gargas, Pech Merle, Rocamadour, La Baume Latrone). In other caves, such as Pech Merle and Las Monedas the scratched scrawls adjoin areas which look highly polished by repeated rubbing, although these areas are not in the narrow passageways where similar polishing from the rubbing of bodies of men and animals occurs frequently. These panels appear also near areas smeared with red ocher, for instance at Gargas or in the amazing little Blanchard rock shelter at Saint-Marcel, recently discovered by Dr. Allain. This shelter had been blocked up since the end of the Middle Magdalenian, and the ground inside is still littered

[39] fig. 529

with reindeer antlers, while horizontal fissures in the walls served as shelves upon which spear points and flint implements were kept in reserve. So far we know only the entrance area, with a horse's head engraved in a network of parallel strokes, spots of black and ocher, and a ceiling entirely smeared with red ocher and covered with strokes running in all directions.

All these facts make us perceive the importance of the front part of the sanctuary and lead to the notion of rites in the course of which figures of the same type as those decorating the walls, but simplified and piled up over one another, were sketched on these zones as they were on the plaquettes. At the same time some light is cast on the significance of the plaquettes; if the sanctuaries themselves do not give the impression of having been much frequented, the plaquettes certainly played a corresponding role at less solemn levels of Paleolithic life.

7. TOWARD A REVISED CHRONOLOGY

7. TOWARD A REVISED CHRONOLOGY

By this time the reader may be growing impatient for this book on Paleolithic art to start discussing the art as art. If so, he will be pleased to learn that we are almost ready to talk about style. Almost ready: before calling to witness any stylistic imponderables, we must provide a solid framework of data that can be verified historically. Quite apart from the Abbé Breuil, who formulated the first coherent system for dating Paleolithic art, a number of writers have discussed cave art as art, in ways sometimes down to earth, sometimes poetic or philosophical. Such discussions have been to the point, no doubt, to the extent that man is universal and eternal, but—and we must stress this—to that extent only. Their real justification is that in the last analysis stylistic criteria alone have thus far supplied a framework for the history of prehistoric cave art. It was not unreasonable for these writers to suppose that the matter of dates had been settled, that the historians had built their chronological structure which other scholars might therefore use for their own explorations. But this is not yet the case: the dates, stages, cycles, and styles of prehistoric art are so many propositions, and nothing else.

Once again I am obliged to take issue with the Abbé Breuil, and this time concerning the very foundation of his chronological system, the sole source of present-day interpretation. It is impossible, however, to propose a system of dating that is fairly radically at variance with his without spelling out very clearly the reasons that make us give up the classical scheme he launched, according to which cave art is divided into two cycles of development. Anything less would display an unjustified disregard for a theory that has inspired the literature of two generations; it would also neglect an opportunity to show that our own aim is not to destroy but to continue.

THE CLASSICAL CHRONOLOGY

The best statement of the Abbé Breuil's system appears in the first part of *Quatre cent siècles d'art pariétal (Four Hundred Centuries of Cave Art)*—a work that is readily accessible, and, since it was published in 1952, may be said to reflect a very advanced stage in his thinking. According to him, cave art went through two successive cycles—the Aurignacian-Perigordian and the Solutrean-Magdalenian. He worked out two separate developments for painting and for engraving.

PAINTING

The order of succession of figures in the Aurignacian-Perigordian cycle of cave art is as follows: at the very beginning we have the *negative hands* and the *series of disks* (Altamira, El Castillo, Gargas, Les Trois Frères, Font-de-Gaume, Pech Merle); then come *positive hands* (La Baume Latrone, La Pileta); then the meanders (La Baume Latrone, Altamira) in which the *first figures* make their appearance. The *claviforms* and the *large animals* painted red, either in broad bands or evenly filled in, are of the same epoch. Next come in turn the *linear outlines*, first in yellow, then in red, accompanied by *simple* *tectiform* signs, and the *broad blurred outlines* accompanied by *large tectiforms* (La Pasiega, Altamira, El Castillo). After these we find the *flat colors* which fill the outlines at first incompletely, later completely, accompanied by the *broad-field tectiforms* (El Castillo, La Pasiega). The next-to-last stage is marked by *bichrome painting* (La Pasiega, Abri Labatut, Lascaux), and continues with the *black linear outlines* (Lascaux); it is followed finally by "the big uniformly red figures with black heads, and others entirely in sepia brown, in which the perspective, generally twisted until now, tends to be corrected."

In the Solutrean-Magdalenian cycle which follows, painting begins (as before) with *simple linear black outlines* (Altamira, El Castillo, Le Portel, Niaux, etc.), accompanied at Altamira by *black tectiforms*. As in the first cycle, we find next the *large blurred black outlines* (El Castillo, Le Portel, Cabrerets, Bernifal, etc.). The parallelism continues with the *incomplete flat black colors* (same caves). Magdalenian IV (which Breuil regards as the Early Magdalenian) would be characterized in the Pyrenees by *thin black outlines with hatched modeling* (Niaux, Le Portel, Cabrerets). During Magdalenian V *black modeling* appears (Font-de-Gaume, Marsoulas, Le Portel, Altamira). The bichrome painting of the first cycle has its counterpart in the *polychrome painting* of the second cycle (Altamira, Font-de-Gaume, Marsoulas, etc.), accompanied at Font-de-Gaume by tectiforms. Finally the black linear outlines of the Aurignacian-Solutrean are balanced by the small *naturalistic red outlines* (Niaux, Ussat, Pech Merle) of the terminal Magdalenian.

The astonishing symmetry of Breuil's two cycles had already struck a few prehistorians, in particular Mme. Laming-Emperaire. There are very few—if any—examples in history of an art that, in its development, exactly retraces the same route twice in all its details. To establish any such development with certainty, we can only rely, in the present case, on the minor arts, on the superimpositions of figures on the walls, and on the style of the figures. The arguments drawn from the minor arts will be fully discussed a little later; for the moment, we may observe that the figures painted on objects are more than exceptional, and the little they contribute coincides so vaguely with cave art that they scarcely have practical use. The stylistic arguments are of very unequal value: the figures on reliably dated "Aurignacian-Perigordian" objects are extremely crude, but we know that in all the arts there are many examples of crude work dating from late epochs. On the other hand, the "primitive" is not always the earliest. Now, taking into account the fact that "linear outlines" reappear four times (at the beginning and end of each of the two cycles), is it always possible to find in the style of such simple figures sufficient guarantee against error?

Is it true that the linear outlines at the beginning of the Aurignacian-Perigordian cycle are red while those at the end of it are black, like the earliest in the Solutrean-Magdalenian cycle, the latest of which are red? Did this distribution of coloring stuffs really have compelling value for the Paleolithic artists, considering that red and black pigments were used in every period, even though the available supply may have varied in amount? At the back of the Axial Gallery at Lascaux there are two facing ibexes, so nearly identical in detail that one cannot tell them apart when tracings of the two are reversed.[1] One is red, painted of fairly widely spaced dots, and the Abbé Breuil places it in Phase IV, among the earliest figures; the other is black with dots linked in a more continuous outline, and he places this in Phase 9 *b*, among the latest figures. The outlines of the two figures do not intersect at any point—which, if they did, would give some basis for thinking one was earlier than the other; but they are executed in the same technique, and their styles are indistinguishable. Thus the early attribution for the reddish figure depends on the "rule" that red linear outlines go back to the Aurignacian proper or to the Gravettian, and the late attribution for the black figure depends on the "rule" that black linear outlines are of more recent date. Now, the oldest linear outlines which are dated stratigraphically, such as the animal forequarters from Aurignacian II at the Abri Castanet, and at La Ferrassie the ibex (?) from Aurignacian III and the two joined heads from Aurignacian IV, have in each case black linear outlines. *A priori*, without citing other examples which will appear in due course, the task of dating figures would seem to be made unduly hard, if we are to

[1] *fig. 112*

189

rely solely on the evidence of style which is impermanent, and of colors which are variable but reduced to two alternatives, black and red. In the example from Lascaux under discussion, the ibexes are obviously of the same period, probably even contemporaneous, and when we compare them with dated finds, neither one can be attributed to the earliest stages of the Upper Paleolithic.

It is hard to distinguish the "blurred" black outlines from the other black outlines and black modelings, and we sense within the examples given by the Abbé Breuil a certain amount of personal interpretation. At Pech Merle, which he cites as an example, the outline can pass from thin to "blurred" within the same figure, depending on which part of the body we are looking at. At Bernifal, also cited, there is only a single very vague figure, hard to distinguish in whatever lighting we devise. In the Cantabrian region, the blurred outlines are the most recognizable: but the comparison among figures seems equally to show that it is hard to distinguish between the process of applying color in closely spaced touches (supposedly identical in the Aurignacian and the Magdalenian) and the style in which the figures are rendered, for that also tends to make them look alike.

Can we rely more confidently on bichromy and polychromy to distinguish between the two cycles of the black-modeled series? A single example, the Altamira ceiling—polychrome composition par excellence—will suffice to show that the progression from "simple linear outlines to modeled black figures to polychrome figures" can hardly be accepted without reservations. Does even the distinction between Perigordian (Gravettian) bichromes and Magdalenian VI polychromes rest on unassailable foundations? In both cases the colors employed are exclusively red and black, so that it is hard to tell what the difference is between a bichrome in red and brown and a "polychrome in red and brown" (Breuil's very words, in *Quatre cents siècles...*, page 76). In other words, what criteria of bichromy and polychromy distinguish a bison in black outline filled in with modeled ocher on the Altamira ceiling, assigned to Magdalenian VI, from a horse in black outline filled in with modeled ocher in the Axial Gallery at Lascaux, assigned to the Perigordian? The distinction is made the more problematical by the fact that the low reliefs dated Magdalenian III at Angles-sur-l'Anglin (where we ought to find simple black linear outlines or, at most, black blurred outlines) were heightened with black and ocher.

For the central figures on the Painted Ceiling at Altamira, the attributions are as follows: the figures executed in black outline, "sometimes slightly modeled," are supposed to belong "to the end of the Solutrean and the beginning of the Magdalenian"; the strongly modeled black figures, to Magdalenian V; the polychromes to Magdalenian VI. Apart from the risk, already mentioned, which we run when we assume that pictorial traditions changed in each stage of the Magdalenian (that is, each time the hunters modified their weapons), does the examination of the evidence compel us to assume such a progression? The strongly modeled black figures, supposedly older than the polychromes by at least two thousand years, are in every respect identical with the "polychromes" except for the ocher filling. When we re-examine the whole ceiling, figure by figure, it is impossible not to acknowledge that apart from the ocher filling all the polychrome figures are identical with the black figures.[2] Furthermore, the few bison in modeled black are squeezed into the few spaces between the large two-color figures and serve as space-fillers in the grand tapestry of animals. The simple linear figures are in even more subordinate positions, many of them being merely heads which, without perceptibly encroaching on the large figures, occupy the small intervals between them. Thus it becomes very difficult to imagine that first there was a scattering of five truncated linear figures, then six modeled figures placed at random four thousand years later, and that finally, two thousand years later still, fifteen large bison were added in such a way that they touch the others only with the tips of their horns and hoofs. It would seem simpler to think of a sequence running in the reverse order.

Examples are fairly numerous of incomplete figures inserted within previously executed groups. At Marsoulas, above the black and red horse, there is the dorsal outline of a bison in modeled black. This is cited as a typical example of a superimposition of supposedly successive figures, the horse on the bison: actually, the images do not overlap, and the shading of the bison becomes less marked the closer it approaches the dorsal line of the horse. Whether the two figures were executed at the same time or centuries apart, the order in which they were executed is the exact opposite of the one proposed. The same circumstance is to be seen in the Rotunda at Lascaux, where one incomplete horse is squeezed in between two large bulls; but Breuil has here recorded the true sequence.

It would be wearisome to make a critique of all the instances where the classical chronology is vulnerable, and the greater part of what remains to be said will be included implicitly or explicitly in the pages that follow. To adopt a two-cycle theory for painting is to introduce inextricable confusion into the period of roughly ten thousand years during which cave art seems to have been practiced as such. The theory, at the beginning, is logical and rational: art apparently began with simple outlines, then developed more elaborate forms to achieve modeling, and then developed polychrome or bichrome painting before it eventually fell into decadence. Another logical idea underlies the chronological division: since the decorated objects seem to go back to the Aurignacian, the art of the caves must have extended from the Aurignacian to the terminal Magdalenian. And yet an evident contradiction arises from the elements presented by superimpositions that are incontestable, or simply by the logical assumptions: the elaborate forms do not all date from the latest period; it is therefore necessary to assume that the identical sequence was repeated all over again in the course of the Upper Paleolithic, each time beginning and ending with linear outlines. The two-cycle theory is needed to avoid what would otherwise appear to be contradictions in the succession of figures in a given panel.

ENGRAVING AND SCULPTURE

In the case of the engravings, stratigraphic data have indirectly imposed restrictions on the two-cycle theory; the development of engraving within each cycle is less clear-cut than that of painting. The low reliefs at Laussel, Le Roc de Sers, Angles, and Le Cap Blanc show clearly that the Aurignacian-Perigordian merges into the Solutrean-Magdalenian. What is surprising is that the Abbé Breuil acknowledged this merging without drawing from it any conclusions affecting his theory concerning painting, even though sculpture provides solid ground because it is dated by excavations—the opposite of painting, whose sequence has to be determined by inference. The reader will perhaps understand now why we devoted so much space to decorated objects prior to discussing the significance of the works and the elements of dating: the direct dating of cave art rests on extremely insecure foundations.

The sequence proposed by Breuil for the two cycles in the development of incised work and sculpture runs as follows: the *digital drawings*—long lines on clay surfaces—are the counterpart of the painted lines of meanders; the first painted figures are contemporaneous with the *primitive animal figures*, but these are followed by *light engravings*, which are the counterpart of the linear drawings. The *deep engravings* correspond to the large blurred outlines, and the *low reliefs* to the modeled blacks and the bichrome paintings. Such are the successive stages of the Aurignacian-Perigordian cycle.

The Solutrean-Magdalenian cycle begins with the *low reliefs*, which correspond this time, oddly enough, to the painted linear figures—a correspondence that is contradicted at Mouthiers and Angles-sur-l'Anglin, where the figures in low relief were painted in monochrome or bichrome. Now follow *fine engravings* which also correspond to the painted linear figures. Actually, at Angles, the fine engravings are of the same epoch as the low reliefs, and neither can possibly belong either to the Gravettian or to Magdalenian VI. The last part of the developmental sequence is constituted by *fine engravings*

(Magdalenian IV), *modeled statues* (Le Tuc d'Audoubert and Montespan), more *low reliefs* (Font-de-Gaume), and another set of *fine engravings* (Magdalenian V–VI).

We can see, because each stage may be established by at least one solid piece of evidence, that the two-cycle theory of engraving is a long way from presenting a very convincing order: the low reliefs are at the middle of its sequence, and the fine engravings turn up everywhere. Only the deep engravings are unique, for, at least in some instances, they correspond to the first stage of low relief. The presence of fine engravings throughout the time span covered by the two cycles is explained by the fact that a notable proportion of them correspond to the panels of unfinished outlines which were discussed in the preceding chapter.

Our criticism of a theory which for several decades provided an explanation of cave art will no doubt seem unduly severe. The reader must bear in mind that this theory existed in its main outlines fifty years ago. Despite the data then already obtained on the basis of stratigraphic evidence (and the Abbé Breuil had been a prime mover in obtaining this), the manifestation of the Aurignacian period (which seemed to have begun suddenly) presupposed a Homo sapiens who was complete from the outset, so to speak, with his art. It was impossible to imagine, in the absence of archaeological proof, that nothing found in the dwelling sites would correspond to the cave works attributed to the Aurignacian. Not until around 1920 were the first dated elements found at La Ferrassie; only around 1930 were these confirmed by finds at Isturitz; together with scattered fragments from a few other sites, these now began to yield an idea of what art was truly like before the second part of the Gravettian. It was even less apparent that people could have entered the caves at a rather late date in order to decorate them. Therefore it was necessary to discover, deep in the cave interiors, evidence that hunters had visited them in every epoch.

In the pages that follow I hope to show that, although the chronology of cave art remains partly hypothetical, hypotheses other than the two-cycle theory are perfectly defensible. A historian (and the prehistorian differs from other historians only in the nature of his sources) has to base the history he writes on historical data; but Paleolithic art presents historical data only from dated objects, from the few cave walls datable by reference to archaeological deposits, and from the intellectual content of the works whose variations must coincide with the general chronological scheme. There is no historical method, properly speaking, that does not base its chronological system upon these elements. We should remember that early in this century such a method was difficult to apply, and that the enormous number of examples of cave art—the collection was already almost complete at the time—called for a system of explanation. The Abbé Breuil's great achievement is to have undertaken and brought to completion the critical inventory of several dozen caves and to have attempted to discover in the figures themselves the order of their development. This order can be understood, for the most part, only on the basis of dated materials, but it was difficult to go far in this direction. Apart from a highly elaborate theoretical apparatus for explaining cave art, stratigraphic chronology, the only instrument for controlling the data, still remained open to the exceedingly haphazard excavation methods practiced by countless collectors among whom there were only two or three outstanding individuals. The resources neither of a penetrating intuition, nor of a prodigious power for deciphering and reconstructing figures, nor of a flexible and ingenious mind—these could not be substituted for the weapons of historical criticism.

CHRONOLOGY AND DISTRIBUTION OF ART AT PALEOLITHIC SITES

In order to establish a chronology of cave art despite the glaring gaps in research methods, we have at our disposal a capital of finds: some part of these is rigorously dated, and the bulk of them is fairly closely datable. These finds consist, primarily, of fragments of walls, decorated blocks, and the walls themselves in those cases where covering deposits make it possible to assign them a minimum age. Not a great deal of this evidence—perhaps thirty examples in all—comes from sites where the works were executed in the dwelling itself.

One fact is obvious at once: that portion of cave art which is directly datable is virtually all contained between the Aurignacian proper (a few slabs) and Magdalenian III (several sites with sculptures from the mature Gravettian, the Solutrean, and Magdalenian III). Few difficulties are raised by the early, exterior wall decorations, but the question arises whether there was a contemporaneous art farther inside the caves. Do we possess any direct material evidence that figures were executed in the dark portions before the beginning of the Magdalenian? Everywhere, prior to that epoch, we find decorated outer walls; but then all such evidence ends. May we not suppose that invasion of the cave interiors began at that moment? In fact, the invasion of these interiors seems to have taken place at a relatively late period; most of the evidence we possess from the period between the terminal Gravettian and the Magdalenian concerns the walls receiving daylight or situated near daylight. There are a very few examples, however, from around the Solutrean, of caves decorated from front to back (Pech Merle, El Castillo, La Pasiega).

From the very moment when the evidence of decorated exterior walls disappears, decorated objects begin to increase proportionately in number and variety: hundreds of engraved plaquettes, as well as hundreds of spear-throwers, pierced staffs, and spatulas, offer elements for stylistic comparison with the works inside the caves. This capital has been exploited haphazardly, single objects striking investigators as "just the same" as one or another work on the cave walls. Although it is legitimate to evaluate these isolated cases of identification, for or against, it is no less necessary to question the whole of the evidence that takes on, when viewed statistically, often startling features.

One example will show what we can ask of the documents of prehistoric art, taken as a whole. The rarity of reindeer on the cave walls struck prehistorians long ago—it is one of the animals least often represented in the caves, although it lived in these regions throughout the Upper Paleolithic. Breuil writes: "The reindeer, which is so abundant in the figures on portable objects, is much less so in cave art and often is not found at all. And yet there is no difference in age between these two arts. The difference is probably simply of a psychological order." The statistical and stratigraphic facts do not entirely support this view. On decorated objects the reindeer becomes perceptibly less common toward Magdalenian III–IV, and is "abundant" only in the mature and terminal Magdalenian. But when we study the sanctuaries containing compositions that are certainly late in the Magdalenian, we find that the reindeer is present (Les Combarelles, Font-de-Gaume, La Mouthe, Les Trois Frères, Las Monedas, Teyjat). Consequently there do not seem to be two unrelated contemporaneous arts—that of decorated objects in which the reindeer is "abundant" and that of cave art in which it is "not found at all"—but two successive series of sanctuaries and objects, the first series without reindeer the second with the reindeer represented in both. Moreover, we may ask whether the sanctuaries without reindeer were not, at least part of them, localized between Magdalenian I and Magdalenian IV—a very short period, geologically speaking.

As we have said, the exploitation of the evidence of decorated objects brings in elements for stylistic criticism. These are elements that deserve priority. We may imagine that during Aurignacian I and II there were artists capable of drawing a bison correctly on a wall, but since the only dated objects bear outlines that are almost formless, it is impossible to prove that a single cave-wall work is reliably Aurignacian. We can credit the mature Gravettian with much more, for on decorated objects of that period are animal outlines both painted and engraved, still crude but perfectly constructed; nonetheless, lacking material proofs, we cannot attribute the large frescoes at Lascaux to artists of the Gravettian.

Between the mature Gravettian and the Solutrean, from the Don Valley to the Pyrenees, we find female figures in frontal view, some engraved, some in low relief, and some in high relief, but no female figure of that type exists in any deep sanctuary. Moreover, the female figures occasionally found in the caves are shown in profile and bending forward, exactly like those on the plaquettes dated from Magdalenian III to V. The chronological interpretation of any compositions including such figures will henceforward be obliged to take this fact into account.

When we examine the decorated objects for such details as the treatment of eyes, manes, and coats of the various species of animals, we become aware that very specific conventions were observed during Magdalenian IV and at least part of Magdalenian V: horses are fairly often represented with two parallel strokes at the base of the mane, and a kind of M extends across the abdomen between the front legs and hind legs; bison have a diagonal which starts at the shoulder joint and runs to the root of the tail; ibexes have a straight line from haunch to knee; reindeer have a row of dots between shoulder and thigh. These details truthfully render features of the modeling or of the coat, and one must admit that they could have been so observed and rendered in every period of the Upper Paleolithic, but in fact these conventions have thus far been found only on decorated objects of the rather late Magdalenian. There are numerous examples of similar modeling in the art of the deep caves—Altamira, Le Portel, and Niaux, among other caves. It is hard not to think that there is a certain chronological relationship between the objects and the cave art.

The signs raise a number of difficult problems. Their sexual meaning has been demonstrated by numerous examples, but only in cave art, for the only small find showing a sign from the Cantabrian group (an engraved pebble from Isturitz) comes from the Passemard excavations and its date may oscillate between the Solutrean and Magdalenian IV. Nevertheless, this find is valuable, inasmuch as all cross-checking tends to place within this time span the developing abstraction of the signs.

Finally, if we were to list each of the arguments upon which chronological placing is based, the result would lead to agreement on a number of points: the sanctuaries seem indeed to have begun outside the caves toward the close of the Aurignacian, to have been elaborated in the daylit zones during the Gravettian, when the technique of low relief was mastered, and to have had their great period of sculpture during the Solutrean and the beginning of the Magdalenian. By that time the interior of the caves relatively close to daylight must already have been invaded, and a few deeper caves; but the movement into the interior did not become general until Magdalenian III–IV. The plaquettes must have been used to preserve sanctuaries on a small scale in the dwelling sites, and the large compositions were moved deeper and deeper into the caves. This movement seems to have been progressive, and we shall try to demonstrate it by such caves as La Mouthe, Les Combarelles, Galleries B and C at La Pasiega, and Le Portel, where the latest compositions are located in the remotest parts of the caves.

Our demonstration of the chronological evolution of the sanctuaries will make use of all the materials that have been discussed in the course of this book. Our point of departure is the fact that the groups of figures are not the result of random accretion, but compositions that have their fundamental basis in the pairing of animals and signs. This is the same basis for our reading of the subjects which makes possible the discovery, in any given composition, of the common origin of the assembled figures or those that were subsequently added to complete it or to amplify it. It also enables us, in caves containing multiple compositions, to determine priorities for the successive groups, both in chronological and topographical order.

At Altamira, for instance, there are four groups of figures that make up the overlapping ensembles. The first, much damaged and no doubt composite, is near the entrance and was probably just beyond the area of half-light at the time it was executed: it comprises one horse deeply incised, some red paintings, and signs in the shape of coats-of-arms. The second group occupies the Painted Ceiling; it is complete in itself, with its unfinished outlines, the bison/horse theme, and the peripheral animals; the signs are claviforms and barbed signs, and the animals' coats have marks like those in other compositions with claviforms at Niaux, Le Portel, and Les Trois Frères. The third group is spread throughout the cave from the entrance to the back, and all of its subjects are painted in black: the ibexes at the entrance, the panels of unfinished outlines, the bison/horse groups, ibexes in recesses with ventral markings, stags, passageway and back-cave signs, signs from the Cantabrian category of brace-shaped signs, and some human faces modeled from the natural relief of the walls. All the correlating elements at our command put the execution of this group between that of the entrance sanctuary and that of the great ceiling. The fourth group is placed in the deep gallery and comprises only engravings that overlap with the last elements of the third group: it treats the bison/mammoth/horse theme. Its character as a late work is emphasized by the fact that the bison's tongue protrudes, a detail that is not found on decorated objects until relatively late. The example of Altamira illustrates the principles of the method I have followed, which consists in constantly bringing to bear every element of data at our disposal.

ARCHAEOLOGICAL EVIDENCE

Examination of the archaeological evidence supplies the chronological foundation upon which the cave works must come to rest. If the most accurate clues, those provided by the tools and implements found at the sites, do not perforce coincide with the clues derived from study of the artistic development, they nevertheless constitute a chronological scale as convenient as that of the "centuries" used by historians. It is, however, essential for the reader to keep in mind that when we speak of "Solutrean" art, we are speaking of works from the period of "flint points in the shape of laurel leaves"; the works are not the productions of a "Solutrean culture," which is a fluid entity.

With these qualifications we can divide prehistoric art into four stylistic periods, simply as a set of guideposts in time:

Period I—all finds with figure representations, from the earliest to the boundaries of the mature Gravettian.

Period II—finds from the terminal Gravettian and the first phase of the Solutrean. In the present state of our sources, the terminal Gravettian and the proto-Solutrean may be considered to form a whole—the period between the Gravettian and the Solutrean, within which the exact divisions are still obscure.

Period III—the (probably) mature Solutrean and the Early Magdalenian (I and II).

Early Period IV—Magdalenian III and IV, of which the archaeological definition is still fairly vague.

Late Period IV—extending to Magdalenian V and VI. Actually, the chronological uncertainties make it impossible to establish formal distinctions for the end of Magdalenian IV and the transition between V and VI.

Terminal Period IV—representing the close of the Magdalenian, which may be considered as mature Magdalenian VI and the transition to the Mesolithic.

This chronological outline is justified only by the succession of dated objects and dated cave works, which doubles the evidence bearing on stylistic development, and on development with respect to thematic content.

The first general conclusion suggested by study of the dated finds is that the same content persists from first to last. The pairing of animal species with signs appears in the Aurignacian and disappears with the terminal Magdalenian. Consequently, the ideological unity of cave art rules out the guideposts that it might provide for us had there been changes in the basic themes. Only variations in the representation of this uniform subject matter are discernible in the course of a stylistic study.

Actually, although human beings of both sexes appear from first to last, their representations vary significantly. The ways of representing the entire body, or the large abstract signs, give us insight into the stylistic tendency of the times and the formation of regional traditions. The same applies to the representations of animals. We have referred to the seeming eclipse of the reindeer and the mammoth during the middle period of the Upper Paleolithic. At the same time, the conclusions drawn from the content of the dated finds are still very scanty and disparate. Even in outline they do not compose a grand design directly applicable to the cave finds; they are simply precious guideposts.

CHRONOLOGY OF CAVE DECORATION

Like the decorated objects, which must determine the actual sequence of styles and the assignment of styles to specific points in time, cave art must be based on such of its works as are dated. If there is a genuine coincidence between the style of dated cave walls and that of the objects, it is safe enough to try to assign undated cave-wall works to a given style and a given period.

We have repeatedly stated that dated cave-wall works are few. It is possible, however, to adduce about twenty examples, some dated with complete certainty, others with a high degree of probability. We must begin, then, by drawing up a list of the available evidence.

Reasonably dated from the period between the Gravettian and the Early Solutrean (Period II) are the wall decorations at La Grèze (Dordogne), at Laussel (Dordogne), and at Pair-non-Pair (Gironde); also the second chamber and a part of the sanctuary at Gargas (Hautes-Pyrénées). The subjects represented in these various caves all belong, by their treatment, in Style II.

The low reliefs at Le Roc de Sers (Charente) and at Bourdeilles (Dordogne) are dated from the Solutrean; they belong to Style III. It is possible to assign to Early Style IV the decorations at Angles-sur-l'Anglin (Vienne), Mouthiers (Charente), and Le Cap Blanc (Dordogne) which are dated from Magdalenian III.

No cave wall is as yet reliably dated from the period corresponding to Magdalenian IV–V, though we have many significant finds of objects from this period. Thanks to the large engraved stalagmite slabs at the Teyjat cave (Dordogne), which date from Magdalenian V–VI, we can determine an advanced stage of this period.

Despite the paucity of dated cave walls, nothing contradicts what we have ascertained from the evidence of the decorated objects. It is regrettable, however, that all the evidence for cave art derives from low reliefs and engravings. Very few paintings have stratigraphic support; we may, however, mention the fragments from the Abri Labatut (Dordogne): a hand in negative, and the forequarters of a stag. These finds are not enough, but they are valuable because they do not contradict the other evidence we possess for hands and figures in Style II during the Gravettian. Finally we must here take into account all the evidence (tools and equipment found *in situ*; carbon–14 dating; climatic factors) which tends to place the majority of the Lascaux figures between the mature Solutrean and the Middle Magdalenian, a date that is in keeping with their pictorial style. Since all the dated evidence is in accord, the undated cave-art evidence can be approached with relative safety; in any case, it seems that style, in conjunction with the other factors, can determine some degree of classification and that, on the other hand, inferences made on the basis of nonstylistic criticism can be followed only in the measure that they agree with those based on style. Such a classification will never be hard and fast since it lacks the decisive element of absolute dating, but it must be attempted, with full recognition of its necessarily conjectural character.

ONCE we are well inside the cave, we must take the figures lining the walls as our only source for a chronological critique. The figures scattered over the walls in seeming disorder may be presumed to date from different epochs, and an appreciable part of the criticism rests on arguments concerning position. If we remember that the arrangement of subjects is a function of the cave's topography, we can first of all investigate whether all the figures, taken as a whole, correspond to a coherent succession of themes —that is, whether the signs or animals at the entrance, those in the central panels, and those at the back of the cave are patently in the same technique and the same style. Thus, among the dozens of painted and engraved figures at Altamira, the "Black Sequence" stands out as a distinct whole, with its signs and animals occurring from the beginning to the end of the cave at the places where theoretically they should be. We can next ascertain the existence of several phases, and make the observations necessary to establish their chronological succession. These observations seem to lead me to three categories of material relevant to discussion, all concerned with aspects of positioning: (1) superimpositions of figures, (2) location of the sanctuaries progressively deep within the caves, and (3) the "annotations" that may have been made by later generations of Paleolithic visitors to an already completed sanctuary.

SUPERIMPOSITIONS

THE idea of a "stratigraphy" that could be applied to the figures incised and painted on the cave walls provided the earliest basis for establishing a chronology of these undated documents. The Abbé Breuil made frequent use of superimpositions and gave convincing examples of their validity, at least in a relative sense. We have already said, however, that the argument based on superimpositions is not always decisive, for two figures may deliberately have been drawn one on top of the other at the same time.

A systematic survey of the superimposed figures leads to a first comprehensive finding. Except for sanctuaries where little space was available (for example, Les Combarelles, La Mouthe, El Castillo), Paleolithic artists showed great respect for old—in the sense of inherited—figures and, whenever they could, avoided covering these with later additions. The number of significant superimpositions seems indeed to have been limited by the artists themselves; in the large caves they chose new areas each time for their compositions.

Superimpositions of figures executed in the same technique cannot be regarded as significant, especially when they strengthen the coherence of a theme. This applies, for instance, to the large black fresco at Pech Merle, in which bison and horses, mammoths and oxen are superimposed in pairs.[3] Close study of the way these subjects were executed, moreover, discloses that the relative position of the superimposed figures is reversed between one end of the fresco and the other, and that the artist, when drawing two figures, has sometimes made the lines of the first one of the pair overlap those of the second, sometimes the other way round. We observe the same thing at Marsoulas (mentioned previously), where a bison reduced to head and dorsal line was, so to speak, slipped underneath the first figure, a completed bichrome horse. We may also cite Le Cap Blanc, where the hindquarters of a bison in low relief were sculptured underneath the forequarters of a horse,[4] and Angles-sur-l'Anglin, where one of the female human figures serves as foreground for the hindquarters of a bison.

Significant superimpositions are rare. At Altamira, in two instances, we find engravings in a later style overlapping passageway signs in the "Black Sequence." In most cases we find "insertions"—blank spaces filled in with figures that add new life to an old composition. At Les Combarelles, the little groups of bison in Compositions 58 and

[3] *fig. 68*

[4] *fig. 69*

96 are inserted within groups of older figures, and in Composition 87 the little painted horses in Late Style IV are effectively superimposed over an antecedent engraving which is, none the less, in the same style.

"ANNOTATIONS" AND REPAINTINGS

Mᴏʀᴇ frequently found than genuine superimposed figures, and more in keeping with the evolution of Paleolithic religious thought, are figures that have been worked over, and additions to old figures. Lascaux is the cave where worked-over figures are most unmistakably in evidence; Abbé Breuil reported a great many examples. As will be seen later, Lascaux discloses two phases of intense frequentation. The earlier phase corresponds to the paintings in the passage of the Apse and the Nave, where alterations are numerous; the later phase is represented by the Rotunda and the Axial Gallery, corresponding to a period when the Apse was covered with engravings, unfinished outlines, and signs. As will also be seen, the abstract signs are gradually changed in their presentation: during the last period "annotations" were made, such as the introduction of claviform signs which played no part in the earlier tradition. Similar evidence is found at El Castillo and La Pasiega.

One of the most characteristic instances of "annotation" is Composition 88 at Les Combarelles, known as the "horned horse" group. Here one of the horses in the mammoth/horse composition was transformed into a bovid by the addition of a pair of horns, which creates a bovid/horse + mammoth. Ebbou in the Ardèche offers an even more striking example, although in their over-all execution its engraved figures exhibit a most homogeneous style,[5] the theme being that of ox/horse with framing ibexes. But toward the end of Early Style IV or the beginning of Late Style IV, near the two main compositions, two engravings were added representing bison that have a completely Pyrenean aspect.[6] Such annotations or later additions are valuable from the chronological point of view; they would be incomprehensible were their meaning not supplied by the thematic content of the sanctuary as a whole. The claviform signs at Lascaux[7] replace the female signs of an earlier tradition; the horned horse at Les Combarelles may be understood only in the light of a composition calling for a bovid; and the bison at Ebbou were added by the Magdalenians to restore a sanctuary that had fallen into disuse.

[5] *fig. 164*

[6] *fig. 723*

[7] *fig. 334*

THE MOVEMENT TOWARD THE INTERIOR OF THE CAVES

Iꜰ we take into account Paleolithic people's respect for the images executed by their ancestors, we are almost naturally led to think that they moved progressively deeper into the caves in search of new surfaces for their figures. This movement would account for the origin of successive sanctuaries in the same cave, and for repetitions in the case of central compositions, where we sometimes find the same or a similar theme treated two, three, or four times.

The actual situation is complicated by the fact that the earliest occupants could have established their sanctuary over the entire length of a cave or even directly at the back of it. The reuse and the freshening up of caves also complicate the study of the phenomena of the repetition of themes and the location of sanctuaries. When we find two or three successive sanctuaries in the same style, it is indeed impossible to determine whether they were executed over the space of a few years or of a few centuries. On the other hand, when the oldest sanctuary is found in the remotest portion of the cave, it is apparent that the usual order in which the sanctuaries were executed could be reversed.

Despite these reservations, we have sufficiently numerous and significant examples to accept the rule of progression toward the interior, not as determined by any deliberate desire to execute works further and further from the daylight, but simply by the using up of the available wall space. At La Mouthe, for example, the first decorated ceiling shows a horse/ox group in Style II; the next chamber has a bison/horse + ibex-and-stag group in Style III, with the big sign shaped like a coat-of-arms; and the chambers at the back have a network of engravings in Style IV. At Le Portel the first accessible gallery is occupied by early figures in Style III, while almost all the figures in the remoter galleries are in Early Style IV. At Saint-Cirq the front of the cave, which receives daylight, is decorated with sculptures in Style III; the rear portion, which is dark, has engravings in Early Style IV. In sanctuaries that have a high density of figures the situation is not so clear-cut: Lascaux, Les Combarelles, Altamira, El Castillo, and La Pasiega all look like especially difficult jigsaw puzzles, and to reconstruct them in their entirety is no easy task. At Lascaux, however, the oldest sanctuary, which is in Style III, does not seem to extend beyond the beginning of the Nave. In the remoter portions of Lascaux we find evidence of a second wave of Style III which brought about a remodeling of the whole cave and the invasion of the Apse by areas of unfinished outlines. The Shaft was decorated in Early Style IV. At Altamira the overlapping is total, from the use of the whole cave for the "Black Sequence" in Style III; although the great ceiling located near the entrance is painted in Early Style IV, the only figures in Late Style IV are found in the remotest portions of the cave. At El Castillo the situation is particularly confused: the shape of the cave, divided into several chambers opening from a central chamber near the entrance, lent itself to a number of separate sanctuaries. At La Pasiega the situation is fairly clear in Gallery C, where the part nearer the entrance is occupied by early figures in Style III, while the remoter part is decorated with figures in Early Style IV.

The positional arguments supply a fairly reliable grasp of the facts, so long as they are not regarded as self-sufficient. It is also necessary to examine the arguments to be drawn from the signs, and finally those that emerge from a study of the caves by regions.

EVIDENCE BASED ON THE EVOLUTION OF THE SIGNS

THE chronological value of the signs at first seems dubious, in view of their rarity on decorated objects and the fact that we have no way of dating stratigraphically their occurrence on the cave walls. Actually, there is a great deal of evidence which, when coordinated, confers upon the signs a perfectly coherent evolutionary scheme. For the primitive phase (Style I and II of the animal figures) we have evidence from objects; for the archaic phase (Style III) and the classical phase (Early Style IV), statistical correlations with the animal figures show the link between the signs and the dated animals; for the late period (Late Style IV), decorated objects again provide guidance. Although some problems remain, the main lines are clearly enough defined.[8]

[8] *chart* xxxv

HANDS. The hands present one of the problems still needing clarification. The Abbé Breuil regarded them as very archaic, and in several cases they do seem to belong to an early phase of cave decoration. At Gargas, the cave contains only figures in Style II and Style III; at Pech Merle, the hands occur in the vicinity of figures in the earliest Style III; at Bernifal, we find them in the first chamber, opposite painted figures that are in an indefinable style, but are *a priori* earlier than the engravings in the remote part. In a few cases, such as Les Combarelles, Font-de-Gaume, and El Castillo, it was hard to place the hands chronologically in relation to a group that is predominantly in Style III.

REALISTIC SIGNS IN STYLE I AND STYLE II. On the Aurignacian slabs we find numerous vulvas, either realistic or stylized as easily identifiable ovals. These figures are normally associated with dots or short strokes; those at the Cellier and Blanchard rock shelters and

⁹ *figs. 263–274*

at Isturitz show all the revolutionary stages leading to abstraction. The latest ones at these sites are in mature Style II, contemporaneous with the "steatopygous" female figures⁹: in fact, the vulvar figures are reduced (as at Pair-non-Pair) to concentric ovals or circles, or (as at Kostienki I) to semicircular "medallions." Cave-art evidence from this period, except for Pair-non-Pair, is practically unknown: at this primitive phase the number of decorated walls is very small.

¹⁰ *fig. 219*

QUADRANGULAR SIGNS. The first major spread of cave art showing animals, corresponding to Style III, comes between the Solutrean and the Early Magdalenian. A fairly large number of sanctuaries in France and in Spain illustrate this period. In most of them we find signs that have the particular feature of being inscribed within a quadrangular outline. The identification of the initial motif is determined by the quadrangular figures with a median line. At Isturitz, from levels dated between the Solutrean and the Middle Magdalenian, we have a half-rounded rod¹⁰ decorated with vulvas, some shaped as triangles, others as rectangles divided by a line. Variants on cave walls are very numerous, ranging from the unfilled rectangle to the checkerboards we find at Lascaux.

¹¹ *figs. 61, 112*

It is interesting to note that the quadrangular signs fall into apparently well-defined regional groups. The rectangles at Lascaux, Le Gabillou, and La Mouthe in the Périgord, are of the vertical type, whereas in Spain those at Las Chimeneas, La Pasiega, El Castillo, and Altamira are of the horizontal type. On the walls they may run in every direction, but in the former region the median division is longitudinal, in the latter transverse.¹¹ The signs at Pech Merle and those at Le Portel are of the quadrangular type, but in shape they rather suggest forks and may be related to the image of the hand. As we have seen, the hand seems to have corresponded to the same function, and ambiguities of form are frequent in the Paleolithic.

BRACE-SHAPED SIGNS. These give a fairly striking example of chronological relationships. In shape they are transitional between the quadrangular and the claviform signs in the Périgord as well as in the Cantabrian region. The animal figures accompanying them, however, no longer quite belong to Style III, nor yet to Early Style IV. Better still, at Lascaux, Le Gabillou, Pech Merle, Le Portel, El Castillo, and La Pasiega, quadrangular signs are associated with figures in the earlier phase of Style III, and brace-shaped signs with those in Style IV. At Lascaux the situation is especially striking: compartmented rectangles are found near the large groups in Style III in the Axial Gallery, the Passageway, and the Nave; the "Chinese" horses in the Axial Gallery, reworked at a later date, are accompanied by one brace-shaped sign; the figures in the Shaft, executed at a still later date, are in the only portion of the cave which contains claviform signs. The signs, provided we do not lose the stylistic control afforded by the animal figures, actually constitute a chronological framework.

CLAVIFORMS AND TECTIFORMS. The chronological framework for these signs is not completely settled in its details, and the period of Style IV still has obscure parts. The claviforms are certainly inspired by the female figure in profile, of which examples occur in the Magdalenian, associated with animal figures in Style IV; but it is equally certain that there are brace-shaped signs whose links with vulvar figures are still discernible. In the Cantabrian region, from the Pyrenees to the Asturias, the intermediate stages are supplied in turn by, first, the brace-shaped signs in the Monte Castillo caves (El Castillo, La Pasiega) and the bird-shaped sign at Le Portel; second, the large claviforms with branches of equal length, found in conjunction with figures in Early Style IV (Marsoulas, the Altamira ceiling, La Pasiega); third, constituting the first indications of Late Style IV, claviforms with asymmetrical branches or otherwise deformed, found in conjunction with animals in that style at Niaux, Les Trois Frères, Las Monedas, and El Pindal. The chronological sequence is thus complete.

In the Périgord the situation is less clear. The "preclaviform" brace-shaped signs turn up in the last phase of Style III at Lascaux, Villars, and Le Gabillou. Claviforms in

Early Style IV are found only at Lascaux. However, female figures in profile are present at Les Combarelles where we find no developed claviforms; in place of them are tectiform signs which accompany figures in Early Style IV resembling those at Font-de-Gaume, Bernifal, Les Combarelles, and Rouffignac, which are close to those of Niaux and Les Trois Frères. The tectiform signs are morphologically related to the brace-shaped signs in the Cantabrian region; the claviforms, apart from those at Lascaux, are all found in the same southern sector. Unfortunately our data are not yet ample enough to make certain that the former and the latter are evidence for a cultural expansion the center of which would be Pyrenean-Cantabrian, nor sufficient even to enable us to say what situation in time the Lascaux signs occupy in relation to the tectiforms we find in the Les Eyzies region.

LATE SIGNS. Signs, most often engraved, which represent vulvas are found on the walls of many caves; their outlines present every stage from the crudest realism to "arrows" or two slightly divergent parallel strokes. Many are incorporated as wound marks on the bodies of animals, often accompanied by parallel strokes. The dating of these figures is rather approximate for many appear to have been later additions to the initial compositions. What seems almost certain is that they are scarce or altogether missing in the caves decorated purely in Style III or Early Style IV, whereas they abound when Late Style IV makes its appearance, as at Bernifal, Les Combarelles, Montespan, and Les Trois Frères. Moreover, these signs also turn up on the late plaquettes, for instance on those from Limeuil. Although we cannot say that all oval and triangular symbols are late, we can assert that they play an important role in the terminal period. Their execution differs from that of the realistic signs of the primitive period, but since it is hard to be sure in every case, it seems necessary to suspend judgment unless we have a specific stratigraphic and stylistic context.

At all events, the primitive realistic signs, the quadrangular signs, the brace-shaped signs, the claviforms, the tectiforms, and the late realistic signs show, by the consistency with which they appear in regional sequences, that they can be used as evidence in formulating a chronological framework.

COMPARISON WITH THE CLASSICAL CHRONOLOGY

IMPLEMENTING the various arguments for dating cave works brings to the fore the relationship obtaining between the signs and the style of the figures. There are no claviforms accompanying archaic figures, or quadrangular signs accompanying figures dating from the last period. Bringing together the evidence supplied by the positioning of the figures and by superimposition (where this occurs), this fundamental relationship gives us a firm grip on the organization, which at first glance seemed to elude us entirely, of the cave images. The chronological breakdown thus arrived at does not, on many points, coincide with that proposed by the Abbé Breuil, yet we must stress that our findings leave a large part of the old master's views still undisturbed.

The main point of divergence is our removal, for lack of specific evidence, of cave art from the Aurignacian proper: some of the works he so classified are moved to the period between the Gravettian and the Solutrean; the rest are included among the unfinished outlines dating from all epochs. Another point of divergence is our dating of the bichrome and polychrome groups traditionally situated at the end of each of the two cycles —that is, in the "Upper Perigordian" and the terminal Magdalenian. In the classification proposed here, the bichrome and polychrome paintings form a single group within Style III and Early Style IV, from Lascaux (the Rotunda and Axial Gallery) to Altamira (the Painted Ceiling)—that is, from the start of the Magdalenian to about Magdalenian IV. This attribution not only maintains the chronological unity of finds which have many points of affinity with one another, but also agrees with the data supplied by the excavations.

The most conspicuous difference lies in our elimination of the two-cycle theory. This difference is perhaps more apparent than real. For the engravings and sculptured works, Breuil, as we have seen, while formulating his theory of two independent cycles, actually ended with a single pattern of development, the low reliefs dating from the end of the Aurignacian-Perigordian cycle taking their place close to those dating from the beginning of the Solutrean-Magdalenian cycle, so that his classification, except for details of attribution, tends on the whole to come close to that proposed here. Real divergence on this score would be surprising because there is no lack of dated works in low relief or of dated decorated objects.

With respect to painting, there is certainly less agreement between the two classifications; more accurately, such agreement as appears is, so to speak, accidental. For when we take the sequence of caves proposed in each division of each of Breuil's two cycles and put the linear figures of the first next to those of the second—and likewise compare the "blurred" outlines, the bichrome painting, and polychrome painting from each sequence—we rediscover, in its general outlines, the classification I have proposed.

Agreement between the classical chronology and that which emerges when we integrate the traditional two cycles into one is not complete for two reasons. First, when Breuil enumerates the caves characteristic of any given evolutionary stage, he does not as a rule specify which works he considers to be typical. When one makes such a list based on detailed study of each cave, one does not always find the most characteristic works; besides, most of the caves contain works from several periods or were long believed to, so that exact proof is almost impossible. At the same time, Breuil's publications contain so many sound observations and he carried out so many sound chronological analyses on a limited scale that had he ever assembled the evidence with a view to an illustrated publication on his chronological theory, he could not have assigned the claviform signs to the beginning of the Aurignacian-Perigordian cycle, nor could he have failed to discover that the brace-shaped signs, the claviforms, and the tectiforms weave around the bichrome and polychrome figures a firm mesh which the two-cycle theory tears asunder.

There is normal agreement on many observations of detail and on the succession of finds which are really dated by stratigraphy; also, in both chronological systems, archaic figures such as the oxen on the first ceiling at La Mouthe are recognized to be earlier than elaborate figures such as those on the Altamira ceiling. I cannot understand why Lascaux was attributed to the Perigordian, but it seems obvious to me that the earliest figures, such as those painted in the Passageway and in one portion of the Nave, are close to the Solutrean, as their treatment and state of preservation alike suggest.

The over-all order of the figures at El Castillo, La Pasiega, and Altamira is practically the same in both chronological systems, despite differences of detail. At Altamira, for instance, the Abbé Breuil assigns the meanders and the deep engravings in the first chamber to the Aurignacian, certain black figures and engravings in the middle portion to the Solutrean and the beginning of the Magdalenian, and the figures on the Painted Ceiling to Magdalenian VI; in my classification all the figures, following the same sequence, belong near the mature Gravettian, near to the Solutrean, and in Magdalenian III (that is, Style II, Style III, and Early Style IV). At Les Combarelles, Breuil distinguishes a phase preceding the Early Magdalenian (hands, painted signs, erased paintings of animals), a phase in the Early Magdalenian, and one in the Middle Magdalenian. This corresponds, in the order of progression at least, to my own classification: painted signs and traces of painted animals, then the majority of animals engraved in Early and Late Style IV, followed by paintings and engravings in Late Style IV. Thus my sequence falls within the period from the Middle Magdalenian to Magdalenian IV–V.

It would be easy to adduce further examples that do not reduce the distance between the chronological extremes of the two systems, yet justify my feeling that I am not gratuitously attacking a system which, at the time it was conceived, represented a great advance.

8. A SURVEY OF PALEOLITHIC ART

8. A SURVEY OF PALEOLITHIC ART

IN the present state of our knowledge, Paleolithic art extends over the greater part of Europe. Outside the Continent, finds are either lacking entirely, scarce, or not reliably dated. Except for one place in southern Siberia (Mal'ta), Asia has so far yielded neither cave walls nor decorated objects that can be reliably assigned to a period preceding the ten millennia which represent the Paleolithic of Western Europe. Africa contains thousands of cave figures, painted as well as engraved, but proof of their age has not yet been supplied. Those dated with certainty do not seem to go very far back of historical times; there are other, earlier ones, but it is not yet known how far back to establish their limits.

In Europe, Paleolithic art is found in two areas, differing greatly as to the density of the finds. The eastern region, from the Rhone valley to the Don valley, as yet provides evidence that is widely scattered and limited to decorated objects found in ancient open-air dwelling sites. The western region, represented by France and Spain, comprises several hundred caves containing paintings or engravings, or decorated objects, or both. Italy up to now has been a special case: exact dates cannot yet be assigned to some decorated caves and some sites at which objects have been found. The USSR has only one decorated cave, near the Ural Mountains, and several sites at which decorated objects have been found.

Relations between the western and eastern regions, between the so-called Franco-Cantabrian area and the territories beyond the Seine and the Rhone, have had no constant character, at least insofar as this can be inferred from the extant evidence. Around 20,000 B.C. the region extending from Russia to the Pyrenees seems to have constituted a vast cultural whole, with Czechoslovakia and Austria providing the transition between east and west. Then the links appear to have been cut or at least considerably weakened. Toward 9,000 B.C., when the climate began to approximate its present form, a tide of Franco-Cantabrian influences flowed toward the north and east: for a short period Switzerland, Germany, the Low Countries, and the British Isles were enriched by the last products of Paleolithic art.

The area in which the artistic finds display the greatest continuity is the Franco-Cantabrian region—more accurately, the basins of the Loire and the Garonne, the right bank of the Rhone, the Pyrenees, the French and the Spanish Basque country, the Cantabrian mountains, and the Asturias. And on the fringes of this region in which caves occur in greatest numbers, a few limestone islets contain caves that show the importance of these for conserving evidence which otherwise would not have survived for us.

The chronological placing of the artistic evidence is secured by two methods. One is concerned with the finds discovered at dwelling sites and correspondingly dated with them; the other is concerned with the figures executed on cave walls and dated by indirect methods. The techniques for directly dating decorated objects are those practiced in prehistoric archaeology: the works of art accompany tools or weapons whose relative age is determined by their position in successively recent layers of deposits. Their absolute age is determined by the carbon-14 method of measuring radioactivity—there being no inscriptions in a period before written characters had appeared. By cross-checking the various methods of direct dating, the decorated objects are found to date between approximately 30,000 and 8,000 B.C.

The development of figurative art occupies a fairly well-defined time span. Evidences from before 20,000 B.C. are scanty, consisting of slabs decorated with extremely crude engraved or painted figures. In their content and style, however, these early finds prove to be the direct ancestors of works produced in the peak period—that is, between 20,000 and 15,000 B.C. After 15,000 B.C. a new phase seems to open up, marked by a profusion of decorated objects and by stylistic developments in the representation of figures. By 8,000 B.C. the whole development seems to be over: other cultures, having no relation to that of the hunters of mammoth and reindeer, had replaced it.

If the stylistic evolution of the figures is remarkably coherent, the invariability of the subjects treated is no less remarkable. Its elements are borrowed from the environment in which the hunters lived, and the apparently normal presence of his quarry casts an illusion over the very conventionalized use of these images. Statistical analysis of the subjects discloses a system of symbolic representation of the living world which persists, with only minor variations, throughout the period of Paleolithic art. This system seems to imply a division of the animal species into two groups which are comparable to the division into male and female of the human world. The horse, the stag, the ibex, and the more dangerous species such as the lion and the rhinoceros belong to the male group; the bison and the aurochs or wild ox belong to the female group. The mammoth, the reindeer, and the hind are sometimes put in the one group, sometimes in the other, in accordance to the given epoch and region. This basic division of living creatures resulted, at the same time, in acts determining separation and in acts determining complementarity or comparison.

On the decorated objects, one characteristic type of decoration seems to have been for male objects and another for female objects, each with its corresponding symbols. In the caves, it is obvious that there are three groups of figures: males at the entrance, males and females at the center, and males at the back. From the earliest period, human figures are schematized by the representation of the reproductive organs, translated into more or less abstract graphic symbols. But the meaning remains intelligible, because complete representations of men and women reappear in various epochs.

Within this general framework, there are numerous combinations. The most frequent is the representation of the bison and the horse accompanied by male and female symbols; variants occur, however, where the female symbol is accompanied by an animal from the male group, and where only signs, or sometimes only animals, are paired. There are also examples of integration where images of the bison and the human female are juxtaposed, or where a man is equipped with a stag's antlers and a horse's tail. With a symbolic intention that is closely related, the spear seems to have been assimilated to the male and the wound to the female: wounded animals are usually found in compositions that do not contain signs, in which the presence of such animals is explained by their taking the place of the signs.

Thanks to the uniformity and the elaboration of this figure symbolism, the study of variants permits us to establish a chronological framework controlled both by the archaeologically dated evidence and by the evolution of style. The results thus obtained differ to a very marked degree, both in the meaning of the figures and in the chronology of Paleolithic art, from the classical theories to which the Abbé Breuil contributed the largest share. In particular, it no longer seems possible to maintain that the figures in the caves are the result of the random accretion, from the Aurignacian to the terminal Magdalenian, of images of animals magically wounded by hunters. The sanctuaries have a well-determined structure of figure composition, corresponding to religious representations linked with the opposition and complementarity of male and female elements.

This summation of the elements discussed in turn in this work introduces, in conclusion, an attempt at an over-all synthesis of Paleolithic art. There is no need to cherish many illusions on the score of this essay. The data presented here are rather coherent, and sufficiently correlated to contain a part of the truth, but they are still insufficiently supported by the only incontestable evidence, that provided by archaeological excavations. Only the data supplied by the most recent excavations meet the requirements of a detailed chronology. The systematic search for significant material at the entrances to the decorated caves and inside them is far from having been carried out in an orderly, scientific manner. It is, however, evident that the deposits in these dwelling sites are related to the sanctuaries: the instances of Altamira, El Castillo, Les Trois Frères, Le Portel, Angles-sur-l'Anglin, Gargas, and several other sites are sufficient to show that the stylistic evidence for cave art is first of all to be sought in the exterior deposits. Until we have genuinely scientific investigations in this field, the picture we can draw must remain somewhat hazy.

The chief problem has been to introduce order into a mass of facts forming one long crowded sequence, within which every fact is transitional in relation to what precedes and what follows it. We have therefore introduced the notion of four major periods to delimit a stylistic evolution which parallels the archaeological divisions no more and no less closely than the evolution of symphonic music, in our own day, parallels that of mechanics: there is the primitive period that comprises Style I and Style II; the archaic period, or Style III; and the mature period, or Style IV.

PERIOD I[1]

[1] figs. 249–256

Period I encompasses all artistic finds that precede the general appearance of Style II—that is to say, the Chatelperronian and Aurignacian scrawls and the first coordinated silhouettes dating from the mature Aurignacian and the early Gravettian. No reliably dated cave decoration exists in this period, nor do any objects whose decoration is explicitly figurative; all we have are crude bone fragments and stone slabs showing the earliest attempts at expression by incised line or the use of colors.

The style of the figures is determinable only by reference to works of Period II. They are most often animal heads, forequarters, and dorsal lines, accompanied by vulvar figures and dots or strokes. The latest works disclose the importance of the head and the frontal part of the body as symbolic of the whole animal, and the fact that the starting point of stylistic evolution is not a primitive realism—this latter idea was a pure invention by nineteenth-century prehistorians—but a mode of representation that focuses first on the traits that particularize an animal species, disregarding the rest.

The themes of Period I, as revealed by the very few documents so far discovered, are the same ones that prevail throughout Paleolithic art: the associations of bovid and horse, of mammoth and horse, and of vulva and dots. Sites are most numerous in the Périgord (La Ferrassie; Belcayre; the Blanchard, Castanet, and Cellier rock shelters; Laugerie Haute); this geographical limitation is probably connected with the fact that excavators were better prepared in this region than elsewhere to look for artistic remains on limestone slabs. The same condition explains the discovery of identical evidence at Isturitz. Because of the paucity and the extreme crudity of the works, it is of course impossible to discern regional tendencies.

PERIOD II[2]

[2] figs. 6–8, 24, 29, 31, 52, 54, 55, 75, 86, 87, 93, 111, 257–304

Style II apparently begins at an already advanced stage of the Upper Perigordian or Gravettian, in a period of close cultural continuity between eastern and western Europe. The Gravettian and the proto-Solutrean which follow are still inadequately known in detail, but it can already be stated that they cover nearly ten thousand years of relatively rapid succession of stages toward technical development. This development concludes in the Solutrean. Over this long period, dominated artistically by Style II, it is hard to establish dividing lines that do not sacrifice the transitions: thus I have not thought it possible, for the time being, to subdivide it. The boundary between Period II and Period III, in art, is hard to establish: only after we are well into Period III do we become aware that the canon has evolved in a new direction.

Period II marks the first development of the great sanctuaries; these reach their peak in Period III and do not decline until Period IV. From the outset there are sanctuaries in the dark interior of caves (Gargas), but in most cases the works are still executed on slabs, on the walls of rock shelters, in the daylight zone at the cave entrances, or in the half-lighted sections just beyond. Beginning with Period III, however, painting and engraving spread out into the depths of the interior.

Style II presents a canon directly inherited from the works of Period I. A sinuous cervico-dorsal curve (resembling a flattened S on its side, the larger loop occupying two-thirds of the whole) serves as a structural frame for an animal with excessively incurved forequarters.[3] This curve, with a few alterations and the addition of particu-larizing details, is used indiscriminately for horse, bison, ox, mammoth, stag, feline, and woman. A great deal of imagination was required to ascribe a realistic character to these works, though they are admirable for many other reasons.

3 *charts* xxxix, xl

The uniformity of procedure from eastern Europe to Spain is very striking and justifies our assigning major value to criteria based on the dorsal line. It will be seen, however, that in Style III the technique does not really change but the elements of the curve gradually become distributed differently. The drawing of the curve seems to have been done automatically, and thus it is rigidly fixed in the styles of each successive genera-tion of engravers and sculptors. The importance that this initial outline held for Paleo-lithic artists is confirmed directly by the existence in cave art of panels of unfinished outlines, where we find, during the periods of Style II and Style III, many single curved lines to which only a few details need be added to obtain an animal figure. These apparently hasty scrawls represent animals reduced to their simplest expression, the cervico-dorsal curve.

The human figures are connected with an identical process. Style II includes almost all the dated female statuettes and low reliefs. As we saw earlier in this book, stylization explains the ample forms of these "steatopygous Aurignacian Venuses": the figures are centered on the torso, breasts, thighs, and abdomen; the rest becomes attenuated without details, face and arms most often barely indicated, the legs dwindling away. In Style III, realistic statuettes seem to disappear: the low reliefs at Angles, the engrav-ings at La Roche, and the figurines from Mezin show that in Style IV the head and legs have been completely eliminated.

Except for the engraved slab at Terme-Pialat (Dordogne), we have no female figures in profile.

Sites containing work in Style II are as yet few in number. In the Périgord, the decorated slabs at the Abri Labatut and at Laussel, and the wall engravings at La Grèze and on the first panel at La Mouthe, all seem to be related to this style. In the Gironde, the engravings at Pair-non-Pair show its characteristic features, as do those at Gargas in the Pyrenees, both sites assigned to the Late Gravettian on the basis of their engraved objects. In the Ardèche, the engravings at Chabot, Le Figuier, and Oulen belong with fair certainty to the proto-Solutrean. All these works are in accord with the small num-ber of decorated objects from the same epoch. The only exception is supposed to be provided by the famous engraved pebbles from La Colombière in the Jura, which were assigned to the Gravettian; however, these pebbles appear to have been incorrectly dated, for the tools which accompanied them seem to belong to the Magdalenian. The animals at La Colombière are, beyond any possible doubt, in Style IV.

⁴ *figs. 10, 25, 58, 60, 61, 64, 65, 67, 68, 72, 73, 76–78, 81, 88, 94–98, 100, 104–109, 112, 113, 305–432*

PERIOD III⁴

Between Style II and Style III, a subtle adjustment takes place in the dorsal curve. The figures of the various animal species lose the uniformity of their initial sinuosity; movement begins to be expressed, and it will continue to be until Style IV, by means of specific conventions. When the intention to represent movement is manifested, it is almost never by a general reshaping of the postures, but by a separate shifting of characteristic details, as in the stereotyped gaits of the Lascaux horses.

In Style III, however, mastery of technical procedure is complete: sculpture attains its peak, and painting already makes use of fillings of ocher and manganese underscored with painted or incised outlines. The violent and unusual character of these works comes from the contrast between the maturity of its techniques and the dependence of its forms upon an archaic canon.

The basic element continues to be the dorsal curve, now more attenuated than in Style II but still giving the impression that the animal is being projected forward and upward. The attenuation is particularly noticeable in the horses, in which the curve of the neck is no longer so pronounced. In addition, details of the body become defined, and manes and legs are more fully executed.

A comparative study of the horses at Le Roc de Sers (Style III) and those at Angles-sur-l'Anglin (Early Style IV) clearly illustrates the evolution that takes place in the construction of the figures. At Le Roc de Sers the archaic canon is still clearly discernible in the disproportion between the huge, strongly arched body and the small head and slender legs with rounded hoofs. Mastery of low-relief technique endows the figures with a remarkable plastic quality; these animals look odd—all belly, like basset hounds —and have something in common with the steatopygous female figures. However, the horses in Early Style IV at Angles-sur-l'Anglin, Mouthiers, or Le Cap Blanc approach a naturalistic canon in their proportions; the various parts of the body are distributed more equitably, the bodies lose their forward thrust, and academism is already perceptible.

The bison dated from the Solutrean and the first part of the Magdalenian continue to be related to Style II because enlarged forequarters are natural in the bison. The hump of the withers is not represented in natural proportions until Style IV. The dorsal curve of the Teyjat bison, in Late Style IV, is such that they could be superimposed on photographs of living European bison, whereas the bison in Style III are still remote from reality. As in the case of the horses, the perfecting of the technical execution brings a wealth of details to a structure that is still close to Style II. The front part of the dorsal curve evolves in a very peculiar way. European bison today have on the forehead a dense mass of hair, the forelock; on the neck, the woolly mane fills out the contour as far as the hump of the withers, which are marked by the protrusions of the vertebrae. These three features—forelock, mane, and withers—merge in the living animal to form a continuous curve, the hairy masses being more marked in the male than in the female. Figures in Style II such as the bison at Vogelherd, despite the enlarged forequarters, respect the regularity of this curve and we meet it again in Late Style IV, restored to its natural proportions. In Style III and Early Style IV, each element of the curve is dissociated from the others and emphasized—the forelock, the mane, and the withers are represented as three successive humps. The mane is especially developed: its progressive overdevelopment and its eventual return to natural proportions can be followed very well, first at Le Roc de Sers (Solutrean), where the hump can only just be made out, then at Angles (Magdalenian III), where the mane forms a voluminous parcel grafted onto the back of the neck, then on the carved and incised bison at Isturitz (Magdalenian IV), and last at Teyjat (Magdalenian V).

Styles II and III display the greatest variety of themes, whereas Early Style IV is almost exclusively dominated by the bison/horse theme. The sanctuaries in the Franco-Cantabrian region give much prominence to the ox/horse theme (Style II: La Mouthe—

first composition, Pair-non-Pair, and Gargas—second chamber; Style III: Bourdeilles, Lascaux, Pech Merle, Ebbou, and La Pasiega—Galleries A and C). Beginning with Early Style IV the bison takes on growing importance, relegating the ox to a "side chapel," so to speak—that is, always present but off by itself. The bison/horse theme, however, is already present in Style III, as are also combinations in which the mammoth sometimes plays the part of male complement (ox/mammoth and bison/mammoth at Pech Merle), sometimes that of female complement (mammoth/horse at La Baume Latrone). The hind/horse theme is found at Covalanas. Moreover, we already find combinations of three animals, such as bison/horse + mammoth and ox/horse + ibex.

The signs corresponding to the animals of Style III are the most elaborate to be found in the Upper Paleolithic, and the most abstract. Forms still close to the vulvas and rows of dots and strokes in Style I, but already stripped and geometrized, accompany the figures in Style II (Gargas, Pair-non-Pair). In Style III the signs take on a frankly decorative aspect: quadrangular "coats-of-arms" at Lascaux, signs in the shape of "birds" at Pech Merle, "huts" at La Mouthe and El Castillo.

The human figures are closely connected with the signs and animals in their corresponding categories, and one may feel that the symbols they incarnate are in some sense interchangeable. The theme of the man carrying a spear and pursued by a bison occurs in this form at Le Roc de Sers, but, allowing for variations of epoch and culture, it seems to be the same theme as that expressed at Pech Merle, where a man pierced by spears is shown next to a sign which seems to be the abstract form for both bison and woman; or the theme at Lascaux of the man lying prone before a bison that is pierced by a spear; or at El Castillo of the horse (male symbol) riddled with wounds, underneath a brace-shaped sign symbolizing the female group.

The imprints of hands, sometimes positive but more often negative, seem more frequent during Period II (Labatut, Gargas) and Period III (Pech Merle, El Castillo, Rocamadour) than during Early Period IV (Font-de-Gaume, Bernifal, Les Combarelles). The symbolism of the hand is still obscure.

The sum total of the elements at our disposal for determining Style III is great enough to enable us to perceive fairly clear regional divisions. Confining ourselves to ensembles represented at two or more sites, we can single out one group in the Périgord, one in the Lot, one in the Cantabrian area, and one in the Ardèche valley. The Perigordian group (Lascaux; Le Gabillou; Villars; Saint-Cirq, entrance; Font-de-Gaume, earliest stage; La Mouthe, second panel) is characterized by Style III animals in monochromatic coloring and by rectangular signs in the form of checkerboards. A second sequence of compositions, close to Style IV, is accompanied by brace-shaped signs. The Lot group is represented by the caves at Pech Merle, Cougnac, and Rocamadour, which are stylistically closer to Style II than are the Perigordian caves. The signs at Pech Merle are of the quadrangular type. There also exists a second sequence of animals in a more developed style accompanied by brace-shaped signs. The brace-shaped signs are found in two combinations: sign with male symbol (Rocamadour; Pech Merle—also at El Castillo), or signs grouped together in a recess (Cougnac; the bison/women panel at Pech Merle—also at La Pasiega). The Spanish group comprises El Castillo, La Pasiega, and Altamira: all of these contain figures from different periods, but the underlying scheme is based on compositions belonging to Style III. At El Castillo there are, from the entrance to the back of the cave, a number of paintings in linear yellow and red, which together form a complete set on the theme of bison/horse accompanied by large quadrangular and brace-shaped signs. Gallery A at La Pasiega also displays a sequence of compositions on the theme of ox/horse with brace-shaped signs grouped together in an underground fissure. At La Pasiega in Gallery C the ox/horse group occupies the front part of the gallery and the signs are placed in a recess. At Altamira, a continuous series on the bison/horse theme in linear black extends from the entrance to the back-cave area; the quadrangular and brace-shaped signs are assembled in the most distant part just before the final signs—short strokes—are reached. The Cantabrian Spanish group is very coherent, but it presents variants which are still hard to classify chronologically. In actual fact, ensembles held to be contemporaneous by the prehistorian may have been spread over several centuries, during which there were perhaps many additions or, on the contrary, none whatever. It is evident that the Périgord, Lot, and Cantabrian groups have a common over-all structure, that the animals are closely related in style and the signs are of the same family and disposed within the caves in comparable locations. Each group, however, clearly displays regional elaborations, since it is possible to subdivide them into closely related "cave families."

The fourth and latest of these families is that of the caves in the Ardèche, which are located close to one another in narrow gorges—Chabot, Figuier, Huchard, Oulen. Here we find deeply incised engravings apparently linked with proto-Solutrean tools and weapons; these engravings are characterized by a profusion of mammoths associated with either the horse or the bison.

Several caves that are cut off from the others in time or in space fill in the blanks (as it were) between the caves that can be placed in natural groups or "families."

One may cite as dated elements the Solutrean low reliefs at Le Roc de Sers and Bourdeilles. The number of caves that can be linked stylistically to Style III, but cannot be otherwise dated, is relatively high. In the Dordogne, the early decorations at Lascaux and Villars are attributable to this stage, and to it probably also belong a portion of the figures at Font-de-Gaume, particularly the painted bovids at the back of the cave—Font-de-Gaume is hard to analyze because many changes were made by the Paleolithic artists themselves, and because the works are in a poor state of preservation. In the Lot, the group formed by Pech Merle, Cougnac, and Rocamadour has already been mentioned. In the Pyrenees, except for the Isturitz figures—low reliefs which according to Passemard go back to the Solutrean—we may mention the figures in Gallery 2 at Le Portel (Ariège). In Spain, apart from the earlier parts of Altamira, of El Castillo, and of La Pasiega, we may include all the figures at Las Chimeneas, the deeply incised figures at the entrance to La Peña de los Hornos, and a considerable number of paintings at La Peña de Candamo. For the Rhone valley, Period III seems to be represented by the set of engravings at the Ebbou cave, with the exception of two bison in Style IV which were added later.

⁵ figs. 2, 3, 5, 9, 11–15, 26–28, 30, 32–37, 45–50, 53, 56, 57, 59, 62, 63, 66, 69–71, 74, 79, 80, 82–85, 89–92, 99, 101, 110, 114–121, 433–709

PERIOD IV⁵

THE evidence of decorated objects and a few dated walls make it possible to delimit Period IV with what appears to be fair accuracy: it begins during Magdalenian III and ends with the termination of Magdalenian VI; the mid-point is somewhere around 12,000 B.C. We have referred earlier to the uncertainties hanging over Magdalenian III and IV, the former very clear from the north down to Les Eyzies, the latter in evidence from Les Eyzies down to Spain. These problems are of relatively little concern to us, since the existence of a "Middle Magdalenian" suffices to relate the works to one another without reference to archaeological evidence (tools and equipment). Greater accuracy, however, would be desirable to reduce, in particular, the uncertainties at Font-de-Gaume and Les Combarelles.

The great majority of the sanctuaries that are situated in unlighted cave areas are dated within Period IV. Some of them are situated at a considerable distance from the cave entrance: at Rouffignac, Villars, Niaux, Les Trois Frères, Le Tuc d'Audoubert, Montespan, Etcheberriko-Karbia, and La Cullalvera, among others. This change is the more noticeable because at the beginning of Period IV we still find sanctuaries in rock shelters and at cave entrances, in keeping with the earliest tradition, and because in the terminal Paleolithic there seems to be a return to entrance sanctuaries.

Thanks to the details of the figures, Period IV can be clearly divided into two sets or sequences which, in all likelihood, are successive. Our chronological uncertainty is due, on the one hand, to the vagueness of archaeologists who date most decorated objects "to within one Magdalenian," and, on the other, to the fact that whereas the low reliefs of Magdalenian III were painted, only vestiges of pigment have come down to us and we cannot determine the exact moment when particular details of modeling were introduced. This uncertainty having been stated, let us review the data in the order which our correlations seem to demand.

Early Style IV further mitigates the features of the primitive canon. Not all traces of disproportion between forequarters and hindquarters, and between belly and legs, have disappeared; in execution the horses are approximately halfway between those at Pech Merle and Lascaux—inflated hides provided with four tiny legs and with minuscule heads atop long curving necks—and the amazingly vivid, well-proportioned silhouettes of the terminal Magdalenian. The sequence we derive from arranging the painted and engraved horses in our chronological order is very convincing in comparison to the errors which can flow from any arrangement based on excessive confidence in the Paleolithic artist's freedom. Convention dominates all these representations, and the labors that have so far been performed to distinguish the "breeds" of horses which served the "artists" as "models" have not led to any coherent results. Like artists in every age, those of the Paleolithic saw with the eyes of their own society—that is, they reproduced not animals, but images of animals. This explains the extraordinary unity of style, the mastery over symbols through the memory of long generations, and the slow evolution of the representational means. More important than investigations into "pregnant mares" and "horses of the Celtic breed" is the appearance of the cross-hatching and shaded applications of color that endow the figures of Early Period IV with such extraordinary intensity. The evolution seems to have been made in two stages and probably under two influences. During Early Period IV, the painted animals are rendered three-dimensionally by a most masterly technique using the interplay of downstrokes and upstrokes; these are completed with areas of flat color, either uniformly applied or applied only to the forequarters. The filled-in outline, sometimes limited to the head, neck, and withers, emphasizes the dilation of the front of the figure. When we consider the best of the figures in Early Style IV at Font-de-Gaume, Le Portel, Marsoulas, Labastide, Santimamine, El Castillo, and Altamira, we can ask ourselves if the sight of low reliefs in the sunshine could have influenced the birth of pictorial modeling in line; the pictorial relief seems to reproduce the sculptures rather than living animals. Now it is during Period III and Early Period IV that the large and small low reliefs are of maximum importance, whether found in the Charente, the Dordogne, or the Basses-Pyrénées. Born of direct observation or filtered through the methods of low relief, the modeling in works from Early Style IV is a modeling of contours.

EARLY STYLE IV

Consequently, Early Style IV is subtly linked with Style III in the evolution of the basic canon, but it is marked by extreme conventionalization of detail. The extraordinary development in the minor arts during the Middle and Upper Magdalenian, especially the advance made in the southwest shortly before harpoons appeared, supplies us with much more evidence. On the spear-throwers and pierced staffs are animals whose proportions become more and more like those of living creatures, and a mounting attention to detail is expressed in microscopic hatchings. These render the movement of the animal, or the play of light on the fur covering different parts of the body. A veritable pictographic code is established for the conventions of modeling, and cheeks, eyes, the roots of the horns, the reflections of light on the flanks—all of these are rendered uniformly throughout a great part of the Franco-Cantabrian region. Where a sufficient number of examples is available from a single site, one notices that not all the cave-wall figures are executed in full detail, that many are represented merely by outlines and a few indispensable features, whereas the objects are meticulously treated and most often elaborately detailed. The cheeks of horses are now rendered in cross-hatched lines that look like a halter, and the regular hatchings of the mane are extended beyond the level of the ears and cut off cleanly. On the shoulder, the line of the mane ends in two vertical parallel strokes which mark the shoulder blade. Starting from the knee joint of the foreleg a line of hatching rises, then sweeps back in a long curve that models the belly and extends downward again along the front of the thigh, forming something like a much-elongated M. The line of the rump, the shanks, and the pasterns are fringed with hatching, and the hoofs are delicately detailed. These details recur in many cave works which tend to be assigned to Early Period IV on the basis of other criteria, and they constitute an important argument for such dating.

The bison undergo a parallel evolution. The introduction of cross-hatching has an influence on the treatment of the dorsal outline, which occurs in two forms. In the first, the mane is still overdeveloped to the point of forming a sort of cockscomb behind the head; in the second, the mane and withers are distinct, their proportions are more modest, and the coat is represented by two areas separated by an unfilled space. The second form of outline seems to be later than the first, but the uncertainty of the archaeological evidence does not permit us to say how much time (relatively little, probably) elapsed between the two conventions. We must also take account of the possibility that these two forms may apply to the male and the female animals, the males being distinguished by their bulkier manes. The filling in of the flanks is very stereotyped, the most constant indication being a line of hatchings running from the knee joint to the tail—a line which faithfully renders the effect of light falling on the flank from above.

There are equivalent conventions for the ibex, the flank of which is marked with a straight line connecting the knee with the thigh joint; the flank of the reindeer is marked with a line of spots which render the darker areas produced in the coat by the rippling movement of the living animal.

Early Style IV corresponds to the direction of the evolution of Style III—that is, represents a sort of medieval period in Paleolithic art, at first still dominated by archaic formulas, then gradually evolving toward an academic canon. From Style I to Early Style IV, representation remains imprisoned between two constraints: the dorsal structure whose basic outline is slightly altered from period to period, and the details which particularize the various species of animal. In Style III, the reconciliation of these features has a baffling quality, for mastery of detail is practiced upon a structure still unreconciled to real-life proportions. In Early Style IV the reconciliation is an accomplished fact; just enough is left of the archaic canon to endow the figures with a certain strangeness, a kind of aerial suspension, but as details proliferate the figures gain substance and become conventionalized.

The advance toward realism thus takes place in two directions which have no real parallel in the experience of the adult modern artist: one is the realization of an almost uniform linear body structure assuring the figure of a living being, and the other is the particularization of this structural framework by the addition of detail. Realistic movement does not have primary importance: on the whole the figures in the first three styles are frozen figures. The curvature of the forequarters endows them with a kind of strong forward thrust, but the limbs do not sustain this illusion. Everything there is to say has already been said concerning the "naturalness" of Paleolithic figures; much perhaps remains to say about the fact that they are symbols, not portraits, "naturalness" being by no means an essential consideration.

The themes of Style IV are divided into two fairly distinct groups, whose precise chronological relationship is still uncertain. The first—represented in particular by Marsoulas, Niaux, the Altamira Ceiling, an important portion of El Castillo (the "polychrome" figures), and Santimamine—is marked by the total eclipse of the mammoth and the reindeer. The great majority of subjects are borrowed from the bison/horse pairing; stags and ibexes play the part of complementary animals in the male group, and the ox occurs in an ox/horse pairing placed in a separate panel. In the second group—represented by Les Combarelles, Font-de-Gaume, Bernifal, Rouffignac, Les Trois Frères, and Las Monedas—the bison/horse pairing is also the main element, but accompanied by the mammoth and the reindeer. At Les Trois Frères, as at La Monedas, only one mammoth is represented, off by itself, but in other caves mammoths are incorporated in the main compositions. At Les Combarelles they most often appear in triple superimposition with the bison/horse, bison/reindeer, and ox/horse pairings; at Font-de-Gaume one whole frieze is made up of reindeer-bison-mammoth-horse super-impositions.

The problem of the chronological place of the different formulas of Early Style IV within so relatively short a period as Magdalenian III–IV (13,000 to 11,000 B.C.) is difficult to resolve, and it is complicated by uncertainty about the exact relationships between the northern and southern phases of the Magdalenian industry in tools and weapons, which serve as references. It seems evident that the Early Style IV sanctuaries in the north (Angles, Mouthiers, Le Cap Blanc, Commarque), where bison/horse without mammoth is the formula, precede in date the mammoths and reindeer at Font-de-Gaume and Les Combarelles, and are more or less contemporaneous with the bison at Niaux. Moreover, the bison at Niaux (bison/horse without mammoth or reindeer) are apparently slightly earlier than those at Les Trois Frères, which are mingled with reindeer that are stylistically close to decorated objects in the late style. By interpolating the figures at Bernifal, Rouffignac, La Mouthe (panels with reindeer), and Las Monedas in Spain (where, besides reindeer, there is one unfinished outline of a mammoth), we arrive at a relatively coherent chronological picture. In one series of caves—Angles, Mouthiers, Le Cap Blanc, Commarque, Niaux, Le Portel, Marsoulas, Labastide, Ussat, Santimamine, Novales, Gallery I B of La Pasiega, Altamira ceiling—bison and horse are associated with stag and ibex; the subjects are in Early Style IV, filled in with bichrome painting or showing conventional details of modeling, and the accompanying signs are "truncated" women, claviforms, or rectangular signs of a late form. In a second series of caves—Font-de-Gaume (except for a portion at the back), La Mouthe (reindeer panels), Bernifal, Les Combarelles, Rouffignac, Les Trois Frères, Las Monedas, El Pindal—the mammoth and the reindeer are added, singly or together, to the initial pairing. These caves clearly belong to Late Style IV and the accompanying signs are tectiforms (in the Périgord), a few claviforms (in the south), and ovals or triangles.

LATE STYLE IV

THE appearance of harpoons in the Magdalenian (Magdalenian V and VI) is accompanied by works having a character noticeably different from the works of the first three styles. Statigraphic data are still too uncertain for us to discern the transitions, or possibly the break; but it is evident that, without having lost all contact with the earlier productions, the face of art has changed. The examples we have are numerous, in France (La Madeleine, Isturitz, Teyjat, Limeuil, and also many sites where decorated objects have been found) as well as in Spain, Switzerland, Germany, Belgium, and even Great Britain.

The line of the basic structure is now completely integrated within a well-proportioned figure—that is to say, it no longer plays a role that is psychologically different from that of other parts of the body. The horses, oxen, bison, mammoths, and reindeer look like excellent photographs, true to life in proportions and movement, and the details occupy a secondary plane of attention. The code of conventions governing modeling becomes progressively freer, and the figures are often devoid of all details except such essential ones as eyes. The frequency with which figures are represented in movement—grazing, galloping, or in herds—is in very striking contrast with the preceding periods, when the intention of portraying movement was not always absent but the effect was obtained by partial means.

Another fact, which seems to have as its corollary the gradual abandonment of the underground sanctuaries, is the abundance of objects bearing compositions of paired animals associated with signs.

Late Style IV evolves without undergoing any profound changes during the latter part of the Magdalenian, and its course is difficult to detect. Most often the caves exhibit this evolved stage only in the form of additions to earlier compositions—the bison/horse/mammoth group in the far gallery at Altamira, one bison in the main panel at Bernifal, a certain number of reindeer and bears at Les Combarelles. The signs accompanying these additions are wounds and more or less stylized vulvas. The caves at Teyjat (Dordogne) and at Sainte-Eulalie (Lot), the decorations on the slabs at Limeuil and Labastide, the "pebbles" from La Colombière (Ain), as well as many more or less isolated slabs found from the Pyrenees to Switzerland, illustrate the evolution in the minor arts after the underground sanctuaries were abandoned.

The value of the time factor has considerably changed between Period I and the point we have now reached. Where terminal Period IV is concerned, it is no longer a question of enclosing an evolution within a few millennia, or even within a few centuries: one or two centuries must now be carefully weighed. The last act in the drama of Paleolithic art takes place between approximately 11,000 and 8,500 B.C. In the course of recent years there have been many systematic excavations that confirm the picture drawn by D. Peyrony on the basis of the Perigordian finds. At the end of Magdalenian IV or the beginning of Magdalenian V, and throughout Magdalenian VI, the reindeer takes on new importance in the kitchen middens no less than in the decoration of objects; it then disappears in the southwest, yielding its place to the stag at the time that present-day climatic conditions were becoming established. Around 9,000 B.C. the replacement becomes definite in the southwest, but in the east and north, from the Jura to Hamburg, the aura of the last Magdalenians and their reindeer lingers on for a few more centuries, while the Franco-Cantabrian region proper adapts itself to the new climate.

The sudden return of the reindeer has already been noted in describing the latest figures that appear on the walls of the Franco-Cantabrian sanctuaries. Sanctuaries with reindeer figures dating from Period IV are not very numerous, but, apart from the Rhone Valley, they are found in each of the major geographical subdivisions (Arcy, Les Combarelles, Font-de-Gaume, Les Trois Frères, Las Monedas). Sanctuaries that date in their entirety from terminal Period IV are even fewer, and if they exist—as at Lascaux, El Castillo, La Pasiega, or in certain other caves—the works are manifestly late, and limited to engravings inserted into older compositions, or signs placed as annotations of older figures; except for Teyjat (Dordogne) and Sainte-Eulalie (Lot), one can hardly cite an ordered composition of cave art in Late Style IV. The works from this period consist essentially of plaquettes or slabs of stone or bone, which were arranged in a manner that permitted a composition to be formed.

The themes become harder to discern because we no longer have cave walls which have remained as Paleolithic man left them, but only slabs on which the figures occur in isolation. Decorated objects such as spears and pierced staffs show that the fundamental principle of dividing the figure into two groups is still respected in Magdalenian V as well as in Magdalenian VI: reindeer, horses, fish, barbed signs—all of them male symbols—decorate male objects. The bone plaquettes of apparently religious character are decorated with paired subjects: for instance, the spatula from Pekarna (Czechoslovakia), both sides showing grouped bison/horse and ibex in a highly traditional composition; the plaquettes from Raymonden and Les Eyzies, which show the head or forequarters of a bison accompanied by human silhouettes carrying spears or forked objects; and a small bone plaquette from Isturitz showing a very schematized horse enframed by an oval and short strokes.

The most coherent evidence on the matter of themes is the set of large slabs of engraved stalagmite at the entrance to the Teyjat cave: about forty figures arranged on them in separate groups attest both to the preservation of the initial scheme and to the evolution that took place in its arrangement. The slabs became shifted in the course of excavation and their original placing was not recorded, so that their order of succession is hypothetical. However, we find four male groups (stag/horse, reindeer/horse/bear repeated twice, and reindeer/horse) and three paired groups (bison/horse/stag, bison/horse/reindeer/bear, ox/horse/reindeer) without signs. During Magdalenian V, consequently, the pairings were still based on the classical form, with two groups on the bison theme and one group on the ox theme. The order of the slabs can be reconstructed with some probability, because the first bison group is accompanied by stags, which occur more often at the entrance than in the back-cave area, and because the second bison group is accompanied by the bear, which, on the other hand, is usually a back-cave subject.

One last piece of evidence which also refers to Magdalenian V is supplied by the Labastide cave. We have already seen that this sanctuary contains one horse in Early Style IV and a few works from Late Period IV. Its decoration constitutes one of the most impressive documents as to the religious habits of Paleolithic people. The first vestiges are found at the exact point from which the entrance to this immense cave may still be seen, a point several hundred yards inside the cave: there we find a block covered with scrawls and unfinished outlines. At a lower level, some large blocks lie opposite a huge monolith which faces the entrance. A big horse is painted on the monolith, and on the blocks there are painted lattice signs, one barbed sign, short strokes, groups of dots, and engraved bison. These constitute the first sanctuary, dating from Period IV. Further on there is a group of engravings in later Style IV—a composition on the bison/horse theme accompanied by oval signs and short strokes and ending with a lion's head. Not far from where the decoration began, near the block with the unfinished outlines, there was a third sanctuary, of still later date, constituted by engraved plaquettes. Unfortunately, in this unique instance of a complete sanctuary of plaquettes, the individual pieces were not kept together and are now scattered among private collections; we cannot be sure that those that have been published are the complete series, and no record of their original position was kept. However, what we do know concerning this little plaquette sanctuary dating from Magdalenian V is very important: there was one bison marked with the "spear and wound" sign, one unmarked bison, one bison marked with red dots (the indications are that this plaquette stood vertically, the bison's muzzle up), some horses, a salmon, and birds. Long-necked birds make their appearance on decorated objects during Period IV; fish become common about the same time. All of this evidence converges to prove that this little group dates from a period when the ancient themes were still alive, although other symbols were taking on growing importance, while at the same time the practice of decorating cave walls was gradually being abandoned.

The engraved slabs at Limeuil in the Dordogne mark one last flare-up: several dozens of them were discovered in close proximity, but unfortunately no detailed observations were made. The inventory shows simply that, except for the abundant reindeer, the fauna is that of temperate present-day Europe. The ox, the stag, the horse, the ibex, and the bear, each subject on a separate slab, could have been arranged to form groups of the classical type.

Small plaquettes and engraved pebbles are common in the last phase of the Magdalenian, and it is not rare to find animals, superimposed or placed on the two faces of a stone, which may have been of the same or of complementary groups.

Beginning with Magdalenian VI we witness a fairly rapid decline of the art. The relatively few extant works found at La Madeleine (Dordogne), Villepin, Bruniquel, and Isturitz attest to a veritable dissolution of the forms during the second part of Magdalenian VI: the figures are reduced to a few curved lines which can sometimes be identified as horns or flanks, occasionally as ovals or fish. The few clear-cut figures are clumsy or incomplete, like the horse and the vague cervids on the engraved pebbles from Villepin.

THE PASSING OF THE ART

And so Paleolithic art in the west comes to an end. As we contemplate the extraordinarily powerful tide that sustained the thought of hunters of horse and bison for more than fifteen thousand years, we ask if it ebbed definitively as the ice retreated? Attempts have been made to discover the places where relics survived. After the disappearance of the last engraved stones, we find in the cultural phase directly following the Magdalenian, at a few Franco-Cantabrian sites, small stones marked with bars or with dots in red ocher. Such stones were found in quantity at Le Mas d'Azil (Ariège) in the so-called Azilian horizon; they show great variety in the arrangement of these marks, and various hypotheses have been advanced concerning their significance. The least implausible is that the Magdalenian figures gradually slipped toward a schematization causing the various subjects to be represented by rows of round spots, jagged lines, and bars breaking up the surface of the stone into compartments. But nothing in the latest Magdalenian examples indicates that such an evolution was under way, and except for the Azilian stones there is nothing to show the path that may have been taken. Whether the same people were creating a new culture or passively taking over an old one, or a new people had come in from the outside, we are now the witnesses of a thought transformed; we have passed the boundaries of the world we had come to know.

The north, too, has been searched for an answer to this mystery. It is certain that as the glaciers retreated to Scandinavia, liberating northern Germany, for example, the reindeer followed them northward and so did the Magdalenian hunters: we find vestiges in the vicinity of Hamburg. As such regions had previously been engulfed by the glaciers, the people there must have come from inhabited regions and preserved, at least for a time, their original culture. But, just as in the south, the change of climate in the north seems to have led to the rapid dissolution of such cultural units as survived for a time: from England to Germany, the Magdalenian culture of circa 9,000 B.C. gives way to other forms in which art holds a far less conspicuous place and has no connection with that of the Paleolithic.

The reindeer came to occupy their present habitats in Scandinavia and Finland; did the Magdalenians follow them there? In the northern USSR and Finland (especially Finno-Karelia), on the one hand, and in Sweden and Norway on the other, we do in fact find a cave-wall art executed on rocks at daylight sites which continues down to the appearance of metals. Does this art, which has been called "Arctic," trace its descent from that of the south? It seems difficult to answer this question, on the basis of present information.

The problems raised in the far south are of great interest. Engravings in the Sicilian caves, given a carbon-14 dating of circa 7,500 B.C., show characteristic groupings (ox/horse/cervid) and human figures in movement; in other words, they must be compared both with Paleolithic art and with the art of the Spanish Levant. The discovery of frescoes in the Neolithic village of Catal Huyuk in Asia Minor reveals that as early as circa 6,000 B.C., scenes with human figures were organized around animal (ox/feline/vulture) themes that were to dominate Eurasian figurative art down to historical times. Here, again, the relationship seems to be that of a new or parallel development.

Thus Paleolithic art seems to have vanished with the Paleolithic itself. Its persistence over some twenty thousand years—from 30,000 to 10,000 B.C.—makes it the longest and the oldest of the artistic adventures of mankind. Its growth is fully as coherent as that of the arts that succeeded it: in its trajectory of development may be seen an unusually extended infancy, an apogee lasting approximately five thousand years, and a decline that accelerates rapidly. This, then, was in every sense a "normal" art, having its clumsy beginnings, its maturity, its tricks of the trade, and even an academism that might sometimes seem tedious were it not so very ancient. The well-nigh incomprehensible miracle is that it should have been so "normal," actually almost commonplace, although no urge toward creating a representational art had existed before it and six thousand years were to pass before the next great art followed it. Paleolithic art, having exhausted its resources of both the concrete and the abstract, left a full catalogue of all the possibilities of the engraver's burin and the painter's brush.

9. THE ANIMALS

OF

CAVE ART:

Stylistic Evolution

HORSE

75 PAIR-NON-PAIR
*Horse in Style II. Compare the
structure with that of the bison in
fig. 86, particularly the proportions of the
body and the line of the neck and back.
About 32 in.*

76 PECH MERLE
*Horse in Early Style III. The
proportions are still close to those of
Style II. About 20 in.*

77 GARGAS
*Horse in Style III, from the bison/horse
group which is at IIb on the plan
(fig. 124). About 8 in.*

78 LASCAUX
*Horse in Style III from the Axial
Gallery. Compare with figs. 76 and 79
to see the development in the proportions
from Style III to Style IV. About 5 ft.*

79 LABASTIDE
*Horse in Early Style IV. Double
shoulder line, modeled body, integration
of the proportions of the different parts.
About 7$^1/_2$ ft.*

80 NIAUX
*Horse in Early Style IV. Note the
shoulder line, hatched modeling, and
wound sign on the flank. The proportions
are completely integrated and the hoofs
rest on the ground. 27$^1/_2$ in.*

75

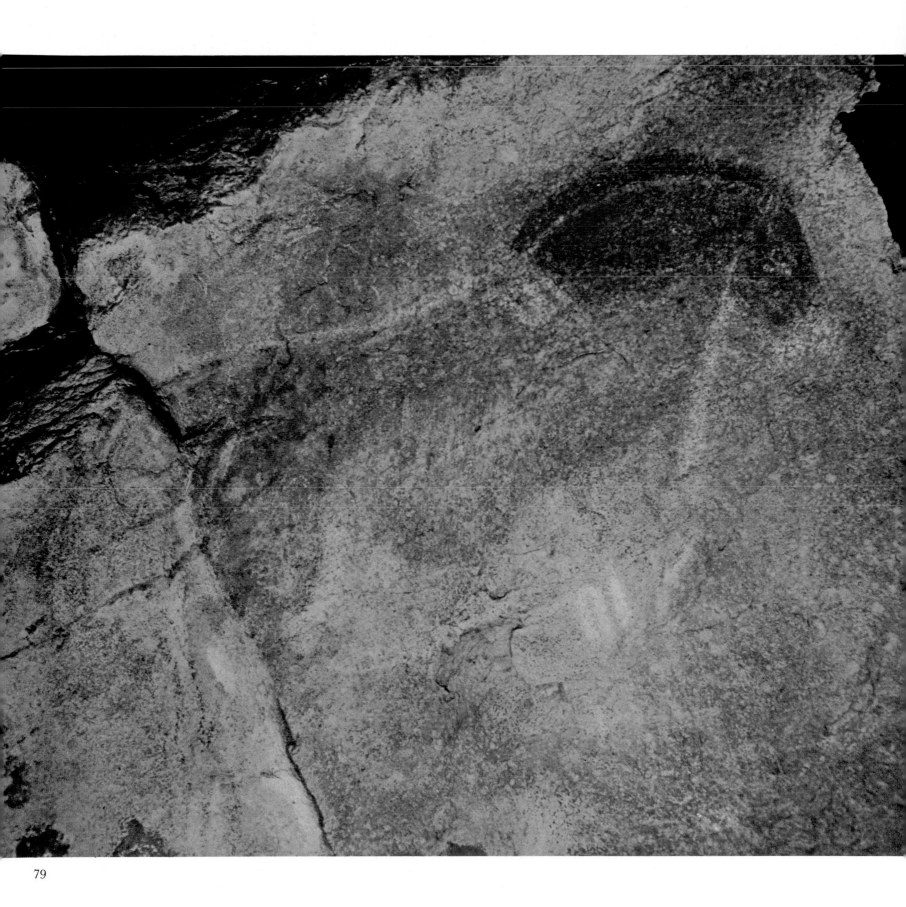

81

82

83

81 LASCAUX
"Chinese" horse in the Axial Gallery. The modeling in Early Style IV is combined with the proportions of Style III. The pacing gait is broken up into separate movements. 59 in.

82 LE PORTEL
Horse in Style IV with conventional modeling. Compare with fig. 81 for the integration of proportions and movement. About 16 in.

83 NIAUX
Horse in Style IV with conventional modeling. The schematic character of this figure derives from its dimensions ($11^3/_4$ in.), tiny in relation to the rest of the panel.

84 LAS MONEDAS
Horse in Style IV. The uncertainty of the lines of modeling in this figure, which is oddly placed on the wall, brings out the conventional character of Early Style IV. About 20 in.

85 LIMEUIL
Horse in Late Style IV (Late Magdalenian). Very sensitive outline and complete integration of movement and expression. Note the close resemblance to fig. 80, which represents the stage immediately preceding this one. Length of plaquette 10 in.

BISON

86   PAIR-NON-PAIR
*Bison in Style II. On a structure that
is vigorous but undefined, the configuration
is obtained by the addition of details:
horns, thick withers, hump. 29$^1/_2$ in.*

87   LA GRÈZE
*Bison in Style II. The figure is of
uncertain date, but it is later than the
Aurignacian and earlier than the
Magdalenian. 23$^5/_8$ in.*

88   LASCAUX
*Bison from the Nave. 7 ft. 10$^1/_2$ in.
Style III; compare with figs. 65 and 68.*

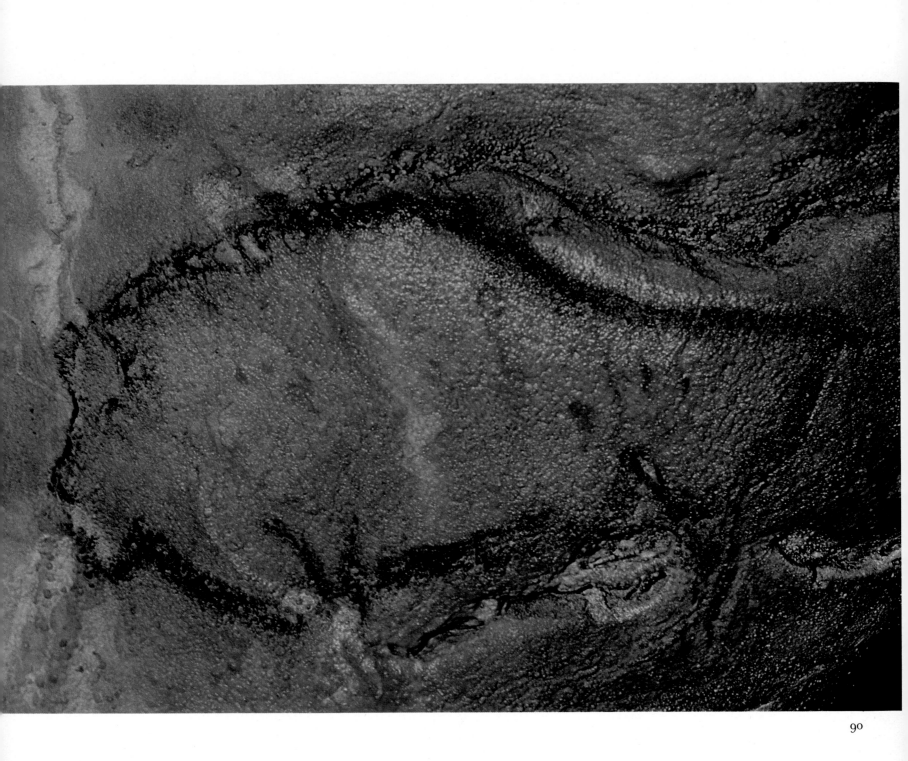

89 NIAUX
Bison in Early Style IV, drawn in the clay floor three-fifths of a mile from the entrance. Three cup-marks made by dropping water from the ceiling have been transformed into wounds. Note the two added strokes on the shoulder. 24 in.

90 LE PORTEL
Bison in Early Style IV. 9½ in. Compare with figs. 86, 88 and 91.

91 NIAUX
Bison in Early Style IV. Modeled with hatching. Note the relative closeness to fig. 90: there is a stronger sense of movement and the hoofs are shown resting on the ground. About 39 in.

92 LE TUC D'AUDOUBERT
Bison in Style IV, modeled in clay. Compare figs. 90 and 91 for the identical balance of proportions and for rendering of detail. 24 in.

AUROCHS

93   GARGAS
      Bovid in Style II, engraved in the
      composition of the semidome.
      About actual size.

94   PECH MERLE
      Aurochs from the side chamber
      with "the wounded man."
      15 in. Style III. Compare with
      fig. 96.

95   BOURDEILLES
      Two aurochs in low relief,
      Style III. Solutrean. About 21 in.

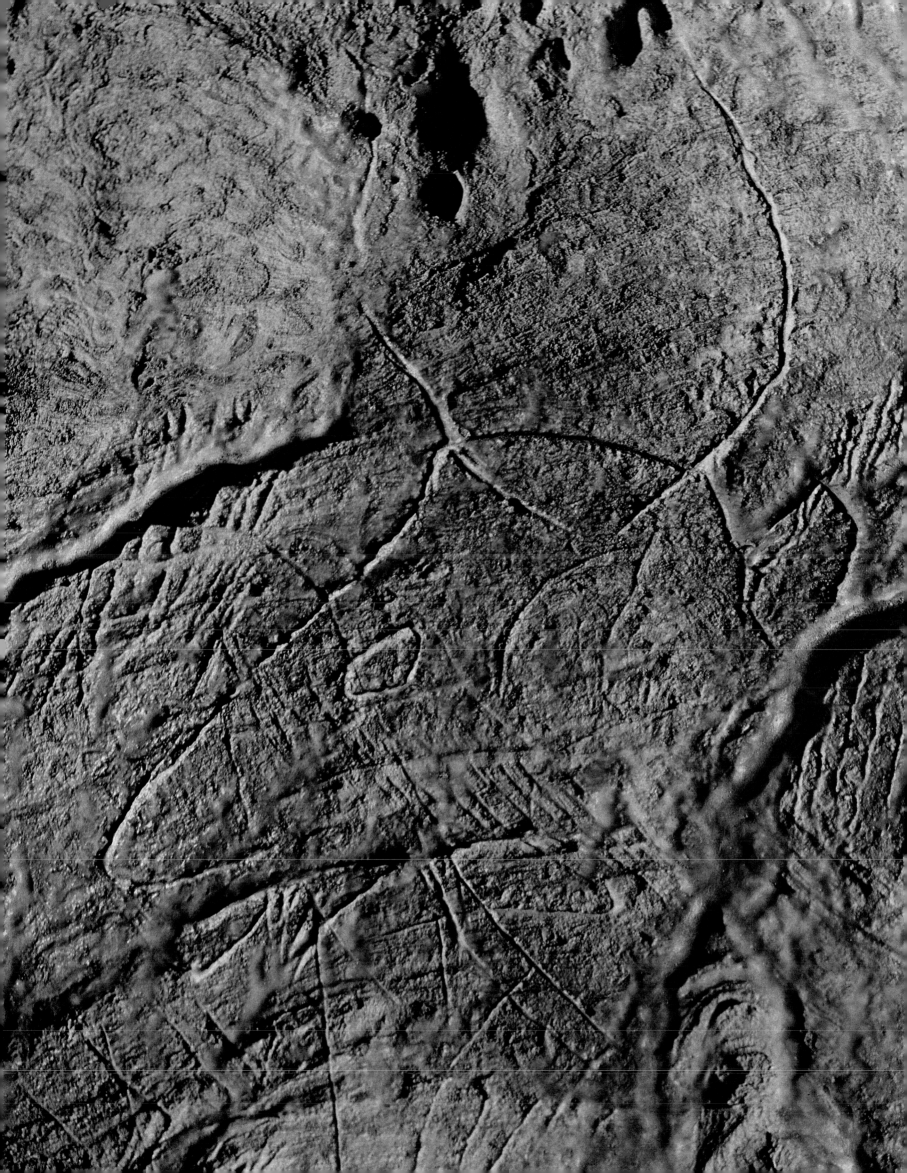

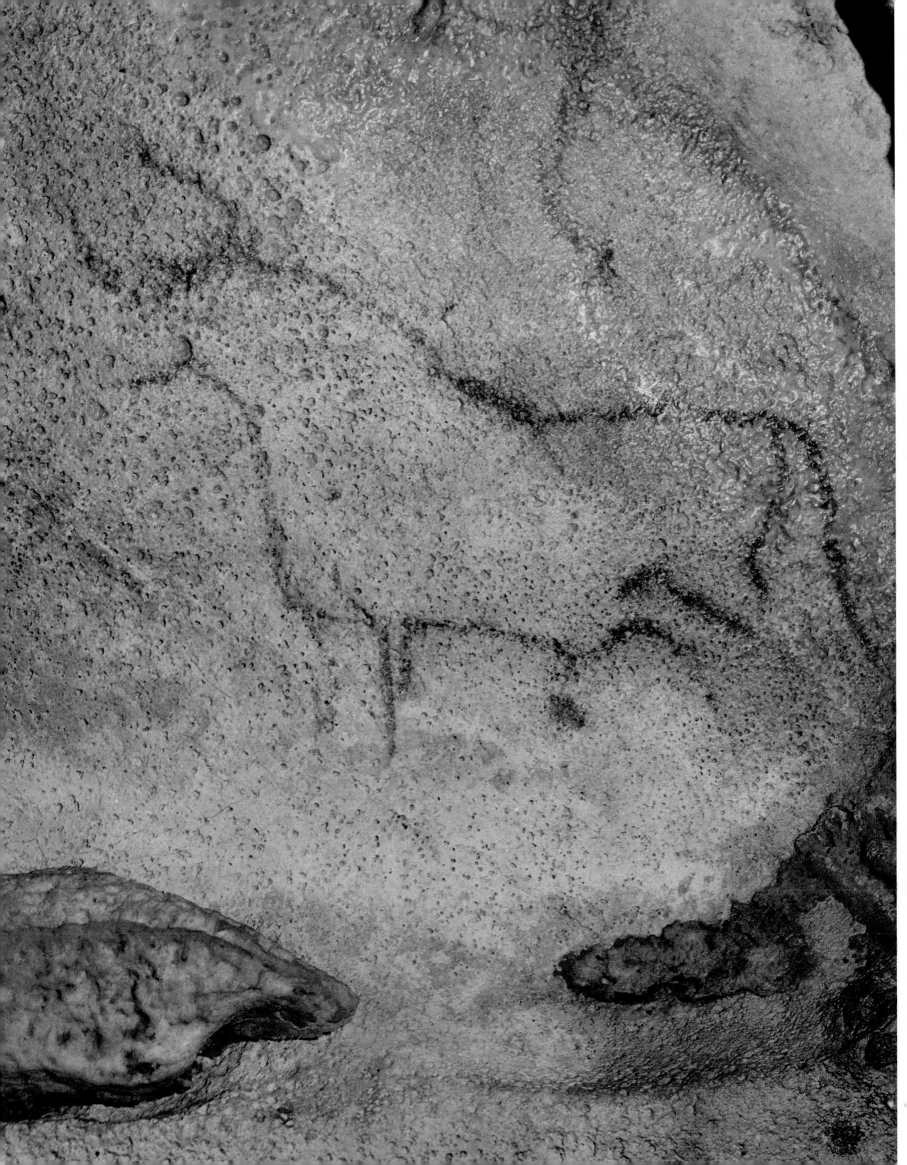

97

98

96 LASCAUX
Aurochs (bull) in the Rotunda.
Style III. About 13 ft.

97 LASCAUX
Aurochs (cow) in the Axial Gallery.
Style III. Red lattice sign and
complementary black stroke in front of
the muzzle and under the neck.
Complementary small black horses.
Cow, 67 in.

98 LASCAUX
Aurochs (bull) opposite the cow in
fig. 97. Style III. A black barbed
sign and a horse are in front of the
muzzle and under the neck.
Complementary red cows superimposed.
About 13 ft.

99 TEYJAT
Aurochs (bull) in Late Style IV.
Compare with the horse in fig. 85 for the
sensitivity of contour, movement, and
expression. Slightly enlarged.

MAMMOTH

100 PECH MERLE

Mammoth in Late Style III from the black fresco (see fig. 68). After the curve of the back was drawn, the legs and trunk were added below without strict concern for proportions or anatomical connections.
About 31¹/₂ in.

101 ARCY-SUR-CURE

Mammoth in Style IV incised on the ceiling. The proportions are better integrated and the outlines are more sensitive than in fig. 100. About 20 in.

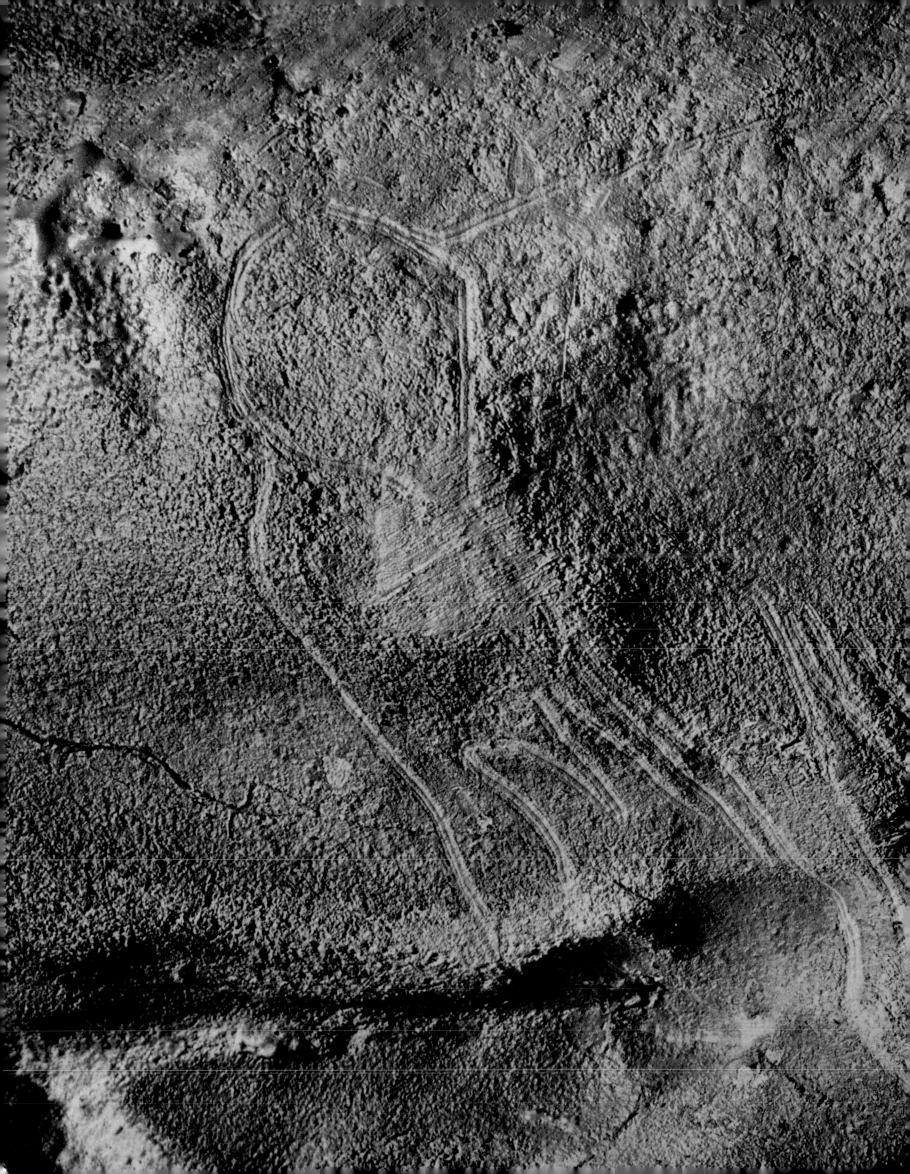

102   EL CASTILLO
*Proboscidian in the terminal gallery,
probably a mammoth. The paucity
of examples in Spanish caves and the
range of periods represented at
El Castillo do not permit a
determination of style. 14 in.*

103   LA BAUME LATRONE
*Mammoth painted with fingers dipped
in clay. The crude execution and the
lack of archaeological context put
this figure beyond the determination
of style. 47 in.*

DEER

104 PECH MERLE
*Stag in Style III. Despite its extreme
schematization, this figure is
stylistically very clear: strongly convex
cervical curve, antlers in semifrontal
perspective. 11 in.*

105 LASCAUX
*Stag in Style III, in the Nave.
Note that the antlers are in the same
perspective as those in fig. 104;
the small brow antler is drawn as a
vertical. Remains of a painted and
engraved horse, also a row of dots.
About 39 in.*

106 LASCAUX
*Stag in Style III, the first subject in
the Axial Gallery. The same stylistic
features as in fig. 105: semifrontal
antlers, ear at the back of the neck.
Quadrangular sign and a
complementary stroke. Row of dots.
About 59 in.*

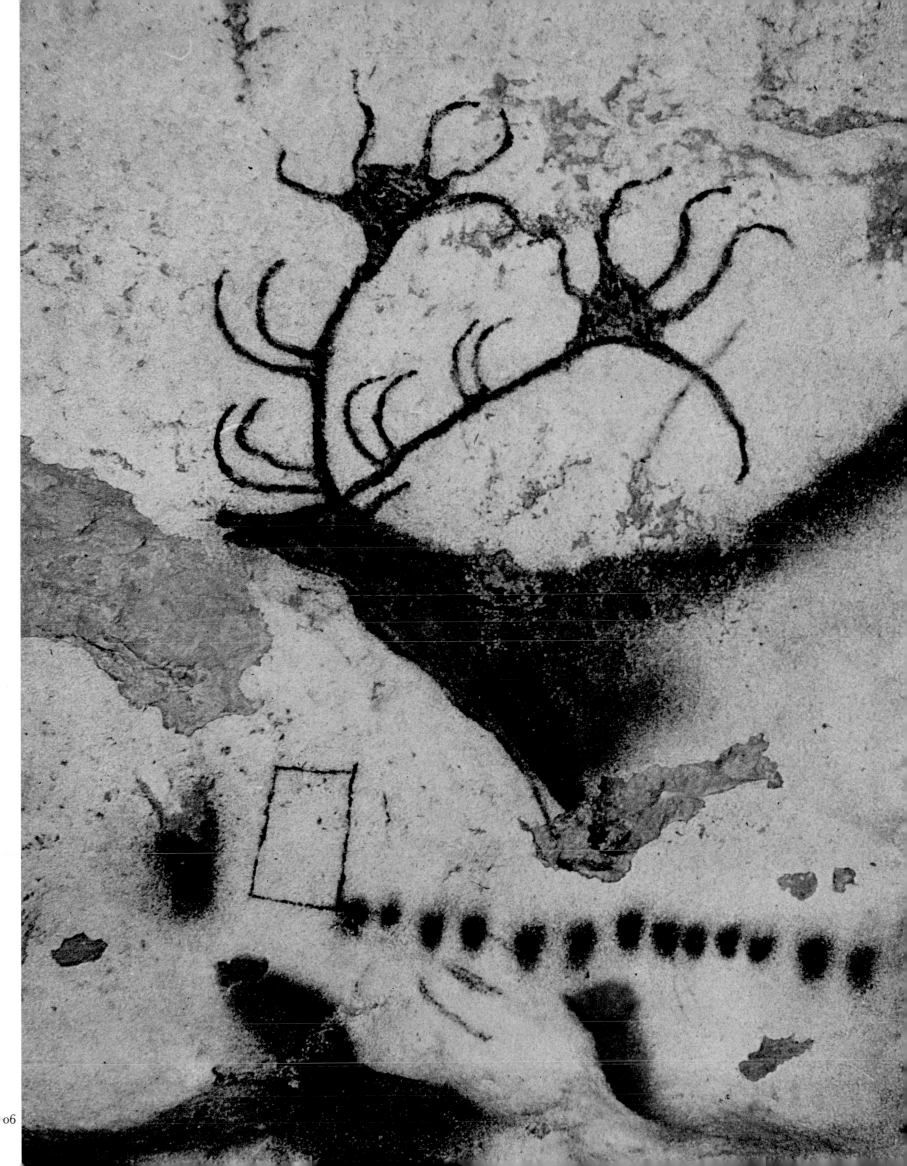

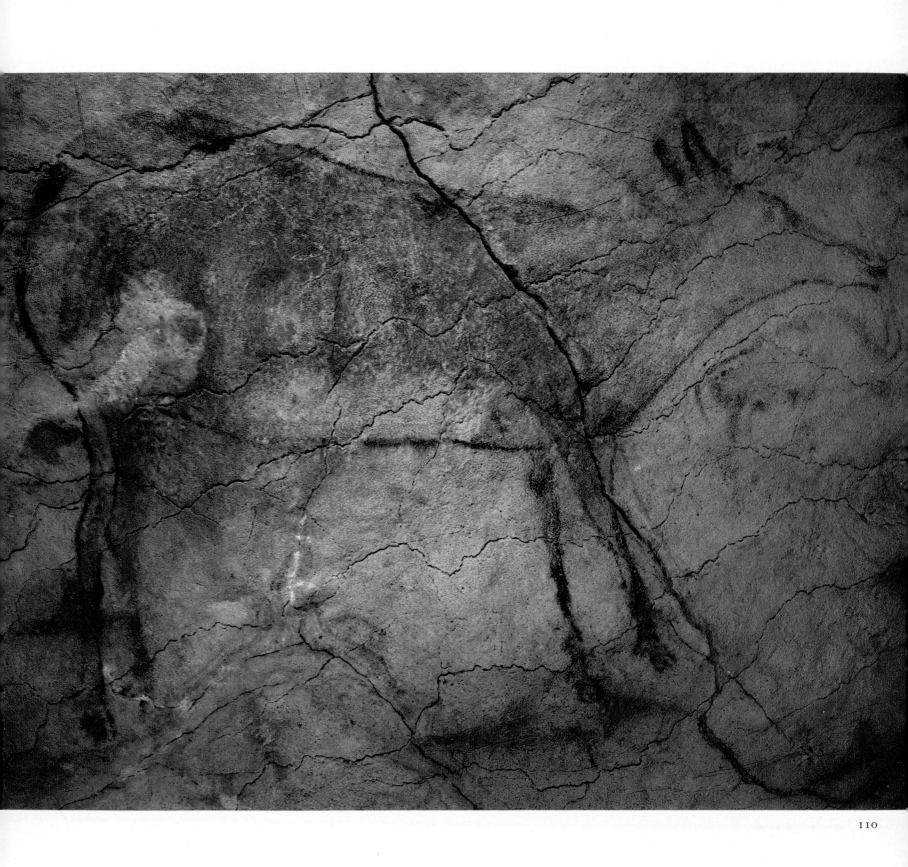

107 LAS CHIMENEAS
Stag in Style III, and accompanying quadrangular signs. About 16 in. Note the stylistic similarity with the stags in figs. 72, 105, and 106.

108 COVALANAS
Hind painted in dotted outline, Style III. 27⁵/₈ in.

109 LA PASIEGA
Painted hind in Gallery A. Style III. 20 in.

110 ALTAMIRA
Hind on the Painted Ceiling, Early Style IV. As at Niaux, a smaller complementary figure (here a bison) is adjacent. 7 ft. 4⁵/₈ in.

IBEX

REINDEER

BOAR

RHINOCEROS

FELINE

FISH

111   PAIR-NON-PAIR
Ibex in Style II. A comparison with fig. 86 shows that the cervico-dorsal, pectoral, and ventral contour lines have the same curves; they are only differentiated at their extremities to indicate the identifying details. About 20 in.

112   LASCAUX
Facing male ibexes in the Axial Gallery. Style III. The horns are in semifrontal perspective. About $6^1/_2$ ft.

113   COUGNAC
Two ibexes in Style III, male and female. The male's horns are in normal perspective, those of the female in semifrontal perspective. Female, $19^5/_8$ in.

114   NIAUX
Ibex in the Black Salon. Early Style IV. Hatched modeling. $19^5/_8$ in.

115   LAS MONEDAS
Female reindeer in Style IV. The horse in fig. 84 appears in foreshortening at the left. Las Monedas is the only Spanish cave containing representations of reindeer. The rendering of proportions and movement is close to Late Style IV. About 15 in.

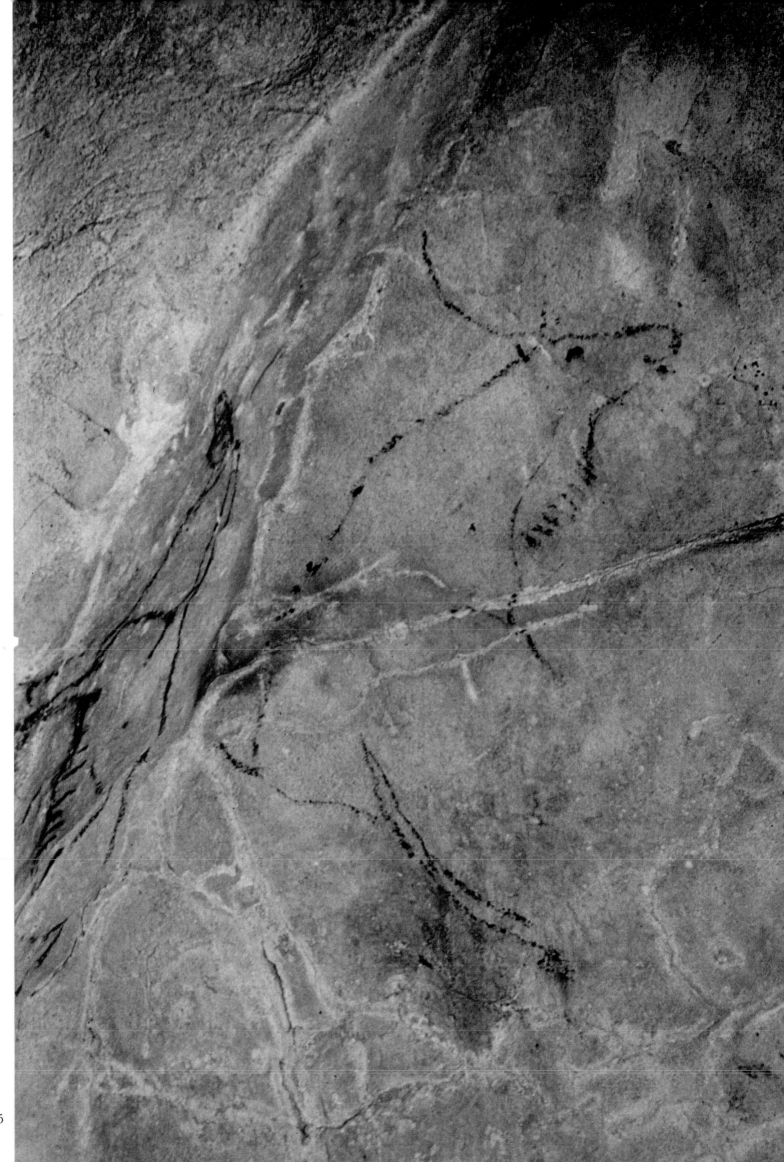

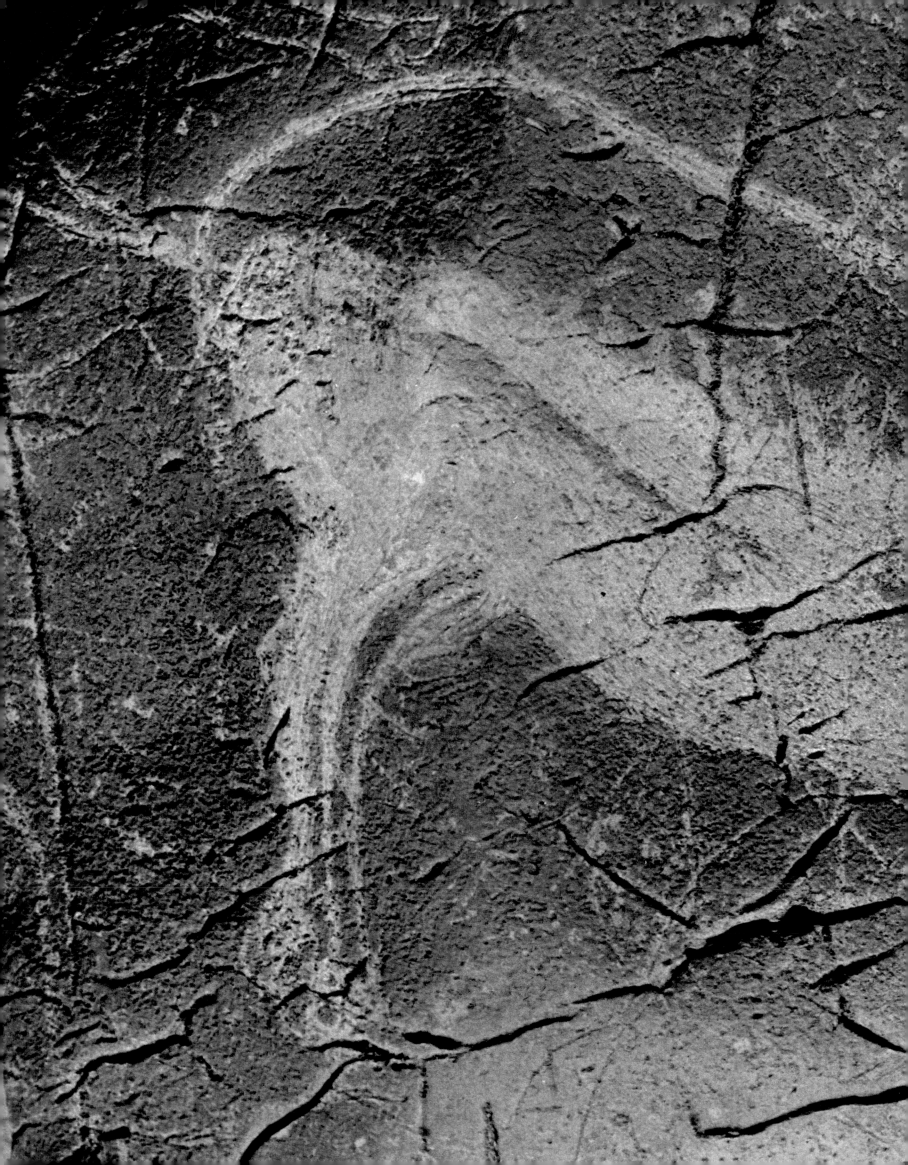

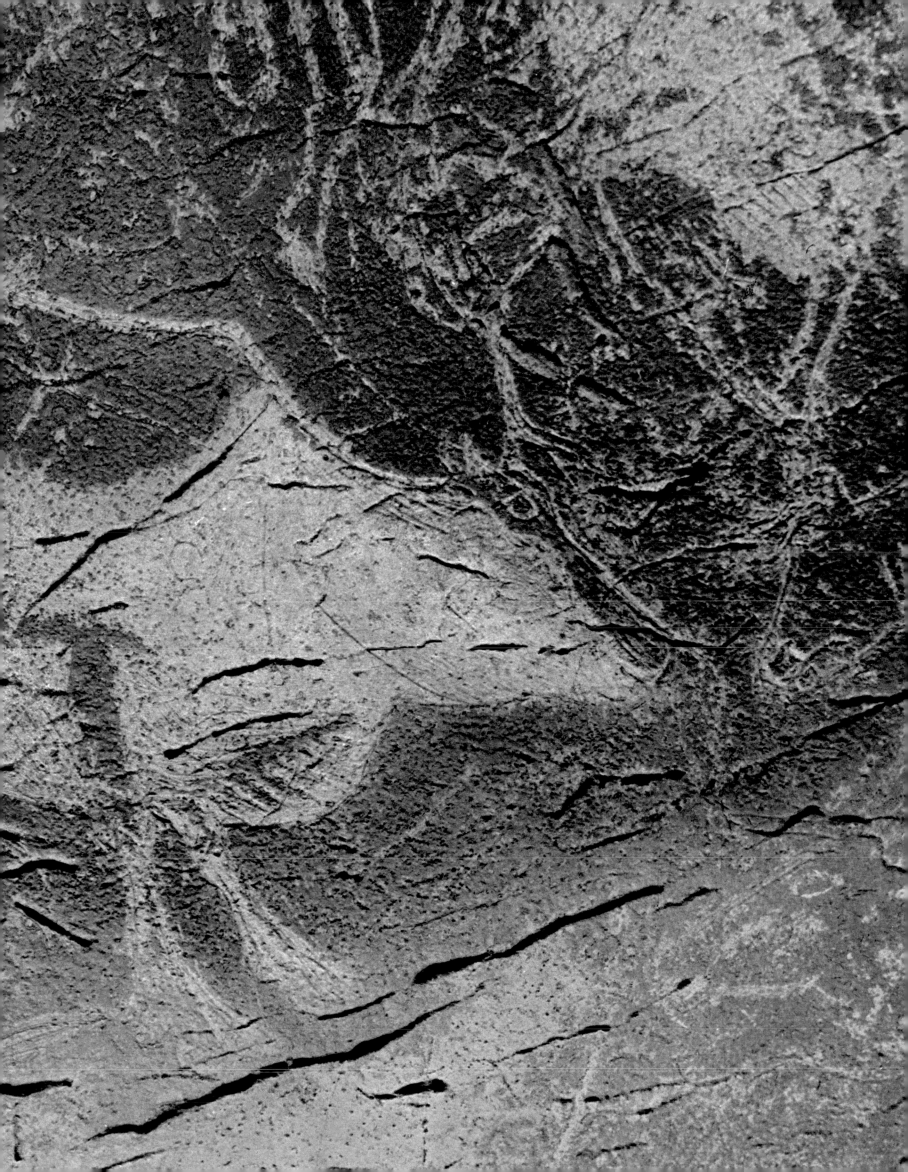

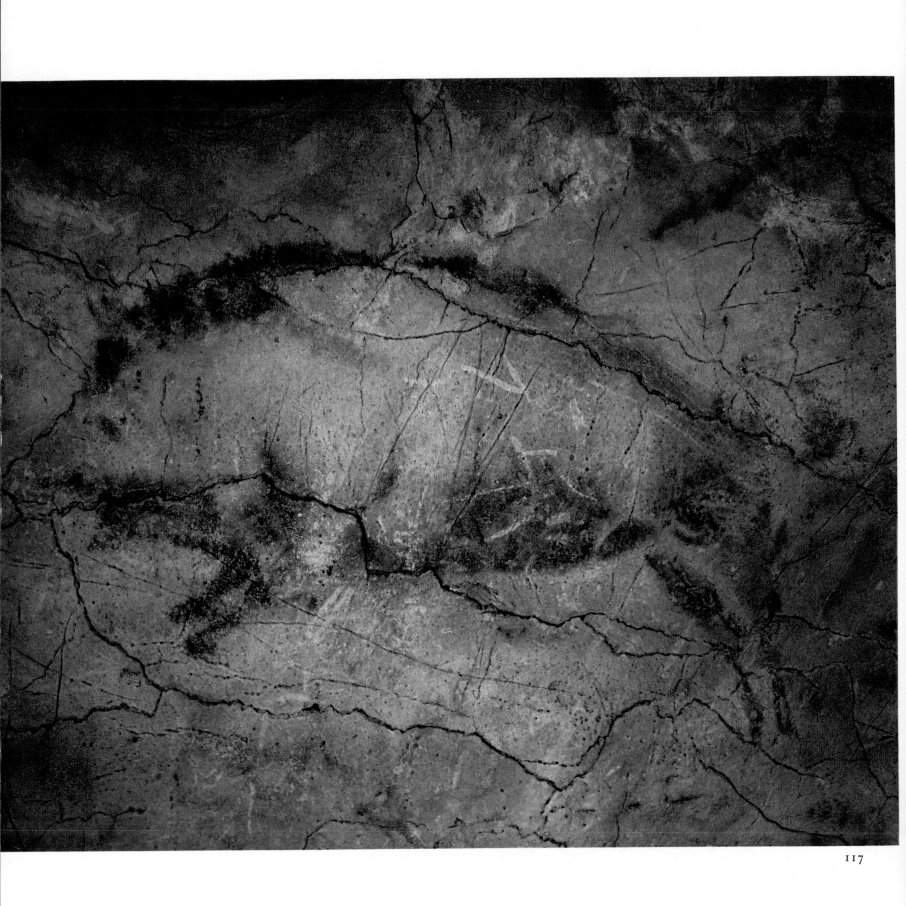

116 LES TROIS FRÈRES
Reindeer in the "sanctuary," modeled
with hatching. Early Style IV.
As at Niaux, the integration of
movement is very advanced, and the feet
rest on the ground. About 16 in.

117 ALTAMIRA
Boar in Early Style IV on the
Painted Ceiling. Altamira is the only
cave in which the boar is unmistakably
represented. 63 in.

118 SANTIMAMINE
Bear painted on a stalagmite. It
accompanies figures in Early Style IV
(see fig. 71). 11⁵/₈ in.

119 ROUFFIGNAC
Woolly rhinoceros. Style IV. The
rhinoceroses in this cave are
incorporated with a composition of
horses and bison in fairly mature
Style IV. 43 in.

120 LES TROIS FRÈRES
Feline in frontal view. Style IV.
The treatment is the same as that of
the figures in the "sanctuary," which
belong to Early Style IV.
About 20 in.

121 NIAUX
Fish of the salmon family, engraved
on the clay floor of the Black Salon.
14 in. Treatment in Style IV.
Compare fig. 36.

Part Two: Documentation

10. DESCRIPTION OF SITES

CONTENTS

STYLE IV (cont.)

MEDITERRANEAN PALEOLITHIC ART

NOTE

In this second and essentially documentary section, the reader may be surprised at the very limited use that has been made of previous publications, the Abbé Breuil's pictorial inventories in particular; I believe that some justification for this should be offered. It would be impossible to make an over-all study of prehistoric art without building upon the foundations laid by Breuil or without making use of the monographs, frequently excellent, which others have published on individual works and sites. I have made every effort to include references to these writings. At the same time, in the course of my own study I have tried to re-examine all the existing evidence—much as one translates an ancient author for one's own comprehension without thereby implying criticism of the eminent philologists who may have previously provided texts.

One of the real problems has been to place the figures in their exact topographical setting. My team members and I have done this on the maps and diagrams that our predecessors have provided, wherever these exist. In the majority of cases, however, I have been obliged to draw on my own field notes, simple sketches which give a picture of the sites but, rather in the manner of maps drawn by early travelers, leave something to be desired in the way of exact proportions and outlines. In a few instances I have simply had recourse to a conventionalized outline as being more appropriate to bring out the over-all composition.

On-the-spot drawings are valuable but they interpose another hand and eye between us and the works of art. Yet figures may be so entangled, and their style or their incompleteness (or the condition of the rock) may be such that I have often been able to understand the principles of a given composition only through statistical analysis. To reproduce on a map the actual tangle of figures at Les Combarelles, for example, would merely be to parody the Abbé Breuil's painstaking pictorial inventory without throwing new light on the meaning of the subjects. Therefore conventionalized representations of the animal species have been adopted to assure an analysis both clear and uncluttered, easily identifiable outlines which reduce the figures to the condition of particles which can be analyzed.

For some panels, and for caves and shelters having few and unambiguous figures, schematic versions of the actual outlines have been supplied. The captions for the maps and diagrams explain the method adopted in each case.

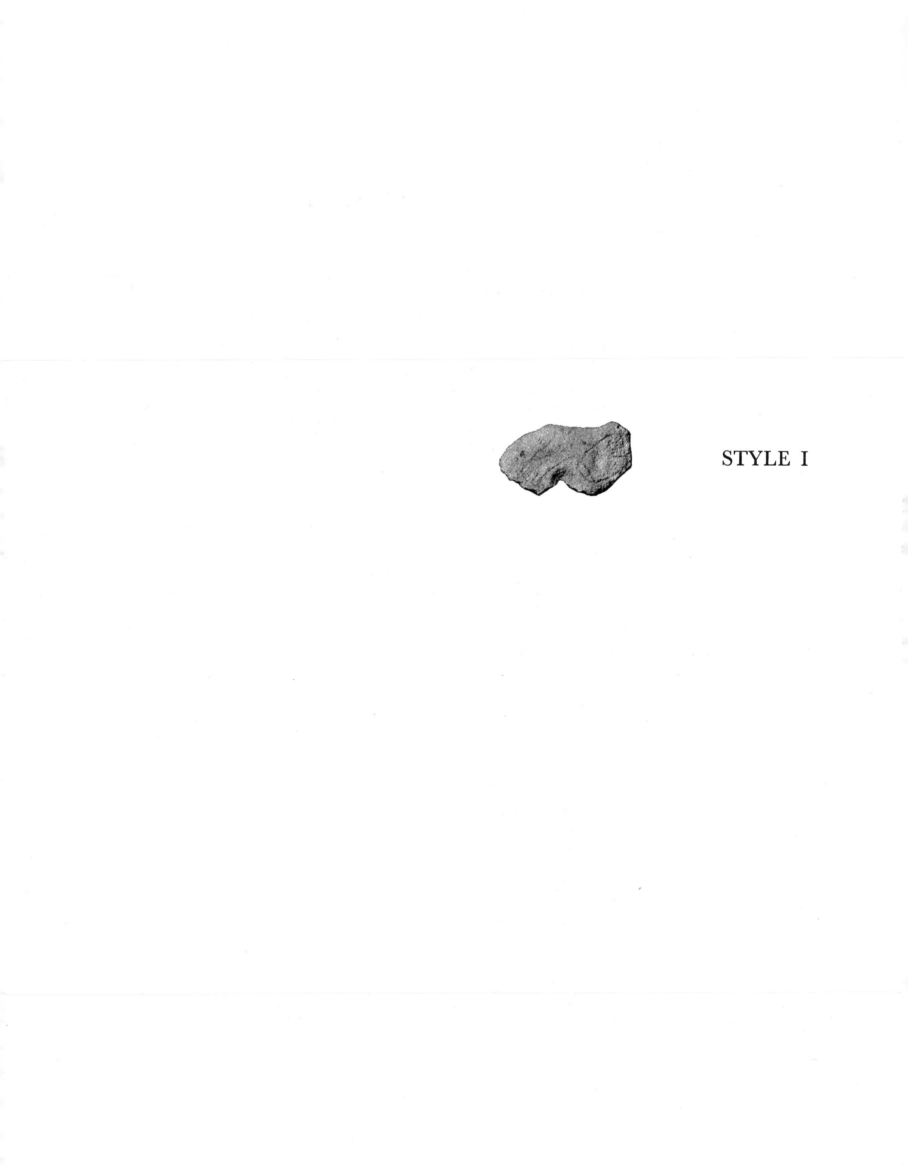

STYLE I

STYLE I

Style I appears in works belonging to the Aurignacian properly so called (Aurignacian I-IV, from 30,000 to 27,000 B.C.). Its themes are sexual symbols realistically represented, and animals extremely crudely rendered. Because of the paucity of reliably dated finds, it is impossible to determine the constant features of this style; however, the stiffness of the outlines obtained by deep incision characterizes most of the animal figures.

The works are executed on plaquettes or blocks; no decorated utilitarian objects, and no works on the walls of unlighted cave areas can be reliably attributed to this period. The most sizable collection of finds is in the Dordogne: the Abri Cellier (Aurignacian I), La Ferrassie (Aurignacian II, III, IV), and the abris of Castanet (Aurignacian II), Belcayre, and Blanchard. Outside the Perigordian area, we might mention the plaquettes from Isturitz (Aurignacian II), and an engraved bone from Arcy-sur-Cure in the Yonne (Aurignacian II).

The realism of the sexual figures must not distract our attention from the elaborate symbolic character of the treatment of such figures. When several representations are grouped on one object, they appear according to the same principles of grouping that were used in later periods: horse/vulva, ibex/vulva, vulva/phallus, vulva/short-strokes, animal/vulva/short-strokes or dots.

ABRI CELLIER

(ALSO KNOWN AS LE RUTH) TURSAC, DORDOGNE, FRANCE

The excavation was conducted in 1927 by Professor Collie of the Logan Museum, Beloit, Wisconsin. The finds were inventoried by D. Peyrony. The works are in the museum of Les Eyzies.

The deposit contained three layers with indications of human occupancy: Aurignacian I, spears split at the base and lozenge-shaped spears; Aurignacian, similar but a bit more recent; Gravettian. The engraved works[1] were found in the lower stratum.

[1] figs. 23, 250–253

CASTANET

SERGEAC, DORDOGNE, FRANCE

Excavated in 1935 by D. Peyrony and Castanet, the owner of the site. The deposit included two levels: Aurignacian I, spears split at the base; and Aurignacian II, lozenge-shaped spears. This latter level contained a few works of art: slabs with stylized vulvas, a slab with an animal's forequarters painted in black, and the slab which is not included in the publication devoted to the site.

ABRI DE BELCAYRE

THONAC, DORDOGNE, FRANCE

Collapsed rock shelter explored by Franck Delage from 1922 on.

[1] fig. 256

Has yielded two Aurignacian levels, between which the engraved flat stone[1] was found.

LA FERRASSIE

LE BUGUE, DORDOGNE, FRANCE

Excavation of this great classic site was begun in 1902, under the supervision of L. Capitan and D. Peyrony; it played an important part in distinguishing the Aurignacian proper and the Perigordian.

The oldest level reached was a Chatelperronian horizon (layers E and E'), which contained no figured works; of the four Aurignacian layers (F, H, H', and H''), however, the three upper ones contained figured works; one Gravettian layer (J) had points of the La Font-Robert type. The Aurignacian layers were christened Aurignacian I (spears split at the base), Aurignacian II (lozenge-shaped spears), Aurignacian III (same spears), and Aurignacian IV (biconic spears). This terminology was coined to suit the local situation; the first two terms have since become generally accepted. The works here presented[1] belong to Aurignacian IV, which already shows some Gravettian characteristics.

[1] figs. 254, 255

STYLE II

STYLE II

THOUGH more numerous than works in Style I, and spread over a much wider area, works in Style II are still not numerous enough to permit arrangement in a well-defined chronological sequence. They turn up in the course of the Gravettian, are reliably attested for the period between the Gravettian and the Solutrean, and probably continue, at least here and there, into the early Solutrean. Their development thus falls between 25,000 and 18,000 B.C., but there is no real break with what precedes and what follows them. Their geographical distribution represents the maximum extension of Paleolithic art, inasmuch as it includes Spain, France, Central Europe, the Ukraine, and Russia as far east as the Don.

The known works belong to every possible genre: among them we encounter the first utilitarian objects decorated with figures; human and animal statuettes; incised figures on blocks, slabs, and plaquettes, as in the preceding period; and the first cave works that can be dated with some certainty.

Among utilitarian objects decorated with figures, we may single out the thick spear of the Upper Gravettian from Isturitz, on which a horse is engraved,[1] and the pierced staff (period between the Gravettian and the Solutrean) from Laugerie Haute, on which two mammoths in low relief appear facing each other.[2] The engraved slabs are found in the Périgord (the Abri Labatut, Terme-Pialat, Laussel, the Abri Pataud, Les Rebières), in the Pyrenees (Gargas, Isturitz, Aussurucq), and in Spain (Parpallo). The human and animal statuettes come from the Périgord (Tursac, Sireuil), the Pyrenees (Lespugue, Brassempouy); Germany (Vogelherd); Central Europe (Willendorf, Petrkovice, Predmosti, Dolni Vestonice); and Russia (Gagarino, Telman, Kostienki). Decorated caves and rock shelters are not very numerous, and the works appear only in the daylight zone and the first dark zone: in France, Pair-non-Pair in the Gironde, Gargas in the Hautes-Pyrénées, probably La Croze at Gontran and La Grèze, both in the Dordogne; and in Spain, the front part of La Peña de los Hornos in Santander. Probably to be ascribed to this period, also, are parts of caves in the Ardèche and the Gard: Chabot, Le Figuier, and the back area of the Oulen cave.

The male and female figures accentuate the two tendencies that appeared in the course of Period I. The statuettes and low reliefs tend toward realism of the type expressed in the so-called Aurignacian Venuses; other works, particularly the engravings on slabs or walls, mark the development toward almost completely abstract stylization.

The animal figures, despite the very great time span (more than seven thousand years) and the geographical spread, exhibit a very striking stylistic unity.[3] They are built upon a strong, sinuous line that defines the neck, withers, and back, and each animal species is characterized by specific details. In the majority of cases, horns or antlers[4] are drawn in absolute profile or in frontal view (twisted perspective); details become more sketchy the greater the distance from the structural line of the trunk, so that legs are merely suggested or not rendered at all and extremities are seldom rendered.

[1] *fig. 257*

[2] *fig. 31*

[3] *charts* XXXIX, XL

[4] *chart* L

The female human figures known in the publications as "Aurignacian Venuses"—or at least such of them as are dated exactly enough—are within the period between the mature Gravettian and the Solutrean. They have been found in southwestern France (Tursac, Laussel, and the Abri Pataud in the Dordogne; Brassempouy and Lespugue in the Pyrenees); in Central and Eastern Europe (Willendorf in Austria; Petrkovice, Dolni Vestonice, and Predmosti in Czechoslovakia; Gagarino, Kostienki, and Telman in Russia). Other discoveries, recognized but less reliably dated, are stylistically akin: at Sireuil in the Dordogne in France, and at Grimaldi and Savignano in Italy.

All these representations are identical in their construction, which bears the same stylistic conventions as the animal representations. The image is centered on the most notable specific characteristics (breasts and pelvic zone), the other parts tapering to such a degree that the head and feet may terminate in a cone.[6] These conventions give to the figures from the period between the Gravettian and the Solutrean, as compared with those from periods III and IV, a "blown-up" look around the middle. The most remarkable feature is the stylistic uniformity of statuettes from Russia, Austria, and the Pyrenees.

STATUETTES

Central Europe and Russia have yielded a great many statuettes carved from the tusks of mammoth (Vogelherd), from soft stone (Kostienki), and from a mixture of clay and bone ash (Dolni Vestonice[7]). These figurines, so far as may be judged from the distribution of the subjects depicted, played the same role as the painted or engraved figures did in the west. In 1951, while undertaking fresh excavations at Dolni Vestonice, B. Klima found a hut surrounded by a low wall of stones deeply marked by fire and, near by, 2,200 pieces of baked clay, including many fragments of figures. Apparently the Czechs of the Paleolithic era knew the lasting properties that firing gives to anything modeled in clay mixed with bone ash. This discovery, as yet an isolated case, nonetheless antedates by about ten thousand years the earliest-known ceramics in the eastern Mediterranean.

LAUSSEL

MARQUAY, DORDOGNE, FRANCE

Excavation was carried out here in 1909 by Dr. Lalanne. The site contained one of the finest stratigraphic sequences in France, extending from the Levallois-Mousterian to the beginning of the Solutrean. The digging was made according to the old technique, with only the over-all chronological divisions respected, and as a result the whole of the Gravettian is thrown together into a single list of finds. Many works of art on slabs were discovered, including the famous low reliefs of human figures. Some of these slabs are from the Middle Aurignacian (the true Aurignacian): these have engraved vulvas on them of a type that is definitely Aurignacian or Early Gravettian. The low reliefs were discovered in the Upper Aurignacian (Gravettian) and in the Lower Solutrean (proto-Solutrean) layers but it is impossible to determine exactly whether they belong in the Gravettian or in the period between the Gravettian and the Solutrean. Among the Gravettian and proto-Solutrean implements there are fairly numerous notched points and some specimens reworked on the flat side, which suggest that the terminal stages (upper Gravettian and the transition to the Solutrean) are well represented.

Four low reliefs with female figures and one with a male figure have been brought to light,[1] as well as a stone phallus and a rudimentary sculpture of an ithyphallic man. A few animal figures were also found: one slab engraved with a ruminant mammal in Style II and a horse's head in Style III.

The principal figure is that of "the woman with the horn," which has traces of ocher. In proportions and technique it belongs to the type from the period between the Gravettian and the Solutrean known through the statuettes from Kostienki, Willendorf, and Lespugue, and the little figure in low relief discovered by H. Movius at the Abri Pataud in Les Eyzies. Like the Russian figures, this one wears a narrow belt. She holds in her right hand an object that can only be a bison horn, and the way she holds it may suggest she is about to drink from it. It is possible that this horn plays the role of complementary element in the symbolic "bison/woman" theme.

A second low relief represents the head and trunk of a woman of the same type: her hair, treated in little squares and falling over the face, is exactly like that of the Willendorf statuette. A third slab, clandestinely acquired by the Berlin Museum, portrays a woman who, like the first, is holding a curved object; the condition of the stone prevents our identifying this, but it might be another bison horn. A fourth slab shows a very curious figure which has given rise to many hypotheses. We see a woman of the customary type, but her legs are tucked under her; and below, in mirror image like the figures on playing cards, is another figure with a roughly sketched head and shoulders exactly like those of the one above. Copulation or childbirth have been discerned here, with the latter the least unlikely.

In the relief of the male figure, part of the head and arms are missing; it is in three-quarter view, tall and slim, and seems to be stretching out its arms; the sexual parts are not specified. If, as seems likely, it was stretching out its arms, the pose would recall a painted figure from Cougnac, a "ghost" with outstretched arms,[2] or still more the two male figures thrown to the ground by bison, from Lascaux and Laugerie Basse.[3] The same theme is known to exist at Le Roc de Sers, which is chronologically close to Laussel. Consequently, it is not out of the question that this male figure from Laussel belonged to the theme of man pitted against animal.

[2] *fig. 386*   [3] *figs. 323, 439*

PAIR-NON-PAIR

MARCAMPS, GIRONDE, FRANCE ·

This important site was excavated by F. Daleau from 1881 on, with, for the period, exceptional care and exactitude. Unfortunately, publication of the data on the industrial finds was very incomplete, and Dr. Cheynier is now preparing Daleau's field notebooks for publication. These will undoubtedly cast much light on the history of the works. The drawings were made at first by Daleau, and then (from 1934 to 1937) by the Abbé Breuil and his assistant, Miss Boyle.

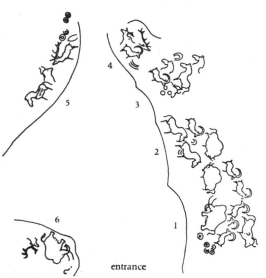

122. PAIR-NON-PAIR. ARRANGEMENT OF THE WALL DECORATIONS
Note the presence of the bovid/horse theme in the three central panels; the signs and ibexes in each group; cervids at the entrance and in the back-cave area; mammoths at the entrance. The statistical probability (based on figures in all the decorated caves) for the various types of animal occupying the locations they occupy here is: 91–92 percent for the bovids, 86 percent for the horses, 65 percent for the ibexes, and 60 percent for the cervids. The over-all decorative arrangement of the sanctuaries seems, from this evidence, already established in the earliest examples (as might have been predicted from Aurignacian decorated slabs).

Pair-non-Pair is a cave about 22 yards deep, the ceiling of which has partly fallen in. The works decorate the walls of a chamber more or less circular in shape which, at the time they were executed, received daylight or was at most shadowed. In this respect Pair-non-Pair resembles the oldest known sanctuaries, which seem to have been placed close to the cave entrances.

The date that should be assigned to the works in Pair-non-Pair is still far from clear, but it is certain that they belong to the archaic period. From what is known of the industries found at the site, the engravings belong, at the latest, between the Aurignacian and the beginning of the Solutrean: they were completely buried under detritus and cave-ins. Although this much is certain, and is supported by the style of the works, it nevertheless leaves a considerable margin of time, about ten thousand years. The walls of the cave are pitted and uneven, the drawings are often hard to make out, the outlines of one work often criss-cross those of another—all of this can lead to differences of opinion. Of all the drawings made at various sites by the Abbé Breuil, those of Pair-non-Pair are the hardest to confirm photographically. Among the interlaced figures, different periods are probably to be found; a few figures may belong to the Aurignacian proper, but the most legible pictures—which, moreover, constitute a coherent whole—seem to belong to the Gravettian. The topography of the cave accounts for the grouping of the works in six rather clearly delimited panels. At the right of the entrance, on Panel 1, it is easy to make out five ibexes,[1] one mammoth, and one aurochs at the upper edge. The figure which Breuil very cautiously proposed as a bear seems to consist of confused lines and of four circular signs that could be taken for the ears and eyes. The ibexes thus dominate this panel, which is normal at the cave entrance.

[1] *figs. 275, 276*

Panel 2 is occupied by two bovids facing each other, probably bison,[2] placed above two horses in single file[3]; an ibex and three or four signs (double circles or ovals) accompany them. The Abbé Breuil identified the bovid on the left as a bear, but appropriate lighting brings out a horn that points ahead of the animal, like that of the bovid on the right. Thus we have a bovid/horse composition, with signs and an ibex on the periphery.

[2] *figs. 86, 278*
[3] *figs. 75, 277*

Panel 3 is very crowded and hard to decipher; the most legible figures are an ox, three horses, and an ibex, along with several double-circle signs. This is the panel on which Daleau thought he could make out a horse with its head turned as though looking back (the "*Agnus Dei*"); G. Malvesin-Fabre has shown that the figures are a horse facing left and an ibex facing right, their superimposed figures giving the impression of a single animal looking over its shoulder.[4] The theme of the panel is ox/horse/signs + ibex.

[4] *fig. 280*

Panel 4 is the farthest from the entrance; it is very confused and includes huge figures whose uncertain outlines run up into the ceiling. However, one group is perfectly legible: two cervids, turned in opposite directions, are superimposed upon one another,[5] and superimposed over both of them is a particularly beautiful ibex. The cervid with its head on the left has a hump above its withers and (as L. Méroc pointed out in connection with figures in the Cougnac cave) is a Megaceros deer, a member of the deer family with very large antlers. This panel is devoted to cervids and ibexes, which corresponds perfectly with its location in the remotest part of the cave.

[5] *fig. 282*

Panel 5, nearly 7 yards long, is an inextricable tangle of unfinished outlines; it is placed directly opposite the compositions on the right-hand wall, as in the Chabot cave and at La Baume Latrone. Out of the jumbled lines a certain number of double-circle signs and three animal figures detach themselves clearly[6]: at the center of the panel an ox and a horse, facing different directions, are superimposed, and farther back, directly opposite the two cervids on Panel 4, there is a stag.

[6] *fig. 281*

Panel 6 is located to the left of the entrance, facing Panel 1. Like the latter, it has one mammoth[7]; there is also the unmistakable head of a cervid facing a large figure that is extremely unprecise, in which Breuil thought could be seen the head of a feline.

[7] *fig. 283*

The signs at Pair-non-Pair are in the archaic form of the abstract signs: Panels 1, 2, 3, and 5 have circles or ovals outlined twice. This is the form that representations of the female sexual parts assume in Period II. Series of male signs—short strokes—appear in every panel; in Panel 5, over the ox/horse group, there is a double line of dots.

All the animal figures correspond to Style II by their common emphasis upon the structural line of the back, the raised withers, and by the fading away of the peripheral details (horns, legs, tails).

LA GRÈZE

MARQUAY, DORDOGNE, FRANCE

The site was hastily excavated in 1904 by Dr. Ampoulange, who discovered the engravings. The Abbé Breuil made a drawing of the engraved bison, and he and D. Peyrony attempted to date the industrial remains.

The works consist of a few deeply incised engravings in the archaic style, plus the extremely damaged remains of a bison of later date. They are all situated in the chamber of a shallow cave that receives daylight, which is true of most works belonging to Style II. The industrial objects seem to have come from at least two strata: one is certainly Magdalenian and no doubt related to the damaged bison in low relief; the other, older level cannot be dated as closely as we should like. Opinion is divided between the Gravettian and the Solutrean. This uncertainty notwithstanding, there is sufficient evidence to assign the works to an early period of cave art. The over-all organization of the figures remains unclear: except for the famous engraved figure of a bison,[1] all we have are incomplete outlines of legs and hindquarters, and one set of lines in which it is perhaps possible to make out an ibex. The engraved bison occupies the most exposed part of the wall, and its state of preservation is in marked contrast to the vague lines around it. It is very characteristic of Style II, the whole figure hung, so to speak, on the very sinuous dorsal line and seemingly thrusting forward. The horns are rendered in frontal view, and details become the more sketchy the farther they are from the line of the back—the extremities of the legs and the tail do not show at all.

[1] *fig. 286*

LA MOUTHE

LES EYZIES, DORDOGNE, FRANCE

The engravings in this cave were discovered in 1895 by a boy named Gaston Bertoumeyrou, who alerted Émile Rivière, the prehistorian. The Abbé Breuil began his pictorial inventory in 1900 and completed it between 1924 and 1930. The removal of detritus from the gallery, which Rivière accomplished for a distance of 142 yards, was resumed in 1959 by a group of speleologists and led to the discovery of new works.

The decoration of La Mouthe is especially rich and complex, with works from Periods II, III, and IV identifiable by stylistic features very much in line with those of other works from the Les Eyzies area. There were extensive evidences of habitation at the entrance; some of these had been scattered about the neighboring fields by the owners of the site, and the rest were cleared away rather than scientifically examined once the engravings were found. As a result it is hard to establish correlations between the works and the industrial objects found at the entrance. The portion of the sanctuary considered here is located more than 100 yards from the entrance in a small chamber, the first in which decorations occur. The engravings on the left-hand wall and the ceiling are very large (5 to 10 feet) and vigorously incised.[1] They form a homogeneous group of four oxen and one horse. Their location well inside the cave would suggest that they should be attributed to a relatively late epoch, but their stylistic character—in this part of the Dordogne, where the relative chronology is based on numerous examples—rules out anything but Style II. The animals exhibit to the highest degree the strong dorsal line that projects them forward; the horns are either in absolute profile or in frontal view; there are no peripheral details. The Abbé Breuil noted with reason their similarity to the figures at Pair-non-Pair. La Mouthe shows clearly how cave decoration was moved progressively farther inside: this first panel is in Style II, the next in Style III, and in the back-cave areas a majority of the figures is in Style IV. *(See also pages 319, 353).*

[1] *figs. 284, 287*

GORGE D'ENFER, ABRI DU POISSON

LES EYZIES, DORDOGNE, FRANCE

The rock shelter was discovered in 1892 by P. Girod; the sculpture was noted in 1912 by J. Marsan.

¹ *fig. 285*

The contents of the shelter, which is about 10 yards long, were subjected to scientific study by D. Peyrony in 1917. The levels included a layer of Aurignacian proper, a barren layer containing traces of extensive peeling from the roof (which rules out the possibility that the sculptures could be Aurignacian), and a layer of mature Gravettian containing Noailles engraving tools (Perigordian V). The figures on the ceiling may thus be reasonably attributed to the last-mentioned period. All the works except the fish for which the shelter is named are in very poor condition; in fact, nothing is left except for fragments found in the layers and very faint marks on the ceiling. Only the fish,¹ which is about 3½ feet in length and executed in raised-field relief, survives in a remarkably good state of preservation. Attempts were made to remove it surreptitiously and convey it to a foreign museum: it shows marks of interrupted cutting around the edges. It is a male salmon, very accurately rendered—we see the hook-shaped jaws of the male that has reached sexual maturity. Under the head, there is another figure in light relief; D. Peyrony thought it might be a bird, the Abbé Breuil a rhinoceros—both suggestions were tentative. I wonder whether it might not be the hindquarters of a bison, slipped under the fish in a manner which can be observed in low reliefs at Le Cap Blanc and Angles-sur-l'Anglin, and in many paintings. The hypothesis is to some extent corroborated by the fact that when we trace, on the basis of the supposed hindquarters, the outline of a bison (using that from the Abri Reverdit, for example), we find the hatched mane in its proper place, in the form of the short strokes which are visible above the salmon. Moreover, on the lower edge of the rock, where vandals attempted to cut away the fish, there is still to be seen the remains of an incision that could be the front edge of the bison's thigh. This salmon seems to date from the end of the Gravettian, but we have no stylistic reference, since it is the only fish from its presumed period. At the same time, the raised-field technique is rather skillfully handled for so early a period; this, in conjunction with the state of preservation of this work on a ceiling otherwise so dilapidated, would suggest a later date. However, there are arguments in favor of an earlier dating; there is an example of raised-field relief (though much more stiff in execution) in the Abri Labatut; and in another connection, even if it is granted that the animal associated with the salmon is a bison, this would not be enough to prove that they constituted a group. Therefore we must leave open the possibility that geological and climatic chance have combined to preserve the fish as the only surviving evidence of a composition the other parts of which have fallen to the ground.

LOS HORNOS

SAN FELICES DE BUELNA, SANTANDER, SPAIN

The cave was discovered in 1903 by H. Alcade del Rio. The mountain in which it is located is called La Peña de los Hornos; "los Hornos" means "the ovens." The Abbé Breuil made excavations there in 1909–10 with the Abbé J. Bouyssonie and Dr. Hugo Obermaier.

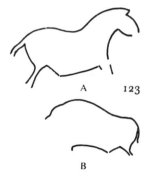

A   123

B

¹ *figs. 687–689*
² *fig. 288; chart* LV

123 *(left)*. LOS HORNOS. The horse (A) and the bison (B) on the wall of the entrance.

The cave consists of a first chamber, into which daylight enters, and several more chambers that form a labyrinth at the end of an intervening corridor 77 yards long. The entrance, which has traces of a daylight sanctuary, is thus separated by that distance from the engravings¹ which decorate the inner chambers and which are in a later style. Here we shall discuss only the engravings at the entrance:² they consist of the remains of a horse and a bison (fig. 123, A and B). The figures are alike in style and treatment; they are deeply incised and are held to be among the most reliably accredited cave figures of the Aurignacian.

During the excavation of 1910, Breuil found among the archaeological deposits a bone plaque (the frontal bone of a horse) on which is deeply incised a horse's hindquarters; this engraving has been compared to that of the animal engraved on the wall. The age of the bone figure would at least appear to be established by the nature of the layer in which it was found. "The filling... included a bottom layer of the Mousterian, above that a typical Aurignacian layer *covering some Solutrean,* and over that some Old Magdalenian" (Breuil, *Quatre cents siècles...,* page 352). According to Breuil, since the horse on the wall is Aurignacian in style and is like the horse engraved on the bone found in the Aurignacian layer, no further proof is needed to date the former. Yet two questions must be asked: first, are the wall engraving and the engraving on the bone plaque really alike? second, is that "Aurignacian" layer really Aurignacian? The merest glance at the two engravings suffices to answer the first question: all they have in common is that both represent part of a horse's body, and both are rather deeply incised.³ The bison in the outer chamber is really like the horse in the same area of the sanctuary; the horse engraved on bone might be compared to a dozen other figures, but not to the one adduced here.

³ *chart* LIV

To answer the second question, we need only turn back to Breuil's 1911 publication (p.88): "Then, over a rather limited part of the corridor, an Early Magdalenian hearth was recognized. It was set over an intermediate clayey level, *very extensively reworked at many spots and without apparent stratification, containing flints, some characteristically Solutrean, others characteristically Aurignacian....* At the very bottom, the frontal bone of a horse was picked up, and engraved on it in broad, deep lines was the hindquarters of a horse, the drawing *absolutely identical* with the one in the entrance way." (Our italics.) How much weight are we to give the archaeological determination? Once the excavation has been completed, nobody can go back over it, and forty-one years later the Solutrean level is still as mixed with the Aurignacian as it was in 1911. Thus the engraving on bone is dated only within a range of 15,000 years. Moreover, it is so far from being characteristic (unlike the horse on the wall) that the matter of its dating is without real significance. The horse at the entrance, like the damaged bison and ibex accompanying it, belongs either to a highly developed Style II or Style III—that is, close to the Solutrean. It has the archaic dorsal line, but already considerably softened: we are reminded of the horses at Le Roc de Sers, Pech Merle, and Lascaux, with their more firmly fixed forequarters and hindquarters, and their accentuated withers. *(See also page 318.)*

GARGAS

AVENTIGNAN, HAUTES-PYRÉNÉES, FRANCE

Known for centuries, the cave was explored at the close of the nineteenth century by Félix Regnault, who discovered the famous cave-bear ossuary and the negative hands outlined in red and black. From 1911 on, E. Cartailhac, H. Neuville, and the Abbé Breuil resumed the excavating and undertook a study of the engravings. Drawings of animals by the Abbé Breuil.

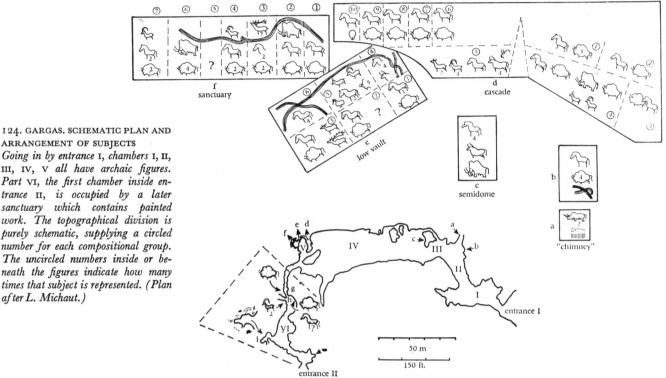

124. GARGAS. SCHEMATIC PLAN AND ARRANGEMENT OF SUBJECTS
Going in by entrance I, *chambers* I, II, III, IV, V *all have archaic figures. Part* VI, *the first chamber inside entrance* II, *is occupied by a later sanctuary which contains painted work. The topographical division is purely schematic, supplying a circled number for each compositional group. The uncircled numbers inside or beneath the figures indicate how many times that subject is represented. (Plan after L. Michaut.)*

The Gargas cave is fairly large, nearly 150 yards long, and varies in width from 22 to 44 yards; it is readily accessible from one end to the other. Daylight enters directly as far as the back of chamber I, and its reflection illuminates the first major turn in the cave, 44 yards from the entrance. These conditions may account for the existence of figures in Style II quite far inside the cave. However, the lack of lighting methods certainly were less important than were psychological reasons in accounting for the fact that the oldest sanctuaries occur close to the cave entrances. The front area of the Gargas cave was occupied by layers containing relics of habitation, part of which belonged to the Late Paleolithic—Chatelperronian, Aurignacian proper, Late and terminal Gravettian. The fact that these different deposits are so chronologically circumscribed is valuable for purposes of dating the works, which for the most part belong to Style II. Moreover, the uppermost Gravettian horizon yielded a few plaquettes engraved with animals, close in style to those on the walls. Topographically, the cave decoration shows extremely interesting subdivisions. Hands in negative[1] (about 150 of them, in all) appear on the walls of chamber I and again in the front part of chamber IV, just past the bend formed by chambers II and III. Following them, the right-side wall of the rear half of the big chamber is filled with meandering lines drawn with the fingers on the clay film. This distribution of hands and meanders may be explained simply by the consistency of the wall surface, but this fact does not permit us to prove that they belong to the same period. Chamber I has a variety of signs in black and red, both short strokes and dots (two short strokes at the left, two at the right, each group in a recess); chamber II has a spread of red dots in a semidome on the left. In chamber IV, a row of short strokes in red marks off roughly the farthest extent of the hands and the meandering lines. Finally, in chamber III, a semidome on the right is completely coated with red.

The animal figures fall within four areas of the cave, seemingly without relation to the decorative scheme outlined above. In chamber II, on the right, an uphill gallery opens containing at the bottom a bison/horse group (*b* on the plan) in Style IV; it is Magdalenian, which proves that the cave was used as a sanctuary much later than the deposits in the entrance would lead us to suppose. Nearly at the top of this steep gallery, in a recess on the left, there are rows of short strokes and dots (*a*), which is normal in a place without egress. The Abbé Breuil discerned a rhinoceros there, which would also be normal, though the unfinished outline may not justify so precise a determination. Passing into chamber IV, in an area (*c*) from which it is still easy to return to the daylit sections, we find archaic figures on the right, some of them engraved on the soft surface of the vault springings near the ceiling,[2] others on the hard wall of a semidome situated to the right of the turning.[3] These figures together form a coherent whole on the bovid/horse/mammoth theme. The third area where figures occur consists of the long spread of meandering lines drawn with fingers, which covers the right-hand wall of the further half of chamber IV: among the meandering lines one can make out a certain number of animal figures. The fourth set of figures[4] is the most important in size and variety, and covers the walls of a recess at the right-hand end of the same chamber (V; *d, e, f*).

[1] *figs. 8, 289–293*

[2] *figs. 24, 304*   [3] *fig. 93*

[4] *figs. 77, 294–303*

Admittedly, the over-all theme of Gargas is not too coherent. The signs at the entrance, at the further end of the ascending gallery, and in the passageway leading to the fourth chamber form a pattern, but one cannot say exactly to which set of figures it refers. The portions covered by meanders and such animal outlines as can be made out among them may have served as the zone of unfinished outlines for the recess in the back and for the semidome at the nearer end of the fourth chamber. The figures in the semidome seem contemporary with some of those in the recess: the entire sanctuary would then be represented by the entrance and passageway signs, and the two areas with engraved animals, between which are located the unfinished outlines—the whole attributable to the Gravettian. The problem of the 150 hands remains untouched.

Negative imprints of hands, surrounded by red or black color, are not numerous in Paleolithic art. They are found in different epochs: in the Gravettian (Abri Labatut, and possibly Gargas and Tibiran); in the course of Period III (Pech Merle, Rocamadour, El Castillo); and in the period of Early Style IV (Marsoulas, Bernifal, Font-de-Gaume, Les Combarelles, Pindal). Those at Gargas have no organic connection with the rest of the decoration and hence cannot be attributed *a priori* to the earliest period. We might give them the benefit of the doubt, statistically speaking, and assume that they date from the same period as most of the rest of the figures—the mature Gravettian: they would then occupy a position definable by the majority of examples found elsewhere. Unfortunately, the examples diverge: at La Baume Latrone, Rocamadour, and Bernifal the hands are at the entrance to the sanctuary; at Les Combarelles, they are in a passage leading to the innermost part of the cave; at Pech Merle they are at the entrance to a side chamber and in the middle part of the cave; at Font-de-Gaume, Marsoulas, the Bayol cave, Pech Merle, El Castillo, and El Pindal they are in the middle area. At Gargas they are found in two areas (chambers I and IV), each leading to groups of animal figures dating from the Gravettian—in the entrance chamber and just before the meandering lines in the fourth chamber. It is possible to see in this arrangement the proof that they were part of the Gravettian sanctuary, but this proof is not based on comparative data. The hands at Gargas are also exceptional in that they occur in compact groups and that they are deformed, or seem to lack parts of some fingers.

⁵ *fig. 93*

The first of the animal groups, in the semidome of chamber IV, is particularly striking because of its archaism. We see heads and indefinite dorsal outlines, a bovid with horns in frontal view,⁵ four horses, a very stiffly drawn mammoth, and numerous hatchings or rows of short strokes. Compositions in which the mammoth plays the part of complementary animal are frequent at different periods (Pech Merle, Rouffignac, Font-de-Gaume, Bernifal, La Croze at Gontran, Altamira, La Mouthe).

The second of the animal groups, in the deep recess (v), is a complex one and reflects at least two periods. On the right-hand portion of the stalagmite near the entrance, and the end of the corridor, also on the right, there are figures fairly close to those in the semidome of chamber IV, which are attributable to the Late Gravettian on the basis of incised pebbles. The left-hand portion of the stalagmite and the ceiling that continues it are covered with a network of figures in a much more mature style, already assimilable to Style III.

Leaving out the hands, whose epoch has still to be determined, Gargas as a whole seems thus to be divisible into three periods. The over-all design of the sanctuary seems to go back to the Gravettian (signs, semidome, meandering lines, a part of the side recess); additions seem to have been made between the terminal Gravettian and the Early Magdalenian in the side recess; lastly, two later Magdalenian figures were engraved in the uphill gallery.

It should be noted that deep in the cave a man-made passage leads to another underground cavity, VI—Gargas II—which was a separate cave in Paleolithic times and is decorated with a badly damaged composition in Early Style IV. Still extant are some entrance signs, a panel of signs in a recess at the left of the former entrance (i), two ibexes (h) at the turning in the chamber known as the Casteret gallery, and two or three bison at the junction with the main cave (g).

 STYLE III

STYLE III

The decorated objects of various kinds in Styles I, II, and III include only 19 percent of the 600 such works that can be dated to within one stratigraphic division, Style IV accounting for the remaining 81 percent. About 30 works, less than 6 percent of the total, can be properly attributed to Period III (Solutrean and Early Magdalenian). Some of these are dated with complete stratigraphic reliability: those from the Solutrean (Les Jean-Blancs, the blocks of Le Roc de Sers, the one at Bourdeilles, a few works from Isturitz, Badegoule, and Altamira), and a few works from the Early Magdalenian (I and II) found at Laugerie Haute and Pech de la Boissière. A good many of these works lend themselves sufficiently to analysis to confirm the characteristics of the two principal sites—Le Roc de Sers and Bourdeilles.

[1] *chart* XLI
What distinguishes Style III and gives it its peculiar character is the survival of the forms of Style II in a technique now completely mastered.[1] From Style II, the construction is retained that is based on a very sinuous dorsal line; the horses' necks and shoulders are high-arched, the bison's humps do not as yet rise as high as the overdeveloped manes of Style IV will later do, and the necks of the bulls and the ibexes are powerfully arched. Limbs are generally detailed right down to the hoofs, but they still keep something of the subordinate character they had in the earlier stages: disproportionately short, they give the animals a low-slung appearance. As a result, the bodies seem huge—a circumstance that gave rise to the theory that artists had a predilection for illustrating Paleolithic pregnant animals, a theory hard to support when the animals represented are obviously males. Another survival of Style II is the manner of individually grafting characteristic details onto the structural line of the withers and body, so that there results a certain strangeness in the positioning of the horns and the ears and in the movement of the legs—a strangeness that will disappear in the following style. More than one angle of perspective is employed for representing horns and antlers: frontal view and absolute profile occur, but the most frequent is the three-quarter view, which the Abbé Breuil termed "half-twisted."

[2] *chart* XLV
The best-dated examples of Style III are low reliefs, and it is known that at Le Roc de Sers, as at Bourdeilles, the modeling exhibits remarkable mastery. The same is true of the paintings, with particularly good examples at Lascaux. It is not impossible that the shadows cast by low reliefs played a part in the conventionalizing of the details in painted modeling. Plenty of examples show that Paleolithic art was anything but "free": the female statuettes in Style II prove that the artists were not making portraits of their wives but copying copies of copies to such a degree that they finally arrived at anatomically absurd figures.[2] It is hard to prove that the wall paintings are a sort of low relief executed in *trompe-l'oeil*, but many of the details suggest that such a possibility should not be ruled out.

[3] *charts* XXXV, XLII
The chronological boundaries of Style III are not precise. It would be astonishing if the opposite were true, for there is no sign of any clean break with the connecting styles. Le Roc de Sers and Bourdeilles fall within the Solutrean (around 17,000 B.C.). Lascaux is dated within the Early Magdalenian (toward 15,000 B.C.), but the cave was frequented over a period of several centuries. We know that the animals in Style III at Lascaux are accompanied by quadrangular signs, and that some later, more developed figures occur in the vicinity of brace-shaped signs and claviforms.[3] Quadrangular and brace-shaped signs are found at Le Gabillou, accompanying animals in Style III and others that tend to Early Style IV. At Villars only brace-shaped signs occur, with animals in mature Style III. At Pech Merle, as also in the Dordogne, the brace-shaped follow the quadrangular signs, and there are animals in two stages of Style III. At La Pasiega and El Castillo we also find brace-shaped in sequence with quadrangular signs (Castillo), brace-shaped and claviform signs (Pasiega), along with animals in two stages of Style III and Early Style IV. At Las Chimeneas we have quadrangular signs with animals in Style III; on the Altamira ceiling we find only claviform signs with animals in Early Style IV. Consequently, it is demonstrated that the sequence of signs—quadrangular to brace-shaped to claviform—corresponds with successive stages in the development from Style III to Style IV. Now, at Le Roc de Sers and Bourdeilles the animals in Style III are Solutrean, while those in Style IV are dated (on the basis of overwhelming evidence supplied by decorated objects) from the Middle Magdalenian. The limits of Style III are thus narrowed down, covering the Solutrean and the Early Magdalenian (Magdalenian I and II), or the period from 17,000 to 13,000 B.C. according to carbon-14 dating.

LE ROC DE SERS

SERS, CHARENTE, FRANCE

The sculptured blocks in low relief at this site were discovered in 1927 by Dr. Henri-Martin. Originally they were lined up to form a frieze along a wall; their dating is reliable thanks to the fact that they were found between two levels of mature Solutrean. Further excavation in 1950 by Mlle. Henri-Martin and R. Lantier led to the discovery of two more sculptured blocks.

The site is a rock shelter at the foot of a cliff. The blocks were aligned on a ledge along the back wall. All but a few had fallen face down before the close of the Solutrean occupancy of the shelter. The original arrangement has been reconstituted as far as possible, but their exact relationships are not yet sure, nor is the fact that we have the complete set. Consequently it is difficult to form a definite idea of the layout of the sanctuary, the only sculptured-block sanctuary that has come under observation so far. In its present state we have, from right to left, the "bison/boar," horses, the "man pursued by a musk ox," horses again, and a man. In addition there is a block with ibexes facing each other, some separate sculptures of ibexes and bison and one head of a bird or snake.[1] These elements are sufficient to indicate the presence of a bison/horse/ibex composition which includes the "wounded man" theme, as at Lascaux and Villars.

[1] *figs. 305–313*

The block with the "bison/boar" is a very interesting example of recutting of the kind known from other low reliefs—at Le Cap Blanc and Angles-sur-l'Anglin, for instance. On it we can see a horse in Style III at its most characteristic, and a bison of the same workmanship, very close to the back-to-back bison at Lascaux or the bison in the last side chamber at Font-de-Gaume, head low and forequarters firmly planted. There is a split in the stone near the head which has been recarved to produce the head of an indefinable animal that some have taken to be a boar.

As for the "man pursued by a musk ox,"[2] I find this identification hard to support. Fossil remains of the musk ox are rare indeed, and the only feature to justify such an identification is that the base of the horns are joined on a median line. This detail is in fact peculiar to the musk ox, but there all resemblance ceases: the rest of the body is that of a charging bison, and there are several examples of bison horns treated much as these are. Moreover, the bison's body has in part been recarved, as at Mouthiers and Le Cap Blanc.

[2] *fig. 305*

The style of the figures is altogether remarkable, and their exact date permits us to make them typify Style III. Their stylistic orginality seems to have escaped the Abbé Breuil, who wrote of them: "The art is consummate, not at all an art at its beginning; it has all the features of the second-cycle art, and there is no difference between this art and that of the Early Magdalenian sculptured sites in the Poitou and the Dordogne. These are very emphatic low reliefs executed by a master's hand. The horses are all pregnant mares with short legs, but the two battling ibexes are old males" (*Quatre cents siècles...*, p. 332). The consummate artistry and the masterful hand are beyond doubt: a good fifteen millennia have gone by since the earliest Aurignacian graffiti, and the statuettes from Kostienki and Lespugue, dating from the period between the Gravettian and the Solutrean, were some four or five thousand years old when these reliefs were made. I cannot agree, however, that their technical excellence is enough to associate them with the Magdalenian works at Le Cap Blanc or Angles. To do this would be like saying a Greek capital and a Gothic capital were contemporary because the men who made them had the same mastery of accentuated low relief. The most pertinent characteristic of these strange animals with distended bodies and very short legs was explained by Breuil with the cliché, "pregnant mares"; but by this criterion, all the animals at Le Roc de Sers are pregnant, including the bison whose great humps and knotted manes attest their maleness, and even the "old male ibexes." This strong contrast between body and limbs is the distinctive feature of Style III wherever it appears (Le Gabillou, Lascaux, Pech Merle, Gallery 2 at Le Portel, and elsewhere). If the style of the figures leads one to think immediately of Lascaux, the groups of the man charged by the bison and of the facing ibexes only strengthen the impression. It was comparison of these figures at Le Roc de Sers and those at Bourdeilles (which date from the Solutrean) with similar ones at Lascaux and Pech Merle that, since 1955, has caused me to date the oldest portions of the latter caves from the Late Solutrean or from a period very close to it.

BOURDEILLES (LE FOURNEAU DU DIABLE)

DORDOGNE, FRANCE

The sculptured block at this site was discovered by D. Peyrony in the course of his excavation in 1924.

The exactness of the chronological location of this block makes it one of the most valuable documents of Paleolithic art. It was found in close association with the Upper Solutrean (layer C of the upper terrace), corresponding to the last period of the "willow leaf" and notched points (16,000–15,000 B.C., according to carbon-14 dating). It shows ten low reliefs and two engravings, representing oxen, one horse, two herbivorous mammals, and ibexes or cervids.[1] Portions of the figures have been damaged, but two of the oxen in low relief are practically intact. With their small heads, pinched necks, and massive bodies with relatively short legs, they are comparable to the Lascaux figures. Although the Abbé Breuil said of them, "The horns are shown in profile and not at all in twisted perspective..." (*Quatre cents siècles...*, p. 315), the design of the undamaged horns corresponds to what he himself called "half-twisted perspective" (that is, the foremost horn has a single curve, the back one is sinuous). This perspective is normal in Style III, and there are dozens of examples of it at Lascaux. No dated figure of an ox comes closer to the oxen at Lascaux than these at Bourdeilles.

[1] *fig. 95*

LASCAUX

MONTIGNAC, DORDOGNE, FRANCE

This famous cave was discovered in 1940, quite accidentally, by two local boys, Ravidat and Marsal. A number of publications have been devoted to it, but none as yet complete. An inventory of the countless engravings, undertaken by the Abbé A. Glory, is in course of preparation.

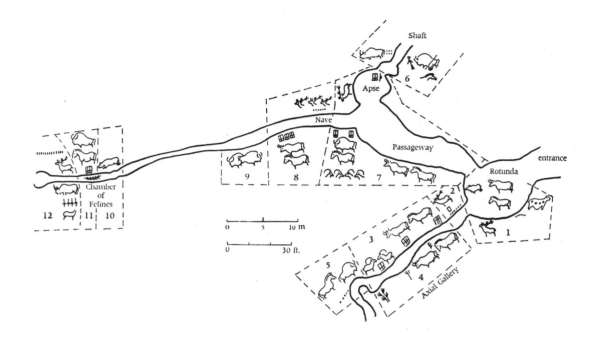

125. LASCAUX. SCHEMATIC PLAN WITH COMPOSITIONS
The numbers 1 to 12 indicate the compositions, which are represented by conventionalized drawings of animals. As may be seen, their topographical distribution is very clear. Note especially the positions of the rows of dots (1, 2, 5, 6, 8), of the cervids (1, 2, 7, 12), of the bison (5, 7, 9, 11), of the ibexes (3, 7), of the rhinoceroses (6, 12), of the felines (10), and of the headless animal (12). Based on a diagram by the Service de l'Architecture.

The cave at Lascaux is about 110 yards long from end to end. It is one long corridor with an axial gallery and a shaft. Except for the latter, the cave presents only minor difficulties of access. If, as seems reasonably certain, the original entrance was about where the present one is, then the earliest paintings must occupy the first zone that did not receive daylight. This location does not rule out the possibility that the sanctuary is an old one, since from the Gravettian through the Early Magdalenian sanctuaries were never far from daylight. It has become customary to study Lascaux chamber by chamber: the decorations are so closely adapted to the shape of the cave that the divisions must have seemed no less natural to Paleolithic men than they do to prehistorians today. These natural divisons are the Rotunda, the Axial Gallery, the Passageway, the Apse, the Shaft, the Nave, and the Chamber of Felines.

[1] *figs. 72, 96, 314, 328*

THE ROTUNDA[1]

Painted in modeled black and in red and black, this group of figures constitutes the most monumental frieze in all Paleolithic art. Some of these figures are more than 17 feet in length, whereas the biggest bison at Altamira are only about 7 feet long, and those at Niaux average about 3 feet. The composition is a remarkably balanced one: its core is constituted by five great bovines, a row of two facing a row of three. Those on the left are accompanied by seven horses headed in the same direction, those on the right by two small horses not fully rendered. This inversion of proportions between the two elements of the main group may not be fortuitous (cf. Niaux, see page 362). Outside the group on the left, bringing up the rear, is the animal that is known as the "unicorn." It is an enigmatic creature that seems to have two long straight horns; from these oddly enough, have come its name. The Abbé Lemozi has noticed that the horns were probably the tail of the bull in front of this animal. If that explanation is not accepted, the animal still remains a mystery. The most extraordinary creatures have been suggested, from the Siberian *elasmotherium* (rhinoceros) and the Tibetan *pantholops* to a disguised man; I myself wrote that it looked like an animal skin with two men inside it. Without the horns and with a longer tail, I should be tempted to suggest a panther painted on the basis of oral tradition. There were panthers in Western Europe during the Upper Paleolithic, though they were rare; this figure shows the rounded head, the sloping back, the belly close to the ground, and the spots characteristic of the beast, rendered in as artificial a manner as the giraffes or rhinoceroses in medieval art. Whether it is a mythological feline or a newly created monster, its subject is that of a back-cave or marginal figure and it is placed correspondingly. The bulls on the right, too, have their marginal animal—a little bear curiously concealed in the black modeling of the next-to-last bull's belly.

The large female signs, so numerous elsewhere in this cave, do not appear in this composition; however, the signs accompanying the bovines on the right are different from those on the left. On the right, the first bull has a barbed sign on the shoulder, the second an equivalent sign (a straight line with two short strokes crossing it at the base) above the withers, the third a single straight line above the withers. Each of the bovines on the left has two small parallel lines against the upper part of its muzzle. The signs in the form of straight lines (which some have seen as spear-throwers) belong to a morphological set so complete that they can safely be identified as virility symbols. The double strokes, on the other hand, are ambiguous; the process of schematic degeneration sometimes led, in different epochs, to a similar representation for male as well as female symbols. At Le Gabillou there are triple strokes that are unmistakably rectangular signs which have lost two sides. Considering that our two groups of bovines are clearly opposed to each other—those on the right show clear indications of their sex, those on the left do not—I wonder whether the short strokes may not be female notations. There are still other signs within this first composition, and they are no less interesting. In front of the forehead of the second beast in the left-hand group there is a composite sign in red: one stroke with two lateral dots/three strokes/one stroke with two lateral dots. I believe this is a case of paired signs; the sign made of one short stroke combined with dots belongs to a series whose complete development can be traced on the walls at Le Gabillou and Lascaux.[2] Archaeology and anthropology, moreover, supply dozens of examples of virility that is represented in this form. On the body of the second bull in the right-hand group we see three groups of double strokes, and a row of dots. There is also a brace-shaped sign, having the particular form that this sign takes at Lascaux. Lastly, above the entrance to the Passageway, a group of red signs seems to confirm the hypothesis that the double short strokes at Lascaux are female signs: there are four of them, plus one barbed sign.

A few figures still remain to be analyzed. There are, in the area of the legs of the bulls on the right, three red bovines that bear the same relation to the larger figures as do the horses in the left-hand composition. Directly in line with the muzzle of the first bovine on the left is a figure vaguely resembling a ghost with two round eyes.[3] Between the two groups of oxen are several little stags; a similar one seems to cross the breast of the second bull on the right. These small animals all move in an opposite direction from the rest of the composition. They frame the exit toward the Axial Gallery and possibly serve as entrance animals to it. The paintings in the Rotunda seem to form two complementary groups: on the right, big bulls and red bovines accompanied by male signs; on the left, cows and horses accompanied by female signs.

THE AXIAL GALLERY[4]

The composition in the Axial Gallery confirms and even enriches what has just been said about that in the Rotunda. The similarity of the formulas used in both is so striking that these compositions served as the starting point of Mme. Laming-Emperaire's theory concerning cave decorations. The two facing walls, taken together, form three groups of figures: the central group consists of two gigantic bovines, a black bull on the left wall, and an enormous head on the right.[5] The decoration as a whole begins and ends with stags. We have just seen that the little stags in the Rotunda may serve as entrance animals to the Axial Gallery. Even if this is not the case, one sees at the right of the entrance a large stag accompanied by paired signs—rectangle and short stroke, row of dots. And at the far end on the left, in front of the horse falling backward, a great spread of antlers has been drawn coming up from the ground.

The first composition includes, on the left-hand wall, four cows and three small, incompletely rendered horses.[6] The accompanying signs—double strokes and crosses—are very odd. There are many crosses at Lascaux and Le Gabillou; the fact that they are often flanked by barbed signs suggests that they are female signs. One of the beasts has what looks like a dart stuck in its chest, as is the case with certain ibexes at Niaux. On the right-hand wall we find an extremely complicated composition.[7] The center is formed by a cow from whose back grow stag antlers treated to look like barbed signs; single, double, and triple strokes accompany the cow, and its flank is marked by a half-barbed line. Underneath is a horse from whose chest emerge not two legs but two rows of dots. Under the horse's belly are the same paired signs that appear in front of the muzzle of one of the beasts in the Rotunda. This piling up of symbols that we find here is somewhat baffling. The Axial Gallery, particularly the first composition, strikes me as Paleolithic art's most elaborate venture into the abstract. The left-hand half of this composition on the right wall is occupied by two of the famous "Chinese horses," which are surrounded with signs: barbed signs or short strokes that might be regarded as arrows, and, close to the first horse, the female signs characteristic of Lascaux's two principal periods—a compartmented rectangle and a brace-shaped sign. The second and principal composition is based, on the left-hand wall, on a huge black bull with a barbed sign in front of its nose[8]; on the right-hand wall, on a black cow with a rectangular sign and a short stroke in front of its nose.[9] Above this cow is a large bovine head. Several little horses accompany the cow, as in the right-hand group in the Rotunda, and several bovines have been drawn inside the body of the black bull opposite, which are like the three red bovines accompanying the bulls in the left-hand composition in the Rotunda. The third composition, on the left, is a procession of horses, one of which is accompanied by a barbed sign[10]; the last horse seems to be falling backward into a recess in the wall.[11] On the right we see two facing ibexes, a theme familiar from other sites, with a rectangular sign between them.[12]

The Axial Gallery gets narrower toward the end; continuing on we find, as we will again in the Nave, a bison/horse group[13] completely cut off from the rest of the composition, the over-all theme of which is ox/horse. Further on, the passage becomes a constricted tunnel where we find a few engraved horses and, at the very end, the red markings that so often indicate the end of the decorated parts of caves. The Axial Gallery as a whole, then, consists of two alternating groups: cow/rectangles/horses, and bull/barbed sign/cows, both groups flanked by stags; there are complementary ibexes, and an isolated bison/horse composition.

THE PASSAGEWAY[14]

This is the least well preserved portion of the cave. The engravings here have still to be inventoried, and the painted figures are extremely faint. From the chronological point of view, this is probably the oldest part of the cave. The decoration seems based upon a large ox/horse+ibex group, with at least one bison/horse composition. The figures link up with those in the Apse.

[2] *charts* XXXIII, XXXVI, XXXVII

[3] *fig. 328*

[4] *figs. 10, 73, 78, 81, 97, 98, 106, 112, 315–317, 319, 320, 325, 326, 329, 330; chart* XXXVIII

[5] *fig. 329*

[6] *fig. 319*

[7] *fig. 317*

[8] *fig. 320*
[9] *fig. 316*

[10] *fig. 325*
[11] *fig. 315*
[12] *fig. 316*

[13] *fig. 330*

[14] *fig. 333*

We must await the complete inventory of the engravings before we can grasp the decorative whole that was constituted by the Passageway, the Apse, and the Nave. At present all we have to go on is four sets of figures: a bison/horse+ibex composition, an ox/horse composition, a group of stags, and two bison. The first composition is on the wall facing the Apse. At the top we find a row of engraved ibexes,[15] separated into two groups, and between the groups a sketchy rectangular sign such as we found in the Axial Gallery. Underneath, we see five horses and one bison.[16] The first horse faces a rectangular sign, and the bison at the other end of the row faces a similar sign. The first horse has a wound mark with a very long median line, and a barbed sign; the second horse has seven wound marks with long median lines and, on the withers, a hooked sign of the Gabillou-Lascaux type: thus, on each animal are paired signs. The bison, in its turn, is marked with seven parallel strokes. There seems, therefore, to be an alternation of symbols between the bison streaked with male signs and the horse marked with an equal number of female signs. The second composition[17] was apparently revised several times, though without changing the orginal ox/horse theme. A large bovine, apparently a cow, is surrounded by little horses which in part she overlaps and by rectangular signs. Disguised by the cow's body is the engraving of a rearing horse. To the left of the composition we notice a brace-shaped sign.

Facing this group is a frieze of five stag heads[18] which must have marked the end of the great decorative whole formed by the Passageway and the Nave. Farther along, as in the Axial Gallery, we find two bison back to back, unusually fine in quality.[19] Beyond the Nave, the cave narrows down to one long passage terminating in the so-called Chamber of Felines.

[15] fig. 338

[16] fig. 318

[17] fig. 321

[18] fig. 322

[19] fig. 331

THE CHAMBER OF FELINES

This chamber, except for its proportions, is comparable to the deep gallery at Niaux: in both cases, the most singular representations have been gathered together. Over a length of eleven yards a perfect maze of animals and signs of every shape constitutes, as it were, Paleolithic man's most concentrated attempt to convince us that his art expresses something other than vague figures of magic. It is extraordinary that so many prehistorians' eyes catch the smallest stumble of a wounded bison and the slightest resemblance of a sign to a fence or a hunter's snare, yet fail to see the shapes or figures that do not fit in with their predetermined view. For if *everything* that can be seen is taken into account, no theory of hunters' magic is tenable—at least not in the summary form which it is likely to be given by an American or European who re-applies his reading about Australian aborigines. It is, of course, unthinkable that Paleolithic people, whose greatest technical achievement was hunting, would not have incorporated hunting images in their metaphysics or that their art would not have been one of wild animals, wounds, and blood, but their minds developed these images within a broader system. It is also unthinkable that Paleolithic men alone of all peoples, should have had a religion in which sexuality did not appear in one form or another, positively or negatively; but nothing about their art is explained by tracking down every hint of copulation between human beings or animals. The facts of subsistence and reproduction being the basis of the preoccupations of any society, it is only normal to find them given expression. The Old Testament and the New lead to the peaks of spirituality through a succession of hundreds of images of sheep, shepherds, and harvests, of barrenness and fertility, yet no one ever questions that these images are integrated into a metaphysical system.

There are about thirty animal figures and a great number of signs in the Chamber of Felines. The narrow entrance passage enlarges to form a series of small bell-shaped "rooms," each about a yard in diameter, occurring successively for a length of about eleven yards. The decoration can be divided into three main groups: (1) the felines, (2) the quadrangular signs, and (3) the rhinoceros and the stag. This arrangement already corresponds by definition to that of a complete sanctuary, with paired signs at the center and lions, stags, and rhinoceros on the periphery. As we are dealing here with the most peripheral composition in the Lascaux cave, we find female subjects poorly represented (three small bison/horse groups), and back-cave male subjects strongly represented (six large felines and one rhinoceros).

Lascaux is the only cave with a complete composition of animals of the feline family.[20] In the first part of the chamber, the two walls and the ceiling display six engravings of felines. These form a real group: one of the animals, a male, is shown tail up in the position of the feline who stakes out his territory with a stream of urine—indicated by a wavy line; on the opposite wall another figure, its sex not indicated, shows several wound marks in the form of hen tracks. Above the three felines on the right are a bison head, a horse's head, a horse in frontal view (this is very rare), and a rectangular sign intersected by a remarkable male sign— barbed, with two strokes at the base. At the end of the composition there is a painted sign that overlaps two engraved ibexes. A number of crosses and barbed signs complete the composition. This first group seems altogether classical, since we find horse and bison, paired signs in the center, and ibexes at one end. Its character as a back-cave composition is attested by the presence of the group of felines, which is itself composed as a group.

The composition of the paired signs divides the chamber into two halves. There are three rectangular signs, one of which is very elaborate.[21] One barbed sign painted in red is exactly like the barbed signs at Marsoulas; numerous lines and barbed signs complete this group, which probably includes the small bison and the horse's head immediately adjacent.

The last composition is a rather complex grouping. We note a sequence of painted and engraved horses

[20] fig. 332

[21] chart XXXVII

and a long row of painted strokes. This grouping includes engraved subjects which perhaps were not originally part of it: a stag's head, a barbed sign with a double arc at the base, and, contiguous with these, a short stroke with a double arc (a virility symbol) and a triangular sign formed of fan-shaped strokes.

On the opposite wall we find, first, a bison and a horse; then a rhinoceros and numerous strokes; finally the last, very unusual group. It contains the headless body of an ibex or stag, the two lines indicating the neck stopping short and leaving no doubt of the intentional character of the omission.[22] Headless animals, which have been found from Russia to Spain (Kostienki I, Les Combarelles, Bédeilhac, Niaux, Altamira), had a meaning that, at the present, cannot be discerned except by conjecture and vague anthropological parallels. The example at Lascaux is not entirely alone on its wall, for just above we find a group of signs having perhaps even greater interest.[23] These consist of four wound marks side by side, in the form of hen tracks, surmounted by four short strokes. It would be hard to find better confirmation of the vulva-wound assimilation, since these "wounds"-without-animals are accompanied, like simpler female signs, with a corresponding number of male strokes. Beyond the last element of the three compositions, we find a few more incised lines and, at the back of the chamber, red dots like those marking the termination of the narrow tunnel at the end of the Axial Gallery.

[22] *chart* XXVII

[23] *chart* XXXVII

THE APSE[24]

[4] *figs. 334–337*

Having drawn up an inventory of the large compositions in the Rotunda, Axial Gallery, Nave, and Chamber of Felines, we turn now to the area known as the Apse and the Shaft. The Apse is a small round chamber about five yards in diameter, covered with thousands of engraved lines. At the back opens the Shaft, approximately thirteen feet deep. There is no doubt that the Apse served for Lascaux as the zone of unfinished outlines and scrawls. Originally, it would seem, this had not been its function, for underneath them there are large painted and engraved figures—oxen, horses, and stags—that must have belonged to the same group as the figures in the Passageway and the Nave. Over these large figures dozens of small animals are superimposed, some fully and carefully rendered, others unfinished, among an extraordinarily confused jumble of parallel lines, barbed signs, and "comets." It has taken the Abbé Glory several years to decipher this inextricable accumulation, which is unprecedented except for certain panels in Les Trois Frères; it includes several quadrangular signs and, remarkably enough, the only claviform signs yet known in the Périgord.

No special problems of interpretation are posed by the contents of the Apse: every decorated cave has its area of unfinished outlines and scrawls, and here we find once more the cave's fundamental themes—ox/ horse/ibex/stag, piled up together with a host of signs. Two of the figures are unusual. The first passes for a musk ox,[25] an animal whose bones are very rare among the remains in Late Paleolithic excavations (and such traces, moreover, should be carefully reviewed); one undated representation is known in a sculpture from Laugerie Haute (and this may quite possibly be a bison, even though the horns do in fact resemble those of a musk ox), and this present instance is merely the result of a fortuitous concatenation of lines. The second figure is incontestably a reindeer[26]—Lascaux's only reindeer—and it resembles one at least of the reindeer at Le Gabillou. This unique reindeer poses serious problems; as it is not a later addition to the rest of the figures at Lascaux, we cannot assume the return of some Late Magdalenians who left it as the sole evidence of their visit. The animal is in Style III, and—I repeat—the reindeer is not excluded from the oldest or the middle-period cave compositions because of any scarcity of the live animal at the time. Since the claviform signs occur only at the approach to the Shaft and one of these is obviously superimposed on a horse in Style III and on a rectangular sign,[27] we may in this case have a later addition to the rest of the cave decorations.

[25] *chart* LIII

[26] *fig. 335*

[27] *fig. 334*

The Apse does not pose many questions of over-all interpretation, but its topographical location is somewhat out of the ordinary. If, as seems likely, we grant that the original entrance to the cave lay in the axis of the present-day entrance, the area of unfinished outlines ought to occur just before we come to the "unicorn," in the Rotunda. Its location in the Apse is hard to explain unless we assume that visitors entered the cave via the Shaft and spontaneously made scrawls at this very spot. This assumption, however, raises one objection: The "scene" in the Shaft is a characteristic back-cave scene, which implies that access to Lascaux was not by way of the Shaft, but via the present-day entrance. My own view—at least for the time being—is that the Apse, first given over on the right-hand side to scrawls corresponding to the compositions in the Nave and the Passageway, was gradually covered with figures as the Shaft came to play an increasingly important part in the sanctuary.

THE SHAFT

Above the Shaft, on the ceiling, there is a compartmented rectangular sign which would indeed seem to indicate that during the principal period of decoration this topographical feature already played an important part. In the course of their unfortunately cursory investigation, the Abbé Breuil and S. Blanc picked up some long spears from the Early Magdalenian at the bottom of the Shaft. Yet on the stone rim of the Shaft, above the empty space, a group of claviform signs is engraved[28] in the most unmistakable Middle Magdalenian tradition (and as at Le Tuc d'Audoubert, Niaux, El Pindal). At the bottom of the Shaft there is a famous group of paintings, which has already given rise to numerous explanations. On the left we find a rhinoceros, under whose tail there are six dots (two rows of three),[29] then a man with outstretched arms thrown to the ground by a bison; the latter has a long spear across its body, and its entrails are escaping.[30] Below this scene there is a barbed sign with two lateral dots near the base and another sign which is similar except that the tip, instead of being hooked, bears a bird figure. Opposite we find an incompletely rendered horse.[31]

[28] *chart* XXXVII

[29] *fig. 323*
[30] *fig. 74*

[31] *fig. 324*

The opinion expressed by the Abbé Breuil fuses, so to speak, all the hypotheses: the rhinoceros has disemboweled the bison and is going away; the man was killed by the bison in the course of a hunt; and the stake with the bird figure, as on an Alaskan shaman's tomb, might represent the soul of the deceased. The general sense of the whole would be commemorative and would mark the burial place of a hunter. This hypothesis led Breuil to look for the hunter's body at the foot of the stone rim above the Shaft, but he did not find it. The reenactment is rational from a certain point of view, although it is not quite clear why the bison, disemboweled by the rhinoceros, turns toward his human victim. Without explaining the scene, it is possible to analyze its elements. The rhinoceros is a back-cave or marginal animal (Les Combarelles, Los Casares, Les Trois Frères): to find it at the bottom of the Shaft, accompanied by aligned dots, is perfectly normal. This fact, moreover, would tend to prove that the Shaft did not serve as an entrance. There is no apparent evidence that the rhinoceros and his dots are directly connected with the adjacent scene: in any case, there is no precedent that we can cite.

32 *fig. 439; chart* xxviii The scene involving the bison, on the other hand, is very familiar indeed.[32] It exactly reproduces the engraved reindeer horn from Laugerie Basse, which has on one side a bison marked with one stroke and an ithyphallic man with outstretched arms, on the other side a horse. The same scene, with the same protagonists, turns up in sculptured form at Le Roc de Sers and in painted form at Villars. Consequently this was a theme known from the Solutrean to the Middle Magdalenian. In treatment, the bison is very close to figures of the latter period; it would be closer still had the head not been so curiously set apart from the beard and dewlap in order to express the movement of the horns.

Then there are the signs. I have thought that the one at the man's feet was his spear-thrower and that the staff with the bird was also a spear-thrower, this one of the headless-animal type (one specimen representing a male grouse was discovered at Le Mas d'Azil). Now I am less sure of this. The first sign falls within a very complete morphological sequence that goes from the realistic phallus to the stroke with two lateral dots; thus it is definitely a male sign. Yet it may not be wholly fortuitous that the intestines spilling from the wounded bison were given the shape of concentric ovals. We might have here a variant form of the assimilation of phallus-to-spear with vulva-to-wound. Does the male sign imply an assimilation of phallus to spear-thrower? We do not have sufficient comparative data to answer this question, for spear-throwers exhibit greater variety in the animals represented on them than any other object. The bird sign is even more awkward. Birds are rare both in cave art and on decorated objects, and their position in symbolism is uncertain. About all we can say is that the lower part of the sign painted here resembles a male sign.

LASCAUX'S CHRONOLOGICAL STATUS

Contrary to widespread opinion, the cave of Lascaux is not altogether isolated, stylistically speaking. Identical or closely related figures are found at Le Gabillou, Font-de-Gaume, La Mouthe, and Villars, and belong, in all their distinctive features, to Style III: animals with swollen bodies and spreading short legs, oxen with the foremost horn rendered as a single curve and the rear horn as a sinuous one, bison horns presented frontally, stag antlers in a special perspective—the rear brow antler parallel to the beam of the foremost antler, with double or triple brow antlers. The animals are those also found at two dated sites—Le Roc de Sers and Bourdeilles—which are both Solutrean. It would, then, be reasonable to suppose Lascaux to be Solutrean, and it is not out of the question that the oldest figures do come from that period. All writers have stressed the fact that the Lascaux decorations passed through numerous successive stages and have noted the extent to which they are painted over; the Abbé Breuil distinguished twenty-two different periods of execution, while recognizing the over-all unity of style and locating the whole in the Perigordian.

33 *fig. 336* To me so many subdivisions hardly seem necessary: we are sure that the decoration was reworked during many centuries, but by no means all the superimposed figures date from different epochs. The Abbé Glory, who lived in the cave for several years while making his inventories, distinguishes two main periods: one in which the horses have one ear on their necks and the other on their cheeks,[33] and a period in which both ears are in a normal position. He has discovered in the Apse several repainted or re-engraved figures which clearly show the transition from the one type of representation to the other. This criterion demonstrates that the figures in the Passageway and the first inside the Apse are the oldest. Such conclusions as I have myself been able to reach are much the same, based on parallels between, on the one hand, Lascaux, Le Gabillou, Villars, and Pech Merle and, on the other, La Pasiega, Altamira, and El Castillo. Like El Castillo and La Pasiega, Le Gabillou, Pech Merle, and Lascaux contain animals in archaic Style III along with animals in a more developed style, already close to Early Style IV; moreover, they have compartmented quadrangular signs and brace-shaped signs of a later date. La Pasiega and Altamira, like Lascaux, contain compositions in Early Style IV with claviform signs. Lascaux would, then, comprise three phases: that of the compartmented rectangular signs (probably subdivided into two according to the Abbé Glory); that of the brace-shaped signs which are few in number and correspond to the period when the "Chinese horses" were executed in a style of modeling already close to that of Early Style IV; and lastly, that of the true claviforms, which belong already to Early Style IV. The absolute dating follows from these observations. The main layer of occupation at Lascaux would seem to be somewhere in the Early Magdalenian, and the carbon-14 dating is c.15,000 B.C., between the Solutrean and the Early Magdalenian. On the other hand, the animals in the earliest Style III are close to those at Bourdeilles and Le Roc de Sers—that is, Late Solutrean. Moreover, the evidence of decorated objects found in the entrances to La Pasiega, El Castillo, and Altamira goes back to periods between the Solutrean and Middle Magdalenian. Thus the tissue of assumptions is woven sufficiently tight to enable us to date the Lascaux decorations between the second half of the Solutrean and the beginning of the Middle Magdalenian (III-IV).

LE GABILLOU

SOURZAC, DORDOGNE, FRANCE

The decorations in the cave were discovered in 1941 by Charmarty and Truffier. Some years later the cave became the property of Dr. Gaussen, who is ensuring that it be preserved and studied.

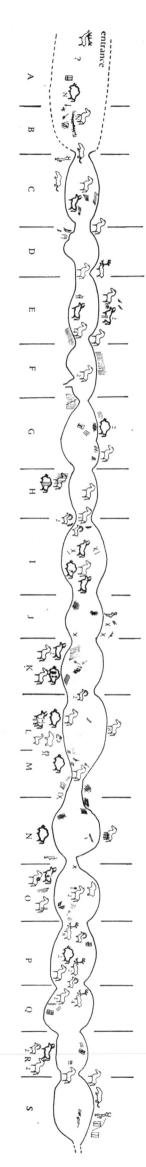

126. LE GABILLOU. SCHEMATIC PLAN WITH FIGURES
The drawings are conventionalized, and the numbers under the figures indicate how many animals of that type are present in a given composition. The bison and oxen are heavily outlined. Note the position of the pairings bison/horse and ox/horse in each of the wider sections of the cave, the presence of felines in B and C at the back of the sections near the entrance, and the repetition of the pairing feline/horned-personage in B-C and in S. Note, too, the cervids in D and P-Q which provide a frame for the innermost gallery, and the presence of ibexes in the passageways H-I, K-L, O-P, and P-Q.

The cave proper is a low, narrow corridor opening out of a small cave of which the walls were cut back within historical times to make a cellar. There are remnants of decoration in the front part, and the whole of the little passage, about 33 yards long, is covered with engravings. Le Gabillou is one of the corridor-sanctuaries, easy of access and of moderate depth. This supplies no definite clue to its date but opens the possibility that the decoration was done prior to the Middle Magdalenian. The quality of the decoration, the state of its preservation, and its contemporaneousness with Lascaux make Le Gabillou one of the most important French caves.[1] *([1] figs. 339–356)*

The decorations are in a series of about twenty little chambers, averaging about a yard in width, separated by narrowings of the walls, an arrangement remarkably similar to that of the Chamber of Felines at Lascaux. The engraving technique, with some areas of ocher here and there, is also the same and the composition is nearly identical—the difference being that the Chamber of Felines at Lascaux is a single back-cave composition whereas Le Gabillou is a complete sanctuary. The fundamental bison/horse theme is taken up over and over again, and, as at Niaux, Le Portel, Santimamine, Altamira, El Castillo, and Les Combarelles, the secondary theme is ox/horse (whereas at Lascaux this formula is oppositely applied). The over-all composition is remarkably balanced, and, to judge by the subjects, there seem to have been two sanctuaries here, the one following the other. The first occupied the entrance and was in large part destroyed when the cellar was made. We find the remains of compositions of bison/horse/compartmented-quadrangular-sign, and a back-area group (corresponding to the first portion of the corridor) which shows two felines[2] and a horned personage (C). This group is an exact counterpart of the composition at the end of the corridor (S), where we meet again feline and horned personages.[3] *([2] figs. 347, 348 [3] fig. 58)*

The second sanctuary is located in the corridor running from chamber D to chamber S. It is framed by cervids (in D and P) very like the one and only reindeer at Lascaux; these represent entrance and back-area animals, as do the stags in the Axial Gallery at Lascaux. About halfway along we come upon the central composition,[4] which occupies chambers I to M. Its general structure is as follows: along the right-hand wall two successive groups of bison/horse/paired-signs with ibexes, then some rather unusual lateral subjects (a hare, a quadruped with a giraffe's neck rather like the "antelopes" at Pech Merle, a bear, and a little feline in frontal view which looks more like something in an animated cartoon than in a Paleolithic sanctuary[5]; along the left-hand wall, before we get to the central group, is "the woman in the parka" (J), who seems to be a woman and is in any case a human being in profile, clothed in a hooded smock,[6] then the sizable group of horses which completes the central composition. Between the first cervid and the "woman in the parka," we find in turn a sizable composition of oxen and horses (E) with a brace-shaped sign of a type different from those at Lascaux and Villars, a bison/horse composition with a quadrangular sign (G), another bison/horse composition, ibexes in a place where the passage narrows (as at other such places), and an ox/bison/horse group with paired signs, crosses, and strokes. *([4] fig. 65 [5] figs. 349, 351 [6] fig. 353)*

Beyond the central composition, back-cave subjects predominate, interrupted by brief reappearances of paired bovids (ox/horse, bison/horse); we find a bear (L), a horned man (N), a profusion of cervids[7] none of which is unmistakably a stag and several of which have reindeer characteristics, and several rectangular signs. Before the last chamber there is one last ox/horse/ibex/rectangular-sign composition (R). The last group of figures comprises a horse, a feline, and a horned man who appears to be dancing and is attached by a long line to two rectangular signs (S). Opposite is a figure hard to make out, which I might regard as a rhinoceros were that not the one animal missing to bring the cave into harmony with my theory about the organization of the sanctuaries. It could be a bison, for in Style III the arc formed by the horn in front of the forehead may look like a rhinoceros horn. *([7] fig. 344)*

The over-all layout of Le Gabillou is that of large sanctuaries like Lascaux, Niaux, Les Combarelles, and La Pasiega, in which we also find sequences of repetitions of the main theme that make full use of the cave's topographical features. Every large surface displays a composition of animals and paired signs; every narrowing of the corridors has passageway signs or ibexes; there are enframing cervids; and men and felines form the ends of each sequence. Despite its limited space Le Gabillou, thanks to a topography favoring succinct organization, offers one of the most remarkable ensembles in all Paleolithic art.

THE SIGNS

[8] *fig. 355*

[9] *chart* XLII

[10] *chart* XXXIII

Though considerable in number and variety, the signs fall within a limited number of specific types. Female signs are represented by more than a dozen compartmented rectangles[8] that are very close to those at Lascaux and enable us, by their variations, to draw up a detailed table of the successive forms. Twice, in connection with oxen, we find the brace-shaped sign of the Perigordian type,[9] slightly different from those at Lascaux and Villars. Crosses occur frequently and, when we compare them with identical signs at Lascaux, persuade us that they may represent an extremely simplified variant of the compartmented sign. Male signs are of three types. There are a great many strokes, single and double, in association with female signs. We also find signs barbed on one side, of a type frequent at Lascaux. The most interesting type is the stroke with smaller strokes on each side.[10] When we collate the different variants from Le Gabillou and Lascaux, we have all the possible Paleolithic ways of rendering the male sexual attributes in abstract form. Finally, in at least two places we encounter parallel rows of dots. Just as everywhere else, the pairing of one or another form of female sign with one or another form of male sign does not seem to obey any regular rule.

THE STYLE AND THE AGE

In style, the animal figures belong to two successive forms of Style III, as at Lascaux and Pech Merle. The bison are of the same type as those at the back of the Nave in Lascaux, except for one with horns like those of the bison in the Shaft which were probably inspired by ox horns. The horses belong to two types. Some are related to the late group of the older horses at Lascaux (distended bodies, spreading legs, oval hoofs, ears on the back of the neck). Others are related to a more recent type, well represented opposite the group of unusual animals in the central compositions; especially noteworthy is a horse whose withers and chest are striped with parallel lines. Their general contours come very close to those of the horse at Commarque and of certain horses at Les Combarelles. Chronologically, Le Gabillou seems to cover the same period as Lascaux and the sanctuaries where quadrangular signs and brace-shaped signs precede the claviform signs; however, unlike Lascaux, the period of the horses with the ear placed on the cheek is not represented. Thus it would seem that the decoration of Le Gabillou can be placed between the Solutrean and the Middle Magdalenian (III–IV).

VILLARS

VILLARS, DORDOGNE, FRANCE

This cave was discovered in 1958 by the Spéléo-Club of Périgueux. As yet there has been no publication devoted to it.

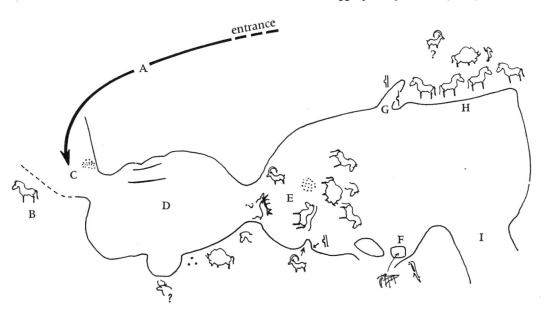

127. VILLARS. SCHEMATIC PLAN WITH FIGURES
The long approach into the cave is indicated by arrow A. *The animals have been conventionalized. Note the female signs behind a stalagmite column at* E *and in a side-chamber at* G.

The cave is a huge one, complicated in structure; one part of it has been decorated as a sanctuary consisting of three contiguous chambers. The original entrance has not been determined with certainty, but the narrow, difficult approach (A) is marked with dots of red ocher here and there and would seem to correspond to the original one. In the main chamber, hearths have been found on the surface of the ground, along with industrial objects, though unfortunately no scientific inventory was taken. Exact excavation is still possible.

The decorated region lies in an area of heavy concretion, and the greater part of the works are veiled or obliterated by the stalagmitic coating. The part marked I on the diagram is, so far at least, totally undecipherable. Thus only a portion of the sanctuary can be analyzed, but it is coherent. At the end of the stretch which is marked out with dots we find one horse by itself (B), then a sequence of paintings in black or red from D to H. An area of dots (C) marks the entrance just beyond a narrow passageway. In chamber D a small recess in the wall contains a barely legible figure which may be the head of an ox. A bit further on, a bison and a horse can be made out. Group E begins just past a narrowing of the walls, with a problematic stag's head and two unquestionable ibexes, one on either side. The ceiling is decorated with two groups of figures: a horse and an unidentified dorsal line, then three horses and a bison. The signs on the ceiling comprise a spread of dots on the left, and, on the right, a female brace-shaped sign of a type found at Lascaux and at Le Gabillou. Group F consists of a schematic figure, which seems to represent a horse with its head down, and a separate block covered with incised lines (vertical strokes and unfinished outlines).[1] Off to the right lies the gallery containing figures barely visible under the calcification. Group G–H, opposite this, is relatively well preserved. It includes brace-shaped signs (G), four horses,[2] an animal with no visible head (which may be an ibex), and a man/bison group[3] very closely related to that in the Shaft at Lascaux.

    The composition in the well-preserved portion of Villars is clear. It is wholly based on the bison/horse theme, repeated three times: in D, in E, and in H. Female brace-shaped signs, set in small recesses, accompany groups E and H, as is fairly often the case. The zone with the unfinished outlines is found opposite the two main groups (F); the man/bison group occupies the most remote portion of the whole decoration; and the ibexes are set at the entrance to the main chamber (E). The decoration is very homogeneous stylistically, and it is scarcely possible to speak of several periods. The schematic character of most of the figures or their poor state of preservation rules out detailed analysis, but the signs and figures of group G–H insure attribution to Style III. The signs belong to the brace-shaped type found at Lascaux, Le Gabillou, Cougnac, and Pech Merle. In three of these caves this type succeeds the quadrangular signs, as it does in Cantabrian Spain: it also precedes the claviform signs in Early Style IV. Thus the figures fall into the second part of Style III, probably corresponding to the Early Magdalenian. One of the horses, with legs stretched stiffly forward and backward like those of the horses in the Rotunda and the Axial Gallery at Lascaux, would seem to confirm this. The resemblance of the man/bison group to that at Lascaux (where it is among the latest figures) further supports the comparative dating.

[1] *fig. 357*

[2] *fig. 359*

[3] *fig. 358*

LA MOUTHE *(continued from page 305)*

FIGURES IN STYLE III

    As one goes down the corridor past the oxen in Style II[1] on the left-hand wall, the gallery enlarges into a broad concave panel on which the Abbé Breuil found twenty-one engraved figures.[2] These are bison, two ibexes (one on each side of the group, as is customary), a stag somewhat apart, and, higher up, close to the ceiling and hard to make out, a horse. The whole group measures about 12 feet. All the animals exhibit a strongly sinuous cervico-dorsal outline of an early form. The bison horns fall into two types. Some are shown in frontal view (in "twisted perspective"), like the horns of the bison at Lascaux, of some of those at Le Gabillou, and of those at Pech Merle. The others are in a closely related perspective, but with the foremost horn rendered as a single curve and the rear one as a wavy incision; this rendering is normal for oxen in Style III and sometimes turns up on bison as well, at Le Gabillou, for example. There are good general reasons for attributing these works to Period III, but the evidence is not sufficient to place them at the beginning rather than at the end, in the Solutrean rather than the Early Magdalenian. In any case they belong with the Lascaux-Gabillou group.

[1] *figs. 284, 287*

[2] *fig. 360*

    Referring to these engravings, the Abbé Breuil expressed an opinion which shows that the distance between his point of view and the chronology proposed in this work may not be as great as appears at first glance. According to him, "There is a considerable analogy with some of the graffiti at Lascaux and the earliest graffiti in the sanctuary at Les Trois Frères; they attest to a transition between the two systems of perspective, attributable to the terminal Perigordian or to the beginning of the Magdalenian" (*Quatre cents siècles* ..., page 293). If the beginning of the Magdalenian follows the terminal Perigordian (which some tend to identify with the Gravettian associated with the Noailles burin), there is nothing to prevent us from viewing Lascaux and the bison at La Mouthe as involved in such a transition; however, Breuil himself has shown that the two periods are separated by the proto-Solutrean and the Solutrean, which cover several thousands of years (five thousand, according to carbon-14 dating). Since, in addition, the Magdalenian of Les Trois Frères is, according to the Abbé himself, Magdalenian IV, there remains a margin of about seven thousand years, ample enough to allow us to propose the mature Solutrean or the Early Magdalenian (Breuil's Magdalenian I–II).

    Beyond the panel of bison, on the right, a side chamber about five yards deep branches off. In the middle of the central panel we find an incised and painted figure—"the hut"—a large rectangular sign with lateral appendages over a tangle of scrawls and unfinished outlines. To the right of this panel is a collection of later figures which are discussed on page 260. The "hut" and the unfinished outlines are an important part of the Style III sanctuary, equivalent to the Apse at Lascaux where the same accumulation of tangled figures and several rectangular signs occurs. The "hut"[3] corresponds to a type of sign different from the types at Lascaux and Le Gabillou; if, as seems not unlikely, it is related to the bison composition, it contributes an important element of dating. It consists of a rectangle divided by eight or nine vertical lines; no horizontal compartments are formed. So far as can be judged from similar figures at Font-de-Gaume (chamber of the small bison) and Les Combarelles (Group 76), it belongs to the end of Style III, just before the tectiform signs make their appearance. Farther on, in the small chamber that was thought to mark the end of the cave before a new gallery was discovered, we find the panel with the so-called rhinoceros, of which we shall speak when we discuss the figures in Style IV. A portion of the decoration belongs to Style III, in particular three horses, one bison, and one ibex, which are in the style of the finest animals at Lascaux. *(See also page 353.)*

[3] *chart LII*

SAINT-CIRQ, NOËL BROUSSE CAVE

SAINT-CIRQ-DU-BUGUE, DORDOGNE, FRANCE

The engravings were discovered in 1952 through information received from Noël Brousse, owner of the cave, by a group working under Blanc and Mortureux, which was subsequently joined by the Abbé Breuil. The drawing of the male human figure shown in fig. 361 was made by the Abbé Glory.

The Noël Brousse cave is a small grotto in the side of a cliff, the walls of which were partially cut out to make a deeper cave. The main chamber, which receives daylight, is approximately 26 feet square; it is in part closed off at the rear by a wall, and beyond this the cave extends a few yards further into a low chamber which can be reached only by crawling on all fours.

The figures belong to two groups, one in the main chamber, the other in the chamber behind it; these groups are distinct both stylistically and topographically. The chamber into which daylight enters has only faint remnants of its original decoration on the portions of the walls not recut by the later hollowing of the cave. To the right of the entrance a small bison in low relief can be made out. Following it, on the sloping rock ledge above, some rather deep-cut lines were read by the Abbé Breuil as a reindeer head. There are actually vague outlines of a head in the eroded calcite, but the lines that should compose the antlers scarcely permit so exact an identification. More lines are added to the right of this. Directly opposite, along the line of the fault that created the cave, remain the traces of a frieze of horses. We can make out, from left to right, a nearly complete body without a head; farther on, a hindquarters; then another horse whose head is worn away, the finest figure; and lastly, the buttocks of a fourth figure. S. Blanc, in the article cited below in the Bibliography, has pointed out the similarity between these remnants (he mentions only two figures of the frieze) and the horses at Lascaux; the stylistic analogy is in fact very striking. To sum up, the first chamber contains extremely scanty remains of a decoration which was destroyed by climatic conditions and by the hollowing out of the cave; these vestiges, however, are of great interest because, apart from Le Roc de Sers and Bourdeilles, they are the only low reliefs in Style III that are so far known. The figures at Lascaux are much less isolated in style than they seemed at first, for gradually we are discovering—at Le Gabillou, among the oldest figures at Font-de-Gaume, at Villars, and now here—works that are contemporary with them. Deep sanctuaries dating from the Solutrean and the Early Magdalenian are very rare, and the majority of works from this period, exposed to the weather, must have disappeared.

The innermost part of this cave is a clear example of the deepening of the sanctuaries inside the caves in subsequent periods. The engravings that decorate the ceiling (unfortunately in fragile condition) in this rear chamber are in a different style, Style IV. On the flat part of the ledge where most of the figures still exposed to daylight are engraved, an ibex head can be seen. Around the ledge to the right, we find a bison head in Early Style IV, with horn, eye, and ears all included within a single outline.[1] In front of the head are several lines difficult to interpret, including a triangle. Farther to the right we find a large male figure. This latter has been christened "the sorcerer"—certain prehistorians so often find it useful to seek in words that have no precise meaning an identification that has no bearing on the figure. All we can say of this completely naked individual (who, in his posture as in the shape of his abdomen, brings to mind rather oddly the "pregnant woman with reindeer" on a famous engraved plaquette from Laugerie Basse), is that he is unmistakably male. A number of lines criss-crossing around the figure might with closer study be resolved as definite signs and figures. The rocky surface below this group of figures is marked with a great many parallel incisions, to the left of which we find a head not easy to identify, which might be related to a bison or to a bestialized human face. Farther to the right there is a small engraved horse whose shoulder seems to be covered by a large oval sign. Lastly, on the ceiling, partly destroyed by the fall of part of the brittle crust, an engraving is visible which seems to have represented a head, perhaps that of a horse.

This little group of figures in the second chamber is hard to interpret. In its present state it includes an ibex, a bovid (probably a bison), a triangular sign similar to certain claviforms, a human figure, a horse marked with an oval, a number of scrawls (strokes), and an unidentifiable head. So far only one other composition has been found to which this one can be compared, the one in the side chamber at Pech Merle containing the wounded man, which shows an ibex, a bovid, a brace-shaped sign, a human figure, and rows of strokes. Group 63–64 at Les Combarelles, which includes two or three human silhouettes near a horse that has a vulva engraved upon it, is comparable to the right-hand part of the Saint-Cirq panel. The other situations in which we find male human figures have different connotations: a man struggling with a bison (Le Roc de Sers, Lascaux, Villars), a horned man (Le Gabillou, Les Trois Frères; the man at Le Gabillou has the same posture as this man at Saint-Cirq, and is associated with quadrangular signs), and men by themselves or included in compositions that are difficult to delimit (Cougnac, Les Combarelles 80–81, Altamira, Los Hornos, La Peña de Candamo, Los Casares). Group 73 at La Pasiega, in Gallery C, perhaps supplies something comparable: on the wall concealing an alcove are a bovid and an ibex; in the alcove, a human bust with horns, a brace-shaped sign, and rows of dots; on the right, a horse, a brace-shaped sign, a few strokes, and some hinds. All of these various groups seem to suggest that the Saint-Cirq panel is a back-cave or at most a passageway composition, rather than a central composition; hence it may be assumed that it is merely a section of the original sanctuary. Does the first chamber, with its horses and bison that have survived destruction, represent the missing part? We might be tempted to think so, were not the two sets of figures different in style: the outer group apparently is in Style III, the inner group in Early Style IV. The panel with the male figure may possibly represent a Middle Magdalenian extension of the sanctuary beyond the entrance, which was completed by the inner chamber: Labastide, La Mouthe, La Pasiega C, Pech Merle, and Le Portel supply examples of one sanctuary succeeding another at a progressively later date.

[1] fig. 361

PECH MERLE

CABRERETS, LOT, FRANCE

The cave and its paintings were first discovered in 1922 by David and Dutertre, who alerted the Abbé Lemozi. In 1949 André David discovered further chambers—the part known as Le Combel—and Lemozi studied these as well. We are indebted to the latter for the pictorial inventory of the entire decoration.

128. PECH MERLE, LE COMBEL, AND MARCENAC. GENERAL LOCATION OF THE CAVES

A *Red Chamber.* B *Natural entrance which may perhaps have been used by Paleolithic men.* C *White Chamber.* D *Gallery with the bear.* E *Main decorated chamber.* F *Ossuary.* G *Gallery with the man-made entrance used today.* H *Le Combel.* I *Rear of Le Combel, which may correspond to the entrance actually used in Paleolithic times. The broken line surrounds the decorated areas.* J *The Marcenac cave. (Plan after the Abbé Lemozi.)*

129. PECH MERLE AND LE COMBEL. ENLARGED PLAN OF THE DECORATED AREAS, WITH FIGURES

1 *Possible entrance at period of the earliest decorations (I in fig. 128).*
2, 3, 4 *Le Combel (II in fig. 128): figures in the earliest style.*
5 *Main decorated chamber of Pech Merle (E in fig. 128): fresco in early style.*
6 *Ossuary (F in fig. 128).*
7 *The large black fresco.*
8 *Area with scraped ceiling.*
9 *Figures just outside the chamber with the women/bison panel.*
10 *The women/bison panel.*
11 *Side chamber with the wounded man.*
12 *Gallery with the bear (D in fig. 128).*
Panels 7–12 constitute the later sanctuary.

Pech Merle consists of a network of underground passages about a mile and a quarter in length. Only one portion of it, that extending 550 yards beyond what must have been the original entrance, contains figures. The large dimensions of the chambers and the arrangement of the works create one of the most impressive displays of cave art. The location of the ancient entrance is not known with certainty, because there are several possible approaches to the main part of the cave; the present entrance has been artificially broken through. General considerations suggest that the Paleolithic entrance must have been through what is today the back of the Combel cave: the figures in Le Combel are stylistically the earliest, they form a whole, and the signs accompanying them are of the quadrangular type. The earliest sanctuary, then, would have been located just inside this former entrance, and the deeper sanctuaries would be of later date; the furthest figure from this entrance, that of the bear, seems to be the latest. Because Pech Merle has so labyrinthine a structure, the successive stages of the sanctuaries are hard to reconstruct. Except for the main decorated chamber, the figures occur in groups within side chambers. Nevertheless, the arrangement within each of these groups is coherent.

LE COMBEL

The walls and the recesses at the foot of the rock slide show vestiges of indecipherable paintings in red (1) which may have embodied the mid-cave compositions: the collection toward the back is in fact typically terminal. On the left, the ceiling of a low gallery is decorated with quadrangular signs formed of dots[1] accompanied by double rows of dots (2). This part of the cave ends in a very small chamber extraordinary in its decoration (3): stalactites come down from the ceiling in the shape of breasts tightly crowded together; two large red dots[2] seem here to play the same role of male signs as the double rows of dots just mentioned. Opposite we find the oddest of all groups, a "procession" of four animals with distended bodies, each one successively borrowing either the back or the belly of the one in front of it.[3] Three necks and shoulders, notably raised, with tiny "antelope" heads atop them, are attached to the four bodies; the rump of the leftmost animal ends in a leg that might be that of a rhinoceros, and a corkscrew tail. It would be idle, at the present time, to attempt to identify these figures. We need only observe that the "unicorn" in the Rotunda at Lascaux, dating from the same epoch, has rhinoceros (?) hindquarters and a distended body, while in the Chamber of Felines in the same cave we find a sort of "giraffe" with horns curving forward. This last figure belongs to an unusual composition that includes a horse in frontal view. At Le Gabillou, among a group of rarely pictured animals (hare, feline in frontal view), we find another "giraffe" with swollen body and the legs of a pachyderm. In other words, these figures at Le Combel are not altogether isolated.

Not far from where Le Combel links up with the main cave there is another side chamber (4), at the end of an impassable corridor connected with the chamber we have been describing; in it the following figures are

[1] *fig. 362*

[2] *fig. 363*

[3] *fig. 364*

321

⁴ fig. 365

found: at the entrance on the right, four dots aligned, and two groups of three dots on the left; these signs serve to introduce a panel⁴ showing two horses in archaic Style III, one feline, one unfinished bison, and rows of dots. Near the present-day entrance in the main gallery, we find red outlines which seem to belong to a group of unfinished outlines at the entrance to the main chamber of the sanctuary.

THE MAIN DECORATED CHAMBER

This chamber contains several panels or decorated areas: on the right are the Ossuary (6), the panel of horses filled with dots (5), the side chamber with the women/bison group (10), and the side chamber with the wounded man (11); on the left is the large black fresco (7); in the center is the scraped area of the ceiling (8); at the far end is the gallery with the bear (12) which also contained some engravings, destroyed in our own time.

THE OSSUARY (6)

The entrance, the corridor, and the rear portion of the large Ossuary chamber show many lines traced on the clay surface of the wall with fingers or a pointed tool; most of these are meanders. At the end of the corridor, in a semidome near the ceiling, we find a cervid with big antlers next to two unfinished hinds: this is Pech Merle's famous engraving of the megaceros, or large-horned deer. Male, with enormous antlers, the figure obeys no stylistic canon, and the outlines are childishly drawn, but two good reasons favor this identification: the antlers are those of the male megaceros deer, and there are other representations of this animal in the Cougnac cave, which is in the same region and the same epoch.

The rear portion of the Ossuary is filled with meandering lines, a spread of red dots, and a very schematic black figure which may be interpreted as either a stag or a horned man of the type found at Le Gabillou. The center of the chamber, greatly altered by excavation of the cave-bear ossuary that was found there, contained (according to the Abbé Lemozi) mounds of clay which may have been the remnants of modeled figures. Actually, none of such great antiquity are known, but it is a striking fact that the only decoration of this chamber is that of the entrance and of the back cave (the megaceros deer, and the stag or horned man); there is no central composition. It is also possible that this side chamber was specially reserved for unfinished outlines, like the large chamber at Gargas or several of the chambers at Rouffignac.

THE PANEL OF THE "DOTTED" HORSES (5)

⁵ figs. 64, 366

This monumental panel⁵ is as enigmatic as that containing the figures of "monsters" in the small side chamber in Le Combel. We find two large horses back to back, in the style of the horses with the feline in Le Combel; they are surrounded by five hands in negative. The animals' bodies are filled in with dots, and more dots run along outside the contours. Furthermore, the spaces under the bellies are filled with vertical and horizontal rows of dots. Lastly, over the right-hand horse we see a fish of the pike family, a circle thinly drawn in red, and the outline of a bison in the same sketchy technique. Above the back of the left-hand horse, moreover, appears (in negative) the stencil of a series of bent fingers.

The stylistic identity of these figures with those in Le Combel leaves no doubt that both groups are contemporaneous: both are archaic compared with the remainder of the cave decoration, and both belong stylistically on the boundary between Style II and Style III. In content, too, these figures are identical with those in Le Combel: we meet again the two horses back to back, the partially rendered bison, the dots inside and around the figures. The feline that would be normal in so prominent a panel is not present. Fish are too rare in cave art to be susceptible of interpretation: on decorated objects, the fish has the value of a male symbol. The main theme, horse/bison, is commonplace; less so is the fact that, here as in Le Combel, the bison is barely suggested with a few lines. It is true there are other instances where the complementary animal is sketchily indicated: at Niaux, for example, the horse is merely indicated in at least two compositions. This practice is not frequent, however; Paleolithic artists themselves may have been aware of this, inasmuch as at the end of the panel of "dotted" horses there is an isolated bison complementary, as it were, to the horses, in the style of Pech Merle's second period.

⁶ fig. 60

The hands and the dots pose another problem. In our discussion of Gargas we saw how varied their placement within the caves may be. At Pech Merle we find hands and dots in the panel of the horses and on a block close to the side chamber with the women/bison group (G). It is striking that both the single hand to the left of the horses and the hand close to the women/bison panel⁶ are accompanied by lines of dots, like female signs accompanied by complementary strokes or dots. No less striking is the fact that, apart from one inconspicuous circle, the customary sexual signs are not found in this panel. We may suppose, then, that the hands and dots in the panel of horses are the equivalents of the quadrangular signs and dots in Le Combel. Hands are too rare in cave art to provide conclusive proof. We can only observe that at Bernifal, Rocamadour, Le Portel, and El Castillo hands occur in the immediate vicinity of rows of strokes or dots; at El Pindal, the hand is in juxtaposition with a horse.

THE WOMEN/BISON PANEL (10)

⁷ fig. 104

At the right of the entrance to the side chamber containing the women/bison panel there is the hand accompanied by dots to which we have just referred. At the left are the forequarters of a stag.⁷ It is hard to tell whether these figures are directly connected with those inside the chamber: the stag, in particular, may belong to the same sequence as the "dotted" horses and constitute a back-cave subject. The panel inside the chamber includes seven figures that exhibit the transitions from the outline of a bison to that of a woman.⁸ Not enough attention has previously been given these figures, which furnish perhaps the most striking evidence of the abstract character of Paleolithic art. Women and bison are both female symbols, and it would be normal to find complementary male symbols, in the form of rows of dots and of a mammoth, dominating this most explicit female representation. We encounter the same theme (mammoth/woman) in the scraped ceiling⁹ just a few yards away; similarly, the theme of the whole right-hand portion of the large black frieze is based on the mammoth/bison pairing. The four female symbols—woman, bison, quadrangular sign, and hand—and the four male symbols—man, mammoth, row of dots, and horse—turn up constantly in pairs of every possible combination.

⁸ figs. 367–371 ; chart XLVIII

⁹ fig. 382

THE WOUNDED MAN (11)

The chamber containing the figure of the wounded man offers a set of subjects painted in red extending more than four yards across the ceiling. First we find an ibex and several rows of strokes; then a branching sign[10] reminiscent of the "spear-throwers" at Lascaux; then further back a bull that is one of the finest figures in the cave,[11] and lastly a group consisting of a man run through with spears, a brace-shaped sign, and some lines and unfinished outlines that resist interpretation.[12] The brace-shaped sign is identical with those at Cougnac, where, moreover, we also find the theme of the wounded man—a circumstance that makes possible exact dating of the two caves with respect to each other. In the figure of the man are combined most of the features exhibited by other male figures. The muzzle-shaped or bird-beak profile is like that of the man in the Shaft at Lascaux; the long tail is like those of the men at Le Gabillou and Les Trois Frères; and the dangling sexual organ is like those at Saint-Cirq and Les Trois Frères. And just as at Le Gabillou, the figure is found right next to a female sign. The meaning of this composition cannot be determined with the slender resources of comparative data at our disposal. The most striking fact is the association of man/threatened-or-wounded-bison (or female-sign/spear); the same association is found at Le Roc de Sers, on the pierced staff from Laugerie Basse (man carrying a spear), at Lascaux (bison run through by spear), at Villars (spear not visible), and at Le Gabillou (long line linking the man with quadrangular signs). The combination wounded-horse/brace-sign at El Castillo may have the same meaning. The combinations man/horse/spear and woman/bison (or ox)/wound are so frequent that we must assume that we are dealing here with a major area of Paleolithic symbolism.

[10] fig. 372
[11] fig. 94
[12] fig. 374

THE LARGE BLACK FRESCO (7)

This monumental panel takes up a full half of the main decorated chamber.[13] From left to right, its three parts are: a composition of ox/horse/mammoth/signs, a composition of bison/horse/mammoth, and a sequence of bison/mammoth pairings. The first group includes three mammoths, four oxen with the remarkable feature of two diverging lines at the tip of their muzzles—representing their "breath," according to the writers—and one horse merely suggested by the dorsal line. One of the oxen is shown in a vertical position, as though falling. We have many examples of animals shown vertically or upside down, and some of them—as here, or the horse at the end of the Axial Gallery at Lascaux—seem to be falling, but the great majority are in the usual position and we may wonder whether the inclusion of a vertical animal in a composition had a special significance or whether it merely concerns an indifference to the rules of perspective as we know them. The ox at the bottom of the panel is marked with several wounds from which blood appears to be spurting. Three groups of signs are represented: the wound marks on the ox just mentioned; on the ox farthest to the right, two double lines of dashes forming a sign similar to those at Le Gabillou and Lascaux, in the series of signs derived from the phallus; and on the mammoth lowest in the composition,[14] a spread of aligned red strokes. Paired signs are present here, though they are less conspicuous than the large signs at Lascaux and Le Gabillou and in the Spanish caves of the same epoch. The frieze merges with and develops into a second composition, the theme of which is the bison. Two bison face the oxen in the preceding group, one horse is superimposed, and five or six mammoths form a wreath around the central theme.[15] Farther along, past the large semidome containing these two compositions, we see a mammoth, then a bison, then a mammoth and a bison that may be marked with a spear, then a bison and a mammoth—and then again the same subject, repeated twice. If the statistics and the numerous examples had not already revealed a systematic pairing of animals of two species, the same stereotyped picture here encountered five times in a row would be sufficient to convince us.

[13] fig. 68

[14] fig. 377

[15] figs. 378, 379, 381

THE SCRAPED CEILING (8)

Toward the upper part of the main chamber, in the chaotic area that separates the right-hand-wall ("dotted" horses, women/bison, wounded man) from the large black fresco, the ceiling covered with a clay surface has been scraped with a stick[16] (like the ceiling of the Nave at Lascaux and the ceilings of certain parts of Rouffignac). Hundreds of lines are tangled together in the best tradition of the zones of unfinished outlines. Here and there a figure can be made out: an ibex, several dorsal outlines of mammoths, and—three times repeated—mammoth/woman groups identical with that in the side chamber with the women/bison panel, which, incidentally, is very close to this spot.

[16] fig. 382

THE BEAR (12)

As we go up toward the fork which leads, in one direction, to the red chamber, and in the other to the gallery with the bear, we first encounter more scrawls in the form of meanders, lattices, and oval figures, and then the gallery of the bear, containing the engraved head of that animal accompanied by a few lines.[17]

[17] fig. 380

Pech Merle is a very important cave, well worth the space we have devoted to it. It is important for its geographical location, for its topographical organization, and for the styles and the subjects represented. Geographically, Pech Merle and Cougnac are situated apart from the Perigordian group and, in several respects, provide a transition to the caves of the Pyrenees and those in Spain. The great similarity between Cougnac and Pech Merle shows that peculiarities of subject and style are not an isolated accident and that we may consider a distinct regional subdivision to exist, at least in Style III. As for the topographical arrangement of the compositions, it is clear that two successive sanctuaries overlap. The earlier one, characterized by the quadrangular signs, includes Le Combel and the right-hand wall of the main chamber, and probably also the red stag, the hand at the entrance to the side chamber with the women/bison panel, and the ibex and ox in the chamber of the wounded man. The second sanctuary is located in the left-hand portion of the main chamber and a portion of the rear; it includes the large black fresco, the scraped ceiling, the women/bison panel, and the wounded man. It is characterized by wound signs and one brace-shaped sign. Its layout along the left-hand wall, from the start of the black fresco, follows a normal scheme of development: large composition with signs and paired animals, zone of unfinished outlines, side chamber with paired signs in which the female element is predominant, side chamber with back-area paired signs, and finally a male figure. Quadrangular signs are followed by brace-shaped signs at Pech Merle exactly as they are at Lascaux and

Le Gabillou, at Le Portel, La Pasiega, and El Castillo; they are always associated with animal figures in Style III. All these caves, then, belong incontestably within the same time span. The animal figures at Pech Merle, like those in the other caves just mentioned, belong to two successive stages of Style III. The earlier stage, accompanied by quadrangular signs (horses in Le Combel and the "dotted" horses), is still close to Style II: the animals have distended bodies, the cervico-dorsal curve is strongly accentuated, the heads are small, the limbs stick out forward and back. In terms of comparative dating, they are situated after the Gravettian and before Magdalenian III, the mid-point lying in the Solutrean or the beginning of the Magdalenian. The later stylistic stage, accompanied by brace-shaped signs (at Pech Merle and also at Cougnac), corresponds to animal figures already approaching those in Early Style IV (the black fresco). Body proportions and limbs come closer to reality, but have not yet attained the aerial stability of the figures at Niaux and on the Altamira ceiling. The brace-shaped signs obviously prefigure the claviforms of Early Style IV, and we have enough data to place this second stage before the Middle Magdalenian.

COUGNAC

PEYRIGNAC, LOT, FRANCE

This cave was discovered in 1949 under unusual circumstances. A dowser named Lagarde pinpointed the location of a sizable cave on the map, and Jean Mazet directed a local team in the work which led to the discovery. So numerous are the failures of divining in the search for caves and in all archaeological prospecting that we hardly know what to think of the true sources of this discovery in a region where caves are not uncommon. However, Lagarde's inspiration has disclosed the existence of one of the most interesting caves in southwestern France. The pictorial inventory was made by Louis Méroc.

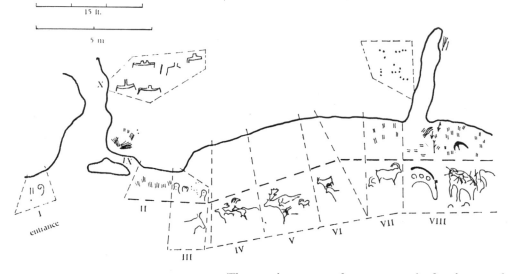

15 ft.

5 m

130. COUGNAC. ARRANGEMENT OF THE PANELS

The numbering is taken from the publication by Louis Méroc and Jean Mazet (see Bibliography). For convenience, the figures and the signs have been separated into different registers; this permits us to note the dense grouping of double strokes at one end of the decorated portion and their absence from the central portion of the fresco.

The cave is one part of a vast network of underground corridors, invaded by a very extensive concretion which had probably already taken place in large measure during the Late Paleolithic. It is possible, however, that, as at Villars, the decorated part is only the surviving portion of a much more extended sanctuary. When the cave was discovered the undisturbed ground contained many remains of animals. A lamp, a quantity of ocher, and a few flints were found just where the Paleolithic men had left them. Unfortunately the flints are not very characteristic. Still, two of the five specimens found are fragments that had been reshaped into regular points having a form most frequently encountered around the Solutrean-that is, within the limits of Style III. All of the works are wholly homogeneous stylistically, and the cave is an especially valuable example of a sanctuary that belongs to a single period. Especially valuable, for it is as necessary to have chronological cross checks for sanctuaries used over a long time span as to have neatly circumscribed examples for each period.

If the surviving portion represents the whole of the Paleolithic decorations, Cougnac contains some altogether untypical pairings. About a hundred yards from the entrance, just before the passage diverges, we find on the left-hand wall, the only one with decorations, a few signs of the type common to the front and rear of sanctuaries as well as in passageways (I). One gallery leads to the left; on its right-hand wall, in a narrow passageway that leads back into the main gallery, we find an area of scrawls such as we may expect in proximity to an important composition (IX). A few yards farther on, in a hollow, we find six brace-shaped signs painted black[1]; despite the variations among them, they are identical with the sign in the chamber of the wounded man at Pech Merle; they are accompanied by one big stroke (X). Such a grouping of signs in a small side chamber occurs frequently (36 percent of the cases).

The remaining decorations in the main gallery extend about 80 feet along the left-hand wall. We first encounter groups of triple strokes (II) drawn with the tips of three fingers, then three "ghosts" (III)[2]—simplified human figures such as we find at Les Combarelles, Les Trois Frères, Le Gabillou, Le Portel, and Font-de-Gaume. Above them is the forequarters of an animal which Méroc interprets tentatively as a wolf; I think that the chest, the withers, and the set of the head are rather those of a stag—we can just make out the antlers as they disappear under the calcareous overlay.

A large curved portion of the wall, about 33 feet long, presents the finest work in this cave.[3] First come three megaceros deer (two males and one female) very soundly identified as such by L. Méroc (IV, V). Surrounding and partly superimposed over them are four unfinished figures: mammoth, ibex, stag, and a man run through by spears. A bit farther on we come to an ibex and his mate (VI). This last has been identified as

[1] *fig. 385*

[2] *fig. 386*

[3] *fig. 383*

a tahr antelope by Koby, a Swiss zoologist, but what we rather have here is a female ibex, of a type by no means extinct, not an Asiatic ruminant. Farther on, we find two more ibexes (VII),[4] one rendered in full, the other a head only, surrounded by double strokes. A low corridor branches off at this point, in which are the signs customary in terminal blind alleys: dots both scattered and in alignment, strokes, and a hooked sign of the type present at Le Gabillou and Lascaux.

[4] fig. 384

Beyond the opening into the narrow corridor, the main decorations resume with two groups of figures (VIII). The first, much encrusted with calcite, has as its principal subject a figure which has been identified as the hindquarters of a mammoth, but which is really the head and withers of a horse of the same type as those in the first sequence at Pech Merle: as at Pech Merle, the withers bear a series of dots. A similar head exists in the Rocamadour cave. Grouped around it are double strokes, two hooked signs, and a branching sign. The final set of figures includes a mammoth, a sign above it with three branches that resembles the wound signs in other caves, and two human male figures run through by spears. The central group is surrounded by three mammoths and an ibex, all incompletely rendered, plus a constellation of strokes and double dots.

The most striking feature at Cougnac is the presence of male themes exclusively. Apart from the signs in the small transverse gallery, and perhaps the three-branched sign in the last group of figures, we find only cervids, ibexes, mammoths, men, double strokes, and hooked or branched signs; it is as though the figures were only the terminal portion of a sanctuary that lacked any central compositions. To be persuaded that the sanctuary is complete as it stands, we have to imagine some utterly unique pairing, either stag/mammoth or mammoth/ibex. Even on the assumption that this is the rear portion of a sanctuary, it is odd not to find some inconspicuous reference to an ox or a bison. The rear portions of other sanctuaries of the same epoch, at Pech Merle and Le Gabillou or at Lascaux, exhibit the same piling up of male symbols (cervids, ibexes, horses, horned men or wounded men), but there is always some final repetition of female animals. The untypical character of the composition brings out even better, perhaps, the stylistic affinities of Cougnac with other caves contemporaneous with it, especially with Pech Merle. The signs fully attest its chronological equivalence with Pech Merle's second period. The men run through with spears bear out the same connotation, since the only two renderings of that theme occur in these two caves. Furthermore, the bodies of the animals, massive but with normal withers, and having vertical legs well integrated within the general structure, similarly suggest the second period at Lascaux and Le Gabillou. The ibex horns have two forms: one shows both horns in two parallel lines (a convention found throughout the Upper Paleolithic) the other shows the horns slightly diverging in "half-twisted" perspective, as at Pech Merle, Lascaux, and Le Gabillou.

The absolute dating of Cougnac will remain uncertain until excavation turns up industrial objects. Its relative dating, on the other hand, is perfectly clear: it corresponds to the second part of Style III—that is, very probably to an already advanced stage of the Early Magdalenian, prior to Magdalenian III.

LE PORTEL

LOUBENS, ARIÈGE, FRANCE

(See fig. 153, page 361, for a diagram of the cave)

Le Portel, also referred to as the Crampagna cave, had long been known when the paintings were discovered in 1908 by R. Jeannel and G. Fauveau. The drawings of the cave were mostly executed by the Abbé Breuil, from 1908 on.

The cave, about 165 yards long, is shaped like a trident (see fig. 153); the present-day entrance is at the base of the handle. Where the three prongs meet the handle there is a rather vast chamber, A, within which a mass of fallen rock indicates a former opening into the cave. Three corridors of nearly equal length form the prongs of the trident. The one at the left has an opening at its far end which seems to have been blocked up before the decoration was executed. In the course of excavations by Vézian, the owner of the property, hearths were discovered at a spot about 100 feet from the present-day entrance, somewhat before the large chamber and at the foot of the fallen rocks. The hearths contained industrial objects and some plaquettes with engravings dating from Magdalenian III–V. These excavations are interesting because they show that here, as elsewhere (Lascaux, Labastide, La Bouiche), Magdalenian man could gain access to the more remote portions of the caves and live there at least temporarily.

Le Portel is a monument of great value not only for the quality and the state of preservation of its works, but also for their arrangement. It was my study of the Abbé Breuil's fine publication of this cave, accompanied by an exact diagram, that initiated all my research into the topographical disposition of figures. One gallery contains eight bison and one horse; another, nine horses and one bison; the large chamber, one bison and one horse; the entrance corridor, again one bison and one horse. These data and such indications, frequently vague, as I found in the few existing topographical studies of sanctuaries determined me to undertake, with the Rev. Hours and Jean Vertut, the topographical analysis of the some seventy caves and rock shelters which are presented in this book.

Two sanctuaries from different epochs occupy the four galleries of Le Portel, clearly separated from each other by the topographical layout. The earlier one seems to begin in the big chamber, and continues along the left-hand gallery 2 (the Jammes Gallery) right up to the blocked-up narrow opening at the end (L–P). The later sanctuary, which corresponds to the hearths discovered by Vézian, begins a few yards from the present-day entrance, runs along gallery 1 (c on plan; Jeannel Gallery), crosses the large chamber and extends into the central and right-hand prongs of the trident: gallery 3 (I–K; Regnault Gallery), where the horses are found, and gallery 4 (D–H; Breuil Gallery), where the bison are found.

THE OLD SANCTUARY

A good many of the black and red paintings that make up the earlier sanctuary are in very poor condition. Starting from the foot of the fallen rocks in the large chamber, on both sides of a fissure are red dots (A); then, on a rocky mass in the middle of the chamber, a composition with about ten more or less incompletely rendered figures, including at least four bison and one horse, and two stags in the upper margin (B). Opposite on the left-hand wall, there are a few red strokes, and in a double recess (L) a four-branched sign in the left and

¹ *fig. 388*   ² *fig. 579*

³ *fig. 387*

⁴ *figs. 390, 391*

an incomplete stag in the right,[1] with horns in Style III. At the corner of Gallery 2 we find a small red horse[2] that is difficult to place stylistically, but delectable for the look it has of a climbing pony and for its eye, supplied by an accidental bump of the wall (i).

On the right-hand wall there follow a few horses in very damaged condition,[3] facing a group of three red dots (M). Then, on the left, we can make out a hollow that is bordered by a few blocks marking out a small recess. In it we find an odd set of figures (N), consisting of a horse's forequarters,[4] a brace-shaped sign, and two small male figures in red whose sexual parts are supplied by stumps of the stalagmite that is part of the wall. Farther on, both walls show a number of red strokes and spots of uncertain shape. Just in front of the blocked-up hole in the back appear groups of dots like those close to the ground in the large chamber, next to the fallen rocks. No other figure in the cave can be reliably assigned to this older sanctuary, which is clearly marked along the course between the rock slide and the blocked-up old opening at the back of Gallery 2. Just where was the entry at the time these oldest figures were done? It is hard to choose between the two blocked-up passages, given the fact that the red dots found at the present entrance and rear are so much alike. I am inclined to opt for the rock fall in the large chamber as the original entrance, since it leads directly to the first composition in the middle of the chamber, then to the recesses containing the first big sign, and from there to the second composition with another big sign and the male human figures (which as a rule are found in the back portions of sanctuaries).

Dating the first set of figures is not made easy by their washed-out condition. The Abbé Breuil held the majority of the works to be Aurignacian, but his arguments are not really convincing. He says of the horses 34–37 in Gallery 1: "They all recall, by the archaic character of their style, the two Aurignacian horses at Les Cabrerets and Sergeac" (see Bibliography). He is unquestionably referring here to the horses at Pech Merle and the horse in the Labatut rock shelter at Sergeac. The former have not been dated directly; the latter has been dated from the very end of the Gravettian (humped points retouched on the flat side), or even from the period between the Gravettian and the Solutrean. Thus the boundary line between Style II and Style III is where we might look for figures related to the horses in gallery 2; on this score, I am entirely in agreement that they should be placed in the time span that extends from Pair-non-Pair to Lascaux. Can we be more exact? The signs suggest that we can, for the four-branched sign in the double recess is in some way intermediate between a stylized vulva and a quadrangular sign, while the sign in the hollowed recess is clearly related to the brace-shaped signs. To settle for the interval between the Solutrean and Early Magdalenian would not be out of line with the chronological system adopted here. At the same time, the figures on the rocky mass in the middle of the large chamber are apparently later than those in gallery 2. *(For description of the rest of the cave, see pages 360–361.)*

ISTURITZ

BASSES-PYRÉNÉES, FRANCE

The low reliefs in the cave were discovered by E. Passemard in 1913.

This site became famous through Passemard's excavations and the separate excavations by R. de Saint-Périer. The large chamber, which contained evidence of an astonishingly long habitation that extended from the Mousterian to the very end of the Magdalenian, slopes steeply down to the lower galleries which were discovered later. At the foot of the slope stands a great stalagmitic mass which prior to the excavations was partly buried under the archaeological deposits. It was on this pillar that Passemard discovered a group of figures in low relief,[1] the upper portion of which, exposed to the air, was greatly damaged. The figures on the left-hand side are nearly intact; those on the right may never have been very clear, and not all of them can be reliably identified. The portions in good condition, however, attest to a very high standard of execution.

¹ *fig. 392*

On the left we readily recognize a reindeer, the upper part of whose antlers are missing; the treatment of the animal is remarkable on every score. Superimposed on the reindeer are two short-tailed ruminants which may be ibexes or stags; they are well executed, but the horns are missing. It is regrettable that we cannot settle the question of their identity; although groupings of stag/ibex and reindeer/ibex are known, a reindeer/stag grouping would be altogether exceptional. The head and withers of the two animals are still faintly visible. The upper part of the right-hand side of the panel shows a reindeer and two horses that are still recognizable, and below is a group of poorly defined figures which are believed to include a mammoth and a bear.

The excavations should have supplied the elements for an exact dating: Passemard found that the Solutrean layer did not come up to the figures, and that the layer that covered them was Magdalenian. The Abbé Breuil, taking into account the fact that in the Pyrenees the "local" Solutrean is immediately followed by Magdalenian IV, assigned the figures to Magdalenian IV. This determination—the Middle or even a more advanced Magdalenian—is based solely on the figures that belong incontestably to Style IV. The conditions give rise to two difficulties. First, if the lower portion of the figures was at the level of the Solutrean deposits, the figures should be more or less Solutrean as well. The style of low reliefs from the Solutrean is rather well known, however, and we have, besides, decorated objects from Isturitz itself: the association with these low reliefs is difficult, if not frankly impossible. So far as this first problem is concerned, it would be very useful to have an exact description of the aspect of the layers of deposits at the foot of the slope and along the stalagmitic mass, so that we could tell whether any sliding had disturbed the order of the layers and thus produced a stratigraphic "aging" of the figures. Unfortunately, the excavations were carried out hurriedly and without scientifically precise apparatus.

The second difficult point concerns the supposedly later date of the Pyrenean Solutrean and the absence of the stages of Magdalenian I, II, and III. Passemard's excavations did not record every stratigraphic sublevel, nor did those of R. de Saint-Périer, whose records were fortunately more complete. Saint-Périer notes, however, at the bottom of Layer II, the presence of some spears characteristic of Magdalenian III, and beneath that, a zone of which the stratigraphy is difficult to make out because it is poor in remains; but it is above the Solutrean, which is also poor. This circumstance leaves room for intermediate stages. Moreover, there is no reason to suppose that the developmental sequence of the Upper Paleolithic, either at Isturitz or in Spain, included an appreciably prolonged Solutrean. Thanks to the analysis of fossil pollens, we know that the successive stages occurred under the same climatic conditions in southern France as in central France. Whether correct or not, the attribution to Magdalenian IV is not based on a critical study of the archaeological evidence. Yet may not this attribution be founded on a postulate other than that of the absence of Early and Middle Magdalenian—namely, on the feeling, perfectly justified, that the style of these figures is late in character? It appears that neither stratigraphic analysis nor the level at which they were buried enables us to determine the date of the Isturitz figures. The fact that they are low reliefs has no special bearing, either, for daylight formerly reached this far into the cave, and low reliefs are to be dated between the Solutrean and the Middle Magdalenian. The composition, if it were really legible, might provide the clue. If the group is based on the reindeer/horse theme, we could conclude that it is very late, inasmuch as this theme only appears in Magdalenian V–VI, and the style would be in keeping with this conclusion. But there are two reasons suggesting caution. First, there may have been bison among the lost figures. On the other hand, although the reappearance of the reindeer is not frequent before the Late Magdalenian, Isturitz had an especially severe climate (as we learn from the pollen analysis); thus the reindeer, at a time when it was disappearing from the cave paintings in the Périgord, may in the Basque country have played a role corresponding to that of the bison. To sum up, the date of the Isturitz figures remains within the Middle Magdalenian, prior to the Late Magdalenian. (*See also page* 380.)

LAS CHIMENEAS

PUENTE VIESGO, SANTANDER, SPAIN

The cave is situated on Monte Castillo, not far from the cave of La Pasiega. It was discovered in 1953 *by Lorenzo Garcia, who was in charge of the Monte Castillo caves.*

131. LAS CHIMENEAS. SCHEMATIC PLAN WITH FIGURES
This is one of the caves in which the layout of the sanctuary presents no ambiguities. The cervids are placed at the entrance and at the very end (1, 2, 10); the large chamber is occupied by an ox/horse + hind/ibex panel (6), and opposite is a panel of rectangular signs (7).

The original entrance to the cave has not been cleared, and it is presently reached through a series of chimneys starting from the way of access into La Pasiega. However, the shape of the original cave is very clear, from the rock slide in front of the original entrance to the end of the decorated portion. The sanctuary begins about twenty yards from the entrance and occupies in turn a small chamber, a passageway, and a rather large chamber; at the back is a deep recess which is reached by passing under successive springings of rock vaults. Its natural layout relates this sanctuary to the corridor-sanctuaries and the least complicated labyrinth-sanctuaries.

The right-hand wall is covered with a soft clay film; the works on it (1–6 in the diagram) are all engravings except for the horse's head on panel 6—a not very successful attempt was made to outline this in black. The harder stalagmite surfaces of the back chamber and its recess are decorated with black outlines having an even thickness, such as might be made with a soft pencil. Both the stylistic characteristics and the over-all unity of the decorations point unmistakably to a single period corresponding to Style III (mature Solutrean and Early Magdalenian). The female signs are of the quadrangular type; the male signs are in the form of double strokes. The accompanying animals are in the most clear-cut Style III—horns, ears, and antlers in "half-twisted" perspective, and the stiff legs of the stags extending forward at the front and backward at the back.

The over-all composition is defined with remarkable clarity. The entrance is marked by two stags and a hind (1, 2, 5). Scrawls and unfinished outlines appear before we reach the large chamber (3, 4). In that chamber, the panel of animals is placed across from a panel of signs; in both panels (6, 7) the springings of the rock vaults were used to advantage to distribute the figures in orderly sequence (as in panel II of the Black Salon at Niaux). On the face of the first springing we find introductory or peripheral animals (hind, ibex) and a horse; on the reverse of that springing, two ox heads; on the face of the second springing the group consists of four oxen accompanied by a hind,[1] and on the other side is the head of an ox all by itself.[2] Scrawls mark the bottom of the various panels. As a whole, then, this composition is based on the ox/horse formula, with accompanying ibex and hind. Except for the hind, a particularly Spanish feature, the formula is that of Lascaux. The prominent position of the stag at the entrance and in the rear of the sanctuary further accentuates this similarity. Group 7 consists of a series of quadrangular signs[3] filled out in different ways, and accompanied by double strokes and a few curving lines of the unfinished-outlines type. The series of signs continues behind the first springing (8), and in the back recess (10) it links up with a series of animals of the male group: a horse and stags (9, 10).[4] A chimney that starts at the left of the panel of stags (10) has a series of scrawls and back-cave signs in the form of double strokes.

All of its stylistic and compositional features relate Las Chimeneas to the sanctuaries having rectangular signs of the ox/horse group, in which cervids play a very important part as back-cave animals (Lascaux, Le Gabillou).

[1] *fig.* 393   [2] *fig.* 394

[3] *fig.* 398

[4] *figs.* 395–397

ALTAMIRA

SANTILLANA, SANTANDER, SPAIN

The decorations at Altamira were discovered in 1879 by the daughter of an archaeologist, the Marquis Marcelino de Sautuola, who was exploring the cave. As is well known, scientific circles did not recognize the authenticity of the figures until twenty years later. Altamira was one of the first caves studied by the Abbé Breuil, who began his inventory in 1902 at the request of Émile Cartailhac.

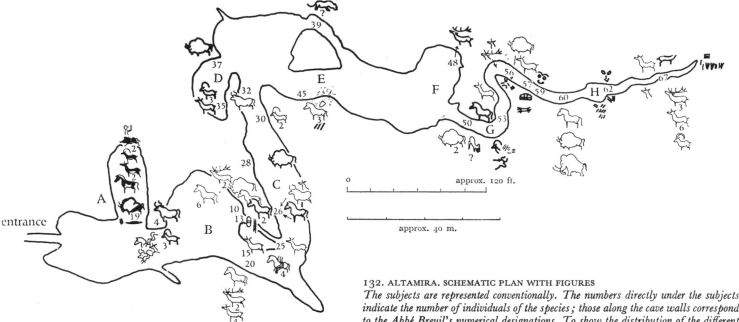

132. ALTAMIRA. SCHEMATIC PLAN WITH FIGURES
The subjects are represented conventionally. The numbers directly under the subjects indicate the number of individuals of the species; those along the cave walls correspond to the Abbé Breuil's numerical designations. To show the distribution of the different series of figures, the polychrome figures are given in modeled form, the figures of the "black sequence" in heavy outline, and the other animals in thin outline. It is obvious that the "black sequence" supplies the pictorial structure of the cave from the entrance to the furthest point, with bison/horse or ox/horse groups accompanied by ibexes; the cervids and ibexes serve as passageway and back-cave animals, while signs mark the topographical transitions. (Diagram after Alberto Corral and Hugo Obermaier.)

The Altamira cave may be divided topographically into three parts: (1) close to the entrance, on the left, the chamber with the Painted Ceiling, situated about 85 feet from daylight in a portion of the cave that must have been dark even in Paleolithic times; (2) the middle portion of the cave, consisting of a large winding gallery with several lateral extensions; (3) the innermost portion of the cave, a narrow corridor about 55 yards long in which are crowded a considerable number of works. These characteristics put Altamira in the category of sanctuaries of average depth and easy access, except for the chamber with the Painted Ceiling which is close to the entrance and may also be classified as of easy access. The topographical features have no decisive chronological value. There have been many excavations at Altamira; unfortunately, not all of them have been well conducted from the stratigraphic point of view. However, the early excavations as well as the most recent ones show that the cave was used with only insignificant interruptions throughout the Upper Paleolithic, from the Solutrean until the mature Magdalenian. The stylistic analysis of the works leads, moreover, to the same conclusion. A recent carbon-14 analysis places Altamira's Early Magdalenian at 13,500 B.C. This date may fairly reasonably be assigned to the figures of the "black sequence."

GENERAL ARRANGEMENT OF THE FIGURES

There are a good many engravings distributed over the walls, from the first figures to those at the back area of the cave. On the basis of stylistic characteristics well attested by decorated objects from El Castillo and from Altamira itself, the Abbé Breuil assigned the oldest engravings to the Solutrean and the Early Magdalenian. The engraved works are scattered among the painted figures that essentially constitute two large groups. One (the "black sequence") begins just a little past the cave entrance, and its figures turn up throughout the middle and back portions of the cave. The other group consists of the figures on the Painted Ceiling near the entrance.

¹ figs. 399–405

THE "BLACK SEQUENCE"¹

The paintings of this series belong to the type which Breuil characterized as having little or no modeling. In chamber B and gallery C (fig. 132) we see a certain number of figures of oxen, bison, and horses; these indicate that the central portion of the sanctuary was located in this area (3, 4, 10, 26, 28, 35, 37); the signs accompanying this group are found inside a narrow side chamber (13). There are four quadrangular signs,

328

and ladderlike lines which play the part of rows of dots. At 39 in chamber E we find, hidden away in a recess, a rather vague figure that might be a feline; it marks the end of the first group of figures. At 35, the back of the dead-end passage D is indicated by two black ibexes[2]; they occupy a position similar in its remoteness to that of the ibexes at the back of Gallery C in La Pasiega (fig. 135). An area extends without figures until the entrance (F) of the long inner gallery, which seems to have played here a part quite analogous to that of the Chamber of Felines at Lascaux. The entrance is signaled by a stag (48); painted or engraved horses[3] and bison occupy the front part of the winding corridor (50, 53, 56). A group of quadrangular signs (57) of a type close to those at La Pasiega and El Castillo,[4] accompanied by some barbed signs, is directly opposite a rough-surfaced patch of wall the irregularities of which have been transformed into human masks (59, 62).[5] Between the cave entrance and its farthest point, some sixty groups of black signs, consisting almost entirely of dots and short strokes, mark the groups of figures or the intervening areas. The entire group of black figures presents stylistic features homogeneous enough to be assigned to a single chronological period, corresponding to Style III. Two of the groups of signs (13, 57) are variations of the same quadrangular type; the ones in the inner gallery seem later than those nearer the entrance. The animals may also belong to two chronologically successive sets, but they are too few in number to provide evidence for a formal evolution. In any case, signs and animals localize the "black sequence" between the Solutrean and the Early Magdalenian, prior to Magdalenian III–IV.

[2] fig. 399

[3] fig. 401

[4] fig. 405
[5] figs. 402–404

THE PAINTED CEILING[6]

[6] figs. 15, 670

The Painted Ceiling at Altamira is the most famous of all Paleolithic works of art; together with certain panels at Lascaux and Niaux it certainly marks the peak of Upper Paleolithic painting. The decoration occupies a space twenty yards long and about ten yards wide, forming a long band that has a most interesting topographical organization.

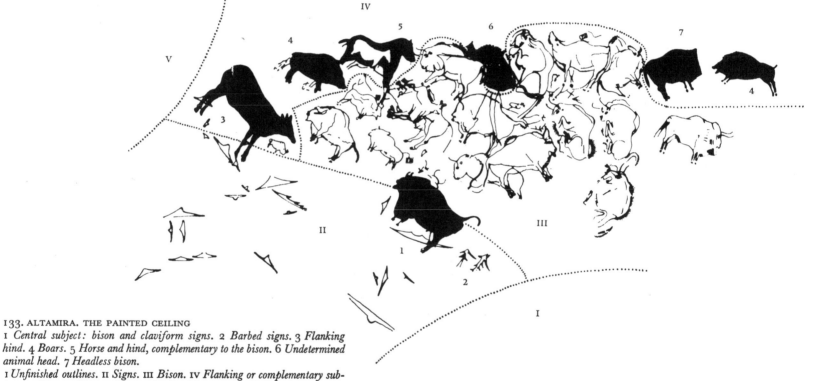

133. ALTAMIRA. THE PAINTED CEILING
1 *Central subject: bison and claviform signs.* 2 *Barbed signs.* 3 *Flanking hind.* 4 *Boars.* 5 *Horse and hind, complementary to the bison.* 6 *Undetermined animal head.* 7 *Headless bison.*
I *Unfinished outlines.* II *Signs.* III *Bison.* IV *Flanking or complementary subjects.* V *Engraved human figures. (Animal figures after H. Breuil.)*

The central portion (III) is occupied by about fifteen bison shown in various attitudes. The largest figure is a male, placed at bottom center; the legs touch a large claviform sign flanked by two barbed signs; the rest of the lower composition is strewn with claviform signs (II). The pairing of symbols, affirmed by the barbed signs adjacent to the claviforms, is correspondingly assured for the animals by the presence of a horse (IV).

The over-all bison/horse theme calls for the addition of a certain number of complementary subjects. A big hind is found at the back (accompanied by a bison which serves as complement to it), another hind complements the horse (IV), and a third hind is placed in front of the big horse's head at top center. The periphery of this monumental composition includes a number of marginal figures which, in a composition for a corridor type of cave, would be placed in the back-cave area. These marginal figures are engravings of male personages (V) near the big hind, two boars (a theme virtually unique in cave art), one on each outer side of the middle, and a headless bison at the end of the group of complete animals. Like the panels in the "sanctuary" of Les Trois Frères, the Altamira ceiling constitutes a whole, including a main bison/horse theme (the horse appears twice toward the edge, as at Les Trois Frères), complementary animals (ibex and hind), and marginal or back-cave themes (boar, headless bison).

From the stylistic point of view, the Altamira ceiling is entirely homogeneous. The points of reference supplied by its variants are found in several other caves, notably El Castillo, Marsoulas, Santimamine, Niaux, Le Portel, Les Trois Frères, and Bédeilhac. Moreover, these stylistic details, which establish the unity of the various caves mentioned, are abundantly in evidence among the decorated objects of Magdalenian III–IV. This makes it hard to account for the Abbé Breuil's attribution of the Painted Ceiling at Altamira to Magdalenian VI.

ENGRAVINGS

[7] fig. 406

Near the entrance to Altamira, we find a broad ceiling-like area covered with meandering lines and figures sketchily drawn with the fingers on a wall lightly coated with soft clay.[7] The Abbé Breuil has attributed these meanders to the earliest phase of the Upper Paleolithic. They are in fact very similar to those at Gargas, which may reasonably be attributed to the stages prior to the Solutrean. It should be borne in mind, however, that meanders on a clay surface have a primitive look no matter when they were executed, and that they are found in decorations dating from the mature Magdalenian (at Rouffignac and Montespan, for example).

[8] figs. 406–408, 666

As previously mentioned, the engravings in the middle portion of the cave and beyond seem to be spaced in different periods of the cave's occupation, filling the intervals between painted areas.[8] In this connection we must mention an interesting group in the inner gallery of the cave, which includes a horse and a bison associated with a mammoth (60). This mammoth is the only proboscidian in Spanish caves that could not possibly be taken for an elephant. The bison it accompanies has fairly late Magdalenian characteristics. It is not unrelated to figures at Le Puy de Lacan, and, like certain figures on Late Magdalenian decorated objects, it has a protruding tongue. The formula bison/horse + mammoth is found at Bernifal, Les Combarelles, Font-de-Gaume, and Rouffignac, and the aspect of the figures in this Altamira composition does not contradict this comparison with caves in which sizable portions of the decoration date from the border line of the Middle and the Late Magdalenian. Nor does the location of these figures in the back part of the Altamira cave involve any inconsistency. Probably the latest work in the cave, this little group constitutes as exceptional a case as does the Las Monedas decoration in which the reindeer appears; it seems to be evidence of a localized influence of figurative traditions from regions much further north.

To sum up, the Altamira cave is relatively coherent in its decorations, as it is in archaeological evidence. Its earliest portions date from the beginning of the Solutrean, the latest from a mature Magdalenian. The topographical and chronological distribution of the figures indicates that during the first important phase of the cave's use as a sanctuary the structure of the decorations was based on the two possibly successive groups of black paintings found in the front and the back portions of the cave. Though these earliest groups cannot be dated with complete accuracy, they would seem to fall into the Solutrean and the Early Magdalenian. The second important phase is marked by the execution of the Painted Ceiling with its polychrome figures; the dating of this is less uncertain, centering upon the Middle Magdalenian (Magdalenian III–IV). Lastly, the small back-cave bison/horse + mammoth group exhibits the influence of a theme that dates from some later phase of the Magdalenian and has heretofore been observed only in Périgord.

LA PASIEGA

PUENTO VIESGO, SANTANDER, SPAIN

La Pasiega is one of the Monte Castillo caves and is situated between Las Chimeneas and Las Monedas. The decorations were discovered in 1911 by Hugo Obermaier and Paul Wernert; the Abbé Breuil made the pictorial inventory. Some excavating, especially in the past few years, has been done near the entrance in an attempt to make access to Gallery B less difficult. So far the only very characteristic finds date from the Solutrean and the Early Magdalenian, which is entirely in keeping with the decoration in this part of the cave. La Pasiega has at least four entrances and comprises several sanctuaries.

The cave consists of a gallery about 110 yards long, running parallel to the hillside. From this gallery five corridors lead, or formerly led, to openings onto the hillside. The middle portion of the gallery and the three corridors leading off from it have little or no decoration. The majority of the figures are grouped at the extremities—Galleries B and A to the east, Gallery C to the west. Within these decorated areas we can distinguish five zones corresponding to different periods of the sanctuary.

GALLERY B

[1] fig. 62

[2] chart LI. Numbers in parentheses refer to the chart

It was at the entrance to Gallery B that some Solutrean remains were found. It contains a small number of figures: bison and horses, stags, and a possible feline, plus a hypothetical hand. Three red claviform signs[1] complete this rather poorly preserved decoration. The so-called inscription of La Pasiega, off by itself on the wall, is in Gallery C.[2] It consists of a number of signs more or less in alignment (1). The sign on the left (2) is reminiscent of certain variants of brace-shaped signs; the ones in the center are like imprints of feet (4); the sign on the right (3) is very like sign No. 15 at El Castillo (5). Various hypotheses have been put forward to interpret this sequence of signs as a real inscription. The least that can be said is that here, as in so many other instances, imagination has been called upon to fill the gaps in research. It would be idle to "read" these signs at La Pasiega, but certain parallels suggest that elsewhere—at El Castillo, Cougnac, Lascaux, and Niaux (5, 6, 7, and 8 respectively on chart LI)—there are variants of quadrangular and brace-shaped signs no less peculiar than these at La Pasiega. As for the alignment, there are enough examples at El Castillo, Las Chimeneas, La Cullalvera, and Lascaux to keep us from considering the very rough alignment here as a unique, especially significant case. More interesting is the presence of an ibex[3] at the back of the side chamber adjoining the place with the "inscription," and of another ibex at the point where Gallery B joins Gallery A. There are also ibexes at the end of every corridor in Gallery C.

[3] *fig. 416*

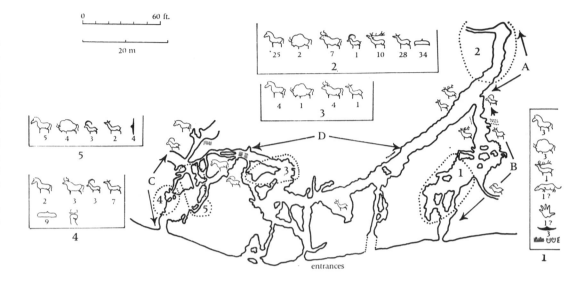

134. LA PASIEGA. SCHEMATIC PLAN AND ARRANGEMENT OF SUBJECTS, WITH INVENTORY OF THE FIGURES
The letters A, B, C, D are the traditional designations of the various parts of the cave (galleries). The large numbers (1–5) indicate the five areas which contain the sanctuaries; the small numbers placed below the conventionalized drawings represent the number of individual animals and signs. Back-cave and passageway subjects are drawn directly on the plan. See also figs. 135–137 below. (Diagram after the official guide to the caves of Monte Castillo.)

GALLERY A

Here we find the figures at La Pasiega which are deservedly the most famous. They constitute a collection of animals and signs painted in red and highly homogeneous in execution. The stylistic unity is matched by the organization of the figures. The gallery (fig. 135) includes a section of the cave (A–F) that ends in a small terminal chamber (G–H), and a fissure (J–K) that cannot be penetrated very far. The whole central part of this layout (D, E, F, G) is occupied by compositions on the ox/horse theme, with stags and hinds as adjuncts. One bison/horse composition occurs at the beginning of the sequence (A), and an identical one occurs toward the end (I). In the cul-de-sac (H) is the only ibex. Apart from two signs accompanying a composition in the center of the gallery (E), the signs—all of which are variants of the brace-shaped type—are grouped at the rear, and in the fissure twenty-five of them are bunched together. The figures[4] are on the whole of excellent quality, and when compared with those of the Périgord caves, exhibit incontestable characteristics of Style III. In particular, we meet again the treatment of bovid horns that we found at Lascaux, Le Gabillou, etc., and the same pattern of cervid antlers. The presence of brace-shaped signs, too, confirms our assignment of Gallery A to the period of Style III—that is, between the mature Solutrean and the end of the Early Magdalenian. On the whole, however, the figures are less archaic than those at Lascaux, which must be more or less contemporary with them. The nearby Las Chimeneas cave contains animal figures that are more closely related to those at Lascaux and associated with signs of the quadrangular type. Thus La Pasiega seems to belong entirely to the second phase of Style III, that of the brace-shaped signs, and it is not surprising that the contours of the animals—like those of certain figures at Le Gabillou and Villars—are already close to Early Style IV.

[4] *figs. 409–415*

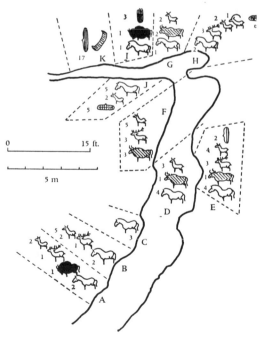

135. LA PASIEGA, GALLERY A. DETAILED PLAN WITH ARRANGEMENT AND INVENTORY OF FIGURES
The subjects are arranged by panel, from A to K. The small numbers near the conventionalized representations indicate the number of individuals of each type.

GALLERY C

Topographically, Gallery C is a rather vast chamber, about eleven yards long, with a labyrinth of little galleries giving off it at the back. The front portion, on the left, is occupied by a collection of animals in Style III almost identical with those in Gallery A. The topographical arrangement of these figures is very striking (see fig. 136). On the wall toward the entrance, the figures include, in particular, one bovid in a vertical position and a very odd group of paired signs that suggest a fenced-off enclosure or an animal trap.[5] Actually it is a sign of the quadrangular type bordered with rows of dots, a common enough subject of which there are

[5] *chart LII (A)*

many examples, but in this case one of the open areas at the ends of the sign contains the hindquarters of a bison, the other the forequarters of a hind. It is probably not by chance that the female sign is here combined with the bison (female symbol par excellence) and the hind into a single group. The remainder of the composition occupies a sort of recess that is reached by two fairly wide openings. The outer entrance wall has a large ox painted in red, accompanied by an ibex. The opening on the left has a hind that seems to be going inside, while the right-hand opening has the head of a hind on each side, facing one another. The panel at the back of the little room, which is closed off by the big blocks of the entrance wall, consists of a large composition of hinds accompanied by a horse, with an ibex in a cranny and several quadrangular and brace-shaped signs. Where the wall recedes on the left we find an odd figure that seems to be a human bust surmounted with an ear and the horns of a bovid (see fig. 134, 4).

The figures deeper inside Gallery C are clearly later in character. The most important group (see fig. 137) is in all but a few details disposed like the one we have just been describing: on a large springing of the cave vault we see a bison, a horse, and an ibex, accompanied by two claviform signs and a series of dots. Two hinds have been placed on either side of the opening of a fissure leading into a small space where we can just make out a horse's head and a vague dorsal line. In style these animals are very different from those in the front part of the chamber. The bison especially, despite the treatment of the horns, clearly belongs to Style IV, as do the ibex and the horse. These characteristics are entirely in keeping with the presence of claviform signs, which place this group in the Middle Magdalenian.[6] Advancing still farther into this gallery, we find some more figures in Style IV—notably, at the very back, two ibexes in a diagonal arrangement, which mark the end of the sequence of figures.

[6] fig. 417

GALLERY D

The middle portion of La Pasiega, Gallery D, is much less richly decorated than the two ends of the cave, and such decoration as it has is less coherent. However, we find a small group on the ox/horse theme, and another on the bison/horse theme.

The figures at La Pasiega attest to two periods of decoration: the older group (Gallery A and the front part of Gallery C) tallies with a probably rather advanced stage of Style III; the later group (back part of Gallery C) belongs to Early Style IV of the claviform period (Middle Magdalenian III–IV). Comparison with what is in the nearby El Castillo cave would be interesting in this connection. Although the signs in Style III at La Pasiega are of a type very like those at El Castillo, they are not exactly similar to the latter (with a few exceptions, such as the brace-shaped signs at El Castillo—group 60 in fig. 139). Nor are the signs in Las Chimeneas, also near by, any more similar to them, and it seems that the three caves were not used simultaneously. Of the three, Las Chimeneas appears to be the oldest, while El Castillo and La Pasiega overlap in time without coinciding completely. If we assign to these three caves the time limits, for Style III, between the Middle Solutrean and Magdalenian III, then the accepted chronology would provide a period of four thousand years (17,000–13,000 B.C.), a time span long enough to account for differences among periods of habitation. The situation is the same for works in Style IV, since the period of the claviform signs is represented only at La Pasiega, while the nearby cave of Las Monedas has a later form of decoration, offering the only example of that style in Spain.

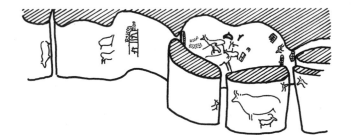

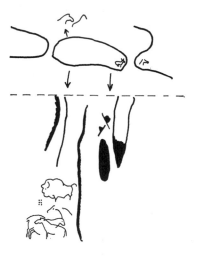

136 (above). LA PASIEGA, GALLERY C.
Arrangement of the group of figures in Style III.

137 (right). LA PASIEGA, GALLERY C.
Arrangement of the group of figures in Style IV;
bison and claviform signs.

EL CASTILLO

PUENTE VIESGO, SANTANDER, SPAIN

The cave's decorations were discovered in 1903 by H. Alcade del Rio, and the Abbé Breuil made the pictorial inventory. Archaeological deposits found in great quantity at the entrance were excavated between 1909 and 1914 by Hugo Obermaier and Paul Wernert. Unfortunately almost nothing has been published about their finding, apart from a short study by Obermaier in 1925. From it we learn that all the horizons of the Upper Paleolithic were represented at El Castillo, some of the levels reaching a depth of nearly six feet. Had a site of this importance been exploited scientifically, we would have answers to some of the elementary questions that have been raised concerning Spanish prehistory. So far as one can tell, works of art turned up only at "the harpoon stage of the Upper Magdalenian"; no such finds were reported from the Solutrean and Gravettian horizons.

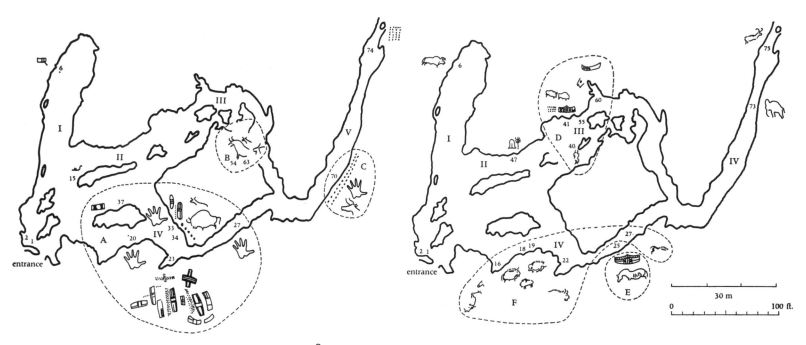

138–139. EL CASTILLO. SCHEMATIC PLANS SHOWING THE DISTRIBUTION OF THE PRINCIPAL FIGURES AT THE VARIOUS PERIODS OF FREQUENTATION
To simplify the diagrams, the animals (horse, stag, ibex, hind) which occur both in the main compositions and elsewhere have not been included. The numbering of the figures is that given in the Abbé Breuil's publication of 1912. (Based on the official guide to the caves of Monte Castillo.)
138 *(left).* PLAN OF THE FIRST OCCUPATION, *corresponding to Style III* (A, B, C).
139 *(right).* PLAN OF THE SECOND (E), THIRD (D), AND FOURTH (F) OCCUPATIONS, *corresponding to terminal Style III and Early Style IV.*

The cave of El Castillo measures about 500 yards from the entrance to its farthest point. It consists of two parallel galleries (I and V) linked by a vast area of fallen rocks forming a labyrinth. Within this labyrinth one large chamber (II) is cut up by blocks and stalagmites. Its lower portion (IV) forms a distinct topographical unit. At its upper end, another distinct area (III) is formed by a number of blocks and winding passages. The terminal gallery (V) is linked to these topographical areas by two separate passages. This conformation explains why different parts of the cave were used as sanctuaries in different epochs, and why, in the course of the cave's lengthy occupation, a number of adventitious figures came to fill up most of the wall space between the main areas.

The Abbé Breuil's 1912 publication on El Castillo, which inaugurated the study of the painted caves, was a topographical analysis of the various subjects; he also published separate diagrams of the hands, the signs, the black figures, the red figures, the polychrome figures, etc. It is to be regretted that this method was not followed in subsequent studies, since a topographical analysis is by far the most suitable for establishing a chronological sequence. On the basis of his topographical study, the Abbé Breuil distinguished two great periods in El Castillo's prehistory, a conclusion which our own labors half a century later confirm. When a topographical analysis is made of the quadrangular signs, the hands, and the animals in Style III, three areas are clearly to be singled out. The most important part of the older sanctuary is to be found in zone IV, the walls of which are completely covered with hands in negative. A group of bison, hinds, and horses is distributed at points 37, 33, 34 (see fig. 138). Some of the signs corresponding to these animals are with the bison at points 33 and 34, but most of them are inside a recess (23) where they are spread about[1] much as are the nearly con-

[1] *figs. 61, 420, 421*

[2] fig. 422

[3] fig. 426

[4] fig. 420

[5] fig. 421

[6] fig. 63

[7] fig. 102

[8] fig. 425

[9] fig. 418

temporary signs in Gallery A at La Pasiega. Another area of this sanctuary is in zone v, where we find more hands,[2] dots, and an ox in Style III; the sanctuary terminates at point 74, where rows of dots are found on a stalagmite that blocks further passage. Thus the earliest painted sanctuary extended from the entrance through points 37, 33, 23, 27, and 70 to point 74. However, a few figures in Style III form an isolated ox/horse group[3] in the labyrinth of zone III, at points 54 and 63.

The painted figures in Style IV are distributed at three main points (fig. 139; D in zone III, E and F in zone IV). A first grouping is found at point 25 (zone IV); it consists of a wounded horse and a brace-shaped sign of the oldest type, very close to the quadrangular signs inside the recess at point 22. This little grouping is reminiscent of the one with the wounded ox at Pech Merle; the horse is nearer to Style III than to Style IV. There is a concentration of figures in Style IV at area D (zone III), where the bison/horse/ibex/stag theme is repeated, now on free-standing portions of the wall, now inside recesses that form, as it were, small side chapels. In one of these, at point 60, a thick stalactite has been transformed into a bison's head by the addition of a few black spots. At point 40 a different use has been made of "natural" reliefs: by the same technique a column of stalagmites has been turned into a bison positioned vertically. A still more recent group is found in area F of zone IV, where some polychrome figures in Early Style IV have been superimposed on figures of the early sanctuary. It is interesting to note that there are no signs corresponding to these polychrome figures. We should expect to find them accompanied by claviform signs, as are figures in this highly developed conventional modeling everywhere else in northern Spain and the Pyrenees. Possibly, those who made the later additions considered the large quandrangular signs nearby in the recess at point 22 to be sufficient. All in all, El Castillo is solidly structured in the topographical sense, so long as the topographical study is limited to the signs and the characteristic animals in the main compositions. This is why we omitted from the diagrams not only horses, for they appear nearly everywhere, but also the ibexes and stags which crowd the passageways, the entrance, and the back of the sanctuary.

STYLISTIC CHARACTERISTICS

The signs at El Castillo supply its chronological as well as its topographical structure. The oldest ones, of the quadrangular type, are concentrated between points 33 and 23 (fig. 138). There are about ten in the recess at point 23, paired with rows of dots. Among these signs are two configurations which neatly confirm what I have said about the sexual character and the pairings of these abstract signs. For what we see here—an instance unique in Paleolithic art—is two signs of the group held to be female, arranged to form a cross.[4] Since these signs normally require their male complements, the painter had to arrange the rows of dots, too, to form a cross; in any case, this is what he did.[5] It would be idle to try to interpret the intention behind this unusual arrangement, but it would have been hard for a Paleolithic painter to find a clearer way of telling us that the signs are paired. At point 25 (fig. 139) in the vicinity of the first collection of signs, there is a brace-shaped sign that is of later date, yet filled out in a manner still closely related to the quadrangular signs. At points 41 and 60 in zone III there are brace-shaped signs nearly identical with those at La Pasiega. The signs at points 6 and 37 (fig. 138) are definitely from one or the other of the two periods (quadrangular or brace-shaped), but it is difficult to settle on either one. A still more special case turns up in group 47 (fig. 139) where rather realistic female signs are accompanied by a branching sign.[6] We have no exact guidelines here: the little group is not from the archaic period of realistic vulvas, nor yet is it from the definitely late period when branching signs are no longer found. On the basis of the painted signs, then, we can narrow down the time span in which the various areas of El Castillo were used to somewhere between the Solutrean (the probable period of the appearance of the rectangular signs) and a time close to the Middle Magdalenian. It may seem surprising not to find claviform signs such as exist at nearby La Pasiega; on the other hand, we find engraved here and there a few more or less realistic oval signs, which seem to supply evidence of the cave's having been visited in the very late Magdalenian.

THE ANIMALS

The distribution of the painted animals is topographically in keeping with that of the different types of signs just described. At points 33 and 34, which seem to have constituted the core of the earliest sanctuary (fig. 138), we find bison not unrelated to the animals in Style III in the Périgord and the Lot. The horse at point 25 (fig. 139) is also quite clearly in Style III. It is harder to assign a chronological place to the proboscidian at point 73.[7] Along with the "elephant" at El Pindal, this figure has given rise to many interpretations which tend to make it an elephant rather than a mammoth. So far as I am concerned, considering that the mammoth is the sole proboscidian of the Upper Paleolithic whose existence, even in Spain, is attested to by skeletal remains, I am inclined to identify this figure with the latter animal. As for the date of this subject at El Castillo, it may correspond either to the earlier or to the later sanctuary, the latter somewhat the more likely, although the "elephant" at El Pindal and the mammoth at Altamira—the only other known examples in Spain—are like this one located at the extreme back of the cave, and obviously later, dating at the earliest from the period of the claviform signs. The animals painted in black are for the most part from the second period, and have all the Style IV characteristics; this is especially true of the two bison at point 41,[8] and to an even greater degree of the small bison off by itself at point 22. We must also mention a black-painted ox at point 6, accompanied by a rectangular sign—the animal looks fairly late in date—and the sequence of red and bichrome figures from points 16 to 19, which are closely related to the figures on the Painted Ceiling at Altamira.

It is more difficult to determine the chronological place of the engravings. There does not seem to have been at El Castillo a group of engravings, properly speaking, such as we find at Les Combarelles, for example; rather, figures were engraved at various epochs to serve as complements, as at Altamira. Immediately inside the entrance we find ibexes and deer[9] which must have belonged among the entrance figures in the sanctuaries of the first period. When we reach chamber I, however, we find later figures, some of which are of the type of unfinished outlines. There are a great many engravings in zones II and III, mostly of the second period— that is, in the areas where the decoration is in Style IV.

To sum up, El Castillo seems to have been in use at periods that correspond only roughly to the periods represented in the other Monte Castillo caves. When we try to place the various sets of figures on the basis of the correlation between the signs and the stylistic characteristics of the animals, we end with producing the following relative order:

(1) Las Chimeneas appears to represent the earliest period, a style comparable to that of Lascaux's first period or Pech Merle's first period.

(2) Area 33–34 at El Castillo would come next and would be related to Lascaux's or Pech Merle's second period.

(3) The front part of La Pasiega (Gallery C) would have to be placed in a period very close to the last-mentioned.

(4) Group 25 at El Castillo exhibits brace-shaped signs of a still early form in association with animals that approach Early Style IV. In time this would correspond more or less with Gallery A at La Pasiega.

(5) Area III at El Castillo would be contemporary with Gallery A at La Pasiega, or a bit later. The animal figures are already in Early Style IV.

(6) The remotest part of La Pasiega brings us to the period of claviform signs contemporaneous with those found in the French Pyrenees.

(7) Area IV at El Castillo (points 16–19) supplies as evidence animals modeled in two colors, of the same period as those at Altamira.

(8) Lastly, Las Monedas brings us to the Late Magdalenian with very deformed claviform signs and the reappearance of the reindeer.

This sequence has only relative value since we lack the statistical certainty required to distribute over a period of six thousand years the several dozen figures concerned. But it is striking that we never find identical groups in any two of these caves, which are at most 650 yards apart. On the other hand, we do find occasionally in La Pasiega and El Castillo isolated animals and signs (such as sign 60 at El Castillo) which show that at any moment of the human occupation of these caves, the inhabitants could in some way comment by adding a single figure to groups that had probably come to seem obsolete.

COVALANAS

RAMALES, SANTANDER, SPAIN

Discovered in 1903 by the Rev. Sierra and H. Alcade del Rio. Drawings by the Abbé Breuil.

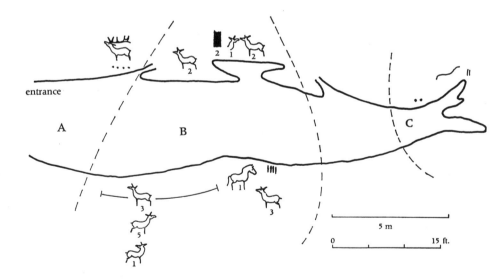

140. COVALANAS. SCHEMATIC PLAN WITH FIGURES
The small numbers under the figures indicate the total number of each species represented.
A *Front part of the sanctuary, marked by dots and a figure probably representing a stag.*
B *Central area: recess with female signs and hinds, opposite a horse and signs in the form of strokes.*
C *Back area: dots, strokes, and an incomplete outline.*

The decorated portion of the cave is situated along a corridor between 250 and 325 feet from the entrance, so that the distribution is especially clear. A recess in the left-hand wall marks the center of the composition and shelters, as is frequently the case, female signs inside it. Covalanas is interesting chiefly for the clarity and simplicity of its arrangement. Before we reach the sanctuary, we find on the right, behind a springing of the ceiling vault, a surface coated with ocher on which no figure can be made out; this surface is situated at a place normally occupied by a panel of scrawls or unfinished outlines. The sequence of figures begins with an animal, the dorsal curve of which is supplied by a natural entablature in the wall (A). The Abbé Breuil thought it was *"un bœuf aux formes légères"* ("an ox of a slender type"); no ox in Paleolithic art, however, possesses such *formes légères*, or the double line of the belly that is clearly drawn here.[1] Two wavy lines, poorly preserved, which may be horns, schematized antlers, or outsize ears, appear over the head. In all likelihood

[1] *fig. 429*

² fig. 431

³ fig. 430

the animal here is a stag, a very frequent entrance animal. This impression is further confirmed by the fact that there is a row of four dots under the belly, which are all the more surely entrance signs because we find them again at the back of the sanctuary and at the end of the main composition (c). After the stag and two hinds we come to the recess (B). Inside it, in the center, is a hind apparently without forelegs, for the line from chest to belly is unbroken.² The shoulder is marked with a spot. On either side are the forequarters of a hind, and in one corner two elongated red signs, very blurred, more or less quadrangular in shape.

Opposite the opening to the recess, on the right wall, we find a horse³ accompanied by rows of strokes and by twelve hinds. One of the latter was identified by the Abbé Breuil as "a male cervid without antlers (reindeer?)." This raises some problems. To begin with, the hinds at Covalanas are extremely varied in their outlines and in the treatment of the ears, and this one is no more peculiar than the others around it. Furthermore, neither the bearing of the head nor the dewlap of this animal points unmistakably to a reindeer. We may add that no incontestable figure of a reindeer that is patently male and without antlers, is known in Paleolithic art. Finally, cases where the reindeer occurs in proximity to the hind are practically unknown either in France or in Spain, where the only cave with reindeer (Las Monedas) is one of the very few Spanish caves without a single hind. These are minor points if the cave-art groupings are assumed to be incoherent, but they take on great importance if these groupings are real compositions. To find an ox at a cave entrance would be highly unexpected and, in fact, unique. A peripheral reindeer would be less surprising, since the reindeer plays that part at Las Monedas, but would supply serious arguments in favor of assigning to Covalanas a date close to the Late Magdalenian—a date completely out of line with the signs and the style of the figures. There is nothing to suggest that we see on this panel anything but a horse, strokes, and hinds; and, as we shall see, this in itself is odd enough. Farther on, the sanctuary comes to its end in an altogether normal fashion with two dots on the left, like the four at the entrance, and, in a recess on the same side, a cervico-dorsal curve, apparently the unfinished outline of a horse, and two small strokes.

The Covalanas composition is remarkable for its simplicity. It is based on the horse/hind theme, with the horse and the strokes (surrounded by hinds) situated directly opposite a hollowed recess in the wall where we find elongated signs and hinds. The hind/horse theme is unusual, like the mammoth/horse theme at La Baume Latrone and the bison/mammoth theme at Arcy-sur-Cure, but there are other examples. At El Castillo, on the panel with the wounded horse (very close in style to this horse at Covalanas), there are hinds and a big brace-shaped sign. Normally, however, the hind does not figure as a leading female subject; it ordinarily appears, as at La Pasiega (Gallery A), as a lateral subject, with or without the stag, in bison/horse compositions. It may also figure as an entrance animal (La Pasiega, Gallery C) on either side of the way into a recess or side chamber. The animals are executed in red pigment applied with a small pad; the resulting spots of color are set at intervals of various lengths, sometimes forming a continuous band. This technique is often used at La Pasiega and La Haza, where, as here, it is accompanied by modeling rendered by heavy lines at throat, shoulder, haunch, rump, flank, belly, and elbow, and by upstrokes and downstrokes. The style of drawing has only a few archaic modulations and is clearly tending toward Early Style IV.

Since we have no archaeological context, we can assign a date to Covalanas only on the basis of comparisons. The signs in the recess are unfortunately blurred. What we see of them cannot, in any case, be classified either with claviforms or ovals; they surely belong among the quadrangular-brace family of signs, both forms of which present very slight variations at El Castillo, La Pasiega, and Altamira. In panels 30 and 34 at La Pasiega (Gallery A) we meet again the Covalanas horse with its peculiar mane, accompanied by brace-shaped signs, and in panel 25 we find the same horse surrounded by the same hinds, next to a quadrangular sign of unusual form which is not filled in. At La Pasiega, with more abundant materials and successive forms of the same sign, we can place these figures between the period of the quadrangular signs and the period of the claviforms—that is, in the Style III that characterizes the second period of Lascaux, as well as Le Gabillou and Pech Merle, which appears to be Early Magdalenian.

LA HAZA

RAMALES, SANTANDER, SPAIN

The cave was discovered in 1903 by the Rev. Sierra and H. Alcade del Rio. Drawings by the Abbé Breuil.

¹ fig. 432

This is a small cave with very worn figures on the walls. The one best preserved and most interesting from the stylistic point of view is a horse executed in red,¹ like those at Covalanas and La Pasiega. Its stylistic affinities with the horses in these two caves, or at least with that of Covalanas, were noted by the Abbé Breuil. The horse at La Haza is interesting primarily for the double line of its shoulder. Apart from the horse at Las Monedas, which bears a single line, this is the only example in Spain of a convention in modeling common in France (Lascaux—period of the brace-shaped signs, Niaux, Le Portel—period of the claviforms, Arcy-sur-Cure, and many decorated objects from the Middle Magdalenian). The stylistic affinity with the horses at La Pasiega and Covalanas is the more normal because the latter date from the period of brace-shaped signs that immediately precede the period of claviforms. Thus we might place the horse at La Haza between the Early Magdalenian and the Middle Magdalenian.

 STYLE IV

STYLE IV

[1] *chart* v

O F all works of prehistoric art 78 percent belong to Style IV. We have seen that most of the decorations on portable objects belong to Style IV,[1] which provides us with more reliable dated evidence than we had for the earlier periods.

[2] *Cf. page 310*

Style IV does not represent a mutation but the normal extension of Style III; this very fact makes it fairly hard to determine where the one stops and the other begins. We have seen that Style III is most conveniently divisible into two periods[2]: that of the rectangular signs and that of the brace-shaped signs, the latter being in some way precursors of the claviform signs. The figures of animals from the second period look much less strange than those from the period of the rectangular signs. At Lascaux, Le Gabillou, Villars, and La Pasiega we can follow very clearly the evolution of the Style III canon, previously described at length, toward a canon closer to normal anatomical proportions. Thus Style IV developed gradually; similarly, the transition from the brace-shaped signs to the true claviforms was gradual and marked by intermediate forms.

[3] *chart* XLIII

Style IV[3] may be broadly defined as follows: Animal outlines are closer to photographic reality, though we still find occasional artistic conventions—for example, in the treatment of bison manes —which are quite extraordinary. Attitudes and movement also tend to be rendered more visually, and apart from some exceptions, horns and antlers are shown in normal perspective. Modeling is rendered by hatchings or spots of color, a convention upheld constantly throughout the Franco-Cantabrian area. Where the figures are completely modeled, the bison show a triangle that descends from the loins, and a strip that runs from the knee of the hind leg to the tip of the buttock; horses have two lines at the shoulder and wavy modeling of the belly; ibexes have a horizontal strip between the hind knee and flank; reindeer have the same strip, with a number of spots aligned on the flank; mammoth heads are wreathed in hair. These details turn up from Arcy-sur-Cure all the way into northern Spain. On the other hand, the signs accompanying animals in Style IV have a pronounced regional character. In the Périgord, the earliest seem to be highly evolved quadrangular signs and truncated female representations; the latest true tectiform signs and wound marks have the form of two converging lines. In the Pyrenees, we can follow the evolution of the claviform signs through three stages, which might be illustrated by Marsoulas, Niaux, and Les Trois Frères. The wound signs appear at Niaux, the oval signs at Les Trois Frères. In Spain, the evolution seems to follow a similar pattern: after the claviforms at Altamira, we come to those at El Pindal and Las Monedas, ending up with the oval signs. In the Périgord, where the datable decorated objects are numerous, we feel clearly that cave art is shifting toward Magdalenian V at the moment when the figures at Les Combarelles come very close to those at Limeuil and Teyjat—all three of these being reliably dated. The same gradual development very probably took place in the Pyrenees, but unfortunately the best evidence from decorated objects comes from Isturitz, in the west, while the best-dated cave art is in the region to the eastward. One gets the feeling, however, that Les Trois Frères must have been created in a cultural climate that is close to, if not identical with, that of the terminal period of Les Combarelles.

In Spain the situation is less clear, and the archaeological evidence is less reliable. The Cantabrian caves are not unlike those in the Pyrenees, and we may assume a rough synchronism between them. North of the Loire, we have only Arcy-sur-Cure, where the signs seem to be very degenerated quadrangulars. The animals there—bison, horse, mammoth—exhibit, along with regional peculiarities, details of modeling of the Perigordian period, corresponding to the last quadrangular signs and the tectiforms. The transition from Early Style IV to Late Style IV is hard to indicate. We feel that the animals at Angles-sur-l'Anglin are sufficiently different from those at Teyjat to justify making a division; over two or three thousand years a certain evolution took place, but it is so slight as to escape the means of our descriptive vocabulary and rests on visual perception. Animals that exhibit traces of Style III outlines (overdeveloped bodies, legs sticking out stiffly forward and backward, humped cervico-dorsal lines), I have assigned to Early Style IV —a designation justified by their synchronism with the signs. Once the outlines become fully photographic, and the attitudes lifelike and often varied (animals trotting or galloping), I have assigned the figures to Late Style IV. However, I trust that no reader will suppose that in the absence of an adequate stratigraphic critical apparatus it is possible to identify the intermediate steps of the development with absolute certainty.

It might seem easy to assign the different phases of Style IV to specific chronological divisions; unfortunately our stratigraphic data are not always sufficient. Thus, in spite of everything it is only in an approximate manner that I suggest Early Style IV as characteristic of Magdalenian III and IV, and Late Style IV as characteristic of Magdalenian V and VI. In fairly numerous cases we can see—for instance, at Les Trois Frères and Les Combarelles—that the evidence overlaps the divisions, and must be clarified by further archaeological research.

LIMEUIL

DORDOGNE, FRANCE

In 1909 several dozen engraved slabs were found by J. Bouyssonie in Magdalenian deposits at the village of Limeuil. They certainly belonged to a sanctuary composed of movable elements. Had diagrams been drawn showing the order in which the finds were made, we might be able to gain some clue to the way the sanctuary was arranged. As it is, we can only guess how the various elements were combined to form compositions, making the most of the slabs involving more than one animal species. The industrial objects are from the Late Magdalenian.

The fauna represented at Limeuil[1] consist of 47 reindeer, 27 horses, 8 oxen, 3 ibexes, 2 stags, 2 bears, 1 hind, 1 feline, and 2 human figures. We find a similar composition at Teyjat where reindeer and horses are dominant, followed by oxen, deer, and bear. Unlike Teyjat, Limeuil has ibexes. The absence of bison from the slabs is noteworthy because this animal appears on a bone plaquette found at Limeuil. From the numerical record we can gather that the normal pairing was of reindeer with horse. The plaquettes with animals of different species confirm this inference; reindeer/horse (10), ox/horse (1), reindeer/ox (1). The signs are very simple, reduced to wounds or ovals for the female category, and to strokes for the male. The majority of the wound marks appear on the flanks of the reindeer.

[1] *figs. 28, 85, 475–477*

TEYJAT, GROTTE DE LA MAIRIE

DORDOGNE, FRANCE

The first engravings in this cave were discovered in 1903 by Denis Peyrony. Subsequent excavations made in collaboration with D. Bourrinet yielded two layers of Late Magdalenian; the lower horizon contained fragments from the engraved decorations. Consequently, the works here date from the beginning of the Late Magdalenian; they supply us with a guidepost all the more valuable because together with the slabs of Limeuil they enable us to define the stylistic features of the late period. The drawings were made by the Abbé Breuil.

141. TEYJAT
ARRANGEMENT OF THE FIGURES
The drawings are based on the publication by E. Capitan, H. Breuil, and D. Peyrony.

The Teyjat works[1] were executed partly on a stalagmitic mass still in place, and partly on large stalagmitic fragments. The latter have been moved, and no record appears to have been kept of their placement prior to the excavations. Consequently it is difficult to reconstruct the original order on the basis of their present positions. On the other hand, the various groups of figures provide material for a highly interesting study of the original composition. The figures break down into three groups: compositions with deer, with reindeer, and with oxen.

[1] *figs. 486–490*

COMPOSITIONS WITH DEER (1, 2)

At present, these occupy the lower section of the front part of the decoration. We make out two groups of figures sketchily rendered in vertical strips. The one on the left, the first that one encounters on entering the cave, includes one bison, one horse, five stags, and two hinds. The second strip includes one horse flanked by a small reindeer, six stags, and two hinds. We surely have here a first bison/horse pairing, and probably a second horse/reindeer pairing (the reindeer in the Late Magdalenian seems to join the family of female symbols that includes the bison and the ox). The stags and hinds serve as complementary animals. The presence of the hinds is noteworthy for the fact that in France they went into a long eclipse in the course of Early Style IV but reappeared in the final period.

COMPOSITIONS WITH REINDEER (3, 4, 5, 6)

² fig. 487

The first evidence of the presence of reindeer is a figure set above the oxen.² Higher up is an incomplete frieze; the surviving figures are three reindeer framing a horse. Still higher, a large slab has a compact group of criss-crossed figures: two bison, two horses, three reindeer, and one bear. To the left of this slab, above the compositions with deer, we find a last slab with a nearly identical grouping: one reindeer, two horses, and one bear. Common to all these groups of figures, the original order of which can only be conjectured, is the double theme bison/horse and reindeer/horse, with the addition of the bear, as at Les Combarelles and on the Limeuil slabs.

COMPOSITION WITH OXEN (7)

The vertical portion of the stalagmitic cascade has the cave's finest figures: three oxen following one another, and beneath them one small horse. The second of the three bovines is obviously a bull; the other two, more slender and without the sheath, are to all appearances cows. As is usually the case in Paleolithic art, sexual characteristics are omitted or discreetly indicated by secondary characteristics.

In spite of its late character, the Teyjat decoration remains classical in composition. Here again are bison compositions and one oxen composition, as at Niaux and Les Combarelles. In addition there are reindeer/horse pairings, such as occur on decorated objects of late date. Stags serve as complementary animals; it is odd to find no ibex.

The style of these figures provided me with a starting point for defining Late Style IV. Conventional filling in of the modeling has been dispensed with, the forms have taken on remarkable flexibility, and the proportions approach photographic truth. The rendering of attitudes and movement is highly sensitive. All these characteristics are found in other dated works of the Late Magdalenian, from Germany to Spain, but in no other collection do they exhibit the same homogeneity. Lastly, it must be noted that Teyjat was so to speak a plaquette sanctuary, located in the dwelling area, in the portion of the cave exposed to daylight; thus it clearly illustrates the return of the zone of executed works to the cave entrances.

SAUT-DU-PERRON

LOIRE, FRANCE

This is a site on the slope of a hill overlooking the Loire River. It was excavated by M. Larue and yielded a dozen plaquettes, mostly of schist, finely engraved. The finds from the excavations here are in the Musée Déchelette at Roanne.

As the nature of the terrain does not lend itself to preservation of bone objects, the deposit yielded only flint implements and works of art on stone. The absence of bone objects makes dating the site a ticklish matter. Writers have assigned it to Magdalenian II, basing this date on the flint tools, which, in the case of the Magdalenian, provide a clue but can rarely be relied upon unless confirmed by spears and harpoons. Moreover, such few decorated objects from Magdalenian II as we possess provide no basis for comparison with the works from Saut-du-Perron. A somewhat later stage of the Magdalenian, however, supplies a few clues which seem to me more reliable.

The oddest work is a pendant with an engraved motif, which, it would seem, can be interpreted only as a schematic female profile, close in some ways to a claviform sign, in other ways resembling figures from Mauern and Mezin. Head and legs dwindle away without detail, and only the rear of the body is rendered with some fullness; the front of the body is indicated only by almost imperceptible modulations of a line that marks off neck, chest, and the beginning of the legs. The most interesting object is a plaquette, one side of which

¹ fig. 478

shows a reindeer and the upside-down hindquarters of a horse.¹ On the other side is an engraving of two horses, plus some scarcely legible lines. Quite apart from the sculptural quality of the figures, the work is remarkable for two reasons. First, it shows a reindeer/horse pairing, such as we also find at the Late Magdalenian sites of Limeuil and Teyjat. Second, the reindeer, treated in a manner characteristic of Style IV, ranks with a great many others from Les Combarelles, Teyjat, Limeuil, and Laugerie Basse, not to mention the reindeer from the terminal Magdalenian in Switzerland. The reindeer/horse grouping is found only in the Middle and Late Magdalenian; it makes its appearance in cave art with Late Style IV at Les Combarelles and Les Trois Frères. Only in this period do the figures exhibit so "photographic" a realism in attitude and detail. Some of the other plaquettes from Saut-du-Perron have lines so sketchily and confusedly drawn as to suggest an earlier date, and we might wonder whether we are not dealing here with two Magdalenian periods, some works belonging to an earlier, others to a later phase. To support this view, however, we would require more exact stratigraphic data, for the reindeer in the late style and the more crudely drawn horses appear on the same plaquette, and we have no reason for supposing that the two are not contemporaneous.

The majority of the engraved plaquettes were discovered at a point of the site called "La Goutte Roffat," among industrial objects recognized as Magdalenian, which I should be inclined to assign to the already mature Magdalenian. But the oddest plaquette² was found at a point of the site called "La vigne Brun," where the

² fig. 479

industrial objects are supposed to be Gravettian. Unfortunately this plaquette is broken and shows no more than the lower portion of an animal that seems to be a rhinoceros. Because of the condition of the site we cannot be sure that this plaquette belongs with the flint tools found in the Gravettian deposit. There is nothing about the treatment of the figure to link it with such dated Gravettian finds as we possess. Rather, the treatment is very like that of the reindeer on the plaquette from La Goutte Roffat: we find here the same exactness of anatomical proportions, the same modeling by means of short lines, that is found only on figures from Magdalenian III onward and reaches its peak in Magdalenian IV–V. There is nothing extraordinary about the presence of a rhinoceros in the mature Magdalenian: the examples at Rouffignac and Les Trois Frères make it perfectly plausible. Consequently, the little collection of works from Saut-du-Perron appears to belong rather with those of the Middle and Late Magdalenian than with those of the Early Magdalenian. The most clearly comparable works are the plaquettes from Limeuil, Laugerie Basse, and Labastide, and the figures engraved on bone matter from Switzerland and southern Germany: this fact is all the more interesting because Saut-du-Perron is situated on the east of the Massif Central, and the works found there mark, so to speak, the boundary between those in the Poitou-Périgord region and those in the eastern Magdalenian sites of the Jura region.

LA COLOMBIÈRE

PONCIN, AIN, FRANCE

The site is a vast rock shelter on the bank of the Ain River. It began to be explored around 1860 and a disorderly pillage continued until 1913 when Lucien Mayet and Jean Pissot undertook the first systematic excavations. By then hardly any-thing was left of the upper horizons: the layers were disturbed, there was no usable publication nor even a collection of objects. The excavations by Mayet and Pissot yielded a substantial body of evidence concerning the industries at the site and also led to discovery of nine pebbles and two fragments of mammoth bone, all of them engraved. In 1948 Hallam Movius of Harvard University made fresh excavations and discovered a tenth engraved pebble. The site was subjected to thorough geological investigation, and samples from the layer where the last pebble was found were measured for carbon-14 radio-activity. The dates thus obtained varied between 9,000 and 13,000 B.C. This was one of the first applications of the carbon-14 method of dating to Upper Paleolithic remains, and the estimate based on it, which leaves a four-thousand-year margin of error, can be regarded as only a very rough approximation. However, two new analyses made in 1956 yielded dates of 12,500 and 12,900 B.C. respectively. The objects discovered by Mayet and Pissot are in the geology laboratory at the University of Lyon; the pebble discovered by Movius is in the museum at Bourg-en-Bresse.

The major problem posed by La Colombière is that of dating. Movius and Bordes, who studied the industrial remains, reviewed the conclusions which Mayet and Pissot had formulated in 1915. The first excavators believed the site to be Upper Aurignacian; the later group assigned it to the Perigordian, associated with the La Gravette points. For various reasons this estimate does not settle the matter. A detailed discussion of typology is outside the scope of the present work, and in any case other prehistorians are already having such a discussion. A summary of Movius' arguments will suffice to show the point at which he left the problem unsolved. Deploring the scarcity of stone implements (about 700 items) and having assigned them to the Gravettian, he then admits that the implements include neither double-shouldered points of the La Font Robert type nor burins of the Noailles type. He suggests some "Solutrean reworking" of a few fragments (while acknowledging that the reworking is not unmistakably Solutrean) and points to some keel-shaped scrapers as evidence that the finds are not Aurignacian (without mentioning that keel-shaped scrapers are well attested in the mature Magdalenian). His dating is based partly on geological data, and partly on specimens with beveled edges of the La Gravette type. As for the La Gravette pieces, 83 percent of them (206) are flakes with beveled edges, not blades. Of these "blades" only one is over two inches, which is very small indeed compared with the usual Gravettian blades. As we know that more careful excavations of Magdalenian sites have since yielded small blades and backed flakes in large quantities, it is not easy to accept a Perigordian dating of the flints from La Colombière. Industrial artifacts of bone, though not abundant, are plentiful enough, and Dr. Allain was able to show that we find just as many of them in the Magdalenian.

There remain the works of art, of which there are a sufficient quantity (10 pebbles and two fragments of mammoth bone, all engraved) to provide a sizable and coherent batch of figures. Since I first examined them in 1946, I have changed my opinion three times. Prior to Movius' excavations, I supposed them to be Magdalenian, without making any special point of it. At the same time, they had for me two unfortunate associations: first, with a counterfeit pebble from La Colombière owned by a collector in Lyon, and second, with the notorious bison from La Genière, a neighboring site. The La Genière bison, which is engraved on lime-stone with a steel implement, was long regarded as a "preliminary sketch" for one of the bison at Font-de-Gaume, whereas it is actually a conscientious copy, not of a bison at Font-de-Gaume, but of the Abbé Breuil's drawing of a bison in that cave. After the American excavations had identified the deposit as Perigordian, it seemed obvious to me that the pebbles, which stylistically have nothing Perigordian about them, were forgeries, and that Movius had been tricked like his predecessors. Since then I have studied the evidence at length and it seems to me (1) that the pebbles are authentic, and (2) that they are not Gravettian.

Finally one might object to the conscientious geological study that was made of the site. This is easy to answer: considering that the Quaternary age is relatively short, the geologist can determine with reasonable certainty the climatic oscillations between cold and temperate periods, and dry and wet periods, but he relies most often on the archaeological evidence (based on industrial objects) to fix the date for an oscillation at a particular point of time. The argument is thus in danger of becoming circular: the geological dating of the La Colombière pebbles is Gravettian because the industrial remains are given as Gravettian. When we add that Movius rejected the carbon-14 dates on the grounds that they did not agree with his attribution based on the fragile evidence of a few short blades with beveled edges, we are left with a big question mark and plenty of room for interpreting the documents differently. The carbon-14 datings are not very exact (9,600, 11,400, 12,500, 12,900, and 13,500 B.C.), but one could, solely on the basis of the fact that the engravings are incontestably in Style IV, date them roughly between 9,000 B.C. (Magdalenian VI) and 13,000 B.C. (Magdalenian III). The middle date of 12,000 B.C., corresponding to Magdalenian IV, is, all told, quite plausible. This rather long discussion has wider relevance then may first appear: uncritical attributions of cave works to remote periods of the Upper Paleolithic, in conjunction with the seemingly reliable dating of the La Colombière pebbles as Gravettian, have produced confusion in the dating of the works of art. The reader need only

¹ figs. 480–485

glance at the plates in P. Graziosi's work on Aurignacian-Perigordian art (see Bibliography) to realize that the La Colombière pebbles have a character very different from the works among which they are placed, and that they really belong later, among the Magdalenian plaquettes.

The range of subjects represented on these pebbles is fairly well defined.[1] Counting only subjects (not individuals), on the eleven decorated items (nine pebbles including one in two halves, and two engraved bones), the horse appears on eight; the reindeer or another cervid is also on eight; the rhinoceros on four; felines on three; the ibex on three; the bear on two; the oval sign on two; a human figure on one; the bison (or the musk ox) on one.

This list brings out the importance of the reindeer and the rhinoceros; the number of rhinoceros is here greater than the total known on all other decorated objects from the Paleolithic.

Is it possible to discern groupings and discover a principle of pairing in these figures? Seven of the items show multiple subjects: the pairing reindeer/horse occurs on six of them. Thus the characteristic association would appear to be of the reindeer with the horse, an association known from many decorated objects, all of which date from the mature or the Late Magdalenian (Limeuil especially), and from a few cave works of equally late date.

Among these six items with reindeer/horse groups, four include the rhinoceros and two the ibex. Only at Rouffignac do we find the rhinoceros as a complementary animal, alternating with the ibex, a circumstance which also suggests an orientation toward the Magdalenian. Thus we arrive at a very coherent formula: reindeer (8/11), horse (8/11) + rhinoceros (4/11) or ibex (2/11), with addition of the feline (3/11) or the bear (2/11).

² fig. 484

Pebble no. 8 has the only large ruminant represented.[2] Mayet and Pissot identified it as a musk ox, and their demonstration is quite persuasive. Without entirely ruling out the identification of this engraved figure as an animal of which the bone remains are, to say the least, extremely rare in the Upper Paleolithic, I am tempted to see it as a bison. When we restore the fragment broken off from the top and later found separately, we obtain the dorsal outline not of a musk ox, but of a bison with the hump and the mane clearly marked. The treatment of the hairy portions follows quite faithfully the classical conventions of Style IV. Only the position of the horn suggests the musk ox, but there are bison (at Le Roc de Sers and at Le Portel, gallery 2) with the horn pointing downward in this fashion. One of the cows at La Loja has horns of an identical shape. In the case under discussion it is hard to see how the horn could be given the normal position on the forehead without curving it down against the cheek. However that may be, either a musk ox or a bison would reasonably belong within the group of habitually dominant symbols, and it is rather extraordinary to find only one big hollow-horned ruminant represented among the forty-odd engraved figures on the eleven finds. To repeat, the closest parallel is with Rouffignac, where bison appear only singly among the engraved compositions; less marked parallels are found at Les Combarelles, Teyjat, and especially at Limeuil where the bison has manifestly been supplanted by the reindeer.

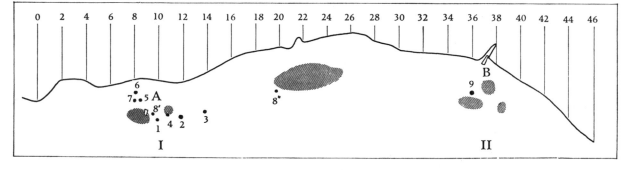

142. LA COLOMBIÈRE. POSITIONS OF THE DECORATED OBJECTS
The numerals indicate distances in meters. Based on Mayet and Pissot (1915), and Movius (1956).

Did the works at La Colombière constitute a sanctuary composed of movable elements? It is the only site for which we have a record of the exact placement of a group of decorated objects. Thanks to the care with which Mayet and Pissot—and Movius, thirty-six years later—drew up their diagrams, we can determine exactly where the various pebbles and engraved bones were found. They lay in the vicinity of hearths, undisturbed since the deposits covered them over. If there was any prior displacement, this could have happened only after they had been abandoned and before they had been speedily buried under the sandy sediments. It would be extraordinary if they had not been moved at all, but judging from the positions in which they were found, no significant shift seems to have occurred. Eight of the pebbles and the engraved fragment of a pelvic bone in the Mayet-Pissot series were found fairly close together, between 8 and 14 meters (A on diagram). inside the shelter. The pebble with the "musk ox" (no. 8) had been broken, and the other part of it was found lying off by itself nearly 20 meters beyond. About 15 meters farther inside, the Movius pebble (no. 9) was found, and in a crevice (the only one in the whole length of the shelter, 46 meters), the fragment of a humerus bone with a reindeer engraved on it (B on diagram). It is hard to be sure whether there were two groups of pebbles, each arranged as a little sanctuary, or whether, on the breaking up of the habitation, some of the pebbles were thrown nearly 30 meters beyond the rest; but it is likely that the two groups corresponded to two separate compositions, for the dispersion would have been greater had the pebbles been thrown at random. The main group must have been between meters 8 and 14 (see diagram); it included various pebbles —one with a horse (no. 2), one with the bison (the "musk ox" of Mayet and Pissot; no. 8), and the fragment of engraved bone (A) that has only figures of the male category (man, reindeer, bear). This first group clearly exhibits a parallelism with certain elements on the slabs at Teyjat: horse/reindeer/bear, and just one motif dedicated to the bison.

The second group was found between meters 36 and 38 (see diagram). It includes the Movius pebble, which has the fullest complement in the whole set (horse/reindeer + rhinoceros/ibex, with feline), and the humerus bone engraved with a reindeer, which Mayet and Pissot found *inside* the crevice at the back of the shelter. It is noteworthy that this second of the two engravings on bone includes only one figure of the male category, a fact that associates it with the other engraved bone (A), and it is also noteworthy that it should have been found in the crevice—that is, in the position where, if this were a cave, we would expect to find a group of dots or strokes, a rhinoceros, an ibex, or a stag. It is hard to say much more without exceeding the bounds of the evidence, but the two groups of figures which were found here undisturbed are readily comparable to the arrangement of a cave sanctuary, such as one of the galleries at Les Combarelles.

The style presents some points of interest. On some of the works the lines are deeply incised, making the animals look massive; not all the legs are rendered in detail, and several of the horses have ball-shaped hoofs, though very different from those in Style III. Most of the fine-line engravings are subtly varied, with the wealth of anatomic detail we expect of the best Style IV. Details of manes and coats are treated in a special manner, the contour line frequently doubled with a more wavy line and the space between filled with hatching. The originality of these details is understandable at a site so far from the center of Franco-Cantabrian art, and does not take away from the over-all impression that these works are fairly late. The fact that one of the horses' hindquarters (pebble no. 3) exhibits, in hatching, the modeling line so characteristic of the treatment of horses that appear on decorated objects in Style IV is a stylistic confirmation of major importance.

As a whole, La Colombière offers affinities with Saut-du-Perron, a less impressive and less well-preserved site where, however, we also encounter bison, horse, reindeer, and rhinoceros (treated very nearly like the rhinoceros on pebble no. 4). The "arrow" signs,[3] if they are really out of the ordinary in having a line linking the oval to the body of the adjacent animal (reindeer, rhinoceros, bear), nonetheless belong clearly to the family of female ovals in Style IV. It does not seem to me that these signs can be interpreted as true arrows planted perpendicularly under the animal's jaw or belly; however, the well-attested vulva-wound assimilation implies, so to speak, the same complementarity that we find on figures with wound marks. In conclusion, neither their style nor their content seems to indicate that these figures at La Colombière are Gravettian works. They are earlier than the Late Magdalenian we find in the Jura region, in Switzerland, and in southern Germany, but they do not diverge from what we expect in Middle Magdalenian finds.

[3] *figs. 481, 482*

ANGLES-SUR-L'ANGLIN, ABRI DU ROC AUX SORCIERS

VIENNE, FRANCE

Excavation of the deposits in this rock shelter had been made long ago. In 1944, Miss Dorothy Garrod and Mlle. Suzanne de Saint-Mathurin, having discovered fragments of sculpture in the excavated material, began a systematic excavation. This led not only to study of a very important layer of the Middle and Late Magdalenian, but also to the discovery of the finest collection of Paleolithic low reliefs apart from those of Le Roc de Sers. Their labors have not ended, and unfortunately Miss Garrod and Mlle. de Saint-Mathurin have not as yet made any substantial publication of the collection of sculptures, so I cannot describe them in detail. However, in an unpublished communication to the Société préhistorique française in 1958, Mlle. de Saint-Mathurin described the general succession of the figures in the frieze, and this entitles me to make use of some of her findings.

The shelter is divided into two sections by a solid mass of rocks that seems to have been in this position in the Paleolithic. The right-hand section, which terminates in a small cave at the right, is greatly damaged; a few fragments of low reliefs are all that survive here. The most important discovery in this section was a slab with a man's bust in profile, a low relief touched up with ocher and black. The left-hand section, over a space of about ten yards, preserves intact a collection of low reliefs consisting of about thirty figures. It is possible to distinguish four portions, from left to right:

(1) A group on the bison/horse theme, with three or four figures of bison and two horses. There may have been more figures farther to the left.

(2) The main group, consisting of the trunks of three women side by side. Above this group appears a small man's face,[1] and higher up a horse. In addition, there are two bison touching the female figures. This is an altogether classical central composition: woman/bison + man/horse.

[1] *chart* XXIX

(3) A bit farther to the left are seven splendid low reliefs of ibexes, some of these recarved from earlier bison, as at Le Roc de Sers and Le Cap Blanc.

(4) Lastly, at the end of the composition, there is a group of engravings, some of them in faint low relief, which include bison and horses, followed by a feline, reindeer, man, and ibex.

The preserved portion seems to correspond to a homogeneous set. The right-hand shelter must have repeated a very similar formula, as so often occurs. The left-hand section, as preserved, comes up to statistical expectations: it shows a central bison/horse + man/woman group with bison and horses on one side and ibexes on the other. Toward the right-hand edge the bison and horses are repeated, and the frieze terminates with a group of figures corresponding to back-cave subjects (felines, cervids, men, ibexes).

The low reliefs at Angles-sur-l'Anglin are reliably dated as Magdalenian III. They are especially valuable as chronological guideposts. The animals exhibit the characteristics of Early Style IV to the greatest possible degree. The bodies are still voluminous, keeping something of the Style III structure, and the limbs often still project stiffly out at front and rear. The bison have pronounced manes, but the horns are in normal perspective. For all these archaic characteristics, there yet comes through an emphasis on realistic detail and a balance that is already of the Middle Magdalenian. Stylistically, the animal figures are between Lascaux and Rouffignac, close to the earlier figures at Les Combarelles. The human figures are perfectly in line with these observations: we find a face in frontal view as at Les Combarelles, and a face in profile with turned-up nose, as also found there. The Middle Magdalenian is the period of truncated human female figures, then the claviforms. The "Venuses" at Angles, which extend from under the breasts to above the knees, are very closely related to the figures from La Roche at Lalinde, and to the three women in profile at Les Combarelles.

MOUTHIERS, LA CHAIRE À CALVIN

CHARENTE, FRANCE

This rock shelter with sculptures was discovered in 1927 by Pierre David.

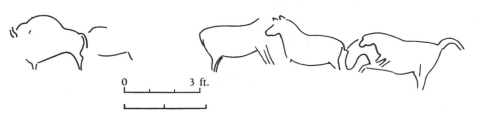

0   3 ft.

1 meter

143. MOUTHIERS. ARRANGEMENT OF THE ANIMALS ON THE SCULPTURED FRIEZE AT LA CHAIRE À CALVIN

The sculptured frieze covers the right-hand portion of a shelter overhung by rock, largely exposed to daylight. Excavation has yielded a great many industrial objects, unfortunately without much detail, from the Solutrean and the Early or Middle Magdalenian. The works which were originally heightened with colors, are in rather flat relief. Their state of preservation is only fair, and has given rise to conflicting interpretations. David sees in the main composition, from left to right, a headless bovid, a horse, then a group of two coupling horses. Mme. Laming-Emperaire sees in the last group a bison, from which a horse has been recut. This interpretation is certainly correct, but it is not complete. The first animal on the left in this group appears to be an ox, the head of which has been lost: the attachment of the tail to the body, the line of the back, the hock, and the belly do not fit either a horse or a bison. The horse in the middle is identifiable without discussion. The right-hand pair[1] consists of a bison of which the dorsal line, position of the tail, thigh, and start of the ventral line are perfectly recognizable, but the head and hump have been recarved to form the withers, head, and forelegs of a horse: in short, a smaller horse, with extended forequarters, has been carved within the middle and hind parts of the bison. Other incisions, remnants of some circular form, give the impression of limbs drawn up for jumping. Such reworkings (or deliberate amalgamations of figures) occur in the frieze at Angles-sur-l'Anglin and in that at Le Cap Blanc. The hypothesis of two coupling horses is based solely on the superimposition of figures, one inside the contours of the hindquarters and the other the outside forequarters of the same bison. About 54 inches to the left of the main frieze a bison is barely visible.[2] The decorations at La Chaire à Calvin, poorly preserved and doubtless incomplete, permit only a few remarks concerning the period to which they belong. The animals are obviously in Style III or Early Style IV; this attribution, though in keeping with the industrial objects found at the site, nonetheless lacks precision. The slimness of the limbs in contrast to the massive body, the clearly separated ears of the horse in the middle, and the way the forequarters of the small horse on the right are thrust forward argue in favor of Style III. The realistic proportions of the central horse's head in relation to its body, and the modeling in the best-preserved portion of the bison's hindquarters argue in favor of Early Style IV. In view of the condition of the figures it would be pointless to wonder whether they could have been executed at two different periods. Nor can the composition provide us with chronological clues; all we can say about it is that its surviving fragment shows a normal subject: ox/horse and bison/horse.

[1] *figs. 492, 493*

[2] *fig. 491*

SAINT-GERMAIN-LA-RIVIÈRE

GIRONDE, FRANCE

The wall of the rock shelter where the tomb of Saint-Germain-la-Rivière was found bears the remains of an engraved composition. On the right is a horse's hindquarters with rectilinear incisions on the flank; on the left, there is an odd personage of the "man bending forward" type, with animalized features. The remains are too scanty for one to be able to grasp the meaning of the composition and it is equally hard to date them exactly. The curving lines of the horse are in Style IV (Middle and Late Magdalenian). The personage bending forward turns up elsewhere in that same period. The incisions could be interpreted as wound marks in the form of two converging lines, which suggest Late rather than Middle Magdalenian.

LE CAP BLANC

MARQUAY, DORDOGNE, FRANCE

The sculptured frieze under the overhanging rock was discovered in the course of Dr. J. G. Lalanne's excavations in 1910, by Peyrille, a member of his team.

This rock shelter is about 50 feet long. The excavations yielded two layers of Magdalenian III in an inhabited site which had paving stones along the wall, and a tomb—such at least is the information that has come down to us. Nothing remains of the observations which could have been made concerning the fitting out of the shelters. The skeleton from the tomb and a portion of the finds are in America, and on neither side of the Atlantic has there been an extensive publication of the finds. The attribution to Magdalenian III, which has the authority of the Abbé Breuil behind it, is surely well founded; it is corroborated by the stylistic identity of the figures here with those at Angles-sur-l'Anglin. The frieze[1] has suffered considerable damage: fragments of it were found in the archaeological layers, and portions of the remaining figures can be made out only with difficulty. For all this, it constitutes one of the most interesting sculptured groups. Close examination of the animals which at first glance seem easily legible reveals a number of anomalies in the modeling and the relief; these are accounted for by reworkings of the figures and vagaries in the forms.

[1] fig. 69

144. LE CAP BLANC. ARRANGEMENT OF THE ANIMALS ON THE SCULPTURED FRIEZE
Dotted lines indicate reconstructions of damaged figures. Note, at 2 and 8, the horses recut from bison, as at Mouthiers.

The frieze begins on the left with a nearly illegible sculpture, probably a horse (not shown on diagram). Then comes a head (1) which has been identified as either a reindeer or an ox, but more nearly resembles a bear. A horse (2) comes next, the best preserved of the figures, with a ring carved out over the back.[2] The withers are rather odd, like the hump of a bison, and we in fact observe that a bison head has been cut away on its cheek, the horse's ear now replacing the bison's horn.[3] When lighted from one side, the rump of a bison can still barely be made out as a continuation from the hump. As at Mouthiers, the figures of the two animals overlap. Directly below the muzzle, just above the lower edge of the frieze, we find the hindquarters of an ibex or a cervid (3). Next comes a horse, the rump of which is behind the head of the preceding animal; its forelegs are well preserved and of normal proportions. Next, at the top of the frieze, appears an odd group which the Abbé Breuil identified as two oxen (5). The hindquarters might suggest a feline; the head on the right is undefinable but seems more nearly that of a carnivore or a cervid than that of an ox. The head that is recarved in the shoulder of that animal can only be that of a cervid, and it is remarkably expressive. The chances are that originally there was a feline here, the head of which was deformed when the cervid was sculptured. The horse (6) underneath this group is the most famous of the animals here; though greatly damaged, it still makes a very impressive figure. When Rev. Hours, Jean Vertut, and I examined it in 1959, using lighting from the side, we noticed traces of a little bison in raised-field relief on the withers, as is also the case with horse no. 2 (both are visible in the photograph, figures 322–323, in the Abbé Breuil's *Quatre cents siècles...*); there were probably other small bison on the flank, but this is hardly more than a guess. Farther on extends a very damaged surface, some broken-off parts of which have been found.

[2] fig. 494

[3] fig. 495

The last group of figures is at the right-hand side of the rock shelter: what survives evinces a great deal of reworking. The main figures are two horses (8 and 9), heads facing to the right, and the hindquarters of a bison (10), the rest of its body lost underneath the horse at 9. The bison hindquarters may be readily identified by the way the tail is attached to the body, the length of the thigh, and the thinness of the abdomen. The horse at 8 is especially odd. On the shoulder, as with horses 2 and 6, a much worn-away bison appears in raised-field relief, just visible enough to disclose its entire outline. The body of the horse is itself peculiar: at the base of the withers there is an entirely unusual oval depression, and the dorsal curve does not even faintly resemble that of a horse—it forms a hump in which one cannot make out backbone, loins, or rump, and it abruptly drops away at the point where the tail should be. In this area the relief is completely incomprehensible, and a second oval depression, which seems to delimit the back of the thigh and the tail, makes this tail preposterously thick. In view of the sculptural excellence of the works at Le Cap Blanc, we cannot write off the anomalies in such a figure as due to clumsiness or carelessness. Gradually we recognize, instead, that the carved masses of the horse's body are those of a bison facing in the opposite direction: what seems to be the tail of the horse is the mane of the bison which extends on to become a perfectly delineated dorsal hump; moreover, in the oval depression of the horse's withers, the thigh of the bison is present. All in all, this is exactly what we saw at Mouthiers, where the form of a bison blends with the two horses recarved upon its mass. Between the legs of the horse at 9, a much-damaged area, we find the dorsal line of a small-sized bison (12).

In its topographical organization, the frieze at Le Cap Blanc is far from complete, but what is left shows that it is much more than the frieze of horses it seems to be at first glance: the lighting in the rock shelter favors the impression of large equines. From one end to the other unrolls a sequence of huge horses, all of them (except the horse at 4) overlaid with small bison; at the left-hand edge of the composition is a figure that might be a bear; on the lower edge, an ibex or cervid; on the upper edge, a figure which is probably that of a feline, and a cervid. The group is commonplace enough in its composition: equivalent groups (central bison/horse, peripheral ibex or cervid, bear or feline) are found at Angles, at Les Combarelles, and at Commarque —to mention only the three cases which are unquestionably contemporaneous.

The reworked figures raise a larger problem, for similar reworked figures are found at Angles and at Mouthiers. Was the reworking contemporaneous with the carving of the figures we have assumed to be earlier? Was a frieze first executed that consisted of the three big horses on the left and the two big bison on the right, with an ibex beneath and a feline above them, and the composition then gone over again to transform the bison on the right into two horses and the feline into a cervid—and the horses overlaid with small bison in raised-field relief to restore a balance between the complementary species? Or was the frieze sculptured from the first with all its ambiguities, as it has come down to us? It is highly probable that really scientific excavations would have supplied the answer. On the basis of what is known, we can only suppose that if two separate Magdalenian III layers existed, the figures could have been altered during the period corresponding to the second layer.

COMMARQUE

SIREUIL, DORDOGNE, FRANCE

The sculptures were discovered in 1915 by the Abbé Breuil and P. Paris.

145. COMMARQUE. SCHEMATIC PLAN WITH FIGURES
At 12, outlines of two undetermined figures, possibly horses; at 4, ibex at the entrance; at 8 and 9, back-cave male figures or carnivores.

This small irregularly shaped cave comprises one chamber about 65 feet long; at the back, two galleries run off at right angles like the top of a T, the longer of the two measuring about 65 feet. No systematic study of the cave has ever been made, and what the deposits may have yielded remains a mystery. The state of preservation of the works is very uneven: most are barely identifiable, but a few are in perfect condition. To the effects of weathering must be added those of inadequate protection, all the more regrettable because, as we shall see, in Commarque is the best relief of a horse's head that survives from the entire Magdalenian. The works are executed in every technique, from low relief to that of deep incision with edges smoothed toward the inside—this latter technique flourished in the Périgord during the Middle Magdalenian. Most of the figures are in such a state that any attempt to reconstruct the original composition in detail would be useless. Near the entrance, on the right, we see the outlines of two completely eroded reliefs; one of them is a horse (1,2). The chamber narrows at the point where the two galleries branch off: here is an area of scrawls, which is a normal feature at the approaches of a major composition.

The left-hand gallery contains vestiges of two reliefs at the entrance (12), and farther on, traces of ocher on the left-hand wall, at the point in side chambers that is normally occupied by signs. The gallery that branches off to the right is better preserved. To the right of the entrance we find an ibex,[1] somewhat worn away but perfectly recognizable (4). For the next few yards, both walls are covered with poorly preserved figures among which horses have been recognized, and, less reliably, a reindeer, a bovid, and a rhinoceros (5, 10, 11). Prolonged examination of these figures and study of many photographs permit me to recognize only horses and zoologically uncertain shapes. The so-called bovid, in particular, is certainly a horse in an advanced stage of erosion. A few yards from the end of the gallery, on the right-hand wall, is an absolutely amazing figure (7): a horse in low relief, the head[2] alone measuring more than 27 inches and the body, which stretches almost 7 feet, fading into the other reliefs on the wall. The work is all the more astonishing because the gallery is less than a yard wide. The quality of the modeling is exceptional and ranks with the finest figures at Angles-sur-l'Anglin, with certain horses at Les Combarelles, and with one or two of the very softly modeled works at Font-de-Gaume.

A smaller horse can be seen within the outlines of the large figure (6). Continuing past the giant horse, over the cornice on the left wall we find a little profile head executed in soft-edge relief.[3] This is held to be a bear's head, which is perfectly plausible although it is rare to find so approximate an execution in the Magdalenian. In position and outline it seems to me closely related to one of the bending men at Les Combarelles, and there is a very similar head at the back of the Saint-Cirq cave. Bear or man, however, it is in the right place at the rear of this gallery. Further on we see a few lines (8), in particular some that actually might have formed the head of a bear.

What is most striking at Commarque is the absence of representations in the female category (bison or ox) —the figures that have been so identified seem doubtful to me. The generally poor state of preservation of the works is probably the best explanation, if we take into account the fact that at the most closely related sites, the overwhelming majority of the figures are horses: at Le Cap Blanc, for example, at first glance only horses seem to be present, and at Les Combarelles there are a hundred horses to fewer than thirty bison. The date of Commarque raises no problem. Its stylistic affinities with Le Cap Blanc and Angles-sur-l'Anglin are such that we are obliged to settle for the Middle Magdalenian. This definite dating is all the more interesting because Commarque adds to the sum of the data that we can bring to bear on some of the works at Les Combarelles and Font-de-Gaume.

ABRI REVERDIT

SERGEAC, DORDOGNE, FRANCE

This shelter under an overhanging rock is about 13 yards long. It was excavated by Reverdit in 1878, and later by several others, among them Didon, D. Peyrony, and F. Delage. The sculptured frieze was noted by Castanet in 1920, and drawings were made of it by the Abbé Breuil.

The decorations here are in very poor condition. The Abbé Breuil made drawings of two horses and three bison[1] which average about a yard in length. At the extreme right there is a head in relief which is not of a horse nor a bison, and may be interpreted as that of a carnivorous animal. It is located in the same position as a feline in the frieze at Angles-sur-l'Anglin, and as the head of the bear (?) on the extreme left of the frieze at Le Cap Blanc. It is to be regretted that the works here should be nearly illegible, since the industrial objects discovered in the shelter are fairly reliably dated as Middle Magdalenian. Among the objects found here is a bone disk engraved with horses, characteristic of finds from the Middle Magdalenian (III–IV).

[1] *fig. 496*

[2] *figs. 13, 497*

[3] *fig. 498; chart* XXIX

[1] *fig. 499*

346

LA MAGDELAINE

PENNE DU TARN, TARN, FRANCE

The results of excavations around 1900 were never published. The sculptures were discovered in 1952, first by Bessac, then by Vesperini and Soulié.

146. LA MAGDELAINE. ARRANGEMENT OF THE FIGURES

The sculptures[1] are in the first chamber of the cave, on both sides of a short corridor in full daylight. What has survived was originally the central portion of more extensive decorations. Around the four figures which are intact we find a few indications of other forms, but they have not yet been deciphered. On the left is the figure of a woman reclining with her head on her hand; the body is partly sculptured, partly supplied by the natural contours of the wall. Below her, on a slanting surface of the rock, is a bison. On the right is another reclining woman; here, too, the sculptor has taken advantage of the natural relief of the wall. To her right is a large horse. All that is missing to complete the composition is an ibex and a small male head. The attitude of the women is unique in Paleolithic art, reflecting a nonchalant freedom of which we know no other example. The style is hard to define. The women's heads and feet are not detailed, which is a typical feature until the Late Magdalenian. The bison and the horse, however, are fully characterized: their massive bodies and relatively short limbs show that they are still close to Style III. This impression is strengthened by the appearance of the bison mane, which forms a voluminous bundle around the neck, a treatment of which there are many examples in Early Style IV. The base of the horns, the eye, and the ear are integrated by one unbroken line, a common device from the Middle Magdalenian onward. Consequently, it is in that period, contemporary with the sculptures at Angles-sur-l'Anglin, that these figures at La Magdelaine are to be placed.

[1] *figs. 500–502*

BERNIFAL

MEYRALS, DORDOGNE, FRANCE

The cave decorations were discovered in 1902 by Denis Peyrony. Drawings by the Abbé Breuil.

This cave, which is about 250 feet in length, is decorated almost from the entrance. The paintings in the first chamber have been preserved because this entrance was blocked up at a very early date. One panel at the right is filled with strokes and negative black hands. A natural relief in the opposite wall was transformed into a bison's head by red lines that indicate the eye and horn. The horn cuts across the belly of a highly schematized mammoth. Nearby we find other figures similar in character, which are at present scarcely legible. A bit further on, we come to a group of black dots in alignment.[1] The passageway narrows, then widens again into a corridor extending to the end of the cave, with side chambers at left and right.

[1] *fig. 503*

A first composition of engraved figures is situated a few yards past the narrow part. At left, just inside a fissure, we find two tectiform signs[2] and a small cervid. These appear on a rocky molding at eye level; the molding continues on the other side of the fissure and along the left side of the corridor, where we find a barbed sign and then a string of tectiform signs, followed by a mammoth and a triangular sign. On the right, beyond this point and at the same level as on the opposite wall, more tectiform signs are seen, extending into the upper portion of the first panel that reaches down to the floor of the cave. This panel is made up of a frieze of mammoths[3] walking toward the left, above, their outlines mingled with signs. Below, in the semi-domes of the wall, we find a bison,[4] noticeable for its late style and the fact that, like many animal bodies on late plaquettes, it has signs on its body—a double oval and two double strokes. Two short lines are set in front of the muzzle. To the right of the bison is an indistinct horse, and a herbivorous animal identified by the Abbé Breuil as a reindeer. Its peripheral location and the late character of the composition justify this identification, but the figure itself could as well be a bovid as a cervid. All the compositions along the corridor are homogeneous in style and content: the tectiform signs bring to mind the incised works at Rouffignac. The bison, however, is completely unlike those at Les Combarelles, Rouffignac, and Font-de-Gaume which are also accompanied by tectiform signs. The head stretched forward, the short mane rendered with small strokes, the two lines at the muzzle indicating "breath," and the signs on the body all constitute a set of characteristics which together, more or less completely, are found occasionally in cave figures (for example, the back-cave bison in the terminal gallery at Altamira), but primarily occur on late plaquettes (Limeuil, Le Puy de Lacan, Labastide).

[2] *fig. 504*

[3] *fig. 506*
[4] *fig. 508*

Continuing past the bison, we come to a wall covered with a grainy stalagmitic growth on which there are "several figures too mediocre to dwell on..." (Breuil, *Quatre cents siècles...*, page 289). They are in fact barely legible, but they can be reduced to a stag, over which is a horse, and over both of them a large oval sign and one long vertical line. The horse is treated exactly like the one[5] in the small chamber just ahead on the right. There, in a recess, we find two horses incised with the same thin line as the preceding animals, and some superimposed red lines. To the left of them is a panel of barely visible bison and horses, incorporating the jagged edge of the rock.

[5] *fig. 509*

The gallery goes on. A recess in the left-hand wall contains groups of lines; then comes an intersection. On the right, a blocked-up side passage forms a small chamber, and there, high up on the stalagmitic wall, we find a very remarkable red tectiform sign[6] made up of tiny colored dots, resembling one of the signs at Font-de-Gaume, with a vertical row of dots coming out of the upper part and a dotted line to the left of it. This sign is directly opposite the other branch of the intersection, an abrupt fissure inside which we find four

[6] *fig. 505*

mammoths engraved with fine lines on the two walls. These mammoths, which the Abbé Breuil copied more than thirty years ago, are identical with the small incised mammoths at Font-de-Gaume and Rouffignac. One detail in the treatment of the latter animals used to bother me: their triangular eyes, which do not appear on the Abbé Breuil's drawings. Looking at the figures under good lighting, we find that at Font-de-Gaume, as at Bernifal, the eyes really are triangular. These mammoths at Bernifal, moreover, possess the "wavy-line" form of tusks exhibited by the "rhinoceros" in the last chamber at La Mouthe and by certain subjects at Rouffignac.

Continuing along the gallery, beneath a low vault we see—or rather, can barely make out—a figure painted in brownish black which may be a bear. Since it is the last figure in the cave, this would be a normal place for a bear. For my part, I confess I have only been able to confirm the presence of the figure, but the Abbé Breuil's identification (incidentally, very cautious) is entirely in line with many other cases of back-cave bears. Lastly, in a small recess close to the ground on the same wall, just before the end of the cave, we find a row of black dots, smaller than those near the entrance. This confirms the fact that entrance signs are usually repeated at the back of a sanctuary (Arcy, Covalanas, La Croze at Gontran, Font-de-Gaume, El Pindal, Niaux).

As a whole—apart, perhaps, from the bison on the first panel of engravings—Bernifal is homogeneous. The red paintings at the entrance include a mammoth no different from the engraved mammoths we find farther inside. Animals and signs alike are so closely related to some of those at Font-de-Gaume and Les Combarelles, and to the engraved decorations at Rouffignac, that it is obvious that they belong to the same cultural complex, that of Style IV.

LES COMBARELLES

LES EYZIES, DORDOGNE, FRANCE

The engravings were discovered in 1901 *by Pomarel, a local resident, who induced Capitan, Breuil, and Peyrony to visit the site. The drawings made by the Abbé Breuil of the figures at Les Combarelles are among his masterpieces.*

The decorated cave is a winding corridor 260 yards long, which makes three hairpin turns in the deeper portion. Scrawls and erratic figures begin about 80 yards from the entrance but the continuously decorated portion does not begin until nearly 100 yards further, and extends to the end of the cave. This innermost part of the cave, about 80 yards long, is covered with hundreds of engraved figures crowded together in an extraordinary tangle. The guided tour permits visitors to see only a limited number of the more conspicuous figures, and no serious study is possible without using the Abbé Breuil's admirable drawings. Les Combarelles, then, is a corridor-sanctuary, relatively easy of access but extending quite far underground. This last fact suggests that its decorations date from the period of Early Style IV, and actually we find no figure there that can be assigned to Style III, let alone to Style II. The only question is whether the cave was used in the Late Magdalenian, for the last figures and some of the signs seem to be of the same age as the slabs at Limeuil and the engravings at Teyjat. Archaeological methods could have dated Les Combarelles long ago if the early excavations had been carried out with a minimum of care, and if reckless pillaging of the intact portions were not still going on. Along with El Castillo, the sanctuary of Les Combarelles is the most complicated of those I have had occasion to study. The dense crowding of the figures and the numerous additions make for extreme confusion. Nonetheless I chose this cave for my first statistical testing, and it was this cave, together with Le Portel and Covalanas, that made me realize the deliberate character of the figure groupings and of their topographical arrangement.

The fundamental theme is the bison/horse theme, which is repeated fourteen times—thirteen times in the large panels of the main corridor, once in a passageway composition (group 44 on plan, fig. 147). The ox/horse theme appears only twice, in two neighboring compositions (37, 39–40). The reindeer appears in seven different groups; six of these enframe the large panels and are either in or close to the hairpin turns, one is in the middle of a composition (15). The bear appears five times, always in passageways. Human figures appear in three places: in the turning just past the first set (27–32, and 62–68 on the opposite wall); at the beginning of the furthest gallery (80–83); and at the end (92). Cervids, too, appear three times: at the beginning of the second set (59 and 61, megaceros deer and hind); at the close of that set (49–50); and at the beginning of the third (113). Felines appear twice: at the end of the second set (51–52), and at the end of the third (105). Among more than 250 identifiable animal figures, this grouping of the species could not be fortuitous; the results of research have confirmed that in its structure Les Combarelles belongs within the general pattern. Its topographical disposition provides a succession of three central compositions, while each of the sharp turnings of the cave assures the localization of passageway and back-cave subjects. Areas of scrawls and unfinished outlines are clear at two spots: before the beginning of the first legible compositions (10 on the right, 78 on the left), and in the first few yards of the innermost gallery (80 on the right, 116 on the left); there are numerous scrawls elsewhere, but they are scattered. At Les Combarelles it is difficult to distinguish the true unfinished outlines, the jumble of the figures being so great that many so qualify without our being able to localize them within a definite zone of scrawls and unfinished outlines.

THE FRONT GALLERY

The figures begin to be organized about halfway in (78–71). On the left-hand wall, a series of horses is strung around two bison. In the first group a human face[1] appears, resembling the one found above the female figures at Angles-sur-l'Anglin. Close to it there are three odd signs: horizontal ovals with lines running through them. I know of no equivalent to these signs, except perhaps the signs bristling with lines that are paired with big brace-shaped signs in the innermost gallery at Altamira. Beside them (on horse 75), there is a quadrangular sign with multiple compartments in vertical latticing: this sign also occurs at Font-de-Gaume, where it is apparently older than the tectiforms, and at Bara-Bahau.[2] Just before the beginning of the figures of the first turning, we find on the left a bison/horse/mammoth group with an oval sign and strokes (69). On the opposite wall the groups are more or less symmetrical with those just described. Two reindeer lead off, then comes a bison/horse + ibex composition with another lattice sign,[3] followed by three mammoths[4]

[1] *fig. 512*

[2] *figs. 534, 690, 691*

[3] *fig. 510*   [4] *fig. 511*

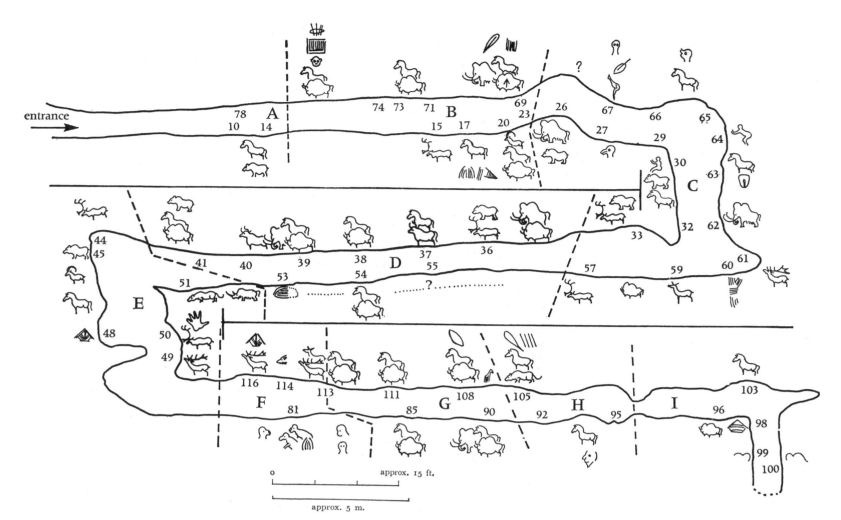

147. LES COMBARELLES. SCHEMATIC PLAN WITH CONVENTIONALIZED REPRESENTATIONS OF THE COMPOSITIONS

A *Figures at the entrance to the Front Gallery: bear, horse.*

B *Main portion of the Front Gallery: paired animals and signs on the bison/horse + mammoth or ibex theme.*

C *Turning which serves as the rear portion of the Front Gallery and the entrance to the Middle Gallery. Human figures, realistic symbols, bears, cervids.*

D *Main portion of the Middle Gallery: paired animals on two themes: bison/horse + mammoth, and ox/horse with signs. At 36, the reindeer/bear group is an extension of figures in the turning (33).*

E *Second turning, which serves as rear portion of the*

Middle Gallery: rhinoceros, feline, bear, reindeer, ibex, human hand. At 48 and 49, the tectiform sign and the stag are an overflow from the Inner Gallery (116).

F *Entrance to the Inner Gallery: signs, carnivore, male figures, and signs.*

G *Main portion of the Inner Gallery: paired animals on the bison/horse + mammoth theme.*

H *Back of the Inner Gallery: feline, man, paired signs.*

I *Terminal tunnel: one last bison/horse composition, tectiform sign.*

Despite their complexity, the figures at Les Combarelles constitute one of the best examples of topographical organization. As at Le Gabillou, this clarity owes much to the cave's structure, a single long corridor with well-defined divisions. The numbers of the compositions are those used in the Abbé Breuil's publication.

corresponding to the mammoth on the other wall. The figures of the turning echo one another from wall to wall. We see several bears and horses, human faces in frontal or profile view, three or four standing personages (30, 64), several more or less schematic vulvas,[5] one phallus, and three small female figures bending forward:[6] these last (67) are identical with the one on the slab at La Roche at Lalinde. We have here an exceptional concentration of human figures and sexual symbols. The three personages at 64, as drawn by Breuil,[7] are not entirely clear.

[5] *fig. 513* [6] *fig. 514*

[7] *chart* LV

THE MIDDLE GALLERY

The figures have the same general arrangement as in the preceding sequence, although the emphasis is on different subjects. On both walls the central portion presents a composition of bison and horses; On the right-hand wall, the bison/horse group is flanked on either side by an ox/horse composition (37, 38, 39). The sequence on the left begins with two cervids, male and female (probably megaceros deer), and some reindeer (61–56). A group of small bison intrudes between them, incised over the reindeer and under the female cervid: the small bison are the same as those at Font-de-Gaume, which are also executed over reindeer. Opposite these figures, on the right wall (33 to 36) are bears, reindeer,[8] a mammoth, and an ibex.[9] Except for the little bison on the left and a bison head on the right, these are all back-cave or framing subjects. Beyond the main compositions of bison/horse and ox/horse,[10] these subjects are taken up again shortly ahead of the turning and in the recesses that mark the turning. On the left we find two felines,[11] one rhinoceros,[12] and an undetermined animal (51–52); farther on, a panel contains two reindeer, one stag, and the only negative hand in the cave. The Abbé Breuil doubted whether this hand is Aurignacian. His doubt on this score is the more

[8] *fig. 516* [9] *fig. 515*

[10] *fig. 517*
[11] *fig. 520* [12] *fig. 518*

understandable because, quite apart from the fact that no properly dated Aurignacian hand has yet been discovered, similar hands are found off by themselves at Bernifal, Font-de-Gaume, Marsoulas, and El Pindal, caves in which all other works are in Style IV. On the right there are a great many figures that represent, apart from one bison head, mainly bears,[13] reindeer,[14] ibexes, and horses (44 to 47).

There are scarcely any signs in the middle portion. Just before we come to the felines there is a painted sign with horizontal latticing (53), of a type unusual in the Périgord; it is incomplete, and seems to be one of the tectiform variants. At the end of the turning (48), we find on the right one clearly identifiable half of a large tectiform sign (mutilated by a crack in the wall), of the type known at Font-de-Gaume, Bernifal, and Rouffignac. There are no human figures or realistic sexual figures such as we found in the first turning.

[13] fig. 519   [14] fig. 521

THE INNER GALLERY

The general theme is here repeated for the third time, with fresh touches. The central portion is exactly the same as before. On the left-hand wall a big bison (109) is balanced on either side by a great number of horses. On the opposite wall, something quite odd seems to have occurred: we find again a string of horses, but, instead of the bison, two mammoths (88, 89). This may correspond to the original intention of the decorators, although the mammoth/horse group is altogether exceptional, the only cases known (Chabot, La Baume Latrone) being in the Rhone basin; however, between the mammoths, lower down, there is a little unfinished bison that may originally have represented the indispensable female symbol. Be that as it may, the Magdalenians were aware of the shortage of bovines, and the great horse (88) is decked out with a pair of horns that Breuil noted as an especially odd detail. Once again, the Paleolithic artists seem truly to have outdone themselves to help along the interpretation, for this is the only case known of a horse masquerading as a bovine. It is also the only case I know of a well-preserved composition in which one of the two main characters seems to be missing.

The portion of the Inner Gallery preceding the large compositions is taken up, first, with an area of scrawls and unfinished outlines. Next, on the left (115–113), we come to two stags and some tectiform signs of the Les Eyzies type (Bernifal, Font-de-Gaume, Rouffignac). On the right (83–80), we see a whole series of human heads in profile, and two or three men bending forward.[15] Nearly all the faces have animalized profiles, and they have greatly contributed to the acceptance of the theory of personages wearing animal masks; I do not reject this theory, but before it is accepted the fact should be explained that when we assemble all known profiles of human heads, we find that they pass almost imperceptibly from the normal profile to that of an animal's head. These stags and men are entirely in order as examples of introductory figures.

The back of the cave is fairly confused. Everything is normal until we come to group 105, where we find a feline[16] and some paired signs; on the opposite wall (92) there is a human face; from this point on, however, we get the impression that a small sanctuary has been tacked on to the others. It is not uncommon to find one last repetition of the main composition among back-cave subjects (Le Gabillou, Lascaux, Marsoulas, La Mouthe, Niaux, etc.). Here we see a group of little horses (93–95); past the narrowing known as the *Bague* ("ring"), is a group of little bison (97) like the intrusive group 58–59 in the Middle Gallery; then, at the last turning, an incised oval and some strokes, a painted tectiform sign, numerous scrawls, and a horse. Apart from some uncertain curved lines, nothing is found after the first six feet beyond the turning. The cave consequently ends in classical fashion before the *Bague* is reached, then has one last surge for a few yards and terminates with some signs and rows of strokes.

[15] fig. 522

[16] fig. 523

STYLE AND DATING

Les Combarelles is based on the classical combination par excellence: bison/horse. Mammoth and reindeer also appear, the ibex less often. The signs are tectiforms and more or less schematic vulvar ovals; there are many rows of strokes but apparently no barbed sign (we cannot be more positive because the outlines are tangled).

The formula bison/horse + mammoth + reindeer is attested at Font-de-Gaume, La Mouthe, and Les Trois Frères. The formula bison/horse + mammoth occurs at Bernifal, La Mouthe, Rouffignac, and Pech Merle, and in the last composition of the inner gallery at Altamira, and at El Pindal. The first three of these caves are in the Les Eyzies region and exhibit tectiforms. Arcy-sur-Cure has a closely related formula: bison/ mammoth + horse.

The caves in which reindeer intervene among bison and horses are Teyjat and Las Monedas.

In all these caves except Pech Merle—Arcy, Bernifal, Font-de-Gaume, La Mouthe, Rouffignac, Teyjat, Les Trois Frères, Altamira, Las Monedas, El Pindal—the figures present incontestable stylistic affinities, between one cave and another, and with decorated objects of the Middle and Late Magdalenian. The Les Eyzies group is especially homogeneous; the greater part of Font-de-Gaume, certain panels at La Mouthe, and the whole of Bernifal and Rouffignac are obviously contemporaneous with at least a majority of the figures at Les Combarelles. The mammoths at all five sites are closely related with respect to details of treatment, and provide us with a very valuable tie-up. If we could date the mammoths on decorated objects as we can date the horses and bison, many problems would be solved at once. The mammoth is extremely rare on Magdalenian objects: there exists one from Raymonden that is very exact in detail, but its date is not reliable. Fortunately, it is an engraving on a bone disk, which localizes it in the Middle Magdalenian. Thus we can accept as a hypothesis that the little mammoths—their eyes frequently triangular, hair hanging down on their foreheads, beards around the lower part of their cheeks, and four legs that peep out from what looks like the fringed upholstery of an armchair—date from the Middle Magdalenian. According to the Abbé Breuil, those at Font-de-Gaume are superimposed over all other decoration; at Les Combarelles, in group 34–35, the mammoth is superimposed on the reindeer: thus they would be dated late in the Middle Magdalenian. However, excavations have not, apparently, turned up any mammoths in France later than the Middle Magdalenian. The mammoth, then, occurs at the latest in decorations dating from Magdalenian IV. What arguments do the other figures supply?

The horses at Les Combarelles, except for the one at 38, show no sign of ventral modeling. Some of them are closely related to the figures at Le Cap Blanc and Commarque; this is especially true of the animals accompanied by lattice signs in the Front Gallery. As for the others—particularly, the small painted horses in the Inner Gallery (86–87 to 107)—they are related to figures at Teyjat and Limeuil. Thus they would fall somewhere between Magdalenian III and Magdalenian V.

The bison at Les Combarelles belong to two main types. The bison that accompany the horse with ventral modeling in group 38, and the one in group 109 all have manes resembling the type found at Angles, high and squarely cut off at the back. The bison in group 20 is exactly like some of the painted bison at Font-de-Gaume and on the painted ceiling at Rouffignac: a very large mane bunched over the shoulder like a knapsack, and a long beard thrust forward. The small bison which intrude in groups 57 to 59 also belong to this type. There is no evidence from decorated objects to provide an exact dating. That they are engraved over the reindeer in group 56–57 provides a clue: they cannot be earlier than the latter. So, once again, they fall somewhere between Magdalenian III and some later stage.

The reindeer do not furnish much information, but the little they do furnish is interesting. Apart from the instance of the small bison, the superimpositions are not significant; but comparisons of style and treatment, on the other hand, lead us toward Teyjat and Limeuil. This would suggest that the reindeer are later, from Magdalenian V. The bears give the same indication; there are many of them, and, though the point has been disputed, they could as well represent brown bears as cave bears. Those figures of bears which are complete have Late Magdalenian outlines and are shown in attitudes otherwise found in that period only on decorated objects.

Consequently, dating Les Combarelles is a delicate matter. The Abbé Breuil places most of the works between the Early Magdalenian and the Middle Magdalenian. I doubt whether one can point to a single work that is reliably dated Magdalenian I–II which resembles any at Les Combarelles, whereas there are a great many such from Magdalenian III-IV. Therefore I believe that the sanctuary was in use in the Middle Magdalenian, around 12,000 B.C., and probably continued to be in use down to the beginning of the Late Magdalenian, around 10,500 B.C. This is the time span that includes Angles, Font-de-Gaume, and at least partly overlaps that of Teyjat.

FONT-DE-GAUME

LES EYZIES, DORDOGNE, FRANCE

The painted and engraved works were discovered by D. Peyrony in 1901. The Abbé Breuil made an especially careful pictorial inventory of them.

148. FONT-DE-GAUME. SCHEMATIC PLAN WITH CONVENTIONALIZED SUBJECTS
The numerals indicate the number of individual representations of each form.
A *First Side Gallery: incomplete figures.*
B *The "Rubicon": composition of bison/horse/ tectiform signs, also unfinished outlines.*
C *First part of Main Gallery: bison/horse + mammoth and reindeer. Tectiform signs and hand. The feline is a little engraving on clay, rather vague in character.*
D *Second Side Gallery: same theme as the preceding. Bear at the back.*
E *Second part of Main Gallery: same theme as C. The wolf may mark the entrance either to this section or to the Side Gallery.*
F *Chamber of Small Bison: composition of bison/ horse/tectiform signs. Quadrangular signs and oxen in Style III.*
G *Low tunnel: humanoid masks.*
H *Style III composition, "ghost."*
I–J *Terminal fissure, back-cave themes: stag, rhinoceros, feline, horses, strokes.*

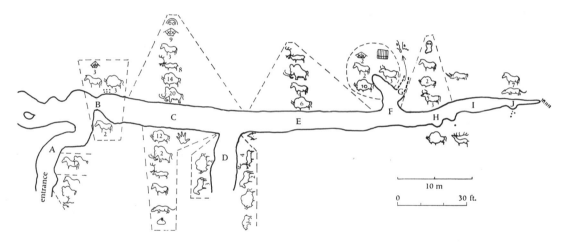

This cave is a good example of a corridor-sanctuary, measuring about 165 yards, with two side galleries. About halfway inside from the entrance a narrowing of the walls, which was named the "Rubicon," marks (as is often the case) the point where the decorated portion begins. The cave terminates in a dead end. Font-de-Gaume, in the simplicity of its structure, could serve as a model of the arrangement of a Paleolithic sanctuary if the poor condition of the walls and the superimpositions did not make for considerable illegibility.

The general framework is fairly clear. Just before the "Rubicon" (B), a side gallery branches to the right in which a few unfinished painted figures appear (A). The first engraved composition (B) occurs at the narrowing of the cave. Immediately beyond there is a group of red dots on the left-hand wall, marking the beginning of the main sanctuary. At the extreme back of the cave is found a matching group of red strokes. The large signs are placed as follows: in the entrance panel (B); in the main composition between the two side galleries A and D; in a small recess (F) to the left of the Main Gallery, known as the Chamber of Small Bison. These details give the Font-de-Gaume sanctuary an especially coherent structure. The innermost portion of the cave is no less a model of the type. First, in a narrow tunnel (G) at ground level, under the Small Bison panel, we find two extremely schematized human profiles resembling those at the rear of the Rouffignac cave, and those at Marsoulas. Just beyond, at H, as one makes one's way through the fissure leading to the dead end, there is a "ghost" painted in black and, on the other wall, a stag facing a rhinoceros; at the very back is one feline and seven horses. With the possible exception of the Chamber of Felines at Lascaux, few decorated caves present so full a complement of figures characteristic of the innermost reaches of a sanctuary.

Analysis of the compositions goes hand in hand with the problem of dating the cave. The Abbé Breuil distinguished six periods ranging from the Aurignacian to the terminal Magdalenian—that is, from red and black linear drawings to polychrome frescoes and very fine engravings, according to the terms of his classification. I find it hard to discover evidence at Font-de-Gaume of anything but Style III and Style IV—that is, a sequence running from the Solutrean to the close of the Middle Magdalenian with, perhaps, a few additions made in the Late Magdalenian. In part, this more restricted dating is based on the signs to be found at Font-de-Gaume, in part on the style and content of the various compositions.

THE SIGNS

Font-de-Gaume is famous for its tectiform signs,[1] nowhere else so numerous and so varied. In the first part of this book we have discussed at length the chronological position of the tectiform signs. There are good reasons to place them in Early Style IV, contemporaneous with the claviforms (particularly those at Les Trois Frères and El Pindal). These late claviforms and the tectiforms of the Perigordian type seem to me to come just before the oval and the realistic female signs that reappear in the terminal period of Paleolithic art. At Font-de-Gaume, as at Les Combarelles, Les Trois Frères, Montespan, and Altamira, we do in fact find many oval signs roughly sketched in particular places or so superimposed as to prove them later additions. At Font-de-Gaume, the Abbé Breuil established that at least some of the tectiform signs appear under bison having exaggeratedly developed manes, of the type encountered at Rouffignac. He was also able to establish that the little engraved mammoths represent one of the latest stages in Font-de-Gaume's decoration. At Rouffignac, mammoths are actually associated with bison having enormous manes; but tectiform signs are also found there, which proves that no very great distance in time separates the two categories. In the Chamber of Small Bison a quadrangular sign[2] which Breuil has reproduced very clearly in his report on the cave is covered over with lines of the type used in tectiforms. The presence of this sign suggests that there should be figures in Style III at Font-de-Gaume, and, indeed, in the Chamber of Small Bison, and a few yards beyond we do find figures of oxen and bison related incontestably to figures at Lascaux, Le Gabillou, Villars, and Pech Merle. Thus, so far as the signs are concerned, Font-de-Gaume seems to contain examples of Style III (quadrangular signs) and of Early Style IV (tectiform signs), as well as evidence of Late Style IV (oval signs). Examination of the compositions will supply a basis for testing this view.

THE COMPOSITIONS

(A) The First Side Gallery, opening off to the right just before we reach the "Rubicon," contains a few figures at two points on the left-hand wall. It is hard to say whether these are unfinished outlines, or figures that have greatly deteriorated. In any case, they comprise the following subjects: horse, mammoth, reindeer —that is, they are beyond question related stylistically to the decorations in the Main Gallery.

(B) Above the narrow passage called the "Rubicon" figures are engraved on the calcareous deposits lining the wall: barely visible at the right, two horses; at the left, a panel on which at first glance three tectiform signs are recognizable.[3] Actually, the panel has a great many figures, including a horse and several bison, as well as numerous strokes in alignment.[4] In view of its placement and the character of the engravings, it would not be implausible to regard this panel as one of the zones of scrawls and unfinished outlines discussed in the first part of this book (see pages 182–186).

(C) The section of the Main Gallery between the "Rubicon" and the Second Side Gallery is covered with a large number of engraved and painted figures. Here only two phases can be reliably discerned. The second of these is represented by the little engraved mammoths with triangular eyes.[5] The first phase comprises in particular, on the left, a long sequence of superimposed mammoths, bison,[6] reindeer, and horses. The superimpositions here do not seem to imply that these figures were painted in very different periods; on the contrary, they seem to constitute coherent compositions on the bison/horse/mammoth theme. The reasons for introducing the reindeer are hard to fathom in the absence of comparative data, but the conditions are analogous to those obtaining at Les Combarelles. On the right are a few figures engraved on clay in the vicinity of black hands in negative. These last do not strike me as dating necessarily from a very early period; I am rather inclined to consider them contemporaneous with the collection of figures accompanied by tectiform signs—a conclusion all the more plausible because at Bernifal and Les Combarelles hands identical in execution are found accompanying the same signs and animals in the same style.

(D and E) The Second Side Gallery and the section of the Main Gallery extending to the Chamber of Small Bison provide a continuation of the preceding group of painted and engraved figures. Here the works are in the same style and built around the same grouping: bison/horse/mammoth/reindeer. We must mention, however, the famous wolf painted in black at the intersection of the side gallery D and section E. This is one of the two incontestable representations of this animal, the other being at Les Combarelles in the vicinity (just as we would expect) of the tectiform signs. At the back of the Second Side Gallery there is a figure that may be a bear.

(F) From the chronological point of view, the Chamber of Small Bison is the most interesting part of the cave. Among the remains of three oxen painted in black, we find a head whose horns and outline are incontestably in Style III, closely related to those of the Lascaux oxen. We also find the quadrangular sign previously mentioned, the tectiform signs which seem to be a later version of the quadrangular sign, and above these the small bison with exaggerated manes and beards. This composition in Style III continues on the left-hand wall of section H.

(G) The short low tunnel off the right-hand side of the Chamber of Small Bison contains two very interesting engraved figures, to which attention has not hitherto been drawn. They are two grotesque profiles, facing each other. The one on the right looks like the well-known profile in the Marsoulas cave; that on the left has a rather surprising nasal appendage in the form of a trunk. One cannot fail to be struck by the repeated occurrence of pairs of human faces such as these in the innermost portions of a number of caves (Rouffignac, Les Combarelles, Marsoulas).

(H) Beyond the Chamber of Small Bison the Main Gallery narrows and becomes a progressively smaller fissure. The most notable figures are two bison, in treatment close to the back-to-back bison in the Nave at Lascaux. In addition there are several bovines in the same style.[7] This portion of the cave appears to contain the remnants of a composition in Style III, probably the oldest decoration in Font-de-Gaume. Moreover, we find here the "ghost" painted in black previously mentioned.

(I) In this part of the gallery, rather high up, we find the well-known "rhinoceros"[8] which is painted in red, and, on the opposite wall, a stag in the same color. These two figures seem to belong to the composition in Early Style IV, in which they, with the feline in section J, represent the back-cave figures. The right-hand wall in sections H, I, and J has some worn remains of a few engraved figures (among them a bison) and some red dots inside two small recesses.

(J) High on the left-hand wall we find a feline and several horses.[9] It is hard to say whether this is a real composition—that is, whether the feline was deliberately placed there to face the group of horses. Considering that felines and horses both belong to the male category and thus are frequently found among the back-cave figures, the fact that both species turn up here may be merely fortuitous. At the very back of the cave's dead end, we find seven red strokes.[10]

In conclusion, the Font-de-Gaume cave seems to contain, first, the remains of a composition in Style III (Solutrean–Early Magdalenian) amounting only to a few animals and one sign. It also contains a large collection of painted and engraved figures (some of the latter almost in low relief) accompanied by tectiform signs, which can be associated stylistically with the animal figures accompanied by tectiforms at Les Combarelles, Rouffignac, and Bernifal. This collection seems to terminate with mammoths identical with those at Bernifal and Rouffignac. From the stylistic point of view, this second collection can be assigned only to Style IV. One portion of it may correspond to Early Style IV, but the influence of Late Style IV already makes itself felt. Consequently, I am tempted to assign the majority of the figures in this cave to Magdalenian IV–V.

[7] figs. 524, 525

[8] fig. 526

[9] fig. 532

[10] fig. 533

LA MOUTHE (*Continued from page 319*)

FIGURES IN STYLE IV

As previously mentioned (pages 305, 319), La Mouthe's earliest composition (ox/horse) is in Style II. The next composition with the "little bison" and the large painted quadrangular sign facing them, is in Style III. The chamber where this "hut" sign appears, on the right as one enters, contains a panel in Style IV comprising a rather jumbled collection of bison, horses, reindeer, mammoths, and a famous large ibex. At the back of the axial corridor, in a recess on the left, we find a panel of reindeer and mammoths with a triangular sign and a barbed sign. At the extreme back, among figures of horses and bison in Style III, we find a few more horses and one poorly preserved mammoth which the Abbé Breuil believed to be a rhinoceros with a pair of preposterous corkscrew horns. The great spiraling tusks of the mammoth have, however, sometimes been represented in this way: a good example can be seen on the painted ceiling at Rouffignac. Until 1959 I thought that the portion of the decorations in Style IV at La Mouthe was ill preserved, incomprehensible, and incomplete: the subsequent discovery of a new chamber at the end of a tunnel has justified that impression, for this chamber contains the main sanctuary, with several mammoths, one reindeer, six bison, one ibex, and one rhinoceros. The painted or engraved figures, in both style and composition, constitute a set closely related to that at Rouffignac.

ROUFFIGNAC

FLEURAC, DORDOGNE, FRANCE

When the painted and engraved works in the Rouffignac cave (also known as Cro-du-Cluzeau, Cro-de-Granville, and Miremont) were first declared prehistoric, in 1956, a passionate controversy ensued. Feeling has since cooled down, and today it seems possible to give a brief objective account of the matter. This enormous cave, which is believed to contain more than 5 miles of galleries, has been known since the sixteenth century from various writings which seem already to have referred, in a rather mythical and obscure manner, to the presence of animal paintings. This early reference to cave art, moreover, is not unique: the Black Salon at Niaux was reported to contain paintings long before the existence of a prehistoric art was discovered. Over the centuries countless travelers and curiosity seekers stopped at Rouffignac and scratched or drew (with charcoal or lampblack) their names and the dates of their visits on the walls. With the same spontaneity that made Paleolithic artists choose certain surfaces for their works, these visitors in turn covered the works of their remote predecessors with inscriptions commemorating their own presence in the cave. For reasons difficult to analyze, Rouffignac was somehow by-passed during the great period of cave exploration at the beginning of the twentieth century; only during the recent vogue for speleology did the works in it begin to attract attention. The first to notice them were members of the Spéléo-club of Périgueux. In a diary kept by one of them (R. de Faccio), I find the following passage, under the date of February 16, 1947: "We're climbing back from the steep drop... a few paintings here and there, we can't judge whether they are prehistoric or not...." Unable to determine the age of the paintings, the speleologists sought the opinion of the district director of prehistoric works who, perhaps rashly, declared them to be forgeries. The amateurs accepted his decision. In June 1956, Louis Nougier and Romain Robert hold the credit not only for returning to look at the pictures, but also for proclaiming their authenticity. Then, for weeks on end, the press published articles on the not-too-cordial relations obtaining among prehistorians, and between prehistorians and speleologists. Adding fuel to the controversy was a remark by the speleological group of Périgueux, who thought in good faith that the frieze of three painted rhinoceroses had appeared at some moment since their previous visit to the cave. It takes long experience with caves to know that it is quite possible to pass certain details a hundred times without actually seeing them until much later, when they suddenly stare you in the face. The quarrel is now a thing of the past. One can only regret that it ever took place, and that the defense of the authenticity of the works was so violent that in the end it may have reflected unfavorably on them.

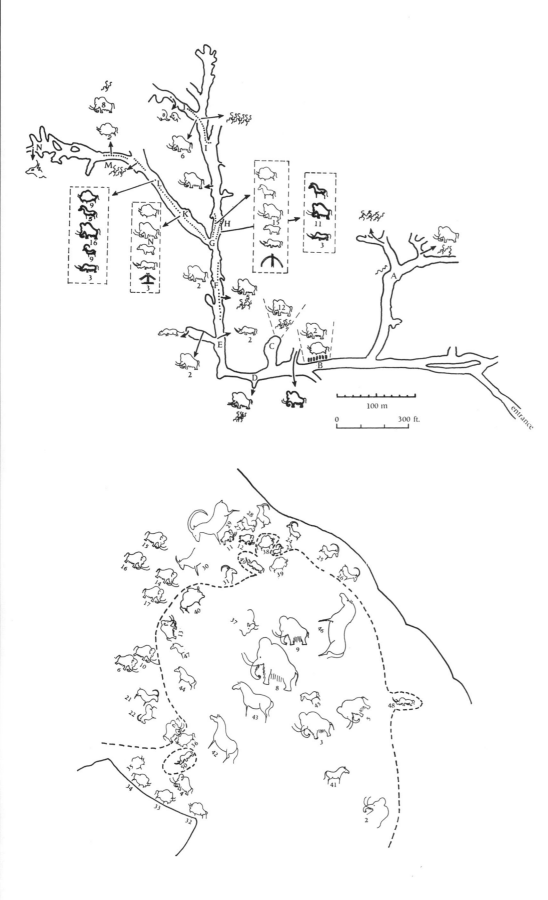

149. ROUFFIGNAC. SCHEMATIC PLAN WITH CONVENTIONALIZED FIGURES

Painted figures are rendered in heavy outline; the other figures are engraved. Small numerals indicate the number of individuals represented.

A *Lateral gallery (Red Ceiling with Serpentines): engraved meanders and a mammoth.*

B *First figures in the Main Gallery: painted mammoth in a recess.*

C *Side chamber with the Red Ceiling: engraved mammoths and meanders.*

D *Side chamber: engraved meanders and a mammoth. Note similarity in content and position of groups A, C, and D.*

E *Gallery of the Two Mammoths.*

F *Continuation of the Main Gallery: engraved mammoths and meanders. Two rhinoceroses are engraved on the ceiling where the gallery forks; a feline is engraved at the back of the gallery.*

G *Fork of the Main Gallery, leading (right) to the Breuil Gallery and (left) to the gallery with the Painted Ceiling.*

H *Breuil Gallery. On the right, painted figures: horse's head, frieze of mammoths, frieze of rhinoceroses. On the left, engraved figures: bison/horse/tectiform-sign + mammoth/bear/rhinoceros.*

I *Last set of mammoths and meanders.*

J *Two facing human profiles, marking the end of the sequence in the right-hand branch of the fork.*

K *Engravings in the left-hand gallery preceding the Painted Ceiling. Note one of the cave's few tectiform signs.*

L *Painted Ceiling. The absence of signs is most unusual. Normally this collection would be complemented by one or several tectiforms (possibly painted red, as at Font-de-Gaume and Bernifal) placed either inside the composition (as at Font-de-Gaume) or in an isolated side chamber (as at Bernifal).*

M *Last composition of the left-branch sequence. Engraved meanders and mammoths. Two bison with no complementary horse—as unusual as the absence of signs on the Painted Ceiling.*

N *Engraving of the so-called saiga antelope, which seems to be a cervid. Either animal would be a plausible back-cave figure of the right-branch sequence.*

150. ROUFFIGNAC. THE COMPOSITION ON THE PAINTED CEILING

(The numbers of the figures are those used by L. R. Nougier and R. Robert.)

The disproportion in the size of the figures is striking, and it will be noted that there is one especially large figure for each of the species included in the basic formula: bison (37), horse (46), mammoth (8), male and female ibex (29, 30). At the center we find one complete bison/horse/mammoth group (37, 8, 43). There is a second complete group (40, 47, 13), and also a third (36, 42, 4). In the first the dominant figure is the mammoth (8), in the second the bison (40), in the third the horse (42). The broken line separates the center, where we find the bison/horse + mammoth groups, from the periphery, around which ibexes and small mammoths face toward the center. The rhinoceroses are distributed along the boundary between center and periphery. At the bottom of the central composition is a group of bison (32–35) which ends at the edge of the drop leading to the lower network of galleries.

Because Nougier and Robert have as yet published only a portion of their findings, I shall limit myself, in this account and in the accompanying plan, to giving a general idea of the sanctuary and its organization. The decorated portion begins about 325 yards from the entrance, and the figures are to be found almost to the very end of the normally accessible parts of the cave, a distance of about 800 yards. This is, then, a typical deep-cave sanctuary, on the order of those listed in chart xx as Early Style IV, which alone would nearly justify the assumption that Rouffignac was decorated between Magdalenian III and the beginning of Magdalenian V. As we shall see, the signs as well as the stylistic analysis confirm this assumption. The sanctuary is laid out on an enormous scale, comparable in size to that at Niaux. It begins in a gallery that opens out on the right about 225 yards from the entrance; about 165 yards inside this gallery is the "Red Ceiling with Serpentines," a surface completely covered with serpentine-shaped signs among which a few figures appear. These serpentine signs are very frequent at Rouffignac, and are invariably found at spots where we would expect a zone of unfinished outlines. Topographically, this first gallery (A) plays the same part as the first right-hand gallery at Font-de-Gaume or the front part of Les Combarelles. Returning to the Main Gallery, at B we find one bison, two mammoths, and a few red strokes, then at C the "Red Ceiling with Mammoths," on which a dozen of these animals are engraved. Before coming to the main fork (G), we find mammoths at various points, two rhinoceroses, and, in the back of a side gallery (E), a feline. At G the cave divides into two branches, one leading ultimately to the human faces, the other toward the "saiga antelope." The large central compositions begin at the fork. At the right, in the Breuil Gallery (H) we have a number of engravings on the theme bison/horse/mammoth accompanied by a bear, rhinoceros, and claviform signs.[1] These engraved figures appear on the left-hand wall, while on the right-hand wall we find a number of black paintings: a horse's head, the frieze of rhinoceroses[2] mentioned above in the historical description, and an astonishing frieze of eleven mammoths arranged in two facing groups.[3] The continuation of the gallery contains more mammoths (I), after which we come to a huge area of scrawls and serpentines, and lastly (J) to two human profiles turned toward each other.[4] This anthropomorphic pair brings to mind the two faces of the same type in the low tunnel under the Chamber of Small Bison at Font-de-Gaume, and those at the back of the Marsoulas cave.

The gallery which forks off to the left at G opens with a long sequence of engravings on the theme bison/mammoth/bear/rhinoceros/tectiform signs. I am surprised not to have found a horse here but there has been no publication as yet of this portion of the cave, and I am relying only on some notes I made myself. Beyond these engravings we come to the large chamber on the ceiling of which is painted Rouffignac's most monumental composition.[5] The theme is bison/horse + mammoth and ibex, accompanied by rhinoceroses. One of the most solidly constructed compositions of the Upper Paleolithic, it is comparable to the Altamira ceiling, the Black Salon at Niaux, and the "sanctuary" at Les Trois Frères. Surprisingly, it contains no signs, and there is no nearby recess such as might contain signs. However, we should note that there are signs in other parts of the sanctuary (H and K), but only one at each point. In this respect Rouffignac is very different from Font-de-Gaume and Bernifal, though not without analogy to Les Combarelles. Beyond the Painted Ceiling we come to a surface covered with serpentines, as at the end of the Breuil Gallery, followed (as is so often the case) by one last bison/mammoth composition (M), and, at the very end of this branch of the cave, to the figure named by its discoverers a "saiga antelope." The horns are acknowledged, however, to curve forward, not back (see "L'antilope 'Saiga' dans l'art pariétal," *Préhistoire et spéléologie ariégeoises*, Société préhistorique de l'Ariège, vol. 13, 1958). I confess I do not understand why this figure has been interpreted as a saiga antelope; apart from a vaguely bulging forehead, it resembles a cervid and, so far as one may judge of so cursory a figure, a reindeer rather than a stag, considering the faint suggestion of hair under the neck. In any case, whether antelope, ibex, or cervid, it is a back-cave or peripheral animal, and just as it was normal that the right-hand gallery should terminate with a human figure, so it is that this one should terminate with a cervid.

The content of the sanctuary raises a few problems. This content is exactly the same as that of Les Combarelles—that is, it consists of a main bison/horse pairing, a third animal intervening frequently (in this case, the mammoth), with the addition of the ibex, the bear, the lion, and the rhinoceros. The signs, too, are the same as those at Les Combarelles—true tectiforms. The odd thing is the numerical imbalance. The engraved portion includes a disconcerting number of mammoths: it is altogether exceptional for the "third animal" to take over the predominance to such an extent from the two main animals. For some time I believed that Rouffignac was built around a bison/mammoth formula, like Arcy-sur-Cure, but the central position of the horse leads me to think that we are presented with the same basic combination as at Bernifal, Font-de-Gaume, and Les Combarelles. The paucity of bison and horses in the engraved portion matches the paucity of signs—according to my notes, there is only one sign in the Breuil Gallery (which seems to have been overlooked in the publication by Nougier and Robert), and another in the gallery of the Painted Ceiling. Both are tectiforms identical with those we find at Font-de-Gaume, Les Combarelles, and Bernifal. This shows that Rouffignac indeed belongs to the same small group of sanctuaries in the vicinity of Les Eyzies.

From the stylistic point of view, Rouffignac is especially unambiguous. Both the painted and the engraved bison are of the type with overdeveloped humps ("knapsacks") and nearly horizontal beards that we find at Font-de-Gaume and Les Combarelles. The mammoths correspond in detail to the small engraved mammoths of Font-de-Gaume and those in the side chamber at the back of Bernifal, particularly in the triangular form of the eye, a form I have found only at these three sites. The horses, especially those on the Painted Ceiling, are very close to those at Les Combarelles; the rhinoceroses, for which we have less comparative data, have a distinct relationship to the single little rhinoceros at Les Combarelles. The same may be said of the ibexes. Thus the decoration of Rouffignac is remarkably homogeneous, and remarkably easy to place among the Perigordian caves. It confirms the existence of a group well defined in both its content and its style, which so far is characteristic only of caves in the vicinity of Les Eyzies. How are we to place it chronologically? The figures are in Style IV; they are closely related to the latest mammoths and bison at Font-de-Gaume and Les Combarelles, just before the reindeer gained preponderance. It is thus highly probable that Rouffignac belongs within the Middle Magdalenian or at the beginning of the Late Magdalenian (Magdalenian IV–V).

[1] *figs. 537, 538, 542*

[2] *fig. 535*
[3] *fig. 536*

[4] *fig. 543*

[5] *figs. 539–541, 544*

ARCY-SUR-CURE

GROTTE DU CHEVAL, YONNE, FRANCE

The Grotte du Cheval ("Horse Cave") was explored and published in 1901 by the Abbé Parat, who had no inkling of the works of art deeper inside, between 200 and 300 feet from the entrance. In 1946 a group of young speleologists, Bourreau, Méraville, and Papon, cleared out the debris blocking off a low-ceilinged gallery and brought the engravings to light.

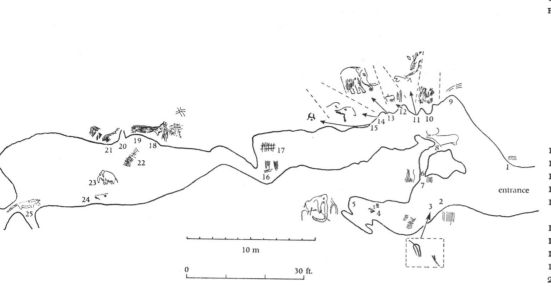

151. ARCY-SUR-CURE. SCHEMATIC PLAN WITH FIGURES

1 *First signs.*
2–3 *Above a short steep drop. Oval sign, barbed sign, and lines.*
4 *Finger marks covered by calcitic deposit.*
5 *Two mammoths and an unidentified figure.*
6–7 *Unfinished outlines and strokes at the entrance to a tunnel.*
8 *Cervid at the entrance to the first chamber.*
8–9 *Two vulvas on the ceiling (not shown on plan).*
9 *Lines at the entrance to the chamber.*
10 *Scrawls.*
11 *Unfinished outlines of mammoths and cervids.*
12 *Sketch of mammoth and strokes.*
13 *Large mammoth.*
14 *Dorsal curve of a bison, barbed sign, and a mammoth's head.*
15 *Bison head.*
16–17 *Strokes and lattice sign.*
18 *Lattice sign and unfinished outlines.*
19 *Bison.*
20–21 *Unfinished outlines and strokes at the entrance to a fissure.*
22 *Lattice sign and strokes.*
23 *Mammoth.*
24 *Head of cervid or ibex.*
25 *Back-cave horses and strokes.*

The Abbé Breuil thought that this cave should be called "Mammoth Cave." It was named "Horse Cave" in 1901 by the Abbé Parat, who made it a rule to name sites after the first animal of which some trace was discovered; I have kept this designation because it has been known as "Horse Cave" for half a century, and because there is another "Mammoth Cave" a few hundred yards away.

The cave entrance yielded very few remains from the Upper Paleolithic, and these are not typical; on the other hand, the nearby caves—Le Trilobite, Le Renne, and Les Fées—yielded rich deposits ranging from the Chatelperronian to the Late Magdalenian.

The sanctuary belongs to the type of corridor-caves, and is far inside and difficult of access; nearly all examples of this type occur within the Middle Magdalenian. Only at a few points is the ceiling more than 40 inches high; Paleolithic men had to crawl on hands and knees for about 200 feet to reach the three small chambers where the works are situated.

The first chamber, to the left, is more like a fissure, at the entrance to which we find an oval sign, a barbed sign, and curves suggesting unfinished outlines. High up in the fissure, opposite finger marks left by the artist, we find two engravings of mammoths. Their arrangement brings to mind the fissure at Bernifal with the four engraved mammoths. To the right are two successive chambers, separated by a very narrow "cat hole." At the entrance to the first we find parallel strokes and a small panel on which is engraved a cervid followed by a hind. In 1962, two vulvas[1] located in a fold of the ceiling were discovered in the vicinity of these two engravings; they are very similar, in treatment, to group 63 at Les Combarelles and to one of the Pergouset figures.[2] They escaped notice for several years because of the calcitic incrustation. The engravings at Arcy were made on a film of soft clay covering the limestone, and except where there have been subsequent limestone deposits, they have conserved such a freshness that their patina can be appreciated only by comparing them with a sample line made in our own time. After these entrance figures, we come to a frieze that consists, first, of two panels of scrawls and unfinished outlines including the head of a cervid which seems to be a reindeer; then come three mammoths,[3] a bison head,[4] and a forked sign. The signs are near the end of the sanctuary, before we reach the cat hole, above a small opening in which a flint blade was found still sticking in the clay; there are two groups of strokes and a ladder-shaped sign which, here at Arcy, seems to stand for a female sign.

Once through the cat hole, we find, in the middle of the last chamber, on the right-hand wall and on the ceiling, a group including scrawls (with many cervico-dorsal curves), a bison,[5] a mammoth,[6] rows of strokes, and a second ladder sign.[7] A bit farther, on the ceiling, we find a head that may be that of a stag or of an ibex.[8] Finally, at the back, there is a horse[9] in Early Style IV with a double shoulder line and a belly modeled in wavy lines; this is accompanied by one last set of strokes.

In composition the Arcy sanctuary is perfectly classical: strokes at the entrance, in passageways, and at the back; panels of scrawls and unfinished outlines; cervids at the beginning and end; paired species (bison/mammoth), paired signs (ladder/strokes, or oval/forked sign). The basic formula, however, is rather ex-

[1] *fig. 548*

[2] *fig. 557*

[3] *figs. 545, 546* [4] *fig. 547*

[5] *fig. 550* [6] *fig. 101*
[7] *fig. 549*
[8] *fig. 552* [9] *fig. 551*

ceptional: the species paired are the bison and the mammoth; this pairing is not found elsewhere except at Pech Merle. Usually, the mammoth appears only as a complementary animal in a bison/horse pairing (Les Combarelles, Font-de-Gaume, Rouffignac, La Mouthe, Gargas, and Altamira—innermost gallery). The appearance of the horse as a back-cave animal is also exceptional—not rare, however, for I know several other examples: at Lascaux (Axial Gallery), Les Combarelles, Ebbou, the Bayol cave, Santimamine, Font-de-Gaume (horse/feline), Le Portel (Gallery 3), El Pindal (horse/stag), Niaux (horse/ibex or headless stag), El Castillo (horse/ibex).

Dating this decoration presents no major difficulties, and I do not share the Abbé Breuil's opinion that the figures at Arcy go back to the Aurignacian-Perigordian. The mammoths, especially the largest ones in the first chamber, are of the type with all four legs fringed with hair, that we know to be Early Style IV; it is also found at Font-de-Gaume, Les Combarelles, Rouffignac, and on a bone disk from Raymonden. The bison head in the second chamber, with eye and horn rendered in a continuous line, belongs to the same style, as a host of examples confirm. The back-cave horse cannot possibly be misconstrued as other than one of the numerous Middle Magdalenian horses with two shoulder lines and wavy-line ventral modeling: we have examples on decorated objects and on cave walls from the Dordogne to Spain. In the Pyrenees or in Spain the signs would be claviforms, and around Les Eyzies they would be tectiforms, but the signs we find here are closer to the lattice signs which precede tectiforms at Les Combarelles and Font-de-Gaume; they are neither Aurignacian-Perigordian vulvas nor the compartmented rectangles of the Solutrean–Early Magdalenian. The presence of two vulvas stresses further the affinities with Les Combarelles. Consequently, it must be within Early Style IV that the "Horse Cave" belongs, and hence it must have been executed during the Middle Magdalenian.

PERGOUSET

BOUZIÈS-BAS, LOT, FRANCE

This cave was discovered in February, 1964, by Astruc and Maury. Thanks to its owner, Mr. Couderc, and members of the Quercy speleological group, I have been able to draw up this brief account based on Jean Vertut's photographs and notes. Not all the figures have been deciphered as yet. In the simplified plan the run from entrance to far end is reduced to a straight line representing 160 yards.

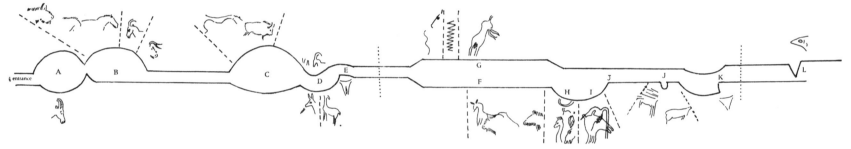

152. PERGOUSET. SCHEMATIC PLAN WITH FIGURES

The Pergouset cave is one of the relatively inaccessible corridor-caves. The greater part can be reached only by crawling on hands and knees. The decoration, which is entirely engraved work, corresponds to Style IV. Both in composition and in some of its figures, this cave presents some interesting data. The layout is fairly clear: the works fall into two sequences (A–E and F–K); beyond these is a spit of rock (L) on which an eye has been engraved—the latter figure is comparable to that engraved at Montespan in a similar location.

The first sequence is introduced by an ibex (A)[1] in front of a low narrow opening. Where the passage widens we find a bison/horse + ibex composition (B).[2] A narrow passage about 20 feet long opens into a small chamber, on the walls of which there is a second bison/horse composition (C); then, in an elbow (D), there are two hinds[3] (a subject seldom found in France, but one which occurs on decorated objects from the Abri Murat, not far from Pergouset). The hinds are placed opposite an ibex.[4] This first group is terminated by a vulva (E).[5] After crawling about 12 yards farther we reach a wider portion of the gallery where it is possible to stand up. The right-hand wall has a third bison/horse + hind composition (F).[6] The wall on the left (G) is covered with lines and presents a highly unusual male figure[7] whose head is replaced with a bison tail, as are the heads in the women/bison panel at Pech Merle. A low chamber follows, with still more surprising figures[8] on the ceiling and right-hand wall (H). One maned head surmounts a disproportionately long neck; this is flanked by an elk head, recognizable as such by its antlers, muzzle, and short beard, and having the same line of a truncated bison tail that replaced the head of the male figure just mentioned. At (I) there are two figures that defy identification: an amoebalike creature with extended pseudopods, and a third "bison tail" with a tuft of oddly placed hairs. In a niche (J), about 30 feet farther on, appear two animal figures (hinds?). Some 80 feet beyond, this sequence ends with a second vulva.

A composition in two sequences on the bison/horse theme is quite common, as is the back-cave figure[9] located at (L) another 80 feet farther inside; this could be a carnivore, a bird, or a fish, without departing from known precedents. The fact that the second sequence incorporates certain more secret subjects into the theme is attested in many other cases. The location of the female signs is more unusual, for they should be found in a more central position, or in a side chamber near the central compositions; their repetition shows that their positions are not fortuitous. There are a few other examples of female signs placed at the back of a cave (Le Gabillou is one of them), and this arrangement at Pergouset recalls signs 48 and 98 at Les Combarelles. The long-necked figure in group H recalls the weird animal in group L at Le Gabillou. The elk near by is extremely rare, if not unique. The headless personage and the "truncated bison tails" confirm the identification of the women/bison at Pech Merle.

[1] *fig. 553*
[2] *fig. 554*

[3] *figs. 555, 556*
[4] *fig. 558*
[5] *fig. 557*
[6] *fig. 559*
[7] *fig. 560*

[8] *figs. 561–563*

[9] *fig. 564*

MARSOULAS

MARSOULAS, HAUTE-GARONNE, FRANCE

This cave has a long scientific history. The Abbé Cau-Durban excavated it in 1883–84, the only one of several investigators who left an account that can be used today; he was followed by many amateur archaeologists who left scarcely any scientific trace. Finally Count Henri Bégouën conducted excavations in the front part of the cave, in the strata that bear only indirectly upon the decorated portion. The paintings on the walls were discovered by Felix Regnault in 1897; they played an important part in the long controversy between partisans and opponents of Paleolithic cave art and, in 1902, they completed Cartailhac's conversion. The study of the cave was made by Cartailhac and Breuil; the latter made drawings of the figures, not all of which have yet been published. New pictorial inventories were made shortly after the Second World War by L. Michaut and M. Ollé; these are valuable for the general guidance they supply, but as renderings of the works most of them are hardly recognizable in the presence of the originals.

It is extraordinary that a cave which had remarkable archaeological deposits at the very foot of the works of art, and which has been the object of so many competent studies, should still present so many problems. The chronological picture, as it emerges from published accounts, is as follows: "... a skimpy lower Perigordian (?) layer, Magdalenian III and IV strata, and even slight traces of later Magdalenian and Azilian" (Breuil, *Quatre cents siècles...*, page 239). As for the works, Breuil assigns a few "very thin" black drawings to Magdalenian III, and the rest to Magdalenian V and VI. The archaeological point of view does not appear to have determined these attributions, since we are told that the only well-represented layer (considered to be Magdalenian III) yielded only a few "thin drawings" buried under the later works, and that the other layers, the surviving traces of which really are "traces," marked the period of intense artistic activity.

As for the findings of the Abbé Cau-Durban, the only explorer to have left us a stratigraphic evaluation (it is cursory, but creditable for the late nineteenth century), they are as follows:

(1) A Magdalenian layer varying in thickness from 10 to 20 inches, containing a great many decorated objects and grooved short spears with single beveling (the Lussac-Angles type). These spears are unanimously regarded as the leading artifact from Magdalenian III. They are occasionally found in the Pyrenees, among decorated objects attributed to Magdalenian IV (Isturitz, layer II). At Marsoulas they coexist with three spear shafts with single ornamental beveling, an artifact that is still more definitely characteristic of the Early Magdalenian and even of the mature Solutrean (Laugerie Haute I'; Jean-Blancs, east, layers A and B; Isturitz IIIa; Bolinkoba, Late Solutrean and Early Magdalenian; Cueto de la Mina, D and E; Chinchon in the Vaucluse, intermediate level between the Solutrean and the "mid"-Magdalenian; and we might add Le Placard, which yielded the spears with ornamental beveling that aided the Abbé Breuil in defining the Early Magdalenian). Thus, contrary to what is thought of the Pyrenean Magdalenian, there existed at Marsoulas evidence from an earlier stage, a fact that will enable us to show that its decoration is not as anomalous as it would be if the date were Late Magdalenian.

(2) A number of small isolated hearths, for which all the reliable evidence has been reduced to fragments of half-rounded rods and a few pendants. Attribution of this layer to Magdalenian IV is founded solely on the fact that it comes above Magdalenian III, and is nothing more than a probable guess.

(3) Traces of Late Magdalenian (one harpoon shaft discovered by L. Méroc) and Azilian (two colored pebbles with no context).

To sum up, the main period of the cave's occupation lies between the Early and the Middle Magdalenian, with scanty indications that it was in use down to the Azilian. The cave might be supposed to have served as a sanctuary at the time when people no longer lived in it, but we also know from Angles and Le Cap Blanc that the men of the Middle Magdalenian had no aversion to living under walls covered with figures.

The cave is about 200 feet long; it is a straight corridor marked by a few recesses. It has works in two sequences that intermingle from beginning to end: the painted set, in very poor condition, and the engraved set. They all belong to Style IV, but at least a majority of the paintings are earlier than the bulk of the engravings. The fact that the Abbé Breuil was unable to publish his pictorial inventory, plus limitations of time, has prevented me from making a complete study of the engravings; I have merely placed them topographically. The paintings, however, have been examined in detail.

Some fifteen fine engravings representing horses, bison, and one cervid (?) take up the first 65 feet. About thirty more engravings, situated between points about 100 and 200 feet from the entrance, occupy the intervals between painted works. Some of the engraved figures in the second sequence seem contemporary with the paintings, or at least to have been incorporated in a sequence of which the meaning was perfectly understood by the artists.

The painted sequence begins, as is normal, with a series of rows of dots about 25 feet from the entrance, on the left-hand wall. The main composition[1] appears on the same wall between 50 and 80 feet from the entrance. At the center we see a large bison and a large horse, both in Early Style IV, accompanied by incomplete animal figures of the same species which look as though they had been slipped in underneath in faded tones. On the bison's flank are two contiguous signs: one is a six-branched sign which seems to belong to the quadrangular group, and the other belongs to the claviforms with large loops (two more specimens of the latter sign are found in the lower portion of the composition). There is a large barbed sign across the bison and the horse. The theme is coherent and complete: bison/horse, quadrangular or claviform female sign, barbed male sign. Below these figures, over a distance of several yards, are numerous barbed signs, rows of dots, and single and double strokes, all drawn in ocher. This tangle corresponds to the customary panel of scrawls. Here it is painted rather than engraved, but so it is at Niaux, for example. At the far end we find a figure unique in Paleolithic art—a bison entirely composed of dots.[2] It is hard to guess the artist's motive for painting this massive figure. The Marsoulas painters were fond of dots in alignment: the entrance sign is distinctly more substantial than usual, and when we go on past the "dotted" bison we find a large sign composed of five rows of dots atop a row of strokes.[3] There are groups of horses and bison,[4] painted or engraved, and accompanied by red signs made up of strokes, up to a point about 50 yards from the entrance. The cave there widens into a small chamber where we find, along with engravings of bison, a certain number of human faces, some in frontal view and some in profile.[5] Beyond them on the right is one last barbed sign accompanied by strokes; opposite, on the right-hand wall, a quadrangular sign appears within the outlines of an engraved bison that seems of later date. At a clayey slope leading down to a small stream, the sequence of figures is terminated with a very fine engraved ibex, an unfinished horse, and opposite these, part of a bison head.

The complete scheme of the decoration at Marsoulas is difficult to establish before we are sure of having all the figures and of their stylistic distribution. What is clear, however, is that the main composition is on the bison/horse theme; that the quadrangular sign occurs twice (in the main composition and past the small chamber); and that the human faces are grouped at a point which seems to have marked the end of the engraved sanctuary—beyond this point there are only three figures, including the back-cave ibex. The barbed signs occur in two areas, apparently matching quadrangular signs in each case. This raises the problem of their date; there is no reason to think that they are not contemporaneous with the set of painted figures.

The Abbé Breuil showed that he was aware of the problem of dating Marsoulas when he applied here, for the first time, his method of analyzing the superimpositions, creating a system of mural stratigraphy. To understand why he was tempted to attribute the paintings to Magdalenian V and VI, we must go back to the scientific climate prevailing at the beginning of the present century. The only large black-and-red figures known were those at Altamira, and the only objects decorated with highly elaborate animals were from the Late Magdalenian. On the other hand, barbed signs were barely known except from the harpoons of Magdalenian VI and the painted pebbles from the Azilian. To my knowledge, barbed signs turn up in nineteen caves; the long "barbed strips" (*"bandes barbelées"*) are much rarer, and the only example I know besides the one at Marsoulas is in the Chamber of Felines at Lascaux, where a long red barbed strip appears directly opposite the only group of quadrangular signs in that narrow chamber. It would be strange that only the Azilians—of all the peoples who lived in the Dordogne and the Haute-Garonne—chose to place their "harpoons" in the vicinity of rectangular signs, and all the stranger in that they did it twice at Marsoulas.

The large bison and the large horse are closely related to the bison and the horse on the Painted Ceiling at Altamira. Moreover, the modeling of the bison is of the same type as that of the bison at Niaux and Le Portel; in these three caves they are accompanied by claviform signs, and there are three claviform signs in the panel at Marsoulas. The treatment of the head, with eye, horn, and ear integrated in the same line, occurs on decorated objects found with industrial remains from Magdalenian III–IV—for example, works from La Madeleine (lower layer) and Isturitz (layer II and the Saint-Martin chamber). At Marsoulas itself the Abbé Cau-Durban discovered a small bison engraved on bone in the same Early Style IV. Consequently, dating the painted portion of Marsoulas seems to present no difficulty: it is Magdalenian III–IV that sets the style. One problem remains, however, in my mind: the rectangular signs and the barbed strips. In all other caves where we find rectangular signs, the animals are in Style III. At Lascaux, where the brace-shaped signs appear after the rectangular signs, we find animals modeled in black and ocher (the "Chinese" horses, the bison in the Shaft) which mark a transition to Early Style IV. Despite the inadequacy of our present knowledge concerning the true divisions of the Magdalenian, I have the feeling that the animals on the Painted Ceiling at Altamira, the horse at Labastide, and the animals at Marsoulas come close to linking up with that period of the Early Magdalenian—Style III— which is continuous with the mature Solutrean. For several years, this strange association at Marsoulas between bison in Early Style IV and signs in Style III has made me go back over the chronological arguments again and again. Frankly, I would rather offer no solution than to spin out an intricate theory of overlappings. It seems wiser to leave the solution of the problem to more thorough and careful study, and to keep in mind that while Marsoulas has quadrangular signs which go perfectly well with the spear shafts with decorated edges from the Early Magdalenian, it also has claviforms with large loops which go well with the grooved spears with unstriated single beveling from the Middle Magdalenian.

LABASTIDE

LABASTIDE, HAUTES-PYRÉNÉES, FRANCE

The wall decorations in this enormous cave were discovered by Norbert Casteret in 1932; subsequently, working with Count Henri Bégouën, he discovered a set of engraved plaquettes. Excavation since 1945 under G. Simonnet has turned up numerous objects that include one engraved plaquette with birds and nineteen carved silhouettes, all of ibex heads except for one bison head.

This cave, on which the published accounts to date are far from complete, is rather unusual for several reasons: Magdalenian objects were discovered at several spots lying uncovered on the ground; hearths existed throughout the interior to the back of the cave, over more than 550 yards; and plaquettes and carved silhouettes were discovered about 200 yards from the entrance, in an inhabited area. A few years ago, vandals altered the engravings beyond hope of restoration, underlining with color the lines cut into the soft walls. In the course of brief visits in 1957 and 1960, I was able to note the topographical details which follow.

As one follows the high ledge around the chasm on the left, one comes to a few black strokes on the wall which seem to mark the beginning of the sanctuary; one then reaches the intersection where the painted horse is found. A few yards farther on, at the edge of the precipice, stands a block covered with fine engravings[1] that consist of unfinished outlines, among which one horse, one bison, and two stag antlers can be distinguished most clearly. It is at this point that the last streaks of daylight are still visible at the entrance. Just beyond are found several more blocks. On one of them is painted in black and ocher one of the finest horses in Early Style IV.[2] Typical in every detail, it has the two shoulder lines and the wavy-line ventral modeling: the execution is very close to that of the horses at Marsoulas and on the Painted Ceiling at Altamira. There are also affinities with the "Chinese" horse in the Axial Gallery at Lascaux, which represents the immediately preceding stage of stylistic development. On another block, opposite the horse, is a group of black-painted signs: from left to right we see a few groups of dots, two surfaces covered with lines forming lozenge shapes like those at Las Monedas (where there is also a horse in Early Style IV modeling), one barbed

[1] *figs. 571, 572*

[2] *figs. 79, 573*

sign of the same type as at Las Monedas, and two double strokes. The surface of the block has numerous traces of very delicate engraving, among which we make out in particular a large bison with legs drawn up. About 100 feet farther on, G. Simonnet and the Abbé Glory saw a patch of painting. Presumably, all these vestiges are only a part of a Middle Magdalenian sanctuary, further traces of which might be discovered with detailed study.

Continuing along the gallery some distance, we come to an important engraved frieze on the right-hand wall that consists, on the left, of five horses and one bison[3]; at the center, under the horse farthest to the left in the right-hand group, a row of strokes; and in a recess, a human face in frontal view with, somewhat below, an oval sign accompanied by a stroke. The right-hand group consists of one bison head, three horses, and, at the edge of the frieze, a very remarkable feline head with the mouth open.[4] At a slight distance is an engraving that seems to represent a goose.[5] The animals in the frieze are in Style IV, the bison having characteristics that are related to Late Style IV (like those on the plaquettes). Incidentally, this opinion is confirmed by the parenthesis-like character of the oval female sign. However, one of the horses has faint indications of wavy-line ventral modeling.

[3] fig. 574

[4] fig. 576
[5] fig. 575

LE PORTEL (Continued from pages 325–326)

THE LATER SANCTUARY

The layout of the later sanctuary is easy to follow because, apart from a few engravings and spots of ocher, all the figures are drawn in black with a firm, even line and the execution is perfectly homogeneous. In gallery 1, just inside the present-day entrance, close to where Vézian discovered the first hearth, we find the entrance (or back-cave) signs. They are small double strokes, spaced a few yards apart. Next comes a "ghost" with a bird body,[1] comparable to the ghosts at Les Trois Frères. The presence of such a figure at the entrance would be very unusual if the owl is merely a human face in frontal view, but we have so few bird figures that opinion on this score must be tentative. Farther on (c) we come to a horse[2] and a bison, and then we reach the large chamber (b) where the old sanctuary occupies the left-hand wall and extends into gallery 2 (m). Galleries 3 (j) and 4 (d) both open off the other side of the chamber and are complementary to each other. Just inside gallery 3 we find a panel of unfinished outlines in black and red, then another panel, in red, which shows a bison drawn vertically (head at the bottom; j on plan), the head of an ox (?), an ibex, and an unidentifiable rump. On the opposite wall there is another group of unfinished outlines and past this, horses painted in black[3] which build up to a veritable herd toward the back of the gallery. Every variant of Early Style IV can be observed, including one horse in full modeling, with the two shoulder lines and the wavy ventral line. Opposite the last of the horses is a "ghost" shown in bust-length, which can be read equally well as a man or as the sketch of a feline head in frontal view. In either case, to find such a figure at the very back is normal. Gallery 3 (i–k), apart from some unfinished outlines, is thus devoted entirely to male themes (horse, lion or man, strokes on the left-hand wall opposite the first horses). It is in the next gallery d–h that the female subjects have been assembled.

Gallery 4 (Breuil Gallery) begins with a bison in Style IV, dubbed the "discovery bison[4]; opposite it there is a black-and-ocher patch. In a recess farther on there are several patches of ocher; at this point the gallery narrows and passage is difficult because of stalagmites, but there is one painting of a horse which is perhaps the counterpart of the bison at the entrance. After about 30 feet without decoration, we come to a panel with the only notable engraved figures in the cave (e). These are scrawls arranged in sheaves ("comets"), a horse with double shoulder line, and a bison. I believe that this panel corresponds to the zone of unfinished outlines which is usually found near important compositions. This is the more likely because just past this point we find, on the left, a small recess decorated at the back with three double strokes in red, and, a bit farther on, an engraved salmon; on the right there is a much larger recess, the "camarin," which contains Le Portel's most interesting collection of figures.[5]

These figures include, first, a horse with a shoulder line and a bison with head extended—a posture we also find in the "Sanctuary" at Les Trois Frères, on the Painted Ceiling at Altamira, on an incised slab at Isturitz, and on one of the spear-throwers from La Madeleine (lower layer). Between the horse and the bison appears a claviform sign of the Les Trois Frères type with a wide loop, and a double row of dots which some observers have seen as outlining the cervico-dorsal curve of a horse—and they may be right. Peripherally, we find one ibex at the bottom, and stag antlers to the right. A few scrawls complete the composition with a motif consisting of an oval and a row of strokes, painted in red. Unquestionably this recess is the core of the later sanctuary and shelters the most complete representation of what the collections of Paleolithic figures were intended to signify. As on the ceiling at Altamira, in the Axial Gallery at Lascaux, in the main composition at Las Monedas, in the recess in Gallery C at La Pasiega, and in the "Sanctuary" at Les Trois Frères, we have here the statistically ideal grouping: bison/horse, female-sign/male-sign, and ibex/stag as complementary animals. Next, grouped at the back like the horses in gallery 3, are seven very fine bison[6] in different variants of Early Style IV, similar to those at Santimamine. The figure farthest inside, deformed by having been executed under the low arch that marks the last accessible point, is that of a stag;[7] though schematized, it is perfectly recognizable.

Up to the present time, the cervids at Le Portel (in the alcove in gallery 2, in the "camarin", and the terminal figure just mentioned) have been supposed to be reindeer. The Abbé Breuil, whose zoological discernment is rarely at fault, seems not to have noticed that the three sets of antlers in this cave all have a double brow-antler. This is never found in reindeer but is a convention which characterizes all figures of stags in

[1] fig. 577

[2] fig. 578

[3] figs. 580–582

[4] fig. 583

[5] fig. 585

[6] figs. 584, 586

[7] fig. 587

Style III and Early Style IV (Altamira, El Castillo, Las Chimeneas, Le Gabillou, Lascaux, La Mouthe, La Pasiega, Pech Merle, Santimamine, Les Trois Frères).

This set of homogeneously executed black figures at Le Portel is dated by abundant evidence. First, the discovery of hearths in the cave attests to its substantial use in the Middle Magdalenian; second, a claviform sign is present; third, the horses show the modeling conventional on decorated objects from Magdalenian III–IV; fourth, the bison have the same characteristics. I would place most of the figures in this set, in agreement with the Abbé Breuil, within the Magdalenian cycle, although I reach this conclusion by a different method. I cannot agree, however, when he assigns some of the horses in gallery 3, for example, to the Aurignacian or the Perigordian on the ground that they are schematized. Actually, every stylistic variant is represented here in a set of figures which are compositionally all of a piece and utterly uniform in technique. He also gives a Perigordian date to the "ghost" on the wall opposite the horses, without any proof. He supposes the ibex in the "*camarin*" to be of the same epoch, on the grounds that its horns are in twisted perspective. This would then be the sole figure in gallery 4 that goes back so far; we must believe that it was executed there, without context, down at the end of a corridor in a favorable position, and that eight thousand years later someone drew figures near by in order to give it the peripheral position occupied by 65 percent of all ibexes. This is just as implausible as it would be to assign Egyptian rams to the Perigordian because of their horns in twisted perspective, or even children's drawings. Dating on the basis of a single detail, such as the treatment of horns, fails to take account of the fact that early forms can be and often are revived.

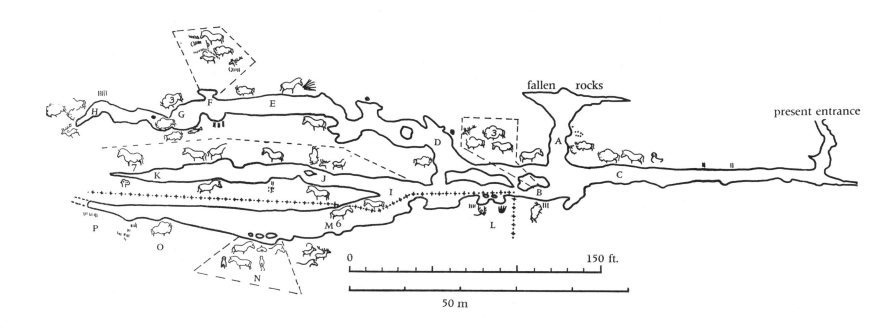

153. LE PORTEL. SCHEMATIC PLAN WITH FIGURES

The rendering of the animals is conventionalized. Numerals on or adjacent to animals indicate number of individuals. (Plan after L. Jammes.)

A *Possibly the entrance in the Upper Paleolithic.*

B *The line of dots and crosses between L and P marks the boundary between the early figures in gallery 2 and those, mostly painted in black, in the decoration in Early Style IV. On the rocky mass at the center of the intersection is a bison/horse + stag group, the first composition in the later sanctuary in B–K–H–C.*

C *Gallery 1, which is the modern entrance but seems to have been a side gallery in the Paleolithic. It contains a bison/horse composition and a bird. A few double strokes terminate the sequence.*

D *Entrance to gallery 4 (Breuil Gallery), where most of the bison are found. A few spots of ocher mark recesses in the front section.*

E *Area of engravings; unfinished outlines and scrawls.*

F *The "camarin," a recess containing a complete composition on the theme bison/horse/paired-signs + ibex and stag. Opposite: double strokes.*

G *Group of bison and a salmon or trout in the small chamber outside the terminal narrow passageway.*

H *Back-cave figures of gallery 4, the right-hand branch of the later sanctuary in Style IV: bison, cervid, and strokes.*

I *Entrance to gallery 3, the left-hand branch of the later sanctuary.*

J *First entrance composition, with the only bison in this gallery. Head of an ox and a damaged ibex. These figures are in ocher.*

K *Group of horses at the back, opposite a humanoid bust.*

L *Figures in Style III begin here, in gallery 2. In wall on left side, twin recesses with paired symbols: four-branched sign in the left-hand recess; antlers and strokes in the right-hand one.*

M *On the right, horses in Style III and figures which are worn away. On the left, in black, a greatly worn group including horse, ibex, stag.*

N *Recessed portion of wall with horses, one sign of the brace-shaped type, and two little male human figures.*

O *Partially obliterated figures among which a bison and strokes can be made out.*

P *Strokes near the terminal dead-end.*

NIAUX

ARIÈGE, FRANCE

One of the Abbé Breuil's "six giants" (together with Altamira, Font-de-Gaume, Les Combarelles, Lascaux, and Les Trois Frères), this cave has been visited during several centuries, the paintings being one of its attractions. Commandant Molard in 1906 recognized the decoration as Paleolithic. Cartailhac and Breuil made known its unusual interest, and the latter made a pictorial inventory of the works.

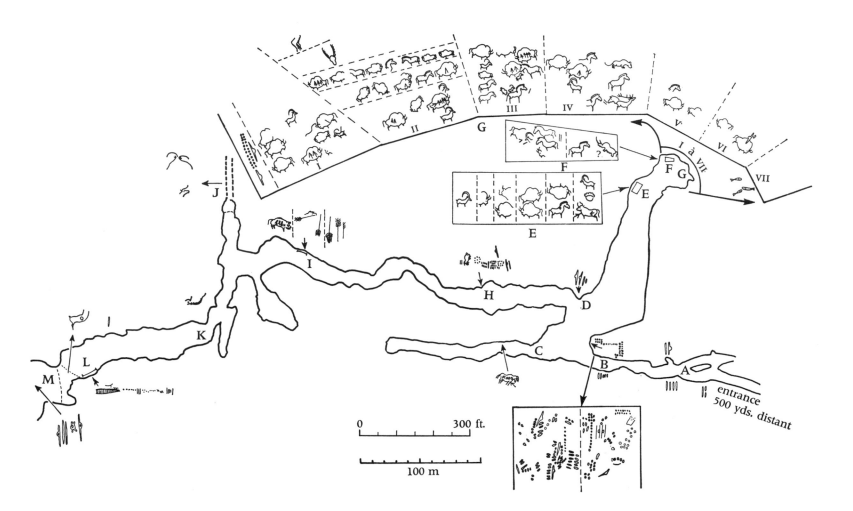

154. NIAUX. SCHEMATIC PLAN AND ARRANGEMENT OF FIGURES

The animal figures in the Black Salon (E, F, G) have been conventionalized. (Plan after Commandant Molard.)

A   *Entrance strokes, paired signs in a recess on the right.*

B   *More strokes, large panel of signs on the right at the turning into the gallery, rows of dots.*

C   *Secondary gallery (Gallery of Cave-Ins) with one ox figure engraved on the ground.*

D   *Strokes and paired signs opposite group B.*

E   *Engravings on the ground at the entrance to the Black Salon: one ox/ibex/isolated-sign composition, and a bison/horse/ibex composition.*

F   *Engravings on the ground in the Black Salon. The first group includes a horse and a rhinoceros (very doubtful), the second a complete composition: bison/horse/paired-signs + ibex.*

G   *The full set of panels in the Black Salon. Note the paired claviform signs at the two sides (I and VI), and the recurrence of the basic bison/horse/ibex theme in*

each panel. On panel II, painted on a recessed part of the wall having several plane surfaces, note that the signs are repeated in clear-cut fashion on each of these; note also the stag and the human figure (?) at the very back. Concerning the composition as a whole, note the stag and feline at the end of the continuous sequence I–II–III–IV, and the fish at the very end of the entire sequence (VII).

H   *Red panel: "the dying bison." The animal is drawn vertically, and there are dots, claviform signs, and strokes.*

I   *Bison engraved on clay floor, marked with paired signs; horse and barbed signs in red on the wall.*

J   *Figures located on the other side of "Green Lake." Facing ibexes and ox, painted black.*

K   *Upside-down horse's head, making use of an irregularity of the wall.*

L   *Composition at the terminal lake: lattice sign of untypical character, dots, and strokes. Headless ibex without forelegs, marked with a red dot.*

M   *On the far side of the terminal lake: paired signs.*

362

Niaux is a monumental corridor-cave with several broad lateral galleries. The decorations begin 500 yards from the entrance, continue for nearly 900 yards, and end at a point about 1,400 yards inside. The cave continues beyond this point, finally merging with the vast Lombrives cave which has its entrance at Ussat. The course of Niaux presents no real difficulties, apart from a little lake ("Green Lake") situated about 1,200 yards inside. However, this is one of the deep-cave sanctuaries, and *a priori* its decoration should belong to the Middle Magdalenian. Every characteristic of the works confirms this. Topographically, the decorations are divided among the Entrance Gallery (in an area 550 to 670 yards from the entrance, A to B), the Gallery of Cave-Ins (c), the Black Salon (E, F, G,), and the Inner Gallery (D to M) which contains the Green Lake and the terminal lake; a few figures are found beyond each of the lakes. The last three galleries are reached from a large chamber at the intersection, 670 yards from the entrance.

ENTRANCE GALLERY

Four groups of red signs (A) are found over a stretch of about 100 yards. The first, consisting of three strokes, is at a point where the gallery narrows: the normal beginning of a sanctuary. A bit farther on, where the gallery widens to form recesses on either side, we find the first of the paired compositions which succeed one another all the way into the Inner Gallery. This gallery contains only one claviform sign and one stroke on the right, and a set of strokes on the left, without animals. Just before the intersection (670 yards from the entrance), five strokes on the right-hand wall mark the transition to the next sequence of figures. The location of the numerous red signs, obviously marking key topographical points, caused the Abbé Breuil to interpret them as road signs or warnings. Certainly the signs could have been used for guidance, but not in the sense of traffic signs; rather, they drew attention to the symbolic significance of the various parts of the cave and in a way "humanized" the trip through the galleries. The intersection at the 670-yard point forms a chamber more than fifty yards in diameter (B–C–D). Three corridors open on to it: the Gallery of Cave-Ins; the huge gallery (some twenty-eight yards wide) which leads into the Black Salon, and the Inner Gallery which ultimately connects with the Lombrives cave.

THE BLACK SALON

The entrance to this ascending gallery is marked on the left (D), at the angle formed with the Inner Gallery, by five strokes nearly identical with those at the end of the Entrance Gallery (B). To the right, on the two dihedral surfaces, there is a group of signs so unusual that Cartailhac likened them to inscriptions.[1] Topographically, this large panel occupies the position of the zones of scrawls and unfinished outlines which are always found near main compositions. At Niaux, engravings were made only on sandy or clayey surfaces, with one exception which will be noted later. The hard rock of the wall has not been scratched, and instead of a tangle of unfinished outlines, we find here a host of devices painted in black and in red. These include no animal outlines; there are exclusively signs, and these can be divided into three categories: (1) dots and strokes, either isolated or disposed in single or double rows running in every direction; (2) three, possibly four, claviform signs; (3) miscellaneous signs—a circle, a "wound" made of two converging lines, and a two-pointed "coat-of-arms." There are nearly two hundred dots and strokes. Thus, apart from miscellaneous signs, the group consists of paired signs like those we find at other locations in the cave—claviform/stroke, claviform/dots. What seems to me remarkable is the absence of unfinished animal outlines. The function of the panels of scrawls and unfinished outlines remains unclear; they are often in the only cave areas that suggest repeated visits. Studying them one cannot help thinking that, whereas the other decorations in sanctuaries were rarely retouched, these panels repeatedly received new figures, often clumsily executed, which sometimes form inextricable tangles.

[1] *figs. 9, 588*

The nearly circular chamber known as the Black Salon[2] lies about 135 yards beyond the large panel of signs. Making the circuit over the uneven ground along the wall at our left, we first come to two groups of engraved figures (E). One[3] consists of four bison, one horse, and an ibex; this formula is applied throughout the cave. The other group[4] is much more interesting. At the very top we see an ibex and below it a five-lobed sign of which I know no other example, unless two of the figures made up of dots on the panel previously described may be considered such. The Abbé Breuil thought of a clenched human fist, and indeed one obtains an effect rather similar to this engraving by pressing a clenched fist into soft clay. One might think also of the footprint of a mammoth, an animal not represented at Niaux, but for the fact that the mammoth is reputed to have had no more than four toes on each foot. Two little lines seem to be coming out of the right-hand side of the figure, which could indicate that we have here another of the numerous variants of tectiform or of coat-of-arms signs. Underneath this sign is an ox accompanied by paired signs: a goose-track "wound" on the flank and a barbed sign in front of the chest. It is almost standard to find a group incorporating the ox in cave decorations based on the bison/horse formula (Altamira, El Castillo, Les Combarelles, Font-de-Gaume, Santimamine), and a bison group in caves on the ox/horse formula. There are only two oxen at Niaux; this one, and a second, almost identical example in the Gallery of Cave-Ins (c). Both are marked with signs of the same character, and each has a barbed sign that seems to stick into the chest; the first has a goose-track wound in the flank, the other has a wound mark (two converging lines) on the shoulder and three circles on the flank. I shall come back to this matter of wounded animals and the associations of vulva/wound, and barbed-sign/spear.

[2] *fig. 70*

[3] *figs. 607, 608*
[4] *fig. 609*

The painted decoration (G) begins beyond the area of engravings on clay.

Side Gallery of Signs

In a cleft in the wall (at left of G, 1 in plan) we find two claviforms and a double row of dots painted in red.[5] Such paired male and female signs placed in small side galleries or recesses near the main compositions account for one-third of all the paired signs in our tabulation (Altamira, Arcy-sur-Cure, Bernifal, El Castillo, Cougnac, Covalanas, La Mouthe, La Pasiega, Le Portel, Villars).

[5] *fig. 590*

First Panel (G, I)

[6] figs. 91, 592

This panel comprises seven bison,[6] two ibexes, and one cervico-dorsal line that may mark the presence of a horse. The first bison, top left, is headless. The number of headless animals (nine at different sites) is sufficient to suggest that this is not a mere matter of oversight. The ibex, at the lower right, seems to be pierced with a line in the back and with a double line on the chest. The two bison that frame this ibex have goose-track or rather "arrow" wound marks; the median line here is very long, as in the wound marks on animals in the Nave at Lascaux. It is to be noted that the signs here seem to harmonize with the symbolic group to which the animals belong (wound marks for the bison, long strokes for the ibex). Depending, then, on which of two points of view (not irreconcilable) we look at them from, we may speak of an ibex run through by spears and two bison with gaping wounds, or of one animal of the symbolic male group bearing male strokes and two animals of the symbolic female group bearing vulvas/wounds.

[7] fig. 610

On the ground between the first and second panels are figures engraved in the clay (F). In the first group are included two horses, one bison head, and one ibex.[7] Signs are limited to a line driven into the chest of the ibex and a two-line wound mark in the space over its muzzle—one is reminded of the "breathing" lines sometimes found in front of the noses of bison or oxen (Altamira—last bison in the Inner Gallery, Bernifal, Pech Merle, for instance). One of the horses has a double shoulder line, a frequent feature of Early Style IV. A bit

[8] fig. 611

farther on we find the second group, consisting of a horse marked with rows of strokes and a queer figure[8] which the Abbé Breuil very tentatively identified as a rhinoceros. Except at Rouffignac, the rhinoceros is very rare and is always placed in male areas (background or periphery), accompanied by male symbols (dots, lion, horse, ibex). Since this is a marginal group involving only strokes and one horse, the position would be normal for a rhinoceros. As for the actual figure outlined, one could hardly see in it more than did the Abbé Breuil, or be more cautious than he.

Second Panel (G, II)

This panel occupies a recess and breaks down into four elements: pediment, arch, entablature, and semidome. Except for one engraved bison on the entablature, these figures are all painted in black. The pediment,

[9] fig. 593   [10] fig. 594

close to the ceiling, has three bison[9] and the head of a fourth. The one on the right is framed by two ibexes,[10] and has five goose-track wounds on the shoulder and flank. Above it are two double wavy lines. There is a rather striking similarity to the first panel (G, I): the bison on the right is again marked with female signs and framed by two ibexes. The arch has three bison and one horse, all painted. There is one painted horse on the entablature, one engraved bison (the only figure engraved on stone in the entire cave), and one painted bison. The semidome is especially interesting: on the left are three bison, two of them headless as in the first panel and in the same relative positions; on the right are two more bison and two heads of horses. Lastly, a

[11] fig. 595

cavity at the back forms the shape of an upside-down gourd which suggests the outline of an animal head in frontal view,[11] with two barbed signs painted at the top—the whole resembling a stag head seen from the front. The stag, an entrance or back-cave animal, is here at its proper place, though geological accident had much to do with the creation of this figure. In a niche beyond there is a black outline that seems to be that of

[12] fig. 602

a human figure, reduced to the trunk and legs.[12]

Third Panel (G, III)

[13] figs. 2, 591, 598
[14] figs. 27, 80, 83
[15] figs. 114, 591, 597

This panel once more takes up the bison/horse + ibex theme, but the horses are more numerous than in the preceding compositions. We see seven bison,[13] five horses,[14] and, as before, two ibexes.[15] The signs fall into two groups: the two bison on the left (as in panels I and II) are marked with goose-track wounds, two black wounds on one animal, two black-and-red ones on the other. A bit farther down, below two horses, there are three double strokes. Thus the compositions are repeated with a regularity which, strangely enough, went unnoticed for half a century.

This panel contains details which confirm the constancy of the symbolical associations. The area of signs or of marked animals, bottom right, presents seven figures: a wounded bison and a horse of the same size, a second wounded bison and a tiny horse placed between its legs, a large horse with a double stroke in front of its nose and its rump superimposed on a tiny schematized bison. Thus we have a kind of reversal of symbolic values: bison complementary to the horse, horse complementary to the bison—exactly as on the Altamira ceiling where a little hind appears over the horse, and the large hind has a little bison under the withers. To make a comparison (dangerous, like all comparisons, but nonetheless useful), the figures here turn up like the male and female principles in Chinese symbolism which show, enclosed within one circle, a white section for the male, black for the female, but also have a white dot in the black section and a black dot in the white section.

Fourth Panel (G, IV)

This panel is in two parts: a pediment dominating the preceding panel (G, III), and a recess. Three bison in single file are painted on the pediment. It seems hardly necessary to remark that the one on the right has a goose-track wound on its shoulder. Above it is sketched a horse, with an ibex between its legs. The repetitions of this theme cease after these four instances, and inside the alcove we find what the second panel would lead us to expect—that is, a set of male symbols, including a stag. And indeed, from top to bottom, we see a big

[16] fig. 600
[17] fig. 601

feline,[16] an incomplete horse overlapping it, and a horse facing a horse's head; between the last two is a double stroke, and at the bottom, on the right, a stag.[17]

Fifth and Sixth Panels (G, V–VII)

Passing the alcove we emerge from the chamber and follow a wall to the left where we find one more horse and four bison; the fourth of these (on the right) is marked with paired red signs, claviforms and strokes. At

[18] figs. 121, 612

the end, two fish of the salmon family are engraved[18] on the ground in a small recess. Though not unusual on decorated objects, where they seem to rank among the male symbols, fish are very rare in the caves.

Having returned to the intersection at the 670-yard point, we leave on our left the Gallery of Cave-Ins containing an ox engraved on the ground (see fig. 154, c), and at D we enter the 880-yard-long gallery leading to the far end of the cave. On the right, some 85 yards down, we come to the panel (H) known as that of "the dying bison."[19] This is not the least peculiar collection of figures in this huge cave, in which the Magdalenians seem to have accumulated problems for future prehistorians to solve. Painted in red on a strip of smooth rock there are, from left to right: two claviform signs surmounting a double row of dots; a bison with folded legs, in a vertical position; and a circle composed of dots, with a dot in the center. Then comes a large claviform sign surmounting a double line of dots, followed by one stroke, one oval composed of dots, and another circle of dots with a dot in the center; these two latter figures surmount another double row of dots. Finally, at the far right, we find one last claviform and one last stroke. On the basis of very logical reasoning, the Abbé Breuil, who saw the claviforms as weapons of the boomerang type, decided that the circles represent the encirclement of the dying bison, and that the whole composition was a kind of hunter's votive offering. Quite apart from the fact that no club or weapon of the boomerang type could fell a bison, it seems to me that we have here a series of female claviform signs paired with male strokes and sets of dots, plus one bison. The close resemblance of this panel to the big panel of paired signs at the entrance to the gallery leading up to the Black Salon makes me think that this is the panel of scrawls and outlines for the rear portion of the sanctuary.

A bit farther on, under the low ceiling of a side chamber on the left, is the spot where imprints of human feet were found in the soft clay. These are boys' footprints: oddly enough, nearly all footprints found in the decorated caves are those of boys. As is well known, this fact led to the hypothesis of initiation rites. Without rejecting this hypothesis, which is as unassailable as it is unprovable in the present state of our knowledge, I wish merely to note that on a road used by people of all age groups, mud puddles and corners off the beaten track would show more footprints of children than of adults. All we can safely infer from the presence of the footprints is that children did frequent the caves.

About 1000 yards inside the cave, still on the right-hand wall, we find the last composition with paired subjects in a slight recess (I): it is quite unusual. To the right are two barbed signs, analogous to one of the signs at El Castillo; one is barbed at the bottom, the other at the top. To the left is a figure in which the painter seems to have done his best to show future generations that he regarded a barbed sign and a horse as equivalent,[20] for it is a sign with a horizontal shaft, feathered like an arrow, the tip of the staff converging with the mouth of a horse that is reduced to a line running from the head to the middle of the back. A bit farther on, engraved in the clay in the ground, we find a complementary composition: a bison marked with three goose-track wounds.[21] Three cup-marks formed in the clay by dripping water have been utilized to suggest the impact of the wounds, and to avoid any doubt on this score, two small strokes are engraved on the shoulder. Horse/barbed-sign for the male group and bison/wounds with two small complementary male signs for the female group sum up, as clearly as possible short of writing it out, the entire system of figures used in Late Paleolithic art. A few dozen yards farther, a gallery runs off to the right; this is the Cartailhac Gallery, at the end of which is the Green Lake. Beyond this lake, which can be crossed only under exceptionally favorable conditions, there are a few painted figures (J), of which Mandement made photographs. Among these are an ox head and a strange figure which the Abbé Breuil identified as an ibex seen from the back in sharply receding perspective. I should be inclined to see it as two facing ibexes, joined at the foreheads, each with one horn, two ears, and the dorsal line. This theme is not unknown: we find it at Le Roc de Sers, at Lascaux, and, closer to Niaux in time and space, on the spear-thrower with ibexes from Les Trois Frères.

Turning back into the Inner Gallery and keeping to the right-hand wall, we notice how an accidental contour of the wall has been used to portray in red the head of a horse fallen on its back (K). Then we reach the terminal lake (L). The left-hand wall and a portion of the ceiling are covered with signs and figures. From left to right we find, in red, a long lattice sign,[22] a row of dots and strokes, then a row of dots in black; this is followed by a row of red strokes and an area of red dots, and finally, in black, a scarcely visible horse's head and an ibex[23] without head or forelegs, having a red spot on its chest. This headless figure is very closely related to the one in the Bédeilhac cave. On the far side of the lake, the cave terminates exactly as it began, with a last group of paired signs (claviforms and strokes) and a final set of strokes (M).

This detailed description was necessary: Niaux is the only cave that vies with Lascaux in the quality of execution of its works, and in the vastness and vigor of its compositions. Elsewhere we find excellent pieces and amply developed sets of figures, but nowhere, except on the Altamira ceiling, the same expressive power. Stylistic analysis reveals the perfect unity of the decorations. We may safely assume that they all belong to the same period. The animal figures are examples of Early Style IV: the bodies filled in with short lines are of the same type as those engraved on decorated objects. We find bison with the dorsal triangle and ventral strip, horses with the double shoulder line and the wavy ventral modeling, and ibexes with ringed horns and with the ventral line found throughout Early Style IV, especially in conjunction with claviform signs. Problems of synchronism arise between caves such as Niaux and Les Trois Frères, where modeling is accomplished by short lines, and caves such as Altamira and Le Portel, where the monochrome and bichrome animals are modeled with spots of color. La Pasiega and Lascaux illustrate the transition from brace-shaped signs to claviforms, with no ovals present; Les Combarelles has tectiforms and ovals; Les Trois Frères, claviforms and ovals. Thus it is probable that Niaux, which has no ovals, can be placed—like the Altamira ceiling and the subjects in the inner portion of Gallery C at La Pasiega—a bit earlier than Les Combarelles and Les Trois Frères. The absence of reindeer at Niaux points in the same direction. All this is in keeping with the Middle Magdalenian, or, to try to pin it down more closely, rather to the beginning or middle than to the end of that epoch—that is, around 12,000 B.C.

[19] figs. 589, 603

[20] fig. 605

[21] fig. 89

[22] fig. 606

[23] fig. 604

LES TROIS FRÈRES AND LE TUC D'AUDOUBERT

MONTESQUIEU-AVENTÈS, ARIÈGE, FRANCE

These two caves together constitute another of the Abbé Breuil's "six giants." Their gradual opening up from 1912 on by Count Henri Bégouën and his three sons (Les Trois Frères is named for the three brothers) forms a major chapter in the literature of prehistory's epic period. Le Tuc contains "the clay bison," the other cave the "Sorcerer"; these, along with the Altamira bison, are probably the most widely known Paleolithic works. I have not had the opportunity of working in these caves; therefore, utilizing the Abbé Breuil's outstanding publication on them, I shall confine myself to making certain points which might serve to guide a study along the lines suggested in this book.

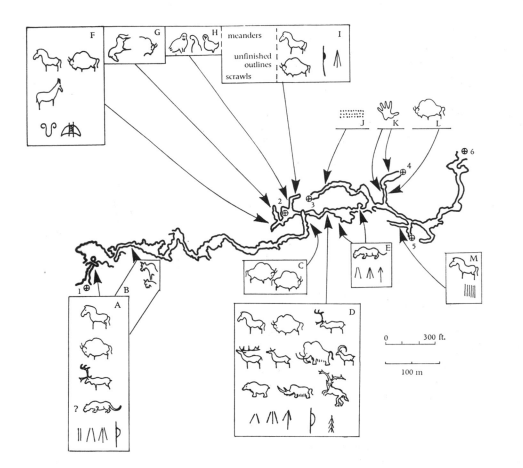

155. LES TROIS FRÈRES AND LE TUC D'AUDOUBERT. *Schematic plan of the caves and arrangement of subjects After H. Bégouën and H. Breuil; the layout of the figures is conventionalized.*

A *Side gallery at the entrance to Le Tuc d'Audoubert. Composition on the basic bison/horse + reindeer theme. Paired signs and a problematic feline.*

B *"Monsters" marking the end of the front part of Le Tuc.*

C *Bison modeled in clay, at the point where Le Tuc overlaps Les Trois Frères.*

D *Conventionalized inventory of the themes in the so-called Sanctuary. Except for the ox, all mammals "normal" in Paleolithic art are represented (felines are near by).*

E *Felines.*

F *Figures in the "Gallery of the Wild Ass." Bison/horse theme.*

G *Bison and horse in the intermediate gallery.*

H *"Owls."*

I *The "Aurignacian" Gallery. Group comprising horses, bison, and signs in Early Style IV.*

J, K, L, M *Isolated figures, the relation of which to the rest has not yet been clearly established.*

1 *Entrance to Le Tuc d'Audoubert.* 2 *Highly probable former entrance to Les Trois Frères in the "Entrance Chamber."* 3 *Mass of fallen earth masking a possible entrance.* 4 *Present-day entrance.* 5 *Entrance through which the discovery of Les Trois Frères was made.* 6 *Entrance to the Enlène cave.*

Looking at the map of the two caves, one is first struck by the way Le Tuc d'Audoubert and Les Trois Frères overlap, and next, by the many entrances that may have been used at various times. One may wonder whether this was a single complex which was frequented by Paleolithic people at different periods, or whether several successive sanctuaries were set up at different points within this enormous underground maze. The most isolated of the decorations, topographically speaking, is that in the front part of Le Tuc d'Audoubert (A, B). It is built around the bison/horse[1] + reindeer theme, with a problematic lion. The accompanying signs are, in the female group, wound marks either of the goose-track type or the type with two converging lines, and the claviform sign; we shall see, however, that Les Trois Frères has, with one exception, the same basic theme and the same signs as Le Tuc.[2] Less than 100 yards from this first set of figures we find two "monsters"[3] which are not, perhaps, without a certain affinity to the pairs of anthropomorphic faces found in other caves of the same epoch (Rouffignac, Font-de-Gaume, Marsoulas). Continuing on into Le Tuc over about 450 yards of rough going, one reaches the famous chamber with the two clay bison and some remnants of modeled figures which have crumbled away.[4] These remnants are scanty enough to discourage any thought that there were once a number of such figures; the bison are certainly the chief element. Next we find ourselves at the back of Le Tuc, at the point where this cave overlaps Les Trois Frères, although the two caves do not actually communicate. The problem arises of why does the decoration of Le Tuc d'Audoubert end with a composition of the central type, without back-cave figures.

Turning to the decoration of Les Trois Frères, we can distinguish ten groups of figures (D to M). Groups D and E are represented by the "Sanctuary" and the felines. The "Sanctuary" has the same basic composition as the entrance to Le Tuc d'Audoubert but it is much richer in complementary figures. It has exactly the same wound signs and the same claviforms: thus there is every reason to assume that it is contemporary with Le Tuc. The two feline groups (E) are accompanied by exactly the same signs. As for the remaining groups of figures, M must be set apart because it is very incomplete and of uncertain style, while the figures at J, K, and L cannot on the basis of our data be related to any group.[5] We are left, then, with four groups, those of the "Wild-Ass Gallery" (F), the "Entrance Chamber" (G), the "Gallery of Owls" (H), and the "Aurignacian Gallery" (I). At all these points we encounter figures or signs that tie up directly with the sets A, B, C, D, and E.

[1] *figs. 613–615*

[2] *figs. 617–618*
[3] *fig. 616*

[4] *figs. 619–621*

[5] *fig. 638*

THE PALEOLITHIC LAYOUT

The first question I asked myself in studying the topography of Les Trois Frères concerned the route followed by the Paleolithic artists who drew the wound signs and claviforms. The route prehistorians have followed since the cave was discovered leads from one of the western entrances to the underground crossroads just before the "Chapel of the Lioness," continuing from there to the engraved lions, the "Sanctuary," and the "Gallery of Owls." Now, lions[6] are back-cave animals; unless we suppose that the western part of the cave once contained a decorated area, since destroyed, in which felines marked the last episode, we have no alternative but to conclude that Paleolithic artists did not follow this route. If we assume that the lions served as back-cave figures for the sanctuary with wound signs and claviforms (D), we realize that the sequence of figures must begin either at the entrance to Le Tuc (1) or in the "Entrance Chamber" (2), continuing from either point to where the lions are located: everything west of the lions is very different in character. Thus there are two possibilities which, however, are not mutually exclusive. The first is that there was only one continuous layout: the entrance was via Le Tuc, at A, where the first group of compositions ends with the "monsters"; after a long interruption come the clay bison, center of a second composition; assuming that the two caves communicated at the time and that the same sequence continued its labyrinthine course toward the "Wild-Ass Gallery" and the "Aurignacian Gallery," it then passed the "Sanctuary" and terminated with the felines. The second possibility, which seems to me more probable, is that the figures at the entrance to Le Tuc constituted a sanctuary contemporary with Les Trois Frères but cut off from the latter, and that the entrance to Les Trois Frères was through the "Entrance Chamber." In this layout, there would have been several entrance compositions: *(a)* the bison/horse group in the "Wild-Ass Gallery," *(b)* the bison/horse group in the gallery at the left of the "Entrance Chamber," *(c)* the "Gallery of Owls," and *(d)* in the "Aurignacian Gallery," a portion of the enormous spread of meandering lines, unfinished outlines, and scrawls which includes a painted bison/horse group and, at the very back, a group composed of one claviform sign and wound signs. This front part of the Trois Frères sanctuary may have linked up with the clay bison (which are less than 20 yards from the "Entrance Chamber" by straight-line measurement). Whether the caves communicated or not, the climax of the decorations was reached in the panels of the "Sanctuary," the heart and core of the whole layout. Beyond that, Paleolithic visitors would not have gone farther than the "Chapel of the Lioness," which would be a normal conclusion to the whole sequence.

"ENTRANCE CHAMBER" AND "AURIGNACIAN GALLERY"

Two further observations seem of some importance: the possibility of linking the "Wild-Ass Gallery" to the "Sanctuary" with claviforms; and the dating of the "Aurignacian Gallery." The figure of the wild ass[7] is not itself especially archaic; there is a faithful replica of it in one panel in the "Sanctuary,"[8] which the Abbé Breuil thinks is Magdalenian. Most peculiar of all are the little signs[9] found in the vicinity of this figure. These signs, which the Abbé Breuil considers to be "probably tectiforms," seem to be variants of the brace-shaped sign, and they are not unrelated to the sign in gallery 2 at Le Portel.[10] Their presence allows us to suppose that some of the figures in the "Entrance Chamber" are definitely older than those in the set with claviforms (end of Style III, Early Magdalenian).

The date of the "Aurignacian Gallery" is another important question. The network of figures, several yards long, drawn on clay is quite baffling: in the strictest sense, these are unfinished outlines drawn on soft walls. Here and there one makes out the head of a bovid or a horse; some silhouettes seem indeed to be fairly old, and several horns occur in Style III. It is not impossible that this part of the sanctuary was frequented from the Gravettian onward; it is only about 100 feet from where we suppose the Paleolithic entrance to have been, and it would have fallen within the first zone of darkness. The location corresponds to that at Gargas.

Assuming that the original entrance was somewhere around the "Entrance Chamber," one would thus find traces of a sanctuary occupying the first zone inaccessible to daylight ("Aurignacian Gallery"), which might date from the Gravettian or the Solutrean. Next, we should expect decorations in Late Style III (brace-shaped signs in the "Wild-Ass Gallery"), and finally Magdalenian additions and overlays (owls, black bison, and signs[11] in the "Aurignacian Gallery"). The group of owls confirms such an expectation, for its position in a side passage near the entrance is analogous to that of the bird at Le Portel.

THE "SANCTUARY"

The so-called Sanctuary is a bell-shaped alcove with overhanging rocks and fissures; panel upon panel, a host of figures are crowded together. The Abbé Breuil's drawings of these, unsurpassed in precision and graphic quality, are surely his supreme achievement. At the top of the "bell," we find the famous engraved and painted figure of the "Sorcerer"[12] which the Abbé Breuil called "the Horned God," now popularized by innumerable reproductions. This personage combines all the male symbols then at the disposal of the artist who executed it: his horns and ears are those of a reindeer, his jaw is that of a horse, and his tail that of a horse, and his penis, though human, is placed where a feline's would be. It is not surprising to find so hypersymbolic a figure at the highest and innermost point of a chamber that is decorated with hundreds of figures, in the arrangement of which Magdalenian symbolism is displayed with a richness unattained elsewhere.

Before summing up what seem to me to be the structural features of the main panels, it is necessary to give a brief account of the figures on the right-hand wall just outside the entrance to the sanctuary. One sees first a panel of unfinished figures of horses, bison, and signs, located, as we should expect, at the approach to the central composition. There are also a few large figures: an ibex, a mammoth,[13] and human masks. The mammoth is the only one in the entire cave and its peripheral position recalls that of the "elephants" at El Castillo and El Pindal, which are also unique examples. The presence of the proboscidian, the ibex, and the human figures at the extreme edge of the decoration is in accordance with the usual pattern.

[6] *figs. 120, 639*

[7] *fig. 624*
[8] *fig. 635*
[9] *fig. 622*

[10] *fig. 390*

[11] *figs. 626–629*

[12] *fig. 57*

[13] *fig. 630*

The Abbé Breuil believed that all the figures in this peripheral composition are Perigordian, but such a view seems to me untenable: some of the bison here are identical, down to the smallest detail, with those on panels he considered Magdalenian. The large ibex is accompanied by a small head (a female or young ibex), the exact equivalent of which turns up at Angles and Rouffignac in the Middle Magdalenian. On the panels in the "Sanctuary," one rhinoceros and a certain number of bison and ibexes[14] have been classified as Perigordian; no detailed reasons are given for this attribution. For most of them, proof of contemporaneity with the rest of the panels can easily be found in figures on some of the most firmly dated Magdalenian objects. The ibexes near the rhinoceros have horns in twisted perspective, but that does not prove them Perigordian; they occupy the same peripheral location as the ibex in the "*camarin*" at Le Portel, whose horns are in the same perspective. In both cases, such an attribution obliges us to suppose that a complicated grouping of main figures was built in the Magdalenian around a single Perigordian ibex placed, as though on purpose, on the far edge of the future panel. Finally, the little rhinoceros does not especially suggest the only reliably dated Perigordian rhinoceros—namely, the one at Les Rebières.

To discern the general organization of the "Sanctuary," we ought to have an exact breakdown of the different panels. However, the publication devoted to it enables us to note, panel by panel, variations in the relative representation of each species in respect to both number and dimension. The fact that such variations occur relates the compositions to those at Niaux, Lascaux, Les Combarelles, and Rouffignac—everywhere that the number of figures is sufficient to bring out their detailed organization. Several panels consist of a compact herd of bison with a single large figure of that animal providing the background.[15] A certain number of horses are slipped in among the countless bison, and the periphery is occupied by complementary figures: ibexes, stags, reindeer, rhinoceroses, humanoid faces. In one of the lateral panels, the largest figure is a horse surrounded by little bison and accompanied by two bears which are sprinkled with circles and V-shaped wound signs. On other panels, the reindeer dominates in size and number; one marginal recess is even occupied by panels in which the reindeer[16] overshadows the other species. In other words, the same principal species (bison, horse, reindeer) keep recurring but each time one of them is emphasized, this emphasis reflecting its position in relation to the whole.

The figures are covered with a real cloud of V-shaped and goose-track signs, and in one isolated area we find a horse[17] with a row of fourteen claviform signs engraved over it.

Dating the group of figures bearing claviform and wound signs presents no special problems. Dozens of bison, horses, and reindeer match dated decorated objects in so many details that the Abbé Breuil had no hesitation in assigning the bulk of them to Magdalenian IV. Thus Les Trois Frères and Le Tuc d'Audoubert belong to the Middle Magdalenian. It is interesting, however, to try to place them chronologically in relation to other sanctuaries of this period. There can be no doubt that they present affinities with sanctuaries containing claviform signs, but at the same time these two Ariège caves have tangible indications that they belong to a somewhat later stage than Altamira. One whole group of caves (Altamira, Gallery C at La Pasiega, Marsoulas, the main chamber at Labastide, Le Portel) exhibits a technique in which polychromy and painted modeling are dominant. The theme in all these sanctuaries comprises bison and horse, stag and ibex; it excludes the reindeer, the mammoth, and the rhinoceros. Niaux has the same subject matter, but there the modeling of the figures by means of short lines brings it closer to Les Trois Frères. The latter and Le Tuc d'Audoubert are contemporaneous with the reappearance on a grand scale of the reindeer; and this reappearance is attested on decorated objects from the second part of the Middle Magdalenian and the first part of the Late Magdalenian. It is at this time that decorated objects and the art in the caves are rich in equivalent forms, and when the mammoth and the rhinoceros are regularly present, even reaching some of the Spanish caves (Altamira, El Pindal, Los Casares). Consequently, we may suppose that Les Trois Frères and Le Tuc d'Audoubert—like Rouffignac, Les Combarelles, and Font-de-Gaume—belong to the latest period of the deep subterranean sanctuaries.

LE MAS D'AZIL

ARIÈGE, FRANCE

This immense cave was excavated at the close of the nineteenth century, notably by Edouard Piette, who discovered there the first evidences of the strata since known as Azilian. The cave's vast network of galleries is situated on the right bank of the Arize River which at this point flows through a natural tunnel. Here various investigators have unearthed prehistoric finds, among which those from the Magdalenian occupy an important place. Between 1901 and 1912 the Abbé Breuil and Count Henri Bégouën discovered the red paintings which mark the entrance of what is now known as the Breuil Gallery. Mandement, at that time curator of the cave, later cleared out the inner portion of that gallery and rendered visible a sizable group of paintings and engravings. Breuil made drawings of some of these, but there has been no publication on Le Mas d'Azil as a whole. Works of art occur at various points on the walls of this vast subterranean maze, but it would require long and careful study to reconstitute the original layout, inasmuch as the former curator considerably altered the topography in the course of years of extensive digging. The following account will be confined to the Breuil Gallery, which contains the only more or less coherent set of figures. It is hard to make much of the data yielded by the excavations. In addition to Piette's very early excavations and those of J. and M. Saint-Just Péquart, Le Mas d'Azil was subjected to a series of utterly reckless excavations by amateur archaeologists and unqualified professionals. While awaiting fresh investigations of what still remains in one of the world's greatest prehistoric sites, all we know is that the Upper Paleolithic was represented in several layers, and that the Middle and Upper Magdalenian layers yielded a most remarkable collection of decorated objects.

THE BREUIL GALLERY

This portion of the underground network, as it now appears after removal and fill-in operations, consists of a fairly wide chamber about 16 feet long and a corridor that tapers off after about 130 feet. The works fall into two clearly distinguishable groups: the chamber with red paintings, and the corridor which contains engraved figures and a few black paintings. It is not absolutely certain that the physical form of the cave in Paleolithic times was just as we find it today. Along the corridor, especially, there were side passages which are now blocked up with debris.

156. LE MAS D'AZIL. BREUIL GALLERY. SCHEMATIC
PLAN WITH FIGURES

The figures at 6 and 7 are conventionalized.

1 to 5   *Red paintings in a style hard to determine; remains of a bison/horse + stag composition.*

6 and 7   *Bison/horse group.*

8   *Side gallery, obstructed with the debris of old excavations. One red dot at the entrance. Across the entrance stands a block covered with lines, on which one can make out two odd figures of fish (sole or European flounder), similar to the little carved silhouette from Lespugue.*

9   *Pebble with a horse engraved on it, found below the bison at 10.*

10   *Bison engraved on an angle of the wall above the location of the pebble at 9.*

11   *Edge of rock turned into the figure of a bison by means of a few lines.*

12   *Illegible figure.*

13   *Natural relief converted into an animal head.*

14   *Red dot at entrance to a side passage.*

15   *Painted bison and red dots.*

16   *Natural relief turned into a horse by means of black paint.*

17   *Black-painted head of bison whose back may be supplied by a ridge of rock.*

18   *Stag head.*

19   *Red dot.*

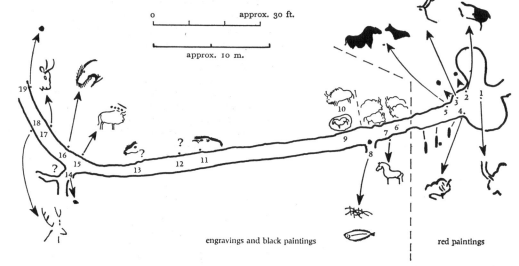

approx. 30 ft.

approx. 10 m.

engravings and black paintings   red paintings

The Chamber

The red paintings discovered by Abbé Breuil and Count Bégouën are in poor condition; several are scarcely legible, and the general organization cannot be made out. At the entrance, in the portion that has been widened, the ceiling seems to have had broad areas covered with red; at the center one can see a bison, depicted from muzzle to just behind the hump. Along the right-hand wall (2 to 5 on fig. 156) several figures can be made out, among them a stag head and a horse; opposite these, on the left-hand wall, we see a bison (4) and a few strokes. In view of the poor condition of the figures, all we can say is that there is a sufficient number to make up a composition on the bison/horse + cervid theme. Nor does the style of the animals lend itself to lengthy considerations; as the Abbé Breuil himself put it, "... though recalling Perigordian figures, they could belong to a later period." (*Quatre cents siècles...*, page 235).

The Corridor

This portion of the cave contains figures that are far more numerous and more interesting than those in the chamber. Near the entrance, at a point where the corridor narrows, we see on the right (6) four engraved bison and on the left (7) an engraved horse. These figures are in Style IV. Past this point, a gallery cluttered with debris opens off to the left; the entrance to it is marked with a red dot on the ceiling. In the accessible portion of this gallery, there is a block on which we find among numerous tangled outlines two representations of flat fish.[1] These have the same characteristics as the carved bone silhouette of a sole from Lespugue.[2] As in the latter case, the fact that we have here a sole or a European flounder is proved conclusively by the continuous fin around the fish and by the presence of both eyes on one side. Apparently no writer so far has called attention to these engravings. On the right-hand side of the corridor, farther on, Mandement very judiciously kept a portion of the Paleolithic ground intact. There we find (9) a pebble[3] lying on the ground exactly underneath a bison (10) engraved on the wall.[4] On this pebble a horse is engraved. Like the animal figures at 6 and 7, these two are in rather advanced Style IV and closely related to those at Montespan and Les Trois Frères.

A few yards farther on, there is a small bison head (11) on the left,[5] engraved over a horizontal ridge that provides the animal's forehead. Next come some vague lines (12), followed by a natural relief (13) which has been converted into an animal head by the addition of a few lines in black paint; the species cannot be clearly identified. Beyond this point the corridor forks: the left branch, which is blocked up, has a red dot on the ceiling; opposite the entrance, on the right-hand wall, is a fine bison painted in black (15) with four red dots in alignment over the the withers. On the same wall, just past this figure, a natural relief was transformed with black paint into an animal's forequarters: this has been interpreted as a feline, but I should rather be tempted to see it as a horse. About 2 yards farther on, still on the right, is a well-executed bison head (17), painted black.[6] Opposite it (18) we see a poorly preserved stag head. Lastly, there is one red dot (19) apparently marking the end of this set of figures.

The figures in the corridor are very homogeneous in style and doubtless belonged to a composition of which we now have only a part. The bison/horse theme recurs several times (6 and 7, 9 and 10, 16 and 17). Group 9 and 10, consisting of the engraving on the wall and the pebble on the ground, is especially interesting because it shows that, in certain cases at least, decorated objects were used in compositions. This collection of figures is in Early Style IV, probably close to Late Style IV: the manner of filling in the figures with hatching brings to mind the decorated objects of Magdalenian IV. At the same time, we must note that this cave, like Niaux, Montespan, and Le Portel, seems to contain no reindeer. The entrance chamber, though probably belonging to an earlier period, cannot be dated on the basis of the data available at present, but the decorations in the corridor clearly belong to the Middle Magdalenian.

[1] *figs. 640–641*
[2] *fig. 234*

[3] *fig. 644*
[4] *fig. 643*

[5] *fig. 645*

[6] *fig. 642*

MONTESPAN

COMMUNE DE MONTESPAN, HAUTE-GARONNE, FRANCE

The Montespan cave, about a mile and a half in length, has two entrances: one at Montespan, at the point where the little stream known as La Houantou goes underground and flows through the cave; the other at Ganties, at the point where the stream re-emerges through a semicircular ceiling. Entrance at the Montespan end is difficult, for the very low ceiling has a projecting ridge which sometimes acts as a short water trap, so that the opening is filled with water. In 1881, an unusually long dry spell made it possible to enter the cave from the Ganties end, and a number of people from the region visited it. Some time later Louis Trombe, the father of Félix Trombe who subsequently explored the cave, had the idea of sinking a shaft above the point where the stream resurfaces at Ganties; this shaft of access was completed in 1923. That same year, Norbert Casteret, after negotiating the difficult Montespan entrance, discovered, with H. Gogin, the famous gallery containing the bear modeled in clay. In 1923 Félix Trombe began systematic exploration of the entire cave and brought to light the rest of the works in the passages beyond the gallery with figures modeled in clay. There is an excellent publication on the cave by F. Trombe and G. Dubuc.

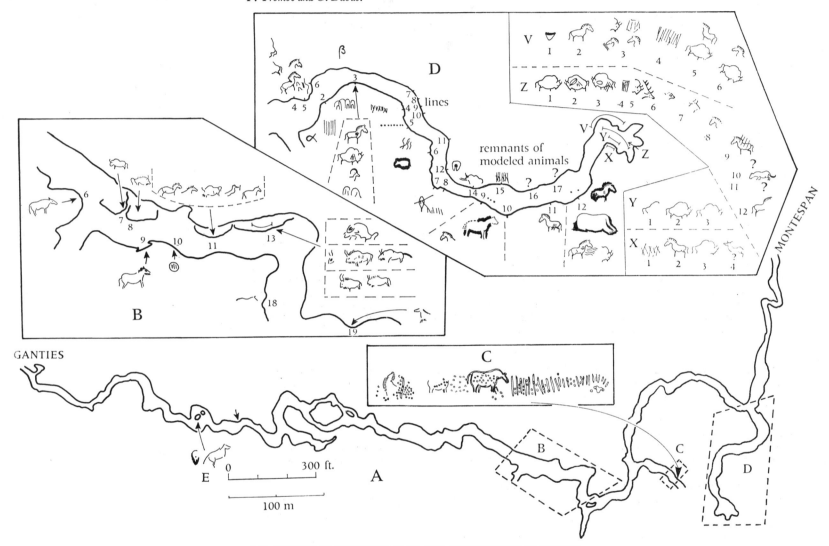

157. MONTESPAN. SCHEMATIC PLAN AND ARRANGEMENT OF FIGURES
Plan after F. Trombe and G. Dubuc; the numbers are theirs. Most of the figures of animals in section
D *(the Casteret Gallery) are conventionalized.*
A   *Over-all plan of the cave. The areas enclosed in broken lines are shown in detail above.*
B   *Trombe-Dubuc Gallery. Composition on the bison/horse theme. At 10: circular sign of aberrant type. At 11: bird (?).*
C   *"Hunting scene" panel.*
D   *Casteret Gallery. As the inventory of figures shows, the over-all theme is bison/horse/ibex.*

The cave consists of a network of underground passages which follow, for the most part, the course of the Houantou stream. Entering at the Montespan end, at a distance of a little over 200 yards one comes to a fork. The axial gallery at the left is the Casteret Gallery (D). It is about 165 yards long and contains, besides the famous bear, a great many works which we will analyze below. Continuing along the main gallery for another 200 yards, one comes to another fork. The side gallery to the left contains the "hunting scene" (C). Proceeding another 200 yards beyond this second fork, along the main passage which follows the little stream, one reaches the Trombe-Dubuc Gallery where there is another set of engravings (B). Beyond these, the little stream continues its underground course; some 330 yards farther on, we come to the last works, a horse and the head of a carnivore (E). From here to the point where the stream re-emerges at Ganties, there are no further signs of human presence. Discoveries of industrial objects and animal remains have been made here and there in the cave, but none of these provides any useful clues for dating the works.

THE CASTERET GALLERY

The Casteret Gallery was originally a carefully organized composition of engravings and figures modeled in clay, part of which has unfortunately disappeared. The over-all arrangement, however, can still be clearly made out. Halfway inside (12), there is a vulva modeled in clay and plastered against the wall, and opposite (7, 8) is an engraved oval and a set of strokes. These are the paired signs that are found, here as elsewhere, at the center of the composition. At the very end of the first segment of the gallery (12), we find the bear and, at the far end of the terminal passage, the figure of a carnivore, the species of which cannot be determined. The general structure (female signs at the center, carnivorous animals at the back) is thus perfectly coherent. The remainder is organized in separate compositions on the dominating bison/horse theme. At the entrance we find a first bison/horse group (4, 5, 6), V-shaped signs, and strokes.[1] A second group (3) follows: bison (with a wound mark), horse (marked with strokes), and ibex.[2] Down to the point where the female signs occur, there are only groups of lines and of dots, and scrawls. Formerly there was also a little figure modeled in clay, carried off by some greedy visitor. Past the female signs we come to the "mammoth" (14). This is a collection of lines that seem to me to have no clear meaning; it would be interesting to see in them the presence of a proboscidian since there are no others in the cave, but I prefer not to be too definite about it. Next come the remnants of several clay figures that formed a frieze; the men who discovered it named it the "frieze of felines." The best preserved of the animals still has its forequarters minus the head.[3] The animal's chest has been pierced in many places with some sharp instrument, like the bear a few yards farther on and the horses in the "hunting scene." I must confess that I do not see in it a feline, but rather a very massive horse, a great portion of which has gradually crumbled away. I have several reasons for this interpretation: the neck and shoulders are equine rather than feline; the elbow is placed where it occurs on a horse; the knee of the foreleg is plainly indicated, whereas this joint is nonexistent in the feline; judging from the imprint surviving on the wall, the hind leg is not positioned like a feline's; and the tail hangs vertically, whereas in all Paleolithic representations of felines it stands up. These arguments should suffice in support of the identification, but I might add that in the central portion of a group of figures one expects to find horses and bison rather than felines, at least in caves of the Franco-Cantabrian region. Farther on we find more remnants of figures modeled in clay, then the group including the bear; this group consists of an engraved horse, an engraved bison, a horse modeled in clay[4] on the ground, and the bear itself.[5] This is a lump of clay about a yard long, very cursorily shaped but impressive in its volume. As is well known, the figure is punctured with holes and has no head; when Casteret found it, the skull of a bear cub lay between the paws. Unfortunately, there is no photographic record and we cannot specify the exact location of this vestige. Prehistorians have very reasonably supposed that the lump of clay was covered with the hide of a freshly skinned bear cub with the head still attached, and that this construction was dealt sharp blows in the course of some magical ceremony.

Past the bear, the gallery narrows and we come to the terminal passage, which contains a number of engravings forming small compositions: bison/horse with a stag, a few oval or wound signs, and strokes. At the far end we find the tiny figure of an undetermined carnivore.

GALLERY WITH THE "HUNTING SCENE"

This is a low gallery—from a certain point on, it is necessary to crawl on hands and knees—on the left-hand wall of which a clay surface (length, 10 feet; average height, 15 inches) has been decorated. The contents of the frieze are sufficiently unusual to have inspired stirring hypotheses concerning the hunting magic practiced by the Magdalenians—hypotheses that are plausible enough, but difficult of demonstration. Objectively, the frieze[6] begins with a very pretty horse's head in a vertical position (A on diagram, fig. 651). Next (B), and scattered throughout the rest of the frieze, there are a large number of holes made with a fairly large cone-shaped tool. Long verticals cut through the round marks on the right-hand side of the frieze. Silhouettes of horses can be made out at two places (C and E). The second of these horses seems to be the most riddled with punctures, like the bear and the figure in the Casteret Gallery which I take to be a horse. Thus we have here three figures of horses, plus dots and strokes. Analyzed in this dry fashion, the frieze seems to be a collection of male symbols (horses and vertical bars) and female symbols (wounds) such as can occur in caves having several compositions. Here at Montespan, however, I think that something more is involved, and that the arrangement of the figures is less abstract than usual. If we consider only the construction of the frieze, we observe a few interesting details: clearly, the figures of the horses were executed earlier than the dots and strokes. The hypothesis of a simulacrum of a hunt might seem confirmed by this first observation. When we analyze the order in which the strokes were made, in relation to the punctures, and, in the case of the latter, imagine how the point of the sharp tool was directed, we notice (1) that some of the punctures were made before the strokes, and some after; and (2) that the punch marks are not scattered over the whole length of the frieze—as would have been the case if they had been made by a weapon hurled at the wall—but form distinct groups. Consequently, it seems that the frieze was executed in successive parts by an artist lying on his side who, after placing the two figures of horses, then made the strokes and the punch marks, the latter by stabbing the wall with some short object held in the hand like a dagger. In view of the execution, and particularly of the cramped quarters where the frieze is placed, there seems no question of a dramatic scene in which hunters might have hurled spears at effigies of horses drawn on the wall. The picture we get, rather, is of one artist executing the symbolic composition, doubtless with much conviction but also with a certain method, taking care not to damage the figures too much. There remains in the hunting scene, as in the bear and the other modeled animal, only the idea of associating symbolic signs with wounds fatal to animals. We have found sufficient evidence of this elsewhere not to be surprised at it here; however, in its interpretation of the idea, the panel provides one of the most moving indications of a way of thinking that cannot be explained by considering it based solely on some sort of imitative magic.

[1] fig. 649
[2] fig. 652

[3] fig. 648

[4] fig. 650   [5] figs. 646, 647

[6] figs. 157 (C), 651

THE TROMBE–DUBUC GALLERY

7 figs. 653, 654

This portion of the cave is decorated with more than a dozen engravings. They show mainly horses and bison,[7] with one very vague figure thought to represent a bird. The sequence terminates (fig. 157, B, 6) with a horse—sometimes described as an "asino-hemionus," but I do not think it is outside the range of possible variations of drawing a horse. There are few signs in this portion of the sanctuary, apart from a circular figure with a few lines cutting across it, and, on the bison, wound marks and strokes.

LAST FIGURES

8 fig. 655

More than three hundred yards farther on (fig. 157, E), we come upon the incomplete drawing of a horse next to a hanging fold of stalactite, the natural shape of which evokes the head of some carnivorous animal, such as a bear—and this resemblance has been brought out by the engraving of an eye and a mouth.[8] The first question that arises is: which entrance did Paleolithic people use? The arrangement of the works seems to me to leave no doubt on this score: as in several deep-cave sanctuaries, the decoration begins with a large number of figures; echoes of them recur farther inside at one or two points, then thin out, and a few back-cave figures bring up the rear. This is the case at Niaux, for example. In all probability, then, the cave was entered from the Montespan end.

STYLE AND DATING

Some of the Montespan engravings were skillfully executed, but the drawing is invariably simple and at times highly schematized. They are far removed from the meticulous execution of the works at Niaux or Les Trois Frères. At the same time, it is incontestable that the figures have much in common with those of Les Trois Frères and Niaux. The subjects include the bison, the horse, the ibex, the stag, the bear, possibly a bird, and an undetermined carnivore; there is no reindeer, no mammoth, no rhinoceros. All of this suggests that Montespan is related to the great sanctuaries with claviforms of the Pyrenean-Cantabrian group. However, Montespan has no claviforms at all, only ovals which are either contemporary with the claviforms or a bit later, and wound signs. The presence of the bear raises a problem. In the Magdalenian the bear, except in rare instances, makes its appearance at a late stage, practically in the Late Magdalenian. It is still absent at Niaux, and already present at Les Trois Frères. In the latter cave, as at Les Combarelles and Teyjat, it is accompanied by the reindeer. Are we to suppose that Montespan is situated chronologically after Niaux and before Les Trois Frères, on the grounds that it already displays the bear, but not yet the reindeer? Although Montespan does correspond to this period, it is no doubt premature to attempt to narrow down the chronological determination so closely. Thus the decorations in this cave, which give every evidence of belonging to a single period, were executed between the end of the Middle and the beginning of the Late Magdalenian, in Early Style IV.

LA CULLALVERA

RAMALES, SANTANDER, SPAIN

The cave is of sizable proportions: it is more than 100 feet high at the entrance, and its explored portion is more than a mile and a quarter long. A few years ago, a regional speleological group discovered in it a number of signs and two painted horses. We visited it in 1957 but for too short a time to be able to locate the few figures that are lacking to make the composition of the sanctuary complete.

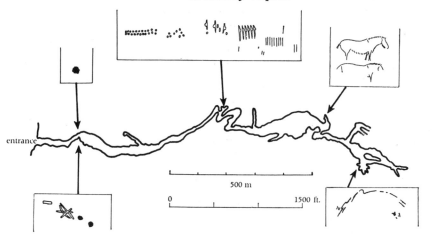

158. LA CULLALVERA. SCHEMATIC PLAN AND ARRANGEMENT OF FIGURES
The scale shows how widely the figures are scattered, yet they form a coherent whole: spots and strokes at the first narrowing of the corridor, paired signs off in a recess, horses, signs at the back.

1 fig. 671
2 fig. 672

Despite all its unusual features, this cave is one of the most typical examples of the organization of a decorated cave. Along a mile and a quarter of immense gallery, the Magdalenians scattered the figures which are absolutely indispensable in setting up a sanctuary. At a point 176 yards from the entrance we come to a narrowing of the corridor from which the entrance is no longer visible. Here we see one black spot and a few red lines on the right, and one black spot on the left: these are the entrance signs. At a distance of nearly 800 yards from the entrance, following the left-hand wall, we come to a wide recess that contains signs; this is in accordance with a formula which is represented in one-third of the caves (Altamira, Arcy, El Castillo, Covalanas, Gargas—upper cave, La Mouthe, Niaux, La Pasiega, Le Portel, Villars, to mention only the chief examples). The groups of red dots in alignment[1] supply a first element, followed by ten red claviforms and ten black strokes; the contrast between male and female signs is particularly sharp.[2] Resuming our course through a rocky chaos of colossal proportions, about 1,000 yards from the entrance, still on the left, we come to another recess just ahead of a bend in the gallery: here we find two black-painted horses.[3] Finally, about 220 yards farther on, in a chamber that marks the end of the main gallery, we again find black strokes, apparently set down at random like the spots at the entrance; they signal the presence of the back-cave signs.[4] What we miss in this remarkably restrained set of decorations is a bison or a group of bison, painted or perhaps engraved, for which we searched in the vicinity of the horses—but they could be dozens of yards from there, hidden in the labyrinth of recesses and blocks. The presence of entrance signs and back-cave signs in their expected places and the classic feature of paired signs in a recess leave little doubt that the cave contains the second element in the pairing of animal species; this element, given the character of the figures, could only be the bison.

Despite the paucity of the figures, the decorations at La Cullalvera can be dated easily by the claviforms and the style of the horses. Both correspond to a probably advanced stage of Early Style IV, close to El Pindal and Las Monedas—that is, mature Magdalenian or beginning of the Late Magdalenian.

[3] *fig. 673*
[4] *fig. 674*

ALTAMIRA

(*See pages 328–330 and figs. 664–670.*)

EL PINDAL

PIMIANGO, OVIEDO, SPAIN

The cave decoration was discovered by H. Alcade del Rio in 1908. The Abbé Breuil made the pictorial inventory. There seems to have been no systematic study of the industrial objects which were found at the entrance, allegedly in considerable quantity.

The figures at El Pindal are not notable for the quality of their execution nor for their state of preservation: most of them demand close, lengthy examination to be grasped at all, and photography gives little assistance. Nonetheless, the cave is very interesting in several respects. Geographically it is one of the outposts at the south and west of the Franco-Cantabrian group; its composition is very regular, the signs it contains supply a valuable chronological marker, and several of the animal figures are stylistically very significant. El Pindal is a corridor-cave about 400 yards long. Most of the figures appear on the right-hand wall in an area about 50 feet long; there are about forty of them, either painted in ocher or engraved.

A first panel shows two vulvar coats-of-arms and one small engraved horse. The second panel constitutes the main composition. It includes a dozen bison, three horses, and one hind.[1] The bison/horse + hind theme is that of the Painted Ceiling at Altamira, and it also occurs as one of the groups at El Castillo (group 20) and in the lower cave at Isturitz. The composition includes numerous signs as well: four groups of claviforms of the type found at Niaux and La Cullalvera, two small oval signs incised under the beard of the largest bison, several wound signs (the type of two converging lines) on the flank or shoulder of the animals. In an outcropping of rock on the wall there is a triangular hollow which has been underlined with ocher. The female category is represented, then, by claviforms and schematized signs of the triangle-oval-wound type. These features recur a bit farther on. Signs in the male category are represented by rows of dots, singly or grouped in pairs or clusters, the arrangement recalling that of the signs at Niaux, La Cullalvera, and Marsoulas. Sequences of strokes have been drawn on the outcroppings of rock that form a canopy above the frieze. The pairing of the male and female signs is very clearly marked: each animal has a corresponding pairing of claviform/dots, wound/dots, or claviform/strokes, in every possible combination. At the end of the panel, near the hollow transformed into a female sign, we find an isolated bison.

[1] *fig. 676*

The next panel includes one bison, one horse's head, one claviform sign, dots and aligned strokes. It would be hard to imagine a more coherent composition. Above the bison is an incised fish. This is a very odd work; if one is to judge by the long, sickle-shaped pectoral and caudal fins, it should represent a tuna but these features have been grafted onto the body of a trout or salmon, with all the details typical of Middle and Late Magdalenian art, including the adipose fin.

Opposite, we find a horse's head in red; a bit farther on, on the right-hand wall, a proboscidian has been drawn in red with a spot on its shoulder. This figure suggests an elephant rather than a mammoth; together with the one at El Castillo and the elephants at La Baume Latrone, it has been advanced as proof that *elephas antiquus* survived in southern Europe down to the close of the Paleolithic. Now, while the presence of the mammoth in Spain at this time is confirmed by the remains of bones, we have not yet found remains of the prehistoric elephant from so late an epoch. At Pech Merle, for instance, we find some mammoths depicted without hair, although nearby figures have hair. In the Ardèche and the Gard (the caves of Chabot and Le Figuier) proboscidians are represented without hair; at the Oulen cave the hair is plainly indicated. While I should not rule out the possibility that *elephas antiquus* survived into the Late Paleolithic, it seems rather farfetched to suppose that the Magdalenians as naturalists were overscrupulous in matters of exact detail. Quite apart from the trout disguised as a tuna, only a few yards from the "mammoth," there are any number of examples of bison figures having variations in treatment which cannot be accounted for as renderings of different species. The remainder of the cave contains representations of a male character spaced some distance apart (sequences of strokes,[2] rows of dots) and a panel of black animals which represent the back-cave figures: a horse's head, one leg of the same animal, a stag, and the hindquarters of a cervid or ibex.[3]

[2] *fig. 677*
[3] *fig. 675*

All the stylistic similarities of the animal figures point to Early Style IV and, more specifically, relate them to caves such as Niaux and Les Trois Frères in which bison are modeled with numerous parallel lines. We might observe here that El Pindal is one of the sites (along with the Abri du Poisson, Pech Merle, Le Mas

373

d'Azil, Le Portel, and Niaux) at which fish are represented. Niaux, Les Trois Frères, Le Tuc d'Audoubert, and La Cullalvera all have the same claviform signs as El Pindal. One of the bison figures, half painted, half engraved (listed by the Abbé Breuil on one occasion as mature Perigordian, on another as Magdalenian), is shown in exactly the same attitude as the bison at Las Monedas. Thus, all these examples suggest that the figures at El Pindal come from around the Middle Magdalenian.

The signs fall into two morphological types: claviforms and schematized vulvar signs. There are caves where we find claviforms only, or tectiforms only (Niaux, La Cullalvera), others where we find both types (Les Trois Frères, Bernifal, Les Combarelles, Font-de-Gaume). The latter caves are those in which the mammoth plays a more or less important part, and where the figures come closest to Late Style IV. In these cases we seem to be dealing with sites that continued to be in use down to the Late Magdalenian. One last detail is of interest: under one of the horses in the second panel on the right, a positive print of a hand was seen (with certain reservations) by Jorda Cerda and Berenguer Alonso. In itself the fact would not be surprising, for there are single hands associated with figures in Style IV at Bernifal, Font-de-Gaume, and Les Combarelles in contexts not unlike that of El Pindal, although those caves do not contain any other figures that can be reliably assigned to the Aurignacian or the Gravettian.

LAS MONEDAS
PUENTE VIESGO, SANTANDER, SPAIN

This cave is situated on Monte Castillo, at the end of the trail leading to the caves of El Castillo, Las Chimeneas, and La Pasiega. It was discovered in 1952 by G. Lorenzo, who was supervising work on the Monte Castillo caves. The full chronological range of the decorated caves is represented within a perimeter of a few hundred yards, from the pure Style III of Las Chimeneas to the very late decoration at Las Monedas. This is the only cave in Spain that exemplifies the last period of the decorated caves.

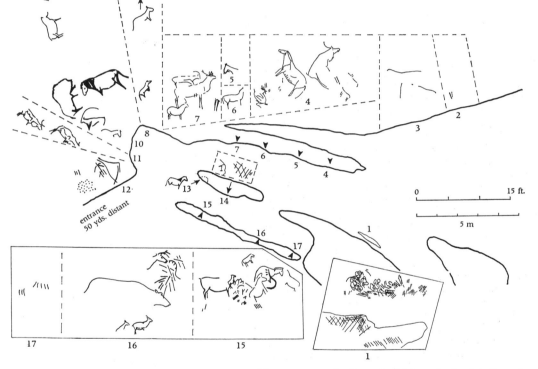

159. LAS MONEDAS. SCHEMATIC PLAN AND ARRANGEMENT OF FIGURES

1 Panel of ovals and strokes in black. Below these is a rock with natural incisions, which has been rubbed smooth along the upper edge.
2 Strokes.
3 Unfinished outlines.
4 Right to left: remnants of two ibexes, double strokes, reindeer, horse, strokes, and remnants of a vertical bison. This is the first major composition.
5 and 6 Horses.
7 Remnants of two reindeer and two ibexes, and strokes.
8 Horse.
9 Feline (?) in a chimney.
10 Bison, horses, ibex, and paired signs from the second major composition.
11 Reindeer peripheral to the preceding composition.
12 Claviforms paired with barbed signs. Dot and strokes.
13 Horse inside a semidome.
14 Panel of crisscrossed lines and headless horse.
15 Panel of horses and signs: at left, a headless ibex.
16 Stag, barbed sign and strokes, bear, and pair of ibexes.
17 Back-cave strokes, on the edge of a fissure.

The sanctuary is situated within a single chamber close to the entrance of a cave having large dimensions. This location is in agreement with attribution of the figures to a period of Late Style IV, when sanctuaries deep inside the caves appear to have been abandoned. As at La Peña de los Hornos, the figures have been placed around a labyrinthine chamber the middle of which is occupied by a stalagmitic mass; the chamber has three approaches. The route that was actually followed is fairly easy to reconstruct. All the works in this cave are painted in black.

The first panel (1) consists of oval figures and sets of strokes forming an incoherent scribble within which it may be possible to distinguish faces with big round eyes[1] The panel is above a large stone marked with natural grooves that form lozenge shapes; the sharp edges of the stone have been polished by a rubbing that does not correspond to that caused by passing bodies. No less odd is the fact that the natural lozenge-shaped striations have been reproduced in the painted panel above it and also beyond, in panel 14. There is no doubt that we have here the panel of scrawls so often found in the vicinity of major compositions. The presence of the striated rock probably accounts for the choice of this approach, rather than the others, as the entrance to the sanctuary. Figures appear in panels 2 and 3 on the opposite wall, rendered in unfinished outline: we can make out a horse, and a mammoth's trunk, head, and back. In the caves of southwestern France, the mammoth makes its reappearance with the reindeer immediately before Late Style IV; in Spain, Las Monedas is the only cave in which the reindeer is represented. Group 4 is the most important from the stylistic point of view,[2] as it includes a horse with M-shaped ventral modeling, which places the figure as Early Style IV (Middle Magdalenian), a remarkably executed reindeer in the spirit of Late Style IV, and remnants of a

[1] fig. 678

[2] figs. 84, 115, 680

bison and an ibex. Farther along the wall we find a horse and a stroke (5), a headless horse (6), and then a remarkable passageway group (7): one reindeer framed by two ibexes.[3] (There is a similar framing of bison at Niaux, from roughly the same epoch.)

A second central composition, the main one, is situated where the wall makes a sweeping curve (8); the composition takes advantage of an incipient corridor and the springings of the ceiling vault. As in the "*camarin*" at Le Portel, we find here a full inventory of associated species and signs. The main subject (10) is represented by a horse[4] and a bison accompanied by an ibex. To their left three reindeer (10–11) follow one another around the edge of a vault-springing.[5] The bison is positioned vertically, but the attitude is not that of a falling animal; rather, it reproduces that of one of the El Pindal bison: head down, left foreleg thrust forward. To the right on the ceiling, and on up toward a chimney, we see a horse and strokes, then a second horse.[6] The highly schematized figure inside the chimney (9) might be that of a feline. To the left, there are signs[7]: a claviform which brings to mind the truncated female figures at Les Combarelles and La Roche is flanked by a barbed sign; to the left of these are three strokes, a scattering of dots, and one spot (12). This composition, which constitutes the center of the sanctuary, is very clear: horse/bison is the theme, with flanking ibex and paired male and female signs; on the periphery, reindeer in the corridor, possibly a feline in the chimney.

The stalagmitic mass in the center of the chamber forms a corridor that completes the circuit. To the left, on the mass itself inside a small semidome, we find (13) a tiny horse,[8] and on the next panel (14) a vertically positioned headless horse, plus some lines reproducing the lozenge shapes of the striated rock previously mentioned. Facing these are the last panels in the sanctuary. Panel 15 is rendered in unfinished outlines, but we see five horses on the right, signs and outlines in the middle and at the bottom, and on the left a well-drawn figure of a headless animal,[9] cervid or ibex. Mme. Laming-Emperaire has called attention to these representations of headless animals, which seem to have constituted a distinct theme. In Early Style IV we find them at the edge of compositions or in remote portions of the sanctuary. The last panel (16), as we should expect, is an accumulation of male subjects: cervid, barbed signs, bear, ibexes. The last decorated portion of the cave (17) shows, as usual, a set of strokes.

The sanctuary at Las Monedas is one of the clearest examples of how the themes are organized. There have been no later additions and the topography of the site lent itself to clear and orderly arrangement with the panel of scrawls (1) and unfinished outlines (2, 3) at the entrance, a first composition (4), passageway figures (7), the second and principal composition (8–12), a second collection of outlines (14), and the back-cave subjects (15, 16, and 17).

Dating Las Monedas gains no support from the discovery of any objects here, which is greatly to be regretted in view of the character of the works. However, there are a number of clues that can be derived from similarities with other caves. Horses and bison are here treated like the animals at Niaux, Le Portel, Les Trois Frères, and El Pindal; all are accompanied by claviform signs and are related to a probably rather advanced stage of the Middle Magdalenian (Magdalenian IV). However, none of those caves except Les Trois Frères has reindeer; yet it is the animals at Les Trois Frères that most closely approach Late Style IV. The mammoth, which is also present at Les Trois Frères and El Pindal, and the bison, which is treated in an anecdotal manner as at El Pindal, complete the series of similarities that lead us to place the decoration of Las Monedas at the approaches to the Late Magdalenian.

SANTIMAMINE

CORTEZUBI, VIZCAYA, SPAIN

The figures were discovered in 1916 by José F. de Bengoecha. Excavation was done by T. de Aranzadi, J. M. Barandiaran, and E. Eguren, and a partial pictorial inventory made by the Abbé Breuil.

This huge cave contains a sanctuary about 20 yards in length, which is reached by climbing over a cascade of stalagmite some fifteen feet high. It consists of a corridor that ends in a round chamber; the best-preserved works are in the latter. In the main corridor, which continues on from the chamber to the remoter portions of the cave, are a few painted and engraved figures. Deposits at the entrance yielded a lavish collection of industrial artifacts extending from the Aurignacian to the Late Magdalenian. In view of these works it is especially interesting to note that the figures in the sanctuary, both those painted in black and those engraved, exhibit a total homogeneity of style.

The sanctuary begins with a few black dots on the left just past the entrance to the corridor at the top of the stalagmite cascade. A small chamber, merely a widening of the corridor, has two bison[1] on the right and, on the left, three bison, two horses, and an ox head. Here, then, we have a first set on the bison/horse theme, with the single ox often found in compositions featuring the bison (at Niaux, for instance). Past the small chamber we find, on the right, a few painted figures hard to make out. On the left is the area of outlines with numerous more or less unfinished engravings of bison and some traces of ocher. Then we come to the rear chamber where we find the second central composition and the back-cave subjects. The main panel is on the left. It includes seven bison, two of which are back-to-back in vertical position, plus one horse, one stroke, and one small rectangle.[2] On the ground in front of this panel is a stalagmitic block covered with engravings of bison, some of them unfinished, and one engraved and painted bison.[3] Opposite this there is a stalagmitic deposit with several figures painted on it—a bear, the hindquarters of a stag or ibex, a stag's head, and an ibex head: all are back-cave or passageway subjects.[4] Turning back toward the entrance, we find three vertically positioned bison[5] painted on the left rim of a fissure, and two ibex heads on the right rim. Lastly, we find a bison head completely upside down. Such vertical and upside-down animal figures are intriguing. A few of them, such as the ox at Pech Merle and the horse at the back of the Axial Gallery at Lascaux, have their limbs in a position which suggests that they are actually falling, but usually the position of the limbs is perfectly normal; we may wonder whether we are dealing with perspective renderings or merely with indifference to the laws of spatial organization as we know them.

The layout of the round chamber is especially clear. One broad composition on the bison/horse theme with paired signs takes up the best panel, with a block of unfinished outlines beneath it. The other wall is

[3] *fig. 681*

[4] *fig. 679*
[5] *fig. 682*

[6] *fig. 683*
[7] *fig. 684*

[8] *fig. 685*

[9] *fig. 686*

[1] *fig. 656*

[2] *figs. 71, 657–660*
[3] *fig. 661*

[4] *figs. 118, 663*
[5] *fig. 662*

occupied by bison and ibexes. It is hard to assign them an exact function, for the ibex is above all a complementary animal and these scattered figures may be related to the main panel. On the other hand, the stalagmite at the back, with the bear, the stag, and the ibex, has the usual position of a back-cave grouping. The
figures in the farther part of the corridor fall into two groups. There are three small paintings—one is certainly a bison, while the other two (barely legible) may represent a bear and a hind; they are accompanied by
three strokes. Farther on, the last work noted is an engraved horse, by no means exceptional as a back-cave
subject (there are seventeen instances, including Les Combarelles, Ebbou, the Bayol cave, Arcy-sur-Cure,
and Font-de-Gaume).

It is easy to find parallels for the Santimamine figures. The bison on the main panel in the round chamber
and on the engraved block exhibit all the variations of the modeling conventions of Early Style IV and tally
in exact detail with examples at Altamira (the Painted Ceiling), Niaux, and Le Portel. These last are closely
related to decorated objects of the period of spear-throwers having broad handles in the shape of animals,
engraved bone disks, and carved silhouettes—that is, the Middle Magdalenian. In particular we find the
triangular shadow between withers and rump, and the strip extending from the tip of the buttocks to the
shoulder. The horses, however, do not exhibit the modeling conventions (shoulder lines and M-shaped ventral line) that we find in figures of horses at the three caves just mentioned.

Signs are especially scanty; this is in marked contrast to caves in Style III like Lascaux and El Castillo but
in accord with sanctuaries in Style IV, where sometimes only one sign is found in a whole cave (Le Portel—
one claviform; Niaux—two claviforms for the whole black sequence). Santimamine's one and only sign is
very discreetly placed at the bottom of the large main panel—a small unfilled rectangle resembling the one
on panel 25 in Gallery A, La Pasiega. Along with the Covalanas rectangles, this gives us three instances in
Spain of quadrangular signs that are unfilled and accompany animals in mature Style III or Early Style IV.
Nevertheless, to find only this small rectangular sign at Santimamine is rather peculiar, for bison of this type,
from Santander to the Ariège, are as a rule accompanied by claviform signs.

LOS HORNOS (Continued from page 306)

FIGURES IN STYLE IV

The part of this cave that is occupied by figures in Style IV has a topographical arrangement which
makes the organization of the figures rather hard to grasp. The sanctuary is in a huge chamber transformed
into a kind of labyrinth by a number of rock masses. At the entrance we find two ibexes[1] and a stag. Entering
the chamber, we see the central composition on the back wall which forms something like a corridor; on the
right are three oxen, on the left are three bison facing two horses. The chamber terminates with a series of
recesses and a blind alley; within these are a panel of signs, a horse group, a figure having a human appearance[2] with lifted arms, and a bison.[3] This decoration thus forms a coherent whole—ibexes and stag at the
entrance, the human figure at the back, bison and oxen in the central panel. However, it is a bit disconcerting
to find oxen and bison side by side: I know of no other instance. The signs, too, are disconcerting: they consist
of meandering lines which suggest no identifiable shape. The style of the animal figures, however, places the
decoration of this chamber in the period of the brace-shaped signs or the earliest claviforms.

Just outside the entrance to this chamber are a few simple drawings that may be prior to Style IV. Most
of the figures inside the chamber belong incontestably to Early Style IV. Treatment of the horns of the oxen,
bison, and ibexes is in the manner normal for the period; in the case of the bison, the eye, horn, and ear are
rendered in one unbroken line. The general aspect is that of Style IV, and two of the bison have little
"breathing" lines in front of their muzzles—a detail familiar from numerous other figures in Style IV. To
sum up, Los Hornos has two sanctuaries which are completely distinct: the one at the entrance is surely very
old and can be assigned to Style II, and the one farther inside is typically Early Style IV—that is, Middle
Magdalenian.

BARA-BAHAU

LE BUGUE, DORDOGNE, FRANCE

The engravings in this cave were discovered by Norbert Casteret in 1951; the drawings of them are by the Abbé André Glory.

This cave is puzzling from the stylistic point of view. The decoration occupies the left-hand wall and the
vaulted ceiling of a huge chamber which lay, in Paleolithic times, in the first zone of darkness. This feature
characterizes the oldest sanctuaries, though we also have several examples from later periods. The engravings,
deeply incised and simple in outline, are executed on friable rock studded with flint nodules. The crudeness
of the works does not necessarily indicate a very early date but does make it difficult to assign them to any
specific style. Their composition, however, is normal.

The decorated area is about 22 yards long and breaks down into three series, to be read from top to bottom
and from left to right. The upper series begins with long lines running in every direction, in the tradition of
the preliminary panels of scrawls and unfinished outlines. However, countless shorter scrawls are found
throughout the decorated surface. Next comes a group including a bison, a horse's head, an indefinable
quadruped supposed to be feline, and—above the bison—a sign that seems to be a rather realistic virility
symbol. The second series begins with strokes and two big signs.[1] The first is very much like an unusual type
of tectiform with several vertical bars. The second, incised on a horse, is a lattice sign with irregular bars
(analogous to that on horse 75 at Les Combarelles and those found at Font-de-Gaume in the chamber with
the little bison)—a type that precedes the tectiforms. The sign is also somewhat similar to the "hut" sign at

1 fig. 688

2 fig. 689   3 fig. 687

1 figs. 690, 691

La Mouthe. Above the sign there are five parallel lines which some have interpreted as a hand, but which seem to me to be strokes corresponding to the preceding signs. These various signs are linked with a group that includes four horses, one bull, and one ibex. The bull,[2] one of the best-executed figures, has no stylistic parallel but its cervico-dorsal line seems to point to Style II. The horses, on the other hand, suggest Style IV. The third series includes a bear and a cervid, the position of whose head is that of a reindeer; both figures are in the middle of a tangle of scrawls. Then appear one horse, one bovid that could be a bison, two horses,[3] and at the end of the frieze, a very uncertain figure that might be an ibex.

The composition is simple: the three series show three bovids accompanied by horses and, in one instance, by an ibex. The middle series includes, in addition, large paired signs and, on the edges, a feline (?), a bear, a cervid, and possibly a last ibex. The set is so unremarkable that we cannot draw arguments from it for dating purposes. If the cervid really is a reindeer, it would relate Bara-Bahau to nearby sites in Style IV. The signs supply our best clues for dating: lattice signs with vertical bars seem to be the last version of the rectangular signs in Style III, and to have slightly preceded tectiforms in the Les Eyzies region. This would put Bara-Bahau in the transitional period between Style III and Early Style IV—that is, at the end of the Early Magdalenian or the beginning of the Middle Magdalenian. Such an attribution will conflict with the much-publicized view that these are "the oldest engravings" from the Paleolithic. I admit that my only argument is based on the signs, but I also maintain that I found here no features unmistakably typical of dated archaic engraving. Like La Clotilde and La Baume Latrone, Bara-Bahau resists stylistic comparison. It may be noted further that the medium or technique in the decoration of each of these three sites is very unusual: at La Clotilde it is incised on soft clay; at La Baume Latrone, painted with fingers dipped in clay; and here at Bara-Bahau it is engraved on what the Abbé Glory called "cottage cheese" studded with flint nodules. Under such conditions, we may suppose that the finer inflections of the linear arabesque necessarily lost a great deal of their typological value, although this in no way detracts from the cave's genuine interest.

MARCENAC

CABRERETS, LOT, FRANCE

Attention was drawn to the figures in the Marcenac cave near Pech Merle by the Abbé André Lémozi, who made the pictorial inventory (see fig. 128).

The entrance to this cave lies only a short distance from what we suppose to be the Paleolithic entrance to Pech Merle. It is a corridor leading to a chamber beyond which the cave has not been explored. The entrance corridor contains a few engravings on the right-hand wall and, opposite them, an area of scrawls and unfinished outlines. The chamber in the back contains only two figures painted in black and placed opposite each other.[1] One is a horse in Style IV, the other a bison with horns in frontal view; despite the horns, the dorsal curve is in Style IV rather than in Style III. Isolated in this fashion, these two works are hard to date. There are horses of a similar general aspect at Les Combarelles, and the bison in low relief at the Abri Reverdit is not unlike this bison at Marcenac. The same treatment of the horns occurs at Lascaux, Le Gabillou, and Villars, and so we presume it to be of early date; but the manner of drawing the animal scarcely suggests great antiquity; we may wonder whether the head is not in frontal view. Lastly, we must observe that the bison at Pech Merle, only a few hundred yards from Marcenac, have horns of a similar shape. With all due caution, then, these figures may be situated close to Early Style IV or the end of Style III; it is not impossible that one day someone will find the brace-shaped or claviform signs that may have accompanied them.

SAINTE-EULALIE

LOT, FRANCE

The engravings here, discovered by the Abbé André Lémozi in 1920, are in the front part of a gallery; at the entrance to it a Magdalenian layer with harpoons was found (Magdalenian V–VI).

The decoration, consisting of fine-line engravings, appears on the left-hand wall in the front part of the cave, adjacent to the area where evidences of habitation were found. Most of the figures are crusted over and barely legible, although several horses and several reindeer can be made out. The Abbé Breuil compared them to figures at Teyjat and Limeuil. The most interesting feature of this small composition is the presence of the reindeer, which is rare among cave-art figures, and the location of the figures so near to the entrance. These facts corroborate what has been said in this book concerning the return, in the Late Magdalenian, of cave decoration toward the daylight zones; at the same time that reindeer reappear on the few decorated walls dating from this epoch, the greater number of them occur on decorated objects of bone or on stone plaquettes.

TIBIRAN

AVENTIGNAN, HAUTES-PYRÉNÉES, FRANCE

This little cave was visited in 1951 by Norbert Casteret, who discovered some painted works; he published photographs and a simplified drawing of the horse.

The cave slopes steeply downward from the entrance to a round chamber about twelve yards in diameter. Above a ledge in this chamber that follows the curving left-hand wall we find nine red hands in negative, with certain of the hands "mutilated" in the manner of the hands of the nearby Gargas cave. The hands are divided into two groups, eight at one place, and a single isolated hand accompanied by four strokes. A corridor opens off the back of the chamber, and at its entrance faint traces of three more hands can still be made out on the right-hand wall. On the opposite wall of this corridor, just before a small steep drop is reached, there is a recess about 2 yards across, in which Casteret discovered a horse, a bear, and "other remnants of black paintings... in such a state of decay as to be almost undecipherable."

[2] *fig. 693*

[3] *fig. 692*

[1] *figs. 694, 695*

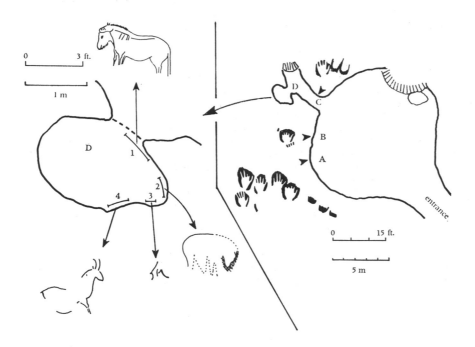

160. TIBIRAN. SCHEMATIC PLAN WITH
FIGURES
A, B, *and* C   *Groups of hands.*
D   *Small chamber with black paintings.*

[1] *fig. 696*

The horse[1] is located above the entrance of the small recess; actually, there are two silhouettes which merge into one: a black-painted horse, apparently in Style III or Early Style IV, and a reworked engraving of a figure whose head seems to be mature Style IV. Both figures have the double shoulder line. To the right of the horse, a dorsal line in black paint has been carried to a stalactite outcropping which quite effectively evokes the shape of a bear's head; I share Casteret's opinion on the identification of this figure.[2] To the right are some black lines, all that remains of a work whose character I was unable to determine. Lastly, still on the right, are faint remains of a rather pretty ibex which appears to be in Style III. However, it is not impossible that the hindquarters belong to a second ibex figure that has faded away. The little group of figures at Tibiran is in an advanced stage of decay. One can only say that a Style III sanctuary probably existed in which the signs were represented (as at Gargas) by hands accompanied by dots. This little composition was touched up in the Magdalenian, at least where the horse is concerned.

[2] *fig. 697*

BÉDEILHAC

TARASCON, ARIÈGE, FRANCE

This enormous cave contained sizable archaeological deposits which have been pillaged by amateurs, especially during the Second World War when the cave was used as an underground airplane factory. Such scraps of evidence concerning chronology as we possess indicate that the Magdalenian played a very important part. Several decorated objects were discovered here, notably a very fine spear-thrower of the type with the animal's head turned back against its body; this was found by Romain Robert.

THE VIDAL GALLERY

About 500 feet inside the cave there is a recess in the right-hand wall of the entrance corridor. It contains some fifteen black- and red-painted figures forming a composition on the bison/horse theme. Most of them are faded, and it is hard to get a clear idea of the original composition. There are quite a few signs in the form of strokes, painted or incised.

MAIN GALLERY

About 440 yards from the entrance, on the left-hand wall of the huge main gallery, a sequence of red dots marks the beginning of the sanctuary, which occupied the entire remaining portion of the cave. Among the better-preserved figures in a mostly very faded composition we notice, in addition to the engravings on the walls, a fair number of engravings on clay and some black paintings. The most interesting of the black paintings is a figure that could pass for a horse's hindquarters prolonged into a body that lacks forelegs and head.[1] This unusual subject has marked affinities with two figures at Niaux. The first of these is the "headless man" painted in panel II in the deepest part of the recess of the Black Salon; the second is the headless ibex without forelegs painted on the ceiling over the terminal lake. Among the figures on clay at Bédeilhac one small modeled bison[2] is worth mentioning; it is near a triangular sign of the female category.

The original arrangement of the figures is hard to discern because of the damage they have suffered; nowhere do we find a really coordinated sequence, except for the little modeled group just mentioned and a number of painted or engraved bison accompanied by horses at the very back of the cave, on the right. The decoration of the Vidal Gallery suggests Early Style IV, its polychrome treatment bordering on that at Marsoulas and Labastide. This would place it in the Middle Magdalenian. The figures at the back of the cave may have been executed at different periods, but all those that are reasonably well preserved belong to Style IV. A few of them[3] are very close to figures at Montespan.

[1] *fig. 701*

[2] *fig. 698*

[3] *figs. 699, 700*

USSAT, GROTTE DES ÉGLISES

ARIÈGE, FRANCE

The engraved and painted works in the Grotte des Églises were discovered in 1921 by Dr. Cuguillère. The Abbé Breuil made the pictorial inventory the same year.

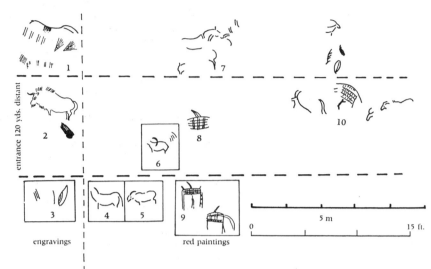

161. USSAT, GROTTE DES ÉGLISES. SCHEMATIC ARRANGEMENT OF FIGURES

The decorated portion lies about 100 yards inside this huge cave, in a recess on the left. In the Abbé Breuil's words, the figures are "modest but interesting vestiges." The decoration covers an area only 10 yards long, and one must know it is there to notice the few small subjects painted in an ocher that has almost completely faded. The decorated portion of the recess begins just a few steps inside, with engravings on the ceiling and on both sides. On the ceiling, the Abbé Breuil discerned one bison and noted the presence of lines. We have definitely found, to the left of the bison, the cervico-dorsal curve of a horse that is above clumps of lines forming "comets" and single and double strokes in alignment. To the right there are a few strokes and an incised oval. This engraved portion may not be linked with the other figures—the bison, the horse, and the paired signs (ovals and strokes) forming a small coherent composition in Style IV. The red-painted portion is a prolongation of the engraved portion, and extends over the ceiling and the side aisles. Even allowing for the fact that some figures have deteriorated or faded to the point of being unrecognizable, the general effect is extremely disjointed and peculiar. However, I do not think that there has been extensive damage; in sanctuaries where that has taken place, such as Sallèles-Cabardès, one always finds a complete figure here and there or readily identifiable fragments. Here, one has the impression of schematization carried to the extreme, where the end result (as in the Bayol cave) is hieroglyphics. The only identifiable animal figures are three horses and six or seven ibexes. One of the horses has the double shoulder line which turns up so often in Style IV. Moreover, there is one oval sign near a barbed sign and a few double strokes. The oddest feature is the presence of very elaborate signs in each group of figures (4–5–9, 6–7–8, 10, in fig. 161): the first group includes one horse, one ibex, and two signs; the second, one horse, two or three ibexes, and one sign[1]; the third, one horse, four ibexes, and one sign. These signs are of a unique type, although plainly referable to brace-shaped signs and tectiforms. Their appendages recall those in the "hut" sign at La Mouthe, the sign at Rocamadour, or the one at the back of the Vidal Gallery at Bédeilhac. The manner of filling in the signs is clearly related to that of the Cantabrian signs (at Altamira, El Castillo, or La Pasiega). Thus they would tend to push back the date of the figures toward the second period of Style III, but in view of the schematization of the animals, it is hard to decide. It is also odd that there is no animal of the female category. In group 10, the Abbé Breuil suggested the presence of one bison head, partly formed by a natural relief, and one bison hindquarters, but I remain undecided about that interpretation. It seems to me that the large signs alone represent the female complements to the animals of the male category.

"Modest but interesting" certainly describes the remains of decoration at Ussat, for they show that within the orderly development of figurative art during each epoch of the Upper Paleolithic, there are exceptions to the general rule not only in peripheral but also in central areas—Arcy-sur-Cure, for instance, where the signs and the bison/mammoth association deviate from the ordinary type; also El Buxu, Etcheberriko-Karbia, La Clotilde, Aldène, and Bayol. The Abbé Breuil assigned the various engraved and painted figures at Ussat to different periods between the Middle Magdalenian and the Azilian, placing the set of red figures at the late boundary of Magdalenian VI. I confess I cannot understand the reasons for this dating. The engraved portion has signs which have exact equivalents in the Breuil Gallery at Le Portel, nor does the bison contradict this chronological association with Early Style IV and the Middle Magdalenian. The painted portion could be somewhat older but certainly not later; to prove it is later, one would have to show the elongated signs with filled-in squares and an appendage at the top to be Magdalenian VI. This would involve moving the figures in Gallery A at La Pasiega up to the same date; the "black sequence" at Altamira would then be of the same epoch, and figures that Breuil himself correctly dated to be earlier would thus become Mesolithic and would imply that the mammoth survived down to the present era. Strange as it may seem, the Abbé Breuil, who so brilliantly demonstrated from the flint implements and the bone fossils that the Upper Paleolithic was a coherent world, did not apply the same principle to its religious and artistic aspects. Even granting that each cave was a tiny world of its own, the figures it contained were certainly governed by the same laws of relationship and similarity that mark all other human accomplishments within a given culture.

[1] *fig. 702*

ETCHEBERRIKO-KARBIA

CAHOUCIHIGUE, BASSES-PYRÉNÉES, FRANCE

The cave was discovered in 1908. Boucher noted the works in 1950; they were studied and inventoried by G. Laplace.

This cave is in the class of those having the sanctuary in the least accessible portion. Not until one has negotiated some 220 yards replete with speleological obstacles (bodies of water, winding passages, low tunnels barely large enough to crawl through), does one find a chamber, of which both walls are decorated with the first group of paintings. The works have greatly deteriorated and they are barely legible and probably incomplete, but extremely interesting. Executed partly in black paint and partly in brown clay, they also have dots and spots of ocher. On the right-hand wall there are horses and dots, along with unidentifiable outlines. The left-hand wall presents two groups of figures, the first composed of a small horse submerged in a spot of ocher, and an ibex painted in clay, the second of a bison painted in clay[1] and a horse rendered partly in black paint and partly in clay. Red and black dots, both scattered and in groups, appear on both walls. For all the gaps in this set, it contains a sufficient number of figures to enable us to discern its basic formula: bison/horse + ibex.

[1] *fig. 703*

Beyond this first decorated chamber, a very steeply sloping mass of stalagmite some 30 feet high leads to a raised terrace; crossing this, one comes to a sheer drop that can only be negotiated inside a narrow fissure with scarcely any handholds or footholds. The second set of figures is located at the bottom of this fissure on two adjoining walls, and consists of black paintings and red dots. Five horses can be seen, one of which is partly engraved, and traces of a sixth, also one ibex and one bison—this last facing a field of red dots, one portion of which forms a circle. The bison is strongly reminiscent of the small red bison placed in front of a circle of dots and various other figures of the same color in the Inner Gallery at Niaux, and the bison in the recess in the Breuil Gallery at Le Portel. The general theme again, is bison/horse + ibex.

The decoration of Etcheberriko-Karbia is classical and very homogeneous: a sanctuary with two identical compositions on the bison/horse + ibex theme. It does not seem to have had entrance, passageway, or back-cave figures, but these may be represented by a few dots placed in inconspicuous spots which have so far escaped observation. Indeed, there is such a dot on a stalagmite column at the exit from the first decorated chamber. Next to this red dot is still to be found a small quantity of ocher where the artist left it. One small flint tool was found near the vertical fissure.

The Abbé Breuil assigned Etcheberriko-Karbia to the Early Magdalenian. Bearing in mind that fairly often he understood "early" to mean Magdalenian III–IV (our Middle Magdalenian), there are serious arguments in favor of this dating. The first argument concerns the type of this sanctuary—far inside the cave and difficult of access. All caves of this type in the Franco-Cantabrian area seem in fact to contain sequences of figures in Early Style IV—Arcy-sur-Cure, Les Combarelles, La Cullalvera, Labastide, Montespan, La Mouthe, Niaux, Rouffignac, Santimamine, Les Trois Frères, Le Tuc d'Audoubert. These caves all present one or more of the following features: lengthy route to be traversed before the sanctuary is reached, places negotiable only by climbing or crawling, or other considerable obstacles.

The second argument is drawn from the type of composition. The bison/horse + ibex theme appears in the compositions of about fifteen caves: Las Monedas, La Pasiega (Gallery C, group 81), Les Combarelles, Angles-sur-l'Anglin, Le Cap Blanc, Niaux, Le Portel (the "*camarin*"), Les Trois Frères, Ussat. The decorations in all these caves—or at least the portions of them considered here—belong to Early Style IV. There are three exceptions: Pair-non-Pair (Style II), La Mouthe (panel with the "rhinoceros," Style III), Villars (Style III).

The third argument is based on style. The horses at Etcheberriko-Karbia, especially the two with a line dividing head from neck and withers, match those at Santimamine and La Cullalvera and those at Isturitz (lower cave), which is the nearest geographically. The bison in the first chamber at Etcheberriko-Karbia has the jutting mane cut off cleanly at the back, one of the most constant features of Early Style IV; the bison at the bottom of the fissure has the lowered head and the mane rendered in hatched lines running to the front which occur on several bison at Niaux and Les Trois Frères. In other words, all features of the Etcheberriko-Karbia figures have parallels in the Middle Magdalenian (III–IV).

ISTURITZ, LOWER CAVE

(*See also pages 326–327*)

Underneath the huge Isturitz cave is a separate lower cave, which is reached today via a man-made opening. One portion of it has walls of veined marble, with a dozen figures on the left-hand side. They were discovered by a group of cave explorers accompanied by G. Laplace.

[1] *figs. 704, 706*

[2] *fig. 705*

The figures are painted or scratched on the marble, forming a short but very coherent sequence. We find, first, three horses,[1] then an unfinished cervico-dorsal curve. The center of the sequence is occupied by an oval sign and a group of forked strokes. After that come the head of a bird (probably a crow), notable for its execution, then a bison in vertical position, a horse, and finally a deeply incised hind.[2] In other words, this set of figures is on the bison/horse + hind theme with an oval sign and strokes. The bison/horse + hind grouping is a Spanish formula; it is applied on the Altamira ceiling, in group 20 at El Castillo, and in El Pindal, which are in Early Style IV. At Altamira the animals are accompanied by claviforms and barbed signs, at El Pindal by claviforms and vulvar coats-of-arms, at El Castillo by a vulvar coat-of arms, and at Isturitz by one oval sign and forked signs. Except for the bird, the Isturitz animals are crudely executed, but the horses have a dividing line between the head and the neck, a feature which seems to characterize Style IV west of the Pyrenees. Consequently, this set of figures would seem to fall within the Middle Magdalenian.

MEDITERRANEAN PALEOLITHIC ART

Paolo Graziosi has created a subdivision of Paleolithic art by uniting eastern Spain, the lower Rhone Valley, and Italy into a separate "province." The distinction seems fully justified: the finds from these regions cannot be identified stylistically with the Franco-Cantabrian complex. It will be seen in the following pages that although the principles of decoration do not differ essentially from what we know elsewhere in the west—not surprising, considering that the basis of the figures and the layout remain the same all the way to Russia—nonetheless the dating criteria patiently developed for Franco-Cantabrian art do not apply here, and the age of the figures still remains a great mystery.

The difficulties of dating arise, first, from the smaller number of sites and excavations, and second, from the different character of the industrial objects found. These fit in with the established Perigordian and Magdalenian chronology only to a limited degree, or not at all. A technological complex known as the Romanellian, the evolution of which is still ill defined, is here substituted for our familiar divisions. The lower Rhone Valley should be especially helpful, for it is situated between the two areas, and indeed in this region several sites are known where western industrial objects apparently belong in the industrial strata of the Mediterranean area and have supplied us with some guideposts. Unfortunately, excavations at the Ardèche and the Gard have barely begun to profit from a modicum of scientific discipline, and most of the sites are still being pillaged more or less on the sly, either by curiosity seekers or by well-meaning individuals without technical training.

Thus it is almost blindfold that we shall examine the sites in the lower Rhone Valley (the Ardèche and the Gard), Italy, eastern Spain, and southern Spain. So far as Spain is concerned, we shall not consider its so-called Levantine art. That its Paleolithic character is in doubt is well known; the Abbé Breuil, long its principal defender on the score of dating, nonetheless omitted it from his *Quatre cents siècles de l'art pariétal,* and the omission appears justified. There is profound disparity between such dated Paleolithic works as are known from a few sites in eastern Spain and the works found in rock shelters in the Spanish Levant. I find among them no trace whatever of the general traditions of Paleolithic art, either in style or in content.

ITALIAN CAVE ART

Fairly numerous engravings have been discovered on the walls of Italian caves. The first set of decorations to become known was reported in 1905 by Paolo Emilio Stasi at the Romanelli cave (Otranto). In addition to several animal figures, among them a bovine, it includes rows of parallel strokes and ovals or "coats-of-arms," some of which are explicitly vulvar representations. Consequently this earliest-known set of figures is in an ambience that corresponds to the most classical features (animals associated with sexual signs) observable elsewhere.

In the course of recent years, important discoveries have been made in Sicily, on Levanzo (an island in the Egadi group), and at Monte Pellegrino (the caves of Addaura and Niscemi, near Palermo). These discoveries were made between 1950 and 1954. Still more recently, engravings were discovered in the Romito shelter, near Cosenza in Calabria.

The Romanelli and the Sicilian figures obviously belong to the same stylistic subdivision and must, at least for the time being, be considered together. The cursory treatment of the bovine figures at Romanelli is also to be found in some of the figures at Addaura, while other, very skillfully executed figures at Addaura have counterparts at Levanzo. The most striking feature of both these types of figure is the treatment of the bovine horns: these are represented by two parallel lines which are not connected with the base. This feature is also found on some engraved bovines on a plaquette from Parpallo (Valencia, Spain) and on others on the walls of the Ebbou cave (Ardèche). Unfortunately, the Parpallo plaquette comes from an undefined, perhaps Solutrean, level, and the Ebbou cave is no more accurately dated. Although the age of the Italian figures has not yet been determined, they are of major importance for understanding the figurative complex of the Upper Paleolithic. We have seen that paired signs were found at Romanelli; at Levanzo there are real compositions including oxen and horses, complemented by the stag. Thus we have here the familiar ox/horse + stag composition, the same that we find at Lascaux, Gargas, Pair-non-Pair, Las Chimeneas, Teyjat, and, in the Mediterranean subgroup, at Ebbou.

The contrasting or complementary animal groups suggest we might look for a second degree of complementarity-or-opposition in a number of the Franco-Cantabrian caves, for at both Levanzo and Monte Pellegrino the ox component is represented by a bull following a cow, and the stag component by stags following hinds; the same may be true of the horse component, for these animals several times appear in pairs.

The Levanzo cave contains a few human figures, one a schematized personage with a bird's beak. The Addaura cave has an extraordinary composition in which we find, among paired animals (deer and equids), a dozen human figures with bird beaks.[1] This group of figures has already provided the subject for many commentaries; it represents a very animated scene or a sequence of events. At the lower left we find a man who seems to be walking and carrying weapons; he is followed by a woman carrying a basket or bulky sack over her shoulder. The rest of the scene shows walking personages, and a man carrying a spear, who is placed just above a large figure of a deer. At the upper right, half a dozen personages in restless attitudes form a ring around two men who seem to be lying on the ground, their feet drawn up over their buttocks; their sexual parts are visible, and there may be a rope pulling up their ankles behind them to neck and shoulders. The scene has been interpreted either as a dance involving possession by spirits, with the possessed dancers rolling on the ground among their companions, or as a scene of ritual strangulation. It is hard to find anything comparable in the Franco-Cantabrian area. The only anecdotal subjects found there are scenes of violence where a human being is attacked by an animal (Lascaux, Le Roc de Sers, etc.). In this respect the Addaura group seems to fall within the general tradition, for to all appearances it is concerned with a violent scene. However, the variety of attitudes and the way some of the personages are shown walking or performing other clearly portrayed actions are not at all in the Franco-Cantabrian tradition, but rather in that of Spanish Levantine or North African art.

_{[1] fig. 710}

THE CHABOT CAVE

AIGUÈZE, GARD, FRANCE

The Chabot cave is the oldest decorated cave in the sense that here, for the first time, a prehistorian noticed the presence of Paleolithic figures. It was in 1878, a year before the discovery of the Altamira figures, that L. Chiron saw the engravings on the left-hand wall and decided they were related to the prehistoric layers he was excavating. The value of this observation was only recognized many years later.

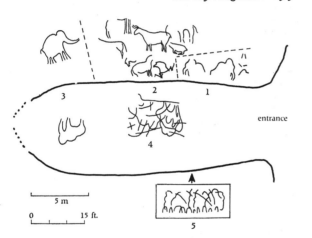

162. THE CHABOT CAVE. SCHEMATIC PLAN AND ARRANGEMENT OF FIGURES

1, 2, and 3 *Main panel, ox/horse + mammoth theme with a possible cervid.*
4 *Ceiling covered with lines, among which several mammoths can be made out.*
5 *Panel of very tangled outlines of mammoths.*

The cave, situated at the exit from the canyon of the Ardèche River, is quite a shallow one, 15 to 20 feet wide at the entrance. The engravings occupy the two walls and the ceiling inside the first few yards of the cave; in other words, they were directly exposed to daylight. In the Franco-Cantabrian domain, this feature, although not ruled out in Magdalenian sanctuaries, characterizes practically all sanctuaries prior to the Early Magdalenian. The engravings are rather deeply incised and their outlines are stiff—a characteristic common to all the caves in the Ardèche canyon. The composition is very clear and almost standard: the right-hand wall is occupied by grouped animal figures, the ceiling is covered with a large number of lines and unfinished outlines, and the left-hand wall presents an extraordinary tangle of unfinished outlines and parallel strokes. Clearly, we have here a panel of animals and signs, and above and opposite it, a large area of scrawls and unfinished outlines. The layout of La Baume Latrone is absolutely identical.

THE PANEL OF FIGURES (1, 2, 3)

The Abbé Breuil, followed by the Abbé Glory and Dr. E. Drouot, deciphered the figures in the right-hand panel. They have been repainted in black, which helps visitors to understand them but distracts attention from some important details.

The central portion is occupied by the large figure of an ox.[1] Around it are several figures, none of them very legible, but in front and at the bottom one recognizes four horses, and in the rear a mammoth and the figure of an animal with legs drawn in, whose head merges with the thigh of the ox. This animal, though much stiffer, brings to mind the deer in the great scene in the Addaura cave in Sicily. Thus the fundamental theme seems to be ox/horse + cervid. This theme is common to almost all the Mediterranean caves (Le

_{[1] fig. 715}

Figuier, Ebbou, Bayol, Levanzo, Addaura, La Pileta), with the addition of the ibex (Ebbou, Bayol, La Pileta) or the mammoth (Le Figuier, Ebbou). Though this arrangement of the central portion is perfectly clear, it is rather paradoxical that there should be so many mammoths. About ten of these animals[2] surround the central composition, and practically the only decipherable figures among the unfinished outlines are also mammoths. The main composition includes paired signs: a large elongated oval, of the type found in the Romanelli cave, is visible above the cervid, and many double strokes appear along the entire frieze.

[2] figs. 712, 713

THE UNFINISHED OUTLINES (4, 5)

On the ceiling there is a network of outlines among which two large mammoths stand out.[3] The left-hand wall offers a real accumulation of mammoths, engraved and re-engraved on top of one another to such a degree that it is only with great difficulty that their mostly unfinished outlines can be made out. This was the wall that so impressed Chiron and other prehistorians of the period; the countless intersections of lines, though purely fortuitous, were interpreted at that time as a host of figures.

[3] fig. 714

The perfect parallelism between the Chabot cave and the other caves in the canyon of the Ardèche precludes any doubt that they were contemporary. The fact that the theme of Chabot is the same as that of other Mediterranean caves, except for its emphasis on the mammoth, is equally striking. On the other hand, the style of the figures is uncommon. We find it again in Le Figuier but not elsewhere, and the only Franco-Cantabrian figures in a somewhat related style are the two mammoths on the pierced staff from Laugerie Haute which belongs to the period between the Gravettian and the Solutrean. Dating the cave is difficult. The figures have an archaic quality which does not necessarily imply great antiquity. However, the horses bring to mind the Franco-Cantabrian Style II. On the other hand, the Chabot cave, like Le Figuier, yielded fairly abundant proto-Solutrean and Solutrean deposits. The so-called "Rhone-basin" Solutrean, like the one in the Pyrenees, has been supposed to be of later date than the Solutrean in the Charente and the Dordogne, but this was merely a working hypothesis which present-day research by no means corroborates. Consequently we may suppose that the Chabot engravings, executed in full daylight, related to Style II, and accompanied by proto-Solutrean deposits, are in fact ancient and go back to that epoch. This agrees with the opinions of Combier, Drouot, and Huchard.

LE FIGUIER

SAINT-MARTIN D'ARDÈCHE, ARDÈCHE, FRANCE

The engravings were discovered in 1890 by L. Chiron and were studied by the Abbé Breuil, the Abbé Glory, and Dr. E. Drouot.

The site is a shelter about 65 feet long at the mouth of the Ardèche canyon, almost directly opposite the Chabot cave. The works were executed in full daylight and are comparable in every respect to those in the Chabot cave.

Six groups of lines are found on the walls. The first group, near the exit from a tunnel to the right of the shelter, consists of lines drawn in every direction, among which we can make out a very crude horse's head. At the left, the second subject is the forequarters of some horned animal, possibly an ox. The third and fourth subjects appear on the wall of a recess; they consist of a mammoth and an uncertain figure behind it; of this last we can make out, clearly enough, a stag's head. The fifth is a group of straight and curved lines; here no identifiable contour can be distinguished. The sixth subject seems to be a mammoth accompanied by a row of vertical lines. What survives of the shelter's decoration is sufficient for us to recognize the same list of animals as at Chabot: ox/horse + stag and mammoth. The best-preserved mammoth so closely resembles the mammoths at Chabot that their contemporaneity is beyond doubt. A small neighboring cave, the Grotte Huchard, contains some unidentifiable remains of engravings.

THE OULEN CAVE

OULEN, ARDÈCHE, FRANCE

The engravings in the front portion of the cave were reported in 1947 by Dr. Paul Raymond, C. de Serres, and Gayte; in 1951 they discovered behind it the chamber with the paintings. The original floor of the chamber, covered with industrial objects and bones, was permitted to be pillaged by visitors. Excavations made at different times yielded several industrial layers corresponding to the proto-Solutrean and the stages immediately following. So far there has been only partial publication of the works. (In the Abbé Breuil's account, mention is made of a cave at Rimousens, La Baume Paschaline, supposedly containing paintings similar to those at Oulen. I have visited it carefully, guided by a local resident who knew where the paintings were located, and I do not believe that they are anything except natural streaks of ocher whose capricious contours could be mistaken for paintings. A few small black dots near the back of the cave and at a few topographically prominent points perhaps indicate that decorations may once have existed.)

The Oulen site consists of a large rock shelter where the engravings were executed in daylight, and a cave behind, low-ceilinged but fairly vast. The chamber is reached by way of a corridor which, according to Gayte, was blocked up with proto-Solutrean deposits when discovered. If no other entrance exists, this would suggest that the figures in the cave proper are prior to the proto-Solutrean—that is, that they date from the period between the Gravettian and the Solutrean, or even from the Gravettian.

THE FRONT SHELTER

The deeply incised engravings are distributed all along the right half of the shelter, in an arrangement similar to that of Le Figuier. Most of the figures are incomplete, the rock having been worn away to some extent, and it is hard to tell how sizable the missing parts may have been. I counted five subjects, from right to left.

The first, to the right of the corridor entrance, is a bison; the middle part of its body is missing; to the left of it there are lines, vestiges of some unknown figure. On the left of the corridor entrance we find first another bison whose head is worn away; continuing left, there is a mammoth which, when intact, must have been a fine figure. The fragments recall the little mammoths in Franco-Cantabrian Style IV much more than the large mammoths in the Chabot cave. Still farther on there is a fifth subject, interesting and well-preserved, consisting of two paired signs—an oval with two rows of small strokes above it. The style of the figures is hard to determine for lack of comparative data: so far as I know, these are the only representations of bison (apart from those at Ebbou, to be discussed later) in the Mediterreanean subgroup. The fundamental theme included the bison, and this is enough to distinguish Oulen from the other caves in the Ardèche canyon. Dating it, however, is impossible because archaeology can furnish only paltry clues from this site, which was once so rich.

THE BACK CAVE

The figures in the cave proper are covered by a calcareous film, and we may imagine there once were some that are invisible today. Those that are there now are sufficiently decipherable to enable us to make out their exact contours. They are certainly the crudest of all known cave paintings—those at Ebbou and La Baume Latrone shine by comparison. These red paintings are aligned along the left-hand wall as far as a small recess, where a few engravings have been added.

We first encounter one line inside a bell-shaped hollow in the ceiling, then the cervico-dorsal line of a mammoth (6–7). If we crawl to the far wall inside a first recess (8), we find two signs more elaborate than the rest; each consists of a brace-shaped sign and two rows of dots. The next bend in the wall shows one red stroke and three black strokes. Next comes the central composition consisting of three small panels (10). The eye is struck first by two cervico-dorsal lines of mammoths (one of which may represent another animal); to the left there is a very sketchy ibex; the panel is completed by three triangles, two groups of strokes, and one spot of color. The second panel, if possible still more meager, contains four triangles, three strokes, and, at the lower left, what I would very tentatively consider to be an ibex. The third panel contains two lines. The recess that comes next (11) contains a triangle reduced to two lines converging at the apex; below it is one dot, and still farther down, three strokes. At the back of the side chamber (12) there is a schematized mammoth, and then a collection of very interesting signs. The ceiling vault forms a springing here, on the back of which are scrawls, some forming the apexes of triangles (13b); the other side shows a group of scratched vertical lines next to another apex of a triangle executed in the same technique (13a). Opposite, on the back wall, there is a red triangle (14).

Despite its distinct meagerness, the cave at Oulen is very interesting. The decoration here is reduced to the indispensable—one entrance mammoth, one mammoth + ibex composition, one back-cave mammoth, and two groups of paired triangle/strokes signs. Dating this chamber will remain pure guesswork until archaeological analysis of what survives at the site provides some light. For my part, I am incapable of choosing between a pre-Solutrean and a post-Solutrean dating.

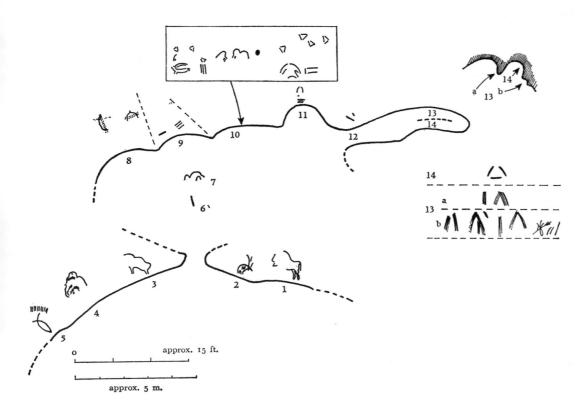

163. THE OULEN CAVE. SCHEMATIC PLAN AND ARRANGEMENT OF FIGURES

1 to 5 *Figures exposed to daylight. From right to left: bison, deteriorated outlines, bison, mammoth, paired signs.*

6 to 14 *Figures in the back cave. Highly schematized figures, among which we can make out a mammoth and an ibex accompanied by paired signs.*

EBBOU

VALLON, ARDÈCHE, FRANCE

This cave, the most important yet discovered in the Rhone Valley, is situated a short distance from the Pont d'Arc, at the entrance to the Ardèche canyon. The more accessible of the engravings were recognized before 1912 by Dr. Jullien; those further inside were discovered in 1946 by the Abbé A. Glory, who also made the drawings. So far there has been no complete publication of the finds.

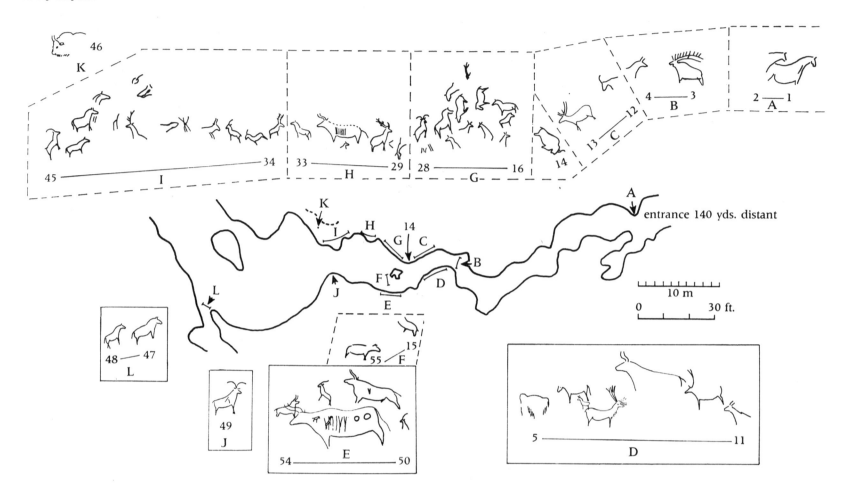

164. EBBOU. SCHEMATIC PLAN AND ARRANGEMENT OF FIGURES

Note, in particular:

1. *The single mammoth at D 5.*
2. *The horse as introductory and back-cave animal (A 1 and L 47–48).*
3. *The predominance of horses in group G, of oxen in panel E opposite.*
4. *The repetition of the ox as central element at E and H.*
5. *The accumulation of male symbols toward the back of the cave, at I and J: stag, ibex, horse.*
6. *The intrusion of two bison of later date, at 14 and K 46.*

The cave consists of one fairly large chamber, with a gallery 275 yards long that opens off at the back. At a point about 150 yards from the entrance there is a shaft (A); just beyond it begins the decoration with entrance animals. Some 20 yards farther on we come to a chamber about 45 yards long (B–L) which contains the remaining figures. All the works at Ebbou are engraved on the soft calcareous film which covers the walls.

The animals at the entrance are two horses, one following the other. The fact is the more interesting because the back-cave animals also consist of two horses similarly arranged. This supplies further verification of the rule we have observed, that entrance and back-cave symbols are often identical. Usually this applies to signs. We find both entrance and back-cave horses, whether or not associated with signs, at El Castillo and Font-de-Gaume, and I have noted a total of fifteen instances of back-cave horses.

The entrance to the decorated chamber is marked by a series of springings of the ceiling vaults. The first figures encountered are a stag and, facing it, the forequarters of an animal which may be a hind (A). Next, following the corridor, we come to a large composition, the center[1] of which is taken up by one ox, one horse, and one ibex, surrounded by four stags and one mammoth (D). Opposite these we see an ibex and a stag (C). As will be made clear later on, the two following compositions are based on the same formula: ox/horse + ibex with lateral stags. This mammoth, however, is the only one in this cave. It may be noted that this

[1] *figs. 716, 717*

385

first portion of the sanctuary contains six cervids, while the rest includes only four. As in the Franco-Cantabrian region, the stag predominates near the entrance, in passageways, and often at the back of caves.

At the top of the climb that brings us to the large decorated chamber, a large table-shaped block of stone lies on the ground. Visitors in our time have trampled it considerably and I did not have time to clean it, but it seems to have lines on it, and it is in the ideal position to serve as an area of scrawls and unfinished outlines (F). The main composition appears on two walls, on either side of the block. On the left (E), we see one bull nearly 2 yards long, bearing paired signs (two circles and eight strokes) on its body, and two small animal figures, at least one of which seems to be a horse. Above them is another bull[2] bearing a V-shaped wound mark, with another bovine ahead of it. The large bull is flanked by ibexes.[3] On the right (G), we find eight horses[4] accompanied by one stag, three hinds, and some ibexes; a few strokes complete the group. Under a small vault (14), close to the ground, there is an engraved bison, of which more will be said later. The second composition is on a smaller scale (H): an ox whose body is marked with strokes is accompanied by a horse and a hind. A stag[5] separates the first composition from the second.

The last group in the sequence is a frieze (I) that shows, in turn, one stag, two ibexes, two signs (apparently a vulva and phallus, both schematized), then one oval vulva extended by a stroke, and next to it a carnivore's head. This last is poorly executed but can only be that of a bear or some animal of the dog family. This group is interesting because it brings to mind a theme known from Magdalenian decorated objects found west of here—namely, male and female symbols placed in front of a bear's head. Then come two horses, one hind (?), and one ibex. In a small recessed vault (K) there is a bison head[6] executed in the same technique as the bison in the big composition. The group terminates with one ibex[7] and the two horses headed in the same direction (L), which have already been mentioned.

The Ebbou decorations are completely orthodox in every respect. The entrance and back-cave figures are male symbols (horses); the stags appear at the entrance and in passages between the compositions. There are three ox/horse groups, the central group being on a larger scale than the others and including paired signs. The last group of figures includes only animals of the male category (stag, horse, ibex) and sexual symbols which come fairly close to realism. Even if these features were not to be observed in other caves of the region, Ebbou would be sufficient to prove that Paleolithic tradition in the Rhone Valley was closely related to that in the Franco-Cantabrian area. The only jarring note is supplied by the bison which intrude (without their complementary horses) into the two compositions in the large chamber. The treatment of these, however, has nothing in common stylistically with that of the other animals. One is scratched; the other is finely engraved, with hair very detailed, in the technique so obviously Franco-Cantabrian that the head would be perfectly at home at Les Trois Frères, Niaux, Rouffignac, or on art objects from any site between Poitou and the Pyrenees. This is plainly a matter of later interpolations among the other figures; viewed in this light, their position is very clear. In fact, the locations of these bison are not fortuitous. We have seen that the first composition is developed on two facing walls, oxen to one side, horses to the other. The Paleolithic visitors who rediscovered this sanctuary must have felt the absence of the female symbol in the panel of horses, and so, following the tradition of Early Style IV farther west, they added a bison, not an ox. Continuing their analysis of the old engravings, they made no additions to the second composition, in which the ox and horse are contiguous, but, because the group at the end comprised only stag, horse, and ibex, they transformed it into a supplementary composition by adding the second bison head. Did the western Magdalenians make other additions? The Ebbou style is so distinctive that the addition of other animals scarcely seems possible; perhaps they were responsible for adding the sexual symbols and the bear's head in the last group, but I find no convincing indications in support of this view.

The engraved bison supply a noteworthy chronological guidepost: the bison/horse group is autochthonous to the Middle Magdalenian. To what period can the figures on the ox/horse theme go back? The Abbé Breuil took no stand on this matter: he reported the special character of the animals with unfinished legs and the ibexes with one horn or two in frontal view, and he correctly noted affinities between the oxen at Ebbou and those in Italian caves. He alluded to possible affinities with the art of Spanish Morocco, which I find less persuasive than affinities with the engraved plaquettes from Parpallo in eastern Spain. Unfortunately the remarkable engraved oxen from Parpallo are of uncertain age, and the related engravings in Italy are associated with Romanellian industrial artifacts, in which Gravettian features persist down to the end of the Upper Paleolithic. When we compare Chabot, Le Figuier, and Oulen, it seems that the Ardèche may have had a period in which the ox/horse theme gave way to the bison/horse theme: at Ebbou the same phenomenon clearly takes place. This succession could have been purely fortuitous, but for the fact that Franco-Cantabrian art exhibits the same sequence. The ox/horse group, as a fundamental theme, occurs at Las Chimeneas, Pair-non-Pair, Bourdeilles, Lascaux, in the earlier work at La Mouthe, and at Font-de-Gaume; elsewhere it appears only as a throwback, in decorations where the compositions are based on the bison/horse theme. Now, in all these caves, the figures belong to Style II or Style III, and are prior to the Middle Magdalenian.

But the parallelism stops here, for the Ebbou figures do not all have the features of Style III. Distended bodies, diverging legs, special treatment of horns such as brow antlers in back parallel to the beam in front—none of these is found here. Except for the horns of some ibexes, the outlines wherever they are simple exhibit the proportions and flexibility of Style IV. In conclusion, we can scarcely arrive at any but a fairly vague dating: the Ebbou figures cannot be later than Early Style IV and may date, within a few centuries, from the same period (13,000–11,000 B.C.). Or, if stylistic traditions in the Rhone Valley were really unrelated to those farther west, the figures may go back to the limits of the Solutrean. I refrain from suggesting so early a date for two reasons: first, we would have to assume that the forms within the Mediterranean subdivision matured precociously, an assumption which the dated evidence from Parpallo does not justify; second, we would have to assume that underground sanctuaries existed in the Mediterranean region before they were known in the Franco-Cantabrian region.

[2] fig. 719
[3] figs. 718, 721
[4] fig. 724

[5] fig. 720

[6] fig. 723
[7] fig. 722

THE BAYOL CAVE

COLLIAS, GARD, FRANCE

The figures were discovered in 1927 by the Abbé Bayol, whose excavations unfortunately cast no light on their age.
Dr. E. Drouot published an excellent description of the decoration.

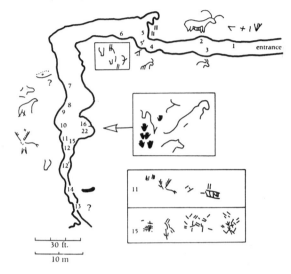

165. THE BAYOL CAVE. SCHEMATIC PLAN AND ARRANGEMENT OF FIGURES
(Plan after Dr. E. Drouot; the numbering of the figures is also his.)
Note, in particular:
1. *The position of the ibexes at the entrance, 2, 3, and 4.*
2. *The double strokes where the cave narrows at the end of the daylight zone (5 and 5′).*
3. *The extreme schematism of the figures, especially the horses (6, 12′, and 16), consisting of no more than partial outlines of heads.*

The Bayol cave has some affinities with the rear portion of the Oulen cave. The painted figures are very poorly executed and considerably abbreviated, but they appear in a rather remarkable order.

The cave has the form of a corridor about 160 yards long. The portion receiving daylight runs straight, then a bend follows where the cave begins to slope downward; at the bottom there is a chamber and beyond it a narrow tunnel which terminates the cave. The daylight portion contains, on the right, first a sequence of signs (goose-track, strokes, cross, apex of triangle) and then an ibex,[1] which is the most elaborate figure in the cave. The horns are in frontal view, and the M-line of ventral modeling is present. Opposite, a bit farther on, two more ibexes are represented by their schematized heads. These are normal entrance figures, like the stag and the horse. In the first narrowing of the bend we find signs in black which are passageway signs of the ordinary type—three strokes and a dot on the left, double strokes on the right. Here the unlighted section begins. Next comes a wall with a panel of animal figures reduced, literally, to signs (6). Dr. Drouot interprets them as a horse, a mammoth, and a bison; there seem, rather, to be two heads of horses indicated by the muzzles, a line showing the forehead and trunk of a mammoth, and a line showing the forehead and horn of a bovid which is not necessarily a bison. In addition there are two double strokes. Bovid/horse/mammoth is the theme at the Chabot cave and the Le Figuier shelter. We need all the comparative data we can get from other Rhone Valley sites to decipher this little group of hieroglyphics.

The chamber at the bottom of the downslope contains some figures that are more explicit, though not all are so. The main composition takes up a large panel at the left. In its upper portion we see side by side the forehead of a highly stylized horse, the head of an ox, an absolutely remarkable feline—its outline drawn like a twisted wire to render with much restraint the chest, head, back, and tail. In the lower portion of the panel[2] we find a horse's head of a more common type, and next to it six hands coated with clay were applied one above the other. Ox/horse + lion and hands thus seem to form the main theme. This theme is similar to that at La Baume Latrone (mammoth/horse + feline and hands); moreover, the Bayol feline enables us to interpret the figure at La Baume Latrone which has hitherto been taken for a snake.

Opposite this central composition are several animals which have been interpreted as a snake's head, a bear, and a horse (16–22); except for the last-mentioned, they seem to me indefinable. Next we come to a baffling set of figures occurring on both walls. Among them there is, beyond question, one stag whose location on the periphery of the central group, near the end of the cave, is normal. The rest (11–15) consist of lines which Dr. Drouot likens to Chinese characters, while the Abbé Breuil sees them as merely stains left by torches and presenting "no artistic or graphic interest." However, they actually are signs which are not unrelated to those in the rear portion of the Oulen site; they are signs that have been extremely simplified in comparison to the usual forms, as are these animal figures compared to the figures in Franco-Cantabrian art. They include several double strokes and two paired signs which we also find at Oulen (converging strokes and single stroke), and there is even a kind of oval with antennae, flanked by a double stroke. I wonder whether these grouped figures may not represent the area of unfinished outlines. Finally, on the right, in a last recess, we find a horse's head in red[3] reduced in outline to the muzzle, and in the terminal tunnel one curved red line. Dr. Drouot saw a figure a bit farther on, but I was unable to find it.

It would be wrong to underestimate the interest of the Bayol cave: like the rear portion of Oulen, it presents evidence that in the art of the Rhone Valley abstraction was carried to a point of unintelligibility for today's prehistorian, who does not possess their oral context. Whereas in Franco-Cantabrian art only the signs achieve graphic abstraction, here the animals themselves tend to become signs. Clues for dating the Bayol cave are extremely scanty, perhaps nonexistent. It has affinities with the rear portion of Oulen and perhaps with La Baume Latrone. Its extreme schematization does not necessarily assign it to a late epoch: the engraved slabs at the Abri Cellier in the Dordogne show that there were highly conventionalized figures

[1] *fig. 725*

[2] *fig. 726*

[3] *fig. 727*

as early as the Aurignacian. The entrance ibex exhibits the ventral modeling line which, in the Franco-Cantabrian region, would point to Early Style IV; but does this apply here? The uncertainties governing all the caves in the Mediterranean area call our attention to the immense amount of work done in the Franco-Cantabrian region over a period of fifty years, and to the wealth of comparative data available there. They also show us—alas!—that although serious excavation has recently been begun in the Ardèche and the Gard, that same half-century, in which there was no scarcity of prehistorians, has yielded virtually no scientific results in this region.

LA BAUME LATRONE

NÎMES, GARD, FRANCE

The paintings at La Baume Latrone were discovered in 1940 by a group of young speleologists; in 1941 the Abbé A. Glory made a pictorial inventory. A number of archaeological excavations were made at the entrance, but no valid scientific results emerged. Colonel Louis made a boring in the chamber containing the paintings; unfortunately, the operation yielded no archaeological data.

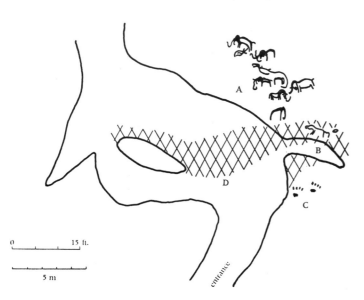

166. LA BAUME LATRONE. SCHEMATIC PLAN WITH ARRANGEMENT OF FIGURES
A   *Painted panel on the theme mammoth/horse + feline, with one oval sign.*
B   *Very sketchy horse and oval sign.*
C   *Positive hands.*
D   *Area where the walls and ceiling are covered with scrawls.*

0   15 ft.

5 m

This is a cave several hundred yards long in which, about 220 yards from the entrance, there is a vast decorated chamber. Getting to it today involves a good deal of trouble: a descent to the bottom of a shaft, followed by a steep slope. A priori, this cave seems to belong to the category of sanctuaries far inside the caves and hard to reach. All examples of this category hitherto known have belonged to the Middle Magdalenian, but the style of these figures rather rules out Magdalenian III–IV. I wonder whether systematic exploration might not lead to the discovery of some easier, shorter route from the surface, blocked up since the Upper Paleolithic.

The layout of the sanctuary is quite remarkable, very similar to that of the Chabot cave. The back of the chamber is taken up by a large fresco several yards long, executed with fingers coated with clay found on the spot. On the ceiling, just above the fresco and extending over nearly the entire chamber, are thousands of meandering lines and scrawls. At the entrance, on the right, several positive hands can barely be made out. In a niche at the bottom to the right of the fresco, there is an engraving which has been believed to represent a young rhinoceros without horns; I am inclined to interpret it as a very sketchily rendered horse, the head of which is closely related to the heads of the horses at La Pileta and some figures at Ebbou.

[1] *figs. 728, 729, 731, 733*

The central composition is highly interesting. It consists of seven proboscidian figures[1] framing an animal which has been interpreted as a snake; the figure which passes as a clumsily executed rhinoceros is at the lower right. These pardonable identifications of the animals at La Baume Latrone surely need reviewing. The proboscidians were regarded as an early species of elephant which had survived in the Mediterranean region longer than elsewhere. Although this paleontological approach has something to be said for it, it is beside the point here. The stylization of the La Baume Latrone elephants is so extreme and so varied that they may equally well be interpreted as mammoths rendered in a fantastic way.[2] I shall keep to this hypothesis, at least for the present. The figure thought to be a snake[3] is so much like that of the feline in the central composition at the Bayol cave that its identification as a feline seems certain. As for the "rhinoceros"[4] (the Abbé Glory's drawing of it is incomplete), there can be no possible doubt that we here have a horse, the tip of whose muzzle is touching a half-oval sign which is perfectly clear on the original. This horse, which has all four legs, also has a dark spot on the withers, and a chest like those we know from many examples in Style III. Its ears are in frontal perspective, on either side of the neck. Consequently, the composition as a whole is definitely on the mammoth/horse + feline theme, with accompanying oval figure.

[2] *charts* XLVII, XLIX
[3] *fig. 730*
[4] *fig. 732*

The style of the La Baume Latrone figures seems to have no parallel among either the Mediterranean or the Franco-Cantabrian caves. What is even more striking about the seven proboscidians than their primitive character is the absence of consistent conventions in their presentation. Except that the tusks of three figures are in frontal perspective, and that three subjects have limply swinging trunks, the treatment of these figures cannot be reduced to a coherent canon. The feline is too schematized to lend itself to lengthy analysis. We can incontestably make out the head and the bared fangs, a rather firm cervico-dorsal line, and the long tail which is flicked around toward the front of the body; the feline in the Bayol cave, though more skillfully rendered, consists of the same elements. It is hard to say whether the other lines represent the feline's body and legs or an entirely different subject. The figure of the horse is scarcely more explicit in style. The spot on the chest is a detail frequently observed in Style III, but there is no parallel anywhere for the other stylistic traits. To sum up, it seems impossible to arrive at any very definite conclusion: the composition as a whole is closely related to that in the Chabot cave which is held to be proto-Solutrean, but the figure of the feline is comparable only to the figure in the Bayol cave, which has not been dated, and there are no stylistic similarities with Franco-Cantabrian art. Before we can attempt to establish the chronological position of La Baume Latrone, we shall have to wait until Mediterranean cave art is better known and better understood.

ALDÈNE

CESSERAS, HÉRAULT, FRANCE

The vast galleries of this enormous cave (also known as the Fauzan cave and the cave of Minerva) formerly sheltered a population of cave bears which, like the human inhabitants, left very extensive remains. All these were to all practical purposes entirely destroyed when the site was mined for phosphate. The loss is irreparable: in view of the cave's geographical position, the rich deposits here could have provided an invaluable guidepost. In 1948 the Abbé M. Cathala discovered in a lower gallery, along with bear and hyena tracks, a long trail of children's footprints made in the soft clay during the Paleolithic.

The known engravings are more than 300 yards from the entrance, in a side gallery. They were discovered by Guerret in 1927.

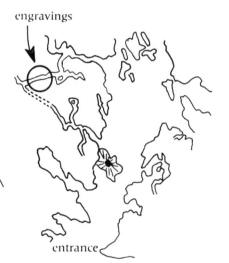

167. ALDÈNE. SCHEMATIC PLAN OF THE FRONT PART OF THE CAVE
(Based on the plan used by the guide.) The portion shown here measures about 325 yards.

In the course of the phosphate mining many obstructions have been cleared away and many former openings blocked up; at present it is hard to say where the gallery with the engravings was situated in Paleolithic times. The area with the engravings seems formerly to have been the back end of a much longer gallery, that is now blocked by debris from the mining operations. The wall on which the engravings were executed has the consistency of chalk, and they look more like scrawls than real engravings. As is usual in caves inhabited by bears, the walls are marked with numerous claw scratches; these were made earlier than the engravings. The figures are strikingly crude in execution and give an impression of great antiquity. Closer examination, however, reveals several skillfully rendered outlines, suggesting an already mature stage of the Upper Paleolithic.

Only seven works are visible today. On the right-hand side of the gallery we see first a large, rather vague figure of an animal (2).[1] Then comes a fairly unusual figure (4) which is believed to represent a rhinoceros: the single horn ends in a shape like a flaming spark, and the eyes (or ears) are rendered by two corkscrew lines. The whole, however, does suggest a rhinoceros more than any other animal.

On the right-hand side, high up (7), there is an incontestable horse's head[2] with mane clearly indicated. The rendering of the muzzle suggests that the animal at 2, on the opposite side, might also be a horse. The remaining four figures are all carnivores. One of them very probably represents a bear; the figure has been touched up with red ocher on the forepart of the body. The figure at 1 is not as easily identifiable as might seem at first sight; photographs necessarily show it in a foreshortening, that, by seemingly lengthening the figure, makes it resemble a bear. Yet when we examine it from the front, we may wonder whether it is perhaps a feline instead. As for the figure at 6,[3] no doubt is possible—the profile is that of one of the finest felines in Quaternary art, the equal in zoological verisimilitude to that at Les Combarelles. The little figure under it (5) cannot be identified with certainty; it is probably a feline, at least judging by the shape and size of the tail. Various signs can be made out over the figures or near them, most of them parallel lines of a later date than the claw scratches; I have not reproduced them on the drawing. On the figure at 6 there is a "comet"-shaped cluster of lines. L. Méroc has also reported a claviform sign drawn across the head of the figure at 2. Although I tried hard to find it—for this sign would furnish a solid dating—I was unable to make it out.

[1] *Numbers refer to fig. 168*

[2] *fig. 736*

[3] *fig. 737*

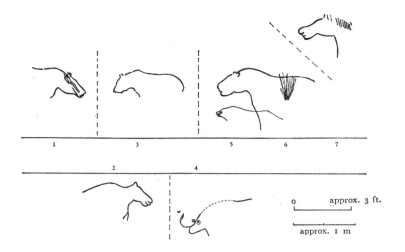

What strikes us in the inventory of the engravings at Aldène is that only back-cave figures are present—bear, feline, horse, rhinoceros—no central figures. This suggests that what we know of this sanctuary is only one portion of the set of figures that once existed. Acting on this impression, we have looked for the figures that would normally precede the present set, but the front part of the gallery was apparently blocked up by the recent mining operations. The dating problem is particularly ticklish. The nature of the chalky rock and the scratching technique used to execute the figures gives them an archaic look that further emphasizes the clumsiness of the figures at 2, 4, and 7. Yet the figures at 1, 3, and 6 (all carnivores) are very skillful. I do not think that a reasonably certain dating can be attained without further points of reference.

SALLÈLES-CABARDÈS, THE GAZEL CAVE

AUDE, FRANCE

This site was excavated as early as 1836—a fact which explains the present condition of the deposits in the inhabited part. In 1947 a speleological group discovered a tunnel leading to a round chamber which contains the first engravings. These were recognized by Dr. M. Cannac and J. Ruffel, who also observed the little panel of goats in the low-ceilinged gallery beyond the round chamber. They made drawings of a number of the figures.

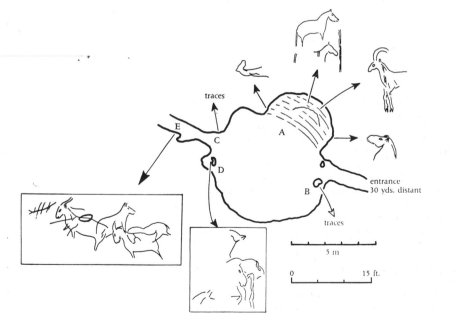

Except for the panel with the goats, the engravings were executed in thin lines on the calcite deposit over the walls of the round chamber. As the calcite has largely crumbled away, all we have left are the ruins of a sanctuary. The most important group seems to have been represented on a rising slope of stalagmite which forms the southern side of the chamber. Figures survive only on the nearly vertical walls surrounding this deposit.

Cannac and Ruffel noticed two horses accompanied by vertical lines, and a fairly well-executed ibex at the back of the south wall. In the other parts of the chamber they could only point out several engraved lines on the north wall.

On the semicircular portion of the south wall containing the horses and the ibex (A), we have been able to make out a horse's head at the right, and the forequarters of a little horse on the left, shown upside down. On a stalagmite at the western side of the chamber are some lines we have been unable to decipher, and the wall above it also has lines very hard to make out. By contrast, on the wall side of a large stalagmite (D), at the left of the entrance to the passage containing the panel of ibexes, there is a set of very fine engravings. We could not interpret the figures on the spot, but photographs taken under a variety of lighting arrangements made it possible to distinguish two horse's heads, the forequarters of a bison, and a few lines. On a vault springing to the left of the gallery leading to the back of the cave is a little panel (30 inches) which displays the masterpiece of the entire cave. It comprises two ibexes, one following the other, the first with the S-shaped horns of the male Pyrenean ibex, the second with the smaller horns of the female.[1] Above them is a vague figure of an animal, and overlapping the hindparts of the female an incomplete figure, possibly a horse. The animals are marked with lines and two signs—one an oval and one a large barbed sign.

What survives of the incised work in this cave seems to have belonged to a small sanctuary; its coherent structure can still be made out. The lines on the column near the entrance may be all that is left of a panel of scrawls and unfinished outlines. The main composition took up the south wall, and only a few of its peripheral figures have survived—three horses, one ibex, and the little upside-down horse which resembles certain figures at Ebbou in position if not in style. A second composition, somewhat abbreviated, as is frequently the case, existed on the stalagmite at the east side of the chamber; it discloses one bison, perhaps the sole survivor of the others that must have been found on these walls. That there was a back-cave group is shown by the panel of ibexes, which are not unlike the pairs of back-cave ibexes at Spanish sites.

The style of the surviving figures supplies a few clues to the possible age of the decorations. The ibex, the bison, and the horses belong unmistakably to Style IV, though it is impossible to pin down this attribution more closely. The back-cave ibexes are rather vague typologically; the heads in normal perspective, and the ears of the male also point to Style IV. The signs, especially the oval one, suggest the same tendency, and toward Late rather than Early Style IV. The large barbed sign which looks something like a parrot's perch occurs on decorated objects from the Late Magdalenian—for instance, on a small bone plaquette from Bruniquel. Consequently, everything points to the Magdalenian, probably somewhere around Magdalenian V, as the period in which these figures were executed. Taken as a whole they are closer in style to Franco-Cantabrian than to Mediterranean works. Like the bison head at Ebbou they show that western influence had reached the Rhone basin around the Middle and Late Magdalenian.

[1] *fig. 737*

LA PILETA

BENAOJAN, MALAGA, SPAIN

The decoration at La Pileta was discovered in 1911 by Colonel Willoughby Verner, who later took part in cave explorations with Hugo Obermaier, Paul Wernert, and the Abbé Breuil. The cave is very vast; only parts of the decoration have been catalogued. Without further study it is hard to work out the general plan of the compositions. Nor is it possible, on the basis of the available archaeological data, to form a very precise idea of the periods represented.

The available documents give only a vague notion of the layout of this sanctuary, which I have not had the opportunity to study on the spot. The Abbé Breuil's drawings, however, show very clearly the same symbolic features as in Franco-Cantabrian caves. The animals represented are the horse, the ox, the ibex, the stag, and the fish. One of the groups (*Quatre cents siècles d'art pariétal*, fig. 514) includes a composition of the classic type. From bottom to top, we find first a cow,[1] then a bull's head associated with a female sign in the form of a goose track, then a horse,[2] under the belly of which is a small stag. Above the horse is a sign that seems to be a variant of the barbed sign from the male category. This, then, would be a composition of the ox/horse + stag type, accompanied by corresponding sexual symbols. It is interesting to note that the female group is represented both by a cow and by a head which is obviously that of a bull; this brings to mind the large compositions in the Rotunda and the Axial Gallery at Lascaux, where a kind of opposition made itself felt between the cows and the bulls within the ox group. The figures are surrounded and marked by numerous double strokes. It should be particularly noted that the cow shows, at the shoulder level, a wound mark formed by two converging lines—beneath which we see a double stroke which seems clearly associated with it; comparable examples are numerous, but we may especially cite the bison engraved in clay in the terminal corridor at Niaux.

As for the other panels, they do not for the time being lend themselves to even partial interpretation. In addition to the animal species mentioned, there are also many signs which may be related to the Franco-Cantabrian quadrangular sign, and meandering lines, scrawls, and numerous groups of strokes. The style of the figures is hard to define; it is fairly close to that of the engravings at Ebbou, hence the figures are probably in Style III. The figures at La Pileta are palpably Mediterranean in character; for them, as for the entire Mediterranean group, a more precise dating would be dangerous.

[1] *fig. 738*
[2] *fig. 739*

11. DOCUMENTARY PHOTOGRAPHS

NOTE ON THE PHOTOGRAPHS

Cave engravings are often thought to defy photography; in any case, they are difficult to read from a single angle of lighting. This fact justifies the use of drawings in all publications on prehistoric art. As a rule, the drawings are made from rubbings on paper applied to the cave wall, or from a sheet of cellophane or other transparent plastic material stretched on a frame. A different method was used for this book. A series of photographs was taken with light from various angles, and at the same time drawings were made on the spot. The tracings were obtained by superimposing the different photographs; in cases where the photographs are hard to interpret, the sight drawings were used and comparisons were made whenever possible with the previous drawings. In the great majority of cases, the final readings agreed completely with previous decipherings; however, some variations have occurred, justifiable by the difficulties of disentangling the cave engravings with complete certainty. In this book drawing is used as a simple process of analysis to aid interpretation by isolating characteristic features: the artistic quality of the works is to be found only in the photographic reproductions.

The captions under the photographs are for identification only; for detailed information, see pages 472–490.

170. LE PLACARD. EARLY MAGDALENIAN

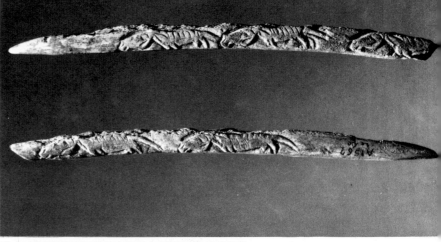

171. LA MADELEINE (DORDOGNE), LATE MAGDALENIAN

172. EL PENDO. MAGDALENIAN

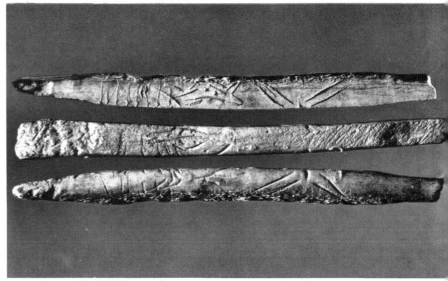

173. LE SENCI. LATE MAGDALENIAN

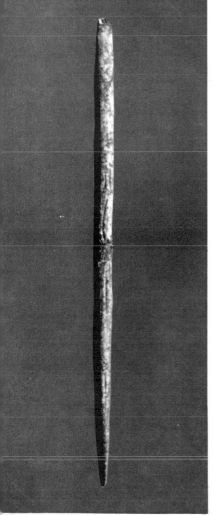

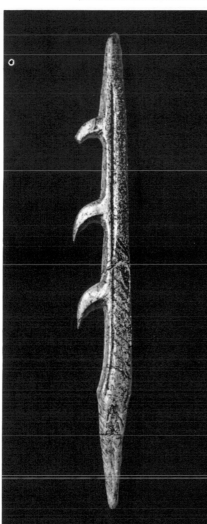

174. ISTURITZ. LATE MAGDALENIAŇ   HARPOONS   175, 176, 177. LE SENCI. LATE MAGDALENIAN

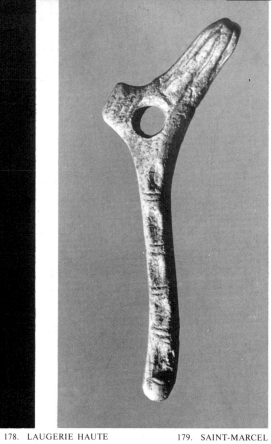

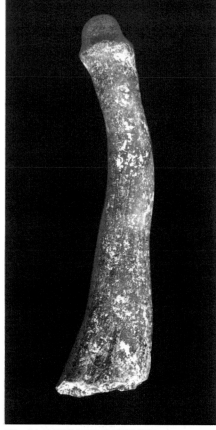

PIERCED STAFFS   178. LAUGERIE HAUTE   179. SAINT-MARCEL   180. LA MADELEINE (DORDOGNE)   181. ARUDY

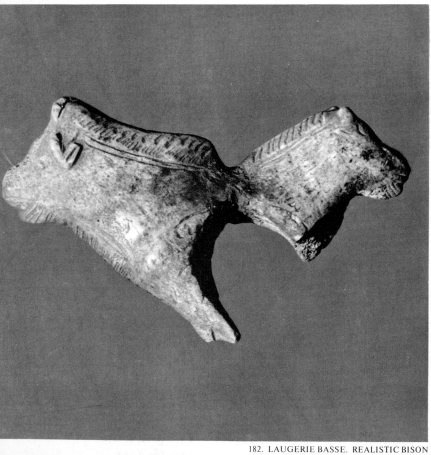

182. LAUGERIE BASSE. REALISTIC BISON   183, 184. LA MADELEINE *(left)*, LAUGERIE BASSE. SCHEMATIC BISON

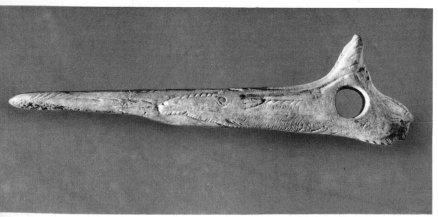

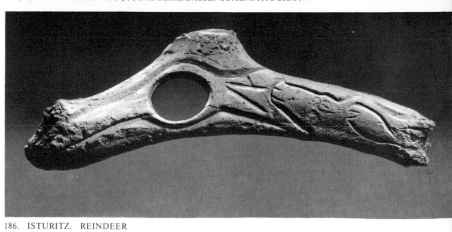

185. LAUGERIE BASSE. REINDEER   186. ISTURITZ. REINDEER

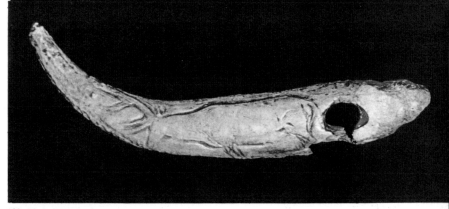

187. THAYNGEN-KESSLERLOCH. REINDEER

188. EL CASTILLO. STAG

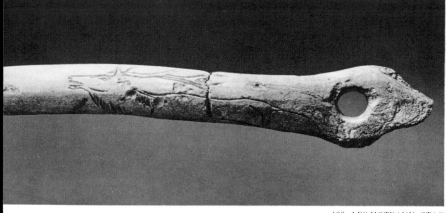

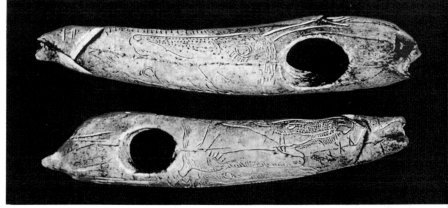

189. LES HOTEAUX. STAG

190. EL PENDO. STAG, HINDS, AND HORSE

192. LA MADELEINE (DORDOGNE). HORSES

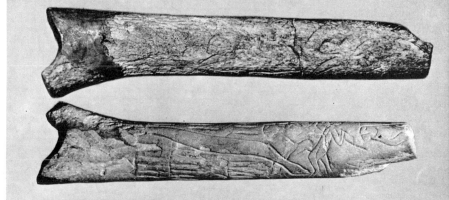

191. SAINT-MARCEL. MALE HUMAN FIGURE

193. LA MADELEINE. BISON, HORSE, MALE HUMAN FIGURE, AND SNAKE

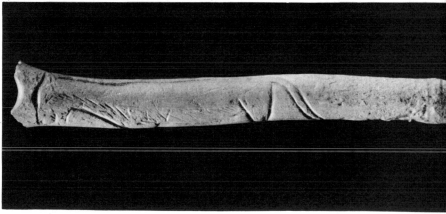

194. SCHWEITZERBILD (SWITZERLAND). HORSE

195. LAUGERIE BASSE. FELINE

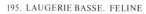

397

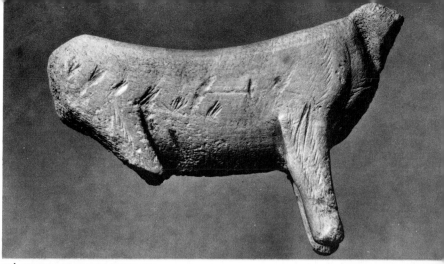

SPEAR THROWERS   196. ENLÈNE. HEADLESS IBEX   197. ARUDY. HEADLESS REINDEER

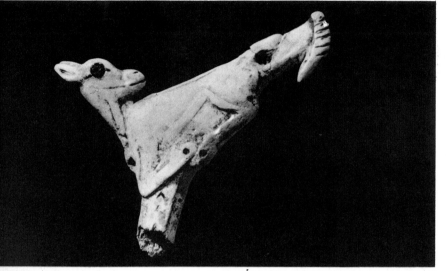

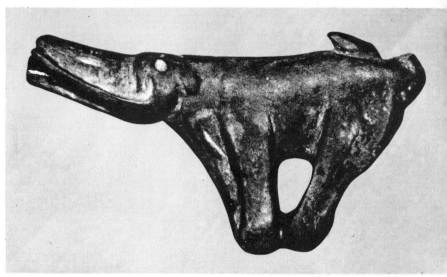

198. BÉDEILHAC. IBEX WITH HEAD TURNED BACK   199. BRUNIQUEL. MAMMOTH

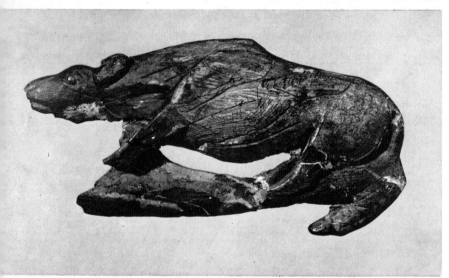

200. LA MADELEINE (DORDOGNE). FELINE   201. LA MADELEINE. BISON WITH HEAD TURNED BACK

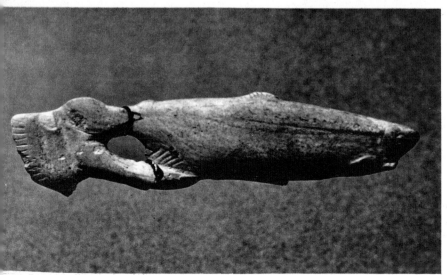

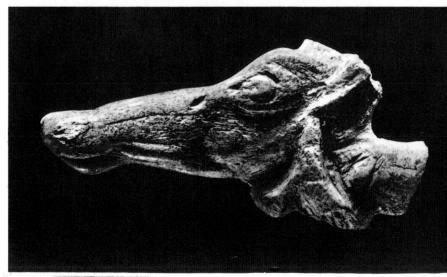

202. LOURDES. FISH OF THE SALMON FAMILY   203. LAUGERIE BASSE. REINDEER

204. LES TROIS FRÈRES. BIRDS

205. LE MAS D'AZIL. IBEX

206. LE MAS D'AZIL. HORSE'S SKULL AND TWO HORSES' HEADS

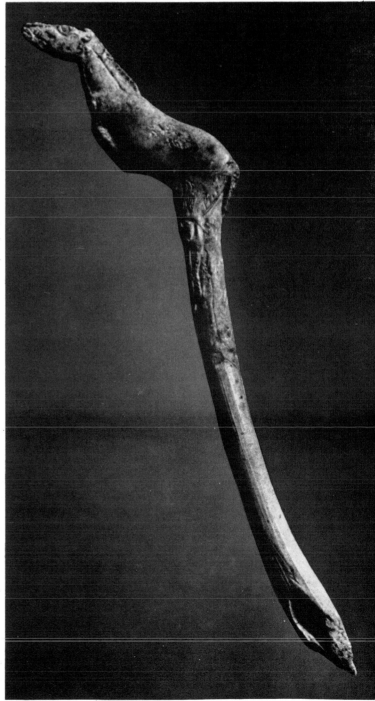

207. BRUNIQUEL. LEAPING HORSE *(see fig. 35)*

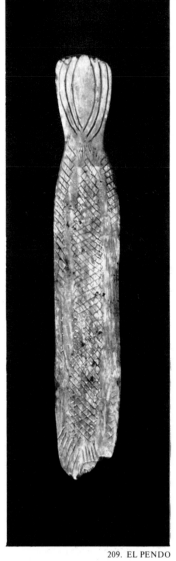

SPATULAS   208. LES EYZIES   209. EL PENDO   210. LAUGERIE BASSE   211. SAINT-MARCEL   212. LAUGERIE BASSE

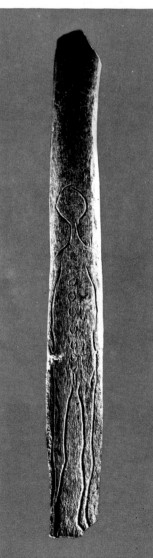

213. ISTURITZ   214. BRUNIQUEL   215. PEKARNA

HALF-ROUNDED RODS 216. LAMADELEINE (DORDOGNE). BEAR AND SEXUAL THEME *(Lower diagram:* PIERCED STAFF FROM MASSAT)

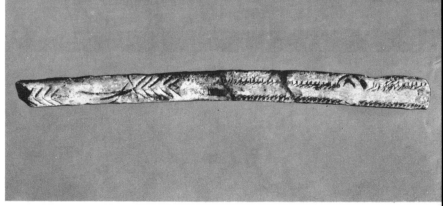

217. LAUGERIE BASSE. CERVIDS 218. LAUGERIE BASSE. GEOMETRIC THEMES

219. ISTURITZ. SCHEMATIC THEMES

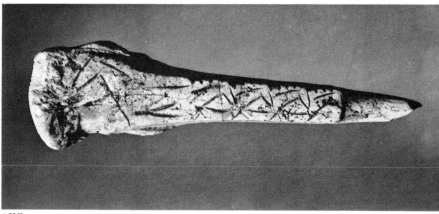

220. ISTURITZ. GEOMETRIC THEMES   AWL   221. LE SENCI. BONE WITH FRIEZE OF HORSES

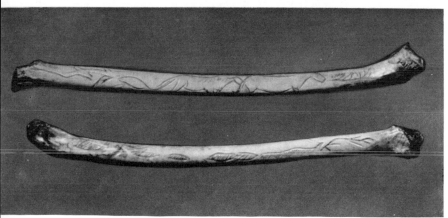

TUBE   222. EL VALLE. HOLLOW BONE WITH STAG, HORSES, AND "FISH"

401

PENDANTS   223, 224, 225. ARCY-SUR-CURE. ANIMAL TEETH AND BONE. COPY AND FOSSIL OF STAG CANINE TOOTH. CARVED AND ENGRAVED BONE   226. ISTURITZ. BEAR

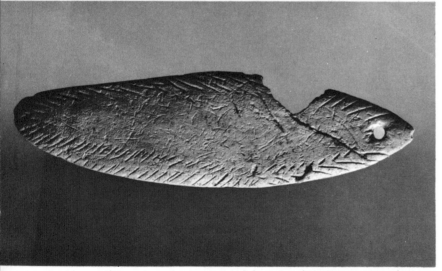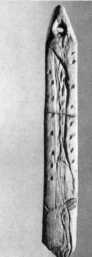

227. SAINT-MARCEL. SEXUAL THEME   228. ISTURITZ. SEXUAL THEMES   229. LESPUGUE. SNAKES   230, 231. LAUGERIE BASSE. GEOMETRIC THEMES   232. ISTURITZ. HORSE

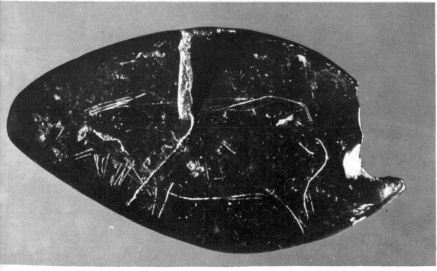

233. ISTURITZ. OVAL PENDANT   234. LESPUGUE. SOLE

235. BOURDEILLES. REINDEER   236. RAYMONDEN. BISON AND MEN

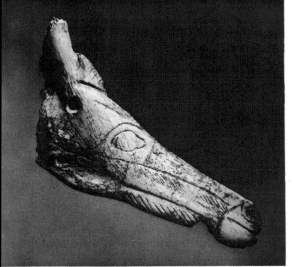

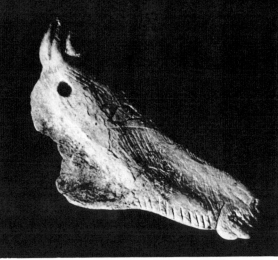

ARVED SILHOUETTES

237, 238, 239. ISTURITZ. HORSES' HEADS

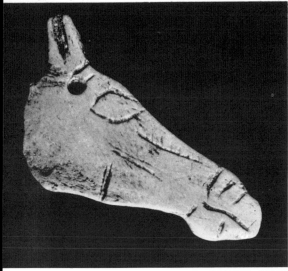

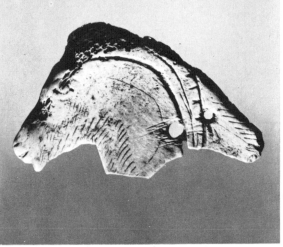

240. LE PORTEL. HORSE

241. ISTURITZ. IBEX

242. ARUDY. HORSE

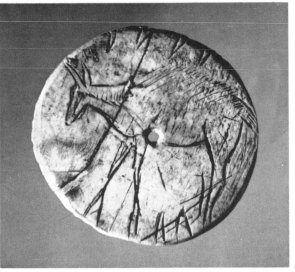

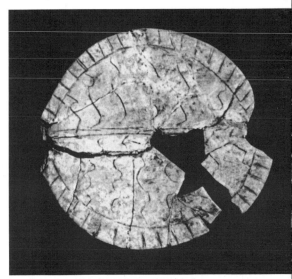

DISKS

243. LAUGERIE BASSE. CALF

245. LAUGERIE BASSE. CHAMOIS (?)

247. LE MAS D'AZIL. GEOMETRIC THEMES

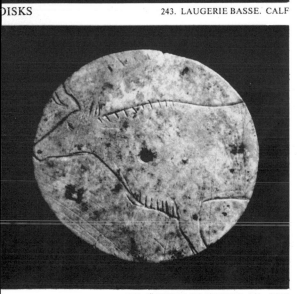

244. REVERSE SIDE OF FIG. 243. COW

246. REVERSE SIDE OF FIG. 245. CHAMOIS

248. BRUNIQUEL. IBEX

STYLE I. ENGRAVED SLABS

249, 250, 251. LA FERRASSIE AND ABRI CELLIER. ENGRAVED VULVAS

252. ABRI CELLIER. IBEX AND OVAL

253. ABRI CELLIER. ANIMAL HEAD, VULVA, AND STROKES

254. LA FERRASSIE. QUADRUPED, VULVA, AND DOTS

256. BELCAYRE. HERBIVORE WITH SHORT TAIL

255. LA FERRASSIE. ANIMAL, OVALS, AND LINES

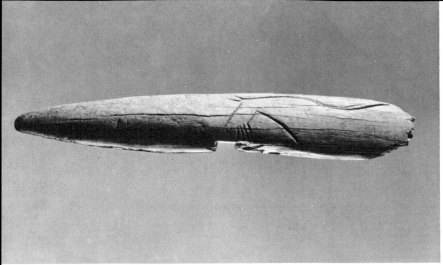

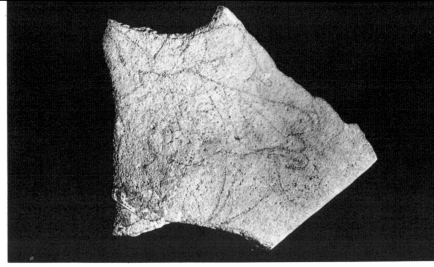

STYLE II. OBJECTS WITH ANIMAL FIGURES   257. ISTURITZ. HORSE   258. LAUGERIE HAUTE. HORSE'S HEAD

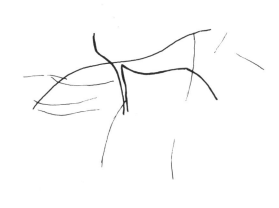

259. ISTURITZ. UNFINISHED OUTLINES

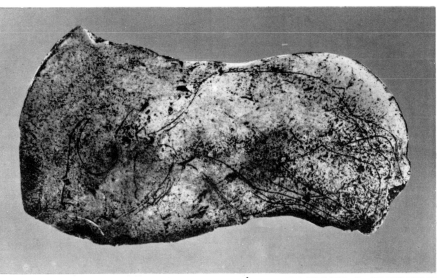

260. LES REBIÈRES. RHINOCEROS HEAD AND HERBIVORE

261. DOLNI VESTONICE. HEAD OF A FELINE   262. DOLNI VESTONICE. HEAD OF A RHINOCEROS

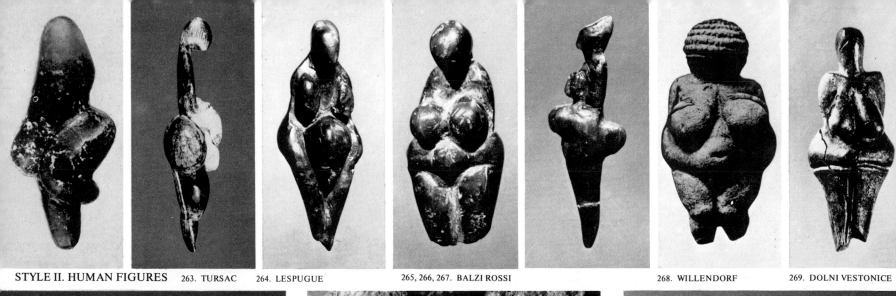

STYLE II. HUMAN FIGURES   263. TURSAC   264. LESPUGUE   265, 266, 267. BALZI ROSSI   268. WILLENDORF   269. DOLNI VESTONICE

270. LAUSSEL. MALE FIGURE   271. LAUSSEL. "WOMAN WITH HORN"   272. LAUSSEL. WOMAN HOLDING AN OBJECT

273. LAUSSEL. THE "SCENE"   274. LAUSSEL. WOMAN HOLDING AN OBJECT

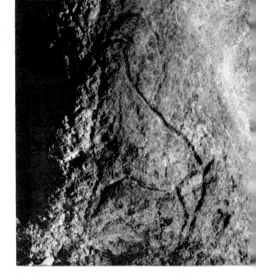

TYLE II. CAVE ART. PAIR-NON-PAIR   275-279. PANELS 1 AND 2   275, 276. IBEXES

277. HORSES   278. BISON   279. MAMMOTH

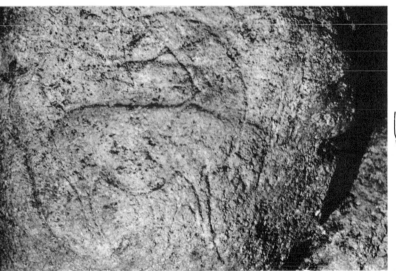

280. PANEL 3. HORSE AND IBEX   281. PANEL 5. AUROCHS

282. PANEL 4. LARGE-HORNED DEER AND TWO IBEXES   283. PANEL 9. MAMMOTH

LA MOUTHE   284. BULLS AND HORSE

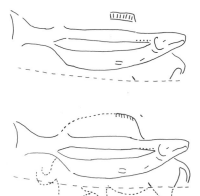

GORGE D'ENFER   285. SALMON

LA GRÈZE   286. BISON

LA MOUTHE   287. BULL

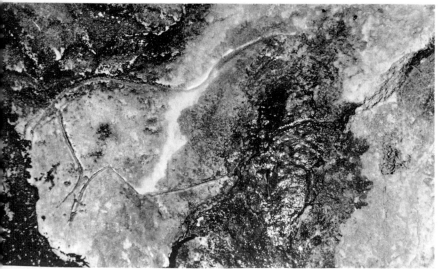

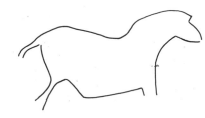

LOS HORNOS   288. HORSE

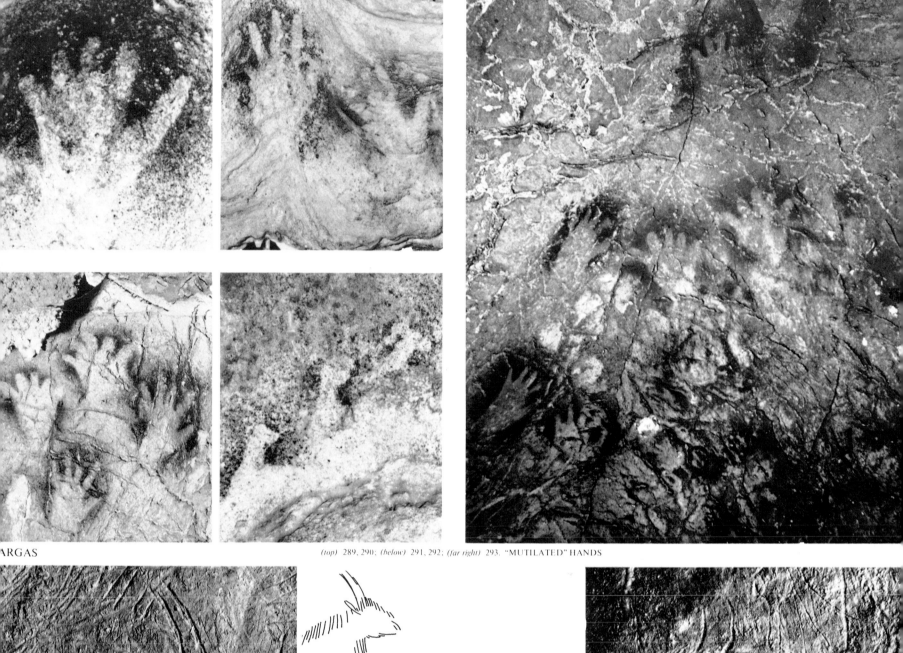

ARGAS   *(top)* 289, 290; *(below)* 291, 292; *(far right)* 293. "MUTILATED" HANDS

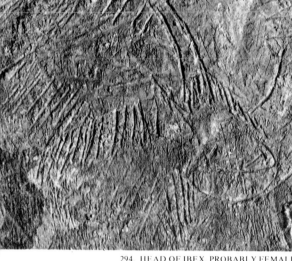

294. HEAD OF IBEX, PROBABLY FEMALE

295. BISON

296. IBEX   297. IBEX

299. FOREQUARTERS OF A HORSE

GARGAS *(cont.)*   298. IBEX

300. HORSE

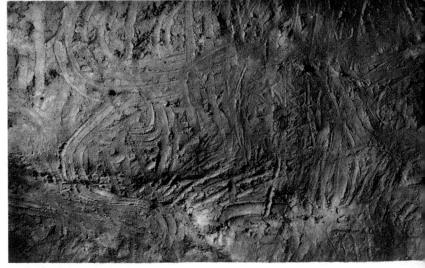

301. BISON

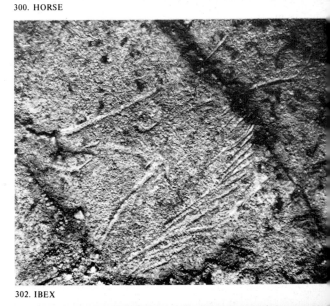

302. IBEX

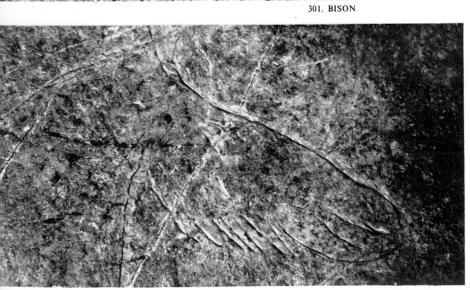

303. HEAD OF A HORSE   304. BISON DRAWN WITH FINGER ON CLAY

410

305. MAN PURSUED BY A BISON   306. HORSE   307. HORSE

308. HORSE SCULPTURED ON A BISON   309. HORSE AND BISON, HEAD OF LATTER REWORKED

310. BIRD   311. FRAGMENTARY LARGE-HORNED DEER (MALE)

312. IBEX   313. FACING IBEXES

LASCAUX

314. ROTUNDA. "UNICORN," COW AND HORSE

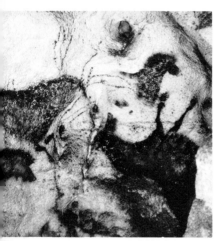

315. AXIAL GALLERY. FALLING HORSE

316. AXIAL GALLERY. COWS AND HORSES. QUADRANGULAR SIGNS. BACK-CAVE IBEXES

318. NAVE. HORSES/BISON COMPOSITION WITH COMPLEMENTARY SIGNS

321. NAVE. COW AND HORSES. QUADRANGULAR SIGNS

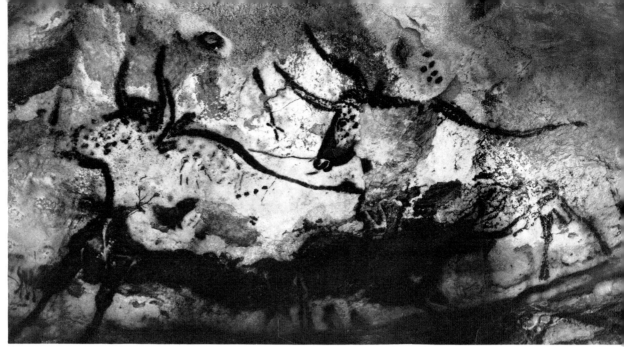

LLS AND RED COWS

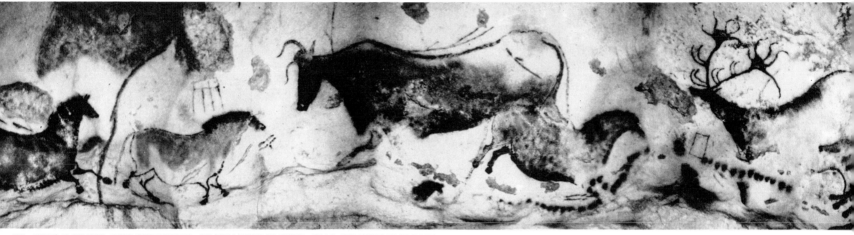

317. AXIAL GALLERY. COW AND HORSES. QUADRANGULAR SIGNS. STAG AND ENTRANCE DOTS

319. AXIAL GALLERY. COWS AND HORSES

320. AXIAL GALLERY. BULL AND COWS

322. NAVE. ENTRANCE STAGS AND DOTS

LASCAUX *(cont.)*   323. SHAFT. RHINOCEROS AND BACK-CAVE DOTS. MAN THROWN TO THE GROUND BY A BISON   324. SHAFT. HORSE COMPLEMENTARY TO

325. AXIAL GALLERY. LARGE HORSE AND BARBED-SIGN

326. AXIAL GALLERY. BACK-CAVE HORSE AND ROW OF DOTS

327. ROTUNDA. ENTRANCE STAG OF THE AXIAL GALLERY

328. ROTUNDA. STAGS BETWEEN TWO SEQUENCES OF AUROCHS

329. AXIAL GALLERY. BULL

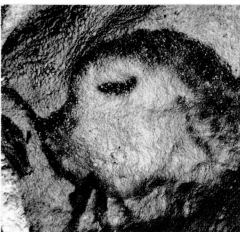

330. AXIAL GALLERY. BACK-CAVE BISON

331. NAVE. BACK-CAVE BISON

332. CHAMBER OF FELINES. IBEXES, TWO FACING FELINES, BARBED SIGNS AND SCRAWLS, HORSE IN FRONTAL VIEW, HEAD OF A BISON

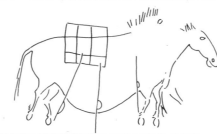

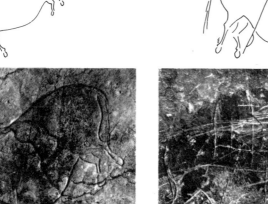

333. PASSAGEWAY. HORSE

334. APSE. HORSE, QUADRANGULAR SIGN, CLAVIFORMS

335. APSE. REINDEER

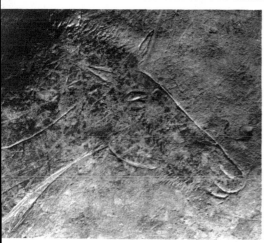

336. APSE. HORSE'S HEAD WITH REWORKED EYES

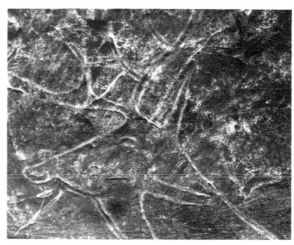

337. APSE. STAG HEAD

338. NAVE. HEADS OF IBEXES

339. HORSE'S HEAD 340. BISON WITH HORNS IN FRONTAL PERSPECTIVE

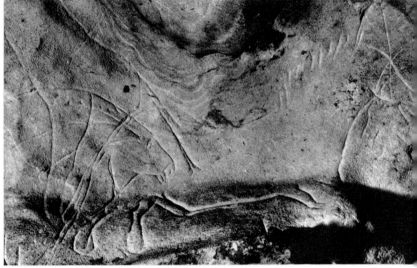

341. BISON WITH HORNS IN SEMIFRONTAL PERSPECTIVE 342. HORSE

343. AUROCHS 344. CERVID

345. HORSE 346. HORSE

347. FELINE HEAD 348. FELINE

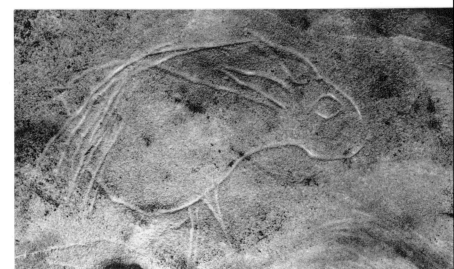

349. FANTASTIC ANIMAL – "GIRAFFE" 350. "HARE"

351. FANTASTIC ANIMAL – FELINE (?) 352. HORSE'S HEAD 353. "WOMAN WITH PARKA"

354. BARBED SIGN 355. QUADRANGULAR SIGN 356. ROWS OF LINES

417

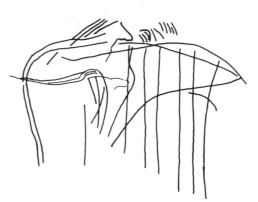

VILLARS   357. UNFINISHED OUTLINES

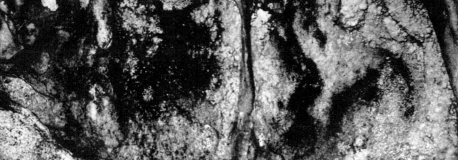

358. MAN AND BISON

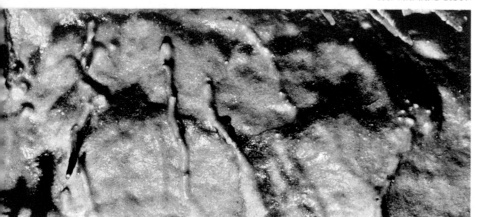

359. HORSE

LA MOUTHE   360. BISON AND IBEXES

SAINT-CIRQ   361. BACK-CAVE PANEL

418

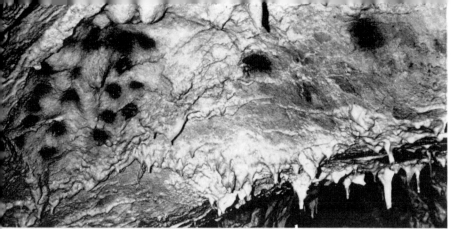

362. LE COMBEL. QUADRANGULAR SIGN AND DOTS

363. LE COMBEL. "CHAMBER OF ANTELOPES." DOTS AND STALACTITES

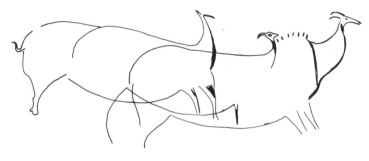

364. LE COMBEL. PANEL OF "ANTELOPES"

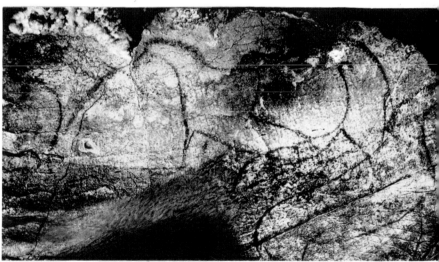

365. LE COMBEL. PANEL WITH "LIONESS"

366. BIG CHAMBER. PANEL OF "DOTTED" HORSES AND HANDS

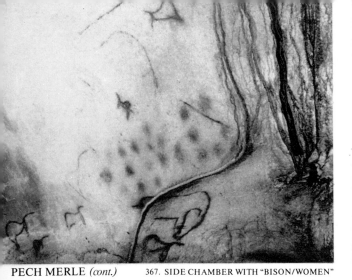
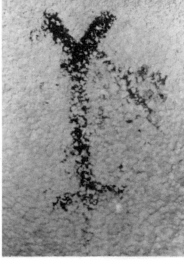

367. SIDE CHAMBER WITH "BISON/WOMEN"   372, 373. SIDE CHAMBER OF "THE WOUNDED MAN." BARBED SIGN AND ROW OF LINES

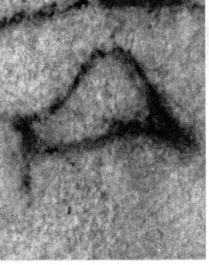
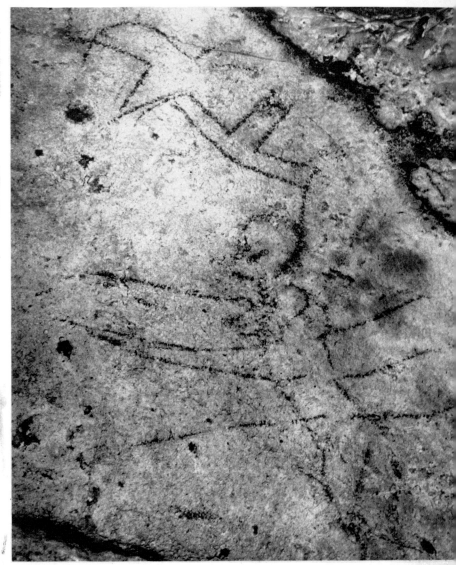

368-371. FROM BISON PROFILE TO FEMALE PROFILE

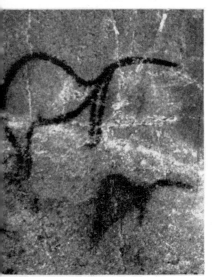

374. MAN PIERCED WITH LINES AND BRACE SIGN

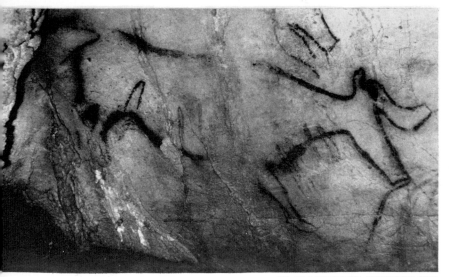
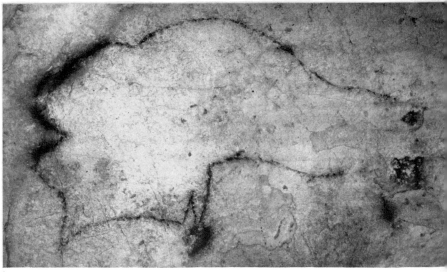

375. BIG CHAMBER. WOUNDED COW   376. BIG CHAMBER. BISON

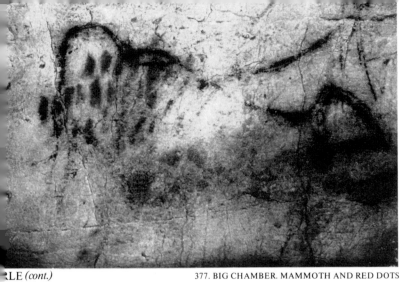

RLE (cont.)

377. BIG CHAMBER. MAMMOTH AND RED DOTS

378. BIG CHAMBER. MAMMOTH

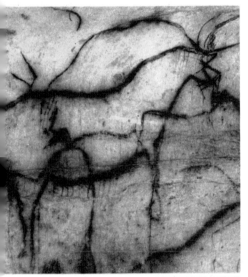

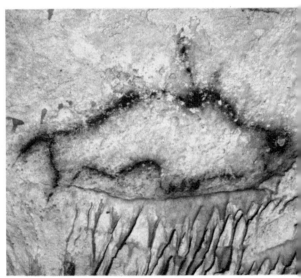

379. BIG CHAMBER. BISON/HORSE GROUP

380. ENGRAVED BEAR IN THE "BEAR CORRIDOR"

381. BIG CHAMBER. BISON AND LINE

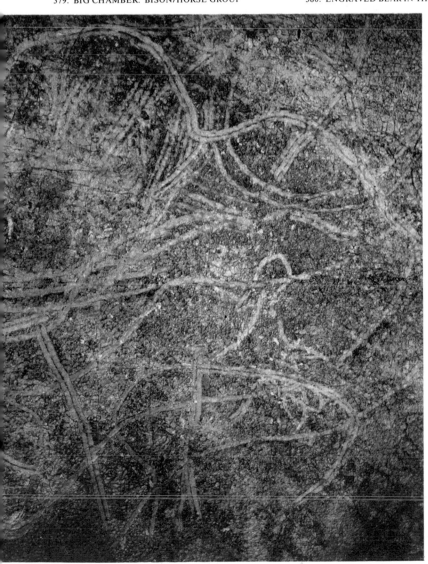

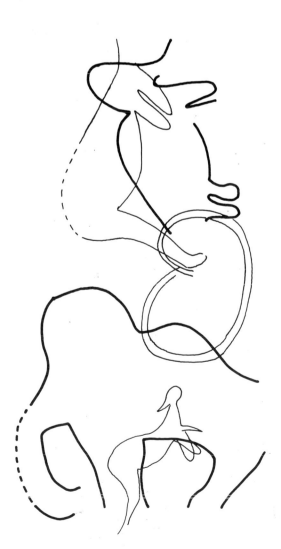

382. CEILING OF BIG CHAMBER. WOMAN AND MAMMOTH

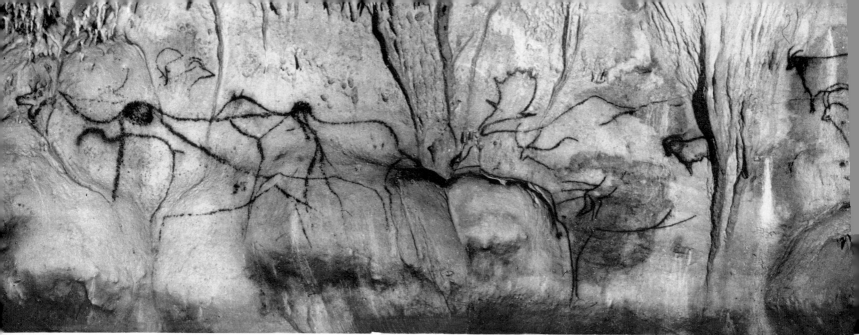

COUGNAC 383. PANEL WITH THREE LARGE-HORNED DEER. MAN PIERCED WITH SPEARS; IBEXES

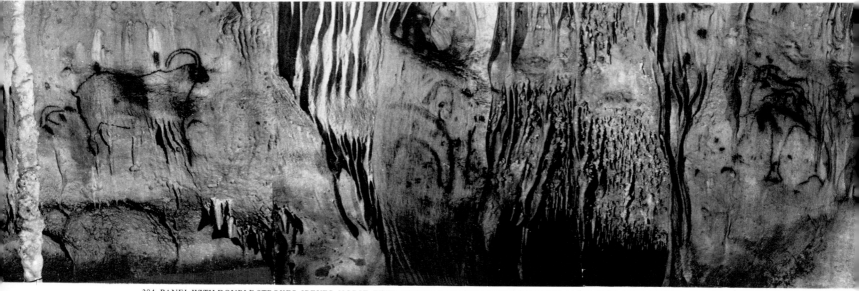

384. PANEL WITH DOUBLE STROKES, IBEXES, HORSE, ENTRANCE TO SIDE CHAMBER WITH DOTS, MAMMOTH, AND MAN PIERCED WITH SPEAR

385. SIDE CHAMBER WITH BRACE SIGNS

386. STAG AND "GHOSTS"

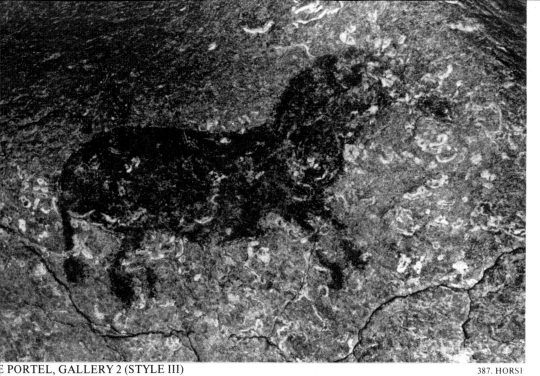

387. HORSE

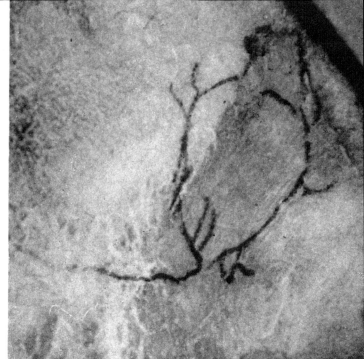

388. STAG ANTLERS IN A NICHE

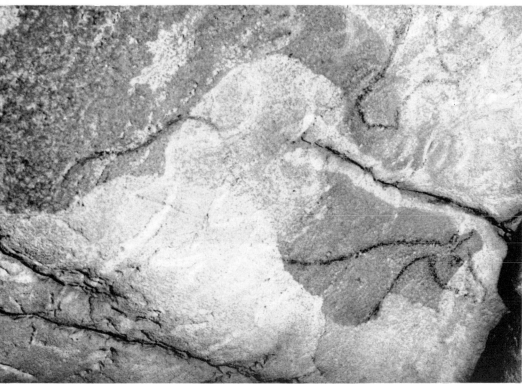

389. BOTTOM OF PANEL M

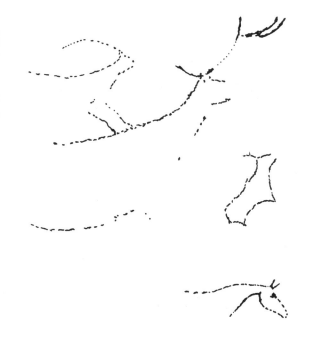

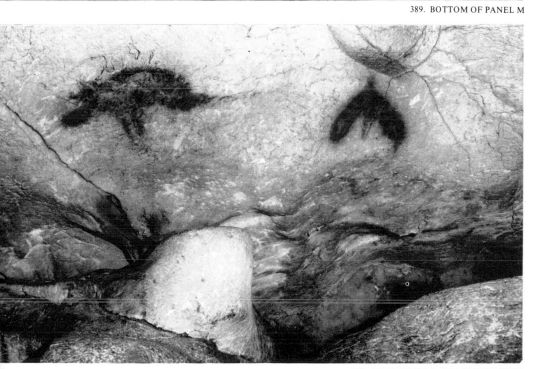

390. HORSE'S HEAD, BRACE SIGN, MAN

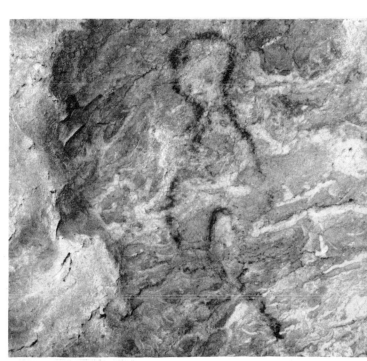

391. MAN FROM PRECEDING PANEL

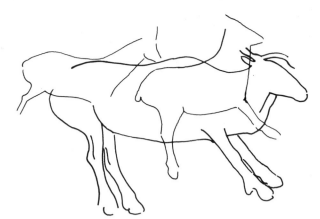

ISTURITZ   392. REINDEER AND IBEXES

LAS CHIMENEAS   393. CENTRAL PANEL. HEADS OF HIND AND COW   396. SIDE CHAMBER. HORSE'S HEAD

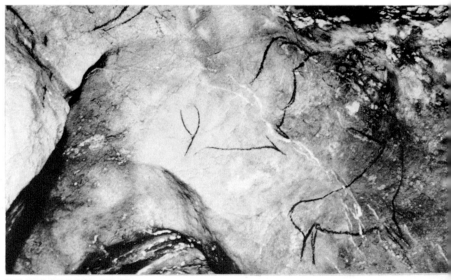

394. CENTRAL PANEL. COW WITH HORNS IN SEMIFRONTAL PERSPECTIVE   397. SIDE CHAMBER. STAGS

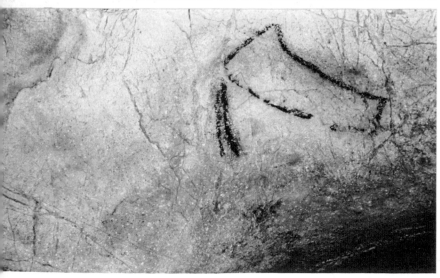

395. SIDE CHAMBER. QUADRANGULAR SIGN, STROKES   398. BIG CHAMBER. QUADRANGULAR SIGNS

ALTAMIRA, BLACK SEQUENCE   399. CHAMBER D. IBEXES   400. CHAMBER D. BISON   401. INNER GALLERY. HORSE

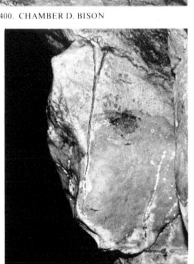

402, 403, 404. IRREGULARITIES OF THE WALL TRANSFORMED INTO MASKS   405. INNER GALLERY. PANEL OF QUADRANGULAR SIGNS

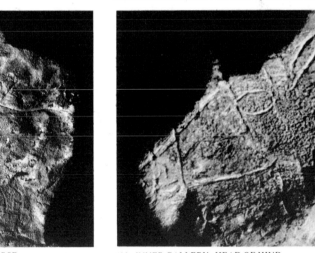

406. ENGRAVED CEILING. HEADS OF AUROCHS AND MEANDERING LINES   407. INNER GALLERY. HORSE   408. INNER GALLERY. HEAD OF HIND

LA PASIEGA   409. GALLERY A. BISON   410. GALLERY A. HORSES AND STAG   411. GALLERY A. HORSE AND STAG

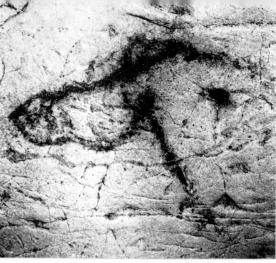

LA PASIEGA *(cont.)*   412. GALLERY A. HIND

413. GALLERY A. HORSE'S HEAD

414. HORSES AND HIND

415. GALLERY A. AUROCHS

416. GALLERY B. IBEX

417. GALLERY C. BISON AND CLAVIFORM SIGNS

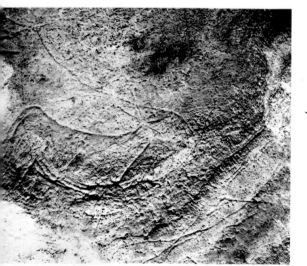

EL CASTILLO   418. STAGS AND HIND

419. HORSE, BARBED SIGN, AND OVAL

420. INTERSECTING QUADRANGULAR SIGNS

421. INTERSECTING ROWS OF DOTS NEAR FIG. 420

422. NEGATIVE HAND

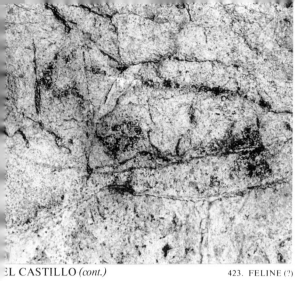

EL CASTILLO *(cont.)*   423. FELINE (?)

424. RHINOCEROS (?)

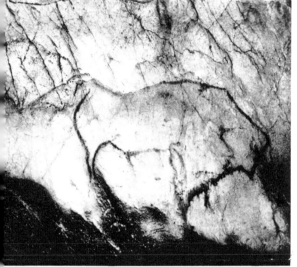

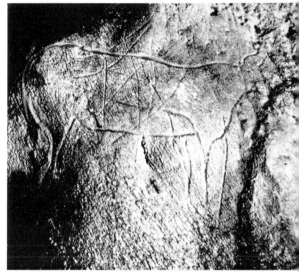

425. PAIR OF BISON

426. AUROCHS

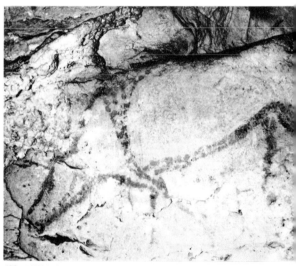

OVALANAS   427. THREE HINDS

428. HINDS WITH DOTTED OUTLINES

429. ANIMAL AT ENTRANCE

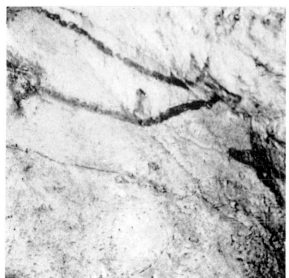

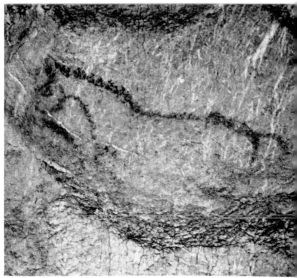

430. PANEL WITH HORSE

431. HINDS IN RECESS

LA HAZA   432. HORSE

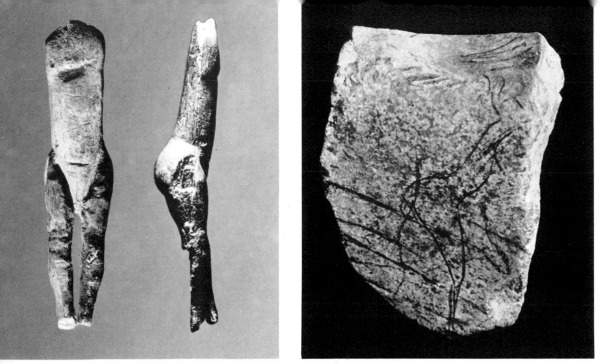

STYLE IV. DECORATED OBJECTS. 433. LAUGERIE BASSE. FEMALE STATUETTE 434. ABRI MURAT. FIGURE, PROBABLY WOMAN 435. LES TROIS FRÈRES. HUMAN FIGURE AND BISON LEG

436. ISTURITZ. BISON AND BARBED SIGNS

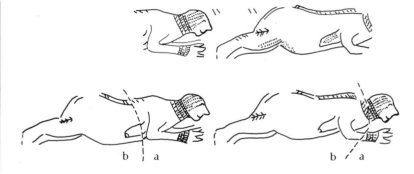

437. REVERSE SIDE OF FIG. 436. WOMAN AND BARBED SIGNS

438. LAUGERIE BASSE. HORSE ON REVERSE SIDE OF FIG. 439 439 WOUNDED BISON AND MAN THROWN TO THE GROUND

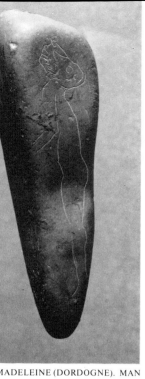

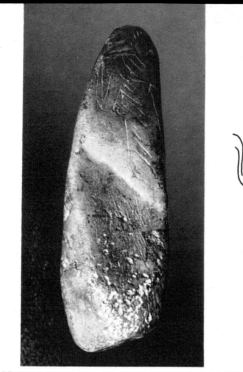

MADELEINE (DORDOGNE). MAN   441. REVERSE SIDE OF FIG. 440. WOMAN WITH ANIMAL HEAD   442. LA MADELEINE. MAN

443. ISTURITZ. MAN AND HEADS OF HORSES   444. PÉCHIALET. MEN AND BEAR

445. ABRI MURAT. HUMAN SILHOUETTES

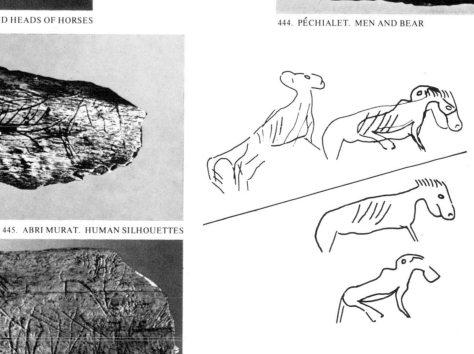

446. LES EYZIES. BISON AND MEN

429

447. LAUGERIE BASSE. HEADS OF HORSES

448. LA MADELEINE (DORDOGNE). HORSE'S HEAD

449. ISTURITZ. HORSE'S HEAD

451. ARUDY. FIVE HEADS OF HORSES

450. ISTURITZ. HORSE'S HEAD

452. REVERSE SIDE OF FIG. 451. AUROCHS' HEAD

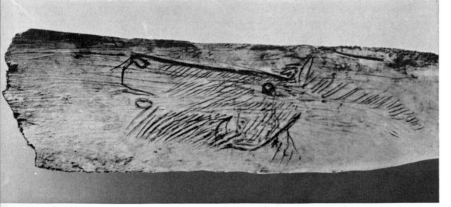

453. LES TROIS FRÈRES. HORSE'S HEAD

454. RAYMONDEN. HORSE'S HEAD

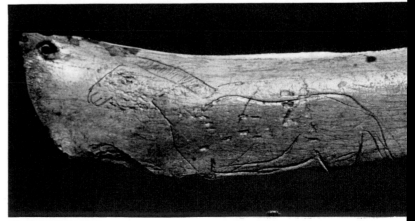

455. LESPUGUE. HORSES

456. EL PENDO. HORSE

430

457. ROBIN HOOD'S CAVE (CRESWELL CRAGS, ENGLAND). HORSE

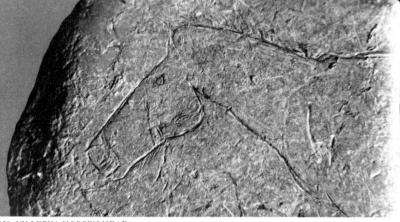

458. VILLEPIN. HORSE'S HEAD

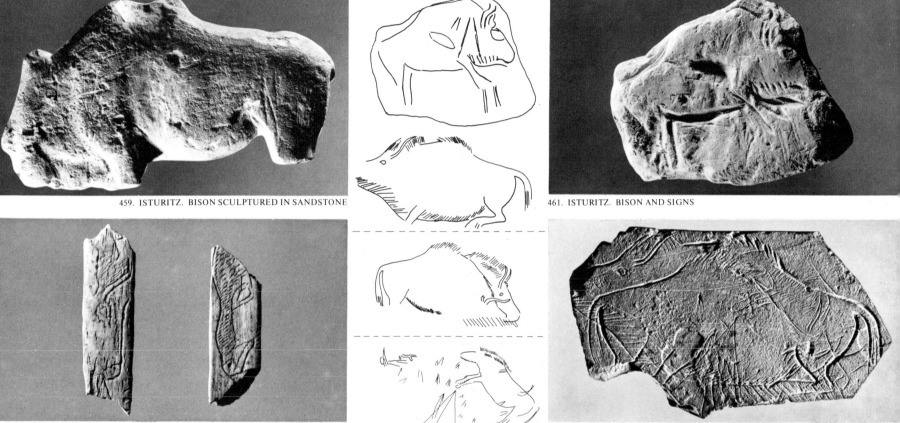

459. ISTURITZ. BISON SCULPTURED IN SANDSTONE

461. ISTURITZ. BISON AND SIGNS

460. ISTURITZ. HEADS OF BISON ON BONE FRAGMENT

462. ISTURITZ. THREE BISON, HORSE, AND SIGNS

463, 464. LE PUY DE LACAN. BISON AND BIRD

465. LE MAS D'AZIL. COW

466. LE MAS D'AZIL. BULL

467. LAUGERIE BASSE. REINDEER

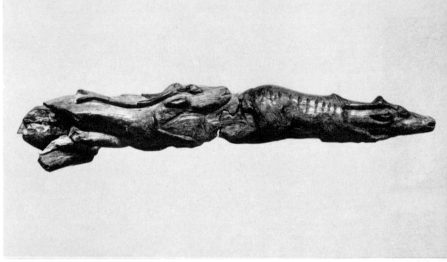

468. BRUNIQUEL. TWO REINDEER

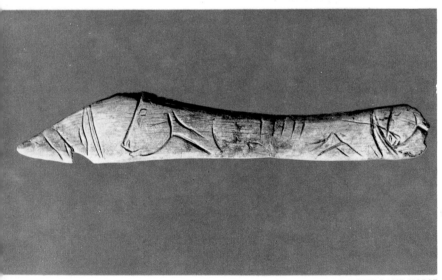

469. LAUGERIE BASSE. BOVIDS AND HORSE

470. ISTURITZ. IBEX

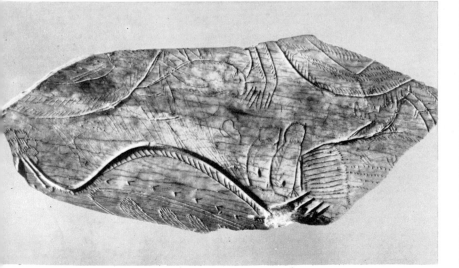

471. LES TROIS FRÈRES. BIRDS AND GRASSHOPPER

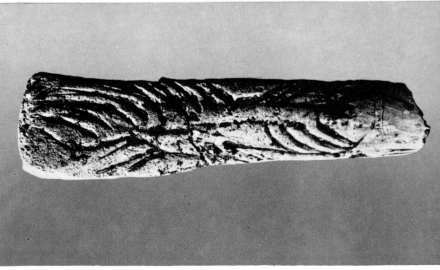

472. RAYMONDEN. BARBED SIGN

432

473, 474. CHALEUX. FLAT STONE, SHOWING ON ONE SIDE AN AUROCHS AND A CERVID; ON THE OTHER SIDE, A HORSE AND TWO IBEXES

475. LIMEUIL. REINDEER

476. LIMEUIL. AUROCHS

477. LIMEUIL. IBEX

478. SAUT-DU-PERRON. REINDEER

479. SAUT-DU-PERRON. LEGS OF RHINOCEROS (?)

433

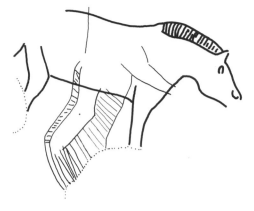

480. HORSE

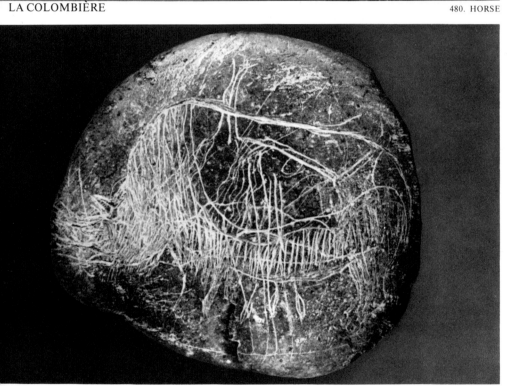

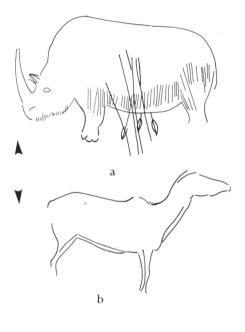

481. RHINOCEROS AND CERVID

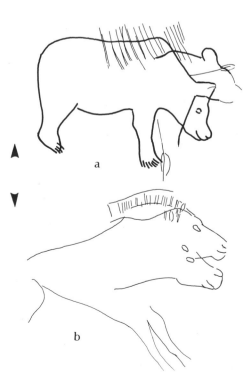

482. REVERSE SIDE OF FIG! 481. BEARS AND HORSES

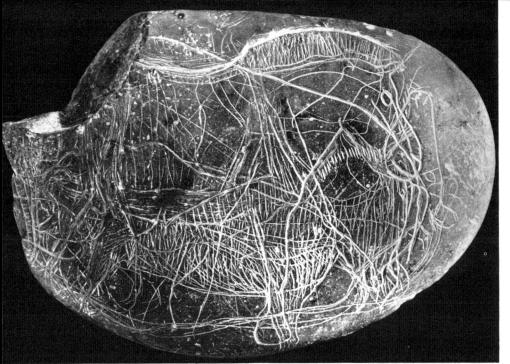

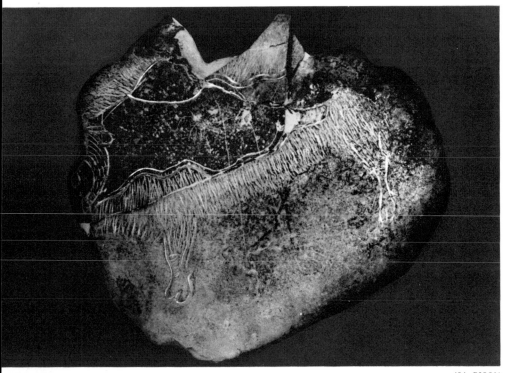

A COLOMBIÈRE (cont.)

483. HORSE, CERVIDS, IBEXES, RHINOCEROS, FELINE

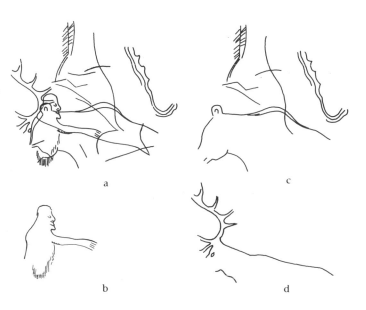

484. BISON

485. MAN, REINDEER, AND BEAR

STYLE IV. CAVE ART. TEYJAT

486. COWS AND BULL

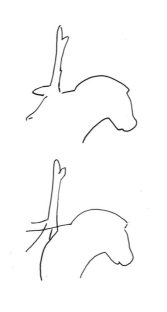

487. HORSE'S HEAD AND LEG OF A REINDEER

489. HEAD OF BISON

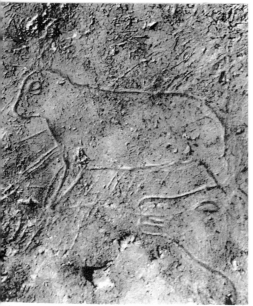

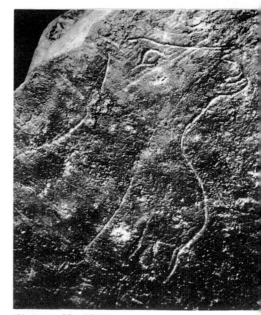

488. FAWN AND HEAD OF REINDEER

490. HEAD OF A REINDEER

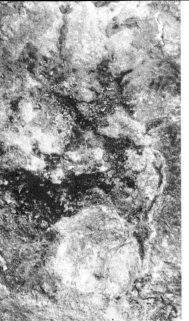

ERS, LA CHAIRE A CALVIN

491, 492. FRIEZE OF BISON AND HORSES

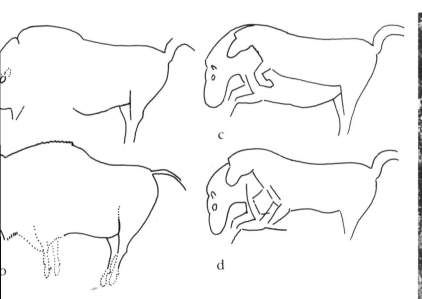

493. HORSES CARVED INSIDE A BISON

LANC

494. HORSES

495. BISON HEAD CARVED ON A HORSE'S HEAD

COMMARQUE   496. HEAD OF AN IBEX   497. HORSE'S HEAD   498. ANIMALIZED HUMAN PROFILE

LA MAGDELAINE (TARN)   500. HORSE   **ABRI REVERDIT**   499. BISON

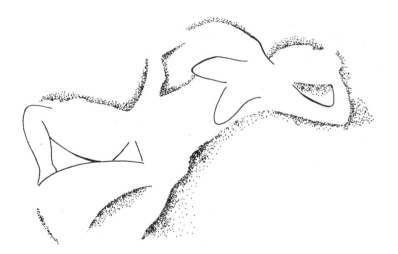

501. FEMALE FIGURE AT LEFT SIDE OF SITE

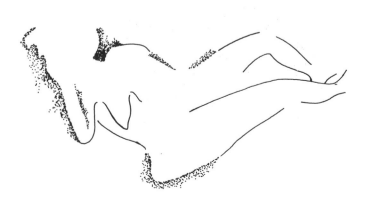

502. FEMALE FIGURE AT RIGHT SIDE OF SITE

438

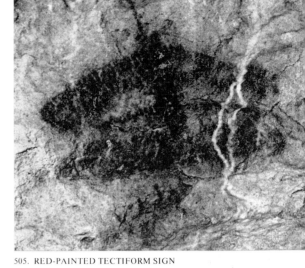

ERNIFAL 503. ROWS OF DOTS AT ENTRANCE

504. TECTIFORM SIGN AND OVAL, SUPERIMPOSED

505. RED-PAINTED TECTIFORM SIGN

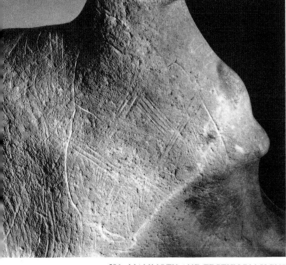

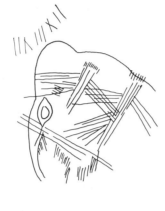

506. MAMMOTH AND TECTIFORM SIGNS

507. HORSE, CERVID, AND SIGNS

508. BISON AND PAIRED SIGNS

509. HORSE

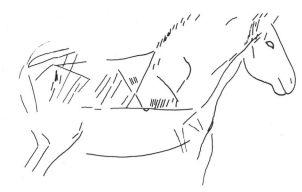

LES COMBARELLES

510. HORSE AND SIGNS

511. MAMMOTH

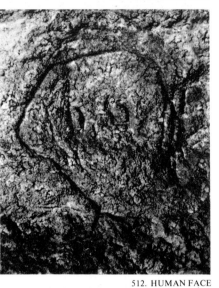

512. HUMAN FACE

513. FEMALE SIGN

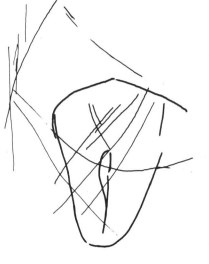

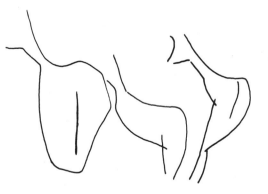

514. FEMALE FIGURES IN PROFILE

515. HEAD OF AN IBEX

516. REINDEER HEAD OVERLAPPING A BISON

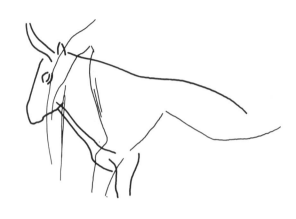

517. AUROCHS OVERLAPPING THE HINDQUARTERS OF A HORSE

518. HEAD OF A RHINOCEROS

519. BEAR

520. FELINE HEAD

521. REINDEER

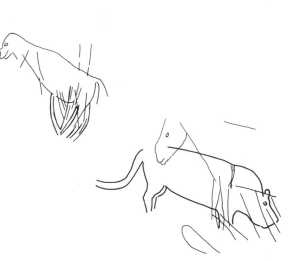

LES COMBARELLES *(cont.)*   522. ANIMALIZED HUMAN FIGURE   523. FELINE

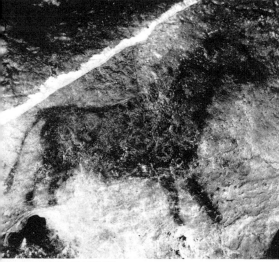

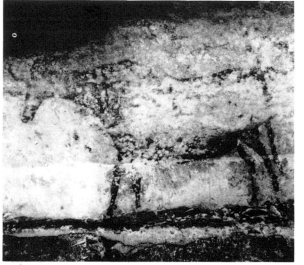

FONT-DE-GAUME   524. BULL IN STYLE III   525. COW IN STYLE III   526. RHINOCEROS

527. FRIEZE OF PAINTED BISON

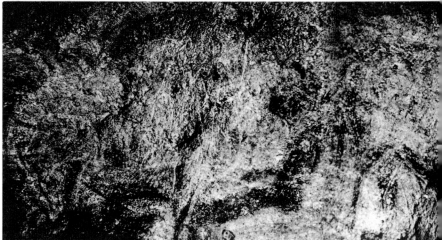

528. BISON

442

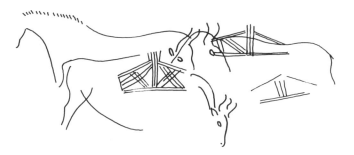

FONT-DE-GAUME *(cont.)*

530. LITTLE MAMMOTH

531. ANTHROPOMORPHIC PROFILES

532. HORSE'S HEAD

533. BACK-CAVE SIGNS

534. QUADRANGULAR SIGN

ROUFFIGNAC   535. BREUIL GALLERY. FRIEZE OF RHINOCEROS

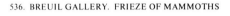

536. BREUIL GALLERY. FRIEZE OF MAMMOTHS

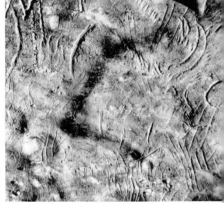

537. BREUIL GALLERY. HORSE AND MAMMOTHS   538. BREUIL GALLERY. BISON

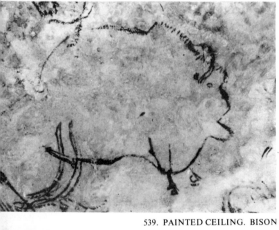

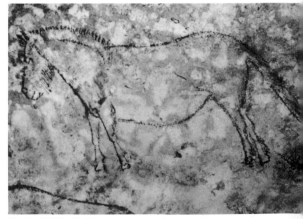

539. PAINTED CEILING. BISON   540. PAINTED CEILING. TWO IBEXES AND MAMMOTH   541. PAINTED CEILING. HORSE

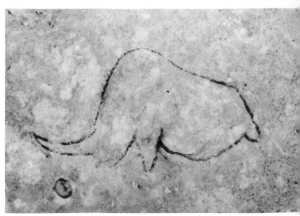

542. LEFT-HAND SIDE, BREUIL GALLERY. BEAR   543. BACK OF RIGHT-HAND SIDE, BREUIL GALLERY. HUMAN PROFILES   544. PAINTED CEILING. RHINOCEROS

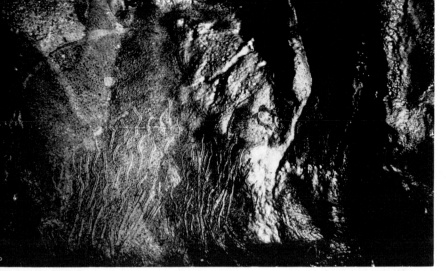

545. MAMMOTH

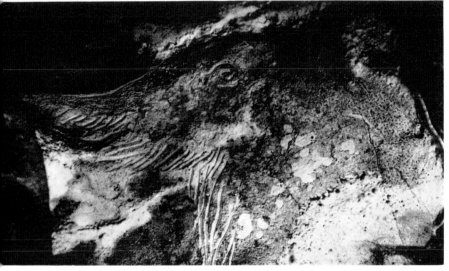

546. HEAD OF A MAMMOTH

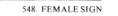

547. BISON HORNS   548. FEMALE SIGN   549. LATTICE SIGN   550. BISON HEAD AND SCRAWLS

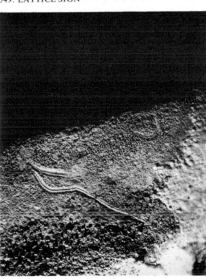

551. BACK-CAVE HORSE   552. CERVID HEAD

445

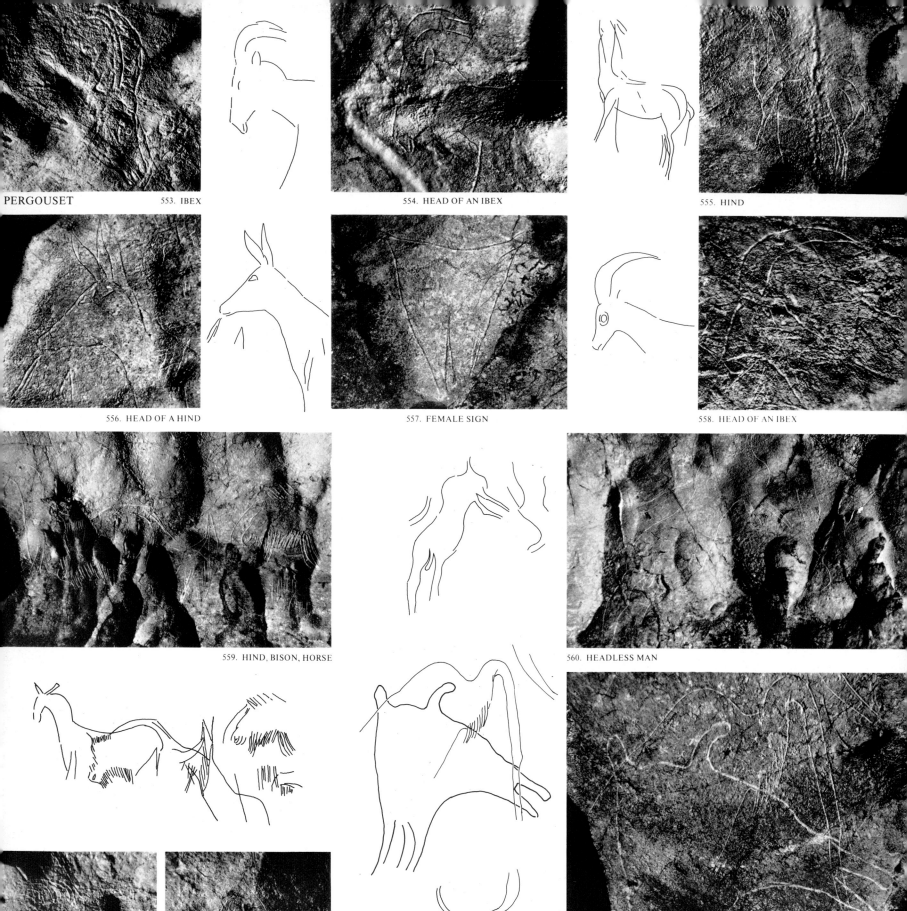

PERGOUSET

553. IBEX

554. HEAD OF AN IBEX

555. HIND

556. HEAD OF A HIND

557. FEMALE SIGN

558. HEAD OF AN IBEX

559. HIND, BISON, HORSE

560. HEADLESS MAN

563. FANTASTIC FIGURES

561. LONG-NECKED ANIMAL

562. HEAD OF AN ELK

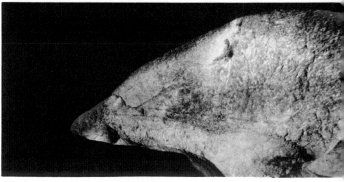

564. POINT OF ROCK MARKED WITH AN EYE

MARSOULAS

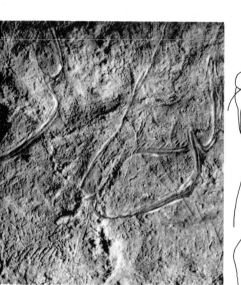

566. BISON HOOFS (DETAIL)

567. FACE IN FRONTAL VIEW

568. FACE IN FRONTAL VIEW

569. ROWS OF DOTS AND OF STROKES

570. BISON PAINTED IN BLACK

LABASTIDE

571. HORSE AND BISON

572. BISON AND CERVID (?)

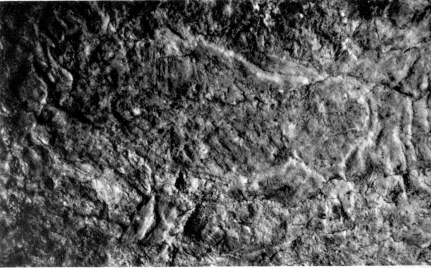

573. BIG POLYCHROME HORSE

574. SMALL ENGRAVED BISON

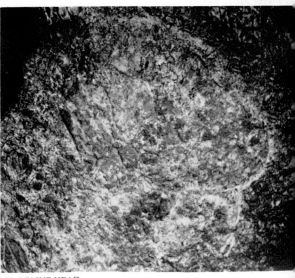

575. LONG-NECKED ANIMAL, CALLED A GOOSE

576. FELINE HEAD

577. GALLERY 1. BIRD

578. GALLERY 2. HORSE

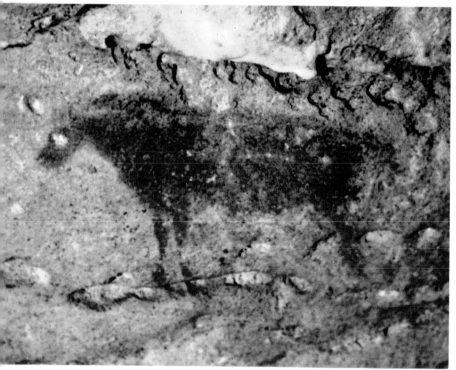

579. GALLERY 3. RED HORSE

580. GALLERY 3. HORSE

581. GALLERY 3. HORSE

582. GALLERY 3. HORSE

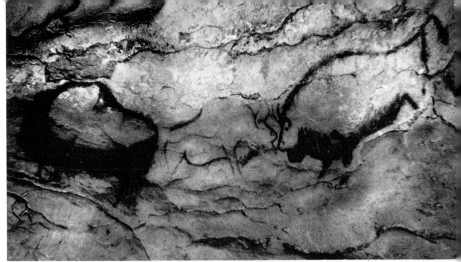

LE PORTEL (STYLE IV, *cont.*)　　　583. GALLERY 4. "DISCOVERY" BISON　　　584. GALLERY 4. GROUP OF THREE BISON

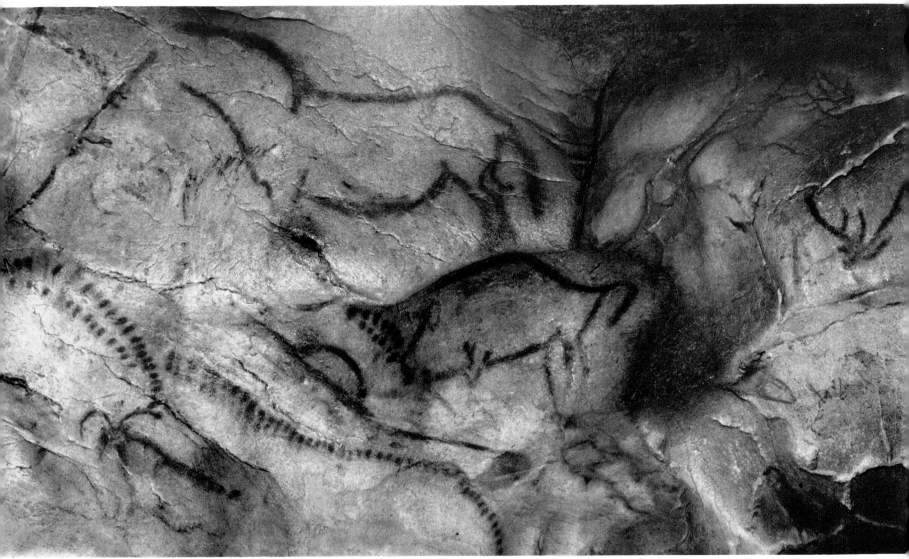

585. GALLERY 4. SET OF FIGURES IN THE *"Camarin,"*　BISON/HORSE/IBEX/STAG, CLAVIFORM SIGN AND DOTS

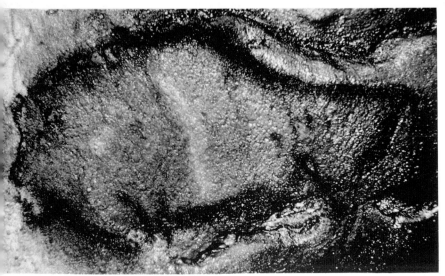

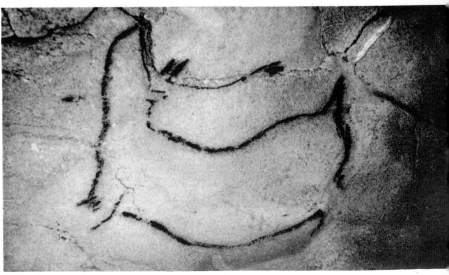

586. GALLERY 4. BISON　　　587. GALLERY 4. BACK-CAVE STAG

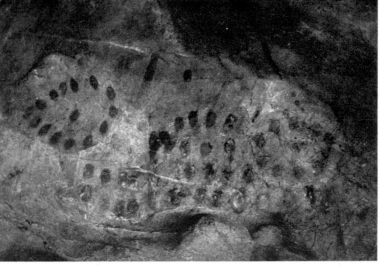

588. PANEL OF SIGNS (AT B ON PLAN)

589. RED DOTS (AT H ON PLAN)

590. CLAVIFORM SIGN IN THE BLACK SALON

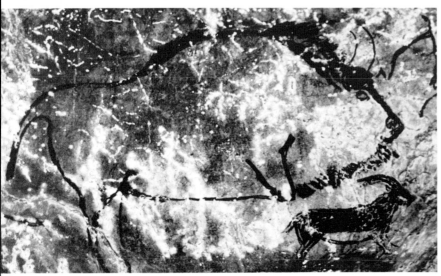

I-597. BLACK SALON

591. BISON AND IBEX, PANEL III

592. BISON AND SIGNS, PANEL I

593. BISON AND SIGNS, PANEL II

594. BISON, SIGNS, AND IBEXES, PANEL II

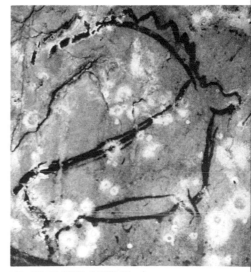

595. STAG ANTLERS, PANEL II

596. SMALL BISON, VERTICAL, PANEL II

597. SMALL IBEX, PANEL III

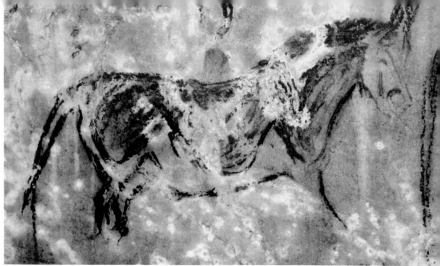

NIAUX *(cont.)*

598. SMALL BISON, PANEL III

599. SMALL HORSE, PANEL III

598-602. BLACK SALON

600. FELINE AND HORSE, PANEL IV

601. STAG AND HORSE, PANEL IV

602. HEADLESS HUMAN FIGURE, BACK OF PANEL II

603. RED BISON, INNER GALLERY

604. HEADLESS IBEX, THE LAST FIGURE IN THE CAVE

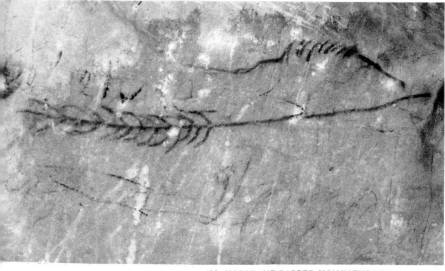

605. HORSE AND BARBED SIGN IN THE INNER GALLERY

606. BACK-CAVE RED SIGN (L ON PLAN)

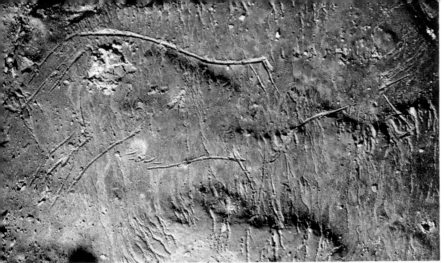

AUX *(cont.)* . ENGRAVINGS ON CLAY

607. HORSE

608. BISON

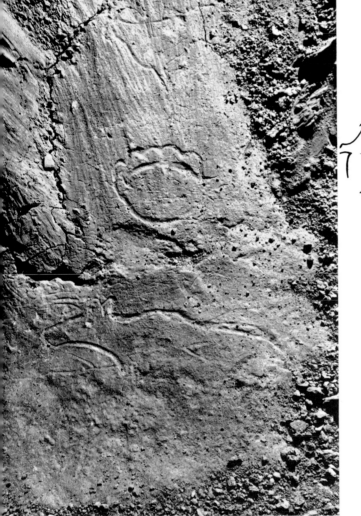

609. IBEX, SIGN, AND AUROCHS

610. BISON/HORSE/IBEX GROUP

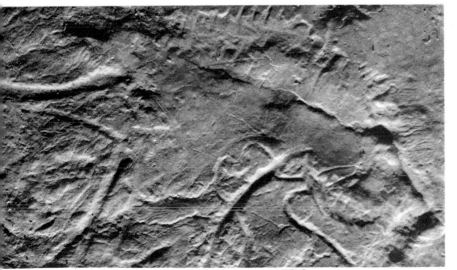

611. HEADS OF HORSE AND OF RHINOCEROS (?)

612. SCHEMATIZED FISH

LE TUC D'AUDOUBERT

613. BISON HEAD

614. HORSE

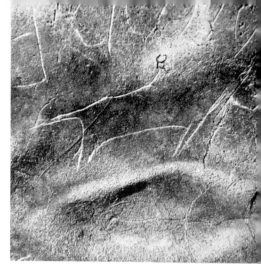

615. SCHEMATIZED HORSE

616. HEAD OF FANTASTIC CREATURE

617. BARBED SIGN ON CLAY

618. OVAL NEAR THE SIGN IN FIG. 617

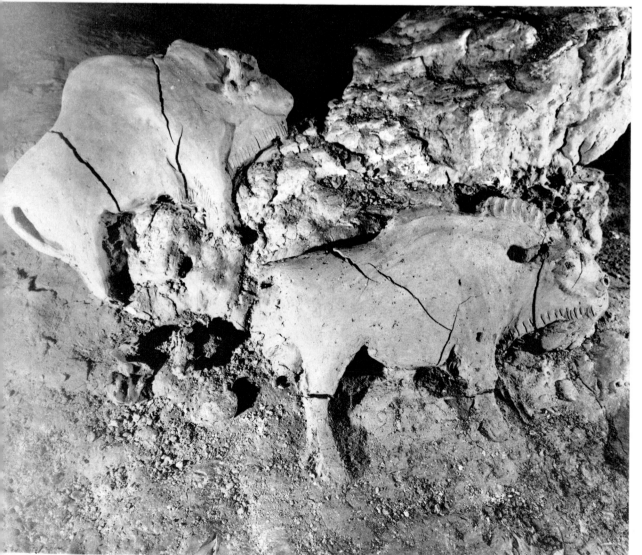

619. TWO BISON MODELED IN CLAY

620. BACK VIEW OF BISON IN FIG. 619

621. PRELIMINARY SKETCH FOR A THIRD BISON

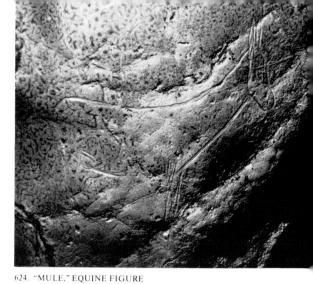

ES TROIS FRÈRES   622. BRACE-SHAPED SIGNS   623. HEAD OF BEAR (?)   624. "MULE." EQUINE FIGURE

625. ENGRAVED AND PAINTED BISON   626. "OWLS"

627. BISON   628. HORSE'S HEAD   629. CLAVIFORM SIGN AND DOTS

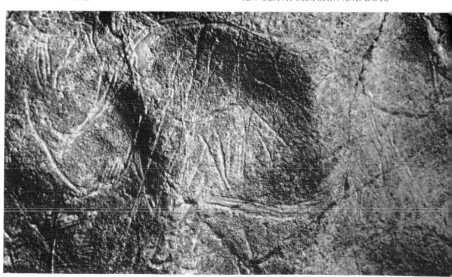

630. MAMMOTH   631. RHINOCEROS

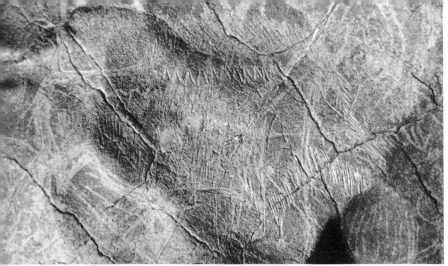

LES TROIS FRÈRES (cont.)

632. BISON AND SIGNS

633. IBEX WITH HORNS IN FRONTAL PERSPECTIVE

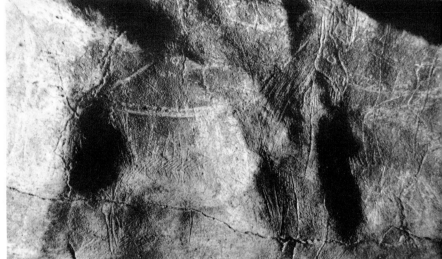

634. HEAD OF BIG BISON IN THE "SANCTUARY"

635. "MULE," EQUINE FIGURE IN THE "SANCTUARY"

636. REINDEER

637. HORSE

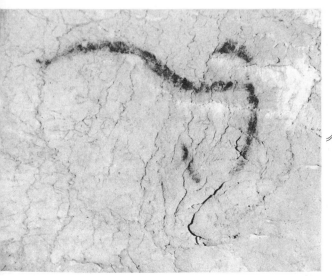

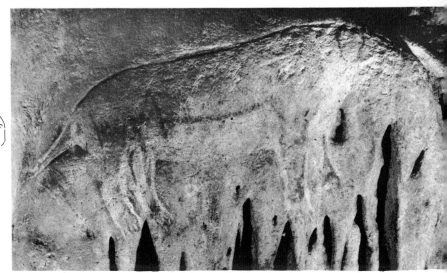

638. BISON PAINTED IN BLACK

639. FELINE

456

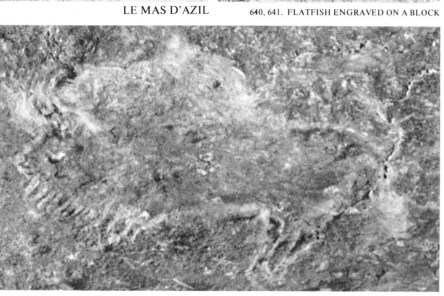
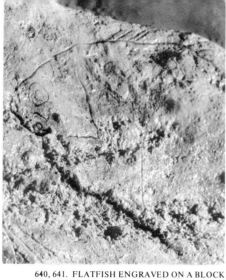

LE MAS D'AZIL   640, 641. FLATFISH ENGRAVED ON A BLOCK   642. HEAD OF BISON IN BLACK

643. SMALL ENGRAVED BISON   645. HEAD OF BISON ON A RELIEF

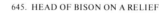

HORSE ENGRAVED ON A PEBBLE, BENEATH BISON IN FIG. 643

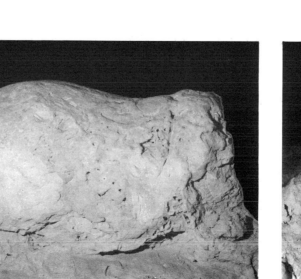

NTESPAN   646. BEAR MODELED IN CLAY, REAR VIEW   647. SIDE VIEW OF THE BEAR IN FIG. 646   648. ANIMAL (FELINE? HORSE?) MODELED IN CLAY

MONTESPAN *(cont.)*   649. HORSE AND SIGNS   650. HORSE MODELED ON THE GROUND

651. PANEL OF THE "HUNT": HORSES, PERFORATIONS, AND LINES

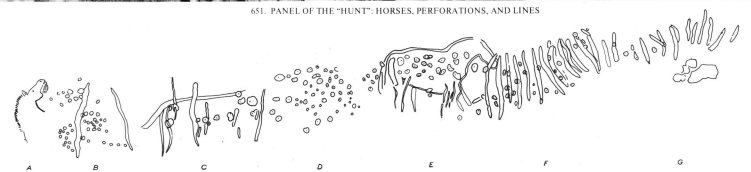

A   B   C   D   E   F   G

652. IBEXES   653. BISON   654. BISON   655. LAST FIGURE IN THE CAVE

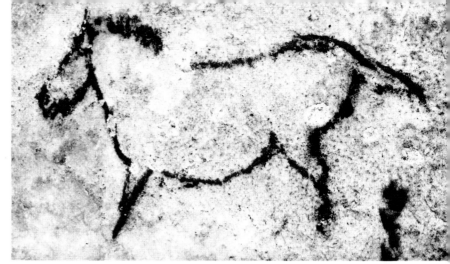

MAMINE

656. BISON

657. HORSE, CENTRAL PANEL

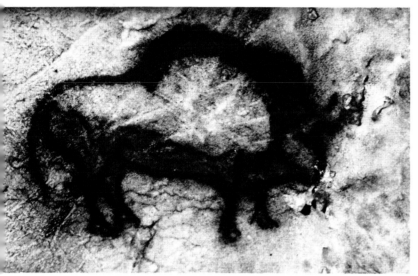

658. BISON, CENTRAL PANEL

659. BISON, CENTRAL PANEL

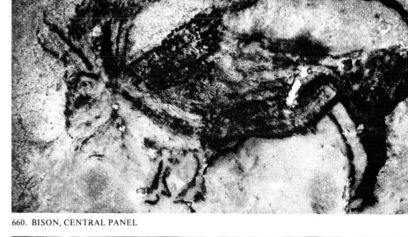

RAVED AND PAINTED BISON ON A BLOCK

662. THREE BISON IN VERTICAL POSITION

660. BISON, CENTRAL PANEL

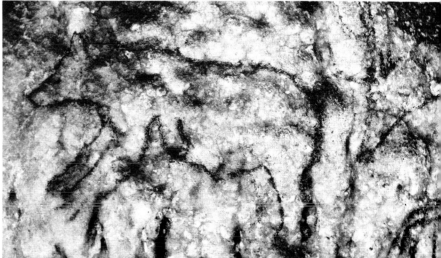

663. BEAR, STAG, AND IBEX

459

ALTAMIRA   664. ENGRAVED BISON   665. HORSE ACCOMPANYING THE BISON IN FIG. 664   666. ENGRAVED HIND

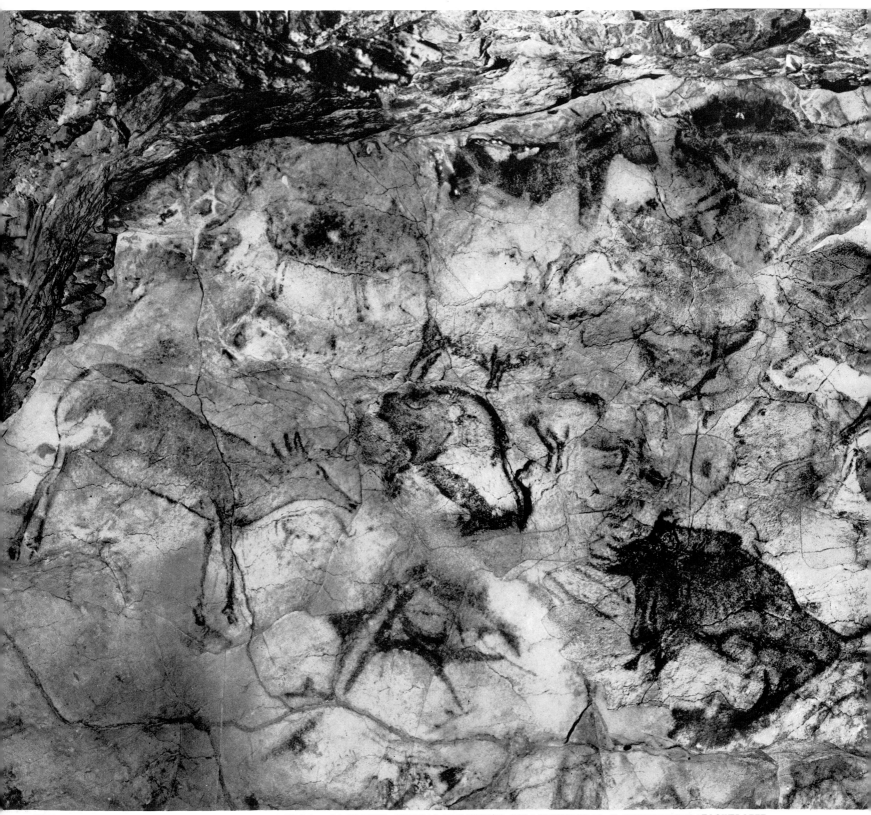

670. PAINTED CEILING. GROUP OF BISON SURROUNDED BY *(left to right)* ONE HIND, ONE BOAR, TWO HORSES, AND A SECOND BOAR. CLAVIFORM SIGNS AT LOWER LEFT

667, 668. HORSES IN STYLE III NEAR THE PAINTED CEILING669. IBEX IN STYLE III

LA CULLALVERA 671. DOTS TO THE LEFT OF PANEL OF SIGNS 672. CLAVIFORM SIGNS AND STROKES

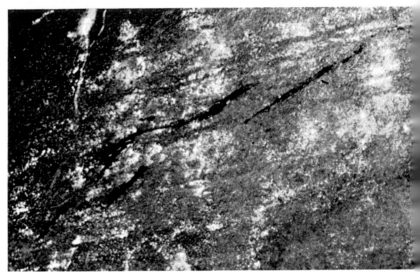

673. HORSE 674. LINES AT THE BACK OF THE CAVE

PINDAL 675. PANEL OF PAINTINGS AT THE BACK OF THE CAVE

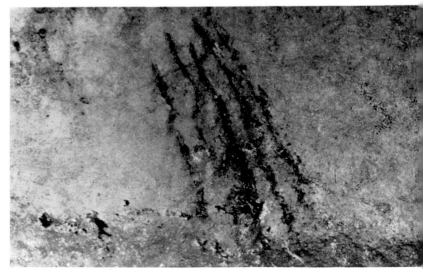

676. RED HIND 677. BLACK STROKES IN ALIGNMENT

462

678. PANEL OF GRAFFITI AT ENTRANCE

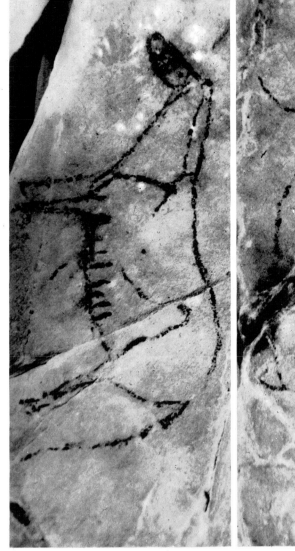

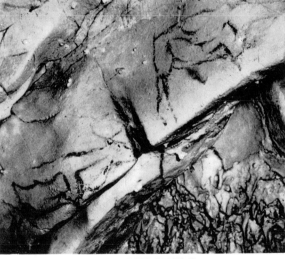

679. HORSE, CENTRAL PANEL   680. HORSE, REINDEER, FIRST COMPOSITION

681. REINDEER AND IBEX, PANEL 7   682. REINDEER, PANEL II   683. LITTLE HORSE ·

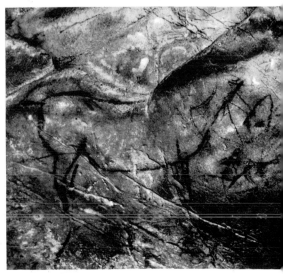

684. PAIRED SIGNS   685. LITTLE HORSE IN A SEMIDOME   686. HEADLESS ANIMAL. LAST PANEL

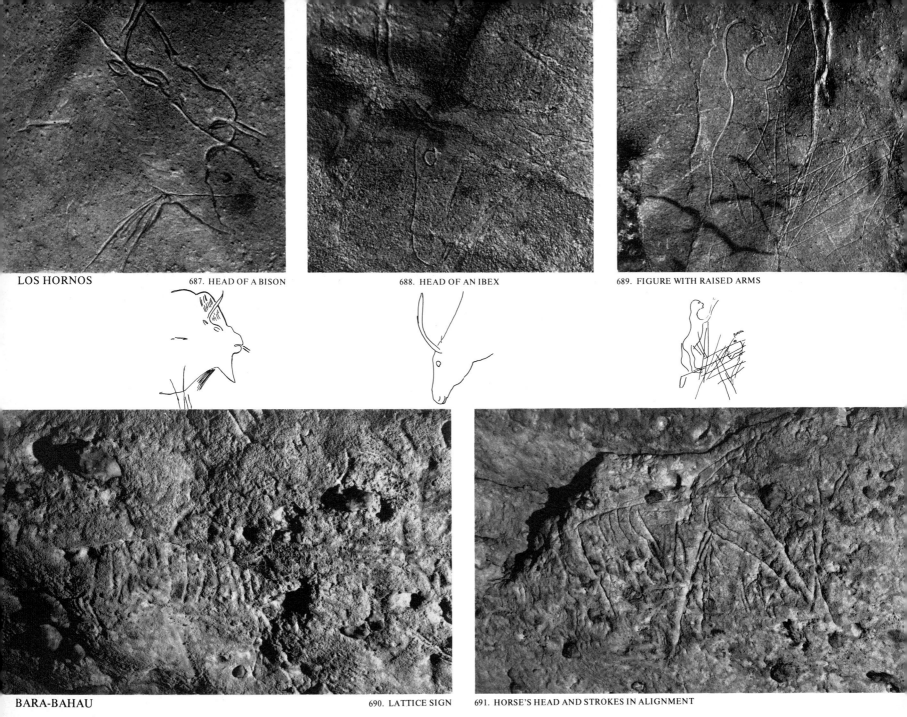

LOS HORNOS

687. HEAD OF A BISON   688. HEAD OF AN IBEX   689. FIGURE WITH RAISED ARMS

BARA-BAHAU

690. LATTICE SIGN   691. HORSE'S HEAD AND STROKES IN ALIGNMENT

692. HORSE   693. HEAD OF A BOVID

C

694. HORSE   695. BISON WITH HORNS IN FRONTAL PERSPECTIVE

696. HORSE WITH DOUBLE OUTLINE   697. BEAR PAINTED ON A NATURAL CONTOUR

AC

698. BISON MODELED ON THE GROUND   699. BISON ENGRAVED ON THE GROUND

700. PAINTED BISON   701. HEADLESS ANIMAL

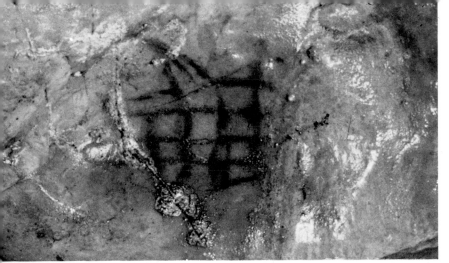

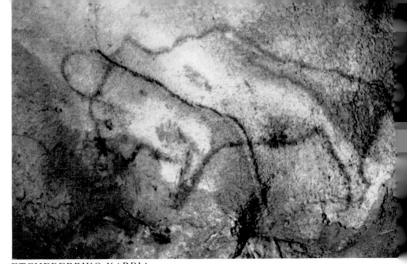

USSAT 702. RED-PAINTED SIGN   ETCHEBERRIKO-KARBIA   703. BISON

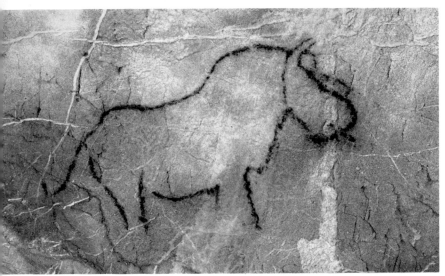

ISTURITZ 704. HORSE   705. HIND

706. HORSE'S HEAD   CANDAMO 707. HORSE

708. HORSE   709. CERVID AND MAN

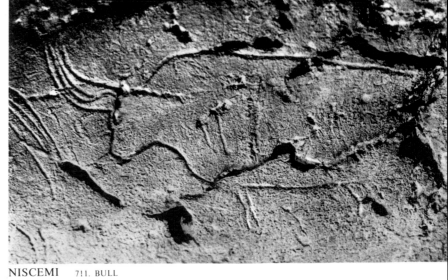

MEDITERRANEAN CAVE ART. ADDAURA 710. SCENE WITH ANIMALS AND HUMAN FIGURES GROTTE CHABOT 712. MAMMOTH

713. MAMMOTH

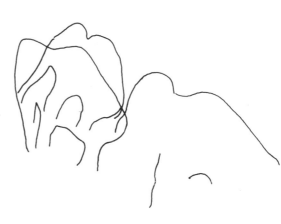

714. UNFINISHED OUTLINES OF MAMMOTHS

GROTTE CHABOT *(cont.)* 715. CENTRAL COMPOSITION: AUROCHS/HORSES/CERVID/MAMMOTH

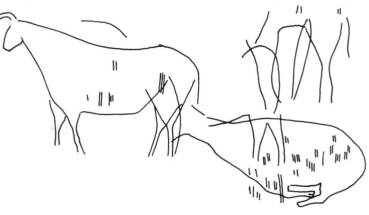

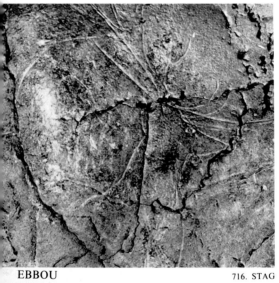

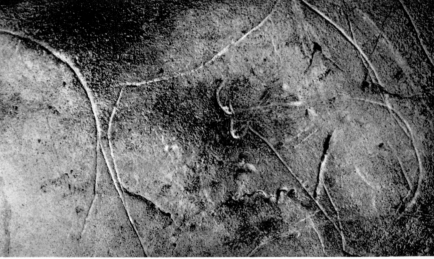

EBBOU 716. STAG 717. IBEX

718. IBEX 719. SMALL BOVID

720. STAG AND HORSE

723. HEAD OF BISON

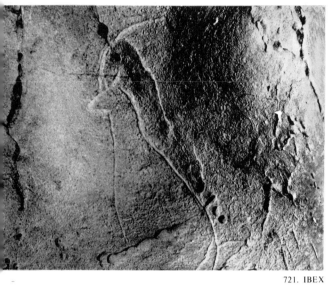

721. IBEX

724. LITTLE HORSE

722. IBEX

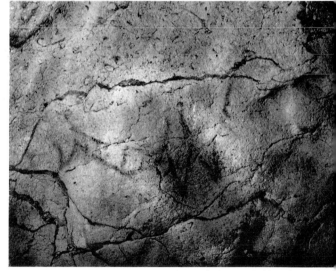

725. IBEX PAINTED IN RED

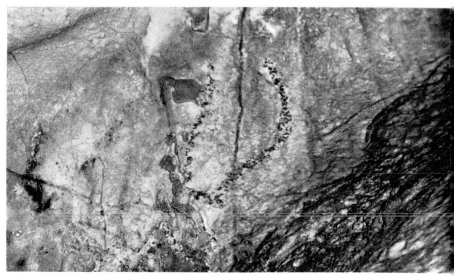

GROTTE BAYOL   726. HORSE'S HEAD IN BLACK   727. SCHEMATIZED HORSE'S HEAD

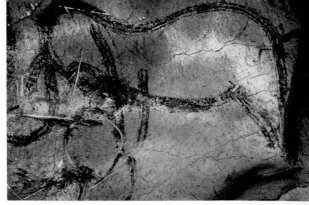

LA BAUME LATRONE 728. TWO MAMMOTHS

731. MAMMOTH

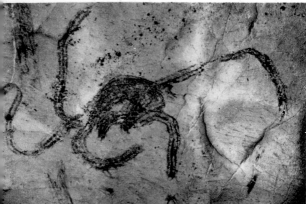

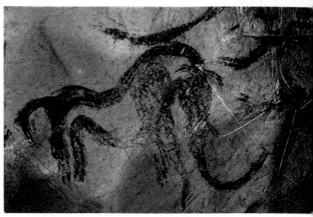

729. MAMMOTH

732. HORSE AND OVAL SIGN

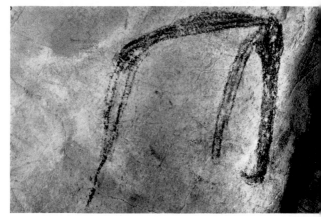

730. FELINE AND MAMMOTH

733. MAMMOTH

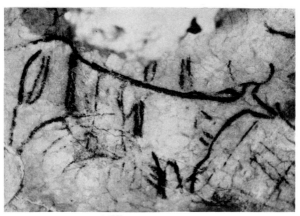

734. HORSE AND SCRAWLS

ALDÈNE 735. FELINE HEAD

736. HORSE'S HEAD

SALLÈLES-CABARDÈS 737. IBEX

LA PILETA 738. COW AND SIGNS

739. HORSE AND SIGNS

470

COMMENTS AND EXPLANATIONS OF THE PHOTOGRAPHS

SPEARS

Decorated spears probably do not appear before the Gravettian or the period between the Gravettian and the Solutrean. On those specimens which are apparently the points of throwing weapons, the representations are schematic, more often even abstract and reduced to mere signs combined into decorative patterns. The plainness of spear decoration may be accounted for by the fact that these weapons were manufactured in quantity and were not expected to last a long time. The earliest and latest specimens show that there was no development toward schematization in the elaborate figures; schematism was determined from the first by the function of the objects (see charts VIII, IX).

170 LE PLACARD
Decorated spear. Early Magdalenian. *Museum, Saint-Germain-en-Laye.*

171 LA MADELEINE (Dordogne)
Spear decorated with horses. Late Magdalenian. *Museum, Périgueux.*

172 EL PENDO
Spear with abstract decoration, including a frieze of highly stylized horses at left. Late Magdalenian. *Museum, Santander.*

173 LE SENCI
Decorated spears. Late Magdalenian. Schematic decoration with all but indecipherable multiple subjects. The central figures seem to be a fish and a horse. *Museum, Périgueux.*

174 ISTURITZ
Spear with geometric decoration. Late Magdalenian. *Collection Saint-Périer, Morigny.*

HARPOONS

Harpoons are found only in the Late Magdalenian. Their decoration, planned to go with the shape of the barbs, seems to derive from the barbed sign or from a stylization of the fish. A few specimens show that the theme of paired animals (cervid/fish) can appear (see chart X).

175–177 LE SENCI
Decorated harpoons. Late Magdalenian. 5–7 in. *Museum, Périgueux (photograph A. Leroi-Gourhan).*

PIERCED STAFFS

Pierced staffs appear from the Aurignacian (c. 28,000 B.C.) to the terminal Magdalenian (c. 9,000 B.C.). Even among the earliest there are some with phalliform handles, and beginning with the period between the Gravettian and the Solutrean (c. 20,000 B.C.) some were elaborately decorated. Their use in the manufacture of spears seems to be proved:

this would account for the symbolic importance of their decoration. The handle and the perforation appear to have stood for a pair of sexual symbols. While the overwhelming majority of the handles have decorations of a male character (phallus, horse, fish, man, feline, stag), some have a bisexual decoration (bison near the perforation plus male symbol on the handle). This is particularly true of the "two bison" motif; its development can be followed from realistic to geometric treatment (see charts XI, XII).

178 LAUGERIE HAUTE
Pierced staff with abstract decoration. Magdalenian III. The hole is framed in double lines. *Museum, Les Eyzies.*

179 SAINT-MARCEL
Pierced staff. Late Magdalenian. Geometric decoration. *Collection Dr. Allain, Museum, Châteauroux.*

180 LA MADELEINE (Dordogne)
Handle of a pierced staff, shaped like a phallus. Middle Magdalenian. *Museum, Les Eyzies.*

181 ARUDY
Handle of pierced staff, decorated with a horse. Magdalenian. 6 1/4 in. *Museum, Saint-Germain-en-Laye.*

182 LAUGERIE BASSE
Head of a pierced staff representing the forequarters of two bison. Judging from the manes and horns, a male and a female seem to be represented. Magdalenian. 5 1/8 in. *Museum, Saint-Germain-en-Laye.*

183 LA MADELEINE (Dordogne)
Head of pierced staff, from the same period as fig. 182. Very schematized representation of the horns and mane of a bison. *Museum, Les Eyzies.*

184 LAUGERIE BASSE
Pierced staff with the "two bison" theme of fig. 182, but more schematically treated. On the handle, aligned strokes; the tip is phalliform. 10 in. *Collection de la Société préhistorique française, Musée de l'Homme, Paris.*

185 LAUGERIE BASSE
Pierced staff with reindeer head. Middle or Late Magdalenian. In front of the muzzle are lines that may be a fish or a branching sign. The tip on the side of the hole bears a carved figure which seems to be a bison head. *Collection de la Société préhistorique française, Musée de l'Homme, Paris.*

186 ISTURITZ
Pierced staff. Late Magdalenian. Very schematic representation of a reindeer and an undecipherable sign. 8 5/8 in. *Collection Saint-Périer, Morigny.*

187 THAYNGEN-KESSLERLOCH
Pierced staff with reindeer, known as "the Thayngen grazing reindeer." In proportions and faithfulness of detail this exhibits Late Magdalenian characteristics like those of the figures from Limeuil (see fig. 475). Reindeer 3 1/8 in. *Rosgarten Museum, Constance (photograph Kabus).*

188 EL CASTILLO
Pierced staff, decorated with a stag. Stag 6 in. *Museum, Santander.*

189 LES HOTEAUX
Pierced staff, decorated with a stag. 9 in. *Museum, Saint-Germain-en-Laye (photograph Musée de l'Homme).*

190 EL PENDO
Pierced staff with complex decoration. 6 1/2 in. Magdalenian, probably late. The object as a whole represents a horse's head; the ears are clearly separated; the other end is both the animal's muzzle and the tip of a phalliform rod. The engraved decoration consists of heads of stags, horses, and hinds, and a filling-in of signs. *Museum, Santander.*

191 SAINT-MARCEL
Pierced staff with a male human figure, the only one of its kind thus far found on this type of implement. The other human figures on pierced staffs are engraved in profile on the handle. *Collection Dr. Allain, Museum, Châteauroux.*

192 LA MADELEINE (Dordogne)
Pierced staff decorated with a string of horses (see figs. 171, 172, and 221). 12 in. Late Magdalenian. *British Museum, London (photograph British Museum).*

193 LA MADELEINE (Dordogne)
Pierced staff with complementary representations. Magdalenian. One side shows two bison (female symbols); the other shows several symbols from the male category: a man; heads of horses; a snake whose tail terminates in a barbed sign; forked signs; and strokes. 6 in. *Museum, Saint-Germain-en-Laye.*

194 SCHWEITZERBILD
Pierced staff showing two horses in single file. The hole has a lozenge-shaped edge; on the tip there are incisions which bring to mind the tips of phalliform staffs. The animals are treated in Late Style IV. *Landesmuseum, Zurich (photograph Landesmuseum).*

195 LAUGERIE BASSE
Layer B (end of the Middle Magdalenian and beginning of the Late Magdalenian). The only pierced staff that is decorated with a feline figure. *Collection de la Société préhistorique française, Musée de l'Homme, Paris (photograph Musée de l'Homme).*

SPEAR-THROWERS

SPEAR-THROWERS, *which are carved out of reindeer antlers, are known only during a relatively brief period, in the Middle Magdalenian and at the beginning of the Late Magdalenian (c. 12,000 B.C.). With a few exceptions, they are found only between the Dordogne and the Pyrenees. The figures on them represent quite a variety of animals: ibex, bison, horse, mammoth, reindeer, feline, bird, fish. Unlike most Paleolithic representations, they show no paired subjects but seem to be divided into a male series and a female series. In style they match Early Style IV as found in cave figures; more particularly, we observe here the richly detailed modeling of the figures at Les Trois Frères, Niaux, Le Portel, and Altamira (Painted Ceiling). A considerable number of spear-throwers show a headless animal. At present we cannot say whether this was a technical device (we have no separate head that can reliably be fitted to a headless figure on a spear-thrower) or the deliberate representation of animals without heads (a theme richly documented in cave art).*

196 ENLÈNE

Spear-thrower of the "headless animal" type. Middle Magdalenian. 3¹/₂ in. The head is cut off rather abruptly: this might suggest that a separate head was sometimes inserted. The state of preservation of this object does not permit reliable zoological identification; in any case, the animal seems to be a cervid or caprid, and the broken lines separating the flank from the belly occur most often on the ibex. *Collection Bégouën excavations, Musée de l'Homme, Paris (photograph J. Oster, Musée de l'Homme).*

197 ARUDY

Spear-thrower exhibiting the same features as fig. 196. A tenon seems to have been supplied onto which a separate head might have been fitted. The clusters of lines on the flank identify the animal as a reindeer. On the shoulder, two lines represent a wound. 2³/₄ in. *Museum, Saint-Germain-en-Laye.*

198 BÉDEILHAC

Spear-thrower of the type with the animal's head turned back. Although known as "the fawn with the birds," like another spear-thrower from Le Mas d'Azil, this represents a young ibex. *Collection Romain Robert (photograph Romain Robert).*

199 BRUNIQUEL

Spear-thrower shaped like a mammoth. The pose is dictated by the shape of the reindeer antler. The raised hook on the back disrupts the animal's contour. 5 in. *British Museum, London (photograph British Museum).*

200 LA MADELEINE (Dordogne)

So-called hyena spear-thrower. This identification is without justification; the animal is a feline, closely related to certain cave figures (see figs. 347, 523). This unusual object is carved in mammoth tusk. 4³/₈ in. *Museum, Saint-Germain-en-Laye.*

201 LA MADELEINE (Dordogne)

Spear-thrower representing bison licking its flank. The pose is dictated by the shape of the reindeer antler. 4 in. *Museum, Saint-Germain-en-Laye.*

202 LOURDES

Spear-thrower decorated with a salmon. The implement's hook (broken) has been grafted onto the tail and abdomen of the fish. 5³/₄ in. *Museum, Saint-Germain-en-Laye.*

203 LAUGERIE BASSE

Reindeer antler. Probably Middle Magdalenian. Fragment of an unidentified object representing a reindeer head—probably the tip of a spear-thrower. Assuming that a normal antler was used, it is clear that this object could have been cut in the same manner as a spear-thrower of the "headless animal" type. 2³/₈ in. *Musée de l'Homme, Paris (photograph R. Pasquino, Musée de l'Homme).*

204 LES TROIS FRÈRES

Spear-thrower decorated with birds in low relief. 3 in. The eye has been hollowed out for inserting a peg of some other material. *Collection Bégouën excavations, Musée de l'Homme, Paris (photograph J. Oster, Musée de l'Homme).*

205 LE MAS D'AZIL

Straight spear-thrower with an ibex in frontal view. Magdalenian. 10⁵/₈ in. *Museum, Saint-Germain-en-Laye.*

206 LE MAS D'AZIL

Fragment, possibly part of a Magdalenian spear-thrower; shows two horses' heads and a horse's skull (the latter seldom represented). 6¹/₄ in. *Museum, Saint-Germain-en-Laye.*

207 BRUNIQUEL

The "leaping horse" spear-thrower. Magdalenian IV. This object has been valuable in dating cave works. Details in the treatment of the coat are found in many painted and engraved figures of horses in Early Style IV. 11 in. *Bétirac excavations, Museum, Saint-Germain-en-Laye.*

SPATULAS

THIS *term is used here to designate every object carved of bony material which could have served as a spatula, smoothing tool, or flat spoon (palette). Examples with decorated handles dating from the terminal Gravettian to the Solutrean have been found from Russia to the Pyrenees. A fish-shaped type occurs frequently in the Middle and Late Magdalenian. In central and western Europe, Late Magdalenian palettes with handles are found, generally elaborately decorated on the flat side—for example, at Pekarna, La Vache, and Fontalès.*

208 GROTTE REY, LES EYZIES

Spatula. Middle or Late Magdalenian. This is the most specific example we have of a "fish" spatula. 7³/₄ in. *Museum, Saint-Germain-en-Laye.*

209 EL PENDO

Part of a spatula. Magdalenian. Very stylized; the species of fish cannot be determined for lack of anatomical detail. 7 in. *Museum, Santander.*

210 LAUGERIE BASSE

Magdalenian spatula. Comparison with figs. 208 and 209 enables us to recognize the fish scales, though they are stylized. The two lateral protuberances correspond to the anal and adipose fins of the Salmon family. The radiating lines of the caudal fin are visible at the tip. *Collection de la Société préhistorique française, Musée de l'Homme, Paris.*

211 SAINT-MARCEL

Fragment of a Late Magdalenian spatula. The scales and what remains of the "handle" end permit identification as an extremely stylized "fish" spatula. About 6 in. *Collection Dr. Allain, Museum, Châteauroux.*

212 LAUGERIE BASSE

Spatula decorated with horse/fish theme. The horse is marked with the double shoulder line common in cave works of Early Style IV. The three lines in front of the muzzle have been interpreted as "breathing" lines. At the tip, the lines render various details of a salmon's tail: adipose fin, caudal fin, scales, the line of the side, and the radiating lines of the caudal fin. About 8 in. *Collection de la Société préhistorique française, Musée de l'Homme, Paris.*

213 ISTURITZ

The themes treated on spatulas (fish and horse) belong to the group of male symbols. This Middle Magdalenian spatula is a good example: it shows a number of parallel strokes, an ibex head (with three "breathing" lines), and a barbed sign. 8 in. *Collection Saint-Périer, Morigny.*

214 BRUNIQUEL

Fragment of spatula. Middle Magdalenian. Incised human figure without indication of sex, showing row of "buttons" down the middle. *Bétirac excavations, Museum, Saint-Germain-en-Laye.*

215 PEKARNA

Broad spatula. Late Magdalenian. 14 in. This work is exceptionally important because it shows the existence in central Europe of the same system of symbols that is found in Franco-Cantabrian art. This implement is more closely related to the engraved plaquettes and cave figures in the west than to the spatulas previously illustrated, which are decorated exclusively with male symbols. One side shows three heads of horses (male symbols); the other side one bison head (female symbol) and one ibex head (the ibex is complementary to the bison at Niaux, for instance). *Moravské Museum, Brno (photograph Moravské Museum).*

HALF-ROUNDED RODS

CARVED *from the firm portion of reindeer antlers, half-rounded rods were glued together, so that two made a spear. They probably also served in the making of other objects. This technique seems to have made its appearance in the Gravettian, though most of the finds come from the Middle and Late Magdalenian. In decoration, they exhibit every stage from the concrete to the abstract, and from extreme elaboration to geometrical simplicity. The most remarkable specimens come from the Pyrenees and are decorated with spirals in relief. Some half-rounded rods show animal figures, and most have paired sexual signs incised on them. In the course of decorative development, the two subjects may well have become related, the vulva/phallus theme and the eye/horn theme gradually working respectively toward the same schematizations (see chart XIII).*

216 LA MADELEINE (Dordogne)
Engraved half-rounded rod. Magdalenian. A very important document in the history of Paleolithic art: the drawing of the three figures (bear, phallus, vulva) shows how far the supposedly "primitive" realism of Paleolithic artists was elaborated and charged with symbolic elements. Phallus and vulva are here treated as a single motif, well on the way to abstraction and not unrelated to the meandering lines on fig. 219 (top). Comparison with the pierced staff

from Massat (diagram at right; bottom) shows the constant oscillation between the expression of realism and of a symbolism that already comes close to the ideographic. The staff from Massat shows exactly the same composition: bear's head, barbed sign (corresponding to the phallus), and vulvar oval. The position of the barbed sign recalls the "breathing" lines in figs. 212 and 213. Note that this is not a portrayal of sexual intercourse (none exists in Paleolithic art) but the juxtaposition of two symbols, a device closer to written than to pictorial description. $5^1/_4$ in. *Museum, Saint-Germain-en-Laye.*

217 LAUGERIE BASSE
Fragment of half-rounded rod with realistic decoration. The animals represented are cervids, one of them apparently a stag growing its first antlers (compare the "hind" in fig. 219). *Collection de la Société préhistorique française, Musée de l'Homme, Paris.*

218 LAUGERIE BASSE
Fragment of decorated half-rounded rod. The decoration is hard to decipher. Recalling the many stages of the decoration of the "fish" spatulas, we realize that these geometric patterns go back to originally realistic themes. *Musée de l'Homme, Paris.*

219 ISTURITZ
Half-rounded rods. Middle Magdalenian. The top one is decorated

with quadrangular and oval vulvas (cf. pendants, figs. 228–233, and cave signs, figs. 316–317, 355, and charts XXXII–XXXVII). The rods with spiral decorations in raised-field relief also seem to have no precise significance; note, however, that the one on the left includes the outline of the head of some herbivorous animal, possibly a hind. The themes we see here, despite their abstract character, may after all have still kept some realistic reference. Largest fragment 8 in. *Collection Saint-Périer, Morigny.*

220 ISTURITZ
Fragment of half-rounded rod. Decoration is devoid of realistic elements. *Collection Saint-Périer, Morigny.*

MISCELLANEOUS OBJECTS

221 LE SENCI
Bone object, pointed. Late Magdalenian. 4 in. This object is very interesting as an example of schematic treatment of horses in the Late Magdalenian (compare figs. 171, 172, and 220). *Museum, Périgueux.*

222 EL VALLE
Engraved bone tube of a bird. Late Magdalenian. 6 in. We make out two horses in single file, one stag, and various symbols which may be related to barbed signs, ovals, and fishes. *Museum, Santander.*

OBJECTS TO BE HUNG

PENDANTS

THESE *make their appearance as early as the Chatelperronian (35,000–30,000 B.C.). Specimens made of pierced teeth, sea shells, and fossils turn up throughout the Upper Paleolithic. Specimens carved from stone and bony matter exhibit variations according to period which deserve closer study. Annular shapes and those with notched edges are the oldest, and seem to last as late as the Solutrean. Notched oval pendants give way gradually to oval pendants with edges marked with parallel incisions; specimens from the Middle Magdalenian often bear an abstract decoration of various signs; others are realistic and incorporate sexual themes (see chart XIV).*

223 ARCY-SUR-CURE
Pendants from the Chatelperronian with hole or groove for hanging. Canine tooth of a fox, reindeer stylet, wolf's canine, and incisor of aurochs or bison. $1^1/_4$ to 2 in. (shown here root down).

224 ARCY-SUR-CURE
Chatelperronian pendants. Reindeer knuckle shaped as a stag canine. 1 in. Fossil from the Secondary Era (Rhynconnella), grooved for hanging.

225 ARCY-SUR-CURE
Pendant carved of bone, with incised lines around edges. $1^1/_2$ in. Aurignacian.

226 ISTURITZ
Bear sculptured in stone. Middle Magdalenian. About 3 in. The size and material make this an altogether unusual pendant. *Collection Saint-Périer, Morigny.*

227 SAINT-MARCEL
Phalliform pendant. Late Magdalenian. 2 in. *J. Allain excavations, Museum, Châteauroux.*

228 ISTURITZ
Magdalenian pendants. The one at the left is phallic in character, that at the right seems to show a number of female signs. 3 in. *Collection Saint-Périer, Morigny.*

229 LESPUGUE
Magdalenian pendant representing two snakes. $5^1/_2$ in. The snake seems to have belonged to the set of male symbols (cf. especially the phalliform pendant in fig. 228; fig. 216; and the snake with tail shaped like a barbed sign in fig. 193). *Collection Saint-Périer, Morigny.*

230–231 LAUGERIE BASSE
Two pendants (fragments). The one at the left is decorated with ovals which may be interpreted as fish or as female signs. The one at the right shows one fish and two X-signs. *Museum, Saint-Germain-en-Laye.*

232 ISTURITZ
Middle Magdalenian pendant with engraved horse. Note that, as on most pendants, the edges are decorated with short lines, here less elaborately than on some others. $3^5/_8$ in. *Collection Saint-Périer, Morigny.*

233 ISTURITZ
Oval pendant. Magdalenian. *Collection Saint-Périer, Morigny.*

234 LESPUGUE
Carved silhouette of an exceptional type, representing a sole. $1^3/_4$ in. The bottom side of the fish is shown here; the eyes are on the other side. Discovered more than 150 miles inland, this carved silhouette is one of the relatively few evidences we have for the circulation of objects (or themes). In the Breuil Gallery at Le Mas d'Azil are two engraved figures identical with this one (see figs. 640–641). *Museum, Saint-Germain-en-Laye.*

235 BOURDEILLES, LE FOURNEAU DU DI-
ABLE

Oval pendant. Stone. Engraving of a reindeer. Late Solutrean. $4^3/_8$ in. *Museum, Les Eyzies.*

236 RAYMONDEN

Fragment of pendant, the ring of which has broken off. $3^1/_4$ in. This object repeats exactly the theme found on an engraved bone from Les Eyzies (see fig. 446). At left, two forelegs and the head of a bison (the bone from Les Eyzies shows the forequarters of a standing bison). Here the head and limbs are truncated, but this may be an effect of perspective; the bison might be in frontal view, head turned to one side. At the right, seven little human figures, lined up on either side of a barbed sign; one of them seems to be holding a branching object. Lastly, three sets of double strokes come together at the top. (On the object from Les Eyzies there are nine human figures filing by, carrying spears over their shoulders, and four barbed signs or branching signs shaped like willows.) This portion of the decoration (bison/barbed sign, man/spear) brings to mind the paired subjects and the man/bison theme in cave art. In both examples the composition suggests a narrative subject, elsewhere found only in scenes where a man is attacked by an animal. Here the arrangement is not clear; moreover, this pendant is of an unusual type: the hatchings which once framed the ring seem related to the salmon theme, customarily found on spatulas (see figs. 208–212). *Museum, Périgueux.*

CARVED SILHOUETTES AND DISKS

So *far as we can judge from the finds, the silhouettes carved out of hyoid bones and the disks carved out of shoulder blades were contemporary, Middle Magdalenian (13,000–11,000 B.C.). Both are decorated with various animal figures and probably were turned out in sets. The only known set (Labastide) consists of one bison and several ibexes, all carved silhouettes.*

237–239 ISTURITZ

Carved silhouettes of horses' heads. $1^3/_4$ to $2^3/_4$ in. The one at the left is the most common type having the stereotyped details of modeling and treatment of the coat which characterize most specimens from southwestern France. The one at the right is of a less common type, but comparison with figs. 237, 238, and 240–242 shows that it has most of the conventional details. *Collection Saint-Périer, Morigny.*

240 LE PORTEL

Horse's head. Carved silhouette. 2 in. The details are the same as in figs. 237–239, but more sketchily executed. *Collection Vézian.*

241 ISTURITZ, SALLE SAINT-MARTIN.

Ibex head. Carved silhouette. $2^1/_2$ in. Middle Magdalenian. The break at the neck and casual placing of the perforations suggest that this is a fragment from a more sizable piece. *Collection Saint-Périer, Morigny.*

242 ARUDY

Horse's head. Carved silhouette. $1^3/_4$ in. The stiff treatment of the coat on this specimen gave rise at the close of the nineteenth century to learned discussions concerning the domestication of the horse in the Magdalenian, the lines of hatchings being thought possibly to represent a halter. Actually what we have here is extreme stylization. *Museum, Saint-Germain-en-Laye.*

243–244 LAUGERIE BASSE

Disk, probably representing a calf on one side and a cow on the other. We have few representations of young animals that cannot be disputed; this example of a female with its young is exceptional. *Museum, Saint-Germain-en-Laye.*

245–246 LAUGERIE BASSE

Disk. $1^1/_8$ in. One side shows a herbivorous animal with the proportions of a hind, or perhaps of a young chamois. The other side shows a crouching herbivore, which might be a chamois. *Museum, Périgueux.*

247 LE MAS D'AZIL

Disk with abstract decoration. *Museum, Saint-Germain-en-Laye.*

248 BRUNIQUEL

Disk, showing an ibex head and the decoration most usual on disks: a border of parallel strokes bounded by a circle and lines radiating from the hole at the center. $1^3/_8$ in. *Collection Bétirac.*

STYLE I

ENGRAVED SLABS

249–251 LA FERRASSIE AND ABRI CELLIER

Vulvas incised on blocks. Fig. 251 also shows a row of strokes and a cup-mark. Block, fig. 251, $21^1/_4$ in. *Museum, Les Eyzies.*

252 ABRI CELLIER

At center, an ibex represented by dorsal line and one horn. At left, curving lines perhaps representing a second ibex. $22^1/_2$ in. *Museum, Les Eyzies.*

253 ABRI CELLIER

Together with figs. 249–252, this slab is one of the earliest known decorated works in human history. They all refute the theory that art began with naturalism. The composition is as abstract as the symbolic compositions in the great Magdalenian sanctuaries: a female sign, already highly stylized; a male sign (row of strokes); association of an animal head (probably a horse) with sexual symbols. As early as 1946, D. Peyrony wrote of this work: "One of the stones... bears a strange drawing. The figure at the left seems to be the head of an equid, that at the right a vulva... The fact

that one line links the two drawings suggests that in the mind of the artist the two were closely associated." $13^3/_4$ in. *Museum, Les Eyzies.*

254 LA FERRASSIE

Layer H″, Aurignacian IV. Slab broken off at the top. We can make out the legs and belly of an animal similar in treatment to the figure at Belcayre (fig. 256). It is accompanied by a stylized vulva and a row of dots. The association we find here between an animal and sexual symbols proves that even at this early stage rows of dots were equivalent to rows of strokes—a correspondence of which there are many later examples. 27 in. *Museum, Les Eyzies.*

255 LA FERRASSIE

Layer H″, Aurignacian IV. Engraved slab generally believed to show the head of a feline. This slab is especially hard to decipher: D. Peyrony's interpretation emphasizes the forepart of the "feline," at the expense of details which appear under different lighting. The engraving is very like most Aurignacian work: juxtaposition of the forequarters of an animal (perhaps a feline) with

strokes and stylized vulvas. One of the vulvas, more deeply incised than the others, gives the impression that the animal has a parrot's beak. $8^3/_4$ in. *Museum, Les Eyzies.*

256 BELCAYRE

Engraving representing a herbivorous animal. Its discoverer supposed it to be a reindeer, but the Abbé Breuil saw it rather as an ibex. The short tail restricts possible identification to the reindeer, the stag, the ibex, the chamois, and the saiga antelope. The two last-named ruminants are so rare in Paleolithic art that they are ruled out statistically. The reindeer, too, is ruled out because we have no other reindeer figure in which the head is positioned so unnaturally. The stag and the ibex, then, remain the only logical possibilities. The work's zoological vagueness gives us no real choice between them. We may note, however, that the stag is usually rendered with a more horizontal muzzle, and consequently Breuil's identification seems justified: slanting muzzle, long neck and withers, and raised tail are usual in renderings of the ibex. 20 in. *Museum, Les Eyzies.*

257 ISTURITZ
Layer IV, mature Gravettian with Noailles burins. Thick pike or spear point engraved with the figure of a horse. 7 in. One of the earliest animal representations on an object of use. The horse exhibits all the features of Style II. *Collection Saint-Périer, Morigny.*

258 LAUGERIE HAUTE
Plaquette incised with several outlines. On the side shown here, we can make out a horse's head. The discoverer filled in the very thin lines with pencil. Two outlines of mammoths appear on the other side. 4³/₄ in. *Museum, Les Eyzies.*

259 ISTURITZ
Layer III, mature Gravettian or the period between the Gravettian and the Solutrean. 6 in. Slab showing unfinished outlines. We make out one

dorsal curve and a deeper line which appears to indicate an animal's chest, foreleg, and belly. *Collection Saint-Périer, Morigny.*

Plaquettes with tangled figures, whether unfinished outlines or superimpositions, which are found in certain parts of caves, are a constant feature of Paleolithic art. The frequent incompleteness of the features, their fineness, and the difficulties they must have posed for the artists, have long intrigued prehistorians. At first, these were taken for something like a modern artist's sketch pads. Dr. Cheynier advanced the theory that these plaquettes were coated with ocher or some other perishable material, before each successive drawing was made. The uneven scratching of the graving tool on these successive surfaces would account for the tangled, incomplete condition of the figures as we see

them. As yet, there is no archaeological evidence in support of this interesting theory.

260 LES REBIÈRES
Engraved pebble found in the Gravettian at the Durand-Ruel site at Les Rebières. 5 in. We make out a herbivorous animal, supposedly an elk, and the forequarters of a rhinoceros. *Collection Pittard, Institut d'Anthropologie de l'Université de Genève (photograph J. Arlaud).*

261 DOLNI VESTONICE
Head of a feline, modeled in clay and bone ash. 2³/₈ in. *Moravske Museum, Brno (photograph Moravske Museum).*

262 DOLNI VESTONICE
Head of a rhinoceros, modeled in clay and bone ash. 1³/₄ in. *Moravske Museum, Brno (photograph Moravske Museum).*

263 TURSAC, ABRI DU FACTEUR
Figurine discovered in 1959 by H. Delporte. 3¹/₄ in. This object is markedly different from the best-known statuettes. Though lacking detail in the head and feet and built up around the abdomen, it is nonetheless in line with Style II (see chart XLIV). The lower appendage gave rise to a number of theories: giving birth, bisexual figure, peg for sticking figurine in the ground. *Museum, Saint-Germain-en-Laye (photograph Artzet).*

264 LESPUGUE
Profile view of female figurine (see fig. 52 and diagram). 5³/₄ in. *Saint-Périer excavations, Musée de l'Homme, Paris.*

265-267 BARMA GRANDE, BALZI ROSSI
Steatite figurines of women. 2 to 2³/₄ in. *Museum, Saint-Germain-en-Laye.*

268 WILLENDORF
Stone statuette. 4³/₈ in. Found among industrial objects similar to those among which the Kostienki statuettes were found, this female figure exhibits the same stereotyped details (see

STYLE II
HUMAN FIGURES

chart XLV). Geographically and morphologically, it is intermediate between Kostienki and Lespugue. *Museum of Natural History, Vienna.*

269 DOLNI VESTONICE
Female statuette modeled in a mixture of clay and powdered bone. 4¹/₂ in. *Moravske Museum, Brno (photograph Moravske Museum).*

270 LAUSSEL
Male figure. 15 in. *Collection Lalanne, Musée d'Aquitaine, Bordeaux (Museum photograph by J. Vertut).*

271 LAUSSEL
Female figure with horn. 17 in. Originally touched up with ocher, the figure seems to be holding a bison horn. *Collection Lalanne, Musée d'Aquitaine, Bordeaux (Museum photograph by J. Vertut).*

272 LAUSSEL
Female figure apparently holding something in her right hand. 11³/₄ in. *Collection Lalanne, Musée d'Aquitaine, Bordeaux (Museum photograph by J. Vertut).*

273 LAUSSEL
Low relief with human figures in inverted mirror image. The hollowed-out portions have been rendered in black in the drawing, to show that there is no anatomical connection between the two subjects, and that the lower figure is limited to a single outline. Interpretations of this work (sexual intercourse, giving birth) are mere conjectures: what we actually see could as well be the sculptured figure of a woman using part of an earlier, unfinished figure. When we carefully place this work over the outlined figures of the woman holding the horn (fig. 271) and that now in the Berlin Museum (fig. 274), we see that its outline exactly corresponds to that of a standing female holding out her left arm. The bending of the legs brings to mind the figurine from Tursac (fig. 263), which also has a lower appendage. 8 in. See chart XLVI. *Collection Lalanne. Musée d'Aquitaine, Bordeaux (Museum photograph by J. Vertut).*

274 LAUSSEL
Female figure holding an object. 8 in. *State Museum, Berlin-Dahlem (photograph Lalanne).*

STYLE II
CAVE ART

PAIR-NON-PAIR

(Plan, fig. 122, page 304)

275-279 PAIR-NON-PAIR
Panels 1 and 2. We make out two facing ibexes (figs. 275-276); in the hollow between them is a third ibex. The largest measures 25⁵/₈ in. The horns are in normal perspective,

which is not the case in certain later figures: in the "*camarin*" at Le Portel, for instance (fig. 585). At lower right is the figure of a mammoth (fig. 279), and in front of it are the hindquarters of a bison (fig. 278), which occupies the center of the right-hand wall. Another bison faces it. Then come two horses (fig. 277) and an ibex. Average length of figures, 30 in.

280 PAIR-NON-PAIR
Panel 3. "*Agnus Dei.*" Height 25 in. It is easy to see how the two figures (ibex and horse) could be interpreted as a single animal having a turned head at the end of a disproportionately long neck.

281 PAIR-NON-PAIR
Panel 5. Aurochs at the center of

the panel with the meandering lines. About 6 ft. We barely make out the figure of a horse of the same size, whose head is pointed in the opposite direction; the figures intersect at the withers.

282 PAIR-NON-PAIR
Panel 4. Two ibexes and one cervid superimposed. On the animal looking to the left we clearly make out the hump marked with a dot, similar to the dot on the Megaceros deer in the Cougnac cave (fig. 383). Length of work about 43 in.

283 PAIR-NON-PAIR
Panel 6. Little mammoth at left of entrance. About 12 in.

LA MOUTHE

284 LA MOUTHE
Group consisting of bulls and one horse. Only the central figure is not distorted by the angle of the photograph: it illustrates the features of Style II. The barely visible horse is below it.

GORGE D'ENFER

285 GORGE D'ENFER, ABRI DU POISSON
Male salmon in raised-field relief. 41³/₈ in. The frame was cut out in recent years, in an attempted theft. The upper drawing shows details visible today; below it is illustrated the possibility that the fish was superimposed on a bison figure, using a figure (reversed) from the Abri Reverdit (see fig. 499).

LA GRÈZE

286 LA GRÈZE
Engraved bison. 23⁵/₈ in.

LA MOUTHE

287 LA MOUTHE
Bull. 47 in.

LOS HORNOS

288 LOS HORNOS
Engraved horse on entrance wall. 15³/₄ in. (see chart LIV).

GARGAS

(Plan, fig. 124, page 307)

289 GARGAS
Black hand in a niche. Executed in a

small, deep concavity, it seems impossible that so clear-cut an outline of a left hand, however mutilated, could have been applied there *(photograph A. Leroi-Gourhan)*.

290 GARGAS
Black hand and red hand. The little finger of the hand at the left appears to have been shortened in the course of execution, but can still be made out through the pigment *(photograph A. Leroi-Gourhan)*.

291 GARGAS
Top and left: two forms of a right hand with fingers bent: *(left)* with palm against the wall; *(top)* with back of hand against the wall. Experiment has verified this reading, accounting for the fact that the fingers of the hand appear mutilated in one instance, and in the other they are crooked.
Bottom and right: one hand imprinted twice. The middle finger is complete on the hand at the right and mutilated on the hand at the left *(photograph A. Leroi-Gourhan; see also fig. 8)*.

292 GARGAS
Prints of a bent right thumb repeated as a frieze. It is possible that this subject, which we find also at Pech Merle (compare fig. 366), represented heads of horses *(photograph A. Leroi-Gourhan)*.

293 GARGAS
Panels such as this show imprints of right hands, fingers bent: *(series at left)* with back of the hand against the wall; *(series at right)* with palm against the wall.

All the hands at Gargas are those of children, or at any rate are smaller than those of an adult male. How the color was applied is not completely clear, but it was certainly done with great care. By experiment, I was able to duplicate these effects of deformed or shortened fingers, with either the back of the hand or the palm against the wall, by using a quite stiff brush ³/₄ in. wide, dipped in a fairly thin ocher, spreading the fingers as wide apart as possible. When the pigment is blown on the wall, there is more blurring and the outlines become more irregular, which is not the case at Gargas.

294 GARGAS
Ibex head, from the same composition as the bison in fig. 295. Probably a female; a male with sketchily executed big horns appears directly below (fig. 297). About 6 in.

295 GARGAS
Bison head, engraved to the right of the cascade. The execution, in parallel hatchings without contour lines, is very characteristic of Gargas.

296 GARGAS
Very schematized ibex head to the left of the cascade. About 20 in.

297 GARGAS
Head of ibex, engraved below fig. 294. About 24 in.

298 GARGAS
Male ibex head engraved on the low vaulted ceiling. This very finely executed figure is much closer to Style III than to Style II. However, the outlines rendered in parallel hatching reflect the same convention as the more primitive-looking figures in the sanctuary. The photograph covers about 16 in. of the figure.

299 GARGAS
Forelegs of a horse engraved to the left of the low vaulted ceiling. About 4 in.

300 GARGAS
Horse's head to the left of the sanctuary. Stylistically close to Style III. About 8 in.

301 GARGAS
Bison head engraved on the right-hand wall at the back of the sanctuary. Photograph covers about 12 in. of the figure.

302 GARGAS
Head of an ibex engraved in the vicinity of fig. 301. About 10 in.

303 GARGAS
Horse's head engraved in the vicinity of figs. 301, 302. About 16 in.

304 GARGAS
Engraving in soft clay on the ceiling of chamber IV. Part of the area of meandering lines drawn with fingers which covers the entire right-hand portion of the chamber between the engraved semidome and the sanctuary (V). The figure is a very schematic bovine head. About 24 in. *(photograph A. Leroi-Gourhan)*.

STYLE III
CAVE ART

LE ROC DE SERS

(All photographs from Museum, St.-Germain-en-Laye)

305 LE ROC DE SERS
Block with the theme "man pursued by bison." The animal has been read as a musk ox, but the detail and proportions are those of a bison. The unusual horns were dictated by ne-

cessity (see fig. 484). The scene is a classic theme in Paleolithic art (see figs. 323, 358, 493). 60 in.

306–308 LE ROC DE SERS
Horses in Style III. Note the proportions of head and limbs, the strongly arched cervico-dorsal line, bowl-shaped hoofs, firmly planted legs—all of which bring to mind Lascaux and Le Gabillou. Fig. 306, 26 in; fig. 307, 16 in.; fig. 308, 34⁵/₈ in. Fig. 308 overlaps a bison, one foreleg of which is visible.

309 LE ROC DE SERS
"Bison-boar" block. Length 64⁵/₈ in. The horse with distended body, exaggeratedly short legs, and bowl-shaped hoofs is very characteristic of Style III. It is closely related to horses at Lascaux and Le Gabillou. The body of the animal which precedes it corresponds in every detail to a bison. The head in front of the break in the stone seems to have been recarved. Anatomically, the head is ambiguous.

310 LE ROC DE SERS

Block with a figure which can be identified as a bird, but is not unrelated to the head of one of the "monsters" at Le Gabillou (see fig. 349). 16 in.

311 LE ROC DE SERS

Fragments of a block on which we make out the body of a deer and the palm of the antlers of a Megaceros deer; there are other examples of this animal at Pech Merle and Cougnac (see fig. 383).

312 LE ROC DE SERS

Ibex in Style III. Note the short legs and the horns in semifrontal perspective.

313 LE ROC DE SERS

Block with facing ibexes. Length about 36 in. Unusually short legs. The theme of facing ibexes is also found in the Axial Gallery at Lascaux.

LASCAUX

(Plan, fig. 125, page 312)

314 LASCAUX

Panorama of figures in the Rotunda (see fig. 72). Perhaps nowhere else in Paleolithic art does the meaning of the composition emerge more clearly in the confrontation of two groups of figures: cows at the left are contrasted with bulls at the right and complemented by the symbolic horses. The horses at the left echo the complementary red bovines accompanying the bulls at the right. The interconnection is provided by the little stags and the large incomplete horse, a replica of which is found in the Axial Gallery in front of the black bull (see fig. 320).
At left: the "unicorn." It is possible that the appendages on the forehead correspond to the tail of the large bovine which precedes it. All the anatomical details are so vague that the most varied theories are possible. Length 65 in. On the rump there is the sketch of a horse which shows that the frieze of horses must have been painted before the "unicorn," but as part of the same composition, inasmuch as the artist refrained from filling in the sketch in order to emphasize the figure of the spotted animal.

315 LASCAUX

Back of the Axial Gallery. Horse positioned upside down, as though falling through space. Complete horse 78 in.

316 LASCAUX

Right-hand wall of the Axial Gallery (see fig. 73). Central composition. Cow and quadrangular sign (see charts XXXVII, XXXVIII), accompanied by little horses. The composition is identical with that on the left-hand portion of fig. 314 and echoes the black bull on the opposite wall (fig. 320). Cow 67 in.

317 LASCAUX

Entrance to Axial Gallery, right-hand wall (see fig. 73). Stag and entrance dots. First paired quadran-

gular sign. Cow and three horses, accompanied by paired signs. The first horse has two rows of dots instead of forelegs. This group runs up onto the ceiling and echoes fig. 319 on the left-hand wall. Cow 9 ft. 2¹/₂ in. The two horses at the left are known as the "Chinese" horses. The treatment of the one nearest the cow is interesting, for it corresponds to the most classic conventions of Early Style IV (double shoulder line and M-shaped ventral modeling). Above its neck and withers is seen a checkerboard quadrangular sign which normally accompanies figures in Style III. In front of its muzzle, there is a variant of the brace-shaped sign which usually accompanies figures in mature Style III or Early Style IV. The arrows accompanying the two horses are complementary barbed signs (see charts XXXVI–XXXVIII). The first horse measures 55 in.

318 LASCAUX

Nave. Composition of horses and bison framed by quadrangular signs. The bison is marked with seven single lines, whereas the two horses are marked with paired signs: one with seven "wounds" and a hooked stroke, the other with one "wound" and a barbed sign. Composition 14 ft. 9 in. For the interpretation of the signs, see chart XXXVI.

319 LASCAUX

Axial Gallery, entrance, left-hand wall. Group of red cows preceding black bull (see fig. 320). Cow at left 9 ft. 2 in.

320 LASCAUX

Axial Gallery. Black bull and barbed sign with complementary horse (see fig. 98). There are two red cows and several sets of horns within the body of the bull. The grouping is the same as that on the right in the Rotunda (fig. 314); the bull echoes the black cow placed opposite (fig. 316). Complete bull about 9 ft. 10 in.

321 LASCAUX

Nave. Composition comprising a cow accompanied by quadrangular signs and little horses, a theme identical with fig. 314 (left) and fig. 316. This group, which corresponds to fig. 314 (right) and fig. 320 (bull and little cows, barbed signs), could have been placed in the Passageway or in the Apse. Cow 63 in.

322 LASCAUX

Frieze of stags at entrance to Nave, accompanied by a row of dots as in fig. 317. The group, 16 ft. 5 in.

323–324 LASCAUX

Scene at the bottom of the Shaft. Actually, there are three groups of figures: (1) a rhinoceros, whose place at the very back is in accord with the usual topographical conventions; (2) six dots, marking one of the extremities of the sanctuary (see figs. 317, 322, 326); (3) scene of the wounded man, comprising the man and the bison and, opposite them, the complementary horse (see figs. 438, 439). The bison seems to be disemboweled, with, in addition, a long spear through its body. A

spear-thrower seems to be lying at the man's feet. These different figures (the concentric ovals of the bowels, the spear, the barbed shaft of the spear-thrower) have also a symbolic significance (see chart XXVIII). The same is true of the hooked staff surmounted by a bird, which has inspired so much conjecture. 9 ft. *(photographs: fig. 323, Hinz; fig. 324, A. Leroi-Gourhan).*

325 LASCAUX

Large horse on the left-hand wall of the Axial Gallery. We see a barbed sign just in front of it (see charts XXXVII, XXXVIII). 9 ft. 10 in.

326 LASCAUX

Back of Axial Gallery. Last horse and row of dots marking the end of the composition.

327 LASCAUX

Rotunda. Little stag at entrance to Axial Gallery. 27⁵/₈ in.

328 LASCAUX

Group of little stags in the Rotunda. Under the legs of the first stag, we see a figure which could be a schematized human face (see chart XXX). Group 67 in.

329 LASCAUX

Axial Gallery, right-hand wall. Head, probably of a bull, above black cow (fig. 316).

330 LASCAUX

Back of Axial Gallery. Bison followed by horse, forming a separate bison/horse group, as at the end of each area of the cave (see figs. 318, 331).

331 LASCAUX

Nave. Black bison, forming the last group of paintings in the cave. 7 ft. 10¹/₂ in.

332 LASCAUX

Chamber of Felines, first portion of right-hand wall. The composition comprises three felines (two of them facing each other), one bison head, a sketch of a horse's head in profile, one horse in frontal view, and several ibexes; a number of barbed signs and parallel strokes are also present (see charts XXXVI–XXVIII). 8 ft. 2 in. *(photographs A. Leroi-Gourhan).*

333 LASCAUX

Passageway. Horse, engraved and painted in the earliest Lascaux manner. Note left ear situated in the middle of the cheek.

334 LASCAUX

Apse. Engraved horse, on which a compartmented quadrangular sign appears, of the type which accompanies figures in Style III. Over this sign have been incised the staffs of two claviforms of the Pyrenean or Cantabrian type, which normally accompany figures in Early Style IV (see chart XXXVII, Apse). These signs are at the entrance to the Shaft, at the bottom of which the scene of the wounded man is located; the bison there is very close to Early Style IV.

335 LASCAUX

Apse. Reindeer engraved on the right-hand wall. This is the only reindeer at Lascaux. In style, it is very close to the figures in the remoter portion of Le Gabillou.

336 LASCAUX
Apse. Horse's head on the ceiling. We can see that the figure was reworked again and again. Ears and eyes in the different versions do not coincide.

337 LASCAUX
Detail of one of the stags engraved in the Apse. Note the left ear placed on the cheek, and the antlers in frontal perspective. Complete stag 39 in.

338 LASCAUX
Nave. Frieze of ibex heads above fig. 318. Height about 12 in.

LE GABILLOU

(Plan, fig. 126, page 317)

339 LE GABILLOU
Horse's head, engraved.

340–341 LE GABILLOU
Bison in small chamber G (see plan). Note that the animals' horns are in Style III; those of the first bison are in the same perspective as those at Lascaux (figs. 318, 331) and at Pech Merle (fig. 376). The horns of the second bison correspond to the perspective that is usual for aurochs; however, the bison in the Shaft at Lascaux (see fig. 323) has the same type of horns.

342 LE GABILLOU
Engraving of small horse. Note the double line at the base of the mane.

343 LE GABILLOU
Aurochs in small chamber E (see plan). Despite the poor quality of the outline, the horns correspond to Style III conventions. Also note the ear, seemingly stuck into the back of the head, a detail with which we are familiar from Lascaux.

344 LE GABILLOU
One of the cervids in chambers P and Q (see plan). It is hard to determine the species. All fourteen of the cervids in this part of the cave lack precision of structure; the details shown could equally indicate stags or reindeer. The antlers and outline of this particular figure could be those of a reindeer, whereas the double-tined antlers, the posture of the head, and the lack of a dewlap are characteristic of a stag.

345 LE GABILLOU
Engraved horse, filled in with red ocher. This is one of the figures at Le Gabillou with obvious affinities to figures at Lascaux (shape of head, arched neck and withers, disproportion between legs and body, ball-shaped hoofs). Note especially the ears and the eye, the abnormal positioning of which is frequently found on the earliest animals at Lascaux.

346 LE GABILLOU
Horse on left-hand wall in chamber L. This is one of the central figures, in style close to the horse in the Shaft

at Lascaux (see fig. 324). It probably falls within the second period of Style III (see chart XLII).

347 LE GABILLOU
Head of feline in area B. This is one of the finest feline figures known, and, except for the one at Labastide (see fig. 576), the only one with bared fangs. The head of a herbivorous animal partly covers the figure.

348 LE GABILLOU
Feline from chamber C; in every feature very close to those in the Chamber of Felines at Lascaux.

349–351 LE GABILLOU
"Monsters" in chamber L. Fig. 349 represents the "giraffe," an animal as hard to identify as the "unicorn" at Lascaux. Fig. 350 suggests a hare with the head and ears treated quite realistically, but the other features do not go with this identification. Fig. 351 shows a creature in frontal view which might perhaps be seen as a feline.

352 LE GABILLOU
Horse's head.

353 LE GABILLOU
"Woman with parka," human figure of indeterminate sex, apparently seated. In view of its topographical position (chamber J) at the very center of the major compositions, it might in fact be female.

354 LE GABILLOU
Sign of undetermined character in chamber N. It brings to mind a few Cantabrian signs (see chart LI).

355 LE GABILLOU
Compartmented quadrangular sign in chamber P. In type, it is closely related to signs at Lascaux (see chart XXXVI).

356 LE GABILLOU
Rows of parallel lines in the vicinity of figures.

VILLARS

(Plan, fig. 127, page 318)

357 VILLARS
Block with unfinished outlines (F). Vertical lines, one horse's head, and several incomplete dorsal curves. When it was discovered, a weekly periodical reproduced this tangle of lines, describing it as a white bear *(sic)* and a hunter armed with a bow and arrow....

358 VILLARS
Group of man and bison (see chart XXVIII). The horns are of an early type. The other details are too vague to permit closer analysis. Bison about 8 in.

359 VILLARS
Horse painted in black, close in style to some of the Lascaux horses (see figs. 314, 325). About 12 in.

LA MOUTHE

360 LA MOUTHE
Bison panel, left-hand portion, ibex at top left. The animals measure between 30 and 40 in.

SAINT-CIRQ

361 SAINT-CIRQ
Main panel in rear chamber. At left, one bison head and one triangular sign; at right, male figure (see chart XXIX). Length of panel about 31 in. Farther to the right, there is a horse and a profile hard to identify.

PECH MERLE

(Plans, figs. 128, 129, page 321)

362 PECH MERLE
Le Combel. Quadrangular signs and dots, painted in red, in the corridor leading to the "Chamber of Antelopes."

363 PECH MERLE
"Chamber of Antelopes." The opening was widened at the time of discovery. On the ceiling are stalactites shaped like breasts, the tips of which seem to have been painted black. On the wall, big red dots. The ceiling is about 40 in. above the ground.

364 PECH MERLE
Panel of "antelopes." About 40 in.

365 PECH MERLE
Le Combel. Panel with "lioness." At left is the head of a feline, at center a horse facing left, and below it a second horse facing right. Note the great stylistic similarity with the dotted horses in the Main Chamber (see fig. 366 and chart XLII). A sketch of a vertically positioned bison visible at center. Scarcely visible dots are scattered through the composition. About 40 in.

366 PECH MERLE
Main Chamber. Fresco of dotted horses. Total length about 11 ft. Note the position of the negative hands surrounding both animals. The hand at top left is accompanied by several dots, the hand at bottom right by two vertical rows of dots. Over the back of the horse on the left, we make out red thumbmarks exactly like those at Gargas. Harder to see from the photograph, there are also a big pike over the right-hand horse (see fig. 64), one circle, and the sketch of a bison.

367 PECH MERLE
Side chamber with "bison/women." At center, a number of dots. At bottom right, one mammoth above a woman, a theme we find repeated at least three times on the ceiling with the meandering lines (see fig. 382). From top to bottom at left, six figures indicate successive transitions from the outline of a bison to that of a woman (see chart XLVIII).

368–371 PECH MERLE
Side chamber with "bison/women." Various statements of the theme. Each figure measures about 4 in.

372 PECH MERLE
Barbed sign in side chamber of "the wounded man."

373 PECH MERLE
Red strokes near the sign in fig. 372.

374 PECH MERLE

Panel with "the wounded man" (see chart XXVIII). The composition measures about 30 in. Note the brace-shaped sign above the male figure. The wavy lines at the top are unexplained.

375 PECH MERLE

Main Chamber. Large panel in black. Wounded cow. Like most Paleolithic figures, this one is without indication of sex, but the outline suggests a cow rather than a bull. Note the treatment of the horns and the straight-line treatment of the muzzle, features found in most Style III aurochs (see figs. 319, 343).

376 PECH MERLE

Bison from the panel in fig. 375, right-hand side. Only one horn is shown, in frontal perspective. 49 in.

377 PECH MERLE

Mammoth with red dots. Under the tail, a disk of fatty matter (anal operculum) can be made out. The frozen bodies of mammoths found in Siberia show that this was a feature peculiar to these proboscidians. 23⁵/₈ in.

378 PECH MERLE

Mammoth at extreme right of the black frieze. The first subject in the sequence of mammoth/bison pairs. 23⁵/₈ in.

379 PECH MERLE

Central theme of the black panel. Horse superimposed over bison (see chart XLII).

380 PECH MERLE

Engraved head of a bear, with vertical lines, in the "bear corridor." About 12 in.

381 PECH MERLE

Bison in right-hand portion of the large frieze. It seems to be run through with a spear. 20 in.

382 PECH MERLE

Right-hand portion of the scraped ceiling. The mammoth/woman theme appears twice. Big oval sign. The woman at the bottom measures 21⁵/₈ in. (see chart XLIX).

COUGNAC

(Plan, fig. 130, page 324)

383–384 COUGNAC

Panels IV, V, VI, VII, VIII. Panoramic view of the large fresco. Total length about 30 ft. *(photographic restitution, J. Vertut).*

383. Panels IV, V, and VI. At the same level as the three Megaceros deer or a little above them, from left to right: sketch of mammoth, ibex head, stag, wounded man, and ibex. Length of panel about 13 ft. The first two Megaceros deer have two diverging lines starting at a spot on the withers. Next to the ibex head on the left is an undetermined figure resembling the antler of a Megaceros deer. At right are male and female ibexes. The female measures 20 in.

384. Panels VII and VIII. Double strokes are scattered through the composition. The opening of the tunnel appears at bottom center; there are dots inside it. Panel VII: male ibex and ibex head. 32 in. Panel VIII *(left)*: horse's head visible through calcite deposit. Double strokes under the neck and withers. Branched sign in front of the forehead. Hooked sign and curving lines appear above the "dotted" neck and withers. This figure has been described as the hindquarters of a mammoth, but it is most probably a horse. Panel VIII *(right)*: at center, mammoth, horns of ibex, and a second figure run through with spears, scarcely visible behind the wounded man. Under the mammoth's trunk and belly, we see the top of the skull and the beginning of the back of two other (unfinished) mammoths. A number of double strokes. Height of central mammoth 29¹/₂ in.

385 COUGNAC

Panel X. Signs in transverse gallery. Two brace-shaped signs and one stroke (at top center).

386 COUGNAC

Panel III. Three schematic human figures (see chart XXX), dots, forequarters of a cervid (at top right). Length of cervid 21 in.

LE PORTEL, GALLERY 2

(Plan, fig. 153, page 361)

387 LE PORTEL

Red-and-black horse in Style III on left-hand wall (M on plan). About 40 in.

388 LE PORTEL

Schematic stag in niche at right (L on plan). As at Lascaux (fig. 322), the antlers are shown in Style III perspective.

389 LE PORTEL

Black and red figures on right-hand wall (M on plan). A horse in Style III can be made out rather clearly at bottom. Above it is a little red stag. At top left (shown in diagram) are a cervid and a black ibex. Total height 31¹/₂ in.

390 LE PORTEL

Group of figures on right-hand wall (N on plan), inside a recess behind a few big stones. At top left, the forequarters of a horse in Style III. At center, a big brace-shaped sign. About 30 in. directly below it is the little male figure shown in fig. 391.

391 LE PORTEL

Male silhouette in red, sexual parts supplied by a small stalagmite. About 14 in.

ISTURITZ

392 ISTURITZ

Engravings on stalagmitic mass in big chamber. Left-hand portion: one reindeer and short-tailed ruminants, most likely ibexes. 59 in.

LAS CHIMENEAS

(Plan, fig. 131, page 327)

393 LAS CHIMENEAS

Large chamber, group 6: front of the second springing of ceiling vault. At left, head of a hind. At center, three heads of oxen.

394 LAS CHIMENEAS

Large chamber, group 6: small engraved head of a cow on right-hand side of second vault springing. Same style as in fig. 393: treatment of horns, placement on head, long thin muzzle, and line of neck and withers are all met with at Lascaux and Pech Merle (see figs. 319, 375).

395 LAS CHIMENEAS

Side recess, group 10: paired signs. The female sign is of the quadrangular type, not filled in. The male sign is a double stroke. Cf. quadrangular sign with single stroke accompanying the stag at the entrance to the Axial Gallery at Lascaux (see fig. 317).

396 LAS CHIMENEAS

Side recess, group 9: head, neck, and withers of horse. The head is small, the neck vigorously arched, and the ears are set separately at the back of the head.

397 LAS CHIMENEAS

Side recess, group 10: stags. The antlers are shown in different stages of schematization, from which one might be tempted to deduce that these animals are of various ages, but the drawings more probably show different degrees of simplification.

398 LAS CHIMENEAS

Large chamber, group 7: black-painted quadrangular signs.

ALTAMIRA, BLACK SEQUENCE

(Plan, fig. 132, page 328)

399 ALTAMIRA

Ibexes (35 on plan). Two males, apparently, with horns characteristic of the Pyrenean variety. This zoological feature, however, does not invariably appear on ibexes in the caves of Spain and the Pyrenees. Over-all length 23⁵/₈ in.

400 ALTAMIRA

Bison (37 on plan). The simplicity of the drawing precludes precise determination of the style, but the figure seems earlier than those with conventional Style IV modeling. 36⁵/₈ in.

401 ALTAMIRA

Horse (53 on plan), accompanied by strokes. The style is hard to define but seems to fall within phase III. 14⁵/₈ in. In front of the horse is a much damaged bison figure.

402–404 ALTAMIRA

Irregularities in the rock transformed into faces by adding two painted eyes and a black patch for a beard. Height about 16 in.

405 ALTAMIRA

Quadrangular signs (57 on plan). Their filled-in character and pronounced curvature along one edge make them transitional to brace-shaped signs. The longest is 16 in.

406 ALTAMIRA
Head of an aurochs on clay portion of ceiling (3 on plan), with meandering lines superimposed. 39³/₈ in.

407 ALTAMIRA
Engraved horse in inner gallery. 11³/₄ in.

408 ALTAMIRA
Engraved head of a hind at back of terminal tunnel (67 on plan).

LA PASIEGA

(Plans, figs. 134–137, pages 331, 332)

409–411 LA PASIEGA
Gallery A. These are figures A and B on fig. 135. The first group, at left, consists of one hind (not shown) and one bison; the central group, of two horses and one stag; the group at the right, of two stags and one horse. Note especially the antlers in Style III perspective. The figures are 12 to 20 in. long.

412 LA PASIEGA
Hind no. 18. 25⁵/₈ in. One of the finest figures in Spanish cave art.

413 LA PASIEGA
Horse's head no. 14. Note its lifted position.

414 LA PASIEGA
Figures in a niche (E on fig. 135). Three horses, one ox, and one hind are accompanied by a quadrangular sign.

415 LA PASIEGA
Aurochs no. 37 (F on fig. 135). Note similarity of horns and head to those of figures at Las Chimeneas (see fig. 394). 31¹/₂ in.

416 LA PASIEGA
Ibex at back of recess in Gallery B. The sketchy figure is very close in execution to the other figures in this gallery.

417 LA PASIEGA
Gallery C. Bison and claviform signs. Bison about 31¹/₂ in. (see fig. 137).

EL CASTILLO

(Plans, figs. 138, 139, page 333)

418 EL CASTILLO
Group of four stags and one hind, engraved near cave entrance (point 2 on both plans). These figures are fairly close to the Las Chimeneas stags and belong to Style III (see fig. 397). Photograph shows about 40 in. of wall.

419 EL CASTILLO
Engraving near entrance (1 on plan). Apparently a horse. There are two engraved signs: an oval on the thigh, a barbed sign at the thorax. The style of this figure is hard to determine. About 20 in.

420 EL CASTILLO
Intersecting red quadrangular signs in side chamber (23 on plan). About 20 in.

421 EL CASTILLO
Intersecting rows of dots near fig. 420. About 20 in.

422 EL CASTILLO
One of the red hands in negative (33–34 on plan). The whole hand is rendered; the space between thumb and index finger is very clear-cut; color continues across the wrist. Obviously, this is a left hand applied palm first to the wall.

423 EL CASTILLO
Black figure (15 on plan.) The Abbé Breuil identified this animal as an equid, but it may well be a feline. About 10 in.

424 EL CASTILLO
Another black figure (rhinoceros?), in a recessed area of the wall (7 on plan). About 12 in.

425 EL CASTILLO
Two bison painted in black (41 on plan). Length 59 in. Although the outline of the first figure is somewhat stiff, both figures belong indisputably to Early Style IV.

426 EL CASTILLO
Engraved aurochs (53-bis, zone D, fig. 139). This figure is in a Style IV area. About 16 in.

COVALANAS

(Plan, fig. 140, page 335)

427 COVALANAS
Right-hand portion of first panel on right-hand wall. Three hinds. Note the exaggeratedly large ears. The hind at center measures 23⁵/₈ in.

428 COVALANAS
Fragment of same panel. Two hinds with dotted outlines. 33¹/₂ in.

429 COVALANAS
Animal at entrance to sanctuary. 55 in. A good example of the way natural reliefs were used to advantage. The rock supplies the outline, from withers to thigh. Note the vagueness of the lines at the top of the head, and the four dots under the belly. Breuil thought this figure was an ox of a slender type, but it is probably a stag.

430 COVALANAS
Panel with the horse, about 67 in.

431 COVALANAS
Two of the three hinds in the recess. About 59 in. The one at the left has no forelegs, and a spot on the shoulder.

LA HAZA

432 LA HAZA
Horse colored with red dots. 17³/₄ in.

STYLE IV

OBJECTS WITH REPRESENTATIONS OF WOMEN

433 LAUGERIE BASSE
Statuette of mammoth tusk; known as the "shameless Venus." 3¹/₈ in. This remarkable statuette has not been dated exactly, since it was excavated prior to modern scientific methods. It belongs to a group of works found in Magdalenian III–IV and V. The head is not present, but the figure may have been headless to begin with. In this respect, the figure would be comparable to several other headless Magdalenian figures (statuettes, engravings, and low reliefs) from Angles-sur-l'Anglin, La Roche at Lalinde (see fig. 56), Les Combarelles (see fig. 514), Petersfels in Germany, and Mezin in the Ukraine. The profile view brings to mind the contour of a claviform sign. *Musée de l'Homme, Paris.*

434 ABRI MURAT
Engraved stone plaquette. Probably a female figure in profile, very close to the figures in group 67 at Les Combarelles (fig. 514) and those on the engraved slab at La Roche (fig. 56). Two lines above the head may represent bison horns. *Lémozi excavations, Museum, Cabrerets.*

435 LES TROIS FRÈRES
Engraved plaquette. 4³/₈ in. The human form here has no indication of sex. The legs are drawn up, and the figure is broken off at the level of the elbow. It is commonly regarded as female, and a number of odd theories have been advanced to account for its bent position. The right foreleg of a bison can also be made out. The theme here may be the frequently encountered woman/bison one. *H. Bégouën excavations, Musée de l'Homme, Paris (photograph J. Oster, Musée de l'Homme).*

436–437 ISTURITZ
Layer II, Middle Magdalenian. Fragment of rib bone. 4 in. From the standpoint of content, this is one of the most interesting of decorated objects. Traditionally, it has been interpreted as follows: one side represents a man crawling toward a woman with a harpoon implanted in her thigh (the harpoon is looked upon as a sign of taking possession); the other side shows two bison, the better-preserved one having two harpoons in its flank. R. de Saint-Périer, when he advanced this interpretation, judiciously noted the fact that harpoons are not found prior to the Late Magdalenian. It is possible, however, to interpret the human figures as two women: the allegedly "male" figure (a on the drawing) has the beginning of a pendulous breast under the arm, and figure b has the same pendulous breast. The part missing from the one figure corresponds exactly to the

preserved portion of the other figure. If so, the scene portrayed belongs to the customary "women with bison" or "women/bison" theme, both elements being represented on the two sides of the bone; their symbolic identity is indicated by complementary male barbed signs and double strokes. *Collection Saint-Périer, Morigny.*

OBJECTS WITH REPRESENTATIONS OF MEN

438–439 LAUGERIE BASSE
Fragment of reindeer antler. $7^1/_2$ in. Not precisely dated. In style, the bison (fig. 439) is Middle Magdalenian. This work, although well known, has not hitherto been compared to the scene in the Shaft at Lascaux (see fig. 323). The two scenes are identical in detail: bison with a spear in the flank, ithyphallic man with outflung arms, and a horse (in this case, the other side of the bone; fig. 438). This scene has been interpreted as a hunter crawling toward the bison he has wounded. Actually, however, its meaning is no clearer than that of similar scenes at Lascaux, Villars (see fig. 358), and Le Roc de Sers (see fig. 305) which treat the same theme. What we have here is obviously a symbolic theme of great durability, since it turns up from the Solutrean to the Middle Magdalenian (see chart XXVIII). *Museum, Saint-Germain-en-Laye.*

440–441 LA MADELEINE (Dordogne)
Engraved pebble. $3^3/_4$ in. This enigmatic work has not been accurately dated. This is the only work, to my knowledge, having on opposite sides a man and a woman. Still, they make a strange couple. The man (fig. 440), whose sexual parts are not shown, has a long, muzzle-shaped face; more normal features are inscribed within this animalized face (see chart XXIX). The latter has been supposed to be a mask. The female figure (fig. 441) is identifiable as such only because she has a human arm and a breast. The head is unmistakably animal and has been interpreted as a reindeer without antlers, although reliable identification seems impossible. Undoubtedly we have here two different sexual entities, with human features for the most part, but Paleolithic symbolism is not so simple as to provide us with masked personages executing some magical hunting dance. The correspondences of man-horse-spear and woman-bison-wound, fully confirmed by statistical analysis, may have led to a host of symbolic allusions, the remoter examples of which are now hopelessly obscure. *Museum, Saint-Germain-en-Laye.*

442 LA MADELEINE (Dordogne)
Fragment of engraved bone. $4^3/_4$ in. Found at lower level (Middle Magdalenian). Ithyphallic figure with raised arms. Representations of men showing the sexual parts account for less than one-third of the total male figures in cave art and among statuettes and decorated objects (about 15 out of about 50). Representation of the human male, there-

fore, did not necessarily involve sexual realism. We may suppose that figures of this type were limited to occasions requiring ithyphallic representation, but this, too, is scarcely susceptible of proof. In representations of the theme "man against bison," some figures are ithyphallic (Lascaux, fig. 323; Laugerie Basse, fig. 439), whereas others show no indication of sexual parts at all (Le Roc de Sers, fig. 305; Villars, fig. 358). At Altamira, six of the human figures on the Painted Ceiling are asexual, one ithyphallic. There are other figures that are not ithyphallic, but have some indication of the sexual parts (Gourdan; Brassempouy; Pech Merle, fig. 374; Saint-Cirq, fig. 361; the "Sorcerer" at Les Trois Frères, fig. 57). There is no reason for systematically "sexualizing" the human figures of the Old Stone Age; as we have seen, there is no indisputable scene of sexual intercourse. Apparently we have merely representations of human beings, with such expressive variations as the subject lends itself to. In this figure the face is thrusting upward, and it has been supposed that the personage is wearing a mask with an animal head. The raised arms, the state of erection, and the animal mask have of course provided good arguments for a theory that this is a dancer in some fertility rite; many male figures have been interpreted in this way. It is a plausible hypothesis, but I do not consider it proved by the figures. As noted, there are scenes showing ithyphallic figures which apparently have little to do with fertility rites. Nor is the theory of the animal masks, although they can hardly not have existed, conclusively proved, especially when we note that representations of the male face exhibit every transition from normal human features to complete bestialization (see chart XXIX). In my opinion, we are dealing with an ideal way of seeing man, a way that no doubt is not wholly purged of zoomorphism, but does not necessarily involve a theory of animal masks. As for the raised arms, we have several other examples: a statuette from Laugerie Basse, a pierced staff from Gourdan, a disk from Le Mas d'Azil, and cave figures from Altamira, Les Combarelles, Los Hornos, Saint-Cirq, and Villars. It is hard to assign a precise meaning to this gesture, which appears on only one-sixth of the male figures. *Museum, Les Eyzies.*

443 ISTURITZ
Salle Saint-Martin. The Magdalenian layer in this chamber seems to have been largely made up of Middle Magdalenian and, perhaps, Early Magdalenian deposits. Engraved plaquette, $2^3/_4$ in. We make out a male figure (see chart XXIX) amid many lines including portions of horses' heads. The eye of one horse has sometimes been interpreted as the man's penis. The association of two male symbols, man and horse, brings to mind the corresponding woman/bison association. *Collection Saint-Périer, Morigny.*

444 PÉCHIALET
This curious engraved slab is believed to be "Perigordian." $7^1/_4$ in. We see a bear at the center of the slab, and on either side of this animal a human silhouette. This engraving seems to treat the theme of man attacked by a bear; the theme also appears on a bone fragment from the Middle Magdalenian found at Le Mas d'Azil (see fig. 50), and is a variation on the over-all theme of men attacked by animals (see chart XXVIII). The exact age of this slab has not been established. *Museum, Saint-Germain-en-Laye.*

445 ABRI MURAT
Engraved bone plaquette. There appear to be three animalized human figures bending forward, with no visible indication of sex. This engraving has sometimes been seen as a representation of sexual intercourse, but nothing supports this view. Actually, the "penis" of the first figure is formed by the legs of the third figure (see chart XXIX). The chief features common to all male Magdalenian figures are the shape of the head—a face elongated like an animal muzzle or a sharply turned-up nose. Less constant features are bent posture, raised arms, and depiction of the sexual parts. *Lémozi excavations, Museum, Cabrerets.*

446 LES EYZIES
Engraved bone plaquette. $3^3/_4$ in. This unusual plaquette shows a "scene" almost identical with the one engraved on a pendant from Raymonden (see fig. 236). At the right can be seen the forequarters of a bison, toward which a procession of nine human figures carrying spears seems to be moving. Four little figures resembling highly stylized trees appear at left and right. *Museum, Les Eyzies.*

OBJECTS WITH REPRESENTATIONS OF ANIMALS

447 LAUGERIE BASSE
Level undefined. Horses' heads engraved on a bone fragment. 6 in. These figures belong to the Middle Magdalenian. They are treated, down to the least details of the coat, like carved silhouettes. *Musée de l'Homme, Paris (photograph R. Pasquino, Musée de l'Homme).*

448 LA MADELEINE (Dordogne)
Level undefined. Horse's head on bone fragment. About $1^5/_8$ in. The treatment is in Style IV, and the details of the coat tend toward Early Style IV (Middle Magdalenian). *Museum, Les Eyzies.*

449 ISTURITZ
Salle Saint-Martin. Middle Magdalenian. Horse's head engraved on schist. $3^1/_2$ in. *Collection Saint-Périer, Morigny.*

450 ISTURITZ
Salle Saint-Martin. Horse's head sculptured in soft sandstone. $3^1/_8$ in. Probably Middle Magdalenian. The

treatment of this figure is unusual. The pose, the closeness of the head to the neck, and the contours of forehead, nostrils, and cheeks all make of this a figure outside stylistic categories. *Collection Saint-Périer, Morigny.*

451–452 ARUDY

Engraved pebble. One side (fig. 451) shows five superimposed heads of horses. The other side (fig. 452) shows the head of a ruminant (aurochs?).

453 LES TROIS FRÈRES

Horse's head engraved on a bone fragment. The treatment is very interesting: the tiny irregular hatchings that model the cheekbone do not follow the conventions we find on carved silhouettes (see figs. 237–242) but correspond exactly to those employed in the horses engraved on the wall of this cave and in the painted horses at Niaux (see figs. 80, 600, 601). *H. Bégouën excavations, Musée de l'Homme, Paris (photograph J. Oster, Musée de l'Homme).*

454 RAYMONDEN

Cylindrical fragment of reindeer antler, with engraved horse. About 4³/₄ in. Late Magdalenian. *Museum, Périgueux.*

455 LESPUGUE

Magdalenian. Horses engraved on bone plaquette. 4³/₄ in. *Collection Saint-Périer, Morigny.*

456 EL PENDO

Probably Magdalenian. Horse engraved on bone plaquette. *Museum, Santander.*

457 ROBIN HOOD'S CAVE, CRESWELL CRAGS

Terminal Magdalenian. Bone fragment showing a horse in Late Style IV and a row of strokes. 3 in. This is the only Paleolithic work yet found in the British Isles. *British Museum, London (photograph British Museum).*

458 VILLEPIN

Engraved pebble. Magdalenian VI. On one side is an engraving of a horse's forequarters; the other side is covered with thin lines, among which we glimpse the forequarters of a ruminant. This is one of the latest Paleolithic works. *Museum, Les Eyzies.*

459 ISTURITZ

Layer II, Middle Magdalenian. Bison sculptured in sandstone. About 6 in. Despite mutilation, the find is interesting for its proportions and the form of the mane, characteristic of Early Style IV. *Collection Saint-Périer, Morigny.*

460 ISTURITZ

Salle Saint-Martin. Middle Magdalenian. Bone fragment showing bison heads. 2 to 2³/₈ in. Note at left how the lines of the ear, eye, and horn are connected, and the modeling in short, regular hatchings on both heads. *Collection Saint-Périer, Morigny.*

461 ISTURITZ

Salle Saint-Martin. Middle Magdalenian. Low relief on sandstone.

Bison with two converging lines (wound mark) on the flank and a big oval cup-mark. At bottom right, two double strokes. *Collection Saint-Périer, Morigny.*

462 ISTURITZ

Salle Saint-Martin. Engraved stone plaquette, showing three bison (two facing in the opposite direction to the third), one horse, and two wound marks on the bison. In treatment and composition this is very close to cave figures at Niaux and Les Trois Frères. Early Style IV. *Collection Saint-Périer, Morigny.*

463–464 LE PUY DE LACAN

Sandstone plaquettes. 8 and 6 in. It is very possible that these are two fragments from a single engraved slab. On the piece at the right we make out heads and forequarters of three bison. On the piece at the left, two hindquarters of bovids, probably bison, and one very remarkable bison head. Below this head is a strange bird, with rump and cloaca visible. There are about ten representations of birds known on decorated objects, most of them poorly dated, but all from Middle or Late Magdalenian. Their symbolic value is not clear. Some are relatively normal: Raymonden—bird of prey(?) on pierced staff; Laugerie Basse, Isturitz, Gourdan—sparrows or gallinaceous birds; Les Trois Frères—sparrows(?); Labastide, Laugerie Basse—waders. There are also figures with a long, wavy, snakelike neck on a bird's body: Bruniquel, Teyjat. The bird shown here brings to mind figures of the men bending forward. These plaquettes are quite reliably dated, for they were found with flint artifacts from the Late Magdalenian. The animals exhibit a flexibility of movement which is fairly in keeping with Late Style IV. *Kidder excavations, Museum, Brive.*

465 LE MAS D'AZIL

Bone fragment. Cow. Found at an undetermined level. *Museum, Saint-Germain-en-Laye.*

466 LE MAS D'AZIL

Bone fragment. Engraved bull in Late Style IV. This excellent figure is close to the one at Teyjat. *Museum, Saint-Germain-en-Laye.*

467 LAUGERIE BASSE

Undetermined level. Schist plaquette. About 6 in. On the side shown are two reindeer in single file; facing in the opposite direction, one reindeer head, one horse's head, and the forequarters of a reindeer. On the other side there is one bison. In style, the animals are Late Style IV, close to that of Limeuil and Teyjat. The plaquette seems to be Late Magdalenian. *Musée de l'Homme, Paris.*

468 BRUNIQUEL

Reindeer antler. 8⁵/₈. Object of undetermined nature, found at an uncertain level. Fairly probably from the Middle Magdalenian. Judging by the proportions of the antlers, the figures are those of a male reindeer following a female

reindeer. The treatment of the coat of the female figure is especially effective. *British Museum, London (photograph British Museum).*

469 LAUGERIE BASSE

Bone plaquette. 6 in. Part of the hindquarters and tail of a bovid (probably an ox). The central figure is another ox. A small head at the right could be that of a horse or of a third ox. The figures seem truncated, because the plaquette was trimmed at the edges. It is apparent, however, that the engraving was made after the trimming, because the lines cut across the beveling. It is not unusual for seemingly incomplete plaquettes to strike us as though they had been designed for a larger area, the lines continuing on beyond their actual boundaries. *Musée de l'Homme, Paris.*

470 ISTURITZ

Engraved bone fragment. Unfinished ibex head: eye and horn were barely begun. *Collection Saint-Périer, Morigny.*

471 LES TROIS FRÈRES

Bone fragment. 3⁷/₈ in. The theme of this little composition, of which only the central portion survives, is absolutely unique in Paleolithic art. At top left we see the wing and belly of a bird, probably a sparrow, beak open to catch a grasshopper. At top right are the legs and lower body of another bird. Turning the object around, we find a third bird at top right: it has the beak of a sparrow, pecking at small round things, perhaps seeds. Its legs are not visible, and under its belly are two little bag-shaped or larva-shaped bodies resembling ant eggs. Lastly, at top left, a fourth bird shows the rear of its body and one leg, possibly a sparrow's. If this scene has a symbolic meaning, we have nothing in the way of comparative data by which to interpret it. *H. Bégouën excavations, Musée de l'Homme, Paris (photograph J. Oster, Musée de l'Homme).*

472 RAYMONDEN

Plaquette of reindeer antler. The Late Magdalenian yielded several plaquettes with barbed signs on them (Arcy-sur-Cure, Bruniquel, Laugerie Basse, Le Mas d'Azil, Teyjat, Veyrier), sometimes rendered as leafy branches. This engraving, which has been thought to represent a crayfish, actually seems to belong to the same type.

473–474 CHALEUX

Engraved sandstone slab. Like the palette from Pekarna (see fig. 215), this geographically remote work illustrates the constancy of Paleolithic themes. One side (fig. 474) shows an aurochs and a cervid; the other (fig. 473) a horse and two ibexes, each animal in the aurochs/horse pairing being accompanied by a complementary species. 31¹/₂ in. *Museum, Brussels (photograph F. Twiesselmann).*

475 LIMEUIL

Single reindeer engraved on corner of a plaquette. About 6 in. *Museum, Périgueux.*

476 LIMEUIL

Forequarters of an aurochs, redrawn several times. $7^7/_8$ in. This is a typical example of reworked outlines. We can see that the animal has several heads and several forelegs. Why this was done is still not known. Reworked cave paintings occur: at Lascaux, for instance, there are painted and engraved horses with the ears differently placed in each version. As the fresh paint obliterated the old engraving, the artist was free to engrave new ears in a different position. A similar procedure may have occurred with the plaquettes. *Museum, Saint-Germain-en-Laye.*

477 LIMEUIL

Forequarters of an ibex. The legs have been reworked. There are double lines at various points on the plaquette. $7^1/_2$ in. *Museum, Saint-Germain-en-Laye.*

478 SAUT-DU-PERRON

Schist slab showing an engraved reindeer and, when turned upside down, the probable outline of the leg and hindquarters of a horse. $3^7/_8$ in. *Musée Déchelette, Roanne (photograph A. Leroi-Gourhan).*

479 SAUT-DU-PERRON

Plaquette with fine-line engraving of a hairy pachyderm (lower part of body) that could be a rhinoceros. *Musée Déchelette, Roanne (photograph A. Leroi-Gourhan).*

LA COLOMBIÈRE
(Plan, fig. 142, page 342)

480 LA COLOMBIÈRE

Pebble no. 2, engraved on one side only. $3^1/_2$ in. The main figure is a horse. Under the belly is something that seems to be the outspread wing of a bird, but actually is the outline of the rump of a quadruped, the foreparts of which are scarcely visible. The hatchings bordered by a double line are frequent in works at La Colombière. *Faculté des Sciences, Lyon (photograph Musée de l'Homme).*

481 LA COLOMBIÈRE

Pebble no. 7. $3^1/_2$ in. On the side shown here, the principal figure is a woolly rhinoceros. When we turn the pebble upside down, we see a cervid without antlers. Under the belly of the rhinoceros are three signs which have been interpreted as arrows stuck in the animal; similar markings appear around the bear on the other side of this pebble. I see these as oval signs, a hypothesis confirmed by the long strokes accompanying them in both cases. *Faculté des Sciences, Lyon (photograph Musée de l'Homme).*

482 LA COLOMBIÈRE

Pebble no. 7, reverse side. The principal figure is a bear, the head of which has been drawn twice. When we turn the pebble upside down, we see a horse with similarly repeated foreparts. This side exhibits the same association of signs (strokes and arrow-shapes) as the side in fig. 481. *Faculté des Sciences, Lyon (photograph Musée de l'Homme).*

483 LA COLOMBIÈRE

Pebble no. 9, discovered by H. L. Movius. $4^3/_4$ in. On one side the principal figure is a deeply incised horse. There are also partial outlines of a rhinoceros and a cervid, pointing in the same direction. Pointing in the opposite direction are a reindeer without antlers, a feline, and two framing ibexes. The other side of the pebble shows a rhinoceros (the head of which was traced three times), a horse, and a reindeer. *Museum, Bourg-en-Bresse (photograph Musée de l'Homme).*

484 LA COLOMBIÈRE

Pebble no. 8. 6 in. One side shows a ruminant, which Mayet and Pissot saw as a musk ox, a plausible hypothesis since bones of the musk ox appear to have been found at a few sites (Abri Castanet, Chaleux in Belgium, Laugerie Haute, Teyjat). To my knowledge, however, there is no representation of this species that could not just as well be interpreted as a bison. Here the only feature that might identify it as a musk ox is the downward and forward sweep of the horns; this feature does, in fact, characterize the musk ox, but in artistic representation this is a perspective device which is used with bison in several instances. *Faculté des Sciences, Lyon (photograph Musée de l'Homme).*

485 LA COLOMBIÈRE

Engraving no. 10. Fragment of pelvic bone of mammoth. $7^1/_8$ in. We make out a human figure with lifted arm (see chart XXIX), the forepart of a bear, and the forepart of a reindeer. The muzzles of the animals have been broken off. Mayet and Pissot interpreted these two outlines as representing a female body. *Faculté des Sciences, Lyon (photograph Musée de l'Homme).*

STYLE IV
CAVE ART

TEYJAT
(Plan, fig. 141, page 339)

486 TEYJAT

Group 7. Cow followed by bull; length of both about 40 in. There is a second cow following the bull.

487 TEYJAT

Small horse's head, with an upside-down reindeer leg over its neck. This figure has been described as representing a reindeer head and a horse's head growing out of the same neck. $7^7/_8$ in. *(photograph A. Leroi-Gourhan).*

488 TEYJAT

Slab no. 2. Young animal, probably a male reindeer. At bottom right, one reindeer head and a number of parallel strokes.

489 TEYJAT

Head of bison, principal figure in group 4. Distance from horns to tip of beard $6^1/_4$ in. Note the repetition of outlines, frequent in the Late Magdalenian *(photograph A. Leroi-Gourhan).*

490 TEYJAT

Reindeer, upside-down at bottom of group 4. Head $2^3/_4$ in.

MOUTHIERS, LA CHAIRE À CALVIN
(Plan, fig. 143, page 344)

491 MOUTHIERS

Very damaged figure of bison, at left of frieze. About 40 in. *(photograph A. Leroi-Gourhan).*

492 MOUTHIERS

Right-hand portion of frieze: horses. Over-all length about 10 ft.

493 MOUTHIERS

Horses carved inside a bison in low relief. About 55 in. Drawings: *(a)* surviving portions of the bison figure shown in continuous line, missing portions in dotted line; *(b)* bison at Altamira—dotted lines indicate the portions missing from the Mouthiers bison; *(c)* relief published as "horses coupling"; *(d)* a drawing of the actual relief—the bent legs are the remnants of a ring carved in the wall.

LE CAP BLANC
(Plan, fig. 144, page 345)

494 LE CAP BLANC

Horses at left side of frieze. The one at the left was probably carved inside a bison; the hump of the latter became the horse's neck and withers. Later, a bison head was carved inside the horse's cheek.

495 LE CAP BLANC

Horse's head inside which a bison head was carved *(photograph J. Vertut).*

COMMARQUE

(Plan, fig. 145, page 346)

496 COMMARQUE
Head of ibex at 4 on plan (entrance to corridor). About 6 in. *(photograph A. Leroi-Gourhan)*.

497 COMMARQUE
Horse at 6 on plan. Head 27⅝ in.

498 COMMARQUE
Head at back of the cave, at 9 on plan. It is generally viewed as a bear, but I think it should be interpreted as a bestialized human profile (see drawing *a*). Very close to the figure at Les Combarelles (see fig. 522, and chart XXIX). About 6 in.

ABRI REVERDIT

499 ABRI REVERDIT
Bison in low relief. Length 43¼ in. *(photograph A. Leroi-Gourhan)*.

LA MAGDELAINE (TARN)

(Plan, fig. 146, page 347)

500 LA MAGDELAINE
Horse at *d* on plan. About 28 in.

501 LA MAGDELAINE
Female figure at *a* on plan. Sculptured portions are rendered in continuous line, the natural relief in shaded dots. About 28 in.

502 LA MAGDELAINE
Female figure at *c* on plan. About 28 in.

BERNIFAL

503 BERNIFAL
Group of big dots, located just before the passage narrows toward the second chamber *(photograph A. Leroi-Gourhan)*.

504 BERNIFAL
Tectiform sign and oval, superimposed *(photograph A. Leroi-Gourhan)*.

505 BERNIFAL
Tectiform sign painted in ocher on one wall of a side chamber. Like some of the tectiforms at Font-de-Gaume, it is composed of small dots in alignment *(photograph A. Leroi-Gourhan)*.

506 BERNIFAL
Mammoth with tectiform signs on it. About 15¾ in.

507 BERNIFAL
Horse, cervid, and signs. About 16 in.

508 BERNIFAL
Bison marked with paired signs. About 20 in.

509 BERNIFAL
Horse on a wall encrusted with calcite. About 12 in. *(photograph A. Leroi-Gourhan)*.

LES COMBARELLES

(Plan, fig. 147, page 349)

Figures in the first gallery

510 LES COMBARELLES
Horse, at 18 on the plan, with body covered by groups of parallel lines.

The treatment of the head is very close to that of the large head at Commarque (see fig. 497). 40 in.

511 LES COMBARELLES
Mammoth, at 26 on the plan. The figure exhibits close affinities with the mammoths at Font-de-Gaume and Rouffignac. 27⅝ in.

512 LES COMBARELLES
Human face, at 76 on plan, near paired signs (see chart XXX). 6 in.

513 LES COMBARELLES
Female sign, at 63 on plan. 8 in.

514 LES COMBARELLES
Group of three schematic female figures, at 67 on plan. Note the absence of head and feet, as at Angles and at La Roche. The figures look like claviform signs (see figs. 585–590). Height 8 in.

Figures in the second gallery

515 LES COMBARELLES
Small ibex head, at 35 on plan, under the reindeer head in fig. 516.

516 LES COMBARELLES
Reindeer head engraved in relief, at 36 on plan. Area of the photograph about 20 in. This reindeer head overlaps a bison head.

517 LES COMBARELLES
Aurochs overlapping the hindquarters of a horse, at 37 on plan. 11⅝ in.
Figures at the second turning

518 LES COMBARELLES
Small rhinoceros head, under the "lioness." About 8 in.

519 LES COMBARELLES
Bear at 47 on plan. 19 in. This figure has been described as a cave bear. In works of art the distinction between the cave bear and the brown bear that we know today (which already frequented this part of the world in the Stone Age) is illusory. The more or less bulging forehead has at best a relative value as a clue to identification. At Les Combarelles alone, we find every stage between this figure and bears with flat foreheads. Thus, the figure here should be referred to simply as a bear.

520 LES COMBARELLES
Forequarters of the "lioness." At 52 on plan. Area in the photograph about 20 in.

521 LES COMBARELLES
Reindeer facing a fissure, at 44 on plan. 15¾ in.

Figures in the third gallery

522 LES COMBARELLES
Bent-over human figure, at 81 on plan. Concentric ovals are superimposed (see chart XXIX). 19½ in.

523 LES COMBARELLES
Last subject in the gallery, at 105 on plan. Feline, horse, and paired signs. Feline 43¼ in.

FONT-DE-GAUME

(Plan, fig. 148, page 351)

524 FONT-DE-GAUME
Black bull in Style III, at H on plan. About 40 in.

525 FONT-DE-GAUME
Black cow in Style III, in the vicinity of fig. 524. Compare with Lascaux (figs. 316, 321, 394). About 40 in.

526 FONT-DE-GAUME
Rhinoceros at the back of the cave, at I on plan. Painted in black. Style IV (see fig. 535). 27⅝ in.

527–528 FONT-DE-GAUME
Figures of bison in ocher and black, at C on plan. 40 to 54 in.

529 FONT-DE-GAUME
Engraved group located at the "Rubicon," E on plan. We make out the silhouette of a horse and several incomplete bison, over which are drawn three big tectiforms and several groups of parallel strokes. Area of photograph about 40 in. wide.

530 FONT-DE-GAUME
Little engraved mammoth. One of the latest figures in the cave. Note the triangular shape of the eye, found also on the mammoths at Rouffignac (see fig. 537). 22½ in.

531 FONT-DE-GAUME
Small engraved human masks, at G on plan. On the wall of the low tunnel leading from the Chamber of Small Bison (see chart XXIX). Height about 8 in. Compare figs. 543, 567.

532 FONT-DE-GAUME
Head of one of the horses in front of the feline at the back of the cave. About 4 in.

533 FONT-DE-GAUME
Seven aligned red strokes in the deepest part of the terminal recess (J on plan). Signs like these, nearly always found in the remotest parts of the caves, seem complementary to the cave itself *(photograph A. Leroi-Gourhan)*.

534 FONT-DE-GAUME
Left-hand wall of the Chamber of Small Bison. At the top we make out the head and belly of one of the small bison. Under the belly are compartmented quadrangular signs.

ROUFFIGNAC

(Plans, figs. 149, 150, page 354)

535 ROUFFIGNAC
Breuil Gallery: frieze with three rhinoceroses. Each figure measures about 40 in.

536 ROUFFIGNAC
Breuil Gallery: central part of frieze of mammoths. Painted in black; at H on plan. Each figure measures 24 to 28 in.

537 ROUFFIGNAC
Breuil Gallery: panel facing figs. 535–536, at H on plan. From left to right: one horse, two facing mammoths. The mammoth at right measures 27⅝ in.

538 ROUFFIGNAC
Breuil Gallery: bison head next to fig. 537. There is a tectiform sign (not shown) at right of the animal, completing the sign/bison/horse + mammoth group.

539 ROUFFIGNAC

Painted Ceiling: bison no. 38. 23⁵/₈ in. Note how the beard is thrust forward, as with the bison at Les Combarelles and Font-de-Gaume (*photograph Romain Robert*).

540 ROUFFIGNAC

Painted Ceiling: ibexes and one mammoth, nos. 23–24. As is often the case (see figs. 294, 383), one of the ibexes has the short horns of a female. About 20 in. (*photograph Romain Robert*).

541 ROUFFIGNAC

Painted Ceiling: horse no. 43. 67 in. (*photograph Romain Robert*).

542 ROUFFIGNAC

Head of a bear, located at left of fig. 537. Length of entire animal 17³/₈ in.

543 ROUFFIGNAC

Back wall of right branch of main gallery. Human faces turned toward each other. See chart XXIX (*photograph Romain Robert*).

544 ROUFFIGNAC

Painted Ceiling: rhinoceros no. 48. Very schematized figure. 27⁵/₈ in. (*photograph Romain Robert*).

ARCY-SUR-CURE, GROTTE DU CHEVAL

(Plan, fig. 151, page 356)

545 ARCY-SUR-CURE

Mammoth no. 13, first chamber of main cave. About 40 in.

546 ARCY-SUR-CURE

Head of mammoth no. 14. The trunk, shown lifted, incorporates an irregularity in the wall. About 20 in.

547 ARCY-SUR-CURE

Upper part of a bison head, no. 15. 6 in. (*photograph Emperaire*).

548 ARCY-SUR-CURE

Female symbol incised on a fold in the ceiling, between 8 and 9 on plan. 4³/₄ in. (*photograph J. D. Lajoux*).

549 ARCY-SUR-CURE

Lattice sign on ceiling of second chamber (no. 22). 11³/₄ in. (*photograph A. Leroi-Gourhan*).

550 ARCY-SUR-CURE

Bison head in second chamber, among meandering lines scrawled on the wall (no. 18). About 16 in. from horn to beard.

551 ARCY-SUR-CURE

Engraved horse at back of cave, over the opening of the terminal dead-end. Note the double shoulder line and wavy ventral modeling (no. 25). Length from muzzle to base of tail 19⁵/₈ in.

552 ARCY-SUR-CURE

Head of a cervid or an ibex, making use of the edge of the rock (no. 24). From eye to tip of muzzle, 4 in.

PERGOUSET

(Plan, fig. 152, page 357)

553 PERGOUSET

Head of ibex at A on plan. About 10 in. This is the first figure in the cave.

554 PERGOUSET

Head of ibex in composition B. Same dimensions as fig. 553.

555 PERGOUSET

Hind at D on plan. The treatment of the body is remarkable (compare fig. 412). About 8 in.

556 PERGOUSET

Head of hind near fig. 555. Under it, a wound sign. Two "breathing" lines at muzzle. The similarity to the wound sign is interesting. About 8 in.

557 PERGOUSET

Female sign in a side chamber at E on plan. Compare figs. 513, 548.

558 PERGOUSET

Ibex head at entrance to the side chamber containing fig. 557. Double strokes to right of ibex head.

559 PERGOUSET

Composition F: hind, bison, horse. The animals are rendered in a fairly stiff Style IV which is to some extent related to the engravings at Rouffignac (see fig. 537).

560 PERGOUSET

Headless man at G on plan. This figure is the only one of its kind so far found in Paleolithic art, but it is obviously related to the women-bison figures at Pech Merle (see figs. 368–371). About 32 in.

561 PERGOUSET

Head of long-necked animal with mane (compare fig. 349); at G on plan.

562 PERGOUSET

Head of a cervid. This is not a stag, but a male Megaceros deer or an elk, both of which have a long brow antler under a broad palm. Favoring identification as an elk are the bulky, hooked profile and the clump of hair under the throat. Compare fig. 616.

563 PERGOUSET

Figures on ceiling at H on plan. They escape all identification, especially the figure at the bottom. The one at the top is not a mammoth, unless it represents the tail and anal operculum of a mammoth; the drawing suggests the tail of a bison when the animal is, for one reason or another, aroused.

564 PERGOUSET

Projecting rock with an eye incised on it. Last figure in the cave.

MARSOULAS

565 MARSOULAS

Big polychrome composition. At top left, the body of a bison marked with a number of signs. To the right of this, a horse modeled in ocher and black. A long barbed sign runs across both animals; and below them is a spread of dots, strokes, and barbed signs. At bottom right there is a bison executed in dots above a big barbed sign (fig. 66). The composition measures about 16 ft. (*photographic restitution, J. Vertut*).

566 MARSOULAS

Hoofs of a large engraved bison. The treatment is in Late Style IV, so far

as the stance is concerned. (*photograph A. Leroi-Gourhan*).

567 MARSOULAS

Group engraved inside a niche in small chamber G (see diagram at left): at top, one human face in frontal view (fig. 59), one of the cave's most famous figures; at right, a figure with an exaggeratedly long nasal appendage; at bottom, a sketch for the upper portion of a feline head. This group has close affinities with the paired faces at Font-de-Gaume and Rouffignac (see figs. 531, 543). Height about 12 in.

568 MARSOULAS

Human face in frontal view, at I on plan. This figure is very close to some of the "ghosts" at Les Combarelles (see fig. 512 and chart XXX). Height 4 in. (*photograph A. Leroi-Gourhan*).

569 MARSOULAS

Group of dots and vertical strokes at bottom right of the big composition. 42¹/₂ in.

570 MARSOULAS

Bison painted in black. 7⁵/₈ in. (*photograph A. Leroi-Gourhan*).

LABASTIDE

571 LABASTIDE

Left-hand portion of the block with engravings. The forequarters of a horse can be seen, also an animal hard to identify, its over-all proportions those of a bison. Length of area shown in photograph about 12 in. (*photograph A. Leroi-Gourhan*).

572 LABASTIDE

Right-hand portion of the block in fig. 571. We make out at left a bison, at right a vague figure which might be a cervid. Both animals positioned vertically. Same proportions as fig. 571. Between the two figures (see drawing), there is a sign which is intermediate between schematized female figures (see fig. 514) and claviform signs (see fig. 590) (*photograph A. Leroi-Gourhan*).

573 LABASTIDE

Big polychrome horse. Length 7 ft. 6¹/₂ in.

574 LABASTIDE

Small engraved bison in inner gallery. About 8 in. (*photograph A. Leroi-Gourhan*).

575 LABASTIDE

"Goose" engraved in a niche. About 12 in. Compare figs. 349 and 561 (*photograph A. Leroi-Gourhan*).

576 LABASTIDE

Feline head in inner gallery. About 16 in. (*photograph A. Leroi-Gourhan*).

LE PORTEL

(Plan, fig. 153, page 361)

577 LE PORTEL

Bird painted in black in gallery I (C). 17⁵/₈ in. See chart XXX.

578 LE PORTEL

Black-painted horse, near fig. 577. 25⁵/₈ in.

579 LE PORTEL

Little red horse at entrance to gallery 2 (I). 7^1/$_4$ in.

580 LE PORTEL

Horse painted in black, from the group at back of gallery 3 (K). About 40 in.

581 LE PORTEL

Horse from the same group. About 24 in.

582 LE PORTEL

Black horse from the same group. This horse is the most complete at Le Portel in respect to detailed modeling. About 16 in.

583 LE PORTEL

Gallery 4 (Breuil Gallery). So-called discovery bison at D on plan. A simple figure, but with all the features of Style IV. 27^5/$_8$ in.

584 LE PORTEL

Group of three bison, painted in black, at G on plan. About 6^1/$_2$ ft. The three figures exhibit various forms of classic Style IV modeling.

585 LE PORTEL

Group of black-painted figures in the "camarin," at F on plan. Horse and bison at center. In front of the bison there are dots and one claviform sign. Under the claviform is a double row of dots vaguely imitating a cervico-dorsal curve. At the very bottom, one ibex. In other words, this is a complete bison/horse (claviform sign/dots) + ibex composition. Opposite it (at right on photograph) are the antlers of a stag; under it one red oval and two or three lines in the same color. The decorated portion extends about 10 ft. (photographic restitution, J. Vertut).

586 LE PORTEL

Black bison marked with a red dot on the flank, at G on plan. 15^3/$_4$ in. (photograph A. Leroi-Gourhan).

587 LE PORTEL

Cervid painted at far end of gallery 3, at H on plan. 11^3/$_4$ in. This figure was identified as a reindeer by the Abbé Breuil. Actually, it has no detail permitting so specific a zoological identification. There is, however, a double brow antler, which is normally characteristic of the stag (photograph A. Leroi-Gourhan).

NIAUX

(Plan, fig. 154, page 362)

588 NIAUX

Panel of red and black signs at B on plan. Area in photograph about 10 in. square.

589 NIAUX

Inner gallery. Group of dots at H on plan, beyond the vertically positioned bison (fig. 603).

590 NIAUX

Claviform sign in a fissure to the left of panel I in the Black Salon.

591 NIAUX

Black Salon, panel III. Bison flanked by ibex. 59 in.

592 NIAUX

Black Salon. Bison at bottom right of panel I. Goose-track wound signs. 36 in.

593 NIAUX

Black Salon. Bison to the left of fig. 594. Wound signs. Observe the clarity of the Early Style IV modeling with dorsal triangle and straight line joining the elbow to the tip of the buttocks. Length 40 in.

594 NIAUX

Black Salon. Panel II. Bison at right on the first ceiling. It is framed by two ibexes and marked by a number of goose-track signs. Length 59 in.

595 NIAUX

Black Salon. Hollow transformed into stag head by adding antlers in black paint. This figure is at the innermost point of panel II. About 16 in.

596 NIAUX

Black Salon. Small vertically positioned bison in deep portion of panel II.

597 NIAUX

Small ibex above the back of the principal horse in panel III (see figs. 27, 70). About 10 in.

598 NIAUX

Small bison at bottom left, panel III. About 24 in.

599 NIAUX

Small horse under fig. 598, panel III. Double shoulder line and ventral modeling 29^1/$_2$ in.

600 NIAUX

Feline and horse in panel IV, superimposed. The feline's cervical curve is wrong, but the head, the thigh, and especially the carriage of the tail make this identification sure. 59 in.

601 NIAUX

Bottom of panel IV. Horse and stag. The treatment of this stag, the only one in the cave, is rather clumsy; it may possibly have been influenced by the outlines of the many ibexes at Niaux. The decorated surface is about 59 in. wide.

602 NIAUX

Small human figure, lacking bust and feet, painted in black in the side chamber that opens behind panel II. About 10 in.

603 NIAUX

Small red bison, positioned vertically at H on plan; known as "the wounded bison." It is among a group of claviforms and dots. 15^3/$_4$ in.

604 NIAUX

Figure painted in black on the vaulted ceiling above the terminal lake. An ibex or a cervid, lacking head and forelegs, with a red spot on the chest (see chart XXVII). About 12 in.

605 NIAUX

Horse and barbed sign, both painted in red (at I on plan). About 28 in. (photograph J. Vertut).

606 NIAUX

Red sign above the terminal lake

(L). 27^5/$_8$ in. This is hard to identify exactly, but it may conceivably be the result of a chance encounter between two horizontal lines and a series of vertical strokes. It can perhaps be related to the ladder signs at Altamira.

607 NIAUX

Horse engraved on clay at E on plan. I has a double mark on the shoulder, and V-shaped wound signs. About 28 in.

608 NIAUX

Bison engraved next to fig. 607 on the clayey ground. About 24 in.

609 NIAUX

Engraving on clay at E on plan. About 40 in. in height. It includes one ibex, one enigmatic sign, and one aurochs marked with a barbed sign and a V-shaped wound.

610 NIAUX

Engraving on clay at F on plan. The decorated area is about 49 in. wide. It is a complete composition, with bison, horse, ibex, strokes, and wounds.

611 NIAUX

Head of rhinoceros (?) overlapping a horse's head, engraved on the clayey ground at F on plan.

612 NIAUX

Fish of the salmon family engraved on clay at VII on plan. About 12 in.

LE TUC D'AUDOUBERT

(Plan, fig. 155, page 366)

613 LE TUC D'AUDOUBERT

Bison head. About 12 in.

614 LE TUC D'AUDOUBERT

Horse marked with double stroke on flank.

615 LE TUC D'AUDOUBERT

Schematized horse surrounded by many claviform signs, in a small side gallery.

616 LE TUC D'AUDOUBERT

Head of fantastic animal, at B on plan. Next to it, another similar figure is engraved. This head is not without analogy to the "elk" at Pergouset (see fig. 562). About 6 in.

617 LE TUC D'AUDOUBERT

Barbed sign engraved on clay ground near the bison modeled in clay (fig. 619). About 28 in.

618 LE TUC D'AUDOUBERT

Oval sign engraved near fig. 617. About 16 in.

619 LE TUC D'AUDOUBERT

Figures of bison modeled in clay and set firmly against the sloping ground. They are the best Paleolithic modeled figures that have come down to us. The largest measures 24 in.

620 LE TUC D'AUDOUBERT

Back view of the bison in fig. 619.

621 LE TUC D'AUDOUBERT

Partially modeled clay figure of bison on the ground. About 6 in.

LES TROIS FRÈRES

(Plan, fig. 155, page 366)

622 LES TROIS FRÈRES
The "Wild-Ass Gallery," F on plan. Brace-shaped signs of a type intermediate between Cantabrian signs and Dordogne tectiforms (see fig. 505). They are akin to one sign at Le Portel (see fig. 390).

623 LES TROIS FRÈRES
Head of bear(?) engraved near the signs in fig. 622 and the "wild-ass" (fig. 624). Within F on plan. About 8 in.

624 LES TROIS FRÈRES
Equid in the "Wild-Ass Gallery." Two other figures like this one are in the cave (see fig. 635); they represent a wild ass rather than a true Hemionus. Here, so close to the Mediterranean, this identification is quite plausible. $15^3/_4$ in.

625 LES TROIS FRÈRES
Painted and engraved bison. In the deepest part of the cave. 59 in.

626 LES TROIS FRÈRES
"Gallery of Owls." Silhouettes of night birds. This theme, also documented at Le Portel (see fig. 577), may have affinities with "ghosts" and faces in frontal view. It occurs in the same topographical conditions (see figs. 351, 386, 402, 512, 568, and chart XXX). $35^1/_4$ in.

627 LES TROIS FRÈRES
Aurignacian Gallery (1 on plan). Bison painted in black, Style IV, superimposed over earlier graffiti. About 67 in.

628 LES TROIS FRÈRES
Aurignacian Gallery. Small horse's head, Style IV, placed in front of the bison in fig. 627. 8 in.

629 LES TROIS FRÈRES
Aurignacian Gallery. Claviform sign and rows of dots at back of gallery.

630 LES TROIS FRÈRES
"Sanctuary." Mammoth. About 36 in.

631 LES TROIS FRÈRES
"Sanctuary." Rhinoceros on the periphery of the panel of bison and horses. About 10 in.

632 LES TROIS FRÈRES
"Sanctuary." Bison. $15^3/_4$ in. Though considered "archaic" by Breuil, it does not depart from the normal features of Style IV.

633 LES TROIS FRÈRES
"Sanctuary." Ibex near fig. 631. Though attributed to the Perigordian, this figure exhibits the same details as many other Magdalenian ibexes in the cave. The horns in twisted perspective turn up in every period (see fig. 585). About 10 in.

634 LES TROIS FRÈRES
"Sanctuary." Head of the big bison which serves as background to one of the main panels. About 20 in. The animal is sticking out its tongue.

635 LES TROIS FRÈRES
"Sanctuary." Second equid ("wild-ass") figure in the cave, more detailed than fig. 624, but otherwise identical. About 16 in.

636 LES TROIS FRÈRES
"Sanctuary." Reindeer with legs bent at the knee. About 24 in. One of a panel of fourteen such cervids (see fig. 116).

637 LES TROIS FRÈRES
"Sanctuary." In the recess, going up the wall toward the "Sorcerer" (see fig. 57). Elaborately detailed horse, superimposed over a bison, the foreleg and dewlap of which are visible in front of the horse. About 16 in.

638 LES TROIS FRÈRES
Bison painted in black in the Gallery of Hands (L on plan).

639 LES TROIS FRÈRES
"Chapel," at A on plan. Engraved and painted feline. $29^1/_2$ in.

LE MAS D'AZIL

(Plan, fig. 156, page 369)

640–641 LE MAS D'AZIL
Engraved fish, at 8 on plan. On a block with very tangled figures, we find two images of soles or European flounders. The sole had already turned up in the Pyrenees on the pendant from Lespugue (see fig. 234). Le Mas d'Azil is 150 miles from the Atlantic and 120 miles from the Mediterranean *(photograph A. Leroi-Gourhan)*.

642 LE MAS D'AZIL
Bison head, painted in black, at 17 on plan *(photograph A. Leroi-Gourhan)*.

643 LE MAS D'AZIL
Small engraved bison, at 10 on plan.

644 LE MAS D'AZIL
Pebble, with horse engraved on it (9). This pebble has been kept at the spot where it was found, directly under the engraved bison in fig. 643 *(photograph A. Leroi-Gourhan)*.

645 LE MAS D'AZIL
Engraved head of bison, in part incorporating an edge of rock (11). The only incised lines are those forming the horn, the ear, the eye, and the muzzle.

MONTESPAN

(Plan, fig. 157, page 370)

646–647 MONTESPAN
Bear modeled in clay. Length about 36 in. Fig. 646, rear view; fig. 647, side view. Note the numerous holes on the flanks and rump *(photograph A. Leroi-Gourhan)*.

648 MONTESPAN
Animal modeled in clay, believed to be a feline. It may be a horse. Note the holes scattered over the chest. Height $27^3/_4$ in. *(photograph A. Leroi-Gourhan)*.

649 MONTESPAN
Casteret Gallery. Engraved horse, with signs, at β4 on plan. About 18 in. *(photograph A. Leroi-Gourhan)*.

650 MONTESPAN
Horse modeled in clay, at α12 on plan, behind the bear (figs. 646, 647). Executed in raised-field relief in clay on the ground, a technique widespread in the Perigord in the Middle Magdalenian. Length $26^3/_4$ in. Note the group of wavy lines in front of the chest *(photograph A. Leroi-Gourhan)*.

651 MONTESPAN
Panorama of "the hunt." About 10 ft. long. At left, a vertically positioned small horse; next to it, a very cursorily rendered horse. At center, a more detailed silhouette of a horse. This half of the frieze comprises mainly perforations, placed around the figures and, in the case of the horse in the middle, on the figure itself. The second half consists mainly of strokes *(photographic restitution, J. Vertut)*.

652 MONTESPAN
Engraved ibex head, at α3 on plan. About 12 in. *(photograph A. Leroi-Gourhan)*.

653 MONTESPAN
Highly schematized engraved bison, at B 13. About 12 in. *(photograph A. Leroi-Gourhan)*.

654 MONTESPAN
Engraved bison, at B 13. About 12 in. The outline comes close to that of some bison at Niaux and Les Trois Frères. Wound marks on flank *(photograph A. Leroi-Gourhan)*.

655 MONTESPAN
Last figure, Trombe-Dubuc Gallery, at E on plan. Head of a carnivorous animal, formed by utilizing a stalagmite. This figure is located about half a mile from the entrance (compare fig. 564) *(photograph A. Leroi-Gourhan)*.

SANTIMAMINE

656 SANTIMAMINE
Bison painted in black in first chamber.

657 SANTIMAMINE
Central panel, horse. $17^3/_4$ in. Exhibits close affinities with the horse at La Cullalvera (see fig. 673).

658 SANTIMAMINE
Central panel, bison. About 16 in. As in fig. 657, the modeling is characteristically Early Style IV.

659 SANTIMAMINE
Central panel, bison. $27^5/_8$ in. Located at extreme right. Rather careless in execution.

660 SANTIMAMINE
Central panel, bison. $23^5/_8$ in. Same modeling features as in figs. 657–659, here filling nearly the whole outline (see fig. 584).

661 SANTIMAMINE
Stalagmitic block covered with very thin incised outlines of bison. They cannot be seen on the photograph. At bottom, a painted and engraved bison in the same style as the figures in the central panel. Only the head is shown here.

662 SANTIMAMINE
Three bison figures, painted in vertical positions on the lip of a

fissure in the round chamber. Total height 31½ in. It is clear the animals are not supposed to be falling. The one at top right has a single line on its flank.

663 SANTIMAMINE
Bear and heads of a stag and an ibex, painted on the cascade of stalagmite. Length of bear 12⅝ in.

ALTAMIRA
(Plans, figs. 132, 133, pages 328, 329)

664–665 ALTAMIRA
Engraved group at 60 on plan, comprising a horse at the right (fig. 665) and a bison on the left (fig. 664), above which there is a mammoth. Only part of the latter can be seen in the photograph. The whole group measures 59 in. Two lines of the withers of the bison overlap an earlier black double line (part of the Black Sequence). Except for the "elephants" at El Pindal and El Castillo (see fig. 102), this mammoth is the only proboscidian represented in a Spanish cave.

666 ALTAMIRA
Engraved hind, at 55 on plan (fig. 132). 21⅝ in. The figure seems to belong to one of the more recent sequences.

667–668 ALTAMIRA
Horses in Style III, in red, near the Painted Ceiling. Each measures more than 40 in. Compare with figs. 314, 317, 326, 342, 359, 387. At lower left in fig. 668 we see the ibex of fig. 669.

669 ALTAMIRA
Red ibex. About 16 in. The treatment is too simplified to assign it a specific style. The horns and general appearance are compatible with the Style III of the horses in figs. 667 and 668. Compare with figs. 313, 316, 416.

670 ALTAMIRA
This is the first photograph ever published of the entire Altamira ceiling (see fig. 133). The area covered is approximately 20 by 10 yards. The over-all composition is brought out clearly. The three main animals are: (1) a bison placed alone, bottom center, next to the spread of claviform signs; (2) the big horse's head, top center, inserted between bison figures; (3) the big hind at left, complemented by a small bison. A second horse, complemented by a hind formed by a reserved area on its flank, is at top left. Directly behind it, on the periphery, is a boar. There is another boar, placed symmetrically at the top right of the ceiling, facing a headless bison (see chart XXVII). The rest of the composition is taken up by about fifteen bison in different postures; four among them (three of which incorporate irregularities in the rock) are shown rolling on the ground *(photographic restitution, J. Vertut)*.

LA CULLALVERA
(Plan, fig. 158, page 372)

671–672 LA CULLALVERA
Group of dots, claviforms, and strokes

located 770 yards from the entrance. Note at right in fig. 672 the row of claviforms (red) and the row of strokes (black).

673 LA CULLALVERA
Black-painted horse, two-thirds of a mile from the entrance. Length about 20 in.

674 LA CULLALVERA
Lines in black, the last sign at the far end of the cave.

EL PINDAL

675 EL PINDAL
Panel of paintings. About 60 in. From left to right: one horse, the hindquarters of a cervid (very faint), a stag facing right, and unidentifiable hindquarters.

676 EL PINDAL
Red hind. 33½ in. Note the series of strokes on the vault springing of the wall above the hind.

677 EL PINDAL
Aligned black strokes marking the end of the sequence of figures. 8 in.

LAS MONEDAS
(Plan, fig. 159, page 374)

678 LAS MONEDAS
Panel 1. Black ovals and strokes, and rock with natural slit. About 40 in.

679 LAS MONEDAS
Panel 10. Horse in central composition.

680 LAS MONEDAS
Panel 4. The main figures are a horse and reindeer back to back. Reindeer measures about 28 in. There is a small, much-damaged bison next to the horse.

681 LAS MONEDAS
Panel 7. Reindeer framed by two ibexes. Length about 24 in.

682 LAS MONEDAS
Panel 11. Sequence of reindeer. With the reindeer on panels 4 and 7, these are the only representations of this cervid known in Spain. Total length 31½ in.

683 LAS MONEDAS
Little horse on panel 8. About 10 in.

684 LAS MONEDAS
Barbed signs and claviforms on panel 12.

685 LAS MONEDAS
Little horse painted on the ceiling o the semidome at 13 on plan. About 8 in.

686 LAS MONEDAS
Left-hand portion of panel 15. It includes several horses, signs, and a headless animal. Only the last is shown here (see chart XXVII). The panel measures about 48 in.

LOS HORNOS
(LA PEÑA DE LOS HORNOS)

687 LOS HORNOS
Head of a bison engraved on ceiling. Area in photograph about 10 in.

688 LOS HORNOS
Engraved ibex head in Style IV. About 10 in.

689 LOS HORNOS
Figure with raised arms. About 18 in.

BARA-BAHAU

690 BARA-BAHAU
Lattice sign. Such signs are especially frequent in Early Style IV compositions (see figs. 549, 565, 606).

691 BARA-BAHAU
We make out the silhouette of a horse, and some parallel lines which may correspond to lattice signs. Compare fig. 510, Les Combarelles.

692 BARA-BAHAU
Equid. Among the last figures in the sequence near the back of the cave.

693 BARA-BAHAU
Front part of an engraving of an unidentifiable bovid. The anatomical details do not indicate definitely whether it is a bison or an ox. Note, however, that the horns and mane are in a late type of perspective *(photograph Laborie)*.

MARCENAC

694 MARCENAC
Black-painted horse. The head is partly covered over with stalagmitic deposits. About 40 in.

695 MARCENAC
Bison in black applied with pad. The horns are drawn in frontal perspective. About 59 in.

TIBIRAN
(Plan, fig. 160, page 378)

696 TIBIRAN
Engraved and painted horse located at D 1 on plan. The figure was re-engraved at a late stage of the Magdalenian *(photograph A. Leroi-Gourhan)*.

697 TIBIRAN
Natural contour painted in black, probably representing a bear. At D 2 on plan *(photograph A. Leroi-Gourhan)*.

BÉDEILHAC

698 BÉDEILHAC
Bison modeled on the ground in clay. Above and in front of this figure are two incised vulvas. 11¾ in.

699 BÉDEILHAC
Bison engraved in the clay of the ground. The execution is close to that of the bison in the Trombe Gallery at Montespan (see fig. 654).

700 BÉDEILHAC
Bison painted in black on an irregular surface. Style IV. 15¾ in.

701 BÉDEILHAC
Animal without head or forelegs, painted in black. Compare with the small figure that is lacking bust and feet in the Black Salon at Niaux (see fig. 602) and with the ibex at the terminal lake in the same cave (see fig. 604 and chart XXVII).

USSAT

(Plan, fig. 161, page 379)

702 USSAT
Sign painted in red, at 8 on plan. About 6 in. *(photograph A. Leroi-Gourhan)*.

ETCHEBERRIKO-KARBIA

703 ETCHEBERRIKO-KARBIA
Bison painted with clay. Length 67 in. *(photograph A. Leroi-Gourhan)*.

ISTURITZ *(Lower Cave)*

704 ISTURITZ
Small painted horse, very cursory in execution. About 8 in.

705 ISTURITZ
Forequarters of a hind, engraved. 6 in.

706 ISTURITZ
Horse's head with the same characteristics as fig. 704.

CANDAMO

707 CANDAMO
Horse painted in reddish brown. About 40 in.

708 CANDAMO
Horse with the same characteristics as fig. 707. 29½ in.

709 CANDAMO
Group of figures. Among others: one cervid and at the top a highly schematized small human figure. Total width about 6½ ft.

MEDITERRANEAN CAVE ART

ADDAURA

710 ADDAURA
Engraved scene. Two human figures are lying on the ground, and around them men with bird beaks are gesticulating. There are also two deer and a pair of equids. Height of panel about 59 in. *(photograph Soprintendenza alle antichità, Palermo)*.

NISCEMI

711 NISCEMI
Bull. The panel as a whole includes another bovid and two equids *(photograph Soprintendenza alle antichità, Palermo)*.

CHABOT

(Plan, fig. 162, page 382)

712 CHABOT
Engraved mammoth, at 1 on plan. 23⅝ in. *(photograph A. Leroi-Gourhan)*.

713 CHABOT
Mammoth engraved on ceiling, at 3 on plan. About 40 in. *(photograph A. Leroi-Gourhan)*.

714 CHABOT
Engraved outlines on ceiling, at 4 on plan; among them we make out a number of more or less complete mammoths *(photograph A. Leroi-Gourhan)*.

715 CHABOT
Central composition, at 2 on plan. At top center, a large figure probably representing a bull; around it, several horses, also mammoths or cervids. The outlines overlap and are hard to read. About 6½ ft. *(photograph A. Leroi-Gourhan)*.

EBBOU

(Plan, fig. 164, page 385)

716 EBBOU
Forequarters of a stag, at D on plan. The head measures about 4 in. *(photograph A. Leroi-Gourhan)*.

717 EBBOU
Ibex to the left of the stag in fig. 716, between the legs of a horse. Length about 8 in. *(photograph A. Leroi-Gourhan)*.

718 EBBOU
Ibex engraved above the withers of the big bull, at E on plan. 10 in. *(photograph A. Leroi-Gourhan)*.

719 EBBOU
Small bovid engraved over the horns of the big bull, at E on plan. Length 11¾ in. *(photograph A. Leroi-Gourhan)*.

720 EBBOU
Stag and small vertically positioned horse, to right of panel H. Height of stag 15¾ in. *(photograph A. Leroi-Gourhan)*.

721 EBBOU
Ibex to right of the big figure in panel E. 10 in. *(photograph A. Leroi-Gourhan)*.

722 EBBOU
Engraved ibex, at J on plan. 10 in. *(photograph A. Leroi-Gourhan)*.

723 EBBOU
Engraved bison head in Franco-Cantabrian style, at K on plan. From tip of horns to muzzle about 8 in. *(photograph A. Leroi-Gourhan)*.

724 EBBOU
Little horse accompanied by strokes. One of the group at left in panel I. About 12 in. *(photograph A. Leroi-Gourhan)*.

BAYOL

(Plan, fig. 165, page 387)

725 BAYOL
Red-painted ibex, at 2 on plan. Total length 23½ in. *(photograph A. Leroi-Gourhan)*.

726 BAYOL
Horse's head painted in black, no. 22 at bottom of main panel. 11¾ in. *(photograph A. Leroi-Gourhan)*.

727 BAYOL
Schematized horse's head at 12′ on plan. 6 in. *(photograph A. Leroi-Gourhan)*.

LA BAUME LATRONE

(Plan, fig. 166, page 388)

728–729 LA BAUME LATRONE
Three mammoths (59 in., 40 in., and 43 in.) in various stages of stylization. Tusks in frontal perspective *(photograph A. Leroi-Gourhan)*.

730 LA BAUME LATRONE
Big feline figure (9 ft. 10 in.). Highly schematized. Where the tail of the feline curves, two mammoths (40 and 31 in.) are placed *(photograph A. Leroi-Gourhan)*.

731 LA BAUME LATRONE
Mammoth. 51 in. *(photograph A. Leroi-Gourhan)*.

732 LA BAUME LATRONE
Horse. An oval sign is placed so close as to touch the nostrils. The figure has been erroneously interpreted as a rhinoceros *(photograph A. Leroi-Gourhan)*.

733 LA BAUME LATRONE
Mammoth. 43 in. On the stylization of the mammoths in this cave, see charts XLVII, XLIX *(photograph A. Leroi-Gourhan)*.

734 LA BAUME LATRONE
Scrawls and a very cursorily executed engraved figure, at B on plan. The figure has been seen as a "hornless rhinoceros," but more probably it is a horse. About 16 in. *(photograph A. Leroi-Gourhan)*.

ALDÈNE

(Plan, fig. 168, page 390)

735 ALDÈNE
Head of big feline, no. 6 on plan. This engraving overlaps a great many scrawls and scratchings. The head measures about 20 in. *(photograph A. Leroi-Gourhan)*.

736 ALDÈNE
Head of horse, no. 7 on plan, at top of frieze. Over-all length about 40 in. *(photograph A. Leroi-Gourhan)*.

SALLÈLES-CABARDÈS

(Plan, fig. 169, page 390)

737 SALLÈLES-CABARDÈS
Central portion of the panel showing ibexes and signs. At E on plan. Width of ibex 28 in. *(photograph A. Leroi-Gourhan)*.

LA PILETA

738–739 LA PILETA
Composition on ox/horse and paired signs theme. At left (fig. 738), a cow with the head of a bull beside it; there is a female goose-track sign in front of the cow's muzzle. At right (fig. 739), a horse with a stag under it; there are many double strokes on both figures. The horse measures 20 in. *(photographs Seminario de Historia Primitiva, Madrid)*.

12. CHARTS

SUPPORTING

THE

HYPOTHESES

CHART I. CHRONOLOGY OF THE UPPER PALEOLITHIC

DATES (CARBON-14)	END OF NINETEENTH CENTURY	BREUIL (first quarter of twentieth century)	DIVISIONS CURRENTLY IN USE	TERMINOLOGY USED IN THIS WORK	STYLES
1965 / 0					
5,000					
10,000		MAGDALENIAN — VI V IV III II I	MAGDALENIAN { UPPER, MIDDLE	MAGDALENIAN { LATE, MIDDLE, EARLY	STYLE IV
15,000			PROTO-MAGDALENIAN (Cheynier) { II I		STYLE III
	SOLUTREAN	SOLUTREAN PROTO-SOLUTREAN	SOLUTREAN PROTO-SOLUTREAN AURIGNACIAN PROTO-MAGDALENIAN (Peyrony)	SOLUTREAN INTER-GRAVETTIAN-SOLUTREAN	
20,000					STYLE II
25,000		AURIGNACIAN — LATE	GRAVETTIAN (Upper Perigordian)	GRAVETTIAN	
30,000		MIDDLE	AURIGNACIAN { II I	AURIGNACIAN	STYLE I
35,000		EARLY	CHATELPERRONIAN (Lower Perigordian)	CHATELPERRONIAN	PREFIGURATIVE PERIOD
40,000	MOUSTERIAN	MOUSTERIAN	MOUSTERIAN	MOUSTERIAN	

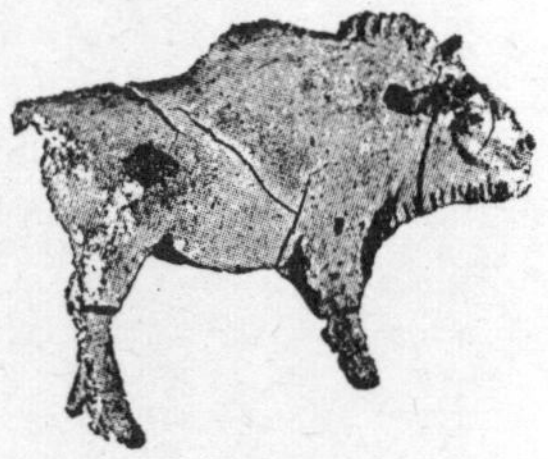

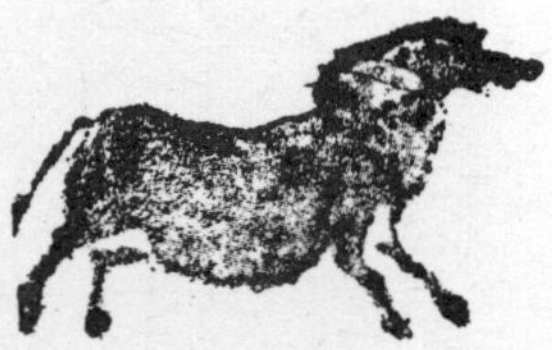

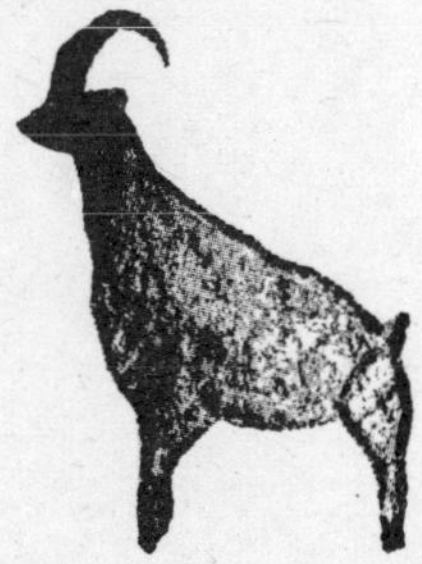

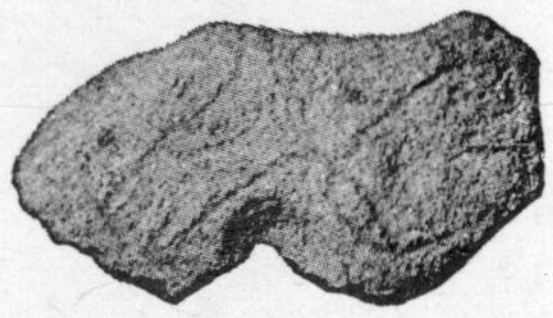

In the last two columns on the right the terminology has been modified to fit the requirements of Paleolithic art. At present it covers a broader time scale than the archaeological breakdown according to industrial objects.

CHART II. PRINCIPAL SITES OF WORKS OF ART RELIABLY DATED OR DATED WITH A HIGH DEGREE OF PROBABILITY

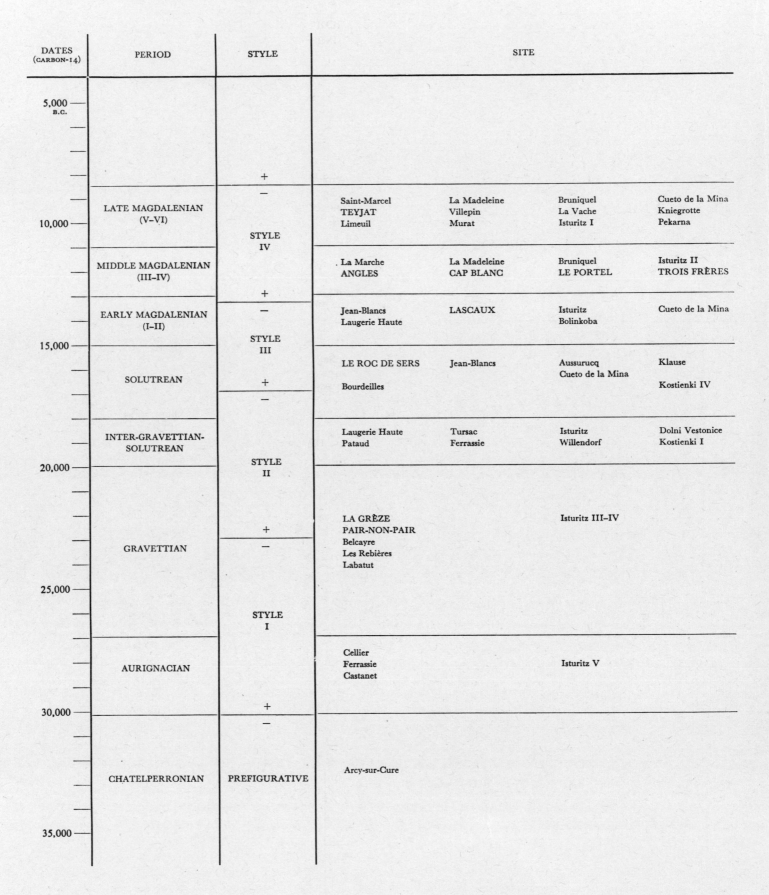

DATES (CARBON-14)	PERIOD	STYLE	SITE			
5,000 B.C.						
		+				
		−				
10,000	LATE MAGDALENIAN (V–VI)		Saint-Marcel TEYJAT Limeuil	La Madeleine Villepin Murat	Bruniquel La Vache Isturitz I	Cueto de la Mina Kniegrotte Pekarna
		STYLE IV				
	MIDDLE MAGDALENIAN (III–IV)		La Marche ANGLES	La Madeleine CAP BLANC	Bruniquel LE PORTEL	Isturitz II TROIS FRÈRES
		+				
	EARLY MAGDALENIAN (I–II)	−	Jean-Blancs Laugerie Haute	LASCAUX	Isturitz Bolinkoba	Cueto de la Mina
15,000		STYLE III				
	SOLUTREAN	+	LE ROC DE SERS Bourdeilles	Jean-Blancs	Aussurucq Cueto de la Mina	Klause Kostienki IV
		−				
	INTER-GRAVETTIAN-SOLUTREAN		Laugerie Haute Pataud	Tursac Ferrassie	Isturitz Willendorf	Dolni Vestonice Kostienki I
20,000		STYLE II				
		+	LA GRÈZE PAIR-NON-PAIR Belcayre Les Rebières Labatut		Isturitz III–IV	
	GRAVETTIAN	−				
25,000						
		STYLE I				
	AURIGNACIAN		Cellier Ferrassie Castanet		Isturitz V	
30,000		+				
		−				
	CHATELPERRONIAN	PREFIGURATIVE	Arcy-sur-Cure			
35,000						

Sites in capital letters contain cave art; other sites are those at which decorated objects have been found.

494

CHART III. LOCATION OF THE PRINCIPAL DECORATED CAVES

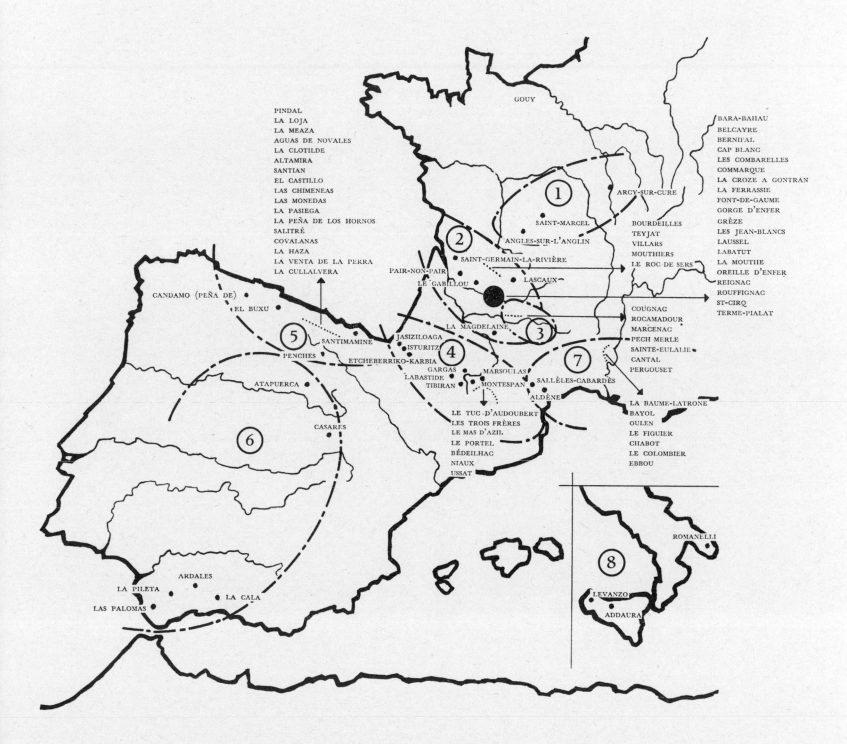

PINDAL
LA LOJA
LA MEAZA
AGUAS DE NOVALES
LA CLOTILDE
ALTAMIRA
SANTIAN
EL CASTILLO
LAS CHIMENEAS
LAS MONEDAS
LA PASIEGA
LA PEÑA DE LOS HORNOS
SALITRÉ
COVALANAS
LA HAZA
LA VENTA DE LA PERRA
LA CULLALVERA

BARA-BAHAU
BELCAYRE
BERNIFAL
CAP BLANC
LES COMBARELLES
COMMARQUE
LA CROZE A GONTRAN
LA FERRASSIE
FONT-DE-GAUME
GORGE D'ENFER
GRÈZE
LES JEAN-BLANCS
LAUSSEL
LABATUT
LA MOUTHE
OREILLE D'ENFER
REIGNAC
ROUFFIGNAC
ST-CIRQ
TERME-PIALAT

GOUY

ARCY-SUR-CURE

SAINT-MARCEL

BOURDEILLES
TEYJAT
VILLARS
MOUTHIERS
LE ROC DE SERS

ANGLES-SUR-L'ANGLIN

SAINT-GERMAIN-LA-RIVIÈRE

PAIR-NON-PAIR
LE GABILLOU
LASCAUX

COUGNAC
ROCAMADOUR
MARCENAC
PECH MERLE
SAINTE-EULALIE
CANTAL
PERGOUSET

CANDAMO (PEÑA DE)
EL BUXU

LA MAGDELAINE

SANTIMAMINE
PENCHES

JASIZILOAGA
ISTURITZ
ETCHEBERRIKO-KARBIA
GARGAS
LABASTIDE
TIBIRAN

MARSOULAS
MONTESPAN
SALLÈLES-CABARDÈS
ALDÈNE

ATAPUERCA

CASARES

LE TUC-D'AUDOUBERT
LES TROIS FRÈRES
LE MAS D'AZIL
LE PORTEL
BÉDEILHAC
NIAUX
USSAT

LA BAUME-LATRONE
BAYOL
OULEN
LE FIGUIER
CHABOT
LE COLOMBIER
EBBOU

ROMANELLI

LEVANZO
ADDAURA

ARDALES
LA PILETA
LA CALA
LAS PALOMAS

The regional subdivisions are based, in the present state of our knowledge, on convenience rather than on thorough study of regional characteristics.

1. NORTHERN AND EASTERN FRANCE. 2. CHARENTE, PÉRIGORD. 3. QUERCY. 4. PYRENEES.
5. CANTABRIAN SPAIN. 6. CENTRAL AND SOUTHERN SPAIN. 7. LANGUEDOC, RHONE, PROVENCE.
8. ITALY.

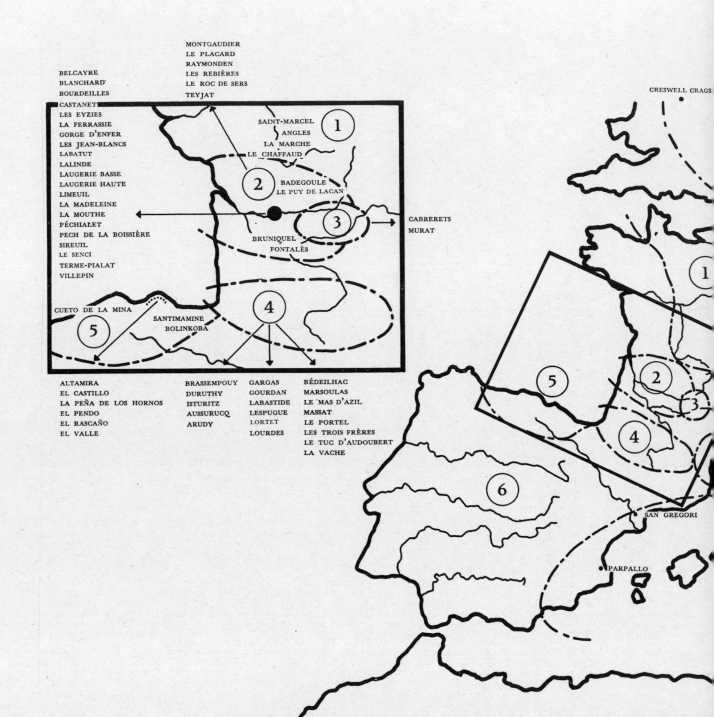

MONTGAUDIER
LE PLACARD
RAYMONDEN
LES REBIÈRES
LE ROC DE SERS
TEYJAT

BELCAYRE
BLANCHARD
BOURDEILLES
CASTANET
LES EYZIES
LA FERRASSIE
GORGE D'ENFER
LES JEAN-BLANCS
LABATUT
LALINDE
LAUGERIE BASSE
LAUGERIE HAUTE
LIMEUIL
LA MADELEINE
LA MOUTHE
PÉCHIALET
PECH DE LA BOISSIÈRE
SIREUIL
LE SENCI
TERME-PIALAT
VILLEPIN

SAINT-MARCEL
ANGLES
LA MARCHE
LE CHAFFAUD

BADEGOULE
LE PUY DE LACAN

CABRERETS
MURAT

BRUNIQUEL
FONTALÈS

CRESWELL CRAGS

CUETO DE LA MINA
SANTIMAMINE
BOLINKOBA

ALTAMIRA
EL CASTILLO
LA PEÑA DE LOS HORNOS
EL PENDO
EL RASCAÑO
EL VALLE

BRASSEMPOUY
DURUTHY
ISTURITZ
AUSSURUCQ
ARUDY

GARGAS
GOURDAN
LABASTIDE
LESPUGUE
LORTET
LOURDES

BÉDEILHAC
MARSOULAS
LE MAS D'AZIL
MASSAT
LE PORTEL
LES TROIS FRÈRES
LE TUC D'AUDOUBERT
LA VACHE

SAN GREGORI

PARPALLO

CHART IV. LOCATION OF PRINCIPAL SITES OF DECORATED OBJECTS

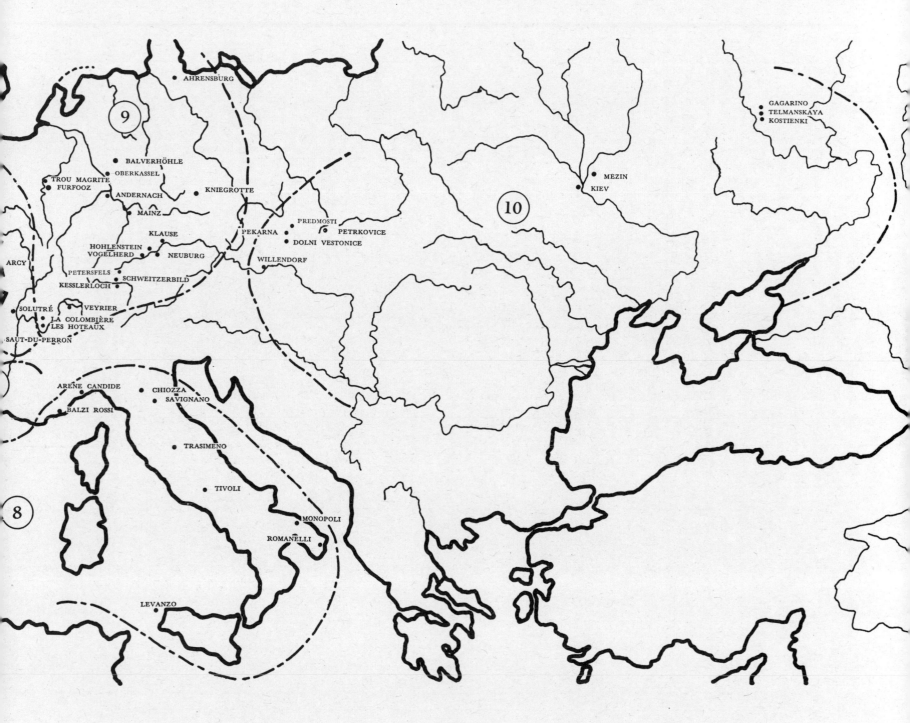

1. NORTHERN AND EASTERN FRANCE. 2. CHARENTE, PÉRIGORD. 3. QUERCY. 4. PYRENEES.
5. CANTABRIAN SPAIN. 6. CENTRAL AND SOUTHERN SPAIN. 7. LANGUEDOC, RHONE, PROVENCE.
8. EASTERN SPAIN, ITALY. 9. GREAT BRITAIN, BELGIUM, GERMANY, SWITZERLAND. 10. CENTRAL
AND EASTERN EUROPE.

CHART V (right).
ANALYSIS OF REALISTIC DECORATED OBJECTS BY TYPE AND STYLE

Note the considerable disproportion between Styles I, II, and III (22 percent) on the one hand, and Style IV (78 percent) on the other. Among other things, this disproportion explains the greater frequency of reindeer and fish on decorated objects than in cave works. Note also that realistic figures appear on decorated tools and weapons; the same is true for objects of personal adornment. By contrast, statuettes and religious art on slabs are to be found in both the early and the late styles. Lastly, non-utilitarian religious works total 65 percent, whereas objects of personal adornment and implements together total 34 percent.

	STYLE I	STYLE II	STYLE III	STYLE IV	
SPEARS		1	3	9	
HARPOONS				8	
PIERCED STAFFS		1		81	
SPEAR-THROWERS				31	
SPATULAS				27	
HALF-ROUNDED RODS				12	
IMPLEMENTS (total)		(2)	(3)	(168)	27%
PENDANTS				13	
CARVED SILHOUETTES				23	
DISKS				13	
OBJECTS OF ADORNMENT (total)				(49)	7%
STATUETTES		29	5	17	
SLABS	19	18	23	306 (109+197)	
OBJECTS OF RELIGIOUS ART (total)	(19)	(47)	(28)	(323)	65%
PERCENTAGE OF RELIGIOUS ART	100%	95%	90%	59%	

22%   78%

	FELINE	BEAR	MAMMOTH	RHINOCEROS	HORSE	STAG	HIND	REINDEER	OX	BISON	IBEX	BIRD	FISH	WOMAN	VULVA	WOUND	MAN	PHALLUS	BARBED SIGN	TOTAL
SPEARS				1	3	1	1						3						3	12
HARPOONS								1					4						2	7
PIERCED STAFFS	1	1	1		12	4	3	7		5	4	2	13				4	13	11	81
SPEAR-THROWERS	1		1		9			3		3	6	2	4						2	31
SPATULAS					3	1	1	1		2	3		8						8	27
HALF-ROUNDED RODS					1	1	2				1		3		2		1	1	2	14
PENDANTS					2						1		1	2	3	2		1	1	13
CARVED SILHOUETTES					19					1	2		1							23
DISKS		2	1		1			1	1	2	1						2		2	13
STATUETTES	5	4	2	1	6					3				26			2	2	1	52
SLABS	6	20	3	4	36	9	14	66	14	36	18	8	6	10	3	12	17		9	291
TOTAL SUBJECTS	13	27	8	6	92	16	21	79	15	52	36	12	43	38	8	14	26	17	41	564

CHART VI (above). FREQUENCY OF SUBJECTS IN DECORATED OBJECTS

The breakdown is based on the subjects represented, regardless of the number of individuals in the same category on any one object.

	FELINE	BEAR	MAMMOTH	RHINOCEROS	HORSE	STAG	HIND	REINDEER	OX	BISON	IBEX	BIRD	FISH	WOMAN	VULVA	WOUND	MAN	PHALLUS	BARBED SIGN	TOTAL
CAVE WALLS	23	24	9	9	313	68	64	36	71	209	78	5	7	7	113	19	47	4	51	1 157
STATUETTES SLABS	11	24	4	4	42	9	16	66	14	39	18	8	6	36	15	6	19	2	10	349
OBJECTS OF ADORNMENT	–	2	–	–	22	–	–	1	1	3	3	–	2	2	5	–	2	1	3	47
WEAPONS, TOOLS	2	–	1	1	28	7	6	12	–	10	14	4	35	–	2	–	5	13	28	168
TOTAL	36	50	14	14	405	84	86	115	86	261	113	17	50	45	135	25	73	20	92	1 721

CHART VII (above). TOTAL FREQUENCY OF SUBJECTS IN CAVE ART AND ON DECORATED OBJECTS

See charts III and IV. The chart above is based on the sites in regions 1 to 5; it does not include regions 6 to 8. As in chart VI, the figures indicate the number of times the subjects are represented, not the number of individuals in each category. The data confirm chart V: horse and bison are poorly represented on decorated objects, reindeer and fish very strongly. These features reflect the upsurge of the decoration of objects and the evolution of some of the basic themes in the Late Magdalenian.

CHART VIII (right).
MAIN TYPES OF SPEARS
IN CHRONOLOGICAL ORDER

(left to right, top row)

CHATELPERRONIAN
    conical-cylindrical

AURIGNACIAN I
    split base

AURIGNACIAN II
    lozenge-shaped

AURIGNACIAN III
    oval in section

AURIGNACIAN V
    single nonstriated beveling

PROTO-SOLUTREAN
    single striated beveling

(left to right, bottom row)

SOLUTREAN
    thin type with single beveling; *left,* beveling
    with rhythmic striations

MAGDALENIAN I
    striated beveling in fern pattern

MAGDALENIAN II
    thin type with groove

MAGDALENIAN III
    short type with single beveling and groove

MAGDALENIAN III–IV
    thin type with single beveling and groove

MAGDALENIAN V–VI
    striated double beveling; *right,* point forked at
    base to lengthen a broken spear

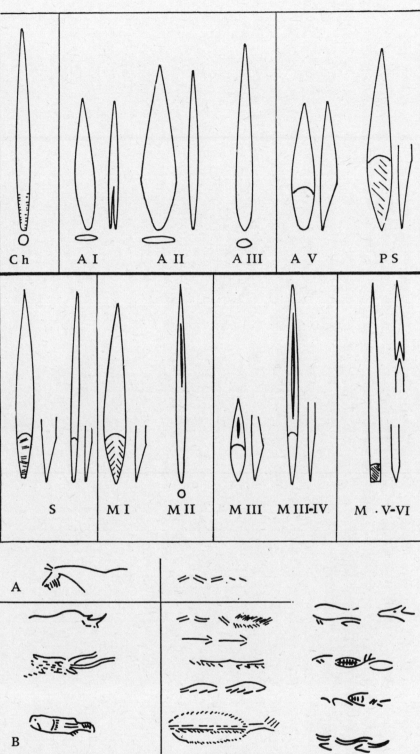

CHART IX (left and center columns).
SPEAR DECORATIONS

The left-hand column shows the less schematized figures; the right-hand column, the highly schematized
figures or the abstractions. A: Gravettian finds; B:
Early Magdalenian; C: Late Magdalenian. It can be
stated that the degree of schematization does not vary
with the epoch: abstract decoration is constantly present, side by side with figure representation. (After
H. Breuil, R. de Saint-Périer, and photographic inventories.)

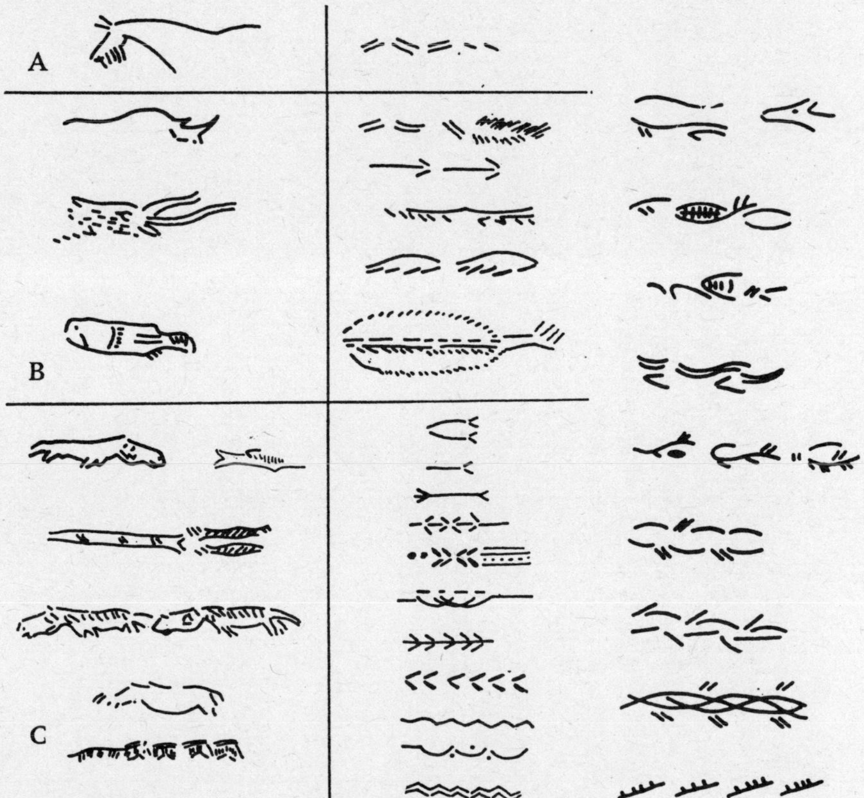

CHART X (far right column).
HARPOON DECORATIONS
(LATE MAGDALENIAN)

Single-line or double-line decoration follows the contours of the object. In most cases (for instance, in the
four lowest drawings), the contours seem merely decorative; but the top five drawings show that the outlines could have a specific meaning. (After H. Breuil
and photographic inventories.)

CHART XI *(below)*.
TYPES OF PHALLIFORM PIERCED STAFFS

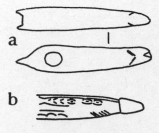

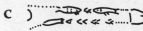

a. EL PENDO

b. LA PILETA
   "Dissociated" decoration from
   the Late Magdalenian; a fish
   can be discerned on it.

c. BRUNIQUEL
   Similar decoration consisting
   of fish and double strokes, but
   more explicit; Late Magdalenian.

d. ISTURITZ
   The incised decorations correspond to the branching sign.

e. LA MADELEINE (Dordogne)

f. FARINCOURT
   Middle Magdalenian. This
   pierced staff was found next
   to a sandstone phallus decorated with a branching sign.

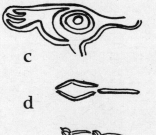

g. ISTURITZ
   Gravettian.

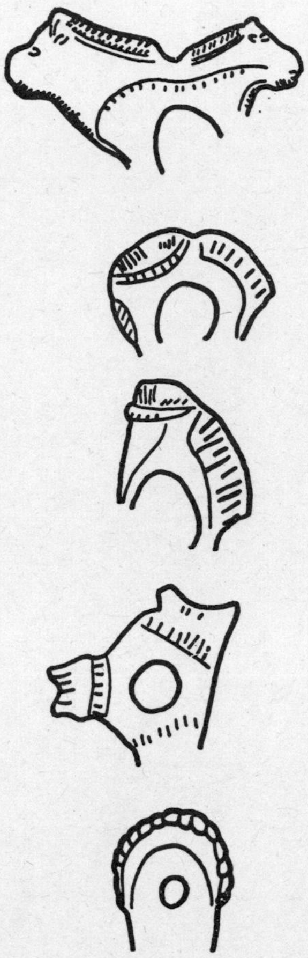

CHART XII *(left)*.
SCHEMATIZATION
OF THE BISON

Schematic representations of bison
over and around the holes in pierced
staffs from the Middle and Late
Magdalenian.

From top to bottom:

LAUGERIE BASSE. Male and female
bison clearly represented.

LA MADELEINE (Dordogne). At left,
the male reduced to horn,
mane, and beard; at right, the
female reduced to mane.

LA MADELEINE. Same theme, a step
nearer to schematization.

LAUGERIE BASSE. Same theme, ab-
stracted.

ISTURITZ. Same theme, completely
abstract.

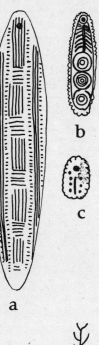

CHART XIII *(below)*. REALISTIC AND SCHEMATIC THEMES
ON HALF-ROUNDED RODS

a. LA MADELEINE (Dordogne)
   At the left of the double sexual
   subject there is an incomplete
   figure which looks like an eye
   (fig. 216).

b. LAUGERIE BASSE
   Head of a herbivorous animal
   (fig. 217).

c. ISTURITZ
   Head of a herbivorous animal
   on a rod decorated with spirals
   (fig. 219).

d. SAINT-MARCEL
   Decorations on a shuttle or a
   half-rounded rod.

e. LA MADELEINE
   Late Magdalenian.

f. LE PLACARD
   Magdalenian (indeterminate).

g. LA MADELEINE
   Late Magdalenian.

CHART XIV *(below)*. THEMES ON OVAL PENDANTS

a. Large pendant from LALINDE with
   elaborate geometric decoration.

b. Notched pendant from SAINT-
   MARCEL which seems to represent
   the same sexual theme as the rod
   from LA MADELEINE (chart XIII,
   a), here expressed by a barbed
   sign and a sequence of circles.

c. "Ladybug" from LAUGERIE BASSE,
   generally believed to represent a
   vulva.

d. Decoration on a fragment of a
   pendant from LE MAS D'AZIL; this
   plantlike motif might actually
   represent a barbed sign placed
   above an oval.

CHART XV. IDEAL ARRANGEMENT OF A PALEOLITHIC SANCTUARY

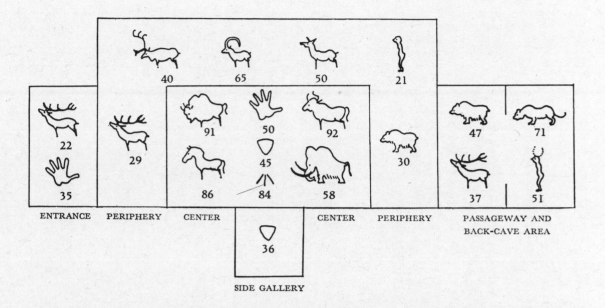

| ENTRANCE | PERIPHERY | CENTER | | CENTER | PERIPHERY | PASSAGEWAY AND BACK-CAVE AREA |

SIDE GALLERY

The percentages have been based on 865 subjects located in 62 caves of which a complete topographical analysis was made. A subject is counted once each time it is represented, regardless of the number of times it is repeated in the same panel (for example, a composition containing 12 bison, 3 horses, 4 ibexes has been counted as bison 1, horse 1, ibex 1). More than 80 percent of the "female" subjects (bison, ox, female signs) occur in a central location. The "male" subjects are more or less evenly distributed in the peripheral locations (for example, the stag 22%+29%+37% = 88%). The only exception is the hand, which is both central and peripheral. Signs from the male category are not shown because their distribution is approximately the same in all locations. Like the horse, they appear on the periphery as elements in the male category and at the center as elements complementary to female signs: entrance 10.9 percent; periphery 20.6 percent; center 25.9 percent; side gallery 9 percent; passageway 19.9 percent; back-cave area 13.5 percent.

CHART XVI.
CAVE ART: GENERAL STATISTICS

The following chart (page 503) gives the breakdown, region by region, for the 72 decorated caves studied. The numerals at the upper left of the squares represent absolute numbers; the underlined numerals express the coefficients obtained by taking as a basis region 2 (Charente and Périgord), for which we have the most abundant and complete data.

In the statistics of *themes*, the basic unit is the presence of a theme, no matter how many times it may be repeated. In the breakdown of *compositional subjects*, the basic unit is the theme present in a distinct composition, no matter how many times repeated. The number of *individuals* is determined on the basis of the total number of repetitions of a theme in a given set. For instance, in region 2, the bison turns up as a theme in 18 caves and rock shelters; at these sites it appears in 72 compositions in which bison are represented by 151 individuals.

The successive breakdowns show that (for instance, in region 2) 18 ensembles out of a total of 22 include the bison in their themes, that the compositions are repeated on the average four times per ensemble, and that there is an average of 2 bison per composition.

The breakdown of themes and compositional subjects, and the working out of the coefficients, restore the balance between the regions. The single mammoth at La Croze at Gontran is, taken absolutely, just as important as the several hundred mammoths at Rouffignac. The method applied, however, involves some inexactness, which is hard to avoid without greatly complicating our presentation. Thus the number of sites in regions 1, 3, 6, and 8 is too low for statistical validity; for these regions our figures have only indicative value. Another inexactness arises from the fact that in a few caves certain themes bulk abnormally large—for instance, the bison at Les Trois Frères and the mammoth at Rouffignac. The distortion is corrected in the table of themes, which shows that the divergences in common themes are relatively small as between one region and another.

CHART XV *cont.)*

THE chart presents a quantitative view of cave art. There are more than 2,000 representations distributed over more than 1,000 compositions in the following 72 caves, which represent for all practical purposes the bulk of cave art:

REGION 1. Angles-sur-l'Anglin, Arcy-sur-Cure, Saint-Marcel

REGION 2. Bara-Bahau, Bernifal, Bourdeilles, Le Cap Blanc, Les Combarelles, Commarque, La Croze at Gontran, Font-de-Gaume, Le Gabillou, Gorge-d'Enfer, La Grèze, Lascaux, Laussel, La Magdelaine, La Mouthe, Mouthiers, Pair-non-Pair, Le Roc de Sers, Rouffignac, Saint-Cirq, Teyjat, Villars

REGION 3. Cougnac, Marcenac, Pech Merle, Rocamadour, Sainte-Eulalie

REGION 4. Bédeilhac, Etcheberriko-Karbia, Gargas, Isturitz, Labastide, Marsoulas, Le Mas d'Azil, Montespan, Niaux, Le Portel, Tibiran, Les Trois Frères, Le Tuc d'Audoubert, Ussat

REGION 5. Altamira, El Buxu, La Peña de Candamo, El Castillo, Las Chimeneas, La Clotilde, Covalanas, La Cullalvera, La Haza, Los Hornos, La Loja, Las Monedas, La Pasiega, El Pindal, Santian, Santimamine, Venta de la Perra

REGION 6. Ardales, Los Casares, La Pileta

REGION 7. Aldène, La Baume Latrone, Bayol, Chabot, Ebbou, Oulen, Sallèles-Cabardès

REGION 8. Addaura, Levanzo, Niscemi

GENERAL VALUES

RELATIVE FREQUENCY OF THEMES

horse/bison		ibex/ox/stag/mammoth/hind				bear/feline/man/reindeer				rhinoceros/fish/woman		
60	45	40	35	31	24	22	18	17	17	16	7	7	6

RELATIVE FREQUENCY OF COMPOSITIONAL SUBJECTS

horse/bison		mammoth/ibex/ox/stag/hind					man/reindeer/bear/feline				rhinoceros/fish/woman		
313	209	79	78	71	68	64	47	36	24	23	9	7	7

RELATIVE FREQUENCY OF INDIVIDUALS

horse/bison		mammoth/ibex/ox/hind/stag					man/reindeer/bear/feline				woman/rhinoceros/fish		
610	510	205	176	137	135	112	88	84	36	29	18	16	8

This breakdown shows that (1) if we disregard exceptional themes, such as megaceros, bird, or monsters (which are no more frequent on decorated objects), horse and bison are the most frequently represented; (2) mammoth, ibex, ox, stag, and hind form a second group much less important; ibex, stag, and hind because they are complementary themes, mammoth and ox because they are themes of pronouncedly regional character. Man, feline, and bear form a third group, together with reindeer. The first three of these are essentially marginal themes, most often appearing by themselves; the reindeer has a markedly regional character, and in addition does not appear during the central period of cave decoration. A last group is constituted by the rare subjects—rhinoceros, fish, and human female. The ratio of subjects to the number of individuals represented is interesting. We find that for some themes this ratio is almost 1:1 (bear, 24:36; feline, 23:29), which shows that these animals are usually isolated. For the majority of themes the ratio is close to 1:2 (horse, bison, ibex, ox, stag, hind, reindeer, rhinoceros, human male, human female). This ratio might be accounted for by the frequency of male/female pairings, if the stag, the hind, and male and female human figures did not contradict or at least complicate such a hypothesis.

The regional frequency of themes shows very interesting variations:

REGION 1. (north of Charente)
horse, reindeer, bison feline, mammoth, stag, ibex, woman, man

REGION 2. (Charente, Périgord)
horse, bison, ibex, man, ox bear, mammoth, stag feline, hind, rhinoceros woman

REGION 3. (Quercy)
horse bear, mammoth, stag, hind, megaceros, bison, ibex, man

REGION 4. (Pyrenees)
bison, horse, ibex feline, stag, mammoth, man

REGION 5. (Cantabria, Asturias)
horse, ox bison, stag, ibex hind

REGION 6. (central and southern Spain)
horse, ox, stag, fish

REGION 7. (Rhone)
horse, mammoth, ibex ox, bison feline

REGION 8. (Italy)
ox, horse, man woman

The picture as a whole discloses two major areas: the first is dominated by the horse/bison pairing (region 1, 2, 4), the second by the horse/ox pairing (regions 5, 6, 8). A third area (regions 3 and 7), where the horse/mammoth pairing is dominant, might be discernible if the scarcity of sites in these regions did not impose caution. This finding is all the more interesting because the four species in question actually turn up almost everywhere. The variation may be accounted for in several ways, especially by bio-climatic reasons, since the bison may have been more exclusively northern than the ox, and the mammoth more abundant at the approaches to the Massif Central. However, another factor should also be considered, without ruling out the bio-climatic one: the ox/horse pairing seems to have been dominant during the period of Style III, and the horse/bison pairing during that of Style IV, at least in regions which have a sufficient number of sites to support such an evaluation (Périgord and Cantabria). Caves in Style III are still almost unknown in the Pyrenees, where the bison is overwhelmingly dominant (13 against 3). Apart from the bison-ox variation, we observe that in central themes the mammoth moves to first place only in the Rhone basin (5 out of 7 caves).

CHART XVI *(cont.)*

REGION / THEME	NUMBER OF CAVES STUDIED	FELINE	BEAR	MAMMOTH	RHINOCEROS	HORSE	STAG	HIND	MEGACEROS	REINDEER	OX	BISON	IBEX	BIRD	FISH	MONSTERS	WOMAN	MAN
THEME																		
1 NORTH	3	1 / 7		1 / 7		3 / 21	1 / 7			2 / 14		2 / 14	1 / 7				1 / 7	1 / 7
2 CHARENTE, PÉRIGORD	22	6 / 6	9 / 9	8 / 9	5 / 5	19 / 19	9 / 9	6 / 6	2 / 2	10 / 10	12 / 12	18 / 18	14 / 14	1 / 1	1 / 1	2 / 2	3 / 3	13 / 13
3 QUERCY	5	1 / 4.5	2 / 9	2 / 9		4 / 18	2 / 9	2 / 9	2 / 9	1 / 4.5	1 / 4.5	2 / 9	2 / 9		1 / 4.5	1 / 4.5	1 / 4.5	2 / 9
4 PYRENEES	13	5 / 8	3 / 3.8	4 / 6.4	1 / 1.6	12 / 17.2	5 / 8	4 / 6.4	1 / 1.6	2 / 3.2	3 / 3.8	13 / 20.8	9 / 14.4	3 / 3.8	2 / 3.2	1 / 1.6		4 / 6.4
5 CANTABRIA	17	1 / 1.3	4 / 5.2	4 / 5.2		13 / 16.9	9 / 11.7	7 / 9.1		1 / 1.3	11 / 14.3	9 / 11.7	9 / 11.7	1 / 1.3	1 / 1.3			4 / 5.2
6 CENTRAL AND SOUTHERN SPAIN	2	1 / 11			1 / 11	2 / 22	2 / 22	1 / 11			2 / 22		1 / 11		2 / 22			1 / 11
7 RHONE	7	2 / 6	1 / 3	5 / 15		5 / 15	2 / 6	1 / 3			3 / 9	3 / 9	4 / 12					
8 ITALY	3					2 / 14	1 / 7	1 / 7	1 / 7		3 / 21						1 / 7	2 / 14
TOTAL THEMES	72	17	19	24	7	60	31	22	6	16	35	47	40	5	7	4	6	27
COMPOSITIONAL SUBJECTS																		
1 NORTH	3	1 / 7		3 / 21		6 / 42	1 / 7			2 / 14		5 / 35	1 / 7				1 / 7	2 / 14
2 CHARENTE, PÉRIGORD	22	10 / 10	13 / 13	47 / 47	8 / 8	136 / 136	11 / 11	7 / 7	2 / 2	24 / 24	26 / 26	72 / 72	27 / 27	1 / 1	1 / 1	3 / 3	4 / 4	19 / 19
3 QUERCY	5	1 / 4.5	1 / 4.5	7 / 31.5		6 / 27	3 / 13.5	2 / 9	2 / 9	1 / 4.5	2 / 9	5 / 22.5	4 / 18		1 / 4.5	1 / 4.5	2 / 9	4 / 18
4 PYRENEES	13	7 / 11.2	5 / 8	5 / 8	1 / 1.6	76 / 121.6	8 / 12.8	5 / 8	1 / 1.6	6 / 9.6	5 / 8	82 / 131.6	24 / 38.4	3 / 4.8	2 / 3.2	1 / 1.6		5 / 8
5 CANTABRIA	17	1 / 1.3	4 / 5.2	4 / 5.2		63 / 81.9	31 / 40.3	47 / 61.1		3 / 3.9	23 / 29.9	41 / 53.3	9 / 11.7	1 / 1.3	1 / 1.3			12 / 15.6
6 CENTRAL AND SOUTHERN SPAIN	2	1 / 11				5 / 55	5 / 55	1 / 11			4 / 44		2 / 22		2 / 22			3 / 33
7 RHONE	7	2 / 6	1 / 3	13 / 39		15 / 45	8 / 24	1 / 3			5 / 15	4 / 12	11 / 33					
8 ITALY	3					6 / 42	1 / 7	1 / 7	1 / 7		6 / 42						1 / 7	2 / 14
TOTAL SUBJECTS	72	23	24	79	9	313	68	64	6	36	71	209	78	5	7	5	8	47
INDIVIDUALS																		
1 NORTH	3	1 / 7		6 / 42		9 / 63	1 / 7			2 / 14		11 / 77	7 / 49				3 / 21	2 / 14
2 CHARENTE, PÉRIGORD	22	15 / 15	23 / 23	145 / 145	15 / 15	304 / 304	29 / 29	10 / 10	2 / 2	57 / 57	60 / 60	151 / 151	58 / 58	1 / 1	1 / 1	3 / 3	7 / 7	35 / 35
3 QUERCY	5	1 / 4.5	1 / 4.5	21 / 94.5		8 / 36	5 / 22.5	2 / 9	4 / 18	1 / 9	6 / 27	13 / 48.5	9 / 40.5		1 / 9	4 / 18	8 / 36	7 / 31.5
4 PYRENEES	13	8 / 12.8	6 / 9.6	6 / 9.6	1 / 1.6	137 / 219.2	8 / 12.8	6 / 9.6	1 / 1.6	20 / 32	6 / 9.6	237 / 379.2	32 / 51.2	4 / 6.4	3 / 3.8	2 / 3.2		8 / 12.8
5 CANTABRIA	17	1 / 1.3	5 / 6.5	4 / 5.2		104 / 135.2	48 / 62.4	111 / 144.3		4 / 5.2	43 / 55.9	94 / 122.2	52 / 67.6	1 / 1.3	1 / 1.3			14 / 18.2
6 CENTRAL AND SOUTHERN SPAIN	2	1 / 11				10 / 110	9 / 99	1 / 11			5 / 55		2 / 22		2 / 22			5 / 55
7 RHONE	7	2 / 6	1 / 3	23 / 69		30 / 90	11 / 33	4 / 12			7 / 21	4 / 12	16 / 48					
8 ITALY	3					8 / 56	1 / 7	1 / 7	1?		10 / 70						1 / 7	17 / 119
TOTAL INDIVIDUALS	72	29	36	205	16	610	112	135	8	84	137	510	176	6	8	9	19	88

GENERAL LISTS OF SITES

1	ADDAURA Sicily	13	23	CAP BLANC, LE Dordogne	2	45	GRÈZE, LA Dordogne	1 (?)
2	ALDÈNE Hérault	?	24	CASARES, LOS Guadalajara	12×13	46	HAZA, LA Santander	?
3	ALTAMIRA Santander	2(11)/4/7	25	CASTILLO, EL Santander	2/3/4(14)	47	HORNOS, LA PEÑA DE LOS Santander	1/11
4	ANGLES Vienne	2	26	CHABOT Gard	17×13	48	HUCHARD Gard	?
5	ARCY-SUR-CURE Yonne	10	27	CHIMENEAS, LAS Santander	12×14	49	ISTURITZ Basses-Pyrénées	32(?)/4
6	ARDALES Malaga	14	28	CLOTILDE, LA Santander	11/(1)	50	LABASTIDE Hautes-Pyrénées	1/5
7	ATAPUERCA Burgos	?	29	COLOMBIER, LE Ardèche	1	51	LABATUT Dordogne	?
8	BARA-BAHAU Dordogne	1/12	30	COMBARELLES, LES Dordogne	1/2/4(11)	52	LASCAUX Dordogne	13/(2)/(3
9	BAUME LATRONE, LA Gard	25	31	COMMARQUE Dordogne	12	53	LAUGERIE HAUTE Dordogne	?
10	BAYOL CAVE Gard	15	32	COUGNAC Lot	?	54	LAUSSEL Dordogne	?
11	BÉDEILHAC Ariège	1 ?	33	COVALANAS Santander	4	55	LEVANZO Sicily	13×14
12	BERNIFAL Dordogne	7	34	CROZE, LA Dordogne	7/11	56	LOJA, LA Santander	11 (?)
13	BERNOUS, LES Dordogne	?	35	CULLALVERA, LA Santander	?	57	MAGDELAINE, LA Tarn	1
14	BERROBERIA Santander	?	36	EBBOU Ardèche	12×13/12/(1)	58	MARCENAC Lot	1
15	BOLADO Asturias	?	37	ETCHEBERRIKO-KARBIA Basses-Pyrénées	2	59	MARSOULAS Haute-Garonne	1
16	BOURDEILLES Dordogne	11	38	FIGUIER, LE Ardèche	17×13	60	MASSAT Ariège	?
17	BUXU, EL Asturias	12×13	39	FONT-DE-GAUME Dordogne	7×8/11	61	MAS D'AZIL Ariège	1
18	CALA, LA Malaga	?	40	FORÊT, LA Dordogne	32	62	MAZACULOS Asturias	0
19	CALEVIE, LA Dordogne	?	41	GABILLOU, LE Dordogne	1/11/2/8/12	63	MEAZA, LA Santander	0
20	CAMBOUS, LE Lot	?	42	GARGAS Hautes-Pyrénées	1/2/7/(12)	64	MILLY Seine-et-Marne	?
21	CANDAMO Asturias	1/11	43	GORGE D'ENFER Dordogne	?	65	MONEDAS, LAS Santander	8×2
22	CANTAL Lot	?	44	GOUY Seine-Maritime	11 (?)	66	MONTESPAN Haute-Garonne	1/2/(11)

CHART XVII *(above)*. SITES OF CAVE ART

CHART XVIII *(below)*. SITES OF DECORATED OBJECTS

1	AHRENSBURG Hamburg	14	BELCAYRE, ABRI Dordogne	27	COLOMBIÈRE, LA Ain	40	FONTALÈS Tarn-et-Garonne	53	KESSLERLOCH Schaffhausen
2	ALTAMIRA Santander	15	BLANCHARD, ABRI Dordogne	28	COUGNAC Dordogne	41	FONTARNAUD Gironde	54	KIEV Ukraine
3	ANDERNACH Coblenz	16	BOLINKOBA Vizcaya	29	CRESWELL CRAGS Derbyshire	42	FURFOOZ Namur	55	KLAUSE Bavaria
4	ANGLES Vienne	17	BOURDEILLES Dordogne	30	CROUZADE, LA Aude	43	GAGARINO Tambov	56	KNIEGROTTE Thuringia
5	ARCY-SUR-CURE Yonne	18	BRASSEMPOUY Landes	31	CUETO DE LA MINA Asturias	44	GARGAS Hautes-Pyrénées	57	KOSTELIK Moravia
6	ARÈNE CANDIDE Liguria	19	BRNO Moravia	32.	DOLNI VESTONICE Moravia	45	GORGE D'ENFER Dordogne	58	KOSTIENKI Tambov
7	ARUDY Basses-Pyrénées	20	BRUNIQUEL Tarn-et-Garonne	33	DURUTHY Landes	46	GOURDAN Haute-Garonne	59	JEAN-BLANCS, LES Dordogne
8	AURENSAN Hautes-Pyrénées	21	CABRERETS Lot	34	ENLÈNE Ariège	47	GOYET Namur	60	LABASTIDE Hautes-Pyrénées
9	ASSURUCCE Basses-Pyrénées	22	CASTANET, ABRI Dordogne	35	EYZIES, LES Dordogne	48	GUDENUSHÖHLE Austria	61	LABATUT Dordogne
10	BADEGOULE Dordogne	23	CASTILLO, EL Santander	36	FACTEUR, ABRI DU Dordogne	49	HOHLENSTEIN Bavaria	62	LALINDE Dordogne
11	BALVERHÖHLE Westphalia	24	CHAFFAUD, LE Vienne	37	FARINCOURT Haute-Marne	50	HORNOS, LA PEÑA DE LOS Santander	63	LARAUX Vienne
12	BALZI ROSSI Ventimiglia	25	CHAISE, LA Charente	38	FERRASSIE, LA Dordogne	51	HOTEAUX, LES Ain	64	LAUGERIE BASSE Dordogne
13	BÉDEILHAC Ariège	26	CHIOZZA Reggio Emilia	39	FIGUIER, LE Ardèche	52	ISTURITZ Basses-Pyrénées	65	LAUGERIE HAUTE Dordogne

67	MOUTHE, LA Dordogne	1 1/2×3/7×2	89	ROC DE SERS, LE Charente	**2**
68	MOUTHIERS Charente	1	90	ROMANELLI Apulia	11 (?)
69	MURAT, ABRI Lot	?	91	ROUFFIGNAC Dordogne	**7**
70	NANCY Dordogne	**2**	92	SAINT-CIRQ Dordogne	1/2
71	NIAUX Ariège	**2/(12)**	93	St-GERMAIN-LA-RIVIÈRE Gironde	?
72	NISCEMI Sicily	11	94	St-MARCEL Indre	?
73	NOVALES, AGUOS DE Santander	1 (?)	95	Ste-EULALIE Lot	?
74	OREILLE D'ENFER Dordogne	?	96	SALLÈLES-CABARDÈS Aude	**2**
75	OULEN Ardèche	7/?	97	SALITRE Santander	?
76	PAIR-NON-PAIR Gironde	2×7/12	98	SANTIAN Santander	0
77	PALOMAS, LAS Cadiz	?	99	SANTIMAMINE Vizcaya	1/11(?)
78	PASIEGA, LA Santander	3/4/13/14	100	SASISILOAGA Basses-Pyrénées	1(?)
79	PECH MERLE Lot	5/7/9	101	SOTTARIZA Santander	?
80	PENCHES Asturias	?	102	SUDRIE, LA Dordogne	?
81	PENDO, EL Santander	?	103	TEYJAT Dordogne	3×**4**/8/31(11)
82	PILETA, LA Malaga	12	104	TIBIRAN Hautes-Pyrénées	?
83	PINDAL, EL Asturias	**4**	105	TOUR, LA Dordogne	?
84	PORTEL, LE Ariège	1/2(12)	106	TROIS FRÈRES, LES Ariège	2×**3**/8
85	QUINTANAL Asturias	?	107	TUC D'AUDOUBERT, LE Ariège	1
86	REIGNAC Dordogne		108	USSAT Ariège	1
87	REVERDIT, ABRI Dordogne	1	109	VENTA DE LA PERRA Vizcaya	1
88	ROCAMADOUR Lot	?	110	VILLARS Dordogne	1

1. bison-horse
2. bison-horse-ibex
3. bison-horse-stag
4. bison-horse-hind
5. bison-horse-lion
6.
7. bison-horse-mammoth
8. bison-horse-reindeer
9. bison-mammoth
10. bison-mammoth-stag

11. ox-horse
12. bison-horse-ibex
13. ox-horse-stag
14. ox-horse-hind
15. ox-horse-lion
16.
17. ox-horse-mammoth
18.
19.
20.

21. mammoth-horse
22. mammoth-horse-ibex
23.
24.
25. mammoth-horse-lion

31. reindeer-horse
32. reindeer-horse-ibex

41. hind-horse

The main themes of the cave art at each site are listed at the far right above. When several themes are present at one site, they are listed by number in topographical order, and separated by a slant bar (/). When a theme includes more than three animals, a multiplication sign (×) is placed between the sets of elements. Compositions in which the bison provides the leading theme are indicated in boldface type. They constitute a majority. The numbers in parentheses refer to complementary compositions (for instance, ox/horse in a cave on the bison/horse theme). The gaps in the list of themes show that by no means all conceivable formulas are represented.

66	LAUSSEL Dordogne	79	MAS D'AZIL Ariège	92	PETERSFELS Baden	105	ROMANELLI Apulia	118	TERME-PIALAT Dordogne
67	LESPUGUE Haute-Garonne	80	MEZIN Kroletz	93	PETRKOVICE Silesia	106	St-MARCEL Indre	119	TEYJAT Dordogne
68	LEVANZO Sicily	81	MONOPOLI Apulia	94	PLACARD, LE Charente	107	St-MIHIEL Meuse	120	TIVOLI Lazio
69	LIMEUIL Dordogne	82	MONTGAUDIER Charente	95	PLANCHETORTE Corrèze	108	SALPÉTRIÈRE Gard	121	TRASIMENO Umbria
70	LORTET Hautes-Pyrénées	83	MOUTHE, LA Dordogne	96	PORTEL, LE Ariège	109	SAN GREGORI Valencia	122	TROIS FRÈRES, LES Ariège
71	LOUBRESSAC Vienne	84	MURAT, ABRI Lot	97	PREDMOSTI Moravia	110	SANTIMAMINE Vizcaya	123	TROU-MAGRITE Namur
72	LOURDES Hautes-Pyrénées	85	NEUBURG Bavaria	98	PUY DE LACAŇ, LE Corrèze	111	SAUT-DU-PERRON Loire	124	TUC D'AUDOUBERT, LE Ariège
73	MADELEINE, LA Dordogne	86	OBERKASSEL Westphalia	99	RASCANO Santander	112	SAVIGNANO Modena	125	VACHE, LA Ariège
74	MAINZ Hesse	87	PARPALLO Valencia	100	RAYMONDEN Dordogne	113	SCHWEIZERBILD Schaffhausen	126	VALLE, EL Santander
75	MARCAMPS Gironde	88	PECH DE LA BOISSIÈRE Dordogne	101	REBIÈRES, LES Dordogne	114	SIREUIL Dordogne	127	VEYRIER Haute-Savoie
76	MARCHE Vienne	89	PÉCHIALET Dordogne	102	REY Dordogne	115	SOLUTRÉ Saône-et-Loire	128	VILLEPIN Dordogne
77	MARSOULAS Haute-Garonne	90	PEKARNA Moravia	103	ROC DE SERS, LE Charente	116	SENCI, LE Dordogne	129	VOGELHERD Würtemberg
78	MASSAT Ariège	91	PENDO, EL Santander	104	ROCHE, LA Dordogne	117	TELMAN Tambov	130	WILLENDORF Krems-

CHART XIX. GENERAL STATISTICS OF SUBJECTS IN CAVE ART

| LOCATION | BISON | OX | HORSE | MAMMOTH | HIND | REINDEER | STAG | IBEX | BEAR | FELINE | RHINOCEROS | TOTAL ANIMALS | FEMALE SIGNS | | | | | | TOTAL FEMALE SIGNS | MALE SIGNS | | | | TOTAL MALE REPRESENTATIONS | HANDS |
													OVAL	QUADRANGULAR	BRACE-SHAPED	CLAVIFORM	TECTIFORM	WOUND		MALE FIGURES	BARBED SIGNS	DOTS	STROKES		
CENTRAL COMPOSITION	148	46	198	29	3	5	4	3	2	2	4	444	15	17	8	5	6	16	67	3	19	11	36	69	7
SIDE CHAMBER	6	2	5	6	4	2	–	7	3	2	1	38	8	11	12	7	3	2	43	4	1	8	11	24	1
PERIPHERY	–	–	–	10	18	10	13	49	7	1	2	110	3	–	–	1	–	–	4	7	15	8	25	55	–
ENTRANCE	–	1	4	–	5	2	10	3	–	–	–	25	2	1	–	–	3	–	6	–	1	15	13	29	5
PASSAGEWAY	2	–	4	2	3	3	3	4	7	5	1	34	1	–	–	–	–	1	2	6	11	7	29	53	1
BACK OF CAVE	5	1	17	3	3	3	14	9	4	8	1	68	4	4	–	1	1	–	10	12	4	6	14	36	–
TOTAL LOCATIONS	161	50	228	50	36	25	44	75	23	18	9	719	33	33	20	14	13	19	132	32	51	55	128	266	14
PERCENTAGE																									
CENTRAL COMPOSITION	91	92	86	58	8	20	9	4	8	11	44	61	45	51	40	35	46	84	50	9	37	20	28	25	50
SIDE CHAMBER	3	4	2	12	11	8	–	9	13	11	11	5	24	33	60	50	23	10	32	12	2	14	8	9	7
PERIPHERY	–	–	–	20	50	40	29	65	30	5	22	14	9	–	–	7	–	–	3	21	29	14	19	20	–
ENTRANCE	–	2	1	–	13	8	22	4	–	–	–	3	6	3	–	–	23	–	4	–	2	27	10	10	35
PASSAGEWAY	1	–	1	4	8	12	6	5	30	27	11	4	3	–	–	–	–	5	1	18	21	12	22	20	7
BACK OF CAVE	3	2	7	6	8	12	31	12	17	44	11	9	12	12	–	7	7	–	7	37	8	10	10	13	–

The numerals do not take into account the number of times individuals in a given category appear in a composition. In other words, the chart does not give the total number of figures, but a topographical breakdown of themes. The frequency of animal figures differs markedly between central subjects on the one hand, and peripheral, entrance, passageway, or back-cave subjects on the other. The frequency of female signs is practically equivalent in central compositions and side chambers.

CHART XX. ANALYSIS OF CAVE-ART SITES BY STYLE AND TOPOGRAPHICAL CHARACTER

STYLE	DAYLIGHT	ENTRANCE	EASY ACCESS		DIFFICULT ACCESS	
			AVERAGE DEPTH	GREAT DEPTH	LESS THAN 100 YDS.	MORE THAN 100 YDS.
II	FIGUIER ○ GORGE D'ENFER ◐ HUCHARD ○ LAUSSEL ◐ OULEN ○ PAIR-NON-PAIR ○	CHABOT ○ LA GRÈZE ○ OULEN ○	LA CROZE ○ GARGAS I ○●			BAUME LATRONE ○●
III	BOURDEILLES ◐ HORNOS I ○ MOUTHIERS ◐ ROC DE SERS ◐ ST-CIRQ I ◐	ALTAMIRA I ○● LA HAZA ●	ALTAMIRA II ○ CASTILLO I ○● CHIMENEAS ● COUGNAC ● COVALANAS ● EBBOU I ○ FONT-DE-GAUME I ● GABILLOU ○ LASCAUX ○● MARCENAC ◐ PASIEGA I ○◐ PECH MERLE I ● PORTEL I ●	PECH MERLE II ●		VILLARS ●
EARLY IV	ANGLES ◐ CAP BLANC ◐ ISTURITZ ◐ LA MAGDELAINE ◐ REVERDIT ◐ ST-GERMAIN-LA-RIVIÈRE ◐	ALTAMIRA ○● ST-CIRQ II ○	BARA-BAHAU ○ BERNIFAL ○● CASTILLO II ○● COMMARQUE ◐○ EBBOU II ○ FONT-DE-GAUME II ○● GARGAS II ● HORNOS II ○ ISTURITZ II ○● MARSOULAS ○● MONÉDAS ● PASIEGA II ○● PINDAL ○● PORTEL II ○● USSAT ●	BÉDEILHAC ○● LABASTIDE ○● NIAUX ○● ROUFFIGNAC ○●	ARCY-SUR-CURE ○ BUXU ○ LA MOUTHE ○● SALLÈLES-CABARDÈS ○ SANTIMAMINE ○●	COMBARELLES ○● CULLALVERA ● ETCHEBERRIKO ● PILETA ● MONTESPAN ◐○ TROIS-FRÈRES ○● TUC D'AUDOU-BERT ◐○
LATE IV		ST-MARCEL ○ STE-EULALIE ○ TEYJAT ○				

SYMBOLS
○ ENGRAVING
◐ SCULPTURE
● PAINTING

From the chronological point of view, we see that, except for La Baume Latrone (which has not been dated), archaic works do not occur at greater than average depth in caves of easy access (in practice from 100 to 165 feet inside, with daylight visibility). Furthermore, except for Pech Merle, only in the period of Style IV do works appear at great depths or in cave areas hard to reach. From the point of view of execution, there seems to be no difference between engraving and painting, except at daylight sites which demonstrably contained paintings that have been destroyed. On the other hand, sculpture is found nowhere but in daylight areas, except for the low reliefs at Commarque and the clay modelings at Montespan and Le Tuc d'Audoubert.

507

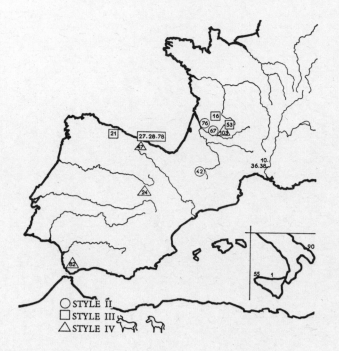

Numbers on the diagrams on this page
refer to Chart XVII.

CHART XXI.

**DISTRIBUTION OF THE OX/HORSE
THEME BY STYLE**

In the Pyrenees-Périgord area the ox appears
as a main theme only in Style II and Style III.
In Style IV it occurs only in complementary
compositions. By contrast, in Spain, the Rhone
valley, and Italy, for what may be climatic
reasons, the ox turns up in Style IV as well as
in Style III.

CHART XXII.

**DISTRIBUTION OF THE BISON/HORSE
THEME BY STYLE**

Only Style III and Style IV are included in
this chart for the geographic area extending
from the Charente in France to Asturias in
Spain.

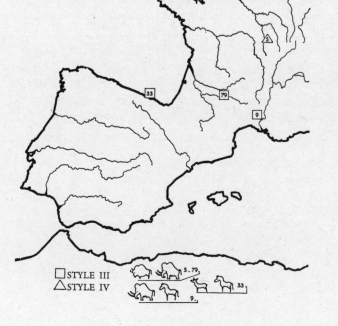
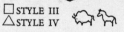

CHART XXIII.

**DISTRIBUTION OF EXCEPTIONAL
THEMES**

(bison/mammoth, mammoth/horse, hind/horse)

The number of sites is too small to enable us
to draw any definite conclusions.

A

D

CHART XXIV.

COMPOSITIONS WITH TWO ANIMALS: MAIN PAIRING

A. LASCAUX
Ox/horse group in the Rotunda.

B. LE GABILLOU
Bison/horse group.
Note paired signs on both animals.

C. ARCY-SUR-CURE
Bison/mammoth.

D. LA BAUME LATRONE
Mammoth/horse group.

E. COVALANAS
Horse/hind group.

B

E

C

CHART XXV.

COMPOSITIONS WITH THREE ANIMALS

A. PECH MERLE
Ox/horse+mammoth.

B. NIAUX
Bison/horse+ibex.

C. EBBOU
Ox/horse+ibex.

D. LAS CHIMENEAS
Ox/horse+hind.

A

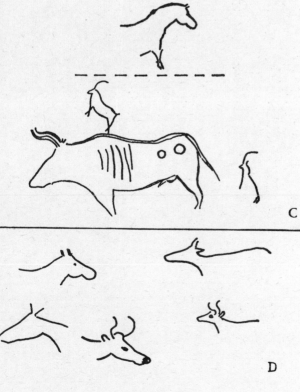

C

B

D

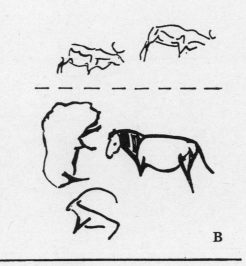

A

B

CHART XXVI.
COMPOSITIONS WITH
TWO CENTRAL AND TWO
COMPLEMENTARY ANIMALS

A. LE PORTEL
　　Bison/horse+ibex and stag.

B. LAS MONEDAS
　　Bison/horse+ibex and reindeer.

C. PAIR-NON-PAIR
　　Bison/horse+ibex and mammoth.

D. LA PASIEGA
　　Bison/horse+stag and hind.

C

D

CHART XXVII.
EXAMPLES OF HEADLESS ANIMALS

1. LASCAUX   Back of the Chamber of Felines.

2. LAS MONEDAS   Last composition.

3. NIAUX   Black Salon, top left of panel I.

4. ALTAMIRA   Painted Ceiling, headless bison at top right.

5. NIAUX   Headless ibex or cervid, last subject in cave.

6. LES TROIS FRÈRES   Spear-thrower of headless animal type.

7. BÉDEILHAC   Headless animal.

8. ADDAURA   Headless animal in panel of oxen and horses.

9. KOSTIENKI I   Headless animal, stone.

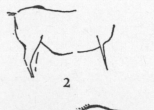

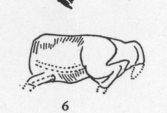
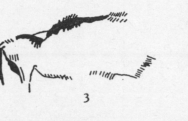

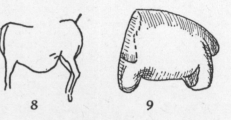

1   2   3   4   5   6   7   8   9

CHART XXVIII.
EXAMPLES OF THE "WOUNDED MAN" THEME

1. LE ROC DE SERS   Man carrying something over his shoulder, pursued by a bison.

2. LASCAUX   Man knocked down by a bison.

3. VILLARS   Man raising arms in front of a charging bison.

4. LAUGERIE BASSE   Man thrown to the ground behind a wounded bison.

5. PÉCHIALET   Man apparently attacked by a bear.

6. LE MAS D'AZIL   Engraving on pierced bone disk, apparently representing a man struck by a bear's paw.

7. PECH MERLE   Man apparently run through with long spears.

8. COUGNAC   Same theme as no. 7.

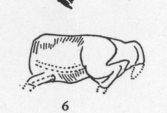

1   5   2   6   3   7   4   8

511

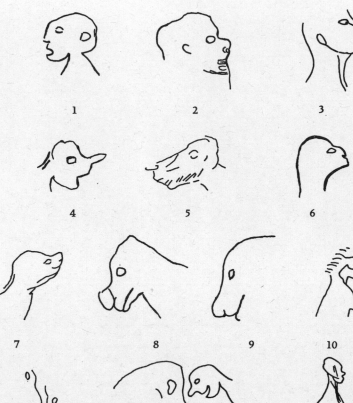

CHART XXIX. MALE PROFILES

We see here every intermediate stage between a normal representation (1) and a completely animalized profile (8 to 10).

1. SAINT-CIRQ

2. ANGLES-SUR-L'ANGLIN

3. LA MARCHE

4. ISTURITZ

5. LA MADELEINE (Dordogne)

6. LOS HORNOS DE LA PEÑA

7. LA MADELEINE (Dordogne)

8. LES COMBARELLES

9. COMMARQUE

10. ABRI MURAT

FACING HUMAN MASKS

11. FONT-DE-GAUME

12. ROUFFIGNAC

13. LES COMBARELLES

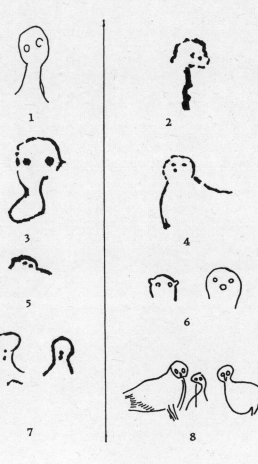

CHART XXX. "GHOSTS"

1. LES COMBARELLES

2. LE PORTEL

3. FONT-DE-GAUME

4. LE PORTEL
   Apparently represents a bird.

5. LASCAUX

6. LES TROIS FRÈRES
   Appears at the edge of one of the panels in the "sanctuary."

7. COUGNAC

8. LES TROIS FRÈRES
   The birds for which the Gallery of Owls was named.

CHART XXXI.

TOPOGRAPHICAL DISTRIBUTION OF MALE AND FEMALE SIGNS

This chart shows that female signs are found almost exclusively in central cave areas, and male signs principally in lateral areas.

			CENTRAL			LATERAL				
			CENTER	SIDE CHAMBER	TOTAL	PERIPHERY	ENTRANCE	PASSAGE	BACK	TOTAL
MALE SIGNS	STROKE		46	11	**57**	25	13	29	14	**81**
	BRANCHING SIGN		19	1	**20**	15	1	11	4	**31**
	DOT		11	8	**19**	8	15	7	6	**36**
	TOTAL		76	20	**96**	48	29	47	24	**148**
FEMALE SIGNS	RECTANGLE		17	11	**28**		1		4	**5**
	BRACE-SHAPED		8	12	**20**					
	TECTIFORM		6	3	**9**		3		1	**4**
	CLAVIFORM		5	7	**12**	1			1	**2**
	OVAL		15	8	**23**	3	2	1	4	**10**
	WOUND		16	2	**18**			1		**1**
	TOTAL		67	43	**110**	4	6	2	10	**22**

CHART XXXII.

TYPOLOGY
OF FEMALE SIGNS

A and B. TRIANGULAR SIGNS

In A 3 and B 3 we see "wound" or "arrow" signs. The forms derived from B correspond to the variants of tectiforms in the Les Eyzies region. Other forms are found among the derivations in E.

C. OVAL SIGNS

D. QUADRANGULAR SIGNS

    1. PÉRIGORD-PYRENEES GROUP

    2. CANTABRIAN GROUP

E. CLAVIFORM SIGNS

This chart shows typological characteristics only. Obviously, in the case of the derived forms (especially for E), there must have occurred borrowings and cross-cultural influences both between epochs and regions.

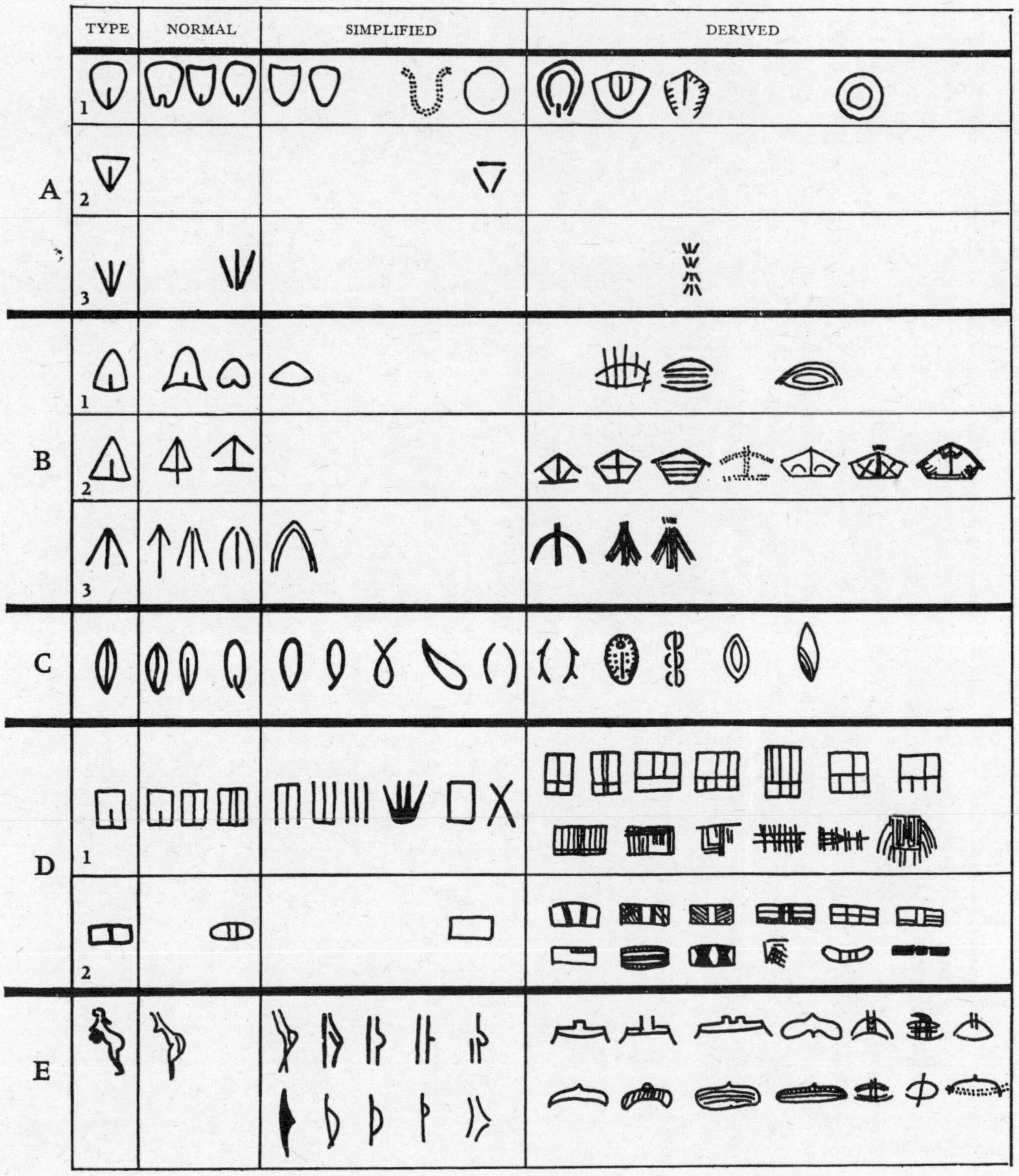

Chart XXXII. Typology of female signs (TYPE / NORMAL / SIMPLIFIED / DERIVED).

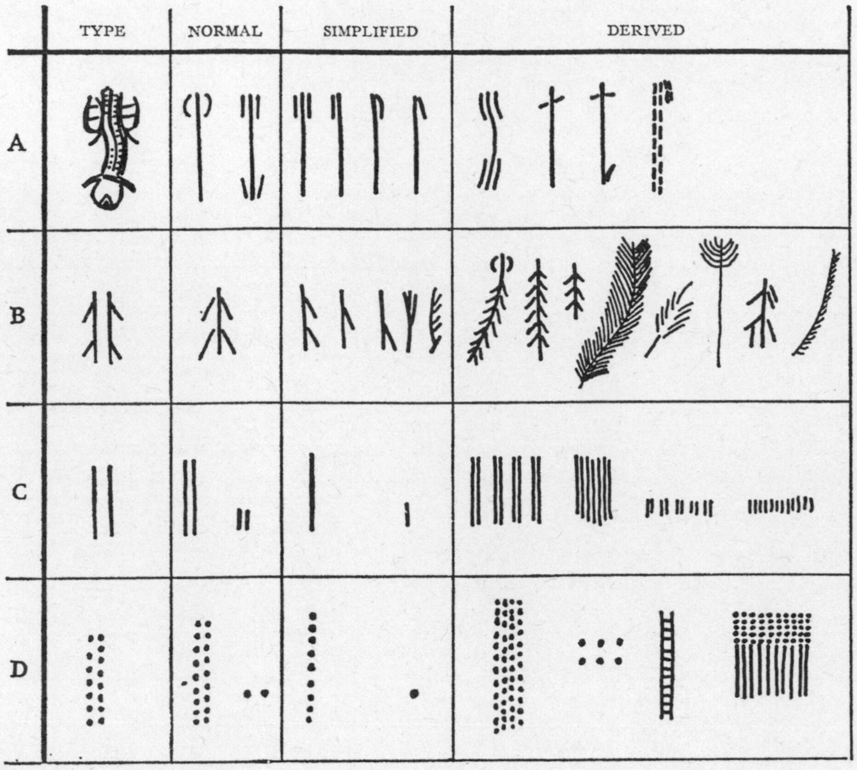

CHART XXXIII. TYPOLOGY OF MALE SIGNS

A. HOOKED OR "SPEAR-THROWER" SIGNS.

B. BARBED SIGNS.

C. SINGLE AND DOUBLE STROKES.

D. DOTS AND ROW OF DOTS, SINGLE AND DOUBLE.

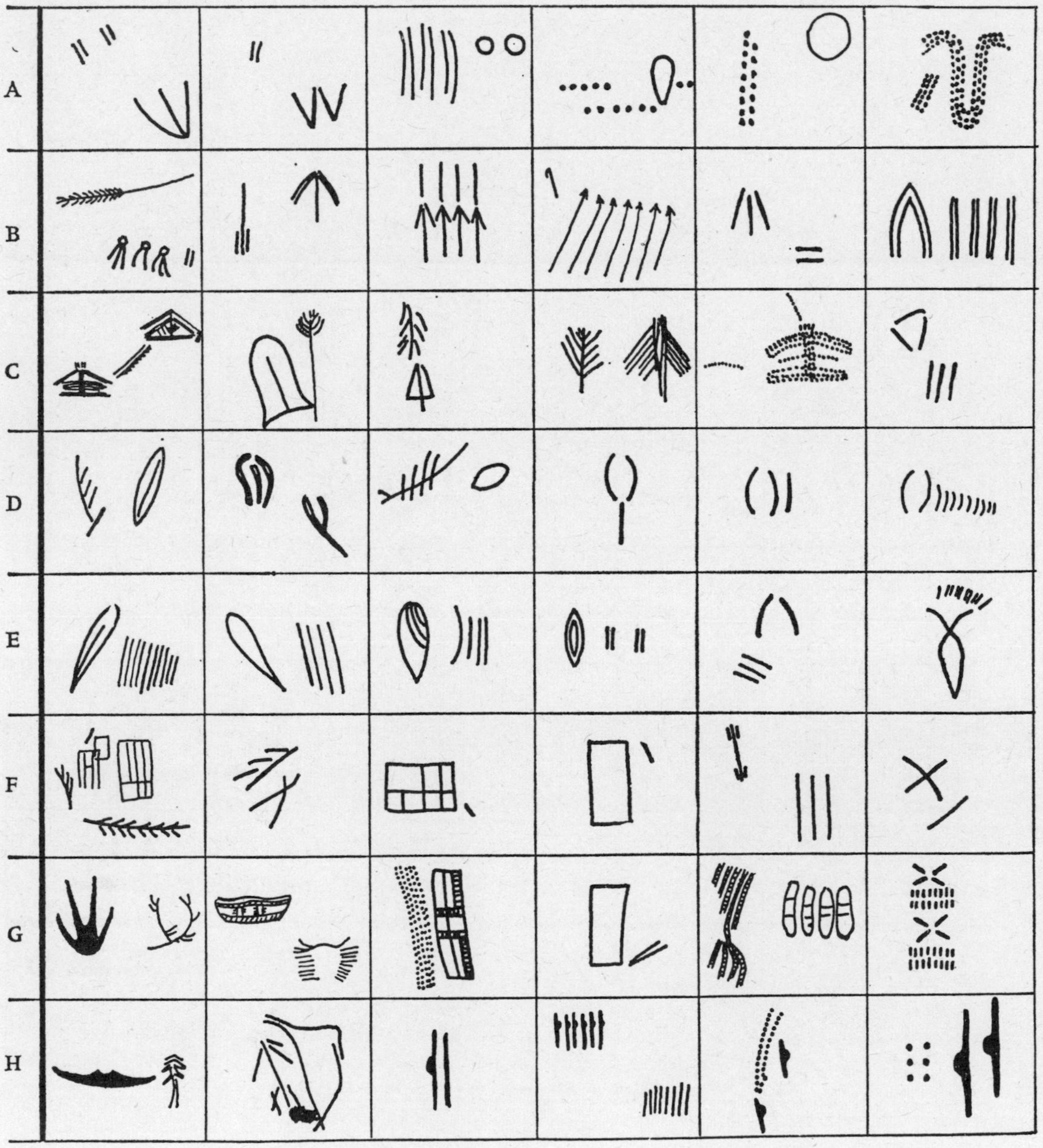

CHART XXXIV.

EXAMPLES OF PAIRED SIGNS

A. From left to right: LA PILETA, FONT-DE-GAUME, EBBOU, LA FERRASSIE, PECH MERLE, LA MEAZA.

B. NIAUX, LE GABILLOU, LASCAUX (Chamber of Felines), LASCAUX (Nave), LAS MONEDAS, LA CROZE.

C. FONT-DE-GAUME, EL CASTILLO, LA MOUTHE, BERNIFAL, OULEN.

D. USSAT, ARCY-SUR-CURE, SALLÈLES-CABARDÈS, SAINT-MARCEL, LABASTIDE, LE PORTEL.

E. LES COMBARELLES (group 69), LES COMBARELLES (group 105), USSAT, BERNIFAL, OULEN, OULEN.

F. LASCAUX (Chamber of Felines), LASCAUX (same), LASCAUX (Axial Gallery), LASCAUX (same), LE GABILLOU, LE GABILLOU.

G. LE PORTEL (Gallery 2), ALTAMIRA (terminal gallery), EL CASTILLO, LAS CHIMENEAS, ALTAMIRA, MARSOULAS (half-rounded rods).

H. ALTAMIRA (Painted Ceiling), LAS MONEDAS, NIAUX, LA CULLULVERA, NIAUX, NIAUX.

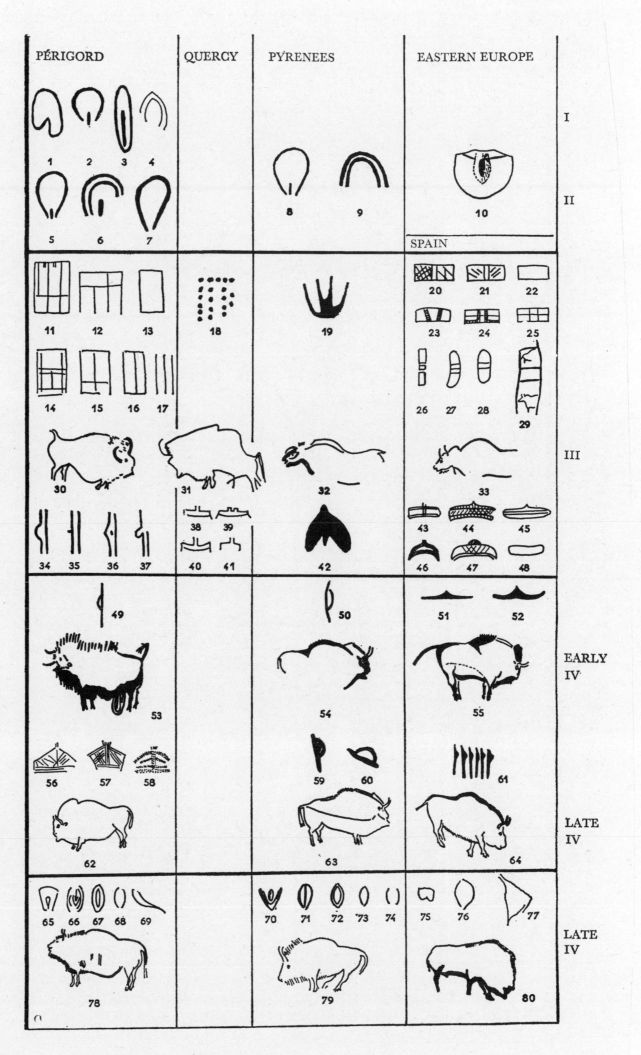

CHART XXXV.
CHRONOLOGICAL AND
GEOGRAPHICAL
DISTRIBUTION
OF SIGNS

STYLE I (Aurignacian)

1–4 ABRI CELLIER.

STYLE II (Gravettian and Late
Aurignacian)

5 LA FERRASSIE; 6 CASTANET; 7 LA
FERRASSIE; 8 GARGAS; 9 ISTURITZ;
10 KOSTIENKI.

STYLE III (Solutrean and Early
Magdalenian)

11–13 LASCAUX; 14–17 LE GABIL-
LOU; 18 PECH MERLE; 19 LE POR-
TEL; 20–22 LAS CHIMENEAS; 23–27
EL CASTILLO; 28 ALTAMIRA; 29 LA
PASIEGA C.

BISON IN STYLE III

30 LE GABILLOU; 31 PECH MERLE;
32 LE PORTEL; 33 LA PASIEGA A.

STYLE III (Early Magdalenian
to Magdalenian IV)

34 VILLARS; 35 LASCAUX; 36–37
LE GABILLOU; 38 PECH MERLE;
39–41 COUGNAC; 42 LE PORTEL;
43–48 LA PASIEGA.

EARLY STYLE IV (Magdale-
nian III—Magdalenian IV)

49 LASCAUX; 50 MARSOULAS; 51
ALTAMIRA; 52 LA PASIEGA; 56 LES
COMBARELLES; 57 FONT-DE-GAUME;
58 BERNIFAL; 59 NIAUX; 60 LE
PORTEL; 61 EL PINDAL.

BISON IN EARLY AND LATE
STYLE IV

53 LASCAUX; 54 MARSOULAS; 55
ALTAMIRA; 62 FONT-DE-GAUME;
63 NIAUX; 64 EL PINDAL; 78 BER-
NIFAL; 79 MONTESPAN; 80 LAS
MONEDAS.

LATE STYLE IV

65–69 LES COMBARELLES; 70 BÉ-
DEILHAC; 71 USSAT; 72–74 LES
TROIS FRÈRES; 75–76 EL PINDAL;
77 LAS MONEDAS.

515

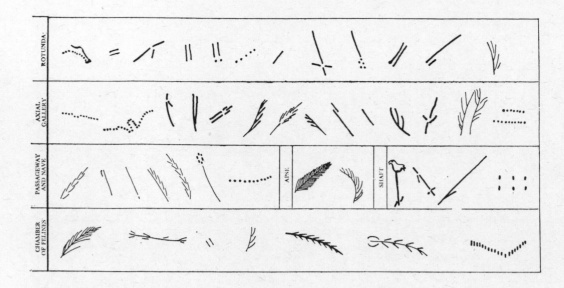

CHART XXXVI (left).

LASCAUX: MALE SIGNS BY
TOPOGRAPHICAL POSITION

This chart shows all possible variations of the stroke, the row of dots,
and the barbed sign.

CHART XXXVII (left).

LASCAUX: FEMALE SIGNS
BY TOPOGRAPHICAL POSITION

(with complementary male signs
in relevant cases)

CHART XXXVIII (below).

LASCAUX: ANALYSIS OF THE
COMPOSITIONS IN THE
AXIAL GALLERY

Bovines and horses are in the top and bottom sections, signs and
complementary animals in the center section. The left-hand
wall is the top section; the right-hand wall is the bottom section.
The stag and the ibexes frame the composition on the right-
hand wall (*see* figs. 316, 317, 319); the quadrangular signs are
also on that side, near their complementaries; most of the barbed
signs are on the other side. The cow/little horses group with the
complementary bull's head on the right-hand wall echoes the
bull/cows group with complementary horses on the other wall.
Note the bison/horse pairing beyond the ibexes, and the entrance and back-cave dots.

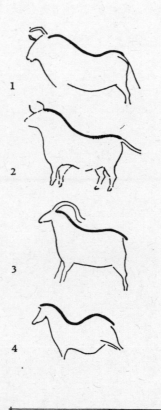

To facilitate comparison, some figures in the diagrams on this page have been reversed.

CHART XXXIX.

CONSTRUCTION OF FIGURES IN STYLE II

The cervico-dorsal line remains the same; details characterizing the species (bison, ibex, and horse) are added.

1. BISON. Pair-non-Pair.

2. OX. La Mouthe.

3. IBEX. Pair-non-Pair.

4. HORSE. Pair-non-Pair.

CHART XL.

EXAMPLES OF FIGURES IN STYLE II

From left to right in each category:

1. SIGNS. Abri Castanet, Pair-non-Pair, Kostienki.

2. STATUETTES AND SLABS WITH FEMALE FIGURES. Terme-Pialat, Kostienki IV, Lespugue.

3. HORSES. Pair-non-Pair, La Croze, Labatut.

4. BISON. Pair-non-Pair, Gargas, La Grèze.

5. OXEN. Pair-non-Pair, La Mouthe, La Croze.

6. MAMMOTHS. Pair-non-Pair, Predmosti, La Croze.

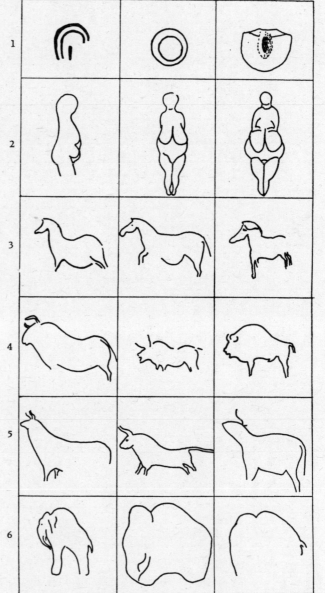

517

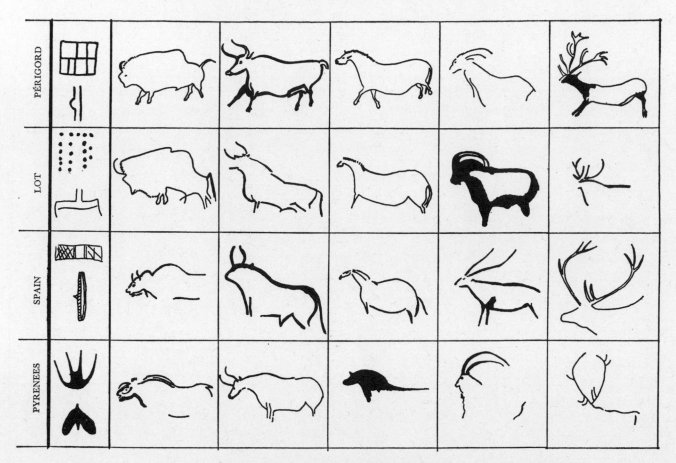

CHART XLI *(above)*. PRINCIPAL FEATURES OF STYLE III

The column at the left shows the signs most commonly associated with animal figures in Style III. Although there are regional differences, these signs are almost identical and seem to indicate that Style III went through two developmental stages. The animal figures shown here (bison, ox, horse, ibex, stag) are from Font-de-Gaume, Lascaux, and Le Gabillou in the Périgord; from Pech Merle and Cougnac in the Lot; from La Pasiega, La Peña de Candamo, and Altamira in Spain; and from Le Portel and Gargas in the Pyrenees. Despite regional variations, bodily proportions and perspective are the same.

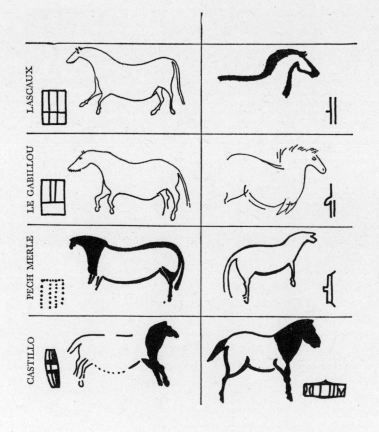

CHART XLII *(left)*.

HORSES AND CORRESPONDING

SIGNS IN STYLE III

It is still hard to define exactly the different phases of Style III. Grouped in this chart are signs and examples of horses corresponding to the probable phases at Lascaux, Le Gabillou, Pach Merle, and El Castillo. Horses very archaic in general appearance, still close to Style II, correspond to the quandrangular sign. Horses of general appearance close to Early Style IV correspond to the brace-shaped sign.

To facilitate comparison, some figures in the diagrams on this page have been reversed.

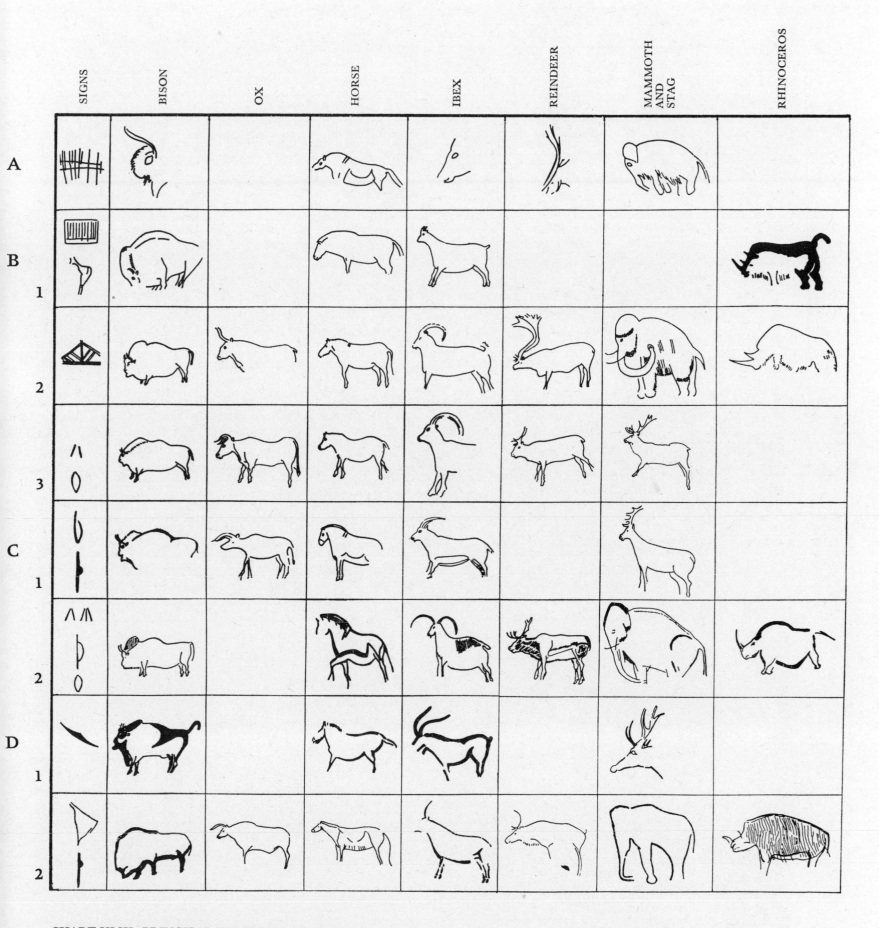

CHART XLIII. PRINCIPAL FEATURES OF STYLE IV

A. NORTHERN FRANCE: Arcy-sur-Cure. B. POITOU-PÉRIGORD: (1) Les Combarelles, Angles-sur-l'Anglin, Le Cap Blanc, Lascaux (Shaft); (2) Les Combarelles, Rouffignac; (3) Teyjat. C. PYRENEES: (1) Marsoulas, Niaux, Labastide; (2) Les Trois Frères, Le Portel. D. SPAIN: (1) Altamira, Santimamine; (2) Las Chimeneas, El Pindal, Los Casares.

Note, in relation to Style III, how the treatment of horns and antlers evolves, and how the over-all proportions, posture, and expression of movement changes.

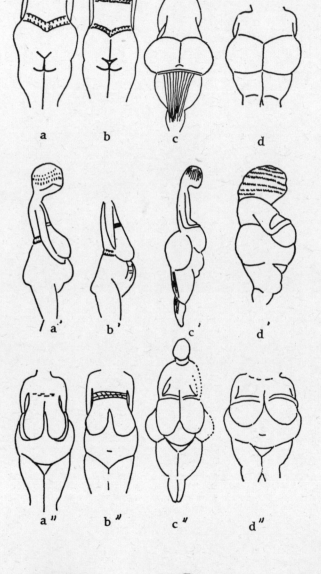

CHART XLIV *(left)*.

FEMALE FIGURES IN PROFILE

PROFILES of figures from TERME-PIALAT (reversed), KOSTIENKI IV, LESPUGUE, GRIMALDI, WILLENDORF, GAGARINO, LAUGERIE HAUTE, MEZIN, LE PORTEL. The figure from Laugerie Haute and the two following, later in date, are included to show the evolution of the canon, which in the end leads to the same contours as those of the claviform signs.

CHART XLV *(left)*.

MODELING OF LOINS AND HIPS IN STATUETTES OF WOMEN

THE evolution of the modeling of loins and hips, which has given rise to theories as to the steatopygia of prehistoric women, is especially interesting.

Statuette 3 from KOSTIENKI (a) has a belt around the waist; the loins are long, the buttocks short and marked at the top with the coccygeal triangle. Statuette 1 from KOSTIENKI (b) presents slightly different features: the loins are separated by a vertical line, the coccygeal triangle is rounded, and the buttocks are very short, so that the fold of the buttocks is rendered by the vertical line of the loins. In the statuette from LESPUGUE (c) the modeling has become incomprehensible: the belt has slipped down to the thighs; loins and buttocks are rendered by two masses without anatomical reality; and a vestige of the coccygeal triangle survives in a completely abnormal position. This last detail, incidentally, has greatly baffled commentators. The WILLENDORF figurine (d) shows the final version of the prototype: loins and buttocks are merged and clumsily linked with the rest.

Treatment of arms and bust is no less revealing. KOSTIENKI 3 (a′, a″), the figurine closest to anatomical reality, has arms placed along the body; KOSTIENKI 1 (b′, b″) has lost the forearms, and there is a band running around the chest above the breasts. LESPUGUE (c′, c″) and WILLENDORF (d′, d″) fuse these two details by inexplicably crossing tiny forearms above the breasts. In every one of its details, from hair to feet, the LESPUGUE statuette defies anatomical common sense. It is precisely because it is a work of art, not an anatomical model, that it has such extraordinary plastic qualities.

CHART XLVI *(left)*.

LAUSSEL: INVERSE FIGURES

IN LOW RELIEF

The hollowed-out portions of the figures are rendered in black in order to show that there is no anatomical connection between the two subjects, and that the lower figure is limited to a single outline. Interpretations of this work (sexual intercourse, giving birth) are mere conjectures; what we actually see could just as well be an attempt to carve the figure of a woman, using part of an earlier, unfinished figure. When we invert this figure and carefully place it over the reversed figures of the woman holding the horn and that in the Berlin museum (center and right), we see that its outline exactly matches these—a standing female holding out her arm.

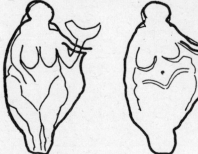

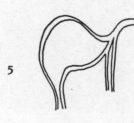

CHART XLVIII *(left)*.

PECH MERLE:

FIGURES SHOWING THE

PERSISTENCE OF THE

SAME FORM OF OUTLINE

1. Horse in "lioness" panel at Le Combel.

2. One of the "monsters" at Le Combel. The construction of figures 1 and 2 reflects considerable reduction in the proportions of the head.

3. Bison in the Large Chamber; the principal masses are transferred to the forequarters, producing a reversal of outline.

4, 5, 6. Stylized figures in the "women/bison" recess. It is hard to tell whether this subject was inspired by woman or bison. Figure 4 is close to a bison; figure 5 seems closer to representations of women. The outline of a human female is clearly suggested in figure 6, where a pendulous breast is formed by the line that turns back on itself.

7. Female figure on "the ceiling with scrawls."

8. Drawing obtained by superimposing woman 7 and horse 1.

CHART XLIX *(above)*.

COMPARISON OF DORSAL

OUTLINES OF PROBOSCIDIANS

(a) Frontal-dorsal contour of one of the "elephants" (the least schematized) in the panel at La Baume Latrone.

(b) Corresponding portion of a mammoth in the black fresco at Pech Merle.

(c) Corresponding portion of the "elephant" at El Pindal.

(d) Corresponding portion of mammoth in the "women/bison" recess at Pech Merle.

These drawings show that in Paleolithic art positive zoological identification cannot be made solely on the basis of outlines.

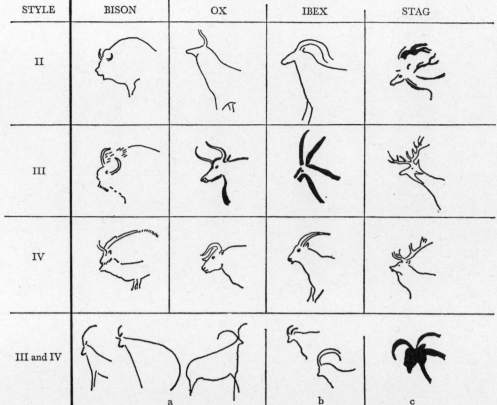

STYLE	BISON	OX	IBEX	STAG
II				
III				
IV				
III and IV	a		b	c

CHART L (*left*).

TREATMENT OF ANTLERS
AND HORNS IN THE VARIOUS STYLES

It is evident that the use of frontal perspective is not invariable in Style II; the horns are sometimes rendered in parallel. In Style III we find both frontal perspective (bison and stag) and semifrontal perspective (ox and ibex). By contrast, in Style IV perspective representations (apart from exceptions) correspond to a "photographic" convention. Thus the clues provided by horns and antlers are valid, though only relatively so. This relativity is demonstrated by the various ibexes in Styles III and IV shown at bottom: (a) Ebbou, three different treatments of horns on contemporaneous figures; (b) Cougnac, two ibexes on the same panel, the male with parallel horns in Style II, and the female with semifrontal horns in Style III; (c) Le Portel, an ibex with horns in frontal perspective, incorporated in a composition in which all subjects are in Style IV.

CHART LI (*below*). LA PASIEGA C: THE "INSCRIPTION"

1. The signs as they appear on the wall. 2, 3, 4. The signs shown separately; we may note similarities in rhythm among the three figures, each built up from a horizontal base, with verticals at the sides, and two or three appendages in the middle. 5. Sign no. 15 at El Castillo. 6. Sign at Cougnac. 7. Sign at Lascaux (Nave). 8. Sign at Niaux (engraving on clay in the Black Salon).

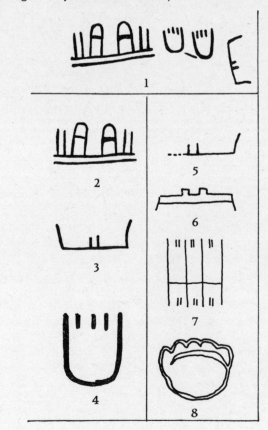

CHART LII (*above*).

SIGNS CAPABLE OF A "MAGIC" INTERPRETATION

THIS chart shows how certain signs could be interpreted as hunters' traps (A), huts (B), and weapons (C). From top to bottom: (A) LASCAUX—cow in front of an enclosure; LA PASIEGA—hind caught by the neck; LA PASIEGA—bison and hind inside an enclosure; NIAUX—bison in front of an enclosure made of stakes; (B) LA MOUTHE—hut shown in perspective; FONT-DE-GAUME—tent with stakes protruding from opening in roof; FONT-DE-GAUME and COUGNAC—huts with chimneys. (C) LASCAUX—harpoon; LASCAUX—spear-thrower; ALTAMIRA—boomerang; NIAUX—throwing club. These cases, selected from hundreds of examples and taken out of context, at one time offered a seemingly plausible explanation of magical art.

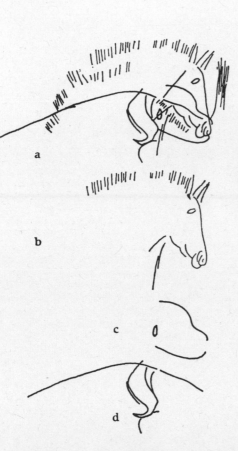

CHART LIII *(left)*.
LASCAUX (Apse):
GROUP OF FIGURES
INTERPRETED AS
REPRESENTING A
MUSK OX

(a) Set of lines producing the appearance of a "musk ox."

(b) Horse's head isolated from this set.

(c) Another horse's head, upside down.

(d) Undeciphered lines.

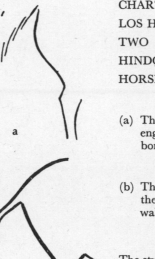

CHART LIV *(left)*.
LOS HORNOS DE LA PEÑA:
TWO VERSIONS OF THE
HINDQUARTERS OF A
HORSE

(a) The hindquarters of a horse engraved on a horse's frontal bone, found in the cave.

(b) The corresponding portion of the horse engraved on the wall outside.

The stylistic treatment of the two figures is obviously totally different (*see* fig. 123).

CHART LV *(below)*. LES COMBARELLES: GROUP 64
(a) The set of lines as shown by photographs taken under various lighting conditions.
(b) The same set as rendered by the Abbé Breuil.
(c) Outlines of the hindquarters of two herbivorous animals and of one horse's head that can be made out with certainty.
(d) Undeciphered lines.
Variously seen and interpreted, this group of figures has fostered several studies on Paleolithic sexuality, whereas there actually seems to be only a series of quadrupeds with tangled outlines.

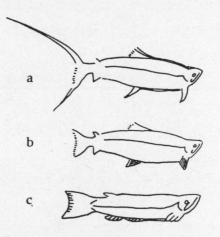

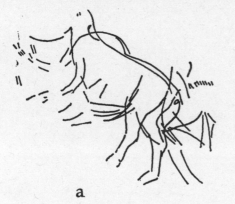

CHART LVI *(above)*. EL PINDAL:
"THE TROUT MASQUERADING AS A TUNA"

(a) The original figure (after H. Breuil, *Les cavernes de la région cantabrique*, 1912).
(b) Removing the sickle-shaped fins, we obtain the outline of what is indisputably a fish of the salmon family (a salmon or trout), recognizable especially by the small adipose fin in front of the caudal fin.
(c) For purposes of comparison: a fish of the salmon family engraved on a spatula from Les Eyzies (*see* fig. 36).

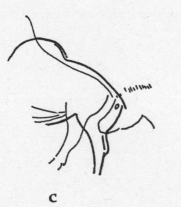

523

BIBLIOGRAPHY

THE *Bibliography has been considerably shortened; otherwise it would merely have repeated, except for a few entries, the bibliographies in* QUATRE CENTS SIÈCLES D'ART PARIÉTAL *by the Abbé Breuil,* L'ARTE DELL'ANTICA ETÀ DELLA-PIETRA *by Paolo Graziosi, and* LA SIGNIFICATION DE L'ART RUPESTRE PALÉOLITHIQUE *by Annette Laming-Emperaire. Here we have followed the principle of giving, for each site, the title of the most complete publication, or of the publication which will direct the reader to a fuller bibliography on the subject.*

GENERAL WORKS

BANDI, HANS GEORG, and MARINGER, JOHANNES, *L'art préhistorique*, Paris, 1955.

GIEDION, SIGFRIED, *The Eternal Present: The Beginnings of Art. A Contribution on Constancy and Change* (Bollingen Series, XXXV, 6, 1), New York, 1962.

GRAZIOSI, PAOLO, *L'arte dell'antica età della pietra*, Florence, 1956.

LEROI-GOURHAN, ANDRÉ, *Documents pour l'art comparé d'Eurasie septentrionale*, Paris, 1943.

————, *Les religions de la préhistoire*, Paris, 1964.

REINACH, SALOMON, *Répertoire de l'art quaternaire*, Paris, 1913.

SAINT-PÉRIER, RENÉ DE, *L'art préhistorique*, Paris, 1932.

ZERVOS, CHRISTIAN, *L'art de l'époque du renne en France. Avec une étude sur la formation de la science préhistorique*, by Henri Breuil, Paris, 1959.

GENERAL WORKS ON DECORATED OBJECTS

BREUIL, HENRI, "La dégénérescence de figures d'animaux en motifs ornementaux à l'époque du renne," *Comptes-rendus de l'Académie des inscriptions et belles-lettres*, 1950, pp. 105–120.

————, and SAINT-PÉRIER, RENÉ DE, "Les poissons, les batraciens et les reptiles dans l'art quaternaire," *Archives de l'Institut de paléontologie humaine, Mémoire 2*, 1927.

GENERAL WORKS ON CAVE ART

ALCADE DEL RIO, HERMILIO, BREUIL, HENRI, and SIERRA, LORENZO, *Les cavernes de la région cantabrique (Espagne)*, Monaco, 1911.

BREUIL, HENRI, "L'évolution de l'art pariétal de l'âge du renne," *Congrès international d'anthropologie et d'archéologie préhistorique*, 13e session, Monaco, 1906, pp. 367–386.

————, "L'évolution de l'art pariétal dans les cavernes et abris ornés de France," *Congrès préhistorique de France*, 11e session, Périgueux, 1934, pp. 102–118.

————, *Four Hundred Centuries of Cave Art*, Montignac, 1952.

LAMING-EMPERAIRE, ANNETTE, *La signification de l'art rupestre paléolithique*, Paris, 1962.

DECORATED OBJECTS IN FRANCE

ANGLES-SUR-L'ANGLIN

    SAINT-MATHURIN, S. DE, and GARROD, DOROTHY, "La frise sculptée de l'abri du Roc aux Sorciers à Angles-sur-l'Anglin (Vienne)," *L'Anthropologie*, t. 55, 1951, pp. 413–424.

ARCY-SUR-CURE

    LEROI-GOURHAN, ANDRÉ and ARL., "Stratigraphie des grottes d'Arcy-sur-Cure (Yonne)," *Gallia-Préhistoire*, t. 7, 1964.

ARLAY

    MILLOTTE, J. P., "Informations archéologiques," *Gallia-Préhistoire*, t. 3, 1960, pp. 182–184.

ARUDY

    CHOLLOT, M., *Collection Piette*, Paris, 1964, pp. 187–222.

    MASCARAUX, F., "La grotte Saint-Michel d'Arudy (Basses-Pyrénées). Fouilles dans une station magdalénienne," *Revue de l'Ecole d'anthropologie*, année 20, 1910, pp. 357–378.

    PIETTE, EDOUARD, *L'art pendant l'âge du renne*, Paris, 1907.

AURENSAN

    FROSSARD, E. and CH., "Etudes sur une grotte renfermant des restes humains de l'époque paléolithique découverte à Bagnières-de-Bigorre," *Bulletin de la Société Ramond*, Jan., 1870, pp. 3–47.

BADEGOULE

    CHEYNIER, ANDRÉ, "Station solutréenne et proto-magdalénienne," *Archives de l'Institut de paléontologie humaine, Mémoire 23*, 1949.

BÉDEILHAC

    MALVESIN-FABRE, G., NOUGIER, LOUIS RENÉ, and ROBERT, ROMAIN, "L'occupation magdalénienne de la grotte de Bédeilhac (Ariège) et découverte d'un nouveau gisement dans la galerie Vidal," *Préhistoire et spéléologie ariégeoises*, t. 8, 1953, pp. 19–48.

    ROBERT, ROMAIN, "Nouvelles fouilles à Bédeilhac," *Bulletin de la Société préhistorique française*, t. 30, 1943, pp. 276–281.

    ———, "Magdalénien de la grotte de Bédeilhac (Ariège)," *Préhistoire et spéléologie ariégoises*, t. 4, 1949, pp. 17–24.

    ———, "'Le faon à l'oiseau.' Tête de propulseur sculpté du magdalénien," *Préhistoire et spéléologie ariégoises*, t. 8, 1953, pp. 11–18.

BELCAYRE

    DELAGE, FRANK, "Gravure aurignacienne de Belcayre (Dordogne)," *Congrès préhistorique de France*, 11e session, Périgueux, 1934, pp. 388–392.

    ———, *Les gisements préhistoriques de Belcayre (Dordogne)*, no place, no date [1951].

BLANCHARD

    DIDON, LOUIS, "L'abri Blanchard des Roches," *Bulletin de la Société historique et archéologique du Périgord*, t. 38, 1911, pp. 246–261, pp. 321–345.

BOURDEILLES (FOURNEAU DU DIABLE)

    PEYRONY, DENIS, "Les gisements préhistoriques de Bourdeilles," *Archives de l'Institut de paléontologie humaine, Mémoire 10*, 1932.

BRASSEMPOUY

    CHOLLOT, M., *Collection Piette*, Paris, 1964, pp. 403–446.

    PIETTE, EDOUARD, "La station de Brassempouy et les statuettes humaines de la période glyptique," *L'Anthropologie*, t. 6, 1895, pp. 129–151.

    ———, and LA PORTERIE, J. DE, "Fouilles à Brassempouy en 1896," *L'Anthropologie*, t. 8, 1897, pp. 163–176.

    ———, and ———, "Fouilles à Brassempouy en 1897," *L'Anthropologie*, t. 9, 1898, pp. 531–555.

BRUNIQUEL

    BÉTIRAC, BERNARD, "L'abri Montastruc à Bruniquel (Tarn-et-Garonne)," *L'Anthropologie*, t. 56, 1952, pp. 213–231.

CASTANET

    PEYRONY, DENIS, "Le gisement Castanet, Vallon de Castelmerle, commune de Sergeac (Dordogne)," *Bulletin de la Société préhistorique française*, t. 32, 1935, pp. 418–443.

CELLIER

    PEYRONY, DENIS, "Le gisement préhistorique de l'abri Cellier au Ruth, commune de Tursac (Dordogne)," *Gallia*, t. 4, 1946, pp. 294–301.

CHAFFAUD, LE

    BERTRAND, ALEXANDRE, "L'os de renne gravé du Musée de Cluny," *Comptes-rendus de l'Académie des inscriptions et belles-lettres*, 1887, p. 221.

    CARTAILHAC, EMILE, "Gravure inédite de l'âge du renne. Grotte du Chaffaud (Vienne), "*L'Anthropologie*, t. 14, 1903, pp. 179–182.

CHAISE, LA

    BOURGEOIS, DELAUNAY, "Notice sur la grotte de La Chaise," *Revue archéologique*, t. 2, 1865, pp. 90–94.

COLOMBIÈRE, LA

    MAYET, LUCIEN, and PISSOT, JEAN, "Abri sous roche préhistorique de La Colombière, près Poncin (Ain)," *Annales de l'Université de Lyon*, t. 39, 1915.

    MOVIUS, HALLAM L., and JUDSON, SHELDON, "The Rock-shelter of La Colombière. Archaeological and Geological Investigations of an Upper Perigordian Site near Poncin," *American School of Prehistoric Research*, 19, 1956.

COUZE RAILWAY STATION

    BORDES, FRANÇOIS, FITTE, P., and LAURENT, P., "Gravure féminine du magdalénien IV, de la Gare de Couze (Dordogne)," *L'Anthropologie*, t. 67, 1963, pp. 269–282.

DURUTHY

    LARTET, LOUIS, and CHAPLAIN DUPARC (comte de), "Sur une sépulture des anciens troglodytes des Pyrénées," *Matériaux pour l'histoire primitive et naturelle de l'homme*, 2e s., t. 9, 1874, pp. 101–167.

ENLÈNE see TROIS FRÈRES, LES

EYZIES, LES

    BÉGOUËN, HENRI, "Un bloc de pierre gravé aux Eyzies," *Prähistorischen Zeitschrift*, 31, 1930, no. 3–4, pp. 264–266.

    CAPITAN, LOUIS, BREUIL, HENRI, and PEYRONY, DENIS, "Les gravures de la grotte des Eyzies," *Revue de l'Ecole d'anthropologie*, année 16, 1906, pp. 429–441.

FACTEUR, LE

    DELPORTE, H., "Une nouvelle statuette paléolithique: la Vénus de Tursac," *L'Anthropologie*, t. 63, 1959, pp. 233–247.

FARINCOURT

MOUTON, P., and JOFFROY, RENÉ, "Précisions nou-
velles sur les stations magdaléniennes de Farincourt
(Haute-Marne)," *Revue archéologique de l'Est et du
Centre-Est*, t. 7, fasc. 3–4, 1956, pp. 193–223.

FERRASSIE, LA

PEYRONY, DENIS, "La Ferrassie," *Préhistoire*, t. 3, 1934,
pp. 1–92.

FONTALÈS

DARASSE, P., "Deux oeuvres d'art magdaléniennes de
l'abri de Fontalès, près Saint-Antonin (Tarn-et-
Garonne)," *Bulletin de la Société préhistorique française*,
t. 52, 1955, pp. 715–718.
———, "L'abri sous roche de Fontalès près Saint-
Antonin (Tarn-et-Garonne)," *Bulletin de la Société méridionale de spéléologie et de préhistoire*, 1948–49.
———, and GUFFROY, S., "Le magdalénien supérieur
de l'abri Fontalès, près Saint-Antonin (Tarn-et-
Garonne)," *L'Anthropologie*, t. 64, 1960, pp. 1–35.

FONTARNAUD

LABRIE, J., "La caverne préhistorique de Fontarnaud
à Lugasson (Gironde)," *Revue historique de Bordeaux*,
1928, pp. 102–113.

GARGAS

BREUIL, HENRI, "Gravures sur schiste périgordiennes
de la caverne de Gargas," *Mélanges en hommage au Prof.
Hamal-Nandrin. Société royale belge d'anthropologie et de
préhistoire*, 1953, pp. 42–50.
———, and CHEYNIER, ANDRÉ, "Les fouilles de Breuil
et Cartailhac dans la grotte de Gargas en 1911 et
1913," *Bulletin de la Société méridionale de spéléologie et de
préhistoire*, t. 5, 1954–55, pp. 341–382.
MALVESIN-FABRE, G., NOUGIER, LOUIS RENÉ, and
ROBERT, ROMAIN, *Gargas*, Toulouse, 1954.
SAHLI, A., "Nouvelles découvertes dans la grotte de
Gargas," *Préhistoire et spéléologie ariégeoises*, t. 18, 1964,
pp. 65–74.

GORGE D'ENFER

PEYRONY, DENIS, "Les abris de Lartet et du Poisson,"
L'Anthropologie, t. 42, 1932, pp. 241–268.

GOURDAN

CHOLLOT, M., *Collection Piette*, Paris, 1964, pp. 39–128.

HOTEAUX, LES

TOURNIER, JEAN, and GUILLON, C., *Les hommes préhistoriques dans l'Ain*, Bourg, 1895.

ISTURITZ

SAINT-PÉRIER, RENÉ DE, "La grotte d'Isturitz," *Archives de l'Institut de paléontologie humaine*, I, "Le magdalénien de la salle Saint-Martin," *Mémoire 7*, 1930;
II, "Le magdalénien de la grande salle," *Mémoire 17*,
1936; III, "Les solutréens, les aurignaciens, et les
mousteriens," *Mémoire 25*, 1952.

JEAN-BLANCS, LES

PEYRONY, DENIS and ELIE, "La station préhistorique
des Champs-Blancs," *Bulletin de la Société historique et
archéologique du Périgord*, t. 61, 1934, pp. 179–202.

LABASTIDE

BÉGOUËN, HENRI, "Les plaquettes de pierre gravées de
la grotte de Labastide (Hautes-Pyrénées)," *Jahrbuch
für prähistorische und ethnographische Kunst*, 1938, pp.
1–10.
SIMONNET, G., "Une nouvelle plaquette de pierre gravée magdalénienne de la grande grotte de Labastide,
commune de Labastide (Hautes-Pyrénées)," *Bulletin
de la Société préhistorique française*, t. 44, 1947, pp. 55–64.

LABATUT

BREUIL, HENRI, "Gravures aurignaciennes supérieures
de l'abri Labatut à Sergeac (Dordogne)," *Revue anthropologique*, année 39, 1929, pp. 147–151.

LALINDE, LA ROCHE AT

PEYRONY, DENIS, "Sur quelques pierres intéressantes
de la grotte de La Roche près de Lalinde (Dordogne)," *L'Anthropologie*, t. 40, 1930, pp. 19–29.

LARAUX

PRADEL, L., and CHOLLET, A., "L'abri périgordien
de Laraux, commune de Lussac-les-Châteaux (Vienne)," *L'Anthropologie*, t. 54, 1950, pp. 214–227.

LAUGERIE BASSE

BREUIL, HENRI, "Les œuvres d'art magdalénien des
fouilles de Le Bel-Maury à Laugerie-Basse," *Congrès
préhistorique de France*, 11e session, Périgueux, 1934, pp.
89–101.
PEYRONY, DENIS, and MAURY, J., "Gisement préhistorique de Laugerie-Basse," *Revue anthropologique*, année
24, 1914, pp. 134–154.

LAUSSEL

LALANNE, J. G., and BOUYSSONIE, JEAN, "Le gisement
paléolithique de Laussel," *L'Anthropologie*, t. 50, 1941–
46, pp. 1–163.
LARTET, EDOUARD, and CHRISTY, HENRY, *Reliquiae
aquitanicae*, London, 1865–75.

LESPUGUE

SAINT-PÉRIER, RENÉ DE, "Statuette de femme stéato-
pyge découverte à Lespugue (Haute-Garonne),"
L'Anthropologie, t. 32, 1922, pp. 361–381.
———, "Les fouilles de 1923 dans la grotte des
Rideaux à Lespugue," *L'Anthropologie*, t. 34, 1924,
pp. 1–15.
———, "La grotte des Scilles à Lespugue," *L'Anthro-
pologie*, t. 36, 1926, pp. 15–40.

LIMEUIL

CAPITAN, LOUIS, and BOUYSSONIE, JEAN, *Limeuil, son
gisement à gravures sur pierre de l'âge du renne* (Institut international d'anthropologie, 1), Paris, 1924.

LORTET

CHOLLET, M., *Collection Piette*, Paris, 1964, pp. 129–
186.
PIETTE, EDOUARD, *L'art pendant l'âge du renne*, Paris,
1907.

LOUBRESSAC

LECLERC, J., and PRADEL, L., "Un bâton orné du
magdalénien final de Loubressac, commune de Maze-
rolles (Vienne)," *Bulletin de la Société préhistorique française*, t. 45, 1948, pp. 401–404.

LOURDES

PIETTE, EDOUARD, "Le chevêtre et la semi-domestica-
tion des animaux aux temps pléistocènes," *L'Anthropologie*, t. 17, 1906, pp. 27–53.
———, *L'art pendant l'âge du renne*, Paris, 1907.

MADELEINE, LA (DORDOGNE)

CAPITAN, LOUIS, and PEYRONY, DENIS, *La Madeleine,
son gisement, ses industries, ses œuvres d'art* (Institut international d'anthropologie, 2), Paris, 1928.

MARCAMPS

LACORRE, FERNAND, "La grotte des fées à Marcamps
(Gironde)," *P.V. de la Société linéenne de Bordeaux*, 1938
(1939).

LAMBERT, A., "Découverte d'une gravure pariétale magdalénienne dans la grotte des Fées à Marcamps," *Bulletin de la Société préhistorique française*, t. 42, 1945, pp. 140–143.

MARCHE, LA

LWOFF, S., "La grotte de La Marche," *Bulletin de la Société préhistorique française*: t. 38, 1941, pp. 145–161; t. 39, 1942, pp. 51–64 and pp. 207–208; t. 40, 1943, pp. 166–169; t. 54, 1957, pp. 622–623; t. 56, 1959, pp. 327–335; t. 59, 1962, pp. 73–91.

PALES, LÉON, and SAINT-PÉROUSE, MARIE TASSIN DE, "Une scène magdalénienne," *Objets et mondes*, t. 4, fasc. 2, 1964, pp. 77–106.

PÉRICARD, LÉON, and LWOFF, S., "La Marche. Premier atelier magdalénien III à dalles gravées mobiles," *Bulletin de la Société préhistorique française*, t. 37, 1940, pp. 155–180.

PRADEL, L., "La grotte magdalénienne de La Marche, commune de Lussac-les-Châteaux (Vienne)," *Mémoires de la Société préhistorique française*, t. 5, 1958, pp. 170–191.

MARSOULAS

CAU DURBAN, D., "La grotte de Marsoulas," *Matériaux pour l'histoire primitive et naturelle de l'homme*, t. 7, 1872, pp. 282–286; t. 19, 1885, pp. 341–349.

MAS D'AZIL, LE

BREUIL, HENRI, "Rapport sur les fouilles dans la grotte du Mas-d'Azil (Ariège), *Bulletin archéologique*, 1902.

CHOLLOT, M., *Collection Piette*, Paris, 1964, pp. 223–402.

PEQUART, SAINT-JUST VICTOR and MARTHE, "Récente découverte de deux œuvres d'art magdalénien du Mas-d'Azil," *La revue scientifique*, No. 3205, Feb., 1942, pp. 91–95.

PIETTE, EDOUARD, *L'art pendant l'âge du renne*, Paris, 1907.

MASSAT

HAMY, THÉODORE J. E., *Précis de paléontologie humaine*, Paris, 1870, pp. 305–309.

MÉROC, LOUIS, "Informations archéologiques," *Gallia-Préhistoire*, t. 2, 1959, p. 148.

NADAILLAC, JEAN FRANÇOIS ALBERT DE, *Les premiers hommes et les temps préhistoriques*, Paris, 1881.

MONTGAUDIER

CARTAILHAC, EMILE, *La France préhistorique*, Paris, 1889, pp. 68–82.

NADAILLAC, JEAN FRANÇOIS ALBERT DE, "Le bâton de commandement de Montgaudier," *Bulletin et mémoires de la Société d'anthropologie de Paris*, 1887, pp. 7–10.

MOUTHE, LA

RIVIÈRE, EMILE, "La grotte de La Mouthe (Dordogne)," *Bulletin et mémoires de la Société d'anthropologie de Paris*, t. 48, s. 4, 1897, pp. 302–329.

MURAT

LÉMOZI, AMÉDÉE, "Fouilles dans l'abri sous roche de Murat," *Bulletin de la Société préhistorique française*, t. 21, 1924, pp. 17–58.

———, "Quelques spécimens de l'art quaternaire (région de Cabrerets, Lot)," *Congrès préhistorique de France*, 12e session, Toulouse-Foix, 1936, pp. 642–659.

PATAUD

MOVIUS, HALLAM LEONARD, "Bas-Relief Carving of a Female Figure Recently Discovered in the Final Perigordian Horizon at the Abri Pataud, Les Eyzies (Dordogne)," *Festschrift für Lothar Zotz*, 1960, pp. 377–387.

PECH DE LA BOISSIÈRE

PEYRONY, DENIS, "La station préhistorique du Pech de la Boissière," *Bulletin de la Société préhistorique française*, t. 31, 1934, pp. 194–213.

PECHIALET

BREUIL, HENRI, "Oeuvres d'art paléolithiques inédites du Périgord et art oriental d'Espagne," *Revue anthropologique*, année 37, 1927, pp. 101–108.

PLACARD, LE

BREUIL, HENRI, "Les subdivisions du paléolithique supérieur et leur signification," *Congrès international d'anthropologie et d'archéologie préhistorique*, 14e session, Geneva, 1912, pp. 165–238.

CHAUVET, C., "Os, ivoires et bois de renne ouvrés de la Charente," *Bulletin de la Société archéologique et historique de la Charente*, 8e s., t. 1, 1910, pp. 1–191.

PIETTE, EDOUARD, *L'art pendant l'âge du renne*, Paris, 1907.

PLANCHETORTE

BOUYSSONIE, JEAN, and BARDON, *La grotte Lacoste*, Brive, 1910.

PORTEL, LE

BREUIL, HENRI, and JEANNEL, RENÉ, "La grotte ornée du Portel à Loubens (Ariège)," *L'Anthropologie*, t. 59, 1955, pp. 184–204.

VÉZIAN, JEAN, "Les foyers magdaléniens de la grotte du Portel (Ariège)," *Préhistoire et spéléologie ariégeoise*, t. 9–10, 1954–55, pp. 13–32.

PUY DE LACAN, LE

KIDDER, LILIA and HOMER H., "Le Puy de Lacan et les gravures magdaléniennes," *Bulletin de la Société archéologique de la Corrèze*, t. 59, 1937, pp. 7–26.

RAYMONDEN

CAPITAN, LOUIS, BREUIL, HENRI, BOURRINET, P., and PEYRONY, DENIS, "Observations sur un bâton de commandement orné de figures animales et de personnages semi-humains," *Revue de l'Ecole d'anthropologie*, année 19, 1909, pp. 62–76.

REBIÈRES, LES

PITTARD, EUGÈNE, "Une gravure sur galet de l'époque aurignacienne," *L'Anthropologie*, t. 23, 1912, pp. 307–311.

REY

RIVIÈRE, EMILE, "Nouvelles récherches dans la Dordogne," *Association française pour l'avancement des sciences, Congrès de Caen*, t. 23, II, 1894, p. 721.

ROCHE, LA see LALINDE

RUTH, LE

PEYRONY, DENIS, "Station préhistorique du Ruth près Le Moustier (Dordogne)," *Revue de l'Ecole d'anthropologie*, année 19, 1909, pp. 156–176.

SAINT-MARCEL

ALLAIN, J., "Premier aperçu d'ensemble sur l'industrie magdalénienne de La Garenne, commune de Saint-Marcel (Indre)," *Bulletin de la Société préhistorique française*, t. 58, 1961, pp. 594–604.

BREUIL, HENRI, "Station de l'âge du renne de Saint-Marcel (Indre) d'après les fouilles de M. Benoist," *L'Anthropologie*, t. 13, 1902, pp. 145–165.

SALPETRIÈRE

Cazalis de Fondouce, Paul, *Les temps préhistoriques dans le Sud-Est de la France*, Montpellier, 1872.

SAUT-DU-PERRON

Larue, M., Combier, Jean, and Roche, Jean, "Les gisements périgordien et magdalénien du Saut-du-Perron (Loire)," *L'Anthropologie;* t. 59, 1955, pp. 401–428; t. 60, 1956, pp. 1–21.

SIREUIL

Breuil, Henri, and Peyrony, Denis, "Statuette féminine aurignacienne de Sireuil (Dordogne)," *La revue anthropologique*, année 40, 1930, pp. 44–47.

SOLUTRÉ

Combier, Jean, "Solutré. Les fouilles de 1907 à 1925. Mise au point stratigraphique et typologique," *Travaux du laboratoire de géologie de la faculté des sciences de Lyon*, n.s., n.2, 1955, pp. 93–222.

TERME-PIALAT

Delugin, A., "Relief sur pierre aurignacien à représentations humaines, découvert au Terme-Pialat, commune de Saint-Avit-Seigneur (Dordogne)," *Bulletin de la Société historique et archéologique du Périgord*, 1914, pp. 3–11.

TEYJAT

Capitan, Louis, Breuil, Henri, Bourrinet, P., and Peyrony, Denis, "Grotte de la Mairie à Teyjat. Fouilles d'un gisement magdalénien," *Revue de l'Ecole d'anthropologie*, année 18, 1908, pp. 153–173, pp. 198–218.
———, ———, ———, and ———, "Observations sur un bâton de commandement orné de figures animales et de personnages semi-humains," *Revue de l'Ecole d'anthropologie*, année 19, 1909, pp. 62–76.

TROIS FRÈRES, LES — TUC D'AUDOUBERT, LE

Bégouën, Henri, "L'art mobilier dans la caverne du Tuc d'Audoubert (Ariège)," *Jahrbuch für prähistorische und ethnographische Kunst*, 1926, pp. 219–228.
———, "Nouvelles fouilles dans les grottes de Montesquieu-Avantès (Ariège)," *Jahrbuch für prähistorische und ethnographische Kunst*, 1928, pp. 98–99.
———, "Notre campagne de fouilles dans la caverne des Trois-Frères (1930–31)," *Congrès international d'anthropologie et d'archéologie préhistorique*, 15ᵉ session, Paris, 1931, pp. 333–340.
Bégouën, Henri and L., "Découvertes nouvelles dans la caverne des Trois-Frères à Montesquieu-Avantès (Ariège)," *Revue anthropologique*, année 38, 1928, pp. 358–364.

VACHE, LA

Malvesin-Fabre, G., Nougier, Louis René, and Robert, Romain, "Engins de chasse et de pêche de la grotte de La Vache (Ariège)," *Préhistoire et spéléologie ariègeoises*, t. 6, 1951, pp. 13–30.
Robert, Romain, "Deux œuvres d'art inédites de la grotte de La Vache (Ariège)," *Bulletin de la Société préhistorique française*, t. 48, 1951, pp. 185–186.
———, "Une gravure inédite de la grotte de La Vache," *L'Anthropologie*, t. 57, 1953, pp. 101–103.
———, and Kühn, Herbert, "Un lissoir gravé inédit de la grotte de La Vache (Ariège)," *Rivista di scienze preistoriche*, v. 7, 1952, pp. 235–238.

VILLEPIN

Peyrony, Denis, "L'abri de Villepin (Dordogne). Magdalénien supérieur et azilien," *Bulletin de la Société préhistorique française*, t. 33, 1936, p. 253.

WESTERN DECORATED OBJECTS

AHRENSBURG

Rust, Alfred, *Altensteinzeitliche Rentierjägerlager Meiendorf*, Holstein, 1937, pp. 73–146.

ALTAMIRA

Sautuola, Marcelino Sanz de, *Breves apuntes sobre algunos objetos prehistoricos de la provincia de Santander*, Santander, 1880.

ANDERNACH

Schmidt, Robert R., *Die Diluviale Vorzeit Deutschlands*, Stuttgart, 1912.

ARENE CANDIDE

Cardini, L., "Nuovi documenti sull'antichità dell' uomo in Italia. Reperto umano del paleolitico superiore nella grotta delle Arene Candide," *Razza e civiltà*, 3, n.1–4, 1942, pp. 5–25.

BALVERHÖHLE

Andrée, Julius, "Die erste Aurignacien Gravierung in Deutschland," *Jahrbuch für prähistorische und ethnographische Kunst*, 1930, pp. 109–110.

BALZI ROSSI

Breuil, Henri, "Renseignements inédits sur les circonstances de trouvaille des statuettes aurignaciennes des Baoussé Roussé," *Archivio per l'antropologia e la etnologia*, v. 58, 1928, pp. 281–286.
Chollot, M., *Collection Piette*, Paris, 1964, pp. 447–460.

BOLINKOBA

Barandíaran, José Miguel de, "Bolinkoba y otros yacimientos paleoliticos en la Sierra de Amboto (Viscaya)," *Cuadernos historia primitiva*, año V, 2, 1950, pp. 73–112.

CASTILLO, EL

Breuil, Henri, and Obermaier, Hugo, "Les premiers travaux de l'Institut de paléontologie humaine," *L'Anthropologie*, t. 23, 1912, pp. 1–27.
———, and ———, "Institut de paléontologie humaine. Travaux exécutés en 1912," *L'Anthropologie*, t. 24, 1913, pp. 1–16.

CHALEUX

Twiesselmann, François, "Les représentations de l'homme et des animaux quaternaires découvertes en Belgique," *Société royale des sciences naturelles de Belgique*, *Mémoires 113*, Brussels, 1951.

CHIOZZA

Graziosi, Paolo, "La Venere di Chiozza," *Studi Etruschi*, v.17, 1943, pp. 371–387.
Degani, Mario, "Una statuetta femminile preistorica e un sepolcreto neolitico scoperto a Chiozza di Scandiano (Reggio Emilia)," *Atti della Società dei naturalisti e matematici di Modena*, v. 71, 1940, pp. 11–22.

CRESWELL CRAGS

Armstrong, H. L., "Notes on Four Examples of Paleolithic Art from Creswell Caves (Derbyshire)," *Jahrbuch für prähistorische und ethnographische Kunst*, 1927, pp. 10–12.

FURFOOZ

Ausselet Lambrechts, C., "L'art et la parure en Belgique pendant le paléolithique supérieur," *Bulletin de la Société préhistorique française*, t. 27, 1930, pp. 468–482.
Overloop, E. van, *Les origines de l'art en Belgique*, Brussels, 1882.

GOYET

Dupont, Edouard, *L'homme pendant les âges de la pierre dans les environs de Dinant-sur-Meuse*, Brussels, 1873.

————, "Etude sur l'ethnographie de l'homme de l'âge du renne dans les cavernes de la Lesse," *Mémoires couronnés et autres mémoires de l'Académie royale de Belgique*, Brussels, 1867.

GUDENUSHÖHLE

Birkner, Ferdinand, "Paläolithische Kunst aus dem Ries im Bayern," *Jahrbuch für prähistorische und ethnographische Kunst*, 1928, p. 97.

Breuil, Henri, and Obermaier, Hugo, "Die Gudenushöhle im Niederösterreich," *Mitteilungen der anthropologische Gesellschaft in Wien*, 1908, pp. 277-294.

KESSLERLOCH

Bandi, Hans Georg, *Die Schweiz zur Rentierzeit*, Frauenfeld, 1947.

Mestorf, J., "La caverne ossifère, dite Kesslerloch, à Thayngen près Schaffhouse," *Matériaux pour l'histoire primitive et naturelle de l'homme*, t. 7, 1876, pp. 97-114.

Schenk, Alexandre, *La Suisse préhistorique*, Lausanne, 1912.

KLAUSE

Obermaier, Hugo, "Institut de paléontologie humaine, Travaux de l'année 1913. Fouilles en Bavière," *L'Anthropologie*, t. 25, 1914, p. 254-262.

————, and Fraunholz, Joseph, "Eine Mammuthdarstellung aus Süddeutschland," *Jahrbuch für prähistorische und ethnographische Kunst*, 1926, pp. 29-32.

————, and ————, "Der skulptierte Rengeweihstab aus der Mittleren Klausenhöhle bei Essing (Niederbayern)," *Jahrbuch für prähistorische und ethnographische Kunst*, 1927, pp. 1-9.

KNIEGROTTE

Richter, M., "Die Jüngere Altsteinzeit im Ostthüringer Orlagau," *Alt-Thüringen*, I, 1955, pp. 11-42.

LEVANZO

Graziosi, Paolo, "Pietra graffita paleolitica e ciottoli dipinti nella grotta di Levanzo (Egadi)," *Rivista di scienze preistoriche*, v. 9, 1954, pp. 79-88.

MAINZ

Neeb, E., "Eine paläolitische Freilandstation bei Mainz," *Prähistorische Zeitschrift*, 15, 1924, pp. 1-8.

MINA, CUETO DE LA

Vega del Sella, Ricardo, Conde de la, "El paleolitico de la Cueto de la Mina," *Comisión de investigaciones paleontológicas y prehistóricas*, n.13, 1916.

MONOPOLI

Anelli, Franco, "Scavi eseguiti nella grotta Mura di Monopoli," *Archivio storico pugliese. Organo soc. storia patria per la Puglia*, 5, fasc. I, 1952.

NEUBURG

Zotz, Lothar Friedrich, "Ein altsteinzeitliches Idol des Zweigeschlechterwesens," *Forschungen und Fortschritte*, 25 Jahr., no. 11-12, 1949, pp. 121-123.

————, "Idoles paléolithiques de l'être androgyne," *Bulletin de la Société préhistorique française*, t. 48, 1951, pp. 333-340.

OBERKASSEL

Breuil, Henri, and Kühn, Herbert, "Die Magdalenien Skulptur von Oberkassel," *Jahrbuch für prähistorische und ethnographische Kunst*, 1927, pp. 193-194.

PARPALLO

Pericot y Garcia, Luis, *La cueva del Parpallo, Gandia; excavacions del Servicio de Investigaciones prehistoricas de la Excma. Diputación provincial de Valencia*, Madrid, 1942.

PENDO, EL

Carvallo, Jesus Maria, and Larin, B., "Exploracion en la gruta de El Pendo," *Junta superior de excavaciones y antiguedades*, 2.

Carvallo, Jesus Maria, and Gonzales Echegaray, Joaquin, "Algunos objetos inéditos de la Cueva de El Pendo," *Ampurias*, 14, 1952, pp. 37-42.

Obermaier, Hugo, "Oeuvres d'art du magdalénien final de la grotte du Pendo près Santander (Asturies, Espagne)," *Préhistoire*, t. 1, 1932, pp. 9-18.

PETERSFELS

Peters, Eduard, *Die Altsteinzeitliche Kulturstätte Petersfels*, Augsburg, 1930.

————, "Die Kunst des Magdalénien vom Petersfels," *Jahrbuch für prähistorische und ethnographische Kunst*, 1930, pp. 1-6.

RASCANO

Obermaier, Hugo, "Escultura cuaternaria de la cueva del Rascano (Santander)," *Boletín de la asociación catalana d'antropologia, etnologia y prehistoria*, v.1, 1923, pp. 7-14.

ROMANELLI

Blanc, G. A., "Grotta Romanelli II," *Archivio per l'antropologia e la etnologia*, v. 58, 1928, pp. 365-411.

————, "Dipinto schematico rinvenuto nel paleolitico superiore della grotta Romanelli in Terra d'Otranto," *Rivista di antropologia*, v.32, 1938-39, pp. 101-113.

SAN GREGORI

Vilaseca, Salvador, "L'estacio taller de silex de San Gregori," *Memorias de la Academia de ciencias y artes de Barcelona*, 3ª epoca, v. 23, n. 21, 1934, pp. 415-439.

SANTIMAMINE

Aranzadi, Telesforo de, Barandiaran, Jose Miguel de, and Eguren, Enrique de, *Exploraciones de la caverna de Santimamiñe. Figuras rupestres*, Bilbao, 1935.

SAVIGNANO

Antonielli, Ugo, "La stauetta femminile steatopigica di Savignano sul Panaro," *Rivista di antropologia*, v. 27, 1926, pp. 283-299.

Graziosi, Paolo, "A proposito della Venere di Savignano," *Archivio per l'antropologia et la etnologia*, v. 55, 1925, pp. 38-46.

Vaufrey, Raymond, "La statuette féminine de Savignano sur le Panaro (Prov. de Modène)," *L'Anthropologie*, t. 36, 1926, pp. 429-435.

SCHWEIZERBILD

Bandi, Hans Georg, *Die Schweiz zur Rentierzeit*, Frauenfeld, 1947.

Schenk, Alexandre, *La Suisse préhistorique*, Lausanne, 1912.

TIVOLI

Radmilli, A. M., "Explorazioni palentologiche nel territoria di Tivoli," *Atti e memorie della Società Tiburtina di storia e d'arte*, v. 26, n. 1-4, pp. 1-20.

————, "La più antica arte del Lazio," *Coluzione artistica della Società Tiburtina di storia e d'arte*, v. 2, 1956.

TRASIMENO

Palma di Cesuola, A., "Nuova statuetta paleolitica rinvenuta in Italia," *Archivio per l'antropologia e la etnologia*, v. 68, 1938, pp. 293-297.

TROU MAGRITE

DUPONT, EDOUARD, "Découvertes d'objets gravés et sculptés dans le trou Magrite à Pont-à-Lesse," *Académie royale de Belgique*, 2ᵉ s., t. 24, n. 8, 1867.

VALLE, EL

BREUIL, HENRI, and OBERMAIER, HUGO, "Les premiers travaux de l'Institut de paléontologie humaine, *L'Anthropologie*, t. 23, 1912, pp. 1–27.
———, and ———, "Institut de paléontologie humaine. Travaux exécutés en 1912," *L'Anthropologie*, t. 24, 1913, pp. 1–16.
CHEYNIER, ANDRÉ, and GONZALEZ ECHEGARAY, JOAQUIN, "La grotte Valle," *Miscelánea en homenaje al Abate Henri Breuil*, Barcelona, 1964, t. 1, pp. 327–345.

VEYRIER

SCHENK, ALEXANDRE, *La Suisse préhistorique*, Lausanne, 1912.

VOGELHERD

RIEK, GUSTAV, "Altsteinzeit Kulturen am Vogelherd bei Stetten ob Lontal (Würtemberg)," *Jahrbuch für prähistorische und Ethnographische Kunst*, 1932–33, pp. 1–26.

EASTERN DECORATED OBJECTS

BRNO

MAKOWSKY, A., "Der Diluviale Mensch in Löss von Brünn. Mit Fünden aus der Mammuthzeit," *Mitteilungen Anthropologische Gesellschaft in Wien*, Bd. 22, 1892, pp. 73–84.

CZECHOSLOVAKIA

NEUSTUPNY, JIRÍ, "Le paléolithique et son art en Bohême," *Artibus Asiae*, 1948.

DOLNI VESTONICE

ABSOLON, KURT, "The Venus of Vestonice, Faceless and Visored," *The Illustrated London News*, Nov. 30, 1929, p. 936.
———, "Nouvelles découvertes de statuettes modelées dans l'aurignacien de Moravie," *Mélanges de préhistoire et d'anthropologie offerts au Prof. Comte H. Bégouën*, Toulouse, 1939, pp. 249–255.

PEKARNA

ABSOLON, KURT, "Les nouvelles fouilles dans la grotte de Pekarna et les poignards faits en mâchoires de cheval," *Mélanges de préhistoire et d'anthropologie offerts au Prof. Comte H. Bégouën*, Toulouse, 1939, pp. 257–262.
———, and CZIZEK, R., "Die Paläolithische Erforschung der Pekarna Höhle in Mähren," *Mitteilungen aus der paläolithischen Abteilung am Mähr, Landesmuseum*, 26, 1932.

PREDMOSTI

BREUIL, HENRI, "Notes de voyage paléolithique en Europe central, II. Les industries paléolithiques du Loess de Moravie et de Bohême," *L'Anthropologie*, t. 34, 1924, pp. 515–552.
KRIZ, MARTIN, *Beitrage zur Kentniss der Quartärzeit in Mähren*, Steinitz, 1903.
MASKA, K. J., OBERMAIER, HUGO, and BREUIL, HENRI, "La statuette de mammouth de Predmost," *L'Anthropologie*, t. 23, 1912, pp. 273–285.

RUSSIA

ABRAMOVA, Z. A., *Paleolititcheskoe iskusstvo na territorii SSSR*, (Paleolithic Art in Russia), Moscow, 1962.

WILLENDORF

SZOMBATHY, JOSEF, "Die Aurignacienschichten im Loess von Willendorf," *Korrespondenzblatt der Deutschen Gesellschaft für Anthropologie, Ethnologie und Urgeschichte*, Bd. 40, nos. 9–12, 1909.

CAVE ART IN FRANCE

ALDÈNE

CATHALA, M., "Découvertes préhistoriques dans la grotte d'Aldène-Minerve, Cesseras (Hérault)," Iʳᵉ *Congrès international de spéléologie*, Paris, 1935, t. 4, pp. 53–59.
GLORY, ANDRÉ, "La grotte ornée d'Aldène ou de Fauzan (Hérault)," *Congrès préhistorique de France*, 15ᵉ session, Poitiers-Angoulême, 1956, pp. 536–541.
GUERRET, MARCEL, "Découverte de dessins préhistoriques dans la grotte d'Aldène," *Bulletin de la Société d'histoire naturel de Toulouse*, 1927, pp. 318–324.

ANGLES-SUR-L'ANGLIN

PATTE, ETIENNE, "Rapport sur les fouilles du Roc aux Sorciers," *Gallia*, t. 7, 1949, pp. 257–258; t. 11, 1953, p. 232; t.14, 1956, pp. 199–200.
SAINT-MATHURIN, S. DE, and GARROD, DOROTHY, "La frise sculptée de l'abri du Roc aux Sorciers à Angles-sur-l'Anglin (Vienne)," *L'Anthropologie*, t. 55, 1951, pp. 413–424.
———, and ———, "L'abri du Roc aux Sorciers à Angles-sur-l'Anglin (Vienne)," *Congrès préhistorique de France*, 15ᵉ session, Poitiers-Angoulême, 1956, pp. 89–94.

ARCY-SUR-CURE

LEROI-GOURHAN, ANDRÉ, "Sanctuaire de la grotte du Cheval à Arcy-sur-Cure (Yonne)," *Mélanges Pittard*, Brive, 1957, pp. 207–215.

BARA-BAHAU

GLORY, ANDRÉ, "La caverne ornée de Bara-Bahau (Le Bugue-sur-Vézère, Dordogne)," *Congrès préhistorique de France*, 15ᵉ session, Poitiers-Angoulême, 1956, pp. 529–535.
———, *Bara-Bahau, Le Bugue-sur-Vézère (Dordogne)*, no place, no date.

BAUME LATRONE, LA

BÉGOUËN, HENRI, "La grotte de La Baume-Latrone à Russan (Sainte-Anastasie)," *Mémoires de la Société archéologique du Midi de la France*, t. 20, 1941, pp. 101–103.
DROUOT, E., "L'art paléolithique à la Baume-Latrone," *Cahiers ligures de préhistoire et d'archéologie*, 2, 1953, pp. 11–46.

BAYOL

BAYOL, J., *Mémoires d'un vieux fouilleur, III. Grotte à peintures de Collias*, Vienne, 1935.
DROUOT, E., "Les peintures de la grotte Bayol à Collias (Gard) et l'art pariétal de la Languedoc méditerranéenne," *Bulletin de la Société préhistorique française*, t. 50, 1953, pp. 392–405.

BÉDEILHAC

BÉGOUËN, HENRI, "Les peintures et dessins de la grotte de Bédeilhac (Ariège)," *Jahrbuch für prähistorische und ethnographische Kunst*, 1929, pp. 1–5.
———, "Les modelages d'argile de la caverne de Bédeilhac (Ariège)," *Jahrbuch für prähistorische und ethnographische Kunst*, 1931, pp. 7–8.
BREUIL, HENRI, and VIDAL, G., "Les fresques de la galerie Vidal à la caverne de Bédeilhac," *Préhistoire et spéléologie ariégeoises*, t. 4, 1949 (1950), pp. 11–16.

Cartailhac, Emile, and Breuil, Henri, "Les peintures et gravures murales des cavernes pyrénéennes," *L'Anthropologie*, t. 21, 1910, pp. 129–150.

BERNIFAL

Capitan, Louis, Breuil, Henri, and Peyrony, Denis, "Les figures gravées à l'époque paléolithique sur les parois de la grotte de Bernifal (Dordogne)," *Comptes-rendus de l'Académie des inscriptions et belles-lettres*, 1903, pp. 202–209.

BERNOUS, LES — BOURDEILLES

Peyrony, Denis and Elie, "Les gisements préhistoriques de Bourdeilles," *Archives de l'Institut de paléontologie humaine, Mémoire 10*, 1932.

CABRERETS

Lémozi, Amédée, "Peintures et gravures découvertes dans les grottes des communes d'Espagnac, de Sainte-Eulalie et de Cabrerets," *Bulletin de la Société préhistorique française*, t. 17, 1920, pp. 256–263.

CALEVIE, LA

Capitan, Louis, Breuil, Henri, and Peyrony, Denis, "Une nouvelle grotte à parois gravées: La Calévie (Dordogne)," *Revue de l'Ecole d'anthropologie*, année 14, 1904, pp. 379–381.

CANTAL

Lémozi, Amédée, "La grotte du Cantal, vallée du Célé près Cabrerets (Lot)," *Bulletin de la Société préhistorique française*, t. 34, 1937, pp. 213–223; t. 54, 1957, pp. 722–723.

CAP BLANC, LE

Lalanne, G., and Breuil, Henri, "L'abri sculpté du Cap-Blanc à Laussel (Dordogne)," *L'Anthropologie*, t. 22, 1911, pp. 385–402.

CHABOT

Combier, Jean, Drouot, E., and Huchard, P., "Les grottes solutréennes à gravures pariétales du cañon inférieur de l'Ardèche," *Mémoires de la Société préhistorique française*, t. 5, 1958, p. 80.

CHAIRE À CALVIN, LA

David, Pierre, "Abri de la Chaire à Calvin," *Congrès préhistorique de France*, 11e session, Périgueux, 1934, pp. 372–373.
Sonneville-Bordes, Denise de, "Etude de la frise sculptée de la Chaire à Calvin (Charente)," *Annales de paléontologie*, t. 49, 1963, pp. 181–193.

COLOMBIER, LE

Glory, André, "Les gravures de la grotte du Colombier à La Bastide-de-Virac (Ardèche)," *Comptes-rendus de l'Académie des inscriptions et belles-lettres*, Nov. 28, 1947.

COMBARELLES, LES

Capitan, Louis, Breuil, Henri, and Peyrony, Denis, *Les Combarelles aux Eyzies (Dordogne)*, Monaco, 1924.
Peyrony, Denis, "Gravures pariétales de la galerie de droite de la grotte des Combarelles," *Bulletin de la Société préhistorique française*, t. 34, 1937, pp. 736–739.

COMMARQUE

Capitan, Louis, Breuil, Henri, and Peyrony, Denis, "Nouvelles grottes ornées de la vallée de la Beune (Dordogne)," *L'Anthropologie*, t. 26, 1915, pp. 505–518.

COUGNAC

Méroc, Louis, and Mazet, Jean, "Les peintures de la grotte de Cougnac (Lot)," *L'Anthropologie*, t. 57, 1953, pp. 490–494.
————, and ————, *Cougnac, grotte peinte*, Stuttgart, 1956.

CROZE, LA

Capitan, Louis, Breuil, Henri, and Peyrony, Denis, "La Croze à Gontran (Tayac), grotte à dessins aurignaciens," *Revue anthropologique*, année 24, 1914, pp. 277–280.

EBBOU

Glory, André, "Les gravures préhistoriques de la grotte d'Ebbou à Vallon (Ardèche)," *La Nature*, 1947, pp. 257–262, 283–285.

ETCHEBERRIKO-KARBIA

Laplace-Jauretche, G., "Les grottes ornées des Arbailles," *Eusko-Jakintza* (Review of Basque Studies), v. 6, 1952.

FIGUIER, LE

Combier, Jean, Drouot, E., and Huchard, P., "Les grottes solutréennes à gravures pariétales du cañon inférieur de l'Ardèche," *Mémoires de la Société préhistorique française*, t. 5, 1958, pp. 61–117.

FONT-DE-GAUME

Capitan, Louis, Breuil, Henri, and Peyrony, Denis, *La caverne de Font-de-Gaume aux Eyzies (Dordogne)*, Monaco, 1910.

FORÊT, LA

Peyrony, Elie, "Les gisements de La Forêt, commune de Tursac (Dordogne)," *Congrès préhistorique de France*, 11e session, Périgueux, 1934, pp. 424–430.

GABILLOU, LE

Gaussen, Jean, *La grotte ornée du Gabillou*, Bordeaux, 1964.

GARGAS

Breuil, Henri, "La décoration pariétale préhistorique de la grotte de Gargas," *Bulletin de la Société méridionale de spéléologie et de préhistoire*, t. 5, 1954–55, pp. 391–416.
Cartailhac, Emile, and Breuil, Henri, "Les peintures et gravures murales des cavernes pyrénéennes. IV. Gargas, Aventignan (Hautes-Pyrenées)," *L'Anthropologie*, 1910, p. 129.
Malvesin-Fabre, G., Nougier, Louis René, and Robert, Romain, *Gargas*, Toulouse, 1954.

GORGE D'ENFER

Peyrony, Denis, "Les abris Lartet et du Poisson," *L'Anthropologie*, t. 42, 1932, pp. 241–268.

GOUY

Graindor, M. J., "Informations archéologiques. Circonscription de Caen," *Gallia-Préhistoire*, t. 2, 1959, pp. 87–88.

GRÈZE, LA

Ampoulange, U., and Pintaud, R.C., "Une nouvelle gravure de la grotte de La Grèze (Dordogne)," *Bulletin de la Société préhistorique française*, t. 52, 1955, pp. 249–251.

HUCHARD

Combier, Jean, Drouot, E., and Huchard, P., "Les grottes solutréennes à gravures pariétales du cañyon inférieur de l'Ardèche," *Mémoires de la Société préhistorique française*, t. 5, 1958, pp. 61–117.

ISTURITZ

PASSEMARD, EMMANUEL, "La caverne d'Isturitz en pays basque," *Préhistoire*, t. 9, 1944, pp. 1–95.

LABASTIDE

BÉGOUËN, HENRI, "Les plaquettes de pierre gravées de la grotte de Labastide (Hautes-Pyrénées)," *Jahrbuch für prähistorische und ethnographische Kunst*, 1938, pp. 1–10.
SIMONNET, G., "Une nouvelle plaquette de pierre gravée magdalénienne de la grande grotte de Labastide (Hautes-Pyrénées)," *Bulletin de la Société préhistorique française*, t. 44, 1947, pp. 55–64.

LABATUT

BREUIL, HENRI, "Oeuvres d'art paléolithique inédites du Périgord et art oriental d'Espagne," *Revue anthropologique*, année 37, 1927, pp. 101–108.

LASCAUX

BATAILLE, GEORGES, *Lascaux*, Lausanne, 1955.
LAMING-EMPERAIRE, ANNETTE, *Lascaux, peintures et gravures* ("Voici", science-information, 48), Paris, 1964.
WINDELS, FERNAND, "Chapelle Sixtine" de la préhistoire," *Centre d'étude et de documentation préhistorique*, Montignac, 1949.

LAUGERIE HAUTE

PEYRONY, DENIS and ELIE, "Laugerie-Haute près des Eyzies (Dordogne)," *Archives de l'Institut de paléontologie humaine, Mémoire 19*, 1938.

LAUSSEL

LALANNE, J. G., and BOUYSSONIE, JEAN, "Le gisement paléolithique de Laussel," *L'Anthropologie*, t. 50, 1941–46, pp. 1–163.

MAGDELAINE, LA (TARN)

BÉTIRAC, BERNARD, "Les vénus de La Magdelaine," *Bulletin de la Société préhistorique française*, t. 51, 1954, pp. 125–126.
BREUIL, HENRI, "Bas-reliefs féminins de La Magdelaine (Penne, Tarn) près Montauban (Tarn-et-Garonne)," *Quaternaria*, t. 1, 1954, pp. 49–53.

MARCENAC

LÉMOZI, AMÉDÉE, "Peintures et gravures paléolithiques découvertes dans les grottes des communes d'Espagnac, de Sainte-Eulalie et de Cabrerets (Lot)," *Bulletin de la Société préhistorique française*, t. 17, 1920, pp. 256–262.
———, "Quelques spécimens de l'art quaternaire (région de Cabrerets, Lot)," *Congrès préhistorique de France*, 12ᵉ session, Toulouse-Foix, 1936, pp. 642–659.

MARSOULAS

CARTAILHAC, EMILE, and BREUIL, HENRI, "Les peintures et gravures murales des cavernes pyrénéennes: II. Marsoulas," *L'Anthropologie*, t. 16, 1905, pp. 431–444.
MÉROC, LOUIS, MICHAUT, L., and OLLE, M., "La grotte de Marsoulas (Haute-Garonne)," *Bulletin de la Société méridionale de spéléologie et de préhistoire*, 1947, pp. 285–320.

MAS D'AZIL, LE

BREUIL, HENRI, and BÉGOUËN, HENRI, "Peintures et gravures préhistoriques dans la grotte du Mas-d'Azil," *Bulletin de la Société archéologique du Midi de la France*, 1913.
NOUGIER, LOUIS, and ROBERT, ROMAIN, *Mas-d'Azil*, Toulouse, 1954.

MILLY

BAUDET, J. L., "Peinture préhistorique inédite découverte dans la vallée de l'Essonne (Seine-et-Marne)," *Bulletin de la Société préhistorique française*, t. 51, 1954, pp. 97–99.

MONTESPAN

TROMBE, FÉLIX, and DUBUC, GABRIEL, "Le centre préhistorique de Ganties-Montespan (Haute-Garonne)," *Archives de l'Institut de paléontologie humaine, Mémoire 22*, 1947.

MOUTHE, LA

RIVIÈRE, EMILE, "La grotte de La Mouthe (Dordogne)," *Bulletin et mémoires de la Société d'anthropologie de Paris*, t. 8, s. 4, 1897, pp. 302–329.

MURAT

PEYRONY, DENIS, "Les peintures murales de la caverne des Merveilles à Rocamadour (Lot)," *L'Anthropologie*, t. 36, 1926, pp. 401–407.

NANCY

CAPITAN, LOUIS, BREUIL, HENRI, and PEYRONY, DENIS, "Nouvelles grottes ornées de la vallée de la Beune (Dordogne)," *L'Anthropologie*, t. 26, 1915, pp. 505–518.

NIAUX

BREUIL, HENRI, "Les peintures et gravures pariétales de la caverne de Niaux (Ariège)," *Préhistoire et spéléologie ariégeoises*, t. 5, 1950, pp. 9–34.
———, "La caverne de Niaux, compléments inédits sur sa decoration," *Préhistoire et spéléologie ariégeoises*, t. 7, 1952, pp. 11–35.
CARTAILHAC, EMILE, and BREUIL, HENRI, "Les peintures et gravures murales des cavernes pyrénéennes. III. Niaux (Ariège)," *L'Anthropologie*, t. 19, 1908, pp. 15–46.

OREILLE D'ENFER

GIRAUD, L., and SCHLEICHER, C., "Travaux et fouilles de Gorge d'Enfer," *Bulletin de la Société préhistorique française*, t. 4, 1907, pp. 164–167.

OULEN

COMBIER, JEAN, DROUOT, E., and HUCHARD, P., "Les grottes solutréennes à gravures pariétales du cañon inférieur de l'Ardèche," *Mémoires de la Société préhistorique française*, t. 5, 1958, p. 70.

PAIR-NON-PAIR

CHEYNIER, ANDRÉ, "La caverne de Pair-non-Pair (Gironde). Description des parois gravées, par H. Breuil," *Documents d'Aquitaine*, 3, Bordeaux, 1963.
DALEAU, FRANÇOIS, "Les gravures sur roche de la caverne de Pair-non-Pair," *Actes de la Société archéologique de Bordeaux*, t. 21, 1896, p. 235.

PECH MERLE

LÉMOZI, AMÉDÉE, *La grotte temple de Pech-Merle. Un nouveau sanctuaire paléolithique*, Paris, 1929.
NOUGIER, LOUIS, and ROBERT, ROMAIN, *Pech Merle de Cabrerets*, Toulouse, 1954.

PORTEL, LE

BREUIL, HENRI, and JEANNEL, RENÉ, "La grotte ornée du Portel à Loubens (Ariège)," *L'Anthropologie*, t. 59, 1955, pp. 184–204.
VÉZIAN, JEAN, "Les utilisations de contours de la roche dans la grotte du Portel," *Préhistoire et spéléologie ariégeoises*, t. 11, 1956, pp. 79–87.

REVERDIT

DELAGE, FRANK, "Les roches de Sergeac," *L'Anthropologie*, t. 46, 1935, pp. 281–317.

ROCAMADOUR

PEYRONY, DENIS, "Les peintures de la caverne des Merveilles à Rocamadour (Lot)," *L'Anthropologie*, t. 15, 1926, pp. 401–407.

ROC DE SERS, LE

LANTIER, RAYMOND, "Les fouilles du sanctuaire solutréen du Roc-de-Sers (Charente) en 1951," *Comptes-rendus de l'Académie des inscriptions et belles-lettres*, 1952, pp. 303–307.
MARTIN, HENRI, "La frise sculptée de l'atelier solutréen du Roc (Charente)," *Archives de l'Institut de paléontologie humaine, Mémoire 5*, 1928.
————, "Les sculptures du Roc," *Préhistoire*, t. 1, 1932, pp. 1–8.

ROUFFIGNAC

NOUGIER, LOUIS RENÉ, and ROBERT, ROMAIN, *Rouffignac, I, Galerie Henri Breuil et grand plafond*, Florence, 1959.

SAINT-CIRQ

BLANC, S., "Une nouvelle grotte ornée près des Eyzies. La grotte Noël Brousse a Saint-Cirq," *Congrès préhistorique de France*, 16e session, Strasbourg-Metz, 1953 (1955).

SAINT-MARCEL

ALLAIN, J., "Nouvelles découvertes dans le gisement magdalénien de La Garenne, commune de Saint-Marcel (Indre). Note préliminaire," *Bulletin de la Société préhistorique française*, t. 54, 1957, pp. 223–227.

SAINTE-EULALIE

LÉMOZI, AMÉDÉE, "Peintures et gravures paléolithiques découvertes dans les grottes des communes d'Espagnac, de Sainte-Eulalie et de Cabrerets," *Bulletin de la Société préhistorique française*, t.17, 1920, pp. 256–263.

SALLÈLES-CABARDÈS

BARRIÈRE, CLAUDE, "Les gravures de la grotte du Gazel, Sallèles-Cabardès (Aude)," *Travaux de l'Institut d'art préhistorique*, V, fasc. 3, 1961, pp. 23–32.
CANNAC, M., "Découverte de poteries de l'âge du bronze et de gravures paléolithiques sur parois dans la grotte de Gazel près Sallèles-Cabardès (Aude)," *Bulletin de la Société préhistorique française*, t. 45, 1948, pp. 152–161.

SASISILOAGA

LAPLACE-JAURETCHE, G., "Les grottes ornées des Arbailles," *Eusko-Jakintza* (Review of Basque Studies), v. 6, 1952.

SUDRIE, LA

GLORY, ANDRÉ, BAY, R., and KOBY, F., "Gravures préhistoriques à l'abri de la Sudrie (Dordogne)," *Rivista di scienze preistoriche*, v. 4, 1949, pp. 97–100.

TEYJAT

CAPITAN, LOUIS, BREUIL, HENRI, and PEYRONY, DENIS, "Les gravures sur cascade stalagmitique de la grotte de la Mairie à Teyjat (Dordogne)," *Congrès international d'anthropologie et d'archéologie préhistorique*, 16e session, Geneva, 1912, pp. 498–514.

TIBIRAN

CASTERET, NORBERT, "Oeuvres d'art pariétales de la grotte de Tibiran," *Bulletin de la Société méridionale de spéléologie et de préhistoire*, t. 5, 1954–55.

TOUR, LA

BREUIL, HENRI, *Four Hundred Centuries of Cave Art*, Montignac, 1952, p. 290.

TROIS FRÈRES, LES — TUC D'AUDOUBERT, LE

BÉGOUËN, HENRI, and BREUIL, HENRI, "Les cavernes du Volp, Trois-Frères, Tuc d'Audoubert," *Arts et métiers graphiques*, 1958.
BÉGOUËN, HENRI, "Une nouvelle grotte à gravures dans l'Ariège. La caverne du Tuc d'Audoubert," *Congrès international d'anthropologie et d'archéologie préhistorique*, 14e session, Geneva, 1912, pp. 489–497.
————, *Les grottes de Montesquieu-Avantès (Ariège). Tuc d'Audoubert, Enléne, Les Trois-Frères, le Musée de Pujol*, Toulouse, 1936.

USSAT

BREUIL, HENRI, "Peintures magdaléniennes de la grotte des églises à Ussat (Ariège)," *Mélanges de préhistoire et d'anthropologie offerts au Prof. Comte H. Bégouën*, Toulouse, 1939, pp. 271–279.

VILLARS

GLORY, ANDRÉ, and PIERRET, B., "La grotte ornée de Villars (Dordogne)," *Bulletin de la Société préhistorique française*, t. 57, 1960, pp. 355–361.

CAVE ART IN SPAIN

ALTAMIRA

BREUIL, HENRI, and OBERMAIER, HUGO, *The Cave of Altamira at Santillana del Mar (Spain)*, Madrid, 1935.
CARTAILHAC, EMILE, and BREUIL, HENRI, *La caverne d'Altamire à Santillane, près Santander (Espagne)*, Monaco, 1906.

ARDALES

BREUIL, HENRI, "Nouvelles cavernes ornées paléolithiques dans la province de Malaga," *L'Anthropologie*, t. 31, 1921, pp. 239–253.

ATAPUERCA

BREUIL, HENRI, *Four Hundred Centuries of Cave Art*, Montignac, 1952, p. 391.

BERROBERIA

LORIANE, D., "Excavaciones arqueologicas realizadas en la gruta y covacho de Berroberia," *Atlantis*, 15, 1936–40, pp. 91–112.

BOLADO

BREUIL, HENRI, *Four Hundred Centuries of Cave Art*, Montignac, 1952, p. 387.

BUXU, EL

OBERMAIER, HUGO, and VEGA DEL SELLA, RICARDO, CONDE DE LA, "La cueva del Buxu (Asturias)," *Comisión de investigaciones paleontológicas y prehistoricas*, 20, 1918.

CALA, LA

BREUIL, HENRI, *Four Hundred Centuries of Cave Art*, Montignac, 1952, p. 395.

CANDAMO, LA

HERNANDEZ-PACHECO, EDUARDO, "La caverna de La Peña de Candamo (Asturias)," *Comisión de investigaciones paleontológicas y prehistóricas*, 24, 1919.

CASARES, LOS

CABRE AGUILO, JUAN, "Las cuevas de Los Casares y de La Hoz," *Archivio español de arte y arqueologia*, t. 30, 1934, p. 30.
————, "Figuras antropomorfas de la cueva de Los Casares (Guadalajara)," *Archivio español de arte y arqueologia*, t. 41, 1940, pp. 81–96.

CASTILLO, EL

ALCADE DEL RIO, HERMILIO, BREUIL, HENRI, and SIERRE, LORENZO, *Les cavernes de la région cantabrique*, Monaco, 1911.
OBERMAIER, HUGO, "El hombre fosil," *Comisión de investigaciones paleontológicas y prehistóricas*, 9, 1925.

CHIMENEAS, LAS

GONZALEZ ECHEGARAY, JOAQUIN, "Les œuvres d'art de 'Las Chimeneas'," *Préhistoire et spéléologie ariégeoises*, t. 8, 1953, pp. 75–77.
———, "Cueva de Las Chimeneas," *Excavaciones arqueológicas en España*, 21, 1963.

CLOTILDE, LA

ALCADE DEL RIO, HERMILIO, BREUIL, HENRI, and SIERRA, LORENZO, *Les cavernes de la région cantabrique*, Monaco, 1911.

COVALANAS

BREUIL, HENRI, *Four Hundred Centuries of Cave Art*, Montignac, 1952, p. 345.

CULLALVERA, LA

GONZALES ECHEGARAY, JOAQUIN, "La cueva de La Cullalvera," *Préhistoire et spéléologie ariégoises*, t. 14, 1959, pp. 18–23.

HAZA, LA

BREUIL, HENRI, *Four Hundred Centuries of Cave Art*, Montignac, 1952, p. 344.

HORNOS, LOS

BREUIL, HENRI, *Four Hundred Centuries of Cave Art*, Montignac, 1952, p. 352.

LOJA, LA

BREUIL, HENRI, *Four Hundred Centuries of Cave Art*, Montignac, 1952, p. 376.

MAZACULOS

BREUIL, HENRI, *Four Hundred Centuries of Cave Art*, Montignac, 1952, p. 382.

MEAZA, LA

BREUIL, HENRI, *Four Hundred Centuries of Cave Art*, Montignac, 1952, p. 375.

MONEDAS, LAS

CARVALLO, J., "Caverne de Las Monedas au Monte Castillo (Puente Viesgo)," *Préhistoire et spéléologie ariégeoises*, t. 8, 1953, pp. 69–74.

NOVALES

BREUIL, HENRI, *Four Hundred Centuries of Cave Art*, Montignac, 1952, p. 375.

PALOMAS, LAS

BREUIL, HENRI, and BURKITT, MILES, *Rock Paintings of Southern Andalusia*, Oxford, 1929.

PASIEGA, LA

BREUIL, HENRI, OBERMAIER, HUGO, and ALCADE DEL RIO, HERMILIO, *La Pasiéga à Puente Viesgo (Santander)*, Monaco, 1913.

PENCHES

HERNANDEZ-PACHECO, EDUARDO, "Los grabados de la cueva de Penches," *Comisión de investigaciones paleontológicas y prehistóricas*, 17, 1917.

PENDO, EL

BREUIL, HENRI, *Four Hundred Centuries of Cave Art*, Montignac, 1952, p. 348.

PILETA, LA

BREUIL, HENRI, OBERMAIER, HUGO, and VERNER, WILLOUGHBY, *La Pileta a Benaojan*, Monaco, 1915.

PINDAL, EL

JORDA CERDA, FRANCISCO, and BERENGUER ALONSO, M., "La Cueva de El Pindal (Asturias)," *Boletín del Instituto de estudios asturianos*, t. 23, 1954, pp. 1–30.

QUINTANAL

BREUIL, HENRI, *Four Hundred Centuries of Cave Art*, Montignac, 1952, p. 382.

SALITRE

BREUIL, HENRI, *Four Hundred Centuries of Cave Art*, Montignac, 1952, p. 348.

SANTIAN

BREUIL, HENRI, *Four Hundred Centuries of Cave Art*, Montignac, 1952, p. 349.

SANTIMAMINE

ARANZADI, TELESFORO DE, BARANDIARAN, JOSE MIGUEL DE, and EGUREN, ENRIQUE DE, *Exploraciones de la caverna de Santimamiñe. Figuras rupestres*, Bilbao, 1935.

SOTTARIZA

BREUIL, HENRI, *Four Hundred Centuries of Cave Art*, Montignac, 1952, p. 343.

VENTA DE LA PERRA

BREUIL, HENRI, *Four Hundred Centuries of Cave Art*, Montignac, 1952, p, 343.

CAVE ART IN ITALY

ADDAURA

GRAZIOSI, PAOLO, "Qualche osservazione sui graffiti rupestri della grotta dell'Addaura presso Palermo," *Bullettino di paletnologia italiana*, v. 65, fasc. 2, 1956, pp. 285–296.
MARCONI BOVIO, JOLE, "Incisione rupestri dell'Addaura (Palermo)," *Bullettino di paletnologia italiana*, n.s. 8, 1952–53, pp. 5–22.

LEVANZO

GRAZIOSI, PAOLO, "Nuovi graffiti della grotta di Levanzo (Egadi)," *Rivista di scienze preistoriche*, v. 8, 1953, pp. 123–137.
———, *Levanzo, pitture e incisioni*, Florence, 1962.

NISCEMI

MARCONI BOVIO, JOLE, "Nuovi grafitti preistorici nelle grotte del Monte Pellegrino (Palermo)," *Bullettino di paletnologia italiana*, s. 9, v. 64, 1955.

ROMANELLI

BLANC, A. C., "Nuove manifestazioni di arte paleolitica superiore nella grotta Romanelli in terra d'Otranto," *Reale Accademia d'Italia*, fasc. 8, s.7, v.1, 1940.
REGALIA, E., and STASI, P. E., "Grotta Romanelli (Castro, Terra d'Otranto). Nota preventiva," *Archivio per l'antropologia et la etnologia*, v. 34, 1904, pp. 17–81.

ROMITO

GRAZIOSI, PAOLO, "La scoperta di incisioni rupestri di tipo paleolitico nella grotta del Romito presso Papasidero in Calabria," *Klearchos*, n. 13–14, 1962, pp. 12–20.

CAVE ART IN RUSSIA

BADER, OTTO NIKOLAEVICH, "Otkrytie paleoliticeskoi pescernoi jivopisi na Urale (Discovery of paleolithic paintings in a cave in the Urals)," *Istoriko arheologic. sbornik*, 1962, pp. 14–23.
———, "Peinture paléolithique dans l'Oural sud," *VIe Congrès international des sciences préhistoriques et protohistoriques*, 1962.

INDEX OF SITES

INDEX OF SITES

*P*AGE *numbers having an asterisk* refer to the main discussion of the particular site. Figure numbers in bold face type indicate colorplates; figure numbers in text type indicate black-and-white illustrations.*